'In a vividly engaging conspectus of the formative ideas of the past century, *The Age of Nothing* shows how Nietzsche's diagnosis [that God is dead] evoked responses in many areas of cultural life, including some surprising parts of the political spectrum. Ranging widely, Watson tracks the pursuit of a convincing response to Nietzsche in philosophers as various as Henri Bergson, William James and G. E. Moore, painters such as Matisse and Kandinsky, futurist composers and modernist poets (notably Mallarmé and Wallace Stevens), movements such as the Beats and the Sixties counterculture and a host of psychotherapeutic cults' John Gray, *New Statesman*

'Intriguing and challenging . . . I recommend this book to anyone who needs to know what the loss of religious faith has meant to the high culture of our civilization . . . a well-informed account' Roger Scruton, *Independent*

'A big, satisfying book . . . Watson has the best witnesses – and most of the best tunes' *Herald*

'Highly readable and immensely wide-ranging . . . Peter Watson has produced what is, in every way, a big book, one that bears reading thoughtfully, with a pencil in hand. For anybody who has wondered about the meaning of life, and that pretty much covers everyone past the age of twelve, discovering *The Age of Nothing* will be an enthralling and mind-expanding experience'
Washington Post

'An exhilarating ride . . . It is a topical book to be sure, but also one that will stand the test of time as a masterful account of its subject' *Boston Globe*

'Watson's encompassing treatment of a difficult subject, in a world growing no less uncertain, is impressive and, ultimately, reassuring'
Booklist (starred review)

'This book matters' *Atlantic Monthly*

'The beauty of this book is Watson's ability to impose order on a riot of ideas . . . even the casual reader will find much to delight and enlighten as Watson elegantly connects the dots from Nietzsche and William James to Bob Dylan and jazz' *Publishers Weekly*

'A rich mixture of cultural, intellectual, political and religious history that demands much of its readers and is in ways a multilayered chronicle of the past 140 years . . . [it moves] seamlessly from literature to art, philosophy, psychology, political movements, world war, drama and popular culture . . . An erudite opus' *Kirkus Reviews*

Peter Watson has been a senior editor at the *Sunday Times*, the New York correspondent for *The Times* and a columnist for the *Observer*. He has published three exposés of the world of art and antiquities, and is the author of several books of cultural and intellectual history. From 1997 to 2007, he was a Research Associate at the McDonald Institute for Archaeological Research at the University of Cambridge.

THE AGE OF NOTHING

How We Have Sought to Live
Since the Death of God

PETER WATSON

WEIDENFELD & NICOLSON

To
Guislane Vincent Morland
and
Nicholas Pearson

A W&N PAPERBACK

First published in Great Britain in 2014
by Weidenfeld & Nicolson
This paperback edition published in 2016
by Weidenfeld & Nicolson,
an imprint of Orion Books Ltd,
Carmelite House, 50 Victoria Embankment,
London EC4Y ODZ

An Hachette UK company

3 5 7 9 10 8 6 4 2

A CIP catalogue record for this book
is available from the British Library.

ISBN 978-0-7538-2810-6

Printed and bound in Great Britain by
CPI Group (UK) Ltd, Croydon, CR0 4YY

The Orion Publishing Group's policy is to use papers that
are natural, renewable and recyclable products and
made from wood grown in sustainable forests. The logging
and manufacturing processes are expected to conform to
the environmental regulations of the country of origin.

www.orionbooks.co.uk

CONTENTS

PART THREE:
Humanity at and after Zero Hour

'The drive to make sense out of experience,
to give it form and order, is evidently as real
and pressing as the more familiar biological needs.'
– CLIFFORD GEERTZ

'We feel that even when *all possible*
scientific questions have been answered,
the problems of life remain completely untouched.'
– LUDWIG WITTGENSTEIN

'Thinking out how to live is a more basic and urgent
use of the human intellect than the discovery
of any fact whatsoever.'
– MARY MIDGLEY

'Man cannot stand a meaningless life.'
– CARL JUNG

'Life cannot wait until the sciences have explained the universe
scientifically. We cannot put off living until we are ready.'
– ORTEGA Y GASSET

'We must wager on meaning's existence.'
– JAMES WOOD, paraphrasing GEORGE STEINER

'Meaning is not a security blanket.'
– SEAMUS HEANEY, paraphrasing W.H. AUDEN

'What is so admirable in being ruled by a need
for peace of mind?'
– JOHN GRAY

'Religion is being replaced by therapy,
with "Christ the saviour" becoming "Christ the counsellor".'
– GEORGE CAREY, when he was Archbishop of Canterbury

'[E]xistence may have no meaning, yet the rage to live
is stronger than the reason for life.'
– JOHN PATRICK DIGGINS

'A meaningful world is one that holds a future that extends
beyond the incomplete personal life of the individual; so that
a life sacrificed at the right moment is well spent, while a life
too carefully hoarded, too ignominiously
preserved, is a life utterly wasted.'
– LEWIS MUMFORD

'. . . the problem of the meaning of life . . . arises because we are
capable of occupying a standpoint from which our most
compelling personal concerns appear insignificant.'
– THOMAS NAGEL

'If God does not exist,
then everything is permitted.'
– FYODOR DOSTOEVSKY

'All religions share the same grievance.'
– OLIVIER ROY

'But is there something where God used to be?'
– IRIS MURDOCH

'There is nothing to express, nothing with which to express,
nothing from which to express, no desire to express –
together with the obligation to express.'
– SAMUEL BECKETT

'We are evolving, in ways that Science cannot measure,
to ends that Theology dares not contemplate.'
– E.M. FORSTER

'We are here on Earth to do good to others.
What the others are here for, I don't know.'
– W.H. AUDEN

'He who has the most toys when he dies wins.'
– MATERIALIST SLOGAN

'A human being is not one in pursuit of happiness,
but rather in search of a reason to become happy.'
– VIKTOR FRANKL

'It isn't just that I don't believe in God and, naturally,
hope there is no God! I don't want
there to be a God; I don't want the universe
to be like that, as I hope to show.'
– THOMAS NAGEL

'The concepts of redness and roundness are as much
imaginative creations as those of God, of the positron,
and of constitutional democracy.'
– RICHARD RORTY

'A life which contains nothing for which one is not
prepared to die is unlikely to be very fruitful.'
– TERRY EAGLETON

'The final value of our lives is adverbial, not adjectival.
It is the value of the performance, not anything that is
left over when the performance is subtracted.'
– RONALD DWORKIN

'Happiness is something we can imagine,
but not experience.'
– LESZEK KOŁAKOWSKI

'There is another world, but it is in this one.'
– PAUL ÉLUARD

'Men should walk as prophecies of the next age, rather
than in the fear of God or the light of reason.'
– RICHARD RORTY

'Philosophers used to speculate about what
they called the meaning of life.
(That is now the job of mystics and comedians.)'
– RONALD DWORKIN

INTRODUCTION

Is There Something Missing in Our Lives? Is Nietzsche to Blame?

By the summer of 1990 the author Salman Rushdie had been living in hiding for more than a year. This had followed a fatwa, an Islamic juristic ruling, issued by the Iranian supreme cleric Ayatollah Khomeini on 14 February 1989, in which he had said, 'I inform the proud Muslim people of the world that the author of the *Satanic Verses* book, which is against Islam, the Prophet and the Quran, and all those involved in its publication who were aware of its content, are sentenced to death. I ask all Muslims to execute them wherever they find them.'

This was by any standard a monstrous event, made all the more terrible by Khomeini's claim of authority over *all* Muslims. But, however wrong, the threat had to be dealt with and Rushdie was given police protection and the use of a bullet-proof Jaguar, though he had to find his safe houses himself. In July of that year, the police had suggested a further refinement for his safety – a wig. 'You'll be able to walk down the street without attracting attention,' he was told. The Metropolitan Police's best wig man was sent to see him and took away a sample of his hair. The wig was made and arrived 'in a brown cardboard box looking like a small sleeping animal'. When he put it on, the police said it 'looked great' and they decided to 'take it for a walk'. They drove to Sloane Street in London's Knightsbridge and parked near the fashionable department store, Harvey Nichols. When he got out of the Jaguar 'every head turned to stare at him and several people burst into wide grins or even laughter. "Look," he heard a man's voice say, "there's that bastard Rushdie in a wig".[1]

It is a funny story, despite the grim circumstances in which it took place, and Rushdie tells it against himself in his memoir, *Joseph Anton* (the cover name he adopted), which he felt safe to publish only in 2012, nearly a quarter of a century after the original fatwa.

There was certainly something missing in his life during those anxious times, the most precious thing of all – his liberty. But that is not exactly what the German philosopher Jürgen Habermas had in mind when he wrote his celebrated essay, 'An Awareness of What Is Missing: Faith and Reason in a Post-secular Age' (2008). He too was concerned with the impact of religion on our lives but meant something no less precious perhaps, and far more difficult to pin down.

No 'Amen': the Terms of Our Existence and the Idea of a Moral Whole

This something had first occurred to him after he attended a memorial service for Max Frisch, the Swiss author and playwright, held in St Peter's Church in Zurich on 9 April 1991. The service began with Karin Pilliod, Frisch's partner, reading out a brief declaration written by the deceased. It said, among other things: 'We let our nearest speak, and without an "amen". I am grateful to the ministers of St Peter's in Zurich . . . for their permission to place the coffin in the church during our memorial service. The ashes will be strewn somewhere.' Two friends spoke, but there was no priest and no blessing. The mourners were mostly people who had little time for church and religion. Frisch himself had drawn up the menu for the meal that followed.

Habermas wrote much later (in 2008) that at the time the ceremony did not strike him as peculiar, but that, as the years passed, he came to the view that the form, place and progression of the service *were* odd. 'Clearly, Max Frisch, an agnostic, who rejected any profession of faith, had sensed the awkwardness of non-religious burial practices and, by his choice of place, publicly declared that the enlightened modern age has failed to find a suitable replacement for a religious way of coping with the final *rite de passage* which brings life to a close.'

And this more than a hundred years since Nietzsche announced the death of God.

Habermas used this event – Frisch's memorial – as the basis for 'An Awareness of What Is Missing'. In that essay he traces the development of thought from the Axial Age to the Modern period and argues that, while 'the cleavage between secular knowledge and revealed knowledge cannot be bridged', the fact that religious traditions are, or were in 2008, an 'unexhausted force', must mean that they are based more on reason than secular critics allow and this 'reason', he thought, lies in the religious appeal to what he calls 'solidarity', the idea of a 'moral whole', a world of collectively binding ideals, 'the idea of the Kingdom of God on earth'. It is this, he said, that contrasts successfully with secular reason, and provides the 'awkward' awareness of something that is missing. In effect, he said that the main monotheisms had taken several ideas from classical Greece – Athens as much as Jerusalem – and based their appeal on Greek reason as much as on faith: this is one reason why they have endured.

Habermas has one of the most fertile, idiosyncratic and provocative minds of the post-Second World War conversation, and his ideas on this score are underlined by the similar notions of his American contemporaries Thomas Nagel and Ronald Dworkin. In his recent book, *Secular Philosophy and the Religious Temperament*, Nagel puts it this way: 'Existence is something tremendous, and day-to-day life, however indispensable, seems an insufficient response to it, a failure of consciousness. Outrageous as it sounds, the religious temperament regards a merely human life as insufficient, as a partial blindness to or rejection of the terms of our existence. It asks for something more encompassing without knowing what it might be.'

The most important question for many people, Nagel says, is this: 'How can one bring into one's individual life a *full* recognition of one's relation to the universe as a whole?' [Italics added] Among atheists, he says, physical science is the primary means whereby we understand the universe as a whole, 'but it will seem unintelligible [as a means] to make sense of human existence altogether . . . We recognize that we are products of the world and its history, generated and sustained in existence in ways we hardly understand, so that in a sense every individual life represents far more than itself.' At the same time he agrees with the British philosopher Bernard Williams that the 'transcendent impulse', which has been with us since at least Plato, 'must be resisted', and that the real object of philosophical reflection must be the ever more accurate description of the world 'independent of perspective'. He goes on: 'The marks of philosophy are reflection and heightened self-awareness, not maximal transcendence of the human perspective ... There is no cosmic point of view, and therefore no test of cosmic significance that we can either pass or fail.'[2]

In a later book, *Mind & Cosmos* (2012), he goes further, arguing that the neo-Darwinian account of the evolution of nature, life, consciousness, reason and moral values – the current scientific orthodoxy – 'is almost certainly false'. As an atheist, he nonetheless felt that both materialism and theism are inadequate as 'transcendent conceptions', but at the same time acknowledged that it is impossible for us to abandon the search 'for a transcendent view of our place in the universe'. And he therefore entertained the possibility (on virtually no evidence, as he conceded) that 'life is not just a physical phenomenon' but includes 'teleological elements'. According to the hypothesis of natural teleology, he wrote, there would be 'a cosmic predisposition to the formation of life, consciousness, and the value that is inseparable from them'. He admitted: that, 'In the present intellectual climate such a possibility is unlikely to be taken seriously'; and indeed, he has been much criticized for this argument.

The argument itself will be discussed more fully in chapter twenty-six but it fits in here because it shows that, one hundred and thirty-odd years after Nietzsche famously announced 'the death of God', many people (though by no means all) are still trying to find other ways to look out upon our world than the traditional religious viewpoints.

Almost simultaneously, Nagel was joined by his fellow American philosopher colleague, Ronald Dworkin, in his *Religion without God* (2013). Here too the main thrust of the argument will be discussed in chapter twenty-six, but Dworkin's chief point was that 'religious atheism' is not an oxymoron (not any more, anyway); that religion, for him and others like him, 'does not necessarily mean a belief in

God' – rather, 'it concerns the meaning of human life and what living well means'; and life's intrinsic meaning and nature's intrinsic beauty are the central ingredients of the fully religious attitude to life. These convictions cannot be isolated from the rest of one's life – they permeate existence, generate pride, remorse and thrill, mystery being an important part of that thrill. And he said that many scientists, when they confront the unimaginable vastness of space and the astounding complexity of atomic particles, have an emotional reaction that many describe in almost traditional religious terms – as 'numinous', for example.

This feels new, though as we shall see in chapter fifteen some of it at least was presaged by John Dewey between the two world wars and hinted at by Michael Polanyi in the late 1950s and early 1960s.[3] The significant factor, for now, is that these three philosophers – on either side of the Atlantic and each at the very peak of his profession – are all saying much the same thing, if in different ways. They share the view that, five hundred and more years after science began to chip away at many of the foundations of Christianity and the other major faiths, there is still an awkwardness, as Habermas put it, or a blindness or 'unsufficiency' (Nagel); a mystery, thrilling and numinous, as Dworkin characterised it, in regard to the relationship between religion and the secular world. All three agree with Bernard Williams that the 'transcendent' impulse must be resisted, but they acknowledge – ironically – that we cannot escape the *search* for transcendence and that, as a result, many people feel 'something' is missing. This is, in effect, they say, the modern secular predicament.

It is in many ways extraordinary that these three individuals – all hugely respected – should, within a few months of each other, but independently, come to similar conclusions: that, depending on where you start counting – from the time of Galileo and Copernicus, four or five hundred years ago, or Nietzsche, 130 years ago, secularization is *still* not fitting the bill, is still seriously lacking in . . . something.

The Canadian philosopher Charles Taylor has no doubt what that something is. In two very long books, *Sources of the Self* (1989) and *A Secular Age* (2007), he repeatedly charges that people today who inhabit a secular world and lack faith are missing out, missing out on something important, vital – perhaps the most important something there is – namely, as he puts it, a sense of wholeness, fulfilment, fullness of meaning, a sense of something higher; they have an incompleteness, that there is in the modern world 'a massive blindness' to the fact that there is 'some purpose in life beyond the utilitarian'.[4]

Human flourishing, Taylor maintains – a fulfilled life – can only be achieved via religion (Christianity, in his case). Otherwise, the world is 'disenchanted', life is a 'subtraction story' with important parts missing. With no sense of 'transcendence', no sense of the 'cosmic sacred', we are left with 'merely human values', which he finds 'woefully inadequate'. The 'higher times', he says, have faded, we are imbued with 'a sense of malaise, emptiness, a need for meaning'; there is a terrible sense of flatness in the everyday, the emptiness of the ordinary, and this need for meaning can be met only 'by a recovery of transcendence'.[5]

Porous v. Buffered Selves

Taylor pursues this argument further than any of the others. He says that humanism has failed, that the 'pursuit of happiness', a current concern, is a much thinner idea or ideal than 'fulfilment' or 'flourishing' or transcendence, that it uses a 'less subtle language', giving rise to less subtle experiences; that it is lacking in 'spiritual insight', spontaneity or immediacy, is devoid of 'harmony' and 'balance', and is ultimately unhealthy.

The modern individual, he says, is a 'buffered' self rather than a 'porous' self. A porous self is open to all the feelings and experiences of the world 'out there', while the modern buffered self is denied these experiences because our scientific education teaches us only concepts, our experiences are intellectual, emotional, sexual and so on, rather than 'whole'. Modern individuals have been denied a 'master narrative' in which they may find their place, and without which their 'sense of loss can perhaps never be stilled'. Without these factors, he goes on, there is no scope for any human life to achieve a 'sense of greatness' out of which a 'higher' view of fulfilment arises. The sense that there is 'something more' presses in on us, and, therefore, we can never be 'comfortable' with unbelief.

Phew. Sceptics may raise their eyebrows at these claims but there is no doubt that they chime with what many people feel or think. And the likes of Taylor find support for their arguments in the statistical fact that, after the highpoint of secularization in the 1960s and 70s, at the beginning of the twenty-first century more and more people are turning – or returning – to religion. Richard Kearney has even given it a name, Anatheism.[6] We shall return to the (ambiguous) meaning of these statistics presently, but it is certainly true that in 2014 the battle between religious thinkers and atheists is as fierce (and indeed as bitter) as it has been for many a year.

For their part, the militant atheists, as they have been described, largely occupy a Darwinian position. Richard Dawkins, Daniel Dennett, Sam Harris and Christopher Hitchens, to name only the best-known, follow Charles Darwin in seeing human beings as an entirely naturally occurring biological species, which has slowly evolved from 'lower' animals, in a universe that has likewise evolved over the past thirteen and a half billion years from a 'singularity', or 'Big Bang', itself a naturally occurring process (albeit where the laws of nature break down) that we shall understand some day. This process has no need of any supernatural entity.

In the latest rounds of this debate, Dawkins and Harris have used Darwinian science to explain the moral landscape in which we live, and Hitchens has described such institutions as the library, or 'lunch with a friend', as episodes in a modern life just as fulfilling as prayer or church- or synagogue- or mosque-going.

The average reader – especially the average *young* reader – could be forgiven for thinking that this is all there is to the debate: either we embrace religion, or we embrace Darwinism and its implications. Steve Stewart-Williams has taken this reasoning to its logical conclusion when he says, in *Darwin, God and the Meaning of Life* (2010), that there *is* no God, that the universe is entirely natural and in that sense accidental, so that there can be no purpose to life, and no ultimate meaning other than that which we work out for ourselves as individuals.

But though it is the Darwinists who, among atheists, are making the most noise at the moment (and with good reason, given the amount of biological research that has accumulated in the past decades), theirs is not the only game in town. The fact is that, since the advance of religious doubt gathered pace in the seventeenth and eighteenth centuries, and in particular since Nietzsche announced 'the death of God' in 1882 (adding, moreover, that it was we humans who had killed him), many people have addressed themselves to the difficult question of how we are to live without a supernatural entity on whom we can rely.

Philosophers, poets, playwrights, painters, psychologists, to name only those whose professions begin with the same letter of the alphabet, have all sought to think through just how we might live, individually and communally, when we have only our own selves to fall back on. Many – one thinks of Dostoevsky, T.S. Eliot, Samuel Beckett – have expressed their horror at what they see as the bleak world that is left once the idea of God leaves it. Perhaps because horror claims all the best tunes, these Jeremiahs have caught the popular imagination, but *The Age of Nothing* will concentrate instead on the other – in some ways braver – souls who, instead of waiting and wallowing in the cold, dark wastelands of a Godless world, have devoted their creative energies to devising ways to live on with self-reliance, invention, hope, wit and *enthusiasm*. Who, in Wordsworth's words, 'grieve not, rather find/ Strength in what remains behind'.

This aspiration, how to live without God, how to find meaning in a secular world, is – once you put your mind to it – a grand theme that has been touched on by a number of the more daring modernist writers, artists and scientists but has never before been gathered together, so far as I know, into a master narrative. When that is done, it provides a rich and colourful story, as I hope to show, a set of original yet overlapping ideas which I am sure many readers will find thrilling, provocative, yet commonsensical and even consoling.

Some consolation is especially called for because the debate over faith, over what is missing in people's lives, has degenerated in recent years into a bizarre mix of the absurd and the deadly.

8

Are We in a Spiritual Recession?
Or, Are We as Furiously Religious as We Ever Were?

Twice in recent years – 21 May 2011 and 21 December 2012 – predictions were made by religious figures that the world would end. Nothing of the kind happened either time, but none of the figures concerned felt a need to acknowledge that their predictions were . . . well, plain wrong. Pakistan has experienced numerous assassinations of individuals seen – by fellow members of the public – to be contravening its relatively new Islamic blasphemy laws. Tunisia has seen two prominent secular politicians assassinated. Sexual and child abuse cases by Muslims in Britain and Holland, or by Catholic priests in a whole raft of countries worldwide, have become virtually part of the furniture of our lives; the abuse of young white girls, by Muslim men, in Britain has been described as a 'tidal wave of offending'.[7]

These events, coming in the wake of other, even more spectacular, atrocities (the devastation of 9/11, the bombings in Bali, Madrid and London, all committed by Muslims), may not have been quite as bloody in terms of the numbers killed. But they do mark an *extension* of religiously motivated criminal behaviour into ever widening areas of human intolerance – and therein lies what is arguably the most important intellectual, political – even existential – paradox facing us in the young twenty-first century.

An atheist observing this set of absurd and deadly behaviours could be forgiven for grimacing in chastened satisfaction. After centuries of religious strife, after more than two hundred years of deconstruction of the factual historical basis of the Bible, after a plethora of new gods has emerged in the most unlikely, mundane and prosaic of ways and places – the Duke of Edinburgh is worshipped as a god on the Pacific island of Vanuatu, a Lee Enfield motorcycle is revered as a deity in parts of India, there is now a website, godchecker.com, listing more than three thousand 'supreme' beings – humans everywhere seem to have learned next to nothing. They are still locked into ancient enmities, still espouse outdated and disproved doctrines, still fall for shabby con tricks, allowing themselves to be manipulated by religious showmen and charlatans.

And yet, and yet ... The blunt (and to many the perplexing) truth appears to be that, despite the manifest horrors and absurdities of many aspects of religion, despite the contradictions, ambiguities and obvious untruths embodied by all major and minor faiths, it is – according to a number of distinguished authorities – atheism that appears to be in retreat today.

One of the first to point this out was the sociologist Peter Berger. His view might be seen as poignant because it had some of the characteristics of a conversion. Berger, an Austrian émigré who became professor of sociology and theology at Boston University, was in the 1950s and 60s a keen advocate of 'secularization theory'. This theory, which was at its strongest in the mid-twentieth century and could be traced back to the Enlightenment, held that modernization 'necessarily' leads to the decline of religion, both in society and in the minds of individuals. On this analysis, secularization was and is a good thing, in that it does away with religious phenomena that are 'backward', 'superstitious' and 'reactionary'.

That was then. In the opening decades of the twenty-first century, however, the picture appears very different, at least to some people. As mentioned above, Peter Berger was one of the first to draw attention to the change which brought about, on his part, a famous recantation. In 1996, he accepted that modernity had, 'for fully understandable reasons', undermined all the traditional certainties, but he insisted that uncertainty 'is a condition that many people find very hard to bear'. Therefore, he pointed out, 'any movement (not only a religious one) that promises to provide or to renew certainty has a ready market'.[8] And, looking about him, he concluded that the world today 'is as furiously religious as it ever was ... is *anything but* the secularized world that had been predicted (whether joyfully or despondently)', that whatever religious colour people have, they are all agreed upon 'the shallowness of a culture that tries to get along without any transcendent point of reference'.[9]

Berger is not alone. There is no question that the spirits of religious authors are on the rise. In 2006 John Millbank, professor of religion at the University of Nottingham, sought to explain how theology can lead us 'beyond secular reason'. In *The Language of God* (2006),

Francis S. Collins, the geneticist who led the American government's effort to decipher the human genome, described his own journey from atheism to 'committed Christianity'. In *God's Universe* (2006) Owen Gingerich, professor emeritus of astronomy at Harvard, explained how he is 'personally persuaded that a superintelligent Creator exists beyond and within the cosmos'. And in *Evolution and Christian Faith*, published the same year, Joan Roughgarden, an evolutionary biologist at Stanford University, recounts her struggles to fit the individual into the evolutionary picture – complicated in her case by the fact that she is transgender and so has views at odds with some conventional Darwinian thinking about sexual identity.

In 2007 Antony Flew, professor of philosophy at various universities in Britain and Canada, in *There Is a God*, explained how 'the world's most notorious atheist [himself] changed his mind'. Also in 2007, Gordon Graham examined whether art, for all its advantages, can ever 're-enchant' the world the way religion did, concluding that it couldn't. In 2008, Dr Eben Alexander suffered bacterial meningitis and went into a deep coma for a week. Recovering, he wrote a best-selling memoir, *Proof of Heaven: A Neurologist's Journey to the Afterlife*, in which he described heaven as full of butterflies, flowers, and blissful souls and angels.[10]

Religion as Sociology, Not Theology

There is another perplexing side to this – namely, that in the past decade some new and sophisticated arguments have been made for understanding religion as a natural phenomenon. Some of these arguments, moreover, have arisen as a result of new scientific findings that have changed the nature of the debate. What are we to make of this state of affairs, in which atheism has the better case, where its evidence involves new elements, which introduces new arguments, but where religion, so its adherents claim, has the numbers, despite its manifest horrors and absurdities?

The most convincing argument I have encountered – certainly the one with the most substantial and systematic evidence to support it

– is that offered by Pippa Norris and Ronald Inglehart in *Sacred and Secular: Religion and Politics Worldwide* (2004). Their book draws on a massive base of empirical evidence generated by the four waves of the World Values Survey, carried out from 1981 to 2001, which has conducted representative and sophisticated national surveys in almost eighty societies, covering all of the world's major faiths. Norris and Inglehart also used Gallup International Polls, the International Social Survey Program and Eurobarometer surveys. While, they say, 'it is obvious that religion has not disappeared from the world, nor does it seem likely to do so', they insist that the concept of secularization 'captures an important part of what is [still] going on'.

Their study identifies a core sociological factor, something they term 'existential security', which they say rests on two simple axioms and which 'prove extremely powerful in accounting for most of the variations in religious practices found across the world'.[11]

The first basic building block in their theory is the assumption that rich and poor nations around the globe differ sharply in their levels of sustainable human development and socioeconomic inequality and thus in the basic living conditions of human security and vulnerability to risks. The idea of human security has emerged in recent years, they say, as an important objective of international development. At its simplest, the core idea of security rejects military strength to ensure territorial integrity and replaces it with freedom from various risks and dangers, ranging from environmental degradation to natural and man-made disasters such as floods, earthquakes, tornadoes and droughts, and to epidemics, violations of human rights, humanitarian crisis and poverty.

The past thirty years have seen dramatic improvements in some parts of the developing world. Nevertheless, the United Nations Development Programme (UNDP) reports that worldwide progress has been erratic during the last decade, with some reversals: fifty-four countries (twenty of them in Africa) are poorer now than in 1990; in thirty-four countries, life expectancy has fallen; in twenty-one, the Human Development Index declined. In Africa, trends in HIV/AIDS and hunger are worsening. The gap between living conditions in rich and poor societies is growing.[12]

Analysis of data from societies around the world has revealed that the extent to which people emphasize religion and engage in religious behaviour could, indeed, be predicted with considerable accuracy from a society's level of economic and other development. Multivariate analysis (a mathematical technique) has demonstrated that a few basic developmental indicators such as per capita GNP, rates of HIV/AIDS, access to improved water sources and the number of doctors per hundred thousand people, predict 'with remarkable precision' how frequently the people of a given society worship or pray. The most crucial explanatory variables are those that differentiate between vulnerable societies and societies in which survival is so secure that people take it for granted during their formative years.[13]

In particular, Norris and Inglehart hypothesize that, all things being equal, the experience of growing up in less secure societies will heighten the importance of religious values, while conversely experience of more secure societies will lessen it. The main reason, they say, is that 'the need for religious reassurance becomes less pressing under conditions of greater security'. It follows that people living in advanced industrial societies will often grow increasingly indifferent to traditional religious leaders and institutions and become less willing to engage in spiritual activities. 'People raised under conditions of relative security can tolerate more ambiguity and have less need for the absolute and rigidly predictable rules that religious sanctions provide.'

It seems plain that improving conditions of existential security erode the importance of religious values but – and here is the rub – at the same time reduce the rates of population growth in postindustrial societies. So rich societies are becoming more secular in their values but *shrinking* in population. In contrast, poorer nations remain deeply religious in their values and will also have much higher fertility rates, producing ever larger populations (and therefore tending to remain poor).[14] A core aim of virtually all traditional religions is to maintain the strength of the family, 'to encourage people to have children, to encourage women to stay home and raise the children, and to forbid abortion, divorce, or anything that interferes with high rates of reproduction'. It should be no surprise, then, that these two interlinked trends mean that rich nations are becoming more secular, but the world as a whole is becoming more religious.

Transcendence v. Poverty

A number of things follow from this analysis. In the first place, we can say that the original secularization theory was right all along but many societies did not follow (or failed to follow) the same industrialization/urbanization path as did the West. Second, and conceivably more important, we can now see that religion is best understood 'as a *sociological* rather than a theological phenomenon'.[15] Far from 'transcendence' being the fundamental ingredient or experience related to belief, as Peter Berger and others claim, poverty and existential insecurity are the most important explanatory factors. Given all this, and combined with the UNDP findings – that the gap between rich and poor countries continues to widen, and 'existential insecurity in some fifty or more countries is likewise growing' – then the 'success' of religion is actually a by-product of the *failure* of some countries to successfully modernize and reduce the insecurities of their people. On this reading, the expansion of religion is nothing for us, as a world community trying to help each other, to be proud of – triumphalism concerning the religious revival is therefore, on this account, misplaced.

A final point is more subtle. When we actually look at the 'flavour' of the religions that are flourishing now, when we look at their theological, intellectual and emotional characteristics, what do we find? We find, first, that it is the established Churches – those with the most elaborately worked out theologies, theologies as often as not about transcendence – that are losing adherents, to be replaced by evangelicals, Pentecostals, 'health-and-wealth' charismatics and fundamentalists of one kind or another. In 1900, 80 per cent of the world's Christians lived in Europe and the United States; today, 60 per cent of them live in the developing world.[16]

What are we to make of evangelical healing and prophecy? If these worked often enough, they would surely take over the world far more than they have done, offering a better explanation for disease, say, than any scientifically derived view. What are we to make of 'speaking in tongues', a biblical phrase that confers a would-be dignity on a phenomenon that, under any rational light, borders on mental illness? When, in February 2011, a reporter on live television in the United States suddenly broke into gibberish for a few moments, it attracted wide interest on other TV stations and on the Internet, and both ribald and sympathetic comment, but no one suggested for a moment that she had had a religious experience (and she didn't say that herself). Discussion centred on which regions of her brain might have caused such an 'epileptic-type' outburst.

What are we to make of health-and-wealth Churches? What role does 'transcendence' play in their ideology? Health and wealth directly address existential insecurity.

To the atheist mind, these developments – the violent intolerance of fundamentalist Islam, the wilful ignorance of the Creationists in certain regions of the United States, speaking in tongues by evangelicals, charismatic 'healing', the worship of motorcycles in India – suggest nothing less than a turning-back of the clock. The simple, obvious and rational sociological explanation for these events only underlines their crudity.

Alongside the sociological explanations for the religious revival, the psychological ones seem – to an extent – almost beside the point. In their book *God Is Back*, John Micklethwait and Adrian Wooldridge hold that there is 'considerable evidence that, regardless of wealth, Christians are healthier and happier than their secular brethren'. David Hall, a doctor at the University of Pittsburgh Medical Center, maintains that weekly church attendance can add two to three years to someone's life. A 1997 study of seven thousand older people by the Duke University Medical Center found that religious observance 'might' enhance immune systems and lower blood pressure. In 1992 there were just three medical schools in the United States that had programmes examining the relationship between spirituality and health; by 2006 the number had increased to 141.[17]

Micklethwait and Wooldridge state: 'One of the most striking results of the Pew Forum [Research Center]'s regular survey of happiness is that Americans who attend religious services once or more a week are happier (43 per cent very happy) than those who attend monthly or less (31 per cent) or seldom or never (26 per cent) . . . The correlation between happiness and church attendance has been fairly steady since Pew started the survey in the 1970s; it is also more robust than the link between happiness and wealth.'[18]

Studies also show, they say, that religion can combat bad behaviour as well as promote well-being. 'Twenty years ago, Richard Freeman, a Harvard economist, found that black youths who attended church were more likely to attend school and less likely to commit crimes or use drugs.' Since then, a host of further studies, including the 1991 report by the National Commission on Children, have concluded that religious participation is associated with lower rates of crime and drug use. James Q. Wilson (1931–2012), perhaps America's pre-eminent criminologist, succinctly summarized 'a mountain of [social-scientific] evidence': 'Religion, independent of social class, reduces deviance.' Finally, Jonathan Gruber, 'a secular-minded economist' at the Massachusetts Institute of Technology, has argued 'on the basis of a mass of evidence' that churchgoing produces a boost in income.

Two observations are pertinent here. The first is that these examples are taken from the USA and, as is becoming clear, that country is exceptional in all sorts of ways and not at all typical of what is happening elsewhere. The second observation is, perhaps, more relevant to our subject. Even if some of these surveys showing the benefits of belief are true, what exactly is being argued here? That God rewards people who go to church regularly and often by making them happier, healthier and, to an extent, richer? But if so, and if God is omnipotent and beneficent, what about the 57 per cent of regular churchgoers who are *not* happy? They go to church – so why has (an omnipotent and benevolent) God discriminated against them? By the same token, why are *any* non-churchgoers happy? Twenty-six per cent say they are, yet seldom or never go to church. How do we know that these people weren't happy or unhappy to begin with, irrespective of their churchgoing behaviour? And in any case, these figures show that, even among the churchgoers, the unhappy outweigh the happy by a significant majority. What, we may ask, is God playing at?

Still more to the point, and revealingly, these are arguments for the *psychological* benefits of faith, not for theological ones. One could argue – theologians in the past *have* argued – that happiness is not the aim for religious people, certainly not for pious Christians, the crux of their belief system being that they can hope for salvation only in the next life. There is thus something in this whole exercise, of trying to prove the benefits of faith at every level, that smacks of . . . well, shaping the evidence to fit the conclusion that was wanted in the first place. Jonathan Haidt in *The Righteous Mind* argues further that 'human flourishing requires social order and embeddedness', which is best obtained by religion, which is the 'handmaiden of groupishness, tribalism and nationalism'. But he also adds that research shows that 'religious people are better neighbours and citizens' not because they pray or read the scriptures or believe in hell ('These beliefs and practices turned out to matter very little') but because they were 'enmeshed' with others of similar religion. Here too religion is conceived of as a psychological phenomenon, not a theological one.

The psychological evidence, however, is really overwhelmed by the much wider picture as described by Norris and Inglehart's sociology. Their conclusion is worth giving in full: 'The critique [of secularization theory] relies too heavily on selected anomalies [and ignores some striking oddities]. And focuses too heavily on the United States (which happens to be a striking deviant case) rather than comparing systematic evidence across a broad range of rich and poor societies . . . Philosophers and theologians have sought to probe into the meaning and purpose of life since the dawn of history; but for the great majority of the population, who lived at the margin of subsistence, the need for reassurance and a sense of certainty was the main function of religion.'[19]

Point one in the argument of this book, then, is that although for some people in the early twenty-first century 'God is back!', the actual situation is rather more complex and considerably more fraught than that simple statement suggests. Contrary to what many religious people would like to believe is happening, that atheism is in retreat, is not true either, at least in the developed world.

At the same time, for many people Charles Taylor had a point when in his 2008 book *A Secular Age* he wrote that modernity involves in some sense a 'subtraction story', a loss or narrowing of experience, a 'disenchantment' with the world that 'leaves us with a universe that is dull, routine, flat, driven by rules rather than thoughts, a process that culminates in bureaucracy run by "specialists without spirit, hedonists without heart"', that atheists lead impoverished lives that are somehow less 'full' than the lives of believers, that atheists 'yearn' for something more than can be provided by the self-sufficient power of reason, and that they are blind and deaf to the miraculous moments when 'God breaks in', in the works of Dante or Bach, or Chartres Cathedral, say.[20]

Many atheists would dismiss Taylor out of hand, but he is not entirely alone in this, either. Here is another raft of books published since the millennium: Luc Ferry, *Man Made God: The Meaning of Life* (2002), John Cottingham, *On the Meaning of Life* (2003), Julian Baggini, *What's It All About? Philosophy and the Meaning of Life* (2004), Richard Holloway, *Looking in the Distance: The Human Search for Meaning* (2004), Roy F. Baumeister, *The Cultural Animal: Human Nature, Meaning and Social Life* (2005), John F. Haught, *Is Nature Enough? Meaning and Truth in the Age of Science* (2006), Terry Eagleton, *The Meaning of Life* (2007), Owen J. Flanagan, *The Really Hard Problem: Meaning in a Material World* (2007), Claire Colebrook, *Deleuze and the Meaning of Life* (2010).

Now, at one stage such a phrase as 'the meaning of life' could have been used only in an ironical or jokey way. Its serious use would have been seen as embarrassing. The 1983 Monty Python film, *The Meaning of Life* had several answers, including 'be kind to fish', 'wear more hats' and 'avoid eating fat'. But 'the meaning of life' is no longer an embarrassing subject, it would seem, in the twenty-first century.

Why should that be? Could it be that Taylor has at least part of a point, in that many of the ways of thought conceived over the past 130 years have proved not to have all the answers? Certainly, many ideologies and 'isms' of the modern world have either collapsed or become dead-ends: imperialism, nationalism, socialism, Marxism, communism, Stalinism, fascism, Maoism, materialism, behaviourism, apartheid. Most recently, with the 'credit crunch' of 2008 and its turbulent wake, even capitalism has come under the spotlight.

'The Things We Have Are Devalued by the Things We Want Next'

The impact of the credit crunch was much more than economic. Writing in *The* [London] *Times*, the author Jeanette Winterson argued that the 'so-called civilized West, at its most materialistic, has failed to deliver the goods . . . we are in a terrible mess'; 'the way out' is through art, she concluded. In a later article in the same newspaper she wrote: 'We have created a society without values, that believes in nothing.' Other aspects of the crisis were highlighted, again in *The Times*, which reported that a survey of Faithbook – a new multi-faith page on Facebook – showed that 71 per cent of those surveyed thought that we are today in a 'spiritual recession' and that that is more worrying than the material recession. (Another survey showed there had been a 27 per cent increase in praying since the credit crunch began, yet more evidence of religious behaviour having to do with existential insecurity.) In November 2008 it was reported that in Britain more people believe in aliens and ghosts than believe in God: of the three thousand surveyed (not a small sample), 58 per cent believed in supernatural entities against 54 per cent who believed in God.* The subscribers to Faithbook hold that 'any faith is better than none'.

Despite some of the cathedrals of capitalism having gone under, or been rescued by nationalization or government bailouts, capitalism hasn't yet, in 2014, collapsed. It certainly got a fright, and is still in intensive care, but its obituary hasn't yet been published. More to the point, all this has provoked, and will continue to provoke, a change of attitude, or perspective: we now appear to be entering a more serious, more reflective time when, as a result of the financial collapse, people are seriously reassessing the values and ideas by which we live. Nigel

---

* Recalling G.K. Chesterton's observation that 'When people stop believing in God, they don't believe in nothing – they believe in anything.'

Biggar, Regius professor of moral and pastoral theology at Oxford, told the *Financial Times* that, having taught many students who went into the City or big law firms, he has observed a recent change. 'I kept in touch with some of them. When they were young, the 24/7 life was stimulating. It became a burden later on when they had a family, but then they were trapped by wealth. I see a move away from that now: more interest in teaching and other forms of public service.'[21]

Several things are conflated here. Religious belief and unbelief are two of them. The failure of science to engage the enthusiasm of many is another. And the psychological dimension is yet another, in which the chief objects of attention have been happiness and loneliness, different sides of the same coin when it comes to fulfilment.

A survey published in Britain in 2008 showed that people across the country were 'increasingly lonely', and that the predicament had been accelerating in the previous decade. The increase in loneliness had started, the survey reported, in the late 1960s, when neighbourhoods had been progressively weakened by increased rates of divorce, immigration, the need to move house for job-related reasons, and the growth of transitory student populations (British universities have increased since 1963 from twenty-three to more than a hundred). Thomas Dumm's *Loneliness as a Way of Life* (2008) characterizes America as the archetypal lonely society of the future, typified by a 'possessive individualism' in which 'personal choice' is a cloak rather than an opportunity.[22]

Happiness, touched on a few pages back, has received, perhaps inevitably, even more attention. Confining ourselves only to twenty-first-century sources, there has been a wave of books exploring happiness – how to achieve it, its links to the latest brain science, what gets in the way of it, how it varies around the world, why women are (in general) less happy than men.

One well publicized finding is that although the developed Western nations have become better off in a financial and material sense, they are not any happier than they were decades ago. In fact, in *The Age of Absurdity: Why Modern Life Makes It Hard to Be Happy* (2010), Michael Foley argues that modern life has made things worse, 'deepening our cravings and at the same time heightening our delusions of importance as individuals. Not only are we rabid in our unsustainable demands for gourmet living, eternal youth, fame and a hundred varieties of sex, we have been encouraged – by a post-1970s "rights" culture that has created a zero-tolerance sensitivity to any perceived inequality, slight or grievance – into believing that to want something is to deserve it.'[23] Moreover, 'the things we have are devalued by the things we want next' – another consequence of capitalism.

On the other hand the latest World Values Survey, published in August 2008, found that over the past twenty-five years, in forty-five out of fifty-two countries where polling took place, happiness *had* risen. But the research also showed that economic growth boosts happiness noticeably only in countries with per capita GDP of less than $12,000. Happiness had fallen in India, China, Australia, Belarus, Hungary, Chile, Switzerland (Switzerland!) and Serbia. Happiness appeared more related to democratization, greater variety and opportunities in the workplace, access to travel and the opportunity to express oneself. Other research showed that individualistic nations, especially in the West, 'were particularly susceptible to negative emotions', whereas Asian or Latin American countries were less so 'because they consider their individual feelings less important than the collective good'.[24]

Let us be honest. These are all fascinating findings, and many of them are salutary and worrying in equal measure. But they are also contradictory and paradoxical. In America it is the churchgoers who are happiest, but worldwide it is those who are existentially insecure (and therefore extremely unlikely to be happy) who most attend church; religion is associated in America with less criminality, but worldwide with more; in America attendance at church boosts income, but worldwide a rise in income fails to increase happiness and it is the poorest who most attend church. Peter Berger says we are as furiously religious as ever but the members of Faithbook think we are in a spiritual recession; Peter Berger says it is the absence of transcendence that people miss but the World Values Survey shows that it is instead the absence of bread, water, decent medication and jobs that people miss, and which leads them to religion.

Despite the contradictions in these findings, amid the atavistic, violent and absurdly incoherent nature of many recent religious manifestations, and although the sociological explanations for both religious and non-religious orientations seem – rationally and convincingly – to outweigh theological ones, it is clear that many religious souls refuse to accept such a state of affairs.

Charles Taylor and the other authors referred to above lead the way in arguing that atheists suffer impoverished lives. But the Norris–Inglehart survey indicates that once existential insecurity is relieved, faith disappears. This sociological transformation is still occurring – it is even beginning to occur in the United States. A Pew Research Center poll published in 2012 reveals that the number in the US with no religious affiliation has risen from 16 per cent in 2008 to 20 per cent four years later. Church attendance has dropped from around 40 per cent in 1965 to under 30 per cent now.[25]

One book cannot hope to have much of an impact when set against the absurd, tragic and horrific dimensions of recent religious history, but this one at least aims to offer something that hasn't, to my knowledge, been done before. It aims to be an extensive survey of the work of those talented people – artists, novelists, dramatists, poets, scientists, psychologists, philosophers – who have embraced atheism, the death of God, and have sought other ways to live, who have discovered or fashioned other forms of meaning in the world, other ways to overcome the great 'subtraction', the dreadful impoverishment that so many appear to think is the inevitable consequence of losing the idea of supernatural transcendence.

I hope to show that such an eventuality is far from inevitable. In fact, when you look at our recent history you encounter quite a lot of surprises in the works of luminaries you thought you knew; you make some unusual (and revealing) juxtapositions, and you discover that the search for other ways to live has been one of the core components – part of the DNA, to use a modern metaphor – of modern culture. You also realize that, far from atheists leading less than full lives, neither God nor the Devil has all the best tunes – and that this book, instead of being called *The Age of Nothing*, could have been called *The Age of Everything*.

One more point, but an important one. Is Nietzsche to blame for our current predicament? Why is it that his intervention has caught our attention above all others? And what does that tell us?

The Phenomenon that was Nietzsche

Towards the end of March 1883 Friedrich Nietzsche, then aged thirty-nine and staying in Genoa, was far from well. He had recently returned from Switzerland to his old lodgings on the Salita delle Battistine but this brought no immediate relief from his migraines, stomach troubles and insomnia. Already upset (but also relieved) by the death the previous month of his erstwhile great friend the composer Richard Wagner, with whom he had fallen out, he came down with a severe attack of influenza for which the Genoese doctor prescribed daily doses of quinine. Unusually, a heavy snowfall had blanketed the city, accompanied by 'incongruous thunderclaps and flashes of lightning', and this too seems to have affected his mood and hindered his recovery. Unable to take the stimulating walks that were part of his routine, and helped his thinking, by the 22nd of the month he was still listless and bedridden.[26]

What added to his 'black melancholy', as he put it, was that it was four weeks since he had sent his latest manuscript to his publisher Ernst Schmeitzner in Chemnitz, who seemed in no hurry to bring out this new book, entitled *Thus Spake Zarathustra*. He sent Schmeitzner a furious letter of reproach, which brought an apologetic reply, but a month later Nietzsche learned the real reason for the delay. As he said in a letter: 'The Leipzig printer, Teubner, has shoved the *Zarathustra* manuscript aside in order to meet a rush order for 500,000 hymnals, which had to be delivered in time for Easter.' This rich irony was not lost on Nietzsche, of course. 'The realization that his fearless Zarathustra, the "madman" who had the nerve to proclaim to the somnambulists around him that "God is dead!", should have been momentarily smothered beneath the collective weight of 500,000 Christian hymnbooks struck Nietzsche as downright "comic".'[27]

The response of the first readers of the work was mixed. Heinrich

Köselitz, Nietzsche's friend, who by long tradition was sent the proofs to read and correct, was rapturous, and he expressed the hope that 'this extraordinary book' would one day be as widely distributed as the Bible. Very different was the reaction of the typesetters in Leipzig, who were so frightened by what they read that they considered refusing to produce the book.

The world has never forgotten – and some have never forgiven – Nietzsche for saying 'God is dead', and then going on to add that 'we have killed him'. He had actually said that before, in *The Gay Science* published the previous year, but the pithy style of *Zarathustra* attracted much more attention.

What *is* it with Nietzsche? Why is it *his* phrase above all others that has been remembered and has stuck? After all, belief in God had been declining for some time. For some, perhaps even many, belief in God – or gods, supernatural entities of any kind – had never seemed right. In most histories of unbelief, or doubt, the account begins in the eighteenth century with Edward Gibbon and David Hume, moving through Voltaire and the French Revolution, taking in Kant, Hegel and the Romantics, German biblical criticism, Auguste Comte and the 'positivist breakthrough'. In the mid-nineteenth century came Ludwig Feuerbach and Karl Marx, Søren Kierkegaard, Arthur Schopenhauer; and the ravages of geological and biological science brought about by Charles Lyell, Robert Owen, Robert Chambers, Herbert Spencer, and above all Charles Darwin.

These accounts, as often as not, add for good measure stories of celebrated individuals who lost their faith – George Eliot, Leslie Stephen, Edmund Gosse. And those who didn't, but who heard the signals, among them Matthew Arnold who, in the decade following Darwin's *Origin*, lamented in his poem *Dover Beach* 'the melancholy, long, withdrawing roar' of the sea of faith. Other accounts stress the sheer antiquity of unbelief, and here the cast includes Epicurus and Lucretius, Socrates and Cicero, Al-Rawandi and Rabelais. Here is not the place to rehearse these narratives. Our concern will be with the timing and the circumstances which culminated in Nietzsche's notably bold proclamation (albeit, we should always remember, one made by a madman).

The Whiff of Danger and the Cargo of Life

One of those circumstances was Nietzsche himself. He was a thoroughly unusual man – quixotic, contradictory, a young meteor who shone with an incandescent writing style but who burned out quickly and went mad at the age of forty-five. His aphoristic style lent itself to easy assimilation, by the public as well as by other philosophers, and was designed to be provocative and incendiary, succeeding only too well as the reservations of those typesetters in Leipzig show. His madness, too, added a colourful salting to his biography, and to the biography of his ideas after his death in 1900. Were his extreme views 'the uninterrupted consequence of his reason', or were they flavoured (distorted?) by his illness, an affliction that has grown more – not less – notorious since his death, as it has become clear that he was suffering from syphilis?

The uses to which his ideas have been put, or are said to have been put, since his death, are also a source of continuing notoriety. Nietzsche's concept of nihilism caught the imagination of the world, one of its consequences being that he is the only person whose ideas, as Steven Aschheim points out, have been blamed for two world wars. This is a burdensome – and enduring – legacy.

His core insight – and the most dangerous – was that there does not exist any perspective external to or higher than life itself. There cannot exist any privileged viewpoint, any abstraction or force outside the world as we know it; there is nothing beyond reality, beyond life itself, nothing 'above'; there is no transcendence, nothing metaphysical. As a result, we can make no judgement on existence that is universally valid or 'objective': 'the value of life cannot be assessed'. As Nietzsche famously insisted, 'There are no facts, only interpretations.'[28]

From this, certain things follow. We are solely the product of historical forces. Contrary to what the scientists say, the world is a chaos of multiple forces and drives 'whose infinite and chaotic multiplicity cannot be reduced to unity'.[29] We must learn to situate ourselves in this multiplicity and chaos and the way we do so is via the 'will to power', by which we seek to gain control over inanimate nature. Our history, especially that of the great religions, Christianity in particular,

us a 'hidden prejudice' in favour of the 'beyond' at the ex-
the 'here and now', and this must be changed. This very
eans that much of our activity will be in *refuting* what has
gone before, a task made no easier by the competing forces within us,
a jostling, which is our natural state and requires us to be spirited in
making sense out of this jostling.[30]

Importantly, Nietzsche tells us that this struggle to achieve mastery
over the chaos that is both outside and inside us – the 'cargo of life' –
leads to a more *intense* form of existence, and it is the only aim we can
have in life, in *this* life here and now. Our ethical stance should be to
achieve this intensity at whatever cost: our only duty is to ourselves.[31]

The role of reason in our lives is to enable us to realize that many of
our urges are irrational, and no less powerful or valuable for that: we
must harness them, and unlock them intelligently, so that they do not
continue to thwart one another. This rationalization of the passions in
our life he defines as the spiritual quality of existence. We should seek
harmony, but we should recognize that some passions are not what the
traditional religions have approved of. For example, enmity is one of
the passions; it should be accepted and lived with as much as any of
the others.[32]

All this naturally affected Nietzsche's idea of salvation. Salvation,
he holds, cannot apply to some ideal 'beyond' the here and now. 'God
becomes the formula for every slander upon the "here and now", and
for every lie about the "hereafter".' And he goes so far as to propose
putting what he called the 'doctrine of eternal recurrence' in the place
of 'metaphysics' and 'religion'. This was his idea that salvation cannot
be other than resolutely *earthly*, 'sewn into the tissue of forces that are
the fabric of life'. The doctrine of eternal recurrence reads that you
must live your life in such a way that you would wish to live it again.
'All joy wants eternity,' he says, and is the criterion for deciding which
moments in a life are worth living and which are not. 'The good life is
that which succeeds in existing for the moment, without reference to
past or future, without condemnation or selection, in a state of absolute lightness, and in the finished conviction that there is no difference
therefore between the instant and eternity.'

We must make a 'Dionysiac affirmation', 'stand in a Dionysian relationship to existence', 'select to live only those instants that we would be willing to live with over and over again, in infinite recession'. In this way we will be saved – saved from fear.

In Nietzsche's new world, without a beyond or a hereafter, life has no purpose other than to live in the grand style, using the will to power to achieve an intensity of experience such that we would like those intense moments to go on and on and on.

All this was as heady as it was dangerous, and a lot is lost in translation, for Nietzsche was a superb stylist of the German language. That language, that style, go some way towards explaining why the world of 1882 picked up on his aphorism – that God is dead – so quickly and so wholeheartedly, even enthusiastically. But it was not the whole picture.

Doubt's Bid for a Better World

A.N. Wilson calls doubt 'the Victorian disease' and Jennifer Michael Hecht, in her history of doubt, says the period 1800–1900 was 'easily the best-documented moment of widespread doubt in human history'. It was, she says, the century of 'doubt's bid for a better world'. 'The best-educated doubters felt that the time for doubting religion was over: it was time to start building something in which one could truly believe, a happy new world. They guessed that it would be a better world because the money and energy once given to religion would be devoted to generating food, clothing, medicine, and ideas. They also thought that they might see farther than ever before, now that their vision was mended.'[33]

Owen Chadwick, who was Regius professor of modern history at Cambridge and one-time President of the British Academy, proposed in his Gifford lectures and subsequently in *The Secularization of Europe in the Nineteenth Century* (1975) that doubt's bid for a better world involved two parallel processes – a social process and an intellectual one. There were, as he put it, two kinds of 'unsettlement' occurring throughout the nineteenth century, 'unsettlement in society, mainly due to new machines, growth of big cities, the massive transfer of populations; and unsettlement in minds, rising out of a heap of new knowledge in science and history, and out of the consequent argument'. And perhaps more important, the two unsettlements merged easily. The crucial twenty years when this 'merger' took place, he pointed out, were 1860–80, exactly the time leading up to Nietzsche's publication of *Zarathustra*.

The Unfitness of Faith and Science

It is important to conclude this Introduction with four qualifications. First, that if we look around, and read our histories of the long twentieth century, we find that by no means everyone has or has had this apocalyptic fear of the death of God, as epitomized by, say, Dostoevsky. In 1980, James Thrower published an account of what he called 'the alternative tradition', the rejection of religious explanations in the ancient world. The German sociologist Wilhelm Dilthey said that everyone has a 'metaphysical impulse', in that we all have within us a theory, however inchoate or incoherent, about the world and our place in it, and about what metaphysical forces may or may not exist. But it would be wrong to say that *everyone* is troubled by the problems that vexed Dostoevsky and Nietzsche so much. Many people *are* troubled by these issues, and troubled deeply, but by no means everyone.[34]

Second, Callum Brown has recently given us a new narrative of secularization. In *The Death of Christian Britain: Understanding Secularisation 1800–2000* (2001) he introduces the notion of 'discursive Christianity', a form of religious identity not captured by the usual sociological categories. Discursive Christianity shapes an individual's personal identity, their private – even secret – selves, which influence morality, personal behaviour (such as saying grace before meals), speech and dress, expectations, the sort of subtle behaviour captured in oral histories. Brown argues that Britain remained a Christian nation until the 1960s, when it collapsed spectacularly, to become thoroughly irreligious. People did not turn to other forms of belief; rather, they stopped regarding themselves as religious.

Brown's statistics are impressive but a number of comments may be made. First, something similar was observed in the United States in the Pew survey report mentioned earlier: there, current religious faith was described as 'mushier' than in the past. Either way, these results flatly contradict the claims of those who argue that 'God is back'. No less important from our point of view, they do not affect this book's argument. Whatever the exact trajectory of secularization, of the collapse of belief in God, the individuals discussed within these pages clearly felt – and feel – that God is indeed dead.

Third, Brown's view overlaps to an extent with the theory of the French analyst Olivier Roy, who in *Holy Ignorance: When Religion and Culture Part Ways* (2010) argues that a parallel process has been recently taking place alongside secularization. Thanks to globalization, religions have become divorced from their cultural homelands – 'deterritorialized'. Christianity is no longer exclusive to Europe and the Middle East, Hinduism in India, or Islam in the desert heartlands, but all are now more or less worldwide.

Consequently, the cultural attributes that once formed an integral part of religious identity and practices have less and less place. Arabs will refer to 'Muslim culture', for example, by which they mean family-related attitudes and practices, segregation of the sexes, modesty, food habits and so on, whereas by 'Islamic culture' is meant art, architecture, the practices of urban life. In order to circulate in a global context, a religious entity must appear universal; for the message to be fully grasped, it must be disconnected from a specific culture as traditionally understood. 'Religion therefore circulates outside knowledge. Salvation does not require people to know, but to believe.' As a result, as they have become 'de-ethnicized', religions have become 'purer', more ideological and, therefore, at the same time, more fundamental. They are, in a very real sense, based more on ignorance than knowledge, Roy says, and, to that extent, and in reply to what Charles Taylor says about secular lives, these religions are thinner.[36]

These various strands come together to show why Nietzsche was the phenomenon he was, why his remarks about the death of God ricocheted around Europe in particular so resoundingly, and why what he said is still so potent today. Although there had always been *some* people who didn't believe in God, and although Doubt with a capital 'D' had been growing since the middle of the eighteenth century, it was only in the 1880s that, again as Owen Chadwick put it, the 'great historical revolution in the human intelligence' became clear to all who took an interest in these matters, and that the act of faith was no longer seen 'to fit the experience of men'. Since then, whatever the adherents of the God-is-back thesis may say, people have continued to lose faith, and religion is evolving in ways that increasingly suggest a rearguard action.

Which leaves us with one issue, the fourth qualification, which is no less important. This is that science, for all its great reputation as the institution that has the capability to acquire all kinds of truth, and despite its undoubted successes, has nonetheless left behind a widespread 'sadness that [it] is not fitted to offer truths about the moral being *and that therefore . . . perhaps truths about the moral being are not to be obtained*'.[37]

However many people have faced up to the fact that we are now living in a world without God, and are troubled by it, just as many have found science wanting as a source of life's meaning. The intertwined nature of these two elements has been in general overlooked, but the link is inescapable, as we shall see, time and again, and has been critical in determining how we have tried to live our lives since Nietzsche wrote what he wrote.

PART ONE

The Avant-Guerre:
When Art Mattered

1

The Nietzsche Generation:
Ecstasy, Eros, Excess

The greatest irony of Nietzsche's life – far greater than *Zarathustra* being held up at the printers by 500,000 hymnals – was surely the fact that he exploded onto the intellectual and cultural scene when he was already insane, catatonic, and knew nothing about what was occurring. It was only in the 1890s that he came to the attention of significantly large audiences.[1] Until that point, he had not been without influence – Steven Aschheim tells us that both Gustav Mahler and Viktor Adler were inspired by Nietzsche, perhaps as early as 1875–8. But this influence was piecemeal and it was not until the 1890s that some sort of 'confrontation' with Nietzsche became virtually obligatory.

His fame spread internationally very quickly, but of course the concern with his ideas was more intense in Germany than elsewhere. Every would-be academic or intellectual was expected to have a 'position' on Nietzsche, or the 'Nietzsche problem' as it was referred to, and among the middle classes in Germany, Nietzsche evenings became commonplace – social gatherings accompanied by music and spoken texts.[2]

As mentioned in the Introduction, part of Nietzsche's appeal lay in the lyrical power of his language, but it wasn't only that. The Germans, many of them, were proud of Nietzsche: he had German roots and was addressing what many people thought were specifically German problems. His opponents stressed his 'Slavic' way of thinking and played down his *Deutschtum*, his Germanness.

Hard Wisdom

Throughout the nineteenth century there had been endless arguments about what actually was and was not German (its borders did keep changing), and Nietzsche was press-ganged into this debate. During the 1890s and thereafter more and more people began to adapt his Germanness and the Nietzsche–German relationship into an ideology. By this account, Germanness was an exclusive precondition for truly understanding him and what he was saying. Here, for example, is Oswald Spengler on Nietzsche: 'Goethe's life was a full life, and that means it brought something to completion. Countless Germans will honor Goethe, live with him, and seek his support; but he can never transform them. Nietzsche's effect is a transformation, for the melody of his vision did not end with his death ... His work is not a part of our past to be enjoyed; it is a task that makes servants of us all ... In an age that does not tolerate otherworldly ideals ... when the only thing of recognizable value is the kind of ruthless action that Nietzsche baptized with the name of Cesare Borgia – in such an age, unless we learn to act as real history wants us to act, we will cease to exist as a people. We cannot live without a form that does not merely console in difficult situations, but helps one get out of them. This kind of hard wisdom made its first appearance in German thought with Nietzsche.'[3]

Carl Jung was no less impressed. He viewed Nietzsche as a development beyond Protestantism, just as Protestantism was itself an outgrowth beyond Catholicism. Nietzsche's idea of the Superman was, he believed, 'the thing in man that takes the place of the God'.[4]

Notwithstanding the enthusiasm of these and other luminaries, it was the youth and avant-garde of the 1890s who made up the bulk of Nietzsche's followers. This had a lot to do with the state of the Kaiserreich, which was perceived then to be both spiritually and politically mediocre. To these people Nietzsche was seen as a pivotal, turn-of-the-century figure, 'a man whose stature was comparable only to Buddha, Zarathustra or Jesus Christ'.[5] Even his madness was endowed by supporters with a spiritual quality. For here was Nietzsche like the madman in his own story, someone who had been driven crazy by his vision and the alienation of a society not yet able to comprehend him. The German Expressionists had a fascination with madness for its allegedly liberating qualities, as they did for all extreme forms of life, and they identified Nietzsche as both a spokesman and an exemplar. Opponents dismissed him, quite wrongly as it turned out, as a 'degenerate' who would 'rave for a season, and then perish'.[6]

Despite the divisions he aroused, his popularity grew. Novels and plays tried to capture and dramatize his already dramatic ideas. People all over Europe started to have 'intoxicating' Zarathustra experiences. Le Corbusier had a *Zarathustra-Erlebnis* (a Zarathustra 'experience' or 'insight') in 1908. Nietzschean concepts like the *will to power* and *Übermensch* entered the vocabulary.[7] Richard Strauss's tone poem *Also Sprach Zarathustra* was premiered in Frankfurt-am-Main in November 1896, the most famous but not the only major artwork stimulated by Nietzsche – Mahler's *Third Symphony* was another, originally entitled *The Gay Science*.

The glossy illustrated magazine *Pan* featured Nietzschean poems in his honour but also printed drawings and sculptures of him, seemingly whenever they got the chance. Between 1890 and 1914 his portrait was everywhere, his bushy moustache becoming a widespread visual symbol, making his face as famous as his aphorisms. From the mid-1890s, encouraged by the Nietzsche archives (under the control of his sister), 'Nietzsche-cult products' were made available in generous amounts, a move that would certainly have maddened him had he been capable of such feelings. Hermann Hesse was just one well known writer who had two images of Nietzsche on his study wall in Tübingen. His face was also a popular device on bookplates, one image showing him as a latter-day Christ, with a crown of thorns. The working-class press appropriated his image as a familiar and succinct way to mock the capitalist commercialization of culture.[8]

Some even adopted what they called Nietzschean 'lifestyles', the most striking example being the designer/architect Peter Behrens. Behrens designed his own 'Zarathustrian' villa as a centrepiece of the experimental Darmstadt artists' colony. The house was adorned with symbols such as the eagle, and Zarathustra's diamond, which radiated 'the virtues of a world that is not yet here'. Behrens surpassed even this in the German pavilion he designed for the Turin 1902 Exposition. In a surreal cavern light flooded the interior in which the industrial might of the Second Reich was on display. Zarathustra, cited explicitly, progresses towards the light.[9]

Bruno Taut (1880–1938), an Expressionist architect, became a prominent exponent of a cult of mountains that emerged and was associated with Nietzsche. Taut's 'Alpine Architecture' attempted to envision an entire chain of mountains transformed into 'landscapes of Grail-shrines and crystal-lined caves', so that, in the end, whole continents would be covered with 'glass and precious stones in the form of "ray-domes" and "sparkling palaces"'.[10]

Nietzschean Kitsch

In a similar vein was the Zarathustrian cult of *Bergeinsamkeit*, 'the longing to escape the crowded cities and to feel the pristine mountain air'. Giovanni Segantini, a painter and another enthusiastic Nietzschean, specialized in views of the Engadine, the mountain region that inspired Nietzsche when he was writing *Thus Spoke Zarathustra*. So popular did his work prove that pilgrims and tourists flocked to these mountains: 'The *Einsamkeitserlebnis* – the experience of being alone – was transformed into a mass business!' The flourishing of a Nietzschean kitsch industry, which would have horrified Nietzsche himself, was another ironic indication of his popularity among the 'philistines'. Paul Friedrich's play *The Third Reich* was one of several that put Zarathustra on stage, in this case clad in a silver and gold costume and a purple coat, a golden ribbon in his blond hair and a leopardskin flung insouciantly over his shoulder. At times people worried that the Nietzsche cult was outdoing Nietzsche himself. In 1893 Max Nordau wrote about the 'Nietzsche Jugend' – the Nietzsche youth – as if they were an identifiable group.[11]

As time went by it became increasingly clear that Germany – and to a lesser extent the rest of Europe – was now populated by Nietzsche generations – in the plural. Thomas Mann was one who recognized this: 'We who were born around 1870 are too close to Nietzsche, we participate too directly in his tragedy, his personal fate (perhaps the most terrible, most awe-inspiring fate in intellectual history). Our Nietzsche is Nietzsche militant. Nietzsche triumphant belongs to those born fifteen years after us. We have from him our psychological sensitivity, our lyrical criticism, the experience of Wagner, the experience of Christianity, the experience of "modernity" – experiences from which we shall never completely break free . . . They are too precious for that, too profound, too fruitful.'[12]

Nietzsche was in particular looked upon as a new type of challenge, paradoxically akin to the forces of socialism, a modern 'seducer', whose advocacy was even more persuasive than the 'odious equalizing of social democracy'. Georg Tantzscher thought Nietzscheanism fitted neatly the needs of the free-floating intelligentsia, trapped as they were 'between isolation and a sense of mission, the drive to withdraw from society and the drive to lead it'. In his 1897 book on the Nietzsche cult, the sociologist Ferdinand Tönnies accused Nietzscheanism of being 'pseudo-liberational'. People, he said, 'were captivated by the promise of the release of creative powers, the appeal to overcome narrow-minded authority and conventional opinions, and free self-expression'. But he condemned Nietzscheanism as superficial, serving elitist, conservative and 'laissez-faire functions' that went quite against the social-democratic spirit of the age.

A little later, in 1908, in *The Nietzsche Cult: A Chapter in the History of Aberrations of the Human Spirit*, the philosopher Wolfgang Becker also appeared puzzled that so many 'cultured luminaries' were attracted to the Nietzschean message, but he agreed with Mann that it meant different things to different people. To the young, Nietzsche's analysis seemed 'deep'; but the German colonial officials in Africa employed his *Herrenmoral* ideal practically every day, as they felt it was suited perfectly to 'the colonial mode of rule'.[13]

The sociologist and philosopher Georg Simmel also took his colour from Nietzsche. His central concept, *Vornehmheit*, the ideal of 'distinction', owed everything to Nietzsche. Simmel looked upon *Vornehmheit* as the defining quality by which individuals 'could be separated from the crowd and endowed with "nobility"'. For Simmel this was a new ideal stemming from the dilemma of how to create personal values in a money economy. Nietzsche had encouraged the pursuit of specific values – *Vornehmheit*, beauty, strength – each of which he said enhanced life and which, 'far from encouraging egoism, demanded greater self-control'.[14]

Marxists thought that Nietzscheanism nakedly served capitalism, imperialism, and afterwards fascism, and that Nietzscheans were no more than the ultimate in bourgeois pseudo-radicalism, never touching on the underlying exploitation, and leaving the socioeconomic class structure intact.

People liked to observe the irony that Nietzsche was dead long before God, but Aschheim maintains that he was simply 'unburiable'. 'Nietzsche was not a piece of learning,' wrote Franz Servis in 1895, 'but a part of life, "the reddest blood of our time". He has not died: "Oh, we shall still all have to drink of his blood! Not one of us will be spared that."'[15] As this book will show, he was right.

Even the choice of Weimar as the location of the Nietzsche archive was intended to emulate – if not surpass – the similar shrine of that other self-styled protector of German spirituality, at Bayreuth. Nietzsche's sister Elizabeth Förster-Nietzsche and her colleagues played a deliberate role in the monumentalization and mythologizing of the philosopher. The place 'was no mere archive but a house of creative powers'. For example, his sister sought to create an 'authorized' Nietzsche, her main object being to 'depathologize' her brother, and in so doing remove the subversive from his ideas making him – as she thought – 'respectable'.

The most grandiose and monumental of plans – much more so than the archive – came from the more enlightened and cosmopolitan adherents. In 1911, for instance, Harry Graf Kessler, the Anglo-German patron of the arts and author of *Berlin in Lights*, envisaged building a huge festival area as a memorial, comprising a temple, a large stadium and an enormous sculpture of Apollo. In this space, intended to hold thousands, art, dance, theatre and sports competitions would be combined into a 'Nietzschean totality'. Aristide Maillol agreed to build the statue, using none other than Vaslav Nijinsky as the model. André Gide, Anatole France, Walther Rathenau, Gabriele d'Annunzio, Gilbert Murray and H.G. Wells joined the fund-raising committee. The project failed only when Elizabeth Förster-Nietzsche withdrew her support in 1913.[16]

Until the First World War, Nietzsche exerted a wide influence on the arts. However, the Great War, as we shall see, totally changed public attitudes to Nietzsche and the impact of his ideas.

Probably, Nietzsche's most explosive and enduring impact was on the intellectual, artistic and literary avant-garde – his invitation 'to *be* something new, to *signify* something new, to *represent* new values' was emblematic of what Steven Aschheim also calls the 'Nietzschean· generation'. Nietzsche gave point to the avant-garde's alienation from the high culture of the establishment.[17] The two forces he favoured were radical, secular self-creation and the Dionysian imperative of self-submersion. This led to several attempts to fuse the individual-istic impulse within a search for new forms of 'total' community, the redemptive community, a theme that recurs throughout this book.[18]

While Nietzsche's identification of the nihilist predicament was a starting point, people swiftly moved on. They sought a transformed civilization that encouraged and reflected a new *übermenschlich* type, creating excitement, authenticity, intensity, and in all ways superior to what had gone before. 'What I was engaged in,' recalled Ernst Blass, the Expressionist poet, referring to café life in imperial Berlin, was 'a war on the gigantic philistinism of those days . . . What was in the air? Above all Van Gogh, Nietzsche, Freud too, and Wedekind. What was wanted was a post-rational Dionysos.'[19]

Freud and Nietzsche had in common that both sought to remove the metaphysical explanation of experience, and both stressed 'self-creation' as the central meaningful activity of life. While Freud strained for respectability, Nietzscheanism revelled in notoriety, but in most ways they were compatible, being stridently anti-scientific and anti-rationalist; and, with its Dionysian rhetoric, the artistic production of the Nietzscheans sought to unlock the wild reaches of the uncon-scious. *Übermensch* strongmen feature prominently in the novels of Gabriele d'Annunzio and Hermann Conradi, where the characters are involved in often brutal searches for innocence and authenticity, as often as not destroying in order to create.[20]

All Are Equal in Regard to Instinct

More than one critic has remarked on the general mood, in the wake of Nietzsche, as being in some ways not unlike that among the 'counterculture' of the 1960s and 70s (see chapter 22). Martin Green, in his book on the Nietzsche generation, concentrates on one noteworthy home, located in the small Swiss village of Ascona. There, a remarkable number of feminists, pacifists, literary figures, anarchists, modern dancers and Surrealists came together to consolidate their radical ideas and initiate certain 'life-experiments'. Green says Ascona was part-Tolstoyan and part-anarchist, with a decidedly naturalist – at times occult – orientation. Among the better-known luminaries who passed through were D.H. Lawrence, Franz Kafka, Carl Gustav Jung and Hermann Hesse.

Nietzscheanism was a pervasive presence, not so much the 'will-to-power' form of Nietzscheanism but the Dionysian kind, where the aim is ecstatic dynamism. 'They sought to create beauty in motion and to affirm life-creating values – above all that of eros. This found its most dynamic physical expression in the idea and development of modern dance.'[21]

Ascona had all the elements of the counterculture that would develop later, mainly in America. Adherents sought intensity through an erotic freedom, which included nudity, sometimes orgies, and at other times embraced a cult of masculinity. There was vegetarianism, sun worship, occultism, black magic, mysticism and Satanism, and a cult of festivals. What united these groupings was a belief in the irrational and in instinct, one unifying idea being that 'all men are equal in regards to instinct'. By the same token, the worship of nature that was so popular in Ascona was practised there because nature worship was understood as meaning 'the worship of the nature to be found in human beings as much as in the nature of animals, plants, the soil, the sea, the sun'. That, says Green, is the Asconan form of piety, 'whether peaceful or ecstatic'.[22]

However, the most important – and best-established – elements of the Asconan idea were its withdrawal from city life in an effort to establish a 'new human type', a post-Christian secular type who expressed a full humanity, together with 'vagabondage' and dance.

A New Human Type: The Vagabond and the Dance

The adoption of Ascona began around the turn of the century when Gusto Gräser, known to history primarily as a vagabond, took part in a meeting in Munich at which seven young people like him decided to withdraw from the world of cities and nations to found a community of their own. In the year of 1900 the Western world had mounted spectacular shows of the technological triumphs that had marked the success of the nineteenth century. But Gräser and the others had a distaste for the world of science, technology and modern medicine. Several of them were craftspeople, in wood, metal or leather, and they wandered through Switzerland in the last months of 1900, looking for the right place to settle and form a community of their own. They found what they were looking for in Ascona.

Ascona was then a backward peasant village of about one thousand people, on the Swiss side of Lake Maggiore, in the canton of Ticino. This area never played much of a role in Switzerland's heroic history. Instead, its attractions included the climate, which allows for both pine and palm trees, snowcaps on the nearby mountains and roses on the lakeshore, and a unique variety of other trees including oak, birch, lime and olive. And then there were the local peasants who, for the artists and intellectuals who came to Ascona, were the complete and joyful antithesis of modern mankind in the cities. The population spoke Italian, practised Roman Catholicism, cultivated vineyards, fished and smuggled (it is near the border). The land was poor and cheap, and people were steadily migrating to the cities or to America.

For the next twenty years Gräser lived in this landscape. He was outdoors and moving all the time; he lived off the land; his lifestyle was his work, his creation, and he worked at it by adapting his needs and his appetites to the climate and the caves, to the fruit and the edible leaves. He was a vegetarian who revered life and refused to eat what had been killed. His principles were assertions of freedom, not renunciations, were humanist, not religious, hearty, not pious.[23] Gräser was in and out of jail for his beliefs (anarchist, radical pacificist, 'theoretical nudist') but found support in Hermann Hesse, who in 1918 wrote an essay based on Jungian ideas, called 'Artists and Psychoanalysis', in which he proclaimed that artists like Gräser have special ways – socially privileged ways – to declare their faith: they are exempt from the ordinary obligations.[24]

Workshops were set up, to manufacture handmade objects – from jewellery to furniture – for people who were dissatisfied with mass-produced factory goods.[25] Activities at Ascona were supposed to be carried out not for economic reasons, or for any particular aim – which might spark ambition – but simply for the joy of activity, for maintaining as much as possible a festival spirit. One needed just enough, it was argued, to support one's *minimal* needs, in that way avoiding being sucked into the social system that was the origin of the malaise in the first place.[26] They enthusiastically embraced concepts like 'full humanity', and followed Nietzsche's Zarathustra: 'The world and man are not here to be improved, but to become themselves.' For example, Eugen Diederichs, Hesse's publisher and publisher of the cultural and political magazine *Die Tat* (The Deed), suggested that 'a third and new stage of human development' might be at hand, which would not just bring with it greater freedom but would bring back dignity (the quality Simmel had made so much of).[27] It was observed that Gräser 'may be said' to have created a new human type, which had its influence mainly on youth movements.[28] For Rudolf Laban, 'the whole meaning of life is to foster the growth of the human, of men (as opposed to mere robots)'.[29]

The idea of vagabondage appears to have crystallized with Gräser (it had been known in the East, of course, since at least the time of the Buddha). It profoundly influenced Hesse, who was himself drawn to the vagabond life. One proof of this is the book that was his most popular before *Demian* was published, which was *Knulp* (1915). The story begins in the 1890s. Knulp is an amiable vagabond who lives in a world of play and sensuality. An erotic venture first sets him on the road, and women always fall for him. But Hesse's stress falls on

Knulp's delicacy, good manners, gaiety, lightness of touch. He refuses to tie himself to any trade, place or person.[30]

Ascona was Gräser's home. He was offered a piece of land by villagers who thought he would attract other vagabonds, but he refused the gift, not wanting to own anything. He had a large number of practical skills, being known around Ascona as a 'plumber' or general fixer. His early 'home' was formed by two slabs of rock, with a few boards to lie on. He is credited with creating the headband and poncho which many vagabonds wore; he made his own tunic and his own rope sandals. He often lived on pick-ups and throw-aways and later inhabited a cave decorated with 'bits and pieces', using twigs for hooks and hollow logs as storage containers. At other times he lived in a caravan, travelling with up to eight children and various women. In 1912 he was the guest of a Leipzig group of *Wandervögel*, young wanderers who were part of the *Jugendbewegung* (the German Youth Movement). Some of his poems appeared in the *Wandervogel* magazine. In 1913 Alfred Daniel, a jurist and an enthusiast for Whitman and Tolstoy, met Gräser in Stuttgart and described him as looking like John the Baptist. Fifty or sixty people at a time, he says, would go to see Gräser and his family in their caravan.[31] In 1922, when mass unemployment returned to Germany as a result of the collapse of credit all over the modern world, people began to turn back to vagabondage. Being a vagabond is not easy, if it is to carry you through winter nights. And at that time there were many attempts to link vagabonds (tramps) with the idle, the perverse, and with revolutionaries.

Laban's Dance Farm

Important as Gräser was for being the first singular – but in his way brave – figure to help fashion Ascona into what it would become, and for the distinctive nature of his post-religious ideas and way of life, it was really the impact of Rudolf Laban that was to kick-start the influence that Ascona would have. In Laban's ethic for a modern, post-Christian civilization one can find the same emphases as in Gräser's. Working in Ascona up to 1919 and in various German cities after that, Laban turned the Ascona experiment into a dance art that won an honoured place in European high culture. He had a vision of life as a kind of perpetual festival, the notion that dance would regenerate life as a whole, where the aim was 'collective ecstasy', 'a mode of putting Nietzsche into practice'.[32]

His father was a soldier but also a butcher, 'middle class at best'. But Laban Jr was far from content with such a life and decided to move his dance pupils to Ascona for the summer of 1913. He returned in subsequent summers, and created a 'dance farm' there. The aim was to have his dancers rehearse and perform in contact with nature – within that lake and mountain landscape. His dancers needed nature, he believed, in order to discover, deep inside themselves, 'the authentic dancer spirit'. He found the perfect place for all this on Monte Verità, and from 1913 on he and his troupe were to be seen on those slopes in the summer months, he with his pipes or his drum, and around him the women (and a few men) leaping and writhing and rushing, each 'evoking' her most hidden impulses. What they enjoyed most, and found most fulfilling, was the wild spontaneity.

A second aspect emerged through Laban's aim to create a feminist modern dance in Ascona, and he gathered around himself a remarkable group. It was Laban who would develop what we call modern dance, and he did so there, with the help of Suzanne Perrottet and Mary Wigman.[33] Laban's work aroused great enthusiasm among those who visited Ascona, including George Bernard Shaw.

Before she joined Laban, Suzanne Perrottet had worked with Émile Jaques-Dalcroze, the Swiss composer, who had developed at Hellerau outside Dresden what he called 'eurhythmics', a method of musical education and appreciation through movement. He concentrated on a kind of dance/art that, he maintained, engaged a different side of the personality and took the form of festival plays, *Festspiele*. This was a kind of civic theatre, popular in French Switzerland, using civic themes and performed on civic or patriotic–historical occasions. Perrottet said she learned a great deal from Jaques-Dalcroze, in particular how to 'listen exactly'. 'But at that time I was looking for dissonance, in order to express my character, and that was not possible with his altogether harmonious structure.' For her, Jaques-Dalcroze was not modern enough. She had to go to Laban for dissonance, 'for a way to express my rebelliousness and the stream of the will-to-deny in me; that he instinctively and most wonderfully did'. He told each pupil to find her own middle C, so that they 'sang together as unco-ordinatedly as the birds in the forest'. And the same was true of their physical movements: each had to discover her own way in her own body and her own emotional self. 'And so with Laban one was reborn, in a bodily way too.'[34]

Perrottet was straightforward in her attitude to the new dancing: 'One had everything to create, it was all so wonderful, so riveting, it was a religion for me, this new art.' As Laban explained in a letter, he had two main ideas: 'first to give Dance and the Dancer their proper value as Art and the Artist, and second to enforce the influence of dance education on the warped psyche of our time'. He did not think, at the time, that dancers got the respect other artists got: 'they always get the *verdammte zweideutiger Lächeln*, "that damned ambiguous smirk"'. (He was a fighting man.) But at root, he insisted, 'every artist is a dancer who speaks, with one or other gesture [*Gebärde*] of his body/soul, of that Highest which philosophers, theologians, dreamers, scientists and sociologists think they have appropriated'.[35]

Others did appreciate what he was trying to do. In her book *My Teacher, Laban* (1954) Mary Wigman described him as 'the magician, the priest of an unknown religion . . . lord and master in a dance-born and yet so real kingdom'. Overwrought? So was Nietzsche. Some of this may have had to do with the fact that Wigman was as sensitive to landscape as was Laban. Like him she fell in love with Ascona, where she always returned to charge her batteries. Modern dancers, she liked to say, 'do not belong in a theatre, but outdoors'.[36]

Martin Green goes so far as to claim that Laban was 'an incarnation of modern dance', like a figure from Nietzsche's *Die Geburt der Tragödie*: 'The original image of the Dionysian is the bearded satyr, in him existence expresses itself more truly, really, fully than in the man of culture . . . and in the festivals of this satyrlike Dionysiac man, Nature mourns her dismembering into individuals.'[37] In Laban's great plan to regenerate life, dancing was primary. He had a many-faceted mind, scientific as well as artistic (he devised an entire notation for his new form of dance). He naturally appreciated that dance was physical and genetic as well as imaginative and organic. 'In the very depths lives the centre of gravity. Around this is deposited the crystal of the skeleton, interconnected and directed by the muscles.'[38] The ambition at Ascona to replace religion was insistent.

Eurhythmics and Ethics: the Dancer Spirit

Laban also embraced the concept of eurhythmics. Because eurhythmics marries music and speed, he believed that one thinks with not just the brain but the whole body, becoming an 'equilibrium of will, feelings and intelligence', thus *intensifying* bodily consciousness and, in so doing, 'preventing any dictatorship by the brain or by the moral conscience'. 'Beauty, aesthetics, good manners, conscience, ethical equilibrium, goodness, are for me synonyms.'

For Laban, the eurhythmist performed a new social function: 'a special profession, which employs the methods of art for ethical ends'. However, eurhythmics did not aim to establish a church, still less a state: instead, 'It awakens a non-religious and non-legal conscience, and *that* will create the new social forms for itself.'[39] For Laban dancing was transcendental, the fusion of thought, feeling, and will. 'Men must rebel against the domination of abstract ideas and fill the world with the dance of the body-soul-spirit. The most significant human creations, in all ages, were born of the *Tänzergeist*, the "dancer spirit".[40]

At the height of his influence in 1913 Laban claimed that perhaps sixty families in the Ascona region were represented among his pupils.[41] This was when Mary Wigman arrived. Born in Hanover in 1886, Wigman came to dance relatively late in life; she insisted that Laban 'was the guide who opened for her the gates to the world she had dreamed of'. She has left us a record of the high spirits she encountered at Ascona. One of the dancers lived in a harmonium crate; and they sometimes danced all night to a gramophone, in grottoes or in taverns.[42]

The high spirits caught on. By 1914, the dance movement was spreading across Europe. There were, for example, seven thousand students enrolled in no fewer than 120 Jaques-Dalcroze schools. The claims made for these schools were ambitious – students were promised much more than the acquisition of rhythm: they would experience there 'the dissolution of both body and soul in harmony'. And the Monte Verità Art of Life School promised each pupil 'the regeneration of his or her life force'.[43]

According to Green, Wigman represented the Asconan values of life-body-gesture-movement-*expression* even more than did Laban. Others 'regarded her as a feminine realization of the Nietzschean programme of autonomous realization'. She studied movement in animals and in nature, and her own choreography tried hard to be anti-erotic, deliberately going beyond dance as 'pretty girls entertaining men'. Fascinated by psychoanalysis and with an abiding interest in Nietzsche, she had more than one affair with the early analysts, Herbert Binswanger being the best-known. She choreographed a version of *Zarathustra* and claimed a role in the origination of Dada, being a good friend of Sophie Taeuber, who was part of the Hugo Ball–Tristan Tzara set. In a notable comparison between Wigman and Isadora Duncan, the author Margaret Lloys related how Wigman would kneel, crawl, crouch, and even lie down on the earth at the close of a dance. 'She was like Isadora Duncan in that both were "womanly" and both danced religiously the faith that was in them, a faith in the dignity and worth of individual man.' Wigman's dance, modern dance, Lloys says, was a matter of wrestling and struggling – a matter of mass, not line – a matter of dynamic, Dionysian ecstatic struggle.[44]

Isadora Duncan, whom the cultural historian Karl Federn described as 'the incarnation of Nietzsche's intuition', was another Asconan habituée. 'The seduction of Nietzsche's philosophy ravished my being,' she admitted in her memoirs, and she called Nietzsche 'the first dancing philosopher'. How much in thrall she was to Nietzsche is clear from her 1903 lecture, 'The Dance of the Future': 'Oh, she is coming, the dancer of the future: more glorious than any woman who has yet been: more beautiful than the Egyptian, than the Greek, than the early Italian, than all the women of past centuries – the highest intelligence in the freest body![45]

But the most extreme examplar of these ideas was Valentine de Saint-Point (1875–1953), author of the 1913 *Futurist Manifesto of Lust*. Respected enough then to have her own creations performed at the Théâtre du Champs-Élysées in Paris and the Metropolitan Opera House in New York, her manifesto was addressed 'to those women who only think what I have dared to say'. It read in part: 'Lust when viewed without moral preconceptions and as an essential part of life's dynamism, is a force. Lust is not, any more than pride, a sin for the race that is strong . . . Lust is . . . the sensory and sensual synthesis that leads to the greatest liberation of spirit . . . Christian morality alone, following on from pagan morality, was fatally drawn to consider lust as a weakness . . . *We must make lust into a work of art*.' For her, Europe and the modern world were going through a feminine historical period: men and women both lacked masculinity. A new doctrine of Dionysian energy was needed in order for 'an epoch of superior humanity' to be achieved. As she said elsewhere, it was 'the brute who must become the model'.[46]

Laban stated that the most significant human creations, at all times, have been 'born of the dancer spirit'. He pointed out that we find danced doctrine – choreosophy – in Plato's *Timaeus* and in the Sufis, for example. For him, the dance instinct consists of a need for change – that's what movement *is*. It follows for him that no religion and no orality can last in its original form. 'We are polytheists and all the gods we know are parts of the daemonic self-changing of the gesture power. A demon is born (or unchained) whenever a roomful of people concentrate their attention on a dancer.' (Green refers to novels by Ascona authors Hesse and Bruno Goetz which contain scenes 'in which a spirit of lawlessness is born among people watching a dancer'.) Laban saw individualism – of mind as well as of behaviour – as a threat to modern culture: this is why dancing *together* is so important. On Laban's sixtieth birthday Kurt Jooss, the German choreographer, wrote a tribute praising his conception of the dance that 'rose above the merely aesthetic to the ethical and metaphysical and gave us images of the various forms of life in their ever-changing interplay'.[47]

Dance is among the most evanescent of art forms (especially when it is the intention of the dance master to create an evanescent form). It is difficult to think ourselves back into that time, when film was in its infancy. But the theatre performances, dance troupes, dance festivals and congresses, and the *Tänzerbund* and the Deutsche Tanz-bühne of Laban together add up to a formidable array of activities and social manifestations, a widespread and coherent effort to put 'life philosophy' into effect during the 1910s, 1920s and 30s and on into the Third Reich. Moreover, the ideals and ideas of Ascona lived on to form elements in such phenomena as Nazism, and the countercultural experiments in North America in the 1960s and later. Laban himself survives among us in, for instance, Joy of Movement, our contemporary cult of the body.[48] Ascona has influenced many people who have never heard of it.

What the Herd Can Never Know

Nor must we forget that, beyond Ascona, up until the First World War, Nietzsche's views were clearly linked with Expressionism. Says Steven Aschheim: 'In virtually every one of its manifold guises – painting, sculpture, architecture, literature, drama and politics – Expressionism and Nietzsche were linked.' Gottfried Benn, arguably the most talented if problematic German Expressionist writer, put it this way: 'Actually, everything that my generation discussed, dissected ... one can say suffered through ... had already found its definitive formulation in Nietzsche; everything thereafter was exegesis ... his ... postulation of a psychology of instinctual behavior as a dialectic – "knowledge as affect", all of psychoanalysis and Existentialism. They were all his achievements.' Nietzsche's fundamental point, Benn maintained, was the replacement of content with expression; the strength or vitality with which views were held was as important as their substance.[49] Life was feeling as much as fact.

Above all, pre-First World War German Expressionism reflected Nietzsche's vision of 'the sublime if painful' role of the elitist, isolated artist–superman, 'who in creating experienced what the herd would never know'. In particular, the Expressionist artist typically subscribed to an elitist, Nietzschean immoralism. Aschheim again: 'In the metaphorical landscape of the lonely Zarathustrian heights, in the shadow of the death of God, stood the artist beyond conventional notions of good and evil: a Nietzschean law unto himself. When Georg Kaiser, the expressionist writer, was sued for debts he had incurred, he proclaimed that the assumption "All are equal before the law" is nonsense.' On this understanding, the act of creativity by a genius, something producing new meaning in itself, was paramount, 'even if his wife and children should perish because of it'.[50] One defining aspect of German Expressionism was that its Dionysian anti-cerebralism was meant to proceed unchecked. In his drama *Ithaka*, Gottfried Benn's spokesman Roenne murders a professor who insists on the unparalleled value of scientific knowledge. Roenne's rant, inciting his fellow students to commit the act, is laid out in terms undeniably Nietzschean. 'We are the youth. Our blood cries out for heaven and earth, and not for cells and worms ... We want to dream. We want ecstasy. We call on Dionysus and Ithaca!'[51]

'More than any other Expressionist ... it was Gottfried Benn who grappled with the consequences of the death of God.' His entire career, says Steven Aschheim, including his short but passionate attachment to Nazism, was an attempt to deal with that Nietzschean predicament.[52] 'He accepted Nietzsche's nihilism,' Michael Hamburger commented, 'as one accepts the weather.' Until 1933 Benn occupied a position of what might be called 'theoretical nihilism', denying the possibility of any metaphysical truth. He preferred what he called a return to the 'preconscious, prelogical, primal and inert state'. This was an attempt to explore what life was like before language and self-consciousness had produced man's 'rift' with nature (others, like Paul Cézanne, pursued similar goals). This was what linked Expressionism and vagabondage as Nietzschean cults.

The Expressionists, like many other Nietzscheans, dithered between a non-political individual stance and a redemptive hunger for union with communities. One prominent example here was Kurt Hiller, a writer and early human rights activist (he was homosexual), and the 'new club' he founded in March 1909, which took Nietzsche as its inspiration. The aim of the club was an 'increased psychic temperature and universal merriment [*Heiterkeit*]', Dionysian evenings of excess. What was now needed, said Hiller, was 'a new post-theist and neohellenic heroism [*Heldentum*]', as Nietzsche had proclaimed it. Has any club ever taken itself so seriously?

The line that runs through many of these developments, and Expressionism in general, is the Nietzschean vision of the self-legislating, creative *Übermensch* artist working in splendid isolation from (and by implication above) the masses. It was, again, ambitious, had its noble elements but was, to our modern sensibility, unattractive all at the same time.

The *Übermensch* Ethic

Around and underlying German Expressionism, both less and more ambitious than poetry, playwriting and philosophy, were a myriad of *Lebensreform* (life-reform) movements that mushroomed in pre-First World War imperial Germany and which more or less shared Nietzsche's views. No doubt these groups also reflected the stresses caused by the rapid industrialization that was then taking place, especially in Germany. 'Naturalist' issues were ever present: vegetarianism, nudism and 'body culture'; and abstinence from alcohol and smoking. They were also animated by strong regenerationist, indeed eugenic, impulses and reflected manifold anarchist, socialist, *völkisch* and racist visions of renewal.[53] This was the Nietzschean key: renewal.

The most important of these movements, both at the time and later, was the German Youth Movement. As reflected in the slogan of one of its prophets, Gustav Wyneken, a philosopher and educational reformer famous for his concept of the attraction between teacher and pupil, 'youth for itself alone' was the watchword. The movement was not just a variant of the Boy Scouts or Girl Guides: it was much more muscular – rejecting, for example, parents, schooling and bourgeois conventions, as it sought 'the free development of the spirit of youth'. Eugen Diederichs was just one who claimed that the Youth Movement 'and its self-redemptive impulses' grew out of Nietzsche's prophecy of the *Übermensch* personality, but added that 'the coming race' could not exist 'in isolated self-absorption'; it needed to be melded into a community. This was a first step in integrating Nietzschean personal realization into a nation (*Volkstum*). It turned out to be a fateful development – later on, Nietzsche would be blamed for two world wars.

A parallel process occurred with Alexander Tille (1866–1912), who was described as a rabid Nietzschean and social Darwinian. Tille was a leading light in the *Alldeutsche Verband* from 1898 on, and an earnest Nietzsche publicist. (He also, incidentally, helped bring Nietzsche to Britain, taught German for ten years at Glasgow University, and in 1895 was appointed editor of an English edition of Nietzsche's works.)[54] As deputy director of the Organization of German Industrialists in Berlin and later as a representative of an employers' association in Saarbrücken, he was not without influence, and his own interpretation of Nietzscheanism emphasized the philosopher's dismissal of equality, Christian ethics, socialism and democracy. And all this combined in Tille's case with an especially brutal form of social Darwinism. Tille expressly advocated 'helping' nature by exterminating 'unproductive elements' of society (cripples, lunatics, the educationally subnormal), and instead favouring its 'efficient and gifted', as they were called then, members. He even believed that slums were beneficial insofar as they 'purged' the nation of its 'useless citizens'.

His *From Darwin to Nietzsche* (1895) made this all very plain. For him a crucial fact was that, unlike Darwin, Nietzsche believed that the new dispensation took society outside and beyond the 'Christian-human-democratic ethic'. Nietzsche's fundamental insight, for Tille, was that people 'did not possess equal worth'. The strong constituted 'upward development', while the weak threatened decay. 'A physiologically high form of human being was the moral goal of mankind.'[55]

The fundamental appeal of Nietzsche, to which the Nietzsche generations responded, was perhaps most clearly put by Karl Joel, a philosopher of a slightly mystical bent, in his *Nietzsche and Romanticism* (1905): 'One sees Nietzsche against the gloomy background of socialism, Darwinism and pessimism from which he freed himself. Without it Nietzsche appears as a fool and a criminal. With it he appears as a hero.' Only the *Übermenschen* were capable of making the future more enchanting and meaningful than the past.[56]

2

No One Way that Life Must Be

For America, the Civil War was a watershed in all sorts of ways. Although not many realized it at the time, her dilemma over slavery had kept the country back, and the war at last allowed the full forces of capitalism and industrialism to flex their muscles. Only after the war ended was the country free to fulfil her early promise.

Her population was still small by European standards, but the frontier was still opening up and there was much uncertainty. The pattern of immigration was changing, and questions of race, tribe, nationality, ethnic affiliation and – not least – religious identity, were ever present. Intellectual life, like everything else, was still in the process of formation, and in this context America had to fashion herself, devising new ideas where they were needed and using ideas from the Old World where they were available and relevant. But America did not lack confidence.

The assimilation of European ideas into the American context was achieved via a small number of nineteenth-century individuals, all New Englanders, who knew each other personally and between them created what we may call the characteristically American tradition of modern thought – Ralph Waldo Emerson, Oliver Wendell Holmes, William James, Benjamin and Charles Peirce, and John Dewey. Their ideas changed the way Americans (and the rest of us) thought and continue to think, about education, democracy, liberty, justice, tolerance – and, of course, about God.

The Limits to Happiness

We can say that what these thinkers had in common was not a group of ideas but, in a sense, a single idea, an idea *about* ideas. 'They all believed that ideas are not "out there" waiting to be discovered, but are tools – like knives and forks and microchips – that people devise to cope with the world in which they find themselves. And they believed that since ideas are *provisional* responses to particular and unreproducible circumstances, their survival depends not on their immutability but on their adaptability . . . There is also, though, implicit in what they wrote, a recognition of the *limits* of what thought can do in the struggle to increase human happiness [italics added].'[1]

The first sighting of what would be called the 'pragmatist' philosophy, and what linked it with the Civil War, came courtesy of Oliver Wendell Holmes. Holmes was a great admirer of Emerson, whom his father had known and befriended. As a freshman at Harvard in 1858, Holmes junior found that Emerson, as he said later, 'set me on fire'. He meant, among other things, Emerson's address to Harvard Divinity School in 1838, when he described how he had been 'bored to distraction' by a recent sermon and had contrasted its artificiality to the wild snowstorm then raging outside the church. This, plus many other musings, had caused him, he said, to renounce his belief in a supernatural Jesus and organized Christianity in favour of more personal revelation. Holmes junior – long-faced and with a distinctive handlebar moustache – agreed with Emerson that it was possible to live in a better relation with one's fellow men outside organized religion than within it.

Holding such views, the Civil War, when it broke out in 1861, provided him with the opportunity to do something practical, and he accepted a commission 'in a spirit of moral obligation' – he hated slavery and found even *The Pickwick Papers* distasteful because of its treatment of West Indians. Holmes suffered no fewer than three injuries during that bloody war – still the war in which most American lives have been lost; and amid the carnage he learned one thing, he said, that was to remain with him all his life. He looked about him and observed that although the abolitionists in 1850 appeared to many Northerners as subversives, by the end of the war 'they were patriots'. He concluded from this, famously: 'There is no one way that life must be.' This guided him and formed him into the wise judge that he became, his wisdom emerging in his great work *The Common Law*, which began life as the Lowell Lectures at Harvard, all twelve given before a full house, where he spoke throughout without notes.[2]

The philosophical brilliance of Holmes was to see that the law has no one overriding aim or idea. (This was the perception he brought from the disaster of the Civil War.) That it had evolved pragmatically, that in any one case there is 'a whole weather pattern' operating – precedence, deterrence, social benefit – in which there are no hard-and-fast distinctions, and whose constituents combine to produce a verdict in individual cases. He wasn't sure that experience is reducible to general abstractions, even though human beings spend so much time trying to do just that. 'All the pleasure of life is in general ideas,' he wrote in 1899, 'but all the use of life is in specific solutions – which cannot be reached through generalities any more than a picture can be painted by knowing some rules of method. They are reached by insight, tact and specific knowledge.' (See pp. 307–10, for a similar argument made by Ludwig Wittgenstein.)

Insight, tact, and specific knowledge. We shall see how important those words are in the story we shall be telling. More, we shall see how those words linked American and European thought, how they became the leading ideas for people who tried to live without God; and how – and this is too often overlooked – they unified people in their opposition to, and criticism of, the scientific world view. It is a fact too little appreciated that the very people who attempted to construct a liveable lifestyle without supernatural or transcendent dimensions, also found the scientific approach not up to the task either.

Holmes's father was a doctor who discovered the causes of puerperal fever, demonstrating conclusively that the disease was transmitted from childbirth to childbirth by doctors themselves. His career culminated as dean of the Harvard Medical School, though he became just as widely known for being what many people regarded as the greatest talker they had ever heard. Partly because of this, he took a founding role in the so-called Metaphysical Club, also known as the

Saturday Club, where literary matters were discussed over dinner and whose other members included Emerson, Hawthorne, Longfellow, James Russell Lowell, Charles Eliot Norton and, later, Holmes Jr, William James, philosopher and psychologist, and Benjamin and Charles Peirce.[3]

'Damn the Absolute!'

Each of these latter figures had impressive credentials. John Jacob Astor aside, William James's grandfather, a dry-goods millionaire, would have been the richest man of the time in New York State. Instead of a formal education William had travelled across Europe with his family, including his brother, the writer Henry, and although William never stayed long at any particular school this travelling gave him *experience*. He did finally settle on a career, in science, at Harvard in 1861, where he formed part of the circle of Louis Agassiz, a deist, the discoverer of the Ice Age and, at the time, one of the most vociferous critics of Charles Darwin. Although Agassiz was a member of the Saturday Club (it was also often referred to as Agassiz's Club), James wasn't so sure about his mentor's opposition to Darwin. He was particularly sceptical of Agassiz's dogmatism, whereas he thought evolutionary theory sparked all sorts of fresh ideas and – what he liked most – revealed biology as acting on very *practical*, even pragmatic, principles. James, like Holmes, was sceptical of certitude, one of his favourite phrases being 'Damn the Absolute!'[4]

At about this time, there was a remarkable development in the so-called new, or experimental, psychology. Edward Thorndike at Berkeley had placed chickens in a box which had a door that could be opened if the birds pecked at a lever. In this way they were given access to a supply of food pellets. Thorndike observed that 'although at first many actions were tried, apparently unsystematically [that is, at random], only successful actions performed by chickens who were hungry were learned'. James wasn't surprised by this, but it confirmed his view, albeit in a mundane way: the chickens had learned that if they pecked at the lever the door would open, leading to food, a reward.

James went one step further. To all intents and purposes, he said, the chickens *believed* that if they pecked at the lever the door would open. As he put it, 'Their beliefs were rules for action.' And he thought that such rules applied more generally. 'If behaving as though we have free will, or as if God exists, gets us the results we want, we will not only come to believe those things; they will be, pragmatically, true . . . "The Truth" is the name of whatever proves itself to be good in the way of belief.' In other words, truth is not 'out there'; it has nothing to do with 'the way things really are'.

Most controversially of all, James applied this reasoning to intuition, to innate ideas. He took Kant's line, for the most part, that many ideas are innate, but he didn't think there was anything mysterious or divine about this. In Darwinian terms, it was clear that 'innate' ideas are just variations that have arisen and been naturally selected. 'Minds that possessed them were preferred [by natural selection] to minds that did not.' But this wasn't because those ideas were more 'true' in an abstract, metaphysical or theological sense; it was because it helped the organisms to adapt. The reason we believed in God (when we did believe in God) was because experience showed that it paid to believe in God. When people stopped believing in God (as they were doing in sizeable numbers when James was alive), it was because such belief no longer paid.[5]

A Core Uneasiness in Us

James's most important, best-known and probably best-loved book on this subject is *The Varieties of Religious Experience*. This remains distinctive in a number of ways. For a start, it began life as a series of Gifford lectures.*

---

*The Gifford Lectures are one of the most distinguished lecture series in the world. They are the legacy of the Scottish judge Adam Gifford who died in 1887, and are intended to encourage a perpetual lively debate on science and 'all questions about man's conception of God or the Infinite'. The legacy provides for annual lectures to be held at one of Scotland's four historic universities – Aberdeen, Edinburgh, Glasgow and St Andrews – and since their inception in 1888 over two hundred books have resulted, by

The Varieties is also distinctive (given the host audience the lectures were intended for) in treading a fine line, managing to be respectful about religion while at the same time telling the stark truth as James saw it. The book takes as its main theme the various psychological states and emotions that he took to be at the centre of religious experience. He considered whether religious leaders in the past had been frankly pathological in their religious concerns and ideas; he noted that 'cranks' often had fixed ideas; he looked at the role of fear in religious belief, at surrender and passivity, at failure in life (in his words, a 'pivotal human experience'). He touched on yoga, Buddhism, Lao-tzu and Vedanta, though he admitted he didn't know much about Eastern religions; he looked at conversion, at saintliness, at mysticism and martyrdom, at the phenomenon of cosmic consciousness. And at root, he said, religion was about 'emotionality', religion was a 'massive chapter' in human egotism, born of a core uneasiness within us, a sense that there is something wrong about us, with religion providing the solution to that unease. He believed that there is always something solemn about religion – solemn, serious and tender – that satisfies a need we have, a solemnity which we feel enlarges us, produces a 'gladness', an inner unity.

At the same time James noted that many people go through the same emotional journey but without turning to religion, so that while religion 'works' for people who are religious, this says nothing about whether any one set of religious beliefs are 'true', and he thought that

---

some of the most distinguished names in theology, philosophy and the sciences. Eight Nobel Laureates are among the names, which include William James, J.G. Frazer, Dean Inge, Arthur Eddington, Alfred North Whitehead, John Dewey, Albert Schweitzer, Karl Barth, Reinhold Niebuhr, Niels Bohr, Arnold Toynbee, Paul Tillich, Rudolf Bultmann, Werner Heisenberg, Raymond Aron, Hannah Arendt, Alfred Ayer, Iris Murdoch, Freeman Dyson, Charles Taylor, Alasdair MacIntyre, Mary Midgley, George Steiner, Hilary Putnam, Martha Nussbaum and Roger Scruton. In his book on the Giffords, Larry Witham describes them as a 'window on a century in which natural science encountered biblical religion with full force'.[6] During that century, he says, the Giffords witnessed four stages: the clash of the great philosophical systems with scientific materialism; the advent of the material sciences – anthropology, psychology, physics, sociology and historical criticism – and their impact on religion; the great rebellion against science and reason in the West – the idea of God as 'wholly other'; and, with the days of one dominant belief system (at least in the West) now over, the resurrection of the rational search for God. Many of the above names and themes will recur in these pages.

mystics have no right to impose their views on the rest of us. In fact, he went so far as to argue that 'we must say goodbye to dogmatic theology'.[7] He made only passing reference to Josef Breuer, Pierre Janet and Freud (*The Interpretation of Dreams* (see pp. 84 ff.) had appeared only in 1900, in German) but he dwelled in detail on what he called 'the subconscious'. He thought that people are dimly aware of subconscious influences on their life, that there is always some part of the self that is, as he put it, 'unmanifested'. It is this, he proposed, that produces the urge to be 'larger', more complete, more unified.

What James was advocating, then, was first the pragmatic argument that, for those who believe in God, he is real because he produces real effects; people believe they achieve a more satisfying life because of religion (and he examined many detailed first-person accounts of religious experiences, most of which, he said, were trustworthy). At the same time, with his aim to create a 'science of religions', he saw religions primarily as a psychological phenomenon, an entirely natural emotional response to the 'misty' ambiguity of life, to fear, and to the conflict within us between assertion and passive surrender as ways to face life, the ever present conflict between the 'yes-function' and the 'no-function'; a response to the very real pragmatic predicament that, in life, lots of ideas negate other ideas. He claimed that many people suffer from what he called 'over-belief', too strong a faith state; that the religious life always risks self-indulgence, and that any attempt to demonstrate the truthfulness of any one set of religious beliefs is 'hopeless'.

In his Gifford Lectures he was pointing out that religion is a natural phenomenon, rooted in our divided self; but he was also saying, indirectly, that advances in understanding the subconscious might well lead to a better understanding of the central uneasiness that we have within us.

'Growth Is the Only Moral End'

More generally, as the American philosopher Richard Rorty has pointed out, James's main accomplishment was of a piece with John

Dewey's. Dewey, though he boasted 'a Vermont drawl', was not a member of the Metaphysical/Saturday/Agassiz Club, since he was based in Chicago, more than seven hundred miles away, where he was a professor. With his rimless eyeglasses and complete lack of fashion sense, he was not the formidable presence that some of the other pragmatists were, but in some ways he was the most successful, or at least the most productive. Through newspaper articles, popular books, and a number of debates with other philosophers such as Bertrand Russell, Dewey became known to the general public in a way that few philosophers are. Like James, Dewey was a convinced Darwinist and for him the start of the twentieth century was an age of 'democracy, science and industrialism'; and this, he argued, had profound consequences.

Dewey, like James, helped us slough off a lot of the misleading intellectual baggage we have inherited from the Platonic tradition, in particular the Aristotelean and Platonic convention that humankind's most 'distinctive and praiseworthy' capacity is 'to know things as they really are – to penetrate behind appearance to reality'. It was this notion that gave rise to the traditional philosophical project of most of the past two thousand years, which has involved trying to find something stable that would serve as a criterion 'for judging the transitory products of our transitory needs and interests'. As a result of what James, Dewey and the others observed, and the conclusions they drew from their observations, Rorty sums up pithily that we now have to 'give up' on the idea that there are unconditional moral obligations, obligations which apply everywhere and at all times because they are rooted in an unchanging ahistorical human nature. Instead, pragmatism replaces the reality–appearance duality with a much less dramatic distinction – that between the more useful and the less useful. This reflects the fact that while the vocabulary of Greek metaphysics and Christian theology was useful for our forebears' purposes, *we* have different purposes, for which we need a different vocabulary.[8]

The same is true of reason. The Enlightenment replaced the idea of supernatural guidance with the idea of what Rorty labels 'a quasi-divine faculty called "reason"'. But Dewey and James thought this was an attempt to keep a special faculty, called 'reason' – something like God – alive in the midst of secular culture. This is tantamount to saying there must be a kind of 'invisible tribunal' of reason overseeing laws which, deep down, everyone acknowledges as binding. Pragmatists argue that such a tribunal does not – cannot – exist.

James and Dewey were both influenced by Emerson's evolutionary sense of history, his awareness that 'democracy is neither a form of government nor a social expediency', but a metaphysic of the relation of man and his *experience in nature* – what he called 'the infinitude of the private man'. When he looked about him, and back through history, Emerson reflected that the great lessons of Nature are variety and freedom. Because of this, he said, all questions of ultimate justification are decided by the future, a future that cannot be definitively predicted, but can be *hoped for*. Ultimately, pragmatism replaces the notion of 'reality', 'reason' and 'nature' with that of a 'better human future'. 'When pragmatists are asked "Better by what criterion?" they have no answer, any more than the first mammals could specify in what respects they were better than the dying dinosaurs. Better in the sense of containing more of what we consider good and less of what we consider bad. And by good they mean "variety and freedom" ... "Growth itself," Dewey said, "is the only moral end."'

A parallel is sometimes drawn between the avant-garde and the aims of pragmatism. In both the search is on for something new, something astonishing in a positive way, rather than any specific expectation. Dewey, for his part, was convinced that European philosophy was held back because it could not shed a world picture that had arisen within – and specifically applied to – the needs of an inegalitarian society. This had bred a dualistic way of thinking which he described as 'baleful', and had led to a fundamental social division between 'contemplators and doers'. In fact, he was of the opinion that philosophy itself began with an attempt to reconcile 'two kinds of mental product' – on the one hand, the products of priests and poets and, on the other, those of the artisans. Dewey believed that, at least until Darwin, the main thrust of Western philosophy had typically reflected the interests of the leisure class, which favoured stability over change. One of the consequences of this had been that philosophy had lent its prestige to the idea of the 'eternal', the aim being to make metaphysics 'a substitute for custom as the source and guarantor of higher moral and social values'. He was determined instead to shift attention from the eternal to the future; philosophy, he maintained, must become an instrument of change rather than one of conservation.[9]

This was radical and so, following Dewey and the other pragmatists, philosophy did indeed change from being the search for some neo-Platonic 'reality', beyond the appearance of things (the idea of God included), to 'How can we make the present into a richer future?'[10]

Alongside this, Dewey wanted to replace the attempt always to achieve certainty with hope. He had little time for the notion of 'truth' in any kind of *certain* sense: he thought that philosophers should confine themselves to 'justification' or, in his words, to 'warranted assertibility' – in much the same way as scientists phrase their findings. Once we realize, as Oliver Wendell Holmes had, that there is no one way that the world is, so it follows that there is no one way it can be accurately represented. Instead, there is a myriad of ways of acting to fulfil human hopes of happiness.[11] Among all this, certainty is unlikely – it is, after all, no longer the aim. James and Dewey thought that the quest for certainty – even as a long-term goal – was an attempt to escape from the world. That quest must be replaced with the demand for imagination. 'One should stop worrying about whether what one believes is well grounded and start worrying about whether one has been imaginative enough to think up interesting alternatives to one's present beliefs. The telos [purpose] of movement and flux is not solely mastery, but also stimulation.'[12]

William James differed from Dewey in that he thought religion and science are *both* 'respectable paths' for acquiring respectable beliefs, so long as we accept that these are beliefs suited to quite different purposes. 'Knowing' is not something at which natural scientists are uniquely skilled. There are simply different ways of justifying beliefs to audiences. None of these audiences is more privileged than any other, or is closer to nature, or a better example of some ahistorical ideal of rationality.[13] A believer in God will always be able to produce justification for his or her beliefs (most of them, anyway) and they will be justifications that meet the requirements of his or her community. At the same time, there is no reason to think that those beliefs, justifiable as they are to the individual and community of which he or she is a part, are those which are most likely to be true. There is no 'higher' aim of inquiry called 'truth', no such thing as ultimate justification – justification before God, or before the tribunal of reason, rather than any merely *finite* human audience. Given a Darwinian picture of the world, there can be no such tribunal. If Darwinian biological evolution has no aim, it continuously produces new species, while cultural evolution produces new audiences; 'but there is no such thing as a species which evolution has in view'.[14]

New Conceptions of Possible Communities

An allied claim of pragmatism is that we live in a world without essences. Because we can never step outside language, there is no such thing as 'reality' unmediated by a linguistic description. Because pragmatists maintain that there is no distinction between knowing things and using them, so there can be no such thing as a description that matches the way an object *really* is apart from its relation to human consciousness or language.[15]

Plato, Aristotle and the main monotheisms all insist on a sense of mystery and wonder in regard to nonhuman powers; that there is, already in existence, 'something better and greater than the human'. Another element in this, also derived from the Greeks, is that humanity itself has an intrinsic nature – there is something essential and unchangeable within us called 'the human', which can be contrasted with what is 'out there' in the rest of the universe. Pragmatism does not subscribe to that view but considers that humanity is an open-ended entity, that whatever it is it is not an unchanging and eternal 'essence'. Pragmatists therefore *redirect* the sense of awe and mystery – which the Greeks and the monotheisms attached to the supernatural – to the future. Pragmatism's guiding spirit, so to speak, is that the humanity of the future, although derived from what we are at present, will be superior in some way, even if in as yet barely imaginable ways.[16]

For pragmatists there is no difference, say, between numbers, tables, stars, electrons, human beings, academic disciplines, social institutions, or anything else. There is nothing *essential* about these entities, nothing to be known about them other than what can be *said* about them. All that can be known about a hard, substantial table, say, is that certain sentences about it are accurate. We can't go 'behind' language to what might be regarded as a more immediate non-linguistic form of acquaintance.[17] For pragmatists it is a waste of effort to concern ourselves with such 'essences' as, say, constellations in the sky or moral values here on earth. These concepts are more or less useful, and this aspect of them is more important than arguing endlessly about their eternal (and therefore essential) nature.

For pragmatists, even the scientists' concern with electrons, with what are called 'fundamental' particles, with essences, is yet another attempt to find something eternal in nature, and this, they suggest, merely reflects a human need; and the trouble with all such attempts is that 'the need to be God is just one more human need'. The point is that nature can be described in any number of ways but *none* of them is the 'inside' way. On this basis, understanding divinity under the aspect of eternity is neither an illusion nor a confusion – it is just one way of describing experience; but it is no more 'inside' (or true) than any other way.

The advantage of anti-essentialism, as we might call it (the term is Rorty's), is that, aligned with Darwinian evolutionary theory, it shows that it is *language* rather than 'mind' that is the distinguishing feature of our species, but one that is continuous with animal behaviour. Together, these have allowed us to move beyond transcendental stories and replace them with empirical – experiential – stories. We have gradually substituted the making of a better future for ourselves for the attempt to see ourselves from outside time and history. As part of this shift, the very idea of philosophy changes: we see it now as an aid in creating ourselves (ourselves in the future) rather than as knowing ourselves.

But the most important element of the anti-essentialist argument is the notion that there is no such thing as a fixed human nature, either generally or as applied to individual people. This view, of the self-contained individual self, what Dewey called the 'belief in the fixity and simplicity of the self', he put down to 'the theologians' ... dogma of the unity and ready-made completeness of the soul'.[18] His insight was to see that, on the contrary, any self may include within it a number of inconsistent selves, which do not necessarily act in harmony. This is an idea that ran throughout the twentieth century in all manner of disciplines, as we shall see. It is, for many, a most liberating doctrine, especially in a world without God.

A New Trinity: Trust, Moral Ambition, Social Hope

It is difficult to exaggerate the importance of this breakthrough. In some ways it aligned Dewey with Freud. With his interest in education, Dewey understood well the importance of the family in helping to socialize individuals – that is, in particular, the role of maternal love in creating non-psychopaths, in creating human selves who find concern for others entirely natural. Freud's notion of the unconscious was in some ways an explanation of, and psychoanalysis a treatment for, individuals with multiple inconsistent and unharmonized selves (and who were disconcerted by it). Historians have located the origin of psychology in numerous places, and this is surely one of them. As Annette Baier, the New Zealand-based moral and feminist philosopher, sums up the pragmatist position, 'the secular equivalent of faith in God . . . is faith in the human community and its evolving procedures – in the prospects for many-handed cognitive ambitions and moral hopes'.[19]

By this account, trust, moral ambition and social hope are the new trinity. In one sense this is not so radical, because more than one historian, or sociologist of religion, has concluded that the root of religious faith ultimately stems from the faith that a child has in its parent. As Rorty sums up Dewey: 'Moral development in the individual, and moral progress in the human species as a whole is a matter of remaking human selves so as to enlarge the variety of the relationships which constitute those selves . . . It is neither irrational nor unintelligent to draw the limits of one's moral community at a national or racial or gender border. But it is . . . best to think of moral progress as a matter of increasing *sensitivity*, increasing responsibility to the needs of a larger and larger variety of people and things.'[20]

Doing away with religious groupings helps this.

Put another way, the pragmatist search is for an ever *wider* inclusion, rather than an exploration of 'depth'; and this applies both to science and in the moral realm. Scientific progress involves integrating more and more data into a coherent overall account, but it is not a matter of penetrating appearance until one arrives at reality. Similarly, moral progress is a matter of seeking/achieving wider and wider sympathy. 'You cannot aim at moral perfection, but you can aim at taking more people's needs into account than you did previously.'[21]

It follows that we should just *give up* the philosophical search for essences, unchanging reality. Moral progress is better understood as like sewing together a complex, multicoloured quilt of different human groups. 'The hope is to sew such groups together with a thousand little stitches.'

Imagination is the final key here, to add to trust, moral ambition and social hope. This amalgam is what will produce new conceptions of possible communities and, in that way, make the human future richer than the human past.[22]

Santayana's Comic Faith

Although he was less than happy with the label of 'pragmatist', George Santayana may be regarded as a maverick member of the species, who was friendly with, much influenced by, and an influence on, William James. Santayana had an unusual career path. Born in Spain, he spent decades in Boston as a professor at Harvard, and then left America, spending a further four decades in Oxford, Paris and Rome. He valued his freedom and, later in life, rejected offers of professorships from many universities on both sides of the Atlantic. Besides producing his many books, he was one of the most influential teachers of modern times – his pupils included Conrad Aiken, Van Wyck Brooks, James B. Conant, T.S. Eliot, Felix Frankfurter, Robert Frost, Walter Lippmann, Samuel Eliot Morison and Wallace Stevens.

Santayana started from the fact, as he saw it, that there is nothing supernatural in life, there is no 'over-soul', as the Germans put it, 'no supernatural more', as William James put it, or, as he himself put it in an early poem: 'No hope of heaven [to] sweeten our few tears'. 'Few' tears because he was convinced that 'the existence and well-being of man upon earth are, from the point of view of the universe, an indifferent incident', that humanity, in terms of the whole, is 'a fragment of a fragment'.[23]

He thought that 'life poses questions we cannot answer', is beset by tragedy, and that transcendentalism adds nothing 'essential'. When religions posed as science, he said, they had misplaced man's hope – 'It was a prodigious delusion to imagine that work could be done by magic . . . Religion, when it has tried to do man's work for him, has not only cheated hope, but consumed energy and drawn away attention from the true means of success.'[24] There is no such thing as a 'timeless soul across the board', no core human nature, which is merely a name for a group of qualities 'found by chance in certain tribes of animals', artificially foregrounded by us, where no such foreground exists in nature itself.[25] As regards absolutism and mysticism, 'all human ideas are being sacrificed to one of them – the idea of an absolute reality'. Mysticism he dismissed as 'a civil war of the mind' that ends 'in the extermination of all parties . . . Absolutism then tyrannously steps in to claim that superhuman Spirit resolves the disharmonies that people cannot.' But 'absolute reality' is no more than a human opinion.[26] Human well-being or salvation, he explained, depends as much on gratuituous external conditions or circumstances that people can neither engineer nor earn, as it does on their own behaviour. Universality, as with the absolute, is like a mechanical rabbit at the dogtrack; it can never be caught.[27]

Santayana accepted that there was a 'spiritual' crisis at the beginning of the twentieth century, but claimed it was not a supernatural problem. Religion, he thought, is an ideal that we would like reality to conform to. Religion should be understood 'poetically'; and it persists 'because more distinctly than any other institution it contributed "moral symbols" to culture that give people a way to live joyfully with the events that threaten meaninglessness: physical extremity or suffering, the limits of intellect or absurdity, and the dark edge of moral comprehension or evil'.[28] Religious rituals create an 'other world' and establish 'a sense of joy' in things, throwing into relief the complex structures of the workaday world. 'Festivity' and not social work, he maintained, was the hallmark of religion as a cultural institution; it was ritual, not certitude, that helped resolve the fear of meaninglessness. Religion lets people break away from social constraints, and religious practices, moreover, underscore the *limit* of human assertion. But he thought it a 'beautiful and good' idea of religion that sin should exist in order to be 'overcomeable' – it gave people a triumphant experience.[29]

He thought, like James, like Dewey, that human beings represent 'chances to make things better', and his solution to the death of God was a new definition of the 'spiritual' and otherworldliness, which was not transcendental and post-mortem but which involved an exploration of the imagination. Philosophy, for Santayana, could not offer 'incorrigible first principles' but was a kind of conversation whose aim was to redescribe the world in ever more imaginatively accurate terms – he called it 'rectification by redescription'.[30] Philosophy, for him, was 'festive, lyrical, rhetorical'. The imagination had to operate with a cosmic sense, but that meant a sense, above all, of our finitude and impotence. The aim of life should be to live triumphantly with finitude.

Santayana had, on the other hand, what he called a 'comic vision' of life ('comic', not 'cosmic'), which 'celebrates the passing joys and victories in the world', and a notion he called 'radical comedy' which involves 'an admission that, in no small part, what links people is the powerlessness and mortality that they share; it is an acceptance of things that resist or defeat self-assertion'; or, put another way, radical comedy occurs when 'everybody acknowledges himself beaten and deceived, yet is happier for the unexpected posture of affairs'. Philosophical meditation and culture, he said, are ways of letting people momentarily break out 'of the shabbiest surroundings in[to] laughter, understanding and small surrenders of folly to reason'. Santayana makes the claim that, 'disregarding the quest for eternal life and transcendent infinitude altogether, both public and private well-being hang on a gracious "love of life in the consciousness of our impotence"'.[31]

A life worth living, he believed, required 'unworldiness': that is to say, in his context, a life away from the workaday world. This is why we need what he called 'a holiday life', a time and place when we can get away from the workaday world and *play*. 'Spirit', for him, is the cultural location for solitary, personal revitalization, a cultural space for the sense of beauty to resolve moral cramps. Santayana thought that the new emphasis on self-realization and technical rationality was 'failing to give sufficient weight to spiritual and moral life'. There was no space for 'spontaneous affirmation', or for appreciating what is 'lovely and lovable'. Well-being – which is the aim of life – occurs in 'reflective episodes of consummate joy that *give point* to things', and giving point to things enables people to 'feel triumphant rather than defeated or brutalized or unreal'.[32]

And this is what cultural space *is*, says Santayana, this is what spirituality is: a playful holiday in which people can depart from the workaday worlds of, say, policy formulation, in order to engage in reflective, imaginative activities that stretch them and discipline them to celebrate and live triumphantly, at least for a time, with finitude. The appreciation of beauty belongs to our holiday life, 'when we are redeemed for the moment'.[33] Beauty – natural beauty or created beauty – is divine in his vocabulary, not in any supernatural sense but simply because of the feelings it engenders in us. Art shows that we can experience varieties of 'finite perfection' without encountering a deity, audiences are made happier by empathizing with characters in unhappy situations, artists render suffering sufferable, tragic characters delight people by letting them identify with images of perfection they approach but miss; imperfection has value as 'incipient perfection'.

Imagination, says Santayana, allows us to realize possibilities not available to experience, and in this the momentum of our imagination will carry us beyond ourselves. There is no absolute reality or supreme good, 'intermittence is intrinsic to life' and so is partiality and finitude, but art allows us to imagine excellence, shows us forms of the 'whole', and apposite endings. Spiritual redemption, in his world, depends on the 'suspension of self-assertion'. 'There is no cure for birth and death save to enjoy the interval by discerning and manifesting the good without attempting to retain it.'[34]

Human self-assertion, he goes on, is indispensable but always falls short. Our salvation is to love life in the consciousness of impotence. We need faith in our intelligence to imagine a future which is a projection of the desirable in the present and to realize that that *is* our salvation. Aesthetic experience discloses a kind of order 'that lets people unify many discrete moments in a harmonious way and carries with it an emotion of perfection, satisfaction or happiness'. Cultural activities and institutions make life significant not because they give direct contact with 'something' above, below or besides culture, but because of the imaginative order they envisage.[35]

Beauty, joy, comedy, play, mirth, humour, laughter – these are what we should aim for, not everlasting bliss. This is what he means by 'comic faith', something less grand and more reasonable than infinite or permanent happiness and blessed immortality. If we can combine this with making a difference – an improvement – to the worlds of our fellow humans, this is the only immortality available. In doing so, we shall not have overcome death, but we shall have overcome death's sting.[36]

Santayana lived on the edge of poetry and it showed, gloriously, in the style of his prose. He is, perhaps, the most understated philosopher of the twentieth century, and a wonderful companion in a world without God, the culmination of the pragmatic approach.

3

The Voluptuousness of Objects

Pragmatism, the subject of the previous chapter, was for the most part an American school of thought. This chapter concerns European thinkers who would not call themselves pragmatists; nevertheless, as will become clear, there is more than a passing similarity in their ideas. The names to conjure with here are Charles Baudelaire, Arthur Rimbaud, Paul Valéry, Paul Cézanne, André Gide and, above all, Edmund Husserl.

Husserl is someone who has not been too kindly treated by history. Partly this has to do with the fact that the brand of philosophy he conceived was given a daunting name, 'phenomenology' – one of those big words, as James Joyce was to say, that 'make us afraid'. In fact, the underlying premise of phenomenology is very straightforward; it is also extremely important, being yet another school of thought that was and is as much anti-science as it was and is anti-religion.

One of its founding elements was summed up by Paul Valéry (1871–1945), the French polymath – poet, essayist, philosopher – who wrote of the late nineteenth century, 'We felt the possibility of a new religion, with poetic emotion as its essential quality.' In fact, Husserl went rather further than this.

Metaphysics of the Concrete

Born Jewish in Moravia but baptized as a Lutheran in Catholic Austria, Husserl – bearded, bespectacled, with a high forehead – may be seen as an outsider twice over. He was a mathematician before he was a philosopher, studying the former subject under Karl Weierstrass in Berlin and the latter under Franz Brentano in Vienna.

Husserl argued that experience is the only form of knowledge and that there are at least two kinds of existence. Ordinary objects exist, out there in the real world, and concepts exist in our consciousness. But consciousness is not a kind of matter, he said: it is what he called an 'intention', not the normal use of that word, but a 'turning toward' the world, a way to meet the world, experience it. Consciousness is not merely an awareness of the world, but also an awareness of that awareness. From this, he said – as the pragmatists said – we cannot go 'behind' consciousness to a more 'inside' view of life or reality. 'The world is not what I think but what I live.'

He also argued that the perception of reality takes place 'entirely without the aid of reason', and that what we think of as primary and secondary qualities of objects are no such thing: objects *are* their appearance and not an aggregate of qualities assembled by the mind. For example, yellowness in a lemon is not a secondary quality, a sort of add-on that the mind attributes to 'lemonness' – it *is* the lemon. There is no 'distance' between consciousness and the table it perceives. We do not have to work out that it is a table by calculating its secondary qualities – the number of legs, the shape of its top, the wood or metal it is made of – we know *immediately* what it is.[1]

Phenomenologists maintain that we need no instruments to understand the world about us: things are what they appear to be, nothing more. Consciousness is not a calculating machine or a camera; it is, in fact, the only absolute, for consciousness is always consciousness *of* something; we cannot just be jealous, we must be jealous *of* someone. There is nothing *in* consciousness.[2] Another example: we are related to the objects around us by their *relationship* to us. The only way to 'understand' utensils is to use them. Pure contemplation or reflection cannot do this for us; a scientist, by analysing the wood and metal of a hammer, for instance, could never arrive at an 'understanding' of it.

The importance of this approach to life was first stressed by Arthur Rimbaud (1854–91), who thought that the world had become 'enslaved' by concepts. It was reinforced by Charles Baudelaire's famous line, *'Je sais l'art d'évoquer les minutes heureuses.'*[3] In a world no longer illumined by God or reason, Husserl wanted a new metaphysic of the concrete, and this is where phenomenology was so influential. By this account, all attempts to reduce the infinite variety of the world (the universe, experience) to concepts, to ideas, to essences, whether those concepts are religious or scientific – whether they are the 'soul', or 'nature', or 'particles' or the 'afterlife' – diminish the actual variety of reality which is part, and maybe the biggest part, or even the whole, of its meaning.

For Rimbaud, Valéry, Gide and others, the real is infinite and so methods of dividing it into comprehensible portions must also be infinite. 'Since matter in its totality is beyond our comprehension, then no method, including that of science, can be the "good" one; no method can ever answer our questions once and for all.' For Valéry, as for others, consciousness was 'the "flaw" in the fullness of being' but it was a flaw in which he rejoiced. 'Certain men, with a certain delicacy of feeling, take a voluptuous pleasure in the *individuality* of objects. They show a delighted preference for that quality in a thing of being unique – a quality all things possess.'[4]

There were two immediate implications of this approach, though there were longer-term influences as well, which we shall come to in due course. One was that the phenomenological view underpinned the artistic approach to life, rather than the scientific *or* the religious. The second was to emphasize that life is made up of a myriad different observations and experiences, epiphanies and insights, and that these accumulate over a lifetime; that fullness, wholeness, is not to be achieved suddenly through some 'transcendent' episode of a religious or therapeutic kind, but is more akin to hard work or education.

'Thingness'

Everett Knight draws our attention to the work of Cézanne who, he says, brought about a new era in art, an art which sought in a number of ways to see objects, as he put it, 'in their full, non-human independence'. Cézanne, in Knight's view (and others'), sought to show that perception is not guided by the intelligence 'but warped by it . . . This is the insight upon which the vision of Cézanne is based. His whole endeavour is to capture objects before his intelligence has organized them into something quite different from what they really are.' He went on: 'As Valéry discovered, the sea is upright, rather than flat as the intelligence would have it. Cézanne draws dishes with several contours, because that is how they actually are before the intervention of the mind.'⁵ Another good example of this phenomenon is the difference between photography and the human eye. It is not uncommon, for instance, for us to experience a hill in the distance as high, as high as we know from experience that it is. In a photograph, however, the hill appears as insignificant.

I.A. Richards, the Cambridge-based philosopher and literary critic, thought that art – poetry in particular, in his case – is 'capable of saving us; it is a perfectly possible means of overcoming chaos'. Others who shared this attitude, after Cézanne, were the Cubists, who had a clear vision and were trying to show that the world of things is 'incommensurate with anything human'.⁶ This led them to a major advance in the arts: the objects they created were not to be regarded as representations, as the traditional understanding had it, but as objects in their own right – their newness, their novelty, was part of their point, part of their *meaning*. Sheer newness, shockability, 'thingness', doesn't sound like much of an alternative to 'salvation', but it proved immensely popular in the twentieth century.

Husserl was also of the same mould as the American pragmatists in that he formed the view that there is no such thing as an unchanging human nature. Since he believed that a person is nothing more than the events of his or her life, it followed that he or she has no 'definition'. This view is profound, and in several ways. It underlines that not only are the objects of the world each unique, but we are too. Each of us has an individual perspective on the world and it can *in no way* be surmounted.[7] So, the only way we can ever come to terms with the world is to abandon any notion that there is, somewhere, an absolute principle (God, for example) and an absolute human nature (God-given) which can be brought together to realize one 'truth'. This view is no less profound in carrying the further implication that science, for all its undeniable successes, is, no less than religion, only one way of understanding the world and not necessarily the one that suits us (some of us) best.

What Valéry and Husserl were both trying to urge on us is a denial of the view that the particular is somehow less consequential than the general. 'In giving our attention to the particular, we fear the risk of fixing ourselves upon an exception to the rule; art by its nature is existential; it is concerned with particulars, while rationalism is interested only in their relationships.' Husserl, in the words of Sartre, 'has given back to us the world of artists and the prophets'. However we approach life, however we deal with it, life will always keep changing and remain beyond the reach of total understanding. We can never formulate an 'exhaustive' explanation in such a way that our quest or our responsibility is 'at an end'.

Assent to the World

Roughly contemporary with Valéry and Cézanne was the philosopher Henri Bergson. Born in Paris of Polish-Jewish descent in 1859, his father was a musician. His early years were spent in London, but after the family moved back to France his first interest was mathematics; then he entered the École Normale Supérieure, where he studied philosophy. Bergson was influenced by the British biologist/philosopher, Herbert Spencer; in London in 1908 he met William James, who helped popularize his ideas in America, while T.E. Hulme did the same in Britain.

Bergson shared many of the ideas of James and the other pragmatists, though in the end he went in a different direction. Like the pragmatists and the phenomenologists, he believed that life consisted of a flux of immediate experience, that 'reality is given immediately to the mind' but that 'life overflows the intelligence' so that 'reality can be recognized but not known completely'. Like the pragmatists and phenomenologists, he thought that reason and logic distorted experience by analysing it into separate elements.[8] For Bergson, reality cannot be represented in the abstract, as science or religion attempt to do, without being distorted, 'because it is always changing'. The world is a plurality, he insisted, implying there is no such thing as an absolute truth; reality always 'escapes' a system, and 'there is no bridge from the finite to the infinite'.

So far, this could all be Dewey, William James, or even Husserl talking. Where Bergson parted company with them, however, was in going further into the workings of the mind. The Victorian era had been obsessed with the so-called scientific idea of the world – or even of the universe – as a *machine*. Bergson's answer was that this was so because it is the way the mind works, the way logic works. Logic is in effect limited – the world, he said, has not been built up in the way that we appreciate it scientifically; science is simply the way we have learned to take the world apart, and the *apparent* scientific unity we (think we) see around us is due to the fact that 'man is a solitary sorting machine'.[9]

He went on to make two proposals, which he saw as advances, and that concern us here. One was his notion of intuition. Around the central intellect, he said, is a 'fringe' of intuition. The intuition acquires forms of knowledge that are 'unseizable' by the intellect; intuition is a form of knowing without analysis, or even being able to state what we know. (Bertrand Russell dismissed this as 'mystical'.) The intuition immerses itself in the flux of life and apprehends experience 'without crystallization'. Bergson thought that there were, in effect, two selves – the logical self and the intuitional self. The poet was the classic example of the intuitional self and metaphor the classic form of intuitional knowledge, a metaphor being 'a new name for a feature of reality for which we previously had no name'.[10] The artist, to be an artist, must be 'free of prose'; poetry is above all the 'grammar of assent' to the world. Others have seen Bergson's concept of intuition as overlapping with Freud's ideas about the unconscious, which we consider shortly.*

Bergson's second advance, as he saw it, and as many influential people did in the early years of the twentieth century, was his notion of creative evolution. Given the nineteenth-century obsession with the world as a machine, Bergson thought that he had observed a crucial way in which the world was *not* a machine and this was in the existence of evolution, the production of new species, new and different forms of organism. It was unthinkable, he said, that any machine could produce – create – a new type of machine, and so here was a fundamental way in which living organisms were different from machines – and this meant the world was not a machine as many scientists implied. But he didn't infer a divine interference in this state of affairs. Instead, he argued that there is a vital impulse, the *élan vital*, which propels evolution and which, over the course of history, has promoted greater and greater mobility in organisms – mobility being, for Bergson, the ultimate expression of freedom. He sought evidence for the *élan vital* in, for example, the fact that the eye has evolved in parallel in quite separate families of animals – this springs, he said, from the same impulse.

This particular belief has been overtaken by evolutionary theory, but at the time the reaction to his ideas was considerable. On his visit to America in 1913, far more people turned out to see and hear him than had for Freud in 1909. This had partly to do with his sponsors – the pragmatists – partly to do with his lecturing style, but mainly to do with the fact that his system was seen as anti-science, or anti scientific determinism, and as offering a non-religious but still mystical explanation for the otherwise fully materialist idea of evolution. It was a little like a replay, albeit it in different clothes, of the moment in the eighteenth century when people couldn't quite shift from Christian belief to atheism in one jump, and so opted for the midway station of deism. Bergson claimed that the *élan vital* was a scientific concept, but for many it had a mystical element, and that was what counted.

---

* The most recent psychological research supports Bergson's division. For example, in *Thinking, Fast and Slow* (2011), the Nobel Prize-winning behavioural economist Daniel Kahneman divides behaviour into System 1 and System 2, the first more instinctive and intuitive, the second reflective and rational.

Spiritual Elitism

George Edward Moore has several claims on our attention. In the first place, as an undergraduate he was elected a member of the Cambridge Conversazione Society, more often remembered as the Apostles, whose other members included such figures as Alfred North Whitehead, G.H. Hardy and Rupert Brooke. If a university may be said to be an ideal community, more devoted to truth and learning and the exploration of philosophy than any other institution, the Apostles were an ideal within the ideal, and afforded many of its distinguished members (or, more accurately, members who would *become* distinguished) a form of spiritual life they rarely found elsewhere.

In existence for more than seventy years when Moore arrived in Cambridge, the size of the society was limited to twelve at any one time (hence its informal name). Members met every Saturday evening during term time, and at these meetings an essay prepared by one of them would be read and discussed, and then a vote taken (this Saturday Club matched the one in Cambridge, Massachusetts). Bertrand Russell, in his *Autobiography*, admitted that 'the greatest happiness of [his] life at Cambridge' resulted from his association with the society; and Moore himself, looking back in 1942 almost fifty years after joining, recalled the 'excitement and admiration' he felt on making the acquaintance of the group of students 'whose conversation seemed to me of a brilliance such as I had never hitherto met with or even imagined ... Until I went to Cambridge I had no idea of how exciting life could be.'[11]

After Cambridge and the Apostles, Moore became, as several Apostles did, a member of the Bloomsbury Group. By the time he joined in 1911 (there was no 'election' as such to the group), Bloomsbury was well established, having begun in 1905 when, after the death of their father Leslie, the Stephen children – Virginia, Vanessa, Thoby and Adrian – moved from Kensington to 46 Gordon Square near the British Museum, in the London district known as Bloomsbury. Here, Thoby introduced his Cambridge friends to his sisters at their weekly 'at homes' on Thursday evenings. These 'at homes' lasted until 1920.

Here is Tom Regan's summary of the group: '[T]he Bloomsbury Group was a powerful force in the artistic and intellectual avant-garde of post-Victorian England, pioneering new forms of expression in fiction and biography, forging new theories in economics and aesthetics. They were the harbingers of "the new", being everywhere – and often contemptuously – against "the old", not only in art and theory, but also in their day-to-day lives. As a matter of deliberate, conscientious decision they chose to live apart from both the very poor and the very rich ... An intellectual aristocracy in the truest sense ... they made no effort to conceal and offered no apology for their shared sense of superiority, their spiritual elitism.'

They were uncommon too in their loves and loyalties, which were often intermixed: Lytton Strachey lost Duncan Grant to Maynard Keynes; Clive Bell lost Vanessa to Roger Fry; Fry lost Vanessa to Grant; Vanessa shared Grant with David Garnett. No wonder, as one wag had it, in Bloomsbury, 'all the couples were triangles'.[12]

In his autobiography *Beginning Again*, Leonard Woolf summed up what Bloomsbury meant and the part in it played by Moore. 'The colour of our minds and thought had been given to us by the climate of Cambridge and Moore's philosophy, much as the climate of England gives one colour to the face of an Englishman.' Keynes agreed, further pointing out that the influence of Moore's philosophy 'was not only overwhelming ... it was the extreme opposite of what Strachey used to call *funeste*, it was exciting, exhilarating, the beginning of a new renaissance, the opening of a new heaven on a new earth, we were the fore-runners of a new dispensation, we were not afraid of anything'. Elsewhere Keynes wrote, 'we accepted Moore's religion ... and discarded his morals'.[13]

But what, then, was this new teaching, which Keynes emphasized, this new dispensation of Moore's, and why was it so overwhelming? This is another case where we have to think ourselves back to a different time, if we are to grasp fully the impact of Moore. Bertrand Russell was aware of this. 'It is surprising how great a change in mental climate those ten years [1904–14] had brought.'

A place to begin lies with Keynes's choice of the word 'religion' to characterize some aspects of Moore's teaching. Keynes took care to add that 'Moore's disciples' would have been 'very angry at the time' with the suggestion that they had a religion. 'We regarded all this as entirely rational and scientific in character.' Moore too would have been unhappy with any suggestion that he had propounded a religion – in his autobiography he described himself as a complete agnostic, and in fact his ethical precepts 'were offered by him as a cognitively and emotionally satisfying substitute for the discarded belief in a supernatural deity – offered, that is, as a religion without god'.[14]

Moore's main work was *Principia Ethica*, published in 1903, but he set out some of his ideas in *Vanity of Vanities* (1899). At one point in his intellectual career he was very melancholic. Belief in God required a leap of faith that he was unable to make and this distressed him – one had to live for nothing, he thought. He began a long struggle to construct a system of ethics that he could live by and that would bring him out of his long melancholic night. He started from the view that, despite the death of God, there are some things in the world that are better in themselves than others, that we can know something about what would be better than what actually exists without having to know everything. Much influenced by Wordsworth and his concept of 'the happy warrior' who works towards creating in himself a 'better' person by actively seeking a more strenuously moral life, Moore first worked his way through art ('art is nothing but a representation of what ought to be').

This doctrine underlay much of what the Bloomsbury Group sought. Moore felt that 'encounters with beautiful art are indistinguishable from those commonly attributed to (alleged) encounters with the Deity'. For Clive Bell, art 'is an expression of and a means to states of mind as holy as any that men are capable of experiencing . . . It is towards art that the modern mind turns, not only for the most perfect expression of transcendent emotion, but for an inspiration by which to live.' Art was the 'queen of endeavours' for Moore. 'Its object – beauty – is something one can care about, something one can strive to bring into the world or encourage others to do so, something by means of which the world can be made better in just the sense in which Moore understands the notion of moral goodness: better in itself.'[15]

What Ought to Exist

And this was Moore's main concern in *Principia Ethica*, that ethics must deal with a notion 'that belongs to it and it alone'. That notion is the Good (with a capital G), 'understood as the property shared by all and only those things that are good in themselves, or that have intrinsic value, or that ought to exist or are worth having for their own sakes'. This was Moore's central notion, that ethics studies an object that is not studied by any other science, that is logically independent of any other activity. For him, in Tom Regan's gloss, the 'good' is not the object of any empirical or natural science, including psychology; and propositions about what things are intrinsically good 'are logically distinct from propositions about any fact that any natural science may discover'.

This led him to his concept of the 'naturalistic fallacy', the name he gave to any attempt to identify the Good with something other than itself. His view was both that the good is indefinable and that some things are good in themselves, and it was the job of ethics to 'fix the nature of this shared property'.[16]

For him, the Good was sometimes a notion, sometimes an idea, sometimes an object, sometimes a practice, but that very idea/notion was not identical with anything other than itself. He thought that everyone was 'aware' of the good; they have a notion of what a better life would be, for example, and they have an idea of what *ought* to exist. The Good exists in the sense that numbers exist, as a useful notion, but numbers – like the Good – cannot exist as entities in the world in the way that trees or rocks or buses exist. For Moore the Good was a 'non-natural' property in that it is neither natural nor metaphysical, and it was his replacement of the word 'non-natural' for the more traditional 'transcendental' that was liberating for so many.

'Ought' being a main focus of *Principia*, what we ought to do, Moore held, 'is what produces the best results'. We might take the view that the 'best result' is equivalent to 'what is more evolved', but this is only one answer. Moore is at pains to point out that, because the Good is indefinable, there can be no one definition of what is Good and therefore no elevated class of 'moral experts', 'whether dressed in the gowns of science or the robes of religion', to impose their views on others – this was clearly very liberating at a time when the sanctimonious Victorian age was coming to an end.[17]

What Moore insisted upon was that individuals judge for themselves what things ought to exist, what things are worth having for their own sake. 'No natural science can do this. No metaphysical system can do this. Every attempt to take this freedom (and this responsibility) away from the individual rests on the same kind of fallacy – the (so-called) naturalistic fallacy. The *raison d'être* of ethics is to prove that there are some things – and these are the most important things in human life – that no science can prove.' Since Moore had a classics background he was temperamentally at home in a polytheistic universe. 'There are many goods, not only one.' It follows from this that the individual must make a leap of faith – faith in what he or she believes to be intrinsically good – not once but many times, and must wrest this freedom from science and religion and give it to 'its rightful bearer: the individual'.

'There is only the [intuitive] judgment itself [after due consideration], hanging suspended in the universe, so to speak, without support from anything other than itself.' Moore was determined to ensure that the moral freedom individuals had only recently grasped from the weakened clutches of an all but deceased religious tradition would not be stolen by the eager hands of evangelical scientists.[18]

Other things flowed from this. For example, that 'no moral law is self-evident'; we can never know with absolute certainty what our duties are (as Kant had said), though if certain rules appear to be useful (to the majority and to common sense), then we should probably follow them; but in this regard we ought to aim at goods affecting oneself and 'those in whom one has a strong personal interest' rather than to 'attempt a more extended beneficence'. And in general we should seek to secure goods that are 'in the present' rather than some more distant future, simply on the grounds of the probability of their realization. Egoism, Moore felt, is 'undoubtedly superior to altruism'. And it was important to distinguish between what we *morally ought* to do and what we have a *moral duty* to do, the former being wider and more encompassing than the latter.

To sum up, then, so long as we do not violate those few rules that are necessary for the stability of any society (such as do not murder, do not steal, do not break your promises), he believed, 'we act as we morally ought if we act with an eye to increasing our store of what is good in this world and sharing this with those for whom we care most – our family and friends'. There need be no more 'extended beneficence'.[19] It was this tightly circumscribed argument for no extended beneficence that appealed so much to the Bloomsbury Group, and it was this 'faith' that Keynes called their 'religion'. Looking back on those years, in a memoir written in 1949 Keynes concluded that 'this religion of ours was a very good one to have grown up under'. He felt that virtue lay in the pleasures of human intercourse and the enjoyment of beauty, but he acknowledged that these things can be maximized only in a stable society.[20]

It has to be said that Moore's doctrine, however well it may have imposed itself among the Bloomsberries, was overtaken by events. What the Bolsheviks and the Nazis thought was 'good', what ought to exist, was scarcely what Moore had in mind. His ideas evolved in a university context – that was their strength and their weakness. Terry Pinkard has noted that, for the most part, British philosophy has been the work of men of the world (Hume, Locke, Mill, Bentham), unlike German philosophy, which was the work of academics (Kant, Fichte, Hegel, Nietzsche, Husserl). Moore was an exception to this rule, and he took a stable society for granted. The twentieth century went against this premise.

Neurosis as a Private Religion

Sigmund Freud needs no introduction. When he died in 1939, W.H. Auden marked his passing with a poem in which he said that the psychoanalyst was 'no more a person/ now but a whole climate of opinion'. Freud was like the weather, Auden went on to say, that 'quietly surrounds all our habits of growth'. Freud was to be criticized – criticized bitterly, relentlessly, and from many different directions before he died, and even more since – but no one can dispute that he exerted an influence over twentieth-century ideas that was second to none. In fact, it is Freud above all who is responsible for the dominant shift in thought in modern times, which has seen a theological understanding of humankind replaced by a psychological one.

One could say that, more broadly speaking, what has actually happened in the modern world is the replacement of a theological understanding of humanity by a *biological* one. Especially in the later decades of the twentieth century, the biological understanding of human nature – especially in its evolutionary context – has been extended and deepened, and these developments and their implications for our theme will be examined in later chapters. But, while it may be the case that the psychological understanding of humanity is *part* of the biological understanding, it is still true that psychology, and psycho*pathology*, have invaded most successfully the territory once occupied exclusively by religion. As we shall see, this is true even among the clergy itself.

Psychoanalysis had been launched, famously, with *The Interpretation of Dreams* in 1900 and had had a mixed reception, frowned upon by the orthodox medical profession but securing a small, devoted, and gradually expanding circle of followers that widened further when Freud and his disciple Carl Jung visited the United States in 1909. The dominant idea of *Dreams* was that, as one observer put it, in sleep the sentry guarding our unconscious is, as it were, off duty; and ideas and emotions that are normally kept buried are let loose, albeit in symbolic and disguised form.

By 1912, when the International Association of Psychoanalysis had surmounted its early problems and the first defections, the journal *Imago* came into existence. Founded by Hanns Sachs, a close friend of Freud and an early psychoanalyst, the journal was to be edited jointly by Freud himself and Otto Rank, a young Viennese psychoanalyst much influenced by Ibsen and Nietzsche. The name, Ronald Clark tells us, was taken from the title of a work by Carl Spitteler, a Swiss poet who won the Nobel Prize for literature in 1919, in which the unconscious is shown both as affecting conscious action and stimulating the creative powers. But, significantly, the word 'imago' also means the final form of an insect after metamorphosis, and the journal was intended to deal not just with any medical aspects of psychoanalysis but with its transformation into a discipline that could confront also the nonmedical possibilities that had emerged from them.[21]

In the first issue Freud stressed the need to extend the scope of psychoanalytic research to fields such as language, customs, religion and the law, mythology, aesthetics, literature, the history of art, and philology; folklore, criminology and moral theory were also to be included. And the journal's ambitions grew still further with time – in the early thirties, Freud was writing that psychoanalysis could 'become indispensable to all the sciences which are concerned with the evolution of human civilization and its major institutions such as art, religion and the social order'.

Imago published the first of four essays representing Freud's application of psychoanalysis to social and anthropological problems, and outlined nothing less than his view of how human society originated, in particular from where the religious beliefs of early man derive.[22] *Totem and Taboo* was published in book form in 1913, though Freud had begun to air his views on religion a few years earlier. In 1907 he began his paper 'Obsessive Actions and Religious Practices' as follows: 'I am certainly not the first person to have been struck by the resemblance between what are called obsessive actions in sufferers from nervous afflictions and the observances by means of which believers give expression to their piety.' To him, he said, the resemblance seemed more than superficial, 'so that an insight into the origin of neurotic ceremonial may embolden us to draw inferences by analogy about the psychological processes of religious life'.

All the same, Freud was careful at that point to stress the differences as much as the similarities between neurosis and religious practice, concluding that 'obsessional neurosis presents a travesty, half comic and half tragic, of a private religion'. At the same time, he went on to say that, just as many patients were unaware of the unconscious reasons for carrying out their obsessional actions, so many religious people were unaware of the motives that impelled them to religious practices. He drew a further parallel in saying that both obsessional neurotics and the pious are motivated by an unconscious sense of guilt, and this sense of guilt 'has its source in certain early mental events, but it is constantly being revived by renewed temptations which arise whenever there is a contemporary provocation'.[23]

Religion, like obsessional neurosis, he said, was based on a suppression of instinct. In the neurotic, the instinct suppressed was invariably sexual, and though that wasn't quite so true of religion, that instinct was 'usually not without a sexual component'. 'Perhaps because of the admixture of sexual components, perhaps because of some general characteristics of the instincts, the suppression of instinct proves to be an inadequate and interminable process in religious life also. Indeed, complete backsliding into sin is more common among pious people than among neurotics and ... give[s] rise to a new form of religious activity, namely acts of penance, which have their counterparts in obsessional neurosis.' And he concluded: 'In view of these similarities and analogies one might venture to regard obsessional neurosis as a pathological counterpart of the formation of a religion, and to describe neurosis as an individual religiosity and religion as a universal obsessional neurosis.'[24]

Although he had begun by trying to sugar-coat the pill he was administering, by the end of his paper Freud had concluded with a message that was bound to be as unpopular as it was controversial: that, in effect, religion was the manifestation of a form of – emotionally equivalent to – mental illness. In the following years he widened the attack. In 1910, in 'Future Prospects of Psychoanalytic Therapy', he went so far as to link secularization with an increase in neurosis. 'You cannot exaggerate the intensity of man's inner resolution and craving for authority. The extraordinary increase in the neuroses since the power of religion has waned may give you some indication of it.' As he was to say later, 'Devout believers are safeguarded in a high degree against the risk of neurotic illness.'[25]

Freud's theory of faith was rooted in his theory of psychology. For him, the anxiety we feel as infants over our helplessness 'is the fundamental feeling which impels a person toward religious faith'. As he put it in a paper on Leonardo da Vinci, published in 1910, 'Biologically speaking, religiousness is to be traced to the small human child's long-drawn-out helplessness and need of help.' Freud discovered (if we set aside the criticisms for a moment) the profound effect of childhood experiences on adult emotional life, and he went on to argue that 'many people are unable to surmount the fear of loss of [parental] love; they never become sufficiently independent of other people's love and in this respect carry on their behavior as infants'. Freud thought that an efficacious religion 'helps the believer master the regressive anxiety that is stirred up by developmental danger-situations when they recur in adult life and become traumas'. 'The roots of the need for religion are in the parental complex; the almighty and just God, and kindly Nature, appear to us as grand sublimations of father and mother.'[26]

Social factors, unique to modernity, have reinforced this dependency. Childhood was extended by the abolition of child labour, while work could call fathers away from home for long periods. In addition, the breakdown of the extended family has tended to isolate the mother–child relationship. All this increases the dependency of the pre-oedipal child on the mother. Many find in religion what they once had in childhood.

Freud went on to say that religion actually contributes to the resolution of the Oedipus complex, thereby protecting believers from neurosis: this is why secularization has been such a painful process for so many people. The religious are unaware of the psychological origins of their religious loyalties. Religion, being in part a substitute for the parents, radiates love and security to the believer – without, however, the anxiety that is usually aroused by intense libidinal ties to the parents. Thus religion helps keep the lid on erotic and aggressive instincts, thereby benefiting society.

So far, Freud had equated religious feelings and behaviour with neurotic behaviour and symptoms, and had rooted religion in the psychodynamics of family life, in what has been called from the child's viewpoint 'the two-parent family love triangle'. Essentially, this subsumed religion as a subset phenomenon of psychology. In *Totem and Taboo*, which he began in the spring of 1911, Freud widened his horizons and sought the anthropological origins of religion in an evolutionary context. He surrounded himself, he told friends, with some 'thick books' that he wasn't really interested in, 'since I already know the results'. He wrote his own book in the Tyrol, well aware of the reception it was likely to provoke – it was 'the most daring enterprise I have ever ventured', he told one friend, an attempt to 'smuggle psychoanalysis into ethnopsychology', as he told another.[27]

The book consisted of four essays: 'The Horror of Incest', 'Taboo and Emotional Ambivalence', 'Animism, Magic and the Omnipotence of Thought' and 'The Return of Totemism in Childhood'. The fourth, which contains the nub of the argument, is of interest here. Freud's hypothesis took as its starting point Darwin's 'primal horde', by which Darwin meant little more than a small self-supporting group under the control of 'the father', who exercised absolute rule over other males in the group, retaining all the women for his own 'use'. Freud argued that eventually the young men revolted, then murdered and consumed the father; and in atonement they forbade the slaughter of a totem animal (which substituted for the father). However, in order to prevent a recurrence of the original crime, under which ran rivalry for the women, marriage within the group was forbidden, as was killing. For Freud this neatly explained the only two crimes with which, he held, primitive society concerned itself – murder and incest.

From our perspective it doesn't matter – for now, at least – that the anthropology on which Freud based his theories has been superseded, shown by more recent studies to have been off-base by some distance, just as Bergson's ideas about the evolution of the eye have been superseded. At the time, Freud's attempts to marry psychology, anthropology and social institutions such as religion and art were seen as advances in the *synthesis* of knowledge, such a synthesis being itself regarded as evidence of advance. And Freud's psycho-anthropological theories invited the view that religion was a natural phenomenon, that there was nothing 'transcendental' about it, that it was to be understood ultimately in anthropological terms. Moreover, since Freud drew attention to the similarities between neurosis and religious practice, it followed that religion was to be regarded, not exactly as a pathological aspect of society (since he acknowledged that some people were helped by it), but certainly as *subordinate* to psychology as a way for humankind to understand itself.[28]

The spread of psychoanalysis 'beyond the couch', as it were, as presaged in the first editorial of *Imago* and confirmed by *Totem and Taboo*, marked what we may call 'the first psychological turn' of the modern era. By offering an explanation for religion, by reconceiving it in psychological terms, and by offering a technology – psychoanalysis – as a way to investigate, understand and resolve unconscious conflicts and pathologies, Freud offered a refuge for people who felt homeless after they had lost their faith.

Peter Gay has examined the early relationship between religion and psychoanalysis in *A Godless Jew: Freud, Atheism and the Making of Psychoanalysis* (1987), where he concludes that a believer could never have founded psychoanalysis, that it needed someone prepared to be iconoclastic, someone who viewed religion as a phenomenon to be studied 'rather than a promise to be prayed for or a supreme reality to worship'.[29] He shows convincingly that Freud resisted all attempts to draw parallels between religion and psychoanalysis. But Gay also makes clear that part of the appeal of psychoanalysis for many, in the early days as later, was the apparent fact that it was deterministic (in terms of the oedipal situation, above all) and yet provided later behaviour with characteristics of 'purpose', 'intention', 'aim'. Whether Freud liked it or not (and he stressed that psychoanalysis was a science, based on 'controlled experience' and susceptible to criticism), these other elements – individual variation and a deterministic teleology – gave it the elements of a substitute faith.

The unconscious – vague, in a sense mystical – became the secular equivalent of the soul. Throughout the twentieth century, as we shall repeatedly see, more and more people entered psychotherapy with what seemed at times religious zeal. And, as the years passed, they sought psychotherapy less and less as a treatment for neurosis and more for a sense of meaning in their lives. This is why Freud became the towering figure that he did, Auden's climate of opinion, despite the legions of his critics.

4

Heaven: Not a Location but a Direction

'Between 1880 and 1930 one of the supreme cultural experiments in the history of the world was enacted in Europe and America.' This is Robert Hughes in *The Shock of the New: Art and the Century of Change*. In explanation he added that, in the time of our grandfathers and great-grandfathers (and grandmothers too, of course), 'the visual arts had a kind of social importance they can no longer claim today'. This was not, he thought, a matter for self-congratulation, and he went on to list what has been lost: 'Ebullience, idealism, confidence, the belief that there was plenty of territory to explore, and above all the sense that art, in the most disinterested and noble way, could find the necessary metaphors by which a radically changing culture could be explained to its inhabitants.'[1]

The Mechanical Paradise

For Europeans in general, not just for the French, the master image, the structure that 'seemed to gather all the meanings of modernity together', was the Eiffel Tower. The focal point of the Paris World's Fair in 1889, the centenary of the French Revolution, it was aptly described as the 'cathedral of the machine age'.[2] One of the main celebrants of what Hughes called 'the mechanical paradise' was Fernand Léger, whose work he saw as 'a sustained confession of modernist hope' – hope, remember, being one of the American Pragmatists' chief ingredients of modern living. Léger's aim was to make images of the machine age that would transcend barriers of class and education, and be 'clear, definite, pragmatic'. One of his greatest paintings, *Three Women*, has as its underlying theme the idea of society-as-a-machine: the composition is geometrically simplified – the women's bodies, the surrounding furniture, the black cat on the sofa, are all formed of tubes and cones and barrels – even the waves in the women's hair are metallic. For Léger, society-as-a-machine was a form of salvation, in that it could bring harmony and an end to cosmic loneliness after the death of God: '[W]e are offered a metaphor of human relationships working as smoothly as a clock, all passion sublimated, with the binding energy of desire transformed into rhythms of shape.'[3]

This idea, that at the turn of the twentieth century art could be important in a way that is no longer possible (and we shall be exploring why this is so), is only half the picture. The other half, from the viewpoint of this book at least, may be found in the work of the Swedish playwright August Strindberg, of whom it has been well said that 'the unit of meaning in his plays is the immediate crisis in the individual soul'.[4] The crucial word here is 'immediate'. Strindberg went through life 'afraid and hurrying' and ridden with guilt, forever reaching out for what it is not in the power of life to grant, his 'metaphysical hunger' causing him at one point or another to occupy every position between believer and atheist and back again.

If we are to fully appreciate the cultural world that existed in the wake of Nietzsche's pronouncements, then we have to allow for these two factors: that at the time art – drama, poetry, painting, the novel – held real promise for making a difference and showing the way forward; and second, that many were convinced the crisis was new, immediate and fundamental, that civilized life was on the edge of an abyss, an abyss that we may not feel as sharply now. The predicament was summed up by H.G. Wells who, in *The Outline of History* (1920), described history as 'a race between education and catastrophe'.

The dominant artistic vehicle of the middle decades of the nineteenth century was the novel, while poetry, drama and the short story were relatively neglected. All three re-emerged in the 1880–90s, coinciding neatly with Nietzsche's interventions. This chapter is concerned with drama which, like painting, possessed an urgency then that it does not quite have now.[5]

'The most important event in the history of modern drama,' Kenneth Muir tells us, 'was Ibsen's abandonment of verse after *Peer Gynt* in order to write prose plays about contemporary problems.'[6] In fact, it could be argued that although Ibsen did indeed tackle a number of social problems that disfigured the late nineteenth century, all of which he claimed he had 'lived through', and that are still with us – the role of women in society (*A Doll's House*), the conflict across the generation gap (*The Master Builder*), the clash between individual liberty and institutionalized authority (*Rosmersholm*), the menace of pollution in a world of material and commercial values (*An Enemy of the People*) – in all of his later plays the dominant theme is the protagonist's search for a moral order *within* him- or herself, to counter the 'cosmic emptiness' and the chaos around him or her.[7]

For this Ibsen there is no order and no God – except insofar as his characters conceive of him. 'Ibsen's centrality to the moral intelligence of the late nineteenth century is derived from Hegel, nothing less than the redemption of man's alienation from himself and from nature by rediscovering "the total human spirit within the conditions of the Present".'[8] His later plays are inevitably dramas of 'spiritual distress', describing his characters' search for consolation in the shadow of death and their attempts to manufacture some form of Paradise in the here and now. 'Redemption from cosmic nothingness, from meaninglessness – this is the nature of the Romantic quest which Ibsen's people share with those of Byron and Stendhal.'[9]

For many years, Ibsen's work was known only in Scandinavia; in the 1890s, however, by which time he was already into his sixties, he suddenly came to the attention of all Europe with the release of *Ghosts*. From then on a new Ibsen play was an international event. 'Never before had a dramatic author so dominated the European theatre or so monopolized public debate.'[10]

Flashes of Spiritual Value

Hardly any of the main characters in Ibsen's later plays fail to conduct themselves on the basis of a *deus absconditus* (a hidden God) or lead lives that are not governed by that awareness. These characters are either pagan acolytes of Dionysus or self-declared apostates, defrocked priests or freethinkers; they are atheist rebels, or agnostics. In *Hedda Gabler* Hedda dreams of being a free spirit, 'irradiated by the orgiastic religion of ancient Greece', living like a deity herself, albeit surrounded by the paraphernalia of a bourgeois existence. In *The Master Builder*, Bygmester Solness brandishes his clenched fist at a deity who allows the pointless deaths of young children, so that Solness abandons himself to a new religion of secular humanism. And in *Little Eyolf* Alfred Allmers, 'the self-styled atheist', first devotes himself to a 'tremendous existential undertaking', a huge book called *Human Responsibility*. 'In many ways,' says Errol Durbach, 'Allmers's predicament seems the paradigm of the romantic dilemma in Ibsen's drama, which, to state in its simplest and crudest terms, is to be trapped between a traumatic sense of existence as process, change and death in a world devoid of consistent value, and a longing for a lost world of static hierarchies where death has no dominion. And in order to resolve this dilemma, the atheist/agnostic/apostate will fashion out of the raw material of existence his analogue of that lost Eden – a symbolic Paradise which promises eternal life, and which he seeks to possess, not as *metaphor* but as *fact*.'[11]

Five of the later plays, *Hedda Gabler*, *The Master Builder*, *Little Eyolf*, *John Gabriel Borkman* and *When We Dead Awaken*, hang together in that their overall theme is a search for a dimension of human existence that is 'forever exempt from the laws of change'.[12] This is highlighted and countered in the plays not just by the lurking presence of death (often in the form of terminal illness – syphilis, tuberculosis, cancer) but in the fact that those who die are the last of their line: this is not just death, but extinction.[13] In a famous article 'Symbols of Eternity: the Victorian Escape from Time', Jerome Buckley grouped Ibsen with Coleridge, Rossetti, Wordsworth, Pater and William Morris in their attempts to 'fashion worlds of artifice beyond the reach of change'. We see these 'symbols of eternity' in Ibsen in, for example, the paradise/kingdom of Orangia/Appelsinia in *The Master Builder*, in Hedda's ancient Greek paganism, in Borkman's mine, in Allmers's search for the unchanging dimension of human responsibility in his great book.

What Ibsen's plays explore are the pain and the tragedy almost inevitably involved in trying to create something of lasting value amid the flux and ceaseless flow of change, the experimental nature of life and reality. That said, his work is guardedly optimistic in its attempt to provide constructive responses to our new predicament, outlined by Nietzsche. '[His work] celebrates joy in the jaws of death, sees in the law of change not decay but continuous transformation of the self, that re-establishes value in an empty world by accepting responsibility for one's actions and decisions, and that creates meaning in the void where none existed.'[14]

Hedda Gabler poses the problem. Hedda has a complex inner life and longs to be 'more' than she is – her bourgeois surroundings do not fulfil her and she aches for a classical world, a culture of higher purposes, of beauty and timeless myth, where she can feel 'upward momentum'. She becomes a 'virtuoso of the eccentric', which helps maintain her feeling of being among the spiritually elect. It is her aim in the play to redeem Løvborg from his wife, who has changed him from being a bohemian into a respectable and abstemious academic. But when he dies in an unseemly scuffle with a prostitute, an ugly accident in a brothel, she realizes that the only way out for her, the only way to impose order – and yes, beauty – on her predicament, is to assert herself by means of her own death in a manner denied Løvborg.

The other later plays are not so uncompromisingly bleak. Salvation, for Ibsen, is not to be achieved in any teleological sense, or by directing ourselves to any God-given 'final cause', but by ethical actions whereby our ideals are reconciled with 'workable human realities'; life is small, and has its ordinary elements – oh, yes – but we must search for dignity where we can find it among those small, mundane lineaments, knowing that the most we can hope for is 'flashes of spiritual value' and that they comprise life's larger purposes.

If this view of flashes of spiritual value overlaps with Santayana's philosophy, Ibsen's idea about 'cosmologies of two' overlaps with D.H. Lawrence (considered later) when he says, 'We lack peace because we are not whole. And we are not whole because we have known only a tithe of the vital relationships we might have had. We live in an age which believes in stripping away the relationships. Strip them away, like an onion, till you come to pure, or blank nothingness. Emptiness. That is where most men have come now: to a knowledge of their complete emptiness. They wanted so badly to be "themselves" that they became nothing at all: or next to nothing.'

In *Little Eyolf* Ibsen gives us an early view of, and an answer to, Lawrence's predicament of isolated individualism. After Eyolf, the crippled and thus half-unwanted son, is drowned, lured into the sea by the Rat-Wife, Alfred and his wife Rita resolve to do more for the poor children in their area. To help these children in a way they never helped their own infirm and less than perfect child brings them together in a way they have not been together before. The value they now see in their lives – to help the children – is an absolute value, in *this* world, the small world that is theirs, that surrounds them. What they are resolved to do may seem unremarkable, may not have the world-wide 'significance' that Alfred's book on *Human Responsibility* might have had, was intended to have had, but it is capable of realization, it is a workable ideal. It may not feel like salvation in a cosmic sense, an otherworldly sense, nor will it confer immortality on Alfred and Rita. But it allows them to take part in something of value – helping others – that in itself can be regarded as immortal.

And finally, it rescues their marriage, no small thing in Ibsen's eyes, and that is because Ibsen has them change. 'Why, oh, why,' says Alfred, 'do we want one another to be always the same, fixed, like a menu card that is never changed . . . life – it keeps renewing itself. Let us hold fast to it, my dear. – We come to the end of it only too soon.' Life *is* change, says Ibsen, echoing the American pragmatists and Henri Bergson, in their different ways.

When We Dead Awaken overlaps with Yeats to an extent. The sculptor Rubek is bored with his wife and at an impasse in his creative life. The fortuitous appearance of a model he once used for his work promises both a revitalized erotic life – desire – and to unlock his creative energies. But this recalls the 'impossible alternatives' in Yeats's poem 'The Choice':

> The intellect of man is forced to choose
> Perfection of the life, or of the work,
> And if it take the second must refuse
> A heavenly mansion . . .

Rubek cannot reconcile these competing forces any better than anyone else can. The central conceit in *When We Dead Awaken* is a quartet – two men and two women – which forms and reforms in a series of alliances, continually seeking, via these realignments, some solution to the individuals' inability to maintain relationships, while leaving them lonely, incomplete, empty and in despair.[15] With Yeats, Ibsen is forcing us to choose and reminding us that the 'absolute' reassurance of art is not life, or not all of life, that it is not in and of itself completion or wholeness.

In *Rosmersholm* can be found similarities with Santayana's work in that the play – bleak and despairing as it is – is about *joy*, about the norm of life being joy, not in the sense that it is the standard, everyday state of man, but *what he is born for*.[16] Rosmer is an apostate, trying to embrace change and effect political reform in Norway, even though it means supporting developments that go against the traditional interests of the aristocracy, of which he is a member. He sees himself as someone innocent and pure who is trying to do good in a disinterested way. Rebekka, the friend of his wife Beata, who committed suicide a year ago, still lives in the Rosmer household because she is in love with Rosmer, sharing his political sympathies and actions. As the play unfolds it becomes clear that Rosmer may not have been quite so pure as he imagines, or pretends to himself to be; that he is and has been in love with Rebekka. When Professor Kroll, Rosmer's brother-in-law, learns of his political plans, he is outraged at the class betrayal and begins to sabotage Rosmer's aims by publishing innuendoes in the local newspaper about what really happened concerning Beata's death – hinting that it wasn't suicide due to mental illness, as originally supposed, but to Rosmer and Rebekka having an affair. Rebekka admits that there is some truth to this, a confession that places a terrible burden on both of them.

Ibsen's message here is that to experience 'goodness', and to value it above personal happiness, 'is to experience the meaning of joy'. He highlights this, typically perhaps, with the encroaching tragedy – the fact that neither Rosmer nor Rebekka can live with the guilt that is now exposed, that their relationship *was* to blame for Beata's suicide. Together they kill themselves, in the same way that Beata died, by jumping into the mill-race. 'They die for the right reasons,' says Durbach, 'to reassert the moral will, to free their love of guilt, and to establish once again the primacy of human values in the world of ordinary experience. They die in joy, in that complete fulfilment and realization of self in the love of the other which, in the language of an earlier dispensation, would be synonymous with blessedness and grace . . . They will die as a fusion of autonomous spiritual powers, a single consciousness, a genuine cosmology of two.' 'Is it you who goes with me, or I with you?' Rebekka asks.[17] 'We go together, Rebekka, I with you, you with me . . . For now we two are one.'

Joy, which is the aim and purpose of life in Ibsen, comes from the power of moral perception. This is the only eternal value in a desolate world, 'even at the cost of life and happiness'.[18] Ibsen's wide range gave his moral vision great authority.

Desire and Cruelty

Of Johan August Strindberg it has been said that 'there is a shorter distance between blood and ink' than with Ibsen. Indeed, Strindberg's dramatizations of what he saw as 'the awful human impasse' were more urgent than either Ibsen's or Chekhov's. As mentioned earlier, Strindberg went through life 'afraid and hurrying' and ridden with guilt. He took personally the moral decay that he saw all around him, and this to an extent fuelled his 'quarrel with God', which was, as Otto Reinert put it, a much more ambiguous enterprise than Ibsen's.[19] Fascinated by the new metapsychologies of Freud and Jung (Strindberg and Freud gained the allegiance of the German literary world at much the same time), his object in his plays was to continually expose the self of the alienated modern man, 'crawling between heaven and earth, desperately trying to pluck some absolutes from a forsaken universe'. He was determined to make war on God – with Nietzsche he shared a contempt for Christianity – while searching for something new, and he identified with the rebels against God – Cain, Prometheus, Ishmael. Yet he admitted at one point, 'I have looked for God and found the devil'; 'Our highest achievement [is] . . . the concealment of our vileness'; and 'My life adds up as a warning for the improvement of others.'[19]

His most characteristic tone is found in his plays *Easter, A Dream Play, Miss Julie* and *The Ghost Sonata*. Each concerns existential revolt directed against the meaninglessness and contradictions of human existence. For Strindberg, in a world of elusive truth, 'only the self has any real validity'.[20] An ardent disciple of Darwin and Nietzsche (he exchanged several letters with the philosopher), Strindberg admitted that 'I myself found the joy of life in its strong and cruel struggles', and in his explorations of the cult of the self he presents us with the argument that it is only Dionysian vitality that carries us along.[21] He himself had a Dionysian vitality, at one stage conducting psychological and drug-induced experiments on his own person, and exploring botany, chemistry and optics in addition to writing sixty plays, thirty works of fiction, autobiography, history and politics, as well as producing the more than sixty paintings exhibited at the Tate Gallery in London in 2005.

He shared certain ideas with the pragmatists and phenomenologists. He was convinced the 'world process' is a whirling chaos of flux and yet more flux, and his work is marked, above all, by his impatience with fixity of character. A fatal error of classical theatre, he felt, was 'its commitment to constant characterization'. The truth is, as revealed in *Miss Julie*, for example, that man never stops developing and contradicting himself, and the only true picture of him is one that reveals 'the multitude of inconsistencies and contradictions' of his soul.[22] Strindberg confirmed that he had lived 'multifariously' the lives of all the people he described in his work, and that his plays were an 'unending dialectic' between his 'many selves'.

At the same time (and contrariwise) he had a 'metaphysical hunger', and though lacking a mystic's temperament he had a mystic's impulse towards some single comprehensive experience of reality, an *Anschluss mit Jenseits*, a union with the beyond. His demands on the 'ultimate' were 'preposterous' but he never learned to reduce them. And this helped bring about a profound change in him. Very possibly the real roots of Strindberg's 'preposterous demands' were sexual and pathological. This is certainly one way of understanding what he called his 'Inferno crisis' in 1894, a number of terrifying paranoiac psychotic episodes lasting two years, after which he rejected his earlier atheistic position and came to accept the semi-mystical views of Emanuel Swedenborg and others, who maintained that life is controlled by 'powers' or supernatural agents, and that there are 'correspondences' between the transcendental world and the real world; that there is, in some mysterious way, an 'Absolute' unifying all experience.

Until that point, however, Strindberg had accepted – more than had Ibsen – the almost classic Nietzschean position: that we are many selves, that we are what we make of these selves, and that is why Dionysian vitality is so important. And only by means of that vitality can we maintain our appetite for experimentally exploring each of these selves until we settle on one that we find fulfilling, always acknowledging that life cannot remain static, either, and that once we find one self that makes us seem whole, life may change again soon enough.

But he also occupied a Freudian position in that he thought that the *expression* of what could be 'dredged up', uncensored, from the unconscious was the only way to achieve wholeness, the only way to 'de-restrict' desire and 'complete' what the self is. But even when these epiphanies occurred, Strindberg didn't expect them to last for ever; the flux of life continued, the Darwinian struggle – as often as not containing cruel elements – never stopped.

'Mozartian Joy Is the Aim'

George Bernard Shaw, the Irish author of some sixty plays, co-founder of the London School of Economics, an early, prominent member of the Fabian Society, and the only person to win both the Nobel Prize for Literature and an Oscar (for his work on *Pygmalion*), both was and wasn't religious – depending on how you define that term. He thought that Darwin had 'dealt a mortal blow to Christianity', but he was much influenced by Bergson's 'creative evolution'. He wrote a book entitled *The Quintessence of Ibsenism* in which he set out a lot of his own interpretations of Ibsen: that he had sought to rescue his generation from materialism, that the aim of life is self-improvement, self-fulfilment; that morality is not fixed but evolves, that standards can never be eternal, that modern European literature is more important in teaching us how to live than the Bible, and that 'Mozartian joy' is the aim.[23]

Shaw thought that life and 'reality' were essentially experimental, that individuals were themselves experiments. Traditional religions, he thought, were intellectually dishonest and inflexible in their inability to take account of evolution and its many implications, the most important of which was and is the indefiniteness and the mutability of reality itself. Given the uncertainty built into reality by evolution, there could be no permanent, unchanging moral imperative built into life, nor could there be any transcendent validity to anything. At the same time, 'We must have a religion if we are to do anything worth doing. If anything is to be done to get our civilization out of the horrible mess in which it is now, it must be done by men who have got a religion.'[24] How he reconciled these two views is part of his achievement.

Shaw was obsessed by change in life, by the possibility – and hope – of improvement, which is why he was as interested and as involved in politics as he was in the theatre. There was no 'golden rule' for him – the way we lead our lives must be judged by its *effect* on life itself, on ourselves and others, rather than by conformity to any rules or ideal. 'Life consists in the fulfilment of the will, which is constantly growing, and cannot be fulfilled today under the conditions which secured its fulfilment yesterday.'[25]

It followed for Shaw that there is more to life than happiness. 'There is nothing so insufferable as happiness, except perhaps unhappiness.' Having the leisure to *bother* about whether you are happy or not, he thought, was a guarantee of miserableness – 'A perpetual holiday is a good working definition of hell.' But he didn't idealize work any more than anything else – because he didn't *trust* idealization. Whereas happiness for him was 'self-centred, transient, sterile and uncreative', he worshipped creativity. With Captain Shotover in *Heartbreak House* he feared 'the accursed happiness . . . of yielding and dreaming, instead of resisting and doing, the sweetness of the fruit that is going rotten'.[26]

If he had any motto or maxim, it was 'Use is life'. He reiterated time and again that 'he could find no mighty purpose' in the pursuit of either personal happiness or personal virtue. But he often spoke about finding his sense of life in 'use'; he even said he believed himself 'used' by an unspecified force for mighty purposes – he was a follower of Bergson and this is how, for him, *élan vital* worked, perhaps. Traditionally, such feelings might originally have involved reverence for some form of deity, but Shaw argued that the conventional understanding of the Christian God was just another form of idealism.

He expressed this better in words he put into Don Juan's mouth in *Man and Superman*: 'Religion [had been reduced] for me to a mere excuse for laziness, since it had set up a God who looked at the world and saw that it was good, against the instinct in me that looked through my eyes at the world and saw that it could be improved.' From this it naturally followed that the life to come, for Shaw, was not 'an eternity spent . . . in a sort of bliss which would bore any active person to a second death', but 'a better life to come for the whole world'.[27] The overlap with the pragmatists here is clear.

In 1895 he wrote to his friend Frederick Evans, a London bookseller and amateur photographer, 'I want to write a big book of devotion for modern people, bringing all the truths latent in the old religious dogmas into contact with real life – a gospel of Shawianity, in fact . . . I have been described as a man laughing in the wilderness. That is correct enough, if you accept me as preparing the way for better things.' This, then, was Shaw's aim, to create 'an awareness of something better and the will to bring it into existence'.[28] And this too is where Bergson came in. In writing the preface to *Back to Methuselah* (1920) Shaw says: 'I had always known that civilization needs a religion as a matter of life or death; and as the concept of Creative Evolution developed I saw that we were at last within reach of a faith which complied with the first condition of all religions that have ever taken hold of humanity;

namely that it must be first and foremost a religion of metabiology. I believe myself to be a servant and instrument of Creative Evolution. God is will ... But will is useless without hands and brain ... That evolutionary process to me is God.'[29]

In looking forward, Shaw was drawn to the superman idea, but his enthusiasm was tempered by two practical concerns: experience showed that if salvation was to be achieved in this world and not the next (which is what he believed, despite his religious feelings), it would have to be available for everyone, not just the Nietzschean few. He also eschewed the Nietzschean apocalyptic view of salvation: Darwin had taught that human progress towards whatever salvation is would come in 'infinitesimal increments'. Here, Shaw's philosophy and his politics came together: in his socialism and his Fabianism he was a gradualist, an evolutionist rather than a revolutionary.

But he wasn't entirely in thrall to Darwin. He accepted that human beings can have no life 'except a share in the life of the community'; but he thought natural selection wasteful and indirect and that politics represented a more direct form of adaptation to our circumstances, nothing less – in his words – than the mechanism we have devised for fulfilling what he saw, in a Hegelian sense, as the will of the world.[30] A whole raft of characters in his plays – Lady Cicely Waynflete, Undershaft, Caesar, Saint Joan, to name a few – identify with some 'essential vitality and will outside themselves'. For Shaw the *giving* of oneself was the central act of faith in life, not as an act of self-abnegation or self-sacrifice, as Christianity would have it, but as a creative duty. The will was central, too, because 'The progress of knowledge and civilization does not mend matters; it simply brings with it new needs and, with them, new sufferings and new forms of selfishness. Therefore, the will is still needed.'[31]

And, as he said elsewhere, 'The world is waiting for Man to redeem it from the lame and cramped government of the gods.'[32] But Shaw frankly acknowledged that 'the precise formula for the Superman ... has not yet been discovered. Until it is, every birth is an experiment in the Great Research which is being conducted by the Life Force to discover that formula.' But he insisted that there is an 'irresistible urge' to achieve an ever higher stage, a desire towards perfectibility: 'In the heaven I seek [there is] no other joy than the work of helping Life in its struggle upward.'[33] In *Don Juan* he wrote, 'I tell you that as long as I can conceive something better than myself I cannot be easy unless I am striving to bring it into existence or clearing the way for it ... I tell you that in the pursuit of my own pleasure ... I have never known happiness.' Or, as Shaw wrote to Tolstoy in 1910: 'To me God does not yet exist ... The current theory that God already exists in perfection involves the belief that God deliberately created something lower than Himself ... To my mind, unless we conceive God as engaged in a continual struggle to surpass himself ... we are conceiving nothing better than an omnipotent snob.' And in the Postscript he added to *Back to Methuselah* as late as 1944: 'God ... is therefore not a Person but an incorporeal Purpose, unable to do anything directly.'[34]

Again, this view informed his politics as much as his plays and ideas. 'The ethic and religion of socialism seek not the ideal society through the ideal individual, but conversely, the ideal individual through the ideal society.' Through politics, society would achieve an ever-widening communal identity by means of an evolutionary process 'in which each new level of development incorporated what was most necessary or "true" from the half-truths of earlier stages'. The 'good' is a process of endless improvement 'that need never stop and is never complete'.[35]

These ideas were incorporated into his plays, where the essential form is one of *movement* that usually carries beyond despair to a synthesis in the shape of a new and firmer grasp on reality, by way of an evolution leading to a more complete self-awareness through a dialectic of action and reaction. In *Candida* the clergyman's wife Candida, asked to choose between her 'weak' husband and her would-be lover, realizes she has learned to live without happiness: 'life is nobler than [happiness]'. As in his other plays, Shaw presents the choice as being between the truer and the less true, not between absolutes.[36]

Shaw's plays focus on superhuman, perceptive models (Don Juan, Caesar, Saint Joan, Undershaft, Henry Higgins, the early long-livers in *Back to Methuselah*), whose function, whether in a 'world historical sense' (à la Hegel) or on a private, mundane, domestic level, is to encourage ordinary individuals (Cleopatra, Barbara Undershaft,

Liza Doolittle, Ellie Dunn) into a larger participation in their own destiny.[37]

Shaw took hope seriously – it is for him, as Robert Whitman has pointed out, a form of moral responsibility. 'To be in hell is to drift (a denial of purpose); heaven is to steer . . . Life is a force which has made innumerable experiments in organizing itself . . . into higher and higher individuals.' Shaw's superman, in contrast to Nietzsche's, is not a goal, an end-product; rather, it is a process, a stage of development: 'Heaven is not a place but a direction.'[38] In *Major Barbara* (1905) Undershaft, a wealthy armaments manufacturer, admits that he would rather be a thief than a pauper, a murderer rather than a slave, because in doing so he would be taking action, and would retain his self-respect. When Cussins, engaged to Barbara, a major in the Salvation Army, asks him innocently what power it is that drives his munitions plant, Undershaft replies enigmatically: 'A will of which I am part', adding, 'I am a millionaire. That is my religion.'

This conformed to Shaw's desire to see an end to the notion that we live for reason instead of for the fulfilment of our will to live. But what emerges from the play is that power and a sense of purpose need each other. If people want a better world, he is saying, they have to create it themselves, not sit back and wait for God to achieve it. 'The end of human existence is not to be "good" and be rewarded in heaven, but to create Heaven on earth.' As he wrote to Lady Gregory: 'My doctrine is that God proceeds by the method of "trial and error" . . . To me the sole hope of human salvation lies in teaching Man to regard himself as an experiment in the realization of God.'[39]

In *Androcles and the Lion* Shaw pits religion against no religion, airing his view that the major form of sin is the status quo, because, as he asserts in the Preface (Shaw was a great one for writing explicatory and often didactic prefaces to his plays), 'the fundamental condition of evolution . . . is, that life, including human life, is continually evolving and must therefore be continually ashamed of itself and its present and past'.[40] Christianity, he believes, is but a stage in moral evolution. And this evolution can only happen via the passionate impulses of life – curiosity, daring, resistance, the 'effort of seeking something better', to be contrasted with what he considered 'the impulses of death', the desire for comfort and happiness, cynical self-serving, and 'dreams of ease'.[41]

For Shaw, vitality, a realistic vision and 'the will to steer' are the trinity we need so as to achieve ever higher organization and 'completer self-consciousness'. The fact that the life force was evolving longer life-spans meant we could achieve even more. 'It is enough that there is a beyond,' says Lilith in *Methuselah*.[42] But Shaw is very quotable. 'The future is to those who prefer surprise and wonder to security.' 'Wrestle with life as it comes. And it never comes as we expect it to come.' 'A faith in life rather than men, in the effort rather than the result, in the process rather than in a utopian vision of The Good.'[43]

In almost all of Shaw's plays the change that comes over the main characters is threefold, and in the direction of 'more'. In one sense 'more' means broader, richer, more complete, more adjusted to reality (more 'adapted' in a Darwinian sense). The second sense is that the characters become more aware that their fulfilment, their salvation, lies outward rather than inside themselves. Third, and allied to this, is the development of *reciprocal enlightenment*, in which each character discovers him- or herself in his opposite.[44] Shaw, like many modern-ists, saw that, if God was dead, if there were no afterlife of bliss, the only alternative was to live this life more intensely. His plays were more didactic than most, more so than Ibsen's, certainly. From the best motives, he wanted to help his public enrich the quality of their lives by nudging them – step by stumbling step – on to an evolutionary road upwards and towards a wider consciousness and a more intense life.

Do Not Look into the Distance

At first sight, there may not seem much of an overlap between Shaw and his Russian contemporary, Anton Chekhov (1860–1904). Chekhov's plays and short stories, his themes, are 'quieter' than Shaw's. But this is deceptive – the Russian was thoroughly immersed in Russian culture and history but his concerns were not at all dissimilar.

Unlike many Russian writers of his generation, Chekhov was not an aristocrat and, in his case, that was important. His father had a small grocery shop in the provincial town of Taganrog. Of his early years Chekhov said: 'In my childhood, I had no childhood.' He was made to work hour upon hour in the grocery shop and was often beaten by his excessively religious father. The young Chekhov particularly objected to being forced to serve as a chorister. Things got worse before they got better. In 1875 the family business virtually went under, his father moved with most of the family to Moscow, and Chekhov – barely fifteen – was left in charge in Taganrog. Yet soon he came to relish the increased freedom (and the lack of beatings, and choirwork). He found he enjoyed the responsibilities that had been thrust upon him and the changed circumstances became altogether emancipating.[45]

Not that the experience was the education he craved. There was a large Greek community in Taganrog and at the school he attended all subjects were taught in Greek. But this did at least have the effect of making him a conscientious autodidact. Eventually he moved on to medical school in Moscow, a choice that he saw as a means of satisfying his humanitarian feelings and that also offered a sense of personal dignity.[46]

Scientific literature always occupied him as much as imaginative writing, but it was from the likes of Tolstoy, Zola, Flaubert and Maupassant that he learned the primacy of a moral dimension in life, his loathing of the philistine world and in particular his view of the colourlessness of everyday life. It was this, as much as anything, that gave him his notorious pessimism.

Only when he moved to St Petersburg in 1885 and met a number of famous writers, who all glimpsed the talent beneath the hack work that was all he had until then allowed himself, did he begin to assert his qualities. His real name appeared for the first time under a short story called 'The Requiem' (1886). Gradually, his views coalesced and 'Ward 6' (1892) marks something of a turning point. He came to accept that art – life in general – was without a unifying core idea, without purpose, was in that sense ultimately trivial; but he also believed that facing the objective truth, describing it in his work, was the first step towards inspiring in the reader or the audience the hope of a better life. In fulfilling this task, hard work, he maintained, was as necessary

as talent.[47] For him the artist was no more than a highly skilled crafts-
man, not a prophet or a high priest. He was frequently attacked for his
failure to depict heroic characters, to which he retorted that he would
gladly depict them, 'if they existed in reality'.

. In some ways Chekhov's style and oeuvre are to be understood as a
reply to Dostoevsky's apocalyptic view of life without God. We are not
in an 'abyss', according to Chekhov; rather, we, or at least the provincial Russians, face a world of *poshlost* – mediocrity, colourlessness and
philistinism – and for the most part a lack of ambition and heroism.
Tolstoy's form of Christianity, Chekhov thought, avoided the issues
facing his fellow Russians, specifically the human misery of many in
the evolving industrial sphere. This is made clear throughout his work,
for example in 'A Boring Story' (1889), 'Ward 6', 'My Life' (1896) and 'A
Doctor's Visit' (1898). Chekhov was in particular conscious of 'how far
life falls short of ideal life', that philistinism destroyed the hope that it
was the purpose of art to create, and that 'no one is very obviously to
blame for what is happening, except that they are all to blame for being
so weak'. These are the culminating themes in his last two plays, *Three
Sisters* and *The Cherry Orchard*.[48]

Chekhov's turning away from Dostoevsky's 'high temperature'
vision, the 'dull prose' of his plays that 'had the precise intention of
reproducing the dull prose of everyday life', his apparent obsession
with the futility of life, the criticism that 'everything ends up seeming
the same' and that his plays are unfocused – all this underlined his
view that grand all-encompassing solutions to life are not to be found,
but that instead we should look for 'rather small-scale and, above all,
practical answers'. It was people's needs that counted, and those needs
could not be fulfilled by great abstract ideas. For him, in marked
contrast to Dostoevsky and Tolstoy, the absence of God did not lead
to moral decline or a moral vacuum: each individual must find the
answer for him- or herself, evolving their morality as they went along.

In fact, Chekhov helped initiate the great change that took place
after Nietzsche, which would echo down the twentieth century:
namely, he was less interested in philosophical (to include religious)
or sociological questions than in the interplay between morality and
(individual) psychology.[49]

Being an autodidact, he was naturally interested in self-improvement and education, and had along the way acquired the view that little could be accomplished without hard work. None of this, however, gave him *direction*. That happened as a result of his visit to the penal colony on the island of Sakhalin in the North Pacific. To him, the penal colony was not just an isolated eyesore, but typified the shortcomings and corruption of the whole Russian Empire. In a seeming instant his sense of purposelessness evaporated, and throughout the rest of his life his writings were devoted to the eradication of the terrible conditions he had seen there. In the early 1890s he extended his activities, forming the view that *practical* innovations, not just art, and however small-scale, were the only way to change Russian society. He sent more than two thousand books to Sakhalin, while directing his critical barbs at his fellow intellectuals who, despite their campaigning words, did little practical to improve matters.[50]

He abhorred the religious revival that took place in Russia at the turn of the century, again because he was convinced that 'there were no great solutions to be had' and because, like capitalism, religion produced a senseless waste of human potential. Like the characters in his plays, people under the sway of religion and/or capitalism 'are too weak and afraid to improve their lot'. 'In his last four plays the only happy characters are those who are smug, self-satisfied or complacent, while the more intelligent, such as Uncle Vanya and Sonya or the three sisters, remain without fulfilment.' Korney Chukovsky, the Russian journalist and poet, summed up Chekhov's belief thus: 'Compassion for the concrete individual was his cult.'

But Joe Andrew, professor of Russian literature at Keele University, adds that this 'cult' went further than compassion, 'for Chekhov believed especially in the individual's potential for heroic action within his own life, which would in turn serve as an example'. He was all too well aware that few among his countrymen would share his views, or aspire to such heights. But he insisted that a start could be made, that there was much that the 'concrete individual' could achieve in his own life. 'First was the absolute necessity to abandon illusion, to realize the truth of one's life and only then could one even think of worthwhile achievements.' As Andrew points out, 'for all the gloominess of the endings of *Uncle Vanya* and *The Three Sisters* the characters left on stage – Vanya and Sonya and the three sisters – have at least made this crucial first step . . . For Chekhov a very genuine form of heroism was to see the world as it is and still love it', very similar to what Santayana was saying. Then, the task is to transform one's life, either by striving for inner freedom, or by *practical* work for one's fellow men. Giving in or giving up is not an option.[51]

For Chekhov, there was no transcendental meaning to life. All one can do is give its arbitrary pattern a coherence by means of one's *work and example* in the cause of humanity. 'One must seek, seek on one's own, all alone with one's conscience' – this was the only faith on offer. He thought the very concept of 'salvation' to be misguided and wrong, distracting us from improving our material conditions, which he found especially backward in Russia. Dostoevskian apocalyptics were for him beside the point. For him, we should not look into the distance, the distant future or the afterlife, but instead concern ourselves with taking that first step *out and away* from our mediocrity. That way heroism lay – the small efforts involved in improving everyday life, for oneself and others; these actions were to be well understood *as* heroisms. At the same time, once that first step had been taken, who knows where else it might lead? His own life was testimony to that. But that first step had to be taken first. This is the beginning of heroism.

5

Visions of Eden:
the Worship of Colour, Metal,
Speed and the Moment

Pablo Picasso, the archetypal modern artist, was born in 1881. The first twenty-five years of his life witnessed the most astounding array of technological innovations the world has ever seen, innovations that shaped war and peace alike: the recoiling machine-gun in 1882; the first synthetic fibre, 1883; the steam turbine, 1884; coated photographic paper, 1885; the electric motor, the Kodak box camera and the Dunlop pneumatic tyre, 1888; cordite, 1889; the Diesel engine, 1892; the Ford car, 1893; the cinematograph and the gramophone record, 1894. The following year Röntgen discovered X-rays, Marconi invented radio telegraphy, the Lumière brothers introduced the movie camera, Freud published the first of his theories on hysteria and the unconscious. And so it went on – the discovery of radium, of the electron, the magnetic recording of sound, the first voice radio transmissions, the first powered flight, the special theory of relativity and the photon theory of light, the discovery of the gene. Together, they amounted to the greatest alteration in man's view of the universe since Isaac Newton. As the French writer Charles Péguy put it in 1913: 'The world has changed less since the time of Jesus Christ than it has in the last thirty years.'[1]

Alongside these revolutionary changes, enacted primarily in Europe and America in the half-century between 1880 and 1930, took place one of the supreme cultural experiments in history. And if we accept that art then had a social importance it can no longer claim today, we should not be surprised to find that it had quite a bit to say about how to live – how to live amid the new technology and the new world it was making, how to live in a world without God. A lot of it was *implied* in the paintings and sculpture of the time, but it was there, and there in abundance.

At the most basic level, with very few exceptions (Chagall, Rouault), the art of modernism was a secular art – religious themes are notable by their absence. In Robert Hughes's seminal book *The Shock of the New*, for example, covering the period 1874–1991, of 268 illustrations only nine could be considered religious (Munch's *Madonna*, Gaudí's cathedral in Barcelona, Rothko's chapel in the grounds of the Menil Collection in Houston). Modern art is a celebration of the secular.

Though important, crucial even, this was not totally new. There had been no shortage of secular painting in the eighteenth or the nineteenth centuries. But what was new, what was a major break, occurred in painting with the innovations of Impressionism, the patchwork compositions of Cézanne, the Pointillism of Seurat and the Cubist works of Braque and Picasso. Here the very foundations of reality – of seeing, of understanding seeing – were being experimented with, just as the experiments in physics taking place at much the same time were yielding – in the X-ray, radio waves and the electron, for instance – new building blocks of nature. Painting was overwhelmed by these innovations: they changed the very idea of art and how we are to understand ourselves.

The Church – God – had no part in this new self-understanding which, taking a leaf out of the new sciences, was *experimental* in approach. Instead, the paintings of this half-century explored the constituent elements of visual experience – colour, light, form – building innovation upon innovation in what was essentially an optimistic adulation of the new world coming into being at that time. Not everyone was equally optimistic, and some not at all, but on balance turn-of-the-century artists were exuberant about their new freedoms and luxuriated in the comforts newly available.

This is easy to overlook. The Impressionists and those who came immediately after them seemed entirely untroubled by the death of God. *This* life, in all its novelty (an inadequate word, trivializing what were transformative innovations), was more than sufficient. For them, as their paintings show, the conditions of the new life were bountiful, and for many that was enough.

An Untroubled Sense of Wholeness

Claude Monet was the most explicit. In 1892, the year Ellis Island became a reception centre for immigrants into the US and Tchaikovsky premiered his *Nutcracker* ballet, Monet rented a room opposite the west front of Rouen Cathedral. Over the following weeks he made around twenty paintings of the same façade under different conditions of light. 'Certainly, he had no religious motive in painting the building. Monet was not a pious Frenchman. Never had so famous a religious object been treated in so secular a way.' Here was a Gothic cathedral, with all the lugubrious associations that went with the Middle Ages. But Monet's brilliantly simple vision and his limpid technique implied that consciousness was more important than religion; his subject was not a view but the act of seeing that view, 'a process of mind, unfolding subjectively, never fixed, always becoming'. The fixed certainties of religion, its fixed beauties, were – by this act – dispelled. Consciousness and the will were what counted. Religion, religious beauty, are a function of the human mind.[2]

Monet's treatment of the great Parisian railway stations was not dissimilar. *His* stations were not the ugly, dirty behemoths of an industrial world, but the locus of the dramas of departure and arrival. Here the excited worship of the locomotive and of the power and beauty of steam, out of which the paintings seem to be constructed, the new experience of travel that railways make possible, confirm the terminus as the new focus of cities, a position that cathedrals once occupied and around which life coalesces.

Later, after Monet moved into his property at Giverny and began to paint what he owned, he concentrated – as the world knows – on water lilies and his pond. The pond, as one critic saw, was a 'slice of infinity'. 'To seize the infinite; to fix what is unstable; to give form and location to sights so evanescent and complex that they could hardly be named – these were the basic ambitions of modernism, and they went against the smug view of determined reality that materialism and positivism give us.'[3] Monet saw what Wallace Stevens was to put into words: that infinity is itself a poetic idea.

The secular world of pleasure – middle-class pleasure, not aristo-cratic – was nowhere better caught than by the Impressionists, whose first show, in 1874, preceded Nietzsche's pronouncements by nearly a decade, though the ascendency of the secular world could already be seen everywhere. Alfred Sisley and Gustave Caillebotte, Degas, Pis-sarro and Renoir were each very different in artistic style, but they did have something in common. 'It was a feeling that the life of the city and the village, the cafés and the bois, the salons and the bedrooms, the boulevards, the seaside and the banks of the Seine, could become a vision of Eden – a world of ripeness and bloom, projecting an un-troubled sense of wholeness.' Yes, wholeness. In the Impressionist world God was not missed. More than that, the Impressionists showed us that pleasures, truths, are fugitive, evanescent, may not outlast the moment. In Impressionism there is no difference between the moment and eternity.

Seurat, however, wasn't satisfied with the inherently fugitive nature of Impressionism. He wanted something more stable, even more monumental; and as a child of the nineteenth century, and in particular of the scientific-positivist nineteenth century, he wanted to bring science – or elements of science – into his art. Particle phys-ics hadn't yet emerged, but the periodic table had been established by the Russian, Dmitri Mendeleev (in 1869), and the elements were regarded as the constituent units of reality – the building blocks of nature. Seurat attempted something parallel in his theory of pointil-lism, based on published theories of colour perception and organized around small dots of pure colour that the eye converted into an image. The stipples were so small – little cells of colour – that all manner of variations could be incorporated; pointillism lent itself to calm, hieratic, luminous subjects rather than dramatic or violent ones.[4]

Robert Hughes describes Seurat's *Port of Gravelines Channel* (1890) as a 'landscape of thought'. This landscape is notable for its complete lack of incident; its subject is light, the hazy luminosity of the north coast of France. A third of the picture is of the sky, the heavens, but for Seurat heaven is Gravelines itself on an afternoon such as this, when nothing moves because everything is in its rightful place. Slow down, Seurat is saying to the spectator, slow down and stop, stop and *look*. Don't let heaven pass you by.

This attitude is developed further in what is arguably his greatest work, *A Sunday Afternoon on the Island of La Grande Jatte* (1884–6). It is afternoon again, a *Sunday* afternoon. People are not at church, not worshipping. They are picknicking, promenading, sailing, playing, walking the dog, enjoying themselves and the weather – what the city and nature have to offer. To the right, near the foreground, stand a very fashionable couple, dressed in grey and black. Have they just been to church? They survey the scene from the (moral?) high ground, taking in the countless people enjoying themselves in very secular ways, most with their backs turned. But there is more context to this picture than in the view of Gravelines. This is a large painting, the size of history paintings in the French tradition, designed essentially for public contemplation. The painting is, if anything, overpopulated, but that only serves to emphasize that all the figures – the dandy with his cane, the girl skipping, the people lounging on the grass – are treated with a monumentality, a nobility and grace that were once reserved for gods and kings. This was an early sighting of what was to be a major theme in twentieth-century art, in writing as much as in painting – namely, the heroism of everyday life, particularly life in the city with all its tensions, antagonisms, brutalities and dirt. In *Sunday Afternoon* there is no tension, no dirt, no brutality.

But this vision of pleasure has a seriousness about it. 'Seurat had grasped that there is something atomized, divided, and analytical about modernist awareness ... To build a unified meaning, in this state of extreme self-consciousness, meant that the subject had to be broken down into molecules and then re-assembled under the eye of formal order. Reality became permanent when it was displayed as a web of tiny, distinct stillnesses.'[5] This prefigures T.S. Eliot's admonition in *Ash Wednesday* (1930): 'Teach us to sit still.'

Colour as Meaning

Matisse's aims coincided with Monet's and Seurat's, and built on them. Born in 1869, the year the *Cutty Sark* was launched, he died in 1954, the year the first hydrogen bomb exploded at Bikini Atoll. He lived through some of the worst political traumas, but you would never know it from his art. Nowhere in Matisse does one feel the alienation or conflict that the modern world seems to have stimulated in so many. His studio was a 'place of equilibrium' that for more than fifty years produced a world within a world, 'images of comfort, refuge, and balanced satisfaction'. Much impressed by Manet and Cézanne (he bought one of the latter's works very early on), he was also influenced by Seurat, becoming friends with Seurat's closest follower, Paul Signac. Signac did several paintings of St Tropez that were instrumental in attracting Matisse to the South of France – and the Mediterranean.

In particular he was very taken with one of Signac's large works, *In the Time of Harmony*, which shows an Arcadia, a scene of 'relaxation and farming by the sea', a visualization of Signac's anarchist beliefs. This seems to have been one of the inspirations for Matisse's own *Luxe, Calme et Volupté* (1904–5), nudists picknicking by the sea near St Tropez. It was, as Hughes has it, Matisse's first attempt to depict the Mediterranean 'as a state of mind'. Not long after, he produced the first of what would become a familiar motif – the sea, the Mediterranean, seen through a window. The bright, discordant – even garish – colours shocked many people to begin with, as did Matisse's depiction of individuals in a pre-civilized world, *Eden before the Fall*, showing figures in their original state, languid as plants or unbridled as animals in the wild. In the two notable works he did for the Russian collector Sergey Shchukin, *The Dance* and *Music*, Matisse takes us back into deep antiquity, before even the red-figure vases of ancient Greece, all the way back to the caves. In the former painting he is showing us the ecstasy the ancients obtained from acts of primitive worship, and in the latter, a group of hunter-gatherers engaging in music and song, one of the basic pleasures of life that may have been born with religion. Here there is an overlap, knowing or not, with Laban.

The sensuality of such works is present in *The Red Studio* of 1911, a closed space in which the 'windows' are provided by Matisse's own paintings dotted about the walls. All have red in them so that, with the flat red of the studio walls which encompasses everything, this is red beyond ordinary experience. The loveliness of the whole is part of the point; this is a self-contained work, celebrating the self-contained world that art can offer, a 'republic of pleasure, a parenthesis within the real world – a paradise'.[6]

During the war years Matisse moved to the South of France – the Mediterranean – and found a large studio in Nice from where he continued to produce paintings in which the common theme was 'the act of contemplating a benevolent world from a position of utter security'.[7] In a painting like *Porte-Fenêtre à Collioure* (1914), ambitiously near-abstract, he was, he admitted, painting his emotions. The purples and blacks and greys, however, are not – as might be conventionally imagined – depressive in their effect. On the contrary, this daring composition – looking forward to Rothko decades later – has a self-confidence about it; it is a perfect example of Matisse's aim, to combine the familiar and the new, to show that the new world of the twentieth century, its innovations, ideas and discoveries, did not have to be worrying and dislocating, that in fact dislocation could be managed, even beautiful.

Many painters would head to the South of France in search of colours and a landscape that would help them *intensify* their pictures. What all these artists had in common was a feeling that colour was the sign of vitality, the emblem of well-being; it extended and sharpened the artist's – and the viewer's – sense of energy, their shared *joie de vivre*. Colour was a gift of nature and the artist's job was to *intensify* the experience of nature, enhancing life. The black habit and biretta of the priest have no place here. Matisse's art never shouts, but it convinces. There is heroism in this.

The Magic of Metal, the Worship of Machines

The sheer *joy* in colour that united so many artists at the turn of the twentieth century radiated, as already noted, an optimism about the emergent new world, an optimism that was shared – trumpeted far and wide – by the Futurists, led by the Italian Filippo Tommaso Marinetti (1876–1944), almost a machine himself, tireless and repetitive. His influence spread far beyond his native country, as far afield as Russia 'where the Futurist worship of the machine and its Promethean sense of technology as the solvent of all social ills became a central issue for Constructivists after 1913'. He devised an approach where every kind of human behaviour could be seen as 'art', thus again intensifying life and in this way spawned the rash of happenings, events and performance pieces later in the century.

Marinetti was convinced that the past – traditional religion as much as anything – was the enemy; that technology had created a new kind of individual – machine visionaries – redrawing the cultural map and creating hitherto undreamed-of experiences and liberties, transforming awareness. 'Machinery was power; it was freedom from historical restraint.' In their manifesto, published in 1909, the Futurists announced: 'We intend to sing the love of danger, the habit of energy and fearlessness. Courage, audacity and revolt will be the essential ingredients of our poetry. We affirm that the world's magnificence has been enriched by a new beauty; the beauty of speed ... We will sing of great crowds excited by work, by pleasure, and by riot.'[8]

This message was rather suborned by the brute fact of the First World War, when the sheer speed of the machine-gun (four hundred rounds a minute) was considerably more lethal than life-enhancing, and when artillery, tanks and U-boats could only underline that the Futurist obsession with the machine was at least somewhat misplaced. But Fernand Léger, who was not strictly speaking a Futurist in his worship of the machine and of metal, was not put off by war. The son of a Normandy farmer, he had fought in the trenches during the war, where he had experienced, he said, a great visual epiphany: 'the breech of a 75-millimetre gun in the sunlight, the magic of light on white metal'.

He first applied this vision to the soldiers he knew in the trenches, painting repetitive rows of bodies and helmets and medals and insignia, all presented as tubes of metal. What interested Léger about metal was not its inhumanity but almost the reverse – its adaptability. In one of his grandest compositions, *Three Women* (1921), introduced earlier, all the bodies and furniture are geometrically simplified, formed as if of metal tubes. 'It is one of the supreme didactic paintings . . . embodying an idea of society-as-a-machine, bringing harmony and an end to loneliness' – in a word, secular redemption. 'We are offered a metaphor of human relationships working smoothly as a clock', everything in its place, the women (and the cat) comfortable with themselves; the scene is placid, even, and though metallic on the surface, far removed from the industrial nightmare often associated with steel and iron. Visually, it is nothing like one of Monet's railway stations, but the sentiment is not dissimilar. Again, this is a world that has left churches behind.

It was wartime, too, that witnessed the movement known as Dada, which built – or tried to build – on the *joy* that the painters in the South of France in the pre-war years had celebrated. One meaning of Dada is that it began with a 'joyous Slavonic affirmation', 'Da da!' – 'Yes! Yes!' – to life. The abstract artist Hans Arp, working in Zurich during the Great War alongside James Joyce and Lenin, said, 'We searched for an elementary art that would, we thought, save mankind from the furious madness of those times . . . we wanted an anonymous and collective art,' collective being the crucial point.[9] The core myth of the avant-garde was that by changing the language of art it could reform the order of experience, and so improve the conditions of social life. The Dadaists subscribed to this view as much as the Futurists did. The Dadaists focused on play as the highest human activity – the antithesis of war – and highlighted *chance* as a way to bring about what it wanted to happen.

Play has a long history in Western philosophy, going back at least to Schiller, who exalted play as the most disinterested – and therefore pure – activity man can aspire to. The new understanding of childhood, since Freud, as the primal battleground of the instincts, was also therefore a pure or original state, which, it was felt – if it could be achieved, or emulated – would release with clarity the simple building blocks of our psychological nature.

No Meaning in the Past

The aim of play and dance was *spontaneity* as a way of letting the un-conscious 'speak' in unadulterated form. Chance allowed this, at least in theory; and in the imitation of play, for instance, paper was torn into random shapes and found objects were let fall where they would; poems were constructed from words randomly drawn out of a bag. 'Every word that is spoken and sung here,' said Hugo Ball, 'represents at least this one thing: that this humiliating age has not succeeded in winning our respect.'

The most lyrical of the Dadaists was Kurt Schwitters, who found beauty in – or at least produced artworks made out of – the detritus of the modern city: old newspapers, bits of wood, the lids of cardboard boxes, used toothpicks: for a world of abundance inevitably produces an abundance of waste. These emphasized, as the Impressionists had done, the fleeting but intense nature of life in the (still relatively new) urban sprawls that cities were becoming, where unrelated strangers were thrown together cheek by jowl in unanticipated, sometimes un-wanted, juxtapositions. One of his best works, *The Cathedral of Erotic Misery* (1923), suggested agglomerations of memories, memories to be discarded along with the materials themselves. There was no meaning to be found in the past; and the new was too new.

So much for the optimists who, as we have seen, were predominantly French and therefore, nominally at least, Catholics, or brought up in that tradition. A far less optimistic reaction came from the Protestant nations: Holland, Scandinavia, Germany.

Expressionism was the art form of those who, unlike the Impres-sionists and Fauvists, *were* bewildered and bothered by the changes taking place, including the death of God. Unlike *Gravelines*, *Grande Jatte* or *The Red Studio*, Expressionism is the art of *struggle*, the art of anxiety, the art of what it means to be alive in an indifferent (rather than a beneficently abundant) universe. What you feel with the Ex-pressionists – and this was an idea that ran through the century and crossed the Atlantic later on – was that the *encounter* with paint, the struggle to make the artwork work, to make it mean what the artist wanted it to mean, is there for all to see. In Expressionist art, above all other forms, what we are told, what we *see*, is that after the death of God all that is left is the self. In some ways the Expressionist artist is *overwhelmed* by life, it rushes in on him, floods his mind to the point where it is all he or she can do to prevent images running away with him or her and descending into chaos. The Expressionist artist feels the responsibility of being an artist, of being human, of showing to the rest of the world the struggle that it is just to live from day to day.

This is shown vividly and foremost in the paintings of the Dutchman Vincent Van Gogh, whose whorls and swirls of heavy impasto – his starry night skies, his writhing mountains, his florid cypresses – almost burst off the canvas with the energy they seek to encapsulate. Van Gogh was less impressed by the colours of the South of France than by the sheer energy that he felt crackling in the atmosphere, the rocks, the vegetation. As if in response to Federico García Lorca's line, 'Who will speak the truths of wheat?', in *The Sower* (1888) Van Gogh does just that. The truth of wheat is that its sowing, growing and reaping are an *encounter* between man and nature, with man as *part* of nature, and without God our encounter with nature is revised: the sun beats mercilessly down, everything in the picture is laid on thick, showing – highlighting – an assertion of man's *will*. A Van Gogh image imposes itself, on the canvas, on the viewer. Here I am, the paintings say, my colours may not be your colours or my shapes your shapes but the composition shows their *force*, in an explosion of ecstasy. The paintings take a vision and push it to the limit. Come with me, says Van Gogh, and I will show you ecstasy in this world, whether it be by sunlight or starlight.

This is not colour as meaning but light and energy as meaning, intensity as meaning, an ecstasy that is available but can only be achieved by effort, physical struggle, the same effort as the sower expends. We must be alive to the energy in the world and use it for our own purposes. And we must *manage* our own energy if we are to live well, to know ecstasy.[10]

But intensity carries risks as well as offering fulfilment. As the world knows, Van Gogh spent just over a year in an asylum in the

South of France in 1889–90. He was not the only one to battle with instability. Edvard Munch wrote in a letter to a friend, 'Disease and insanity were the black angels on guard at my cradle.'[11] Though neither Van Gogh nor Munch, probably, had read the latest physics of the day (energy as a concept dated from the 1850s), energy in nature, its effect on the *perception* of nature, the potentially explosive, destabilizing effects of that energy, are rendered visible in paintings, which invite us to understand nature in a new way, suggesting that we must redefine our relationship with nature after the death of God.

Munch's was a much darker vision than Van Gogh's. In *Death in the Sickroom* (1895) Munch painted his family in the room where his sister died. Their grief is intense, so palpable in the painting that we are invited to ask whether, religious or not, they are totally convinced that there is an afterlife. In *Puberty* (1894–5), a young woman contemplates her own naked body and her budding sexuality – adult life, the future – with a mixture of horror and bewilderment. Horror and bewilderment run through several of Munch's other works, such as *The Voice* (1893) in which a woman dressed in pure white, but with her brown hair arranged around her head like a dead halo, is trapped in a lakeside (or fjord-side) forest, where all the trees and even the reflection of the sun on water are represented as virile, implacable, imprisoning vertical bars. This is the modern condition – we are both estranged from, and yet trapped in, nature; alone. The other people in the painting, aboard a canoe on the water, are likewise locked into a different cell, wedged tightly between two trees, two more confining bars, not allowing them to move.

And then there is *The Scream* (also of 1893), the main image of which has been much commented upon. Less remarked on is the fact that the two figures further along the bridge over the fjord or chasm *do not appear to hear* the scream. They are ciphers for a world that doesn't care. They are far away and indistinct, but given that one is dressed in a long dark cloak or coat, they could be clerics.

Munch in many ways defined Expressionism: insecurity and unease become so strong that the artist has no choice but to recoil upon himself, treating that Self as the one secure point in an otherwise indifferent universe. Munch thought that 'Salvation shall come from

Symbolism', by which he meant that mood and thought were placed above everything, becoming the grounds of reality.[12]

If we examine the works of the other leading Expressionist painters – the spiky, jerky figures of Ernst Ludwig Kirchner, the emaciated, flagrantly naked victims of Erich Heckel, the stiff elongations and violent awkwardnesses of Max Beckmann, the bloody, fleshy impasto of Chaim Soutine – we see, as one critic put it, 'the sluices of the self' opened in the process that would become known as 'expressive individualism'. In other words, the artist's struggle to realize himself is defined in part as *difference from others*, and is achieved only with great difficulty by exploring distortion, violence, sickness, a sort of *via negativa* that cannot help but fasten together individuality and apartness, with the inevitable disappointment of which Valéry spoke. (See chapter 6.) In Expressionism, the Freudian visceral depths have replaced the soul as the ultimate reality in which we find meaning. Essentially we struggle to civilize our instincts which, as Nietzsche foresaw, can be as destructive as creative. As a result it is a reality we are apt to beware of as much as embrace. Intensity cuts both ways.

The Four Traits of the 'New Spirit' in Art

Roger Shattuck who, so far as I know, is the populariser of the useful phrase 'the avant-guerre' in English, distinguished 'a new spirit', in France especially, between 1885 and 1918. These were 'the Banquet Years' which, he said, carried the arts wholesale, not just the visual arts, into the 'ultimate modern heresy: the belief that God no longer exists'. He went on: 'It implies further that after God 'died', man himself became the supreme person, the only divinity . . . With the field thus cleared of supernatural encumbrances, the true approach to the divine came to consist in man's probing of his own most innermost states. For this century, everything from dream analysis to the perception of relativity, became self-knowledge as the first stage to self-assumption. The ancient sin of *hubris*, man's too-great arrogance in the face of the cosmos, disappeared when divine powers no longer existed outside of man. Evil was confined to failure in confronting oneself.'[13]

Shattuck thought that the avant-garde began in France because of its tradition of protest, established back in the Revolution; and he identified the 'New Spirit' in the arts as consisting of four traits, each one different and each epitomized by one of four remarkable individuals – the actor-playwright, Alfred Jarry, the 'primitivist' painter, Henri Rousseau, the composer Erik Satie and the painter-poet-impresario, Guillaume Apollinaire (the phrase 'New Spirit' was first used by Apollinaire, in a lecture).

The four traits Shattuck identified as crucial to the New Spirit began, he said, with a revaluation (in Nietzschean mode) of the very idea of *maturity* – who is the complete man? Throughout history, Shattuck said, the adult qualities of self-control have preponderated over those of the anarchic child. But after Romanticism, and even more after Rimbaud, a new personage emerges: the 'child-man'. Artists became increasingly willing to accept the child's 'wonder and spontaneity and destructiveness' as not inferior to adulthood.[14]

The second trait is a pervading note of humour. 'Humour, a genre that can command the directness of comedy and the subtler moods of irony, became a method and a style.' And Shattuck refers (and defers) to Bergson on the distinction between comedy and irony. 'Humour describes the world exhaustively and scientifically *just as it is*, as if that were just the way things are. Irony haughtily describes the world *as it should be*, as if that were just the way things are.' And this leads us into the device of absurdity, '*the absence of any a priori values in the world, of any given truths*'. Whereas Rousseau was indifferent – or even oblivious – to the mirth his work often provoked, Satie was not – instead, he made use of it. 'Why attack God? He is as unhappy as we are. Since his son's death he has no appetite for anything and barely nibbles at his food.'[15] Faced with this, we no longer know how to react and this is the point: this absence of value becomes itself a value. In particular in the work of Jarry, the 'baseness and incongruity' of life must be understood not as a source of disgust but of joy.

The third trait of the New Spirit is the attachment of meaning to dreams. Dreams have always had some sort of oracular meaning, but it was in the avant-guerre that artists 'abandoned themselves' to a 'second life' of dreams. This was not necessarily Freudian in context

– in fact, it was the ready preoccupation with dreams that helped Freud's book have the impact it did (though it sold very few copies to begin with). 'The employment of dream techniques in the arts implied an effort to reach beyond the bounds of waking consciousness towards faculties that could grapple with unrestricted intuitions . . . These new realms of consciousness and expression were pursued with something approaching religious conviction by Bergson and Proust, Redon and Gauguin. Without relying on the existence of a "higher" or spiritual world apart from our own inner being, dream can endow ordinary experience with an aura of ritual and the supernatural.'[16]

Dream and humour lent themselves to the fourth trait that Shattuck identified – ambiguity. 'Ambiguity here means neither meaninglessness nor obscurity – though both dangers are present. It means simply the expression of two or more meanings of a single symbol or sound.' By this account, there is no single true meaning banishing others that are faulty. Works can be at the same time beautiful and ugly, all meanings are possible, and the extraction of one alone 'infeasible'.

These four traits, Shattuck insists, reveal a profound unity. 'They manifest an unrelenting desire to dredge up new material from within, from the subconscious, and in order to do so they attempt to forge a new and all-important mode of thought, the logic of the child, of dream, of humour, of ambiguity', and this frees the artist from the need to make a work with a single, explicit meaning. This deep preoccupation with the subconscious, he says, is symptomatic of man's belief that he can surpass himself, to reach into himself to extract what education and society have buried. 'The blending of art and life represents an attempt to preserve spiritual meaning in a godless universe. In refusing a dualistic order of earthly and divine, the twentieth century has attempted to have its cake and eat it, too.'[17]

Thus twentieth-century art – and this applies to Impressionism, Cubism, Futurism, Dada – *seeks not so much to represent reality as to rival it*; it strives to be its own subject. The boundaries, the frameworks, were overrun, the two universes, art and not-art, engaged in 'mutual interference', a major device whose lineaments have never been properly assimilated. 'When the distinction between art and reality has broken down, we are ourselves incorporated into the structure of a work of art. Its very form importunes us to enter an *expanded community* of creation which now includes artist and spectator, art and reality.'[18]

Wholeness via Juxtaposition

This, Shattuck says, has profound implications for the very concept of unity, of unifying wholeness. In the Romantic period, immediately preceding modernism, only the privileged personality of the artist could hope for the fulfilment of the yearnings for wholeness, for unity; but the modern sensibility, dispensing with frameworks and boundaries, sought new ideas of unity through dislocation. In the new aesthetic – also a new ethic, as it turned out – the approach to unity, even to wholeness, was to be achieved by *juxtaposition*.

'The arts of juxtaposition offer difficult, disconcerting, fragmented works whose disjunct sequence has neither beginning nor end. They happen without transition and scorn symmetry.' The world is recorded, in effect, 'in the still-scrambled order of sensation' (Ezra Pound, Wyndham Lewis, Virginia Woolf, James Joyce); there is no fusion or synthesis, such wholeness as is formed is beyond the reach or grasp of logic, and represents a desire to respond to the voice within. These works, Shattuck says, have abandoned the possibility of meaning in the classical sense.[19]

The point of juxtaposition is that 'we cannot expect to reach a point of rest or understanding' in the conventional sense. The absurd is, essentially, an expression of the *lack* of connectivity in experiencing the world – play, nonsense, abruptness, surprise now become the order of the arts, rather than *verification* of certain general truths in the old tradition. 'We can no longer expect to find in the arts only verification of knowledge or values deeply rooted within us. We will, instead, be surprised or dismayed.' The search for the subconscious functions by sudden leaps, 'the way a spark jumps a gap', which brings the spectator closer than ever before to the abruptness of the creative process. It is as if the spectator is now watching from the wings rather than the auditorium; there is a closeness, an *intimacy* of form in modern art that stems from this yearning for the subconsciousness shared by all, but which exposes the 'jumpy' nature of the mind, the profound 'unsteadiness' within us – 'Few men ever attain the equilibrium necessary to live fully with what they have.'

Juxtaposition arranges fragments of experience, perishable rather than possessing the stability of monuments, in which the (often) conflicting elements are to be experienced/understood *simultaneously* rather than successively, as was traditionally the case. 'The aspiration of simultanism is to grasp the moment in its total significance or, more ambitiously, to manufacture a moment which surpasses our usual perception of time and space.' Simultanism establishes sources of meaning other than causal sequence, and seizes upon what is, for us in the twenty-first century, a new kind of coherence, a new unity of experience, not progression but intensification – intensification by standing still.[20]

Juxtaposition requires assimilation without synthesis, directness free of conventional order, the compression and condensation of mental processes, freedom from the taboos of logic, potential unity at a moment in time, fixity. 'Only by achieving rest, *arrest*, can we perceive what is happening outside ourselves.'[21] The figures in this chapter, though diverse, were united in their *daring*.

6

The Insistence of Desire

Did André Gide's life owe its shape to the fact that he came from a Protestant family in Catholic France? Or that his father died when he was still a boy and his life at home (he was born in Paris but grew up in Normandy and the Languedoc) was largely influenced by the women of the family? Or that he was an only child? Can such questions ever be answered satisfactorily? Whatever motivation governed Gide's make-up, he was able to end his last major creative effort, *Thésée*, with words that were to become famous: 'I have lived.'[1]

In fact, arguably the most important influence on Gide was the landscape that he explored with the family's Swiss maid, a woman of the mountains, who shared – and fostered – his passion for wild flowers. Later, he was 'intoxicated' by the beauties of the countryside around Uzès, near Nîmes in the Languedoc, the valley of the Fontane d'Ure and above all the *garrigue*, scrubland, where the wild flowers dazzled in the spring. Here, the not overwhelmingly lush surroundings permitted him to appreciate the heroic and dignified qualities of individual flowers. His reaction to natural beauty was never passive, and that fact was to play an important role in his view of life.

Stirred by Self-loss

Devotedly religious in his teens, Gide's faith failed in his twentieth year. He had come to the conclusion that Christianity was 'deadly' to culture.[2] At more or less the same time, he inherited enough money for him not to need to work, so he moved back to Paris and began to mix there with the avant-garde, particularly the writers gathered around Stéphane Mallarmé, whose aestheticism and love of the music of words Gide shared. Like many an only child, he craved company and found a home among the circle that formed around the literary magazine he helped to found, the *Nouvelle Revue Française*.

But he was alive not only to French writers. He was much influenced by Nietzsche, Dostoevsky, Browning, Yeats and Blake, and liked to quote the latter's lines:

> Thou art a man, God is no more
> Thy own humanity learn to adore.[3]

Perhaps because of his upbringing, Gide was temperamentally suited to the phenomenologists' central idea, which was a reaction against the view that the particular is somehow of less consequence than the general. Husserl had said (see chapter 3) that, in giving our attention to the particular, 'we fear the risk of fixing ourselves upon an exception to the rule', but that was never Gide's worry.[4] He shared with Shaw the idea that life is not a possession but an experiment and, as a consequence, he quickly formed the view that a man's greatest task must be 'an exemplary existence'. More specifically, he said that salvation cannot depend on human organization, that man is whatever he will eventually make of himself, limited only by his 'unfortunate eagerness' to accept ready-made definitions which 'permit him to substitute contemplation for action'.

God, Gide thought, is one of these ready-made definitions. Moreover, we should not 'spoil' our life for any one objective; there is no one to pray to, and 'a man must play the cards he has'.[5] Sooner or later we must make a choice, in order to act, but one choice does not necessarily predetermine another. We must realize there is nothing beyond man, except what he can make for himself.[6]

Gide used the word 'spiritual' as Valéry did, as Mallarmé did, as Santayana did, not as something that concerned another realm, a mystical world elsewhere, but as an important part of *this* life that stemmed from the phenomenologists' understanding, the poetic approach to the particular. He came to believe that it is the 'duty' of man to 'surpass' himself, strive not towards any specific goal but simply towards the *enrichment* of existence itself. Life is its own meaning, he concluded, and that meaning has been realized if you can look back on your life and say something like, 'All things considered, I have won the game I played.'

Gide claimed that the particular is itself meaningful, from which it follows that 'truth' is not to be attained by any procedure – artistic, scientific, philosophical – but only by those experiences which are *immediately* accessible to perception and sensation. Nothing, he insists, can trump the argument of the individual who says, 'I saw it' or 'I felt it'. All attempts to systematize experience succeed only in 'denaturing, distorting and impoverishing'.[7]

One consequence of this was that Gide consciously tried to develop his senses, and showed this in his work. Travel, he thought, was an important element here (he was an early visitor to North Africa) – the stranger in the land, taking nothing for granted, is alive in a way that the native inhabitants are not.[8] This is, in essence, what his 1897 book *Les Nourritures terrestres* (Fruits of the Earth) was about, emptying the mind of its contents, so that 'there is no longer anything between us and things'. 'There were merchants of aromatics. We bought different kinds of resins from them. Some were for sniffing. Some were for chewing. Yet others were burned . . . Sheer being grew for me into something hugely voluptuous.' For Gide, touch was the most immediate of the senses, underlining that '[o]nly individual things exist . . . things in themselves hold forth, accessible to everyone, all that life has to offer. Objects are neither "symbols" nor manifestations of "laws" more important than themselves, but independent entities that have successfully resisted all of man's attempts to organize them into other things that can be neither seen, heard nor touched.'[9]

The independence of things, he warned, can be terrible, but it can also be exhilarating, an opportunity; and we should beware explanations, which, he said, were 'necessarily inadequate'. 'Existence is not something that may be thought of at a distance; it has to invade you abruptly, fix itself upon you.'[10] For him, logic was a kind of mental barrier, stopping us from realizing the chaos 'on the other side' – a chaos, he thought, that Baudelaire, Cézanne and his friend Valéry had tried hard to show. For Gide, 'wonder at the world' should replace philosophy which attempts to 'explain' the world. Philosophies, ideologies – and that includes religion – get in the way of wonder.

More than that, Gide believed that all systems of organization – science, religion, philosophy, theories of art – are egoistical impositions on the chaotic reality that is life; and that the *self-loss*, or self-forgetting, involved in wonder, in the immediacy of experience, in the taking of decisions and acting, is, in effect, what salvation is, removing the difference between us and things.

By the same token, he maintained that the idea of the self as a unity is false. The words he used were in fact that the self is a 'superstition'. 'If we look inside ourselves we discover no fixed unchanging thing we can call the self, but only the aimless passage of memories, perceptions and emotions.' That, he thought, was Montaigne's great innovation, to recognize the 'non-stability' of the human personality, 'which never *is*, but is conscious of itself only in a becoming that cannot be pinned down'. As he liked to say, 'I am never; I become.' He shared with Yeats, and many others at the turn of the century, a view of human nature that was in many ways quite at variance with Freud, a view which insisted that there is no single self but as many selves as we want there to be, a new one every day. 'We are no more "determined" from within than from without.'[11]

We are 'condemned' to freedom, Gide said, and the verb was appropriate in that, unless we understand freedom, the complete lack of guidance, the total absence of ready-made solutions, can be fearsome. Rather, he said, 'events should find us ready to exchange one self for another and better one', we have to stand ready to recognize a better self (how we do that is considered later). Everett Knight put it this way: 'The greatness of Gide is to have resisted throughout his life the temptation *to be* – to enter into the "repose" of thinghood.' In other words, he never thought of himself as one thing rather than another, he never resisted change. He thought it was the dread of being nothing very much that made men do dreadful things.[12]

All this was the context for his famous concept of the 'gratuitous act'. Gide's 'philosophy' – though he eschewed that word – his approach to life and experience, was that if man possesses no internal principles, then he exists only through his actions, and when he is acting, behaving, it is the suddenest actions that are the most authentic, because then a man is behaving without allowing himself time to think and his performance will not be tarnished by self-interest. 'A gratuitous act is not dictated by self-interest.' (This was to be strongly substantiated years later by Dietrich Bonhoeffer.) Since there are no eternal goals or truths, 'the only incentive to action is one which leaves man with dignity and autonomy'. This is what establishes value; it is in effect an ethic, which may be summarized as follows: 'You must follow your bent, provided it leads upward. Self-imposed discipline; self-abnegation is the noblest form of self-realization.'[13]

Gide's emphasis on the particular led him to the view that we should strive to bring to 'the fullest fruition' that which is unique in us, and through our actions we must surpass ourselves – that is, seek to achieve more than we thought we could at the outset. And the way to achieve *this*, he thought, was not the old religious idea of 'a contemplative life', but holding ourselves in constant readiness to discover experience through action. And action involving self-loss is the most fulfilling and complete of experiences.

Lies and Shared Fictions

More than one critic has drawn attention to the lines of influence between William James and his 'younger and shallower and vainer' brother, Henry. The older brother stayed with the younger one in the spring of 1901 while the former was writing *The Varieties of Religious Experience*, making use of Henry's typist, Mary Weld.[14] Henry read his brother's finished book in 1902, while finishing his own novel,

The Wings of the Dove. At times their creative lives were so intertwined (both were fascinated by mental illness, for example) that wags described William as the better writer and Henry as the better psychologist.

What concerns us most is Henry's concern with, and approach to, religious experience and how it is to be understood – and possibly replaced – in the modern world. At one level his novels notably reflect the distinction William makes in *Varieties* when describing Lutheran and Calvinist theology as faiths which appeal to 'sick souls', and Catholicism, by contrast, as 'healthy-minded'. This centres most on the problem of evil. 'The healthy-minded individual tends toward pluralism and a view of evil as not central to human experience, but rather "a waste element" . . . so much "dirt", as it were. The sick soul, by contrast, regards the problem of evil as the essential fact of this world, something to be surmounted only by appeal to supernatural forces.'[15] This is not exactly how it is played in Henry's books: 'Bereft of the possibility of a direct encounter with the supernatural, James's protagonists must accept the world in its fallen state.'[16]

The Golden Bowl is the most explicit of Henry's books with regard to religion and what comes after. At one level, the book is about Evil – evil, as the protagonist Maggie Verver puts it, with 'a very big E'. At another level, and even more fundamentally, it is about the problem that, for James, lay before us in a secular world: namely, the problem of desire. It is desire that is at the root of all evil, and the ways in which desire can be expressed and controlled in a world without the traditional rituals of organized religion are for him both the core predicament and the main opportunity. It is the *institutions* of religion that concern James, and how we are to live without them.

The story of *The Golden Bowl* follows the theological conceit of the Fall, which accompanies Maggie's acquisition of self-knowledge. What begins in *The Golden Bowl* is continued in James's later fiction, but religious themes are there transformed into broader concerns. This is because, as Pericles Lewis has observed, 'The characters in James's novels seem to pay little heed to articulated religious belief. Indeed, they often seem to inhabit a moral world in which absolute measures of value such as those associated with God are no longer available.'[17]

Instead, they try to tailor their former ethical views to a new way of living together, still taxed and vexed by the problem of (and solution to) Evil, always manifested through desire.

Henry recognized that he was living in a 'radically new spiritual situation', one in which the organized churches had little role left to play and where, increasingly, religion became a matter of personal experience.[18] As Louis Menand has observed, in *Varieties* William argued that 'God is real because he produces real effects' (see chapter 2 for a wider discussion). More fully: 'The unseen order is, in a sense, the product of our beliefs, and its truth consists neither in the possibility of proving it scientifically nor in the possibility of having an unmediated access to it, but in the fact that it influences our actions in this world.' In effect, Lewis says, William James interpreted transcendental ideas as 'shared fictions', and it was *this* that Henry picked up on in his later works, from *The Golden Bowl* onward.

In those works he explored the mechanisms by which individuals try to obtain from others particular beliefs, and the phenomenon that, in order to belong to a certain group, one must 'accept certain beliefs, and accept them so wholeheartedly as to experience them as one's own ... For James, shared fictions take the place of more traditional religious beliefs; he often describes them as "sacred".' These beliefs may involve believing in someone's goodwill, that one character really loves another, that someone is virtuous; or negative shared beliefs such as suspecting the nature of someone's illness, thinking the worst concerning the origin of another's fortune. This leads, perhaps inevitably, to the point where James suggests that even *lying* might be a moral duty, 'when the lie is in good faith'. The dénouements of his three last completed novels (*The Wings of the Dove* (1902), *The Ambassadors* (1903), *The Golden Bowl* (1904)) turn – like the final scene in Conrad's *Heart of Darkness* – 'on the question of whether the protagonist will tell a "necessary lie" in order to maintain an illusion in which a community would prefer to live'.[19] As Lewis goes on to say, the phrase 'as if' recurs throughout the last three books, echoing William James's recasting of Kant in *Varieties*: 'We can act *as if* there were a God.'[20]

In other words, faced with a world without God and at the same time an ostensible moral base deriving from God, if we are to live together we must maintain fictions – even if, on occasion, they are lies – if they oil the wheels of the community to which we wish to belong. Maintaining community is the all-important priority (this is Habermas's 'solidarity'). More than that, we must treat these shared fictions as sacred. 'In the fallen world of James's novels, the shared fiction seems to be the only remnant of faith that can allow James's characters to live together. The problem for James, his characters, and his readers is that these shared fictions can hardly be distinguished from lies.'

James's characters, especially in *The Golden Bowl*, are both conscious of evil and aware of the absence of supernatural intervention in the modern world. *The Golden Bowl* probes this dilemma and explores what fictions might allow us to overcome it. In the book Maggie Verver, the only child of Adam, a very rich American moneyman and art collector, is set to marry, in London, an impoverished but stylish Italian nobleman, Prince Amerigo. In the run-up to the marriage the prince encounters Maggie's lifelong friend, Charlotte Stant. It is in fact a re-encounter from years before: without Maggie being aware of it, Charlotte and the prince had enjoyed an affair in his native Rome. Before the marriage, Charlotte and the prince go shopping for a wedding present for Maggie and in an antique shop they inspect a golden bowl which, in the end, they don't buy because the prince suspects it has a hidden flaw. Following the marriage (at which point the prince's debts are paid off by Adam), Maggie begins to worry that her father is lonely and she persuades Charlotte to marry him. This brings all four characters closer and, while Maggie seems more interested in her father than in her new husband, Amerigo and Charlotte are again thrown together and re-consummate their affair.

Maggie, all innocence at the beginning of the book, is now acquiring some European sophistication and polish, and she begins to suspect the affair between Charlotte and Amerigo. Her suspicions are soon to be confirmed. She visits the same antique shop where Charlotte and the prince discovered the golden bowl, is shown the very object they didn't buy, and acquires it for her father. However, the shopkeeper has overcharged her and is feeling remorse, so he goes to her house to confess. There he sees photographs of the prince and

Charlotte and tells Maggie about their earlier visit to his shop. They had spoken Italian in front of him, not knowing that he understood every word they were saying.

In the last part of the book, crucial from our point of view, Maggie sets about separating Charlotte and Amerigo, but without letting her father know what's been going on. She persuades him to return to America, taking Charlotte with him. Impressed by Maggie's new-found sophistication and guile, Amerigo warms to his wife and goes along with her plans.

The symbolism of the bowl has been criticized as heavy-handed, but it successfully fulfils several functions. Its potential flaw draws attention to the shortcomings of the characters, each of whom is either a gift or the recipient of a gift, though those shortcomings are never discussed – as so much is not discussed, in particular the affair and Maggie's plotting to induce her father to return to America, thereby taking Charlotte away from the prince. The point is that everyone colludes in *not* discussing these issues. The weather pattern of general well-being is on the surface of things, while underneath the weather is anything but pleasant – and is in fact a collectively shared fiction. 'Although the characters constantly deceive one another, they do so in order to make their lives together bearable.'

James's point is that we need to feel some things are sacred and, in a secular world, there is still this need, but notions of *what exactly* is to be kept sacred have changed: since transcendence is no longer possible – transcendence with a supernatural meaning – then to live in this secular world, as a community, means living with, *accepting*, the fictions of the others 'among whom one is thrown'. Any form of the sacred appropriate to this modern age will be, as for William James, one that is effective because people accept it.[21]

Henry James's novels are, at root, about the intransigence – the insistence – of desire to manifest itself, and its ability to disrupt a social cohesion that traditionally was kept in place by the evolved rituals of organized religion (marriage, above all). In the modern world where ideas of transcendence, of an afterlife, of the sense of community offered by the rituals of organized religions, are no longer open to us, the only way to live, to *have* a community, James is saying, is to act 'as if' the disruptions of desire are not taking place, 'as if' social cohesion is not being disturbed. This gives us the best means of attaining such social cohesion – a sense of community – and of maintaining it. James has identified what for him (and for many others) is the most substantial threat arising from the death of God – the threat to our social sense of who we are. He also recognized that traditional religious organizations had been devoted, in large part, to coping with desire.

For him, belief in God has been replaced – is to be replaced – by the belief that shared fictions are more than just a form of lying: they are a way of living together, of living with and containing desire, and therefore both a shared flaw, a tacit acknowledgement that we are all fallen, and a consolation.

The Collective Mind and the General Purpose

There was an 'as if' element in H.G. Wells's thinking, as we shall see. At the same time, he thought that lying was 'the blackest crime'. There was not much common ground as between Wells and Henry James (indeed, they had had an acrimonious debate) and although he shared *some* of the views of Shaw, Valéry and Wallace Stevens, Wells found it hard to accept beauty and art as self-justifying, as ends in themselves. He thought artists had 'abundant but uneducated brains', that their activities were essentially arbitrary and uncoordinated. In his view, aesthetics was pointless if it had no use, and 'art for art's sake' would eventually lead to the neglect of its original inspiration. His books, including his novels, were purely functional, as he put it, designed specifically to produce social and ethical reform.[22]

Wells decided to become a writer after breaking his leg in 1874, when he was forced to spend some weeks in bed. His father, a part-time professional cricketer (for Kent), brought him a succession of books that fired his enthusiasm, an enthusiasm that survived an early unhappy spell as an apprentice draper, then as a teacher.

Wells's real calling, however, was science. He attended Midhurst Grammar School for a while as a boy, where he was taught science by T.H. Huxley, famously known as 'Darwin's bulldog' for his robust espousal of the theory of evolution. Wells was inspired specifically by Huxley and by evolution but also by science generally. He concluded that, given the way science operated, revealing new possibilities as it solved old problems, we should always remain sceptical that a 'final reality' would ever become known. He thought that ideas of Right and God were only 'attempts to simplify and so bring into the compass of human reactions what is otherwise humanly inexpressible'. Writing at the time that he did, and having the background that he did, Wells recognized around him a process of cultural, intellectual and political evolution of which science and socialism were both parts and that would lead, he thought, to the emergence of what he called a 'Synthetic Collective Mind', 'arising out of and using and passing on beyond our individual minds'. In 1900 there was a widespread feeling that capitalism had run its course, and many people, especially in the Western democracies, assumed that some form of socialism would triumph and spread across the world in the new century.[23]

These ideas were developed in, among other publications, *A Modern Utopia* (1905), *New World for Old* (1908), and *Mankind in the Making* (1903), in which he argued that a more scientific and socialistic society would be brought about through the creation and institutionalization of a caste of philosopher-kings, called Samurai, a 'voluntary nobility'. All political power was to be in their hands; they would be the sole administrators, lawyers, doctors, public officials, and also the only voters. The privileges were considerable but the positions were to be open to all. By means of this caste, Wells felt, society could look forward to an orderly and efficient administration. The Samurai would be international and cosmopolitan in outlook, intellectually open and, crucially, would base their activities and innovations on scientific research. The best science, he maintained, offered the only form of 'universalism' that overcomes – indeed at times abolishes – the difference between *is* and *ought*.[24]

Taking the name Samurai from the upper-class Japanese military caste was an eye-catching tactic, and by it he implied that this caste would, above all, be educated in science and would therefore know how to learn from experience, keep society developing and changing – in effect, this is how the collective mind would operate in reality.

As one reviewer in the science journal *Nature* put it, speaking of *A Modern Utopia*, 'He aims rather at laying down this principle of an order which shall be capable of progressively growing toward perfection; and so it may well be that in his ideal society men will be less reluctant than now to learn from experience.'

Wells thought that Christianity and the other major religions had failed 'to subordinate the individual', that they had in fact 'usually offered rewards' for individuality, punishing only the really deviant and 'vile' exceptions and even then offering absolution. However, 'The essential fact in man's history to my sense is the slow unfolding of a sense of community with his kind, of the possibilities of cooperation leading to scarce dreamt-of collective powers, of a synthesis of the species, of the development of a common general idea, a common general purpose out of a present confusion.' Wells argued that man is perfectible 'within the great instinctual drives of life', and 'it is to that goal that we should strive, incidentally improving the race, and cutting down on the distortions and the prismatic views which most humans accept so easily'.[25]

He conceived of 'perfectibility' not in a theological way, therefore, but as a three-pronged process – perfectibility of the individual but within the greater structure of the state and of the race. 'The continuation of the species, and the acceptance of the duties that go with it, must rank as the highest of all goals; and if they are not so ranked, it is the fault of others in the state who downgraded them for their own purposes ... We live in the world as it is and not as it should be ... The normal modern married woman has to make the best of a bad position, to do her best under the old conditions, to live as though [as if] she were under the new conditions, to make good citizens, to give her spare energies as far as she can to bringing about a better state of affairs. Like the private property owner and the official in a privately conducted business, her best method of conduct is to consider herself [as if she were] an unrecognized public official, irregularly commanded and improperly paid. There is no good in flagrant rebellion. She has to study her particular circumstances and make what good she can out of them, *keeping her face towards the coming time* ... We have to be wise as well as loyal; *discretion itself is loyalty to the coming state* ...

We live for experience and the race; the individual interludes are just helps to that; the warm inn in which we lovers met and refreshed was but a halt on the journey. When we have loved to the intensest point we have done our best with each other. To keep to that image of the inn, we must not sit overlong at our wine beside the fire. We must go on to new experiences and new adventures [Italics added].'[26]

Wells had a mystical side, which we shall come to, but religion 'does not work' for me, he said, a cathedral being no more 'real' for him than a Swiss chalet. Instead, he believed that perfection for society, for the race (which for him came before perfection for the individual), lay in the marriage of science and socialism. 'The fundamental idea upon which socialism rests is the same fundamental idea as that upon which all real scientific work is carried on. It is the denial that chance impulse and individual will and happening constitute the only possible methods by which things may be done in the world. It is an assertion that things are, in their nature, orderly; that things may be computed, may be calculated upon and foreseen. In the spirit of this belief, science aims at systematic knowledge of material things ... the socialist has just that same faith in the order, the knowableness of things, and the power of men in co-operation to overcome chance.'

Science, he liked to say, is the mind of the race.[27]

Wells agreed with Huxley that the process of evolution was basically amoral and 'could not be expected in itself either to produce a more moral species than *Homo sapiens*, or to provide the principles for an ethically conscious society. Thus, there being no inherent virtue in nature, man must strive to correct and control his own evolution, including the evolution of society, and not merely accept or blindly follow the Darwinian process.' He really did think, as many socialists with him, that science and technology would bring an end to toil and shortage. He thought eugenics could help perfect mankind, and that proved controversial too.

Within this general context of science and socialism, Wells thought that fulfilment (of society first, then the individual within it) depended on 'five principles of liberty ... without which civilization is impossible'.[28] These were the principles of privacy, of free movement and of unlimited knowledge, the view that lying is 'the blackest crime', and free discussion and criticism. And underlying all was a sixth principle, that of scientific research. Research produced rational results, their very rationality and impartiality giving them an authority beyond all other claims to knowledge.

In a chapter in *Anticipations of the Results of Mechanical and Scientific Progress* (1901) dealing with 'faith, morals and public policy in the twentieth century', he foresees the spread of a vaguely pantheistic humanism as the religion 'of all sane and educated men'. They will have no definite idea of God, being well aware of the 'self-contradictory absurdities of an obstinately anthropomorphic theology'. This might leave them with a vague, non-anthropomorphic idea, a God who 'comprehends and cannot be comprehended', but for Wells such a God is useless because he plays no part, offers no guidance, as regards the efficient running of society, and therefore has no role, that Wells can see, in the development of the race.[29] For such a God, 'perfection' is an anomaly.

The one element of mysticism to which he confessed was his belief in a 'sense of community', one embracing all of mankind. 'The essential fact in man's history to my sense is the slow unfolding of a sense of community with his kind . . . between us and the rest of mankind there is *something*, something real, something that rises through us and is neither you nor me, that comprehends us, and that is thinking and using me and you to play against each other.' He repeated these sentiments in the preface to the 1914 edition of *Anticipations*, again in a discussion of the 'Collective Mind': 'I saw then [during his period in the Fabian Society] what hitherto I had merely felt, – that there was in the affairs of mankind something unorganized which is greater than any organization. This unorganized power is the ultimate Sovereign in the world . . . It is something transcending persons . . . This Collective Mind is essentially an extension of the spirit of science to all human affairs, its method is to seek and speak and serve the truth and to subordinate oneself to one's conception of a general purpose . . . We are episodes in an experience greater than ourselves . . . I believe in the great and growing being of the species, from which I rise, to which I return, and which, it may be, will ultimately even transcend the limitation of the species and grow into the conscious Being of all things . . .

what the scheme as a whole is I do not clearly know; with my limited mind I cannot know. There I become a mystic.'[30]

Some of these later ideas do not sit comfortably with his earlier position. But he argues in both his non-fiction and his novels that individuals, nations and ethnic groups were aspects of what he terms the 'continuing stream of the race'. At one stage he had a plan to write a history of the world which 'should be as free as possible of any national bias, and hence acceptable everywhere as a common textbook'. This unrealized project reflected his view that 'We are all experiments in the growing consciousness of the race' – a 'great opening out of life', as one of the characters says in *The World Set Free* (1914). It is in this novel too that the main character, Marcus Karenin, who after two operations is near death, still has the energy to cry out defiantly: 'And you, old Sun ... beware of me ... I shall launch myself at you and I shall reach you and I shall put my foot on your spotted face and tug you about by your fiery locks. One step I shall take to the moon, and then I shall leap at you ... Old Sun, I gather myself together out of the pools of the individual that have held me dispersed so long. I gather my billion thoughts into science and my million wills into a common purpose.'[31]

In *The Food of the Gods* (1904) Wells also talks about a mystic 'ongoing force', the narrative being a parable of growth, when an experiment in developing a growth-encouraging substance gets out of hand and generates races of giants (giant humans, giant chickens, giant vermin, giant mosquitoes) all over the countryside. At the close of the novel, the civil engineer Cossar addresses the Giant children who have been raised as an experiment by the protagonists: 'Tomorrow, whether we live or die, the growth will conquer through us. That is the law of the spirit for evermore. To grow according to the Will of God! ... Greater ... greater, my Brothers! ... growing ... Till the earth is no more than a footstool.'[32]

Wells was himself criticized for not having 'a metaphysical dimension', a complaint also directed against his fictional characters. 'His figures do not have the inner life so typical of nineteenth-century novels.' But that is to ignore the fact that these same characters are nonetheless exhaustively analysed into other components, and as often as not, as with Wells himself, a social conscience was replacing religion as the arbiter of their morality.

The fundamental idea behind Wells's approach was that science, and especially scientific *research*, would produce new knowledge that would replace *ought* with *is*. When that happened, morality would be rational, not religious. Some of his ideas were uncannily echoed by physicists of the late twentieth century (see chapter 24).

Memory and Desire

The title *À la recherche du temps perdu*, Marcel Proust's life's work, contains a word that means 'search' or 'research', if not necessarily scientific. At the same time the book has religious overtones throughout, right from the start where the famous episode of the madeleine echoes parts of the Catholic mass. Here the narrator, savouring the mixture of cake and tea, experiences a rush of 'all-powerful joy' that was transcendental: 'I sensed that [this joy] was connected with the taste of the tea and the cake, but that it infinitely transcended these savours, could not, indeed, be of the same nature.'

The very name *petite madeleine* derives from Mary Magdelene, and echoes of Catholic theology continue throughout the book, leading several critics to suggest that Proust's 'religion of art' is to an extent modelled on the Christian theological tradition of confessional writing.

Pericles Lewis has a different and more original notion. He argues that Proust drew heavily on the ideas of the early French sociologist Émile Durkheim in his *Elementary Forms of the Religious Life* which appeared in 1912, just a year before *Swann's Way*, the first of the seven volumes that comprise *À la recherche*.[33] Durkheim, who based a lot of his theories on the study of 'primitive' religions among the aborigines of Australia, argued that totemism was/is the basic form of religion, containing all the essences of later religious forms. Totemism refers to the worship by a clan or tribe of a specific animal or plant, which is sacred, and acknowledges an anonymous and impersonal force that is immanent in the natural world. In totemism, a primitive clan or tribe worships *itself* as a 'power' that exerts a moral force on fellow members, keeping the community intact and confirming and sacralizing its *communal* identity.

By this account, Proust's novel is itself a kind of sociology, regarding the clan as the source of all values – Madame Verdurin's salon, for example, is referred to as a *petit clan*. Proust's story alights throughout on objects that are regarded – by one character or another – as sacred, totemic, in a secular way; or they have 'magical' properties to transport us to another place and time (the way shamans do, in primitive clans). The episode with the madeleine is only the best-known of these: 'such sacred objects restore to the narrator the kind of communion he can no longer, even in his most intimate relations, achieve'.[34]

The profound influence of Durkheim on Proust has been more or less overlooked, Lewis argues, but some links are plain. For example, at the École Normale Supérieure Durkheim was a classmate of Henri Bergson, who married Proust's cousin. At the ENS Durkheim studied philosophy and then received his doctorate from the Sorbonne. Proust also studied philosophy at the Sorbonne, where his professors included two who examined Bergson for his PhD. One of these men, Émile Boutroux, who wrote an influential work on William James and also wrote on spiritualism, was described by Proust as one of his heroes, and he made specific reference to Boutroux's work in *À la recherche*. There is no evidence that Durkheim and Proust ever met or, for that matter, that Proust ever read Durkheim's great book, but their social and intellectual lives undoubtedly overlapped, says Lewis, adding that Proust's high-school teacher, Alphonse Darlu, founded a journal in which Durkheim's introduction to *The Elementary Forms of the Religious Life* first appeared.[35]

Furthermore, both Proust and Durkheim came from Alsatian Jewish families, at a time when Judaism was supposed to be a private matter with no political or social dimension. But that stability didn't last: as in the novel, conflict between Church and state erupted in France itself – with the Dreyfus affair, a scandal following the wrongful conviction for treason of a Jewish army officer. Both Proust and Durkheim took active roles in supporting Dreyfus's case; it became a highly public matter, secularists pitted against believers in traditional religion. The sociologist in Durkheim saw that, with the enormous forces of modernity coming together – urbanization, industrialization, materialism, massification and the growth of technology – it was more necessary than ever to view the individual as sacred: the individual is 'the touchstone according to which good must be distinguished from evil, is considered as sacred . . . It has something of that transcendental majesty which the churches of all times have given to their Gods.'[36] The individual life thus becomes the focus of social forces.

And this, of course, aptly describes the aims of Proust's massive work, in which the narrator is searching for a 'genuine community' such as that which was available in the early Church (and in his early childhood) but 'which today is available in neither institutional religion nor in the social groups that present themselves as alternative religions. Proust also understands the technological and social forces controlling modern life on a religious analogy, not with an omniscient God, but with the variety of powers, spirits, fairies, and gods [with a small g] that populate primitive and folk religions.'[37] Proust laces his work with anthropological metaphors and references – totemism, animism, paganism, magic. Even the form of the narration can be seen as a post-monotheistic phenomenon, a search for sacred, magical, transcendental moments. The narrator moves through the book, attaching himself to various clans, observing the myths and stories they tell themselves – their shared fictions, as Henry James would say – in order to keep their clans together. He is constantly disappointed, but finds salvation in what Proust called *les moments bienheureux* – 'blissful' moments brought about by *involuntary* memories which, he shows, are the royal road to the past, and to our unconscious.

What Durkheim and Proust share, according to Lewis, is not a concern with the individual's relationship with God, but rather 'the sacred power [that] bonds the individual to modern society and to its new gods'. These new sacred universal principles are, for Durkheim, such things as 'Fatherland', 'Liberty', 'Reason' (especially powerful in France after the Enlightenment and the Revolution). While not denying these, Proust shows that *les moments bienheureux* are invariably individual, even solitary, but 'each one opens up a portal to a whole social world'. In his book Proust focuses on the painstaking reconstruction of a coherent self 'from the competing impulses [desires] of an unconscious life'. Theodor Adorno emphasized that Proust was obsessed 'with the concrete and the unique, with the taste of a madeleine or the colour of the shoes of a lady worn at a certain party', through which he shows that our most private self is not self-generating or isolated from society, 'but rather begins its journey shaped by forces that precede and control it'.[38]

The narrator shows, for instance, that to be admitted to Madame Verdurin's 'little clan', you had to share her view that the pianist she had discovered was better than all others then available – her clan shows elements of a sect, admission to which requires full participation in its rituals and commitment to its beliefs. Madame Verdurin is even described as 'an "ecclesiastical power" who brooks no disagreement with her religion of art, in which Beethoven's *Ninth* and the operas of Wagner are "the most sublime of prayers"'. Those of a critical disposition, the heretics, are scapegoated.

Another feature of *À la recherche* is the narrator's repeated experience of disillusionment, his discovery that the sacred rituals of the communities he joins turn out, invariably, to have no transcendent power; they are social forces, no more, and salvation, the bliss of *les moments bienheureux*, is the only transcendence on offer.

Although critics thought that Proust made a religion of art, in fact he was arguing that both religion *and* art have social cohesion as their primary social function. 'When the faithful believe that they are worshipping Wagner, Beethoven or Vinteuil, they are in fact worshipping the standards of the clan itself . . . Specific works of art thus serve for the little clan something of the function that the totem does for Durkheim's Australians.'[39]

Proust is observing that, with the death of God, the death of a monotheistic Christian God, more primitive forms of religious ritual – totemism – may fill the gap. This is because humans like the *experience* of the sacred: 'the modern sacred is still sacred'. But he is also saying that such experiences are essentially hollow: they offer no transcendence, but merely confirm our membership of communities. This may be no small thing, but it is not a big thing either; it is experienced, for the narrator, as a disappointment.

And at this point Proust joins forces with Henry James. What the episodes of involuntary memory build up to in the book is the explanation of desire in the narrator. And he observes, and is drawn to, desire in others. It is the unconscious that explains desire, it is desire that enchants our world, desire that makes us feel 'full' or 'whole'. After the death of Albertine, the narrator muses on the afterlife. 'Desire is powerful indeed; it engenders belief . . . I began to believe in the immortality of the soul. But that did not suffice me. I required that, after my own death, I should find her again in her body, as though eternity were like life.' This echoes James: 'Belief in an afterlife isn't really a question of belief . . . it is on the other hand a question of desire.'[40]

It is the power of desire that binds us to other people. And for that reason, it is desire that is sacred. The desire to be part of a community is one thing, an important thing, but *desire*, of one individual for another, is a very different experience. Communal life, Proust is saying, no matter how desirable from the community's point of view, to establish stability, identity and all the rest, is nowhere near as interesting, fulfilling, enchanting, as the private experience of desire. Desire is particular, just as involuntary memory is particular. The insistence of desire, as Henry James and Proust, and the established Churches well recognised, is disruptive and dangerous, and that is why it becomes the basis of the sacred.

7

The Angel in Our Cheek

'After one has abandoned a belief in God, poetry is the essence which takes its place as life's redemption.' 'The major poetic idea in the world is and always has been the idea of God.' 'The poet becomes "the priest of the invisible".' Each of these statements was made by Wallace Stevens. 'After I had found nothingness, I found beauty' (Stéphane Mallarmé). 'We felt the possibility of a new religion, with poetic emotion as its essential quality' (Paul Valéry). 'Poetry . . . is capable of saving us; it is a perfectly possible means of overcoming chaos' (I.A. Richards). 'What angel do you carry hidden in your cheek?/ What perfect voice will tell the truths of wheat?' (Federico García Lorca).

As has already been emphasized, in the immediate wake of Nietzsche's apocalyptic pronouncements the arts were regarded as important in a way that is no longer true in our own day. This is not to say that the arts are not important now, but that they were felt to be much more important then. Without imagining ourselves back into that epoch, many of the arguments in this part of the book will lack the force they appeared to possess at the time. Something will have been lost in the historical translation.

This was especially true of poetry. Now, in the early years of the twenty-first century, poetry is very much a minority interest, albeit of a very passionate minority. To an extent, it has always been a minority activity, but in late Victorian and Edwardian times, in the decades leading up to the First World War and during the war itself, there were those who had very big ambitions for poetry, who were convinced that it was the natural heir to religion. For figures like Mallarmé and Valéry in France, for Stefan George and his circle in Germany, for Yeats and Wallace Stevens in the Anglophone countries, poetry was 'the realization of a destiny' that brought into being a second, 'higher' self, which offered an 'enlarged world'. As Stevens put it:

> Poetry
> Exceeding music must take the place
> Of empty heaven and its hymns.

God's Orphans

But the place to start is with Mallarmé, because although he didn't set out any specific views, in a specific work or a specific poem, about how to live without God, his entire approach shaped the way a whole raft of followers thought. Indeed, there are those, such as the historian of Symbolism Anna Balakian, who place Mallarmé on a level with Freud and Marx for the role he played in reshaping the way we think. Certainly, Mallarmé was a decisive influence on Valéry, Yeats, Rainer Maria Rilke and Wallace Stevens.

Jean-Paul Sartre, in *Mallarmé, or the Poet of Nothingness* (English edition 1988, French original two years earlier), places the poet centrally in the death-of-God narrative, at least in France. He explains what other influences were in operation at the time, and how they acted together on the mid-nineteenth-century sensibility. All the poets of the mid-century (in France, that is) were unbelievers, he says, though not without a nostalgia 'for the reassuring symmetry of a God-ordered universe'. Many thought that the stature of poetry had been reduced – previously, a poem had been something providentially inspired: 'The poet was only the trumpet; God supplied the breath. The post-Romantics, however, tended to view themselves as a "grotesque tin horn that echoes the discordant noises of Nature".' They therefore established a quixotic elite with aristocratic and idealistic pretensions, and Mallarmé was 'the nerve centre' of this higher culture. In the days of faith, Sartre wrote, 'the gift of poetry had been the sign of the nat-ural aristocrat . . . one was a poet by divine will. Inspiration was the secular term for Grace.'[1]

But science had ravaged that view; it had destroyed the hier-archy among humans by showing that all forms of existence are equal. Moreover, and possibly worse, the second law of thermodynamics, published by Rudolf Clausius in 1854, had demonstrated that 'nothing is created or destroyed' and that the universe would ultimately end in a heat death. This confirmed for many that a perfect God did not exist in Nature, nor did he have the power to create.

Sartre therefore concluded that poets, more than anyone, were 'God's orphans', and even here Mallarmé stood out because his mother had died when he was five and his sister when he was fifteen, so that they 'fused' together into a single absence – absence being the cru-cial term. There was, then, in Mallarmé's life more than in anyone else's, a 'commanding absence', or a 'hovering absence', as Sartre says elsewhere.[2] For Mallarmé, says Sartre, 'his mother never stops dying', and it left a 'pathological gap in his "being-in-the-world"'. This was important for Sartre, who saw Mallarmé as the herald of the twen-tieth century and someone who, '[m]ore profoundly than Nietzsche, experienced the death of God . . . At the very time Taylor conceived of mobilizing men so as to render their work more efficient, he mobilized language so as to assure the optimal yield from Words.'[3]*

And this helps put Mallarmé's achievement in context. What he sought to do, in Anna Balakian's words, was to construct or achieve a 'semantic transcendentalism to compensate for the waning of meta-physical yearnings'.[4] If religions are found ineffective, as they clearly were for many people when Mallarmé was alive, 'then language be-comes the recourse, the mainstay . . . serving the imagination'. This is the basis for his famous dictum that the poet must no longer nar-rate, narrative implying continuity, a sequence that structures reality. Mallarmé sought something new, 'a universe where nothing can be

* Taylorism, named after Frederick Winslow Taylor (1856–1914), referred to the intro-duction of scientifically calculated synthetic workflows into factory management. Intended to improve efficiency, it was sometimes called Fordism.

foreseen or determined in the natural context', where, as Rilke would say later, 'the interpreted world' (this world, here and now) usurps 'the place of heaven as the site of survival in an augmented parameter for the arts'. What this means, in effect, is that the poet does not seek representation, in the traditional way, but looks instead for 'fresh presentation' at the 'absolute moment in time' that can never again be duplicated. More, language in the new poetic sense 'becomes a place of encounter for analogies that are to the enrichment of personality what an interlining is to a simple cloth garment'; images, ideas, are implicit rather than explicit, so that the reader shares a sense of achievement with the poet.[5] Implicitness was to be a feature of twentieth-century thought, as we shall see.

Mallarmé and his enthusiastic followers saw this as a method that highlighted human resistance to spiritual annihilation, the identification (but only hinted at) of '*les mots sans rides*', 'words [and therefore ideas, moments] without wrinkles', the poetic communication of 'the well of meaning', because the well of meaning is inexhaustible, and is not linear 'but rather a circular vortex in perpetual motion'.[6]

A core aspect of this (and it would dominate much poetry of the twentieth century) is 'naming' – naming the world around us, not introspection as such but naming the 'redemptive features of an unconcerned universe'; naming, as he said in a famous quote, flowers 'absent from all bouquets'. Naming, Mallarmé said more plainly, 'does not evoke a return of any particular contour of which we have empirical knowledge and that is specifically recognisable to us in its natural environment'. Put another way, 'The perception of the imperceptible occurs not through a distorting lens but by a rational adaptation to an unexpected linguistic association': word seepage, as he also described it. This is, in effect, what Symbolism is, the creation of an 'other' world, an 'interspace', which depends only on the powers of language and brings us intensely experienced moments in real time, here and now.[7] For Mallarmé, as he explicitly said, this approach would replace a theological teleology 'with a much more practical vision of life on this planet'.[8] For him and his followers, poetry must rid itself of its narrative and mimetic traditions to create its own fiction, its own reality, 'an ontology separate from theological perceptions'.[9]

This is what his poems such as *Hérodiade* and 'L'Après-midi d'un faune' seek to do – he saw them as part of a new 'cohesive mentality': a mentality of naming, but naming not just new contours but also new mysteries, given that the world is inexhaustible and open-ended and because there is among humanity a universal desire for 'the second chance', the second chance not to waste the legacy we have inherited, not to settle just for the life we have lived thus far. The world consists, he said, of a pool of second chances, self-transcending promises we make to ourselves to struggle with fate to invent such things as 'nonspecifiable spaces' or 'indeterminable time perceptions', to 'divest nature of its decaying processes'; these are forms of imaginative naming that only language can bring about.

In these ways, Mallarmé sought nothing less than to reground, reform, reshape poetry for a secular world, maintaining its ambition. A whole raft of first-rate twentieth-century poets responded to his call.

Praise and the Vertical Axis

Before we come to them, however, we need to consider the one man who could rival Mallarmé in his ambitions for poetry, a man who very nearly changed poets from, as Shelley famously put it, 'the unacknowledged legislators of the world' into political demagogues. This was the German, Stefan George. The word 'demagogue' is not too strong.

> The eyes · narrow and only when they rule wide ·
> Were illuminated from behind as if by candles ·
> The pain from some old cruelty.
> Etched in his cheeks.
>
> His face fell steeply down from his dark hair
> As if in princely terraces
> Down to his chin · which only concealed
> And was full of violence · that was deadly in hate.

Around the immobile lips there was the trace
Of conquered temptation ·
And gravely his brow carried
The noble curse like a chosen jewel.

This poem – vivid still in Robert Norton's translation – is not by George but about him. Ernst Bertram, a poet and professor of literature and an authority on Nietzsche, called his poem 'Portrait of a Master', though he elsewhere characterized George as a 'werewolf'.[10] That might be going a bit far, but there is no question that George did have an extraordinary career, as extraordinary as any poet in history; he was a man who carried the ethic of 'art for art's sake' further than anyone else, and who sought energetically to replace religion with poetry.

That extraordinary career began in the early 1890s when George – who had visited Mallarmé in Paris and had been accepted by that master's circle – emerged as a lyric poet along the lines of the French Symbolists. Beginning with his poetry, as Norton, his biographer says, '[t]o an extraordinary and perhaps even singular degree, George sought to submit every aspect of his life to his will . . . His desire to control the perception others had of him was only one more form of the tendency toward radical self-invention that marked his entire life' (something that he shared with W.B. Yeats, though in a very different way).[11] Paradoxically, although he was scarcely seen outside the small coterie of about thirty followers, his influence spread steadily until it encompassed the entire German nation.

George found the Symbolists congenial, in particular their conviction that science had not improved the world but *impoverished* it, by reducing it to what could be measured and calculated, removing even the possibility of transcendental meaning. The Symbolists thought that Nature was but a veneer, obscuring an invisible realm that was the real one; and one to which, moreover, the poet had privileged access. Norton again: 'The words of a poem act, rather, as a kind of conduit, leading not to an appreciation of the things they describe, or even to a specific emotion they might evoke, but through an ultimately inexplicable alignment the poem makes possible a sort of spiritual attunement to the poet's vision, and, ultimately, an encounter with what was variously called the "Idea", the "Infinite" or the "Absolute". And it is the poet, and the poet alone, who can supply the medium enabling this encounter to occur.'[12]

At this distance, in the second decade of the twenty-first century, the idea of the poet having 'privileged' access to anything at all goes against the whole ethos of the postmodern, post-colonial, democratic world, but if we are to fully understand George's aims and impact we have to think ourselves back into that time, when – as reiterated at the beginning of this chapter – art was felt to be far more important than it is now, and artists were looked upon in a different light. Four of George's main collections of poems, for example, were published under revealing titles: *Hymns*, *Pilgrimages*, *The Year of the Soul* and *The Star of the Covenant*.

George was intransigent in his view that art – and artists – took priority in life, even over life. This is shown nowhere more clearly than in a verse in *Hymns* about Fra Angelico, who in George's view had appropriated his materials from the world he lived in:

> He took the gold from holy chalices ·
> For blond hair the straw of ripening wheat ·
> The pink from children who draw with brick ·
> From the washerwoman at the stream the indigo.

Nature here is placed in the service of art and, implicitly at least, the artist is being positioned on the same level as God. Throughout the collection it is the accomplishment of the poet that is foregrounded. Part of the aim here, as elsewhere with the Symbolists, is to subdue and even overthrow the outside world, the physical world we inhabit, which is considered 'irretrievably debased, tawdry and malignant' and which is to be replaced by the creations of this privileged group of initiates.

This privileged group also congregated around George via *Blätter für die Kunst* (Pages for Art), which was more than a journal but a standard-bearer to which George's followers could rally and extend his message. This was all the more important because, early on and for some time afterwards, his books of poems were printed in editions of very few copies (206 for *The Year of the Soul*), and distributed only to hand-picked followers. This privileged view was not confined to George. Hugo von Hofmannsthal wrote to him, confiding: 'I am completely agreed with everything you say; I also have no concern for the "paper", nor for publicity, rather I am concerned solely about coming into contact with a *necessarily small* circle of people searching as I am and to get to know related works of art that are otherwise inaccessible [italics added].' To underscore their task, the journal proclaimed that its central aim was to promote a 'spiritual art' – *eine geistige Kunst* – 'on the basis of the new sensibility and manner – an art for art'.[13]

The most accessible of George's verse is probably *The Year of the Soul*, which Norton describes as 'a melancholy wash spread over the interior landscape of the poet's mind'.

> You stepped up to the hearth
> Where all embers have died ·
> The only light on the earth
> Was the moon's cadaveric colour.
>
> You dipped your pallid fingers
> Deep into the ashes
> Searching feeling groping –
> That there may be a glow again!
>
> See what the moon advises you
> With a gesture of consolation:
> Step away from the hearth ·
> It has become late.

Throughout the book everything is bathed in this 'twilight glow', not unlike the deliquescent, placeless, sensual women in some of Gustav Klimt's paintings, who seem to float past the viewer, where the sheer beauty of the creation outweighs any other form of meaning. (This quality is the one most challenging to the translator.)

George initially wanted to use poetry to create an alternative world, but with *Blätter* he also developed the idea of a circle, a small, privileged group of people to surround him. And in this idea, of a circle of initiates, was embedded the issue of hierarchy that took on increasing importance as a way to live, as a viable alternative to bourgeois society. George and his followers saw a circle of like minds as the best way for great ideas, beautiful ideas, to emerge and coalesce. Even within this circle, there was never any claim that all were equal. Indeed, it was stated that 'small' ideas of the lesser members could help generate larger, more beautiful ideas in the leaders (George himself, of course, was at the top). For the lesser members, it was regarded as consolation enough to have played a part in the higher life of the leaders. As one of them put it, the lesser members gathered the flowers which a leader would later 'weave into his wreath'. The circle always presupposed a centre that gave stability, direction and purpose to the whole.[14]

Such a view, such a set-up, made sense only alongside another characteristic of George's circle – a determined attack on the value of reason and rationality. One can see why. The critical faculty creates doubt, calls things into question, does not recognize sanctioned authority, and therefore tends to be isolating. Belief is best sustained in the absence of criticism. George's group valued above all the 'ecstatic celebration that erases all distinctions among individual beings'.[15]

Various alternatives to reason were offered by members of the circle. Ludwig Klages, a philosopher who thought the modern world 'degenerate' and who founded the German graphologists' association, proposed that 'enthusiasm' drives the artist. 'Creative natures are characterized by the deep love of life. From it flows enthusiasm – that is the power of self-sacrifice, of dissolving into the object of veneration. Belief and adoration are in the soul of the creative one. Art is not created out of objective knowledge, but out of an enthusiastic embrace of illusions and dreams.'

As Leonard Woolf said, there have been countless artistic 'circles' of all colours held together more or less loosely by common assumptions, but there has been nothing quite like George's 'secret Germany', as it would come to be called.[16]

The Tapestry of Life did not have a religious-sounding title, like some of George's other books, but it nonetheless had qualities of a sacred text. Its language recalls the Bible and takes the form of a gospel with an angel, the bearer of the doctrine of 'the beautiful life', George's own idiosyncratic vision. The most important lesson the angel teaches the poet is 'the value and importance of submitting to a superior being', the angel giving the poet leave to adopt a similar position in regard to his own followers.

> A small flock going quietly along its way
> Proudly remote from the working bustle
> And on their flags the slogan stands:
> To Hellas forever our love.

The Greek ideal would eventually congeal for George into a coherent doctrine, inside which he offered the shelter of meaning and certainty, and asked in return absolute loyalty.

> We march at the side of our severe lord
> Who carefully examines his fighters
> No weeping keeps us back from following our star
> No friend's arm and no bride's kiss.

George's followers were, in effect, his disciples. He had adopted the Christian model, but in the service of beauty, to which he alone had ultimate access. This may seem anachronistic to us, but it is at least fairly straightforward. However, there were to be complications.

Shakespeare, Not Yahweh

Some of George's disciples were young men, boys even. At first they were chosen under the pretext of a search for poetic talent, but that was gradually dropped. There were two who were to be especially notable. The first, in 1898, was Friedrich Gundelfinger. So handsome that women sent *him* flowers, he was a mesmerizing conversationalist and a brilliant mimic. Gundelfinger was obsessed with George and George with him. George called him 'Gundolf'.[17]

Even in this we see George's views evolving, in that his personal agenda was gradually raised to the level of a dogma, which had two elements. The George doctrine was for art and against Protestantism, Prussia and the bourgeoisie. Everyone in his circle held to these views with an intensity that is probably beyond us today. Gundolf said it plainly: 'I want to serve Shakespeare and not Yahweh or Baal.' The members regarded themselves as 'a higher form of being' and regarded art not as a game but as sacred. Without exaggeration, it was for them a matter of life or death.[18]

The second of the young men who was to have a profound influence on George was in fact a mere boy. In 1903 when George met Maximilian Kronberger, the former was thirty-five and the latter had just turned fifteeen. And it was the premature death of Maximilian (Maximin, as he became to George) that sparked a crucial new phase in George's own life, partly because Maximin died unexpectedly from meningitis the day after his sixteenth birthday. Until that point, the exceptionalness of the George circle had not gone much beyond their shared sense of aesthetic superiority. But Maximin's death changed everything.

It appears that, at this juncture, George had some kind of mystical experience. As his biographer says, 'The nonrational, immaterial sphere had always been associated with poetry for George. He [now] made a straight-faced claim for Maximin's divinity and himself as a secular priest, in a private religion.' This takes some swallowing, but the poet and translator Friedrich Wolters, who was one of George's most devoted followers, agreed that the master felt himself touched by a miracle – 'that God had decided to appear in human form, as Maximin'.[19] From now on, George saw himself not just as a poet but as a kind of Jesus figure. What distinguished him from others in history who have adopted such a pose (and often received psychiatric treatment as a result) is that his acolytes treated him in the way that he wished to be treated.

By 1910 there were some thirty people in George's entourage, which represented, in their own eyes at least, a distinct alternative to the bourgeois (Christian) way of life. They had a well defined purpose and unity; unlike the loose agglomeration of bourgeois society, the group offered a new way of living *against* society, of sharing a profound hatred for modernity. In his book *The Seventh Ring* (1907) George went so far as to outline a private eschatology, signifying the end of the old way of living together and announcing a new one in which the disciples surround a master. Discipleship, which some among the circle openly acknowledged, would seem a very foreign and even ridiculous idea; nonetheless it liberated the disciple from 'the arrogant isolation of the ego' and allowed him to lead his (hardly ever her) life in the act of adoration and praise, this being the purpose and salvation for the members.

'The duty of disciples is not imitation,' Gundolf claimed. 'Their pride is that the master is unique. They should not *make* his images – but rather *be* his work – not put on and display his petrified traits and gestures – but rather absorb into their being his blood and his breath, his light and his warmth.' 'The *Führer's* disciples,' Gundolf went on (in an unfortunate metaphor), 'should be walking ovens that he has heated, matter he has animated etc ... Only a *Führer* or master can properly be said to be a "personality" ... Whoever knows himself not to be a master should learn to be a servant or disciple – [which is] better than a hyperactive vanity.'[20]

Secret Germany: a Spiritual State

All this was so at variance with the common European tradition of Enlightenment and liberalism that the question has often been asked as to whether some sort of private pathology was involved here, either on George's part or that of his followers (Ludwig Klages certainly showed signs of schizophrenia). But over time, George's influence would grow, not diminish. By then he was the centre of a quasi-religious cultural crusade, 'a circle of disciples [that] was to find its fulfilment in forming a spiritual state, which could gradually penetrate the outlying regions in ever farther reaches'.[21]

One of the reasons why George was not dismissed as deranged undoubtedly stemmed from the uncanny effect he had on others. Alexander von Bernus (1880–1965) was a poet and editor of *Die*

Freistatt, a magazine which published such authors as Frank Wedekind, Rainer Maria Rilke, Stefan Zweig, Thomas Mann and Hermann Hesse. Many of his contributors became his friends, so he was not easily overawed. But when George stayed with him at Stift Neuburg, von Bernus's country residence near Heidelberg, in the summer of 1909, even he admitted that 'what was convincing and compelling about Stefan George was not so much his poetry . . . as the fascination of a great personality who had mastered his passions . . . a personality that was much more that of a Roman Caesar than that of a poet . . . In the years before World War One an almost mythical nimbus surrounded him.'

Gundolf carried this further. He believed 'in spiritual impregnation, in the resurrection and rebirth of the pupil through the master, in the implanting of the spirit, like the priest of a primitive tribe'. All this gained further momentum when, in November 1909, George announced that he was founding a new journal, the *Jahrbuch für die geistige Bewegung* (Yearbook for the Spiritual Movement).[22] According to Karl Wolfskehl, another of George's entourage, 'the group had an agreed view of life itself'. As opposed to the 'overheated cult of individuality of our time', which fed on the empty slogans of 'reason', 'freedom' and 'humanity', George's disciples 'represented the only unity of people, works, and desires to have arisen organically' during the previous two decades. It was only among circle members, Wolfskehl wrote, that 'personal envy and resentment, all striving among one another, all craving to steal or swindle each other's status', were absent. For him and the others, 'the true driving force of the time' should be sought 'not in that infertile wasteland known as the modern world but somewhere else: in the constellation gathered around George that Wolfskehl for the first time gave a name to – "Secret Germany"'. George was felt by his disciples to be the leader of a spiritual war 'that can no longer be avoided'.[23]

Nor was this the end of such claims. Gundolf again: 'Professing one's faith in George is not professing faith in a person. Stefan George is the most important person in Germany today . . . He wields his power by creating the linguistic body of the coming spirit and forming souls for the coming faith.' Gundolf even suggested that the Germans were, in effect, a modern form of chosen people, 'fortunate to have had the miracle of potential rescue dropped in their midst'. Not everyone was chosen, of course. Salvation would be granted to very few, even among the Germans. The others would perish unredeemed. 'With George, those Germans who are still able to experience a poet at all are beginning to have the premonition of a new day and the lifting of an ancient anguish.'[24] For Wolters, 'We should esteem instead the "great man", follow him where he leads us, no matter what sacrifices he may demand.' For those lucky enough to be admitted to the circle, they should 'look for the man who would provide meaning and a model for your will'. It went without saying that members of the circle should keep themselves free from all 'contamination' of a physical or spiritual nature. 'The healthy man turns his eye from suffering and keeps himself fit for battle with his enemy.'[25]

In November 1913 George published *The Star of the Covenant* (Der Stern des Bundes), in an edition of ten copies. It contains a hundred poems that need to be read several times if they are to be understood. It is the testament of 'Secret Germany', its aims being to show that the poet is, in effect, a priest, drawing the attention of his followers to the beauty that has replaced God; to identify the poverty and unworthiness of the present world, which must be eradicated before the new age can begin; and to show followers how to conduct their lives in this new age, in the shadow of the great man who leads them.[26] George's aims in this work are nothing less than breathtaking.

Marianne Weber spoke for many when she said: 'The deification of mortal people and the foundation of a religion based on George . . . seemed to us to be the self-deception of a people who are not entirely up to the modern world.'[27] Nonetheless, when the First World War broke out there were many who came to share George's views about leadership and followership. Georg Lukács thought that the poet was a prototype of Hitler. And many soldiers took *The Star of the Covenant* (by then widely available) with them to the Front and used it 'as a breviary'. This aspect will be examined in chapter 9.

The central unity of George's work is, then, the establishment of a new religion founded on the power of poetry, where it is the *form* that takes precedence over the content of any specific poem or body of poems: it is the form of poetry that *intensifies* sensation. This is to be viewed in the German tradition of *Bildung*, the process of self-cultivation and refinement in which *Dichtung*, the practice and experience of poetry, was seen as a highly valued critical corrective to the progressive domination of intellectual life by scientific research and dispassionate scholarship (*Wissenschaft*). Poetry, on this reading, is superior to the rational idioms of science 'because it is imbued with the power of synthesis' [28] (Remember that Freud had been applauded for *his* synthesis).

All this comes together, for George, in the centrality of the idea of praise. Praise, for him, is the foremost aspect of worship; praise establishes a relationship between the great man and his followers, between in effect a deity and his worshippers. People need both axes, George is saying, in order to be fulfilled. They need a vertical axis, someone to look up to and learn from, and a horizontal axis, where members of the worshipping community live together according to shared ideals obtained by worship. The notion that 'poetry is praise' was adopted by George for his later work. In 1928 Max Kommerell would publish *The Poet as Leader in the Age of German Classicism*.

Living with Disappointment

Paul Valéry, the French poet and man of letters, was born, he said, in one of the places where he would have wished to be born – Sète, in the South of France, 'where my first impressions came from the sea and the activities of a seaport'. Sensitive and highly intelligent, Valéry grew up constantly anxious about making mistakes in his schoolwork and about competition (though there were only four pupils in his class). This may well have coloured his attitudes in later life. Always self-disciplined (Nietzsche's works formed his bedside reading early on), he began to write poetry in his teens, before he did his military service. In 1890, aged nineteen, he met the poet Pierre Louÿs at a festival to celebrate the sixth centenary of the University of Montpellier, Louÿs being a student delegate from Paris. A friendship blossomed, and the Parisian, who mixed in the circle centring on Mallarmé, Paul Verlaine and André Gide, offered to show them some of Valéry's work. These early friendships no doubt helped propel Valéry's talent.

That talent included a lifelong interest in mathematics, and from that stemmed an interest in *order*, which in turn fuelled an interest in music and architecture, major concerns of Mallarmé's. For Valéry, music and architecture were the greatest art forms, for they were 'pure intention'. It was this interest in order that shaped at least part of his philosophy: he thought our main concern should be the attempt to go beyond our organic/biological nature. For him, the processes of organic nature were no guide to the desirable issues of human evolution – as he pointed out, morbidity is as natural as healthiness.[29] What separated humans from other animals was our ability to break free from our biological inheritance, and he insisted that 'the various things that we are' may be best understood as discontinuous from one another, casting doubt on the idea of the *moi pur* because we have many successive selves, some of which exist simultaneously.

Evolutionary fitness was for him a sort of red herring. He thought that our highest destiny is to be other than – outside – our biological urges; that 'the soul's reward is outside evolution, evolution and art [being] totally different', the former achieving its results by imperceptible increments over long timespans, art achieving its effects, usually, by one magnificent urge, or surge. Valéry believed that the imperceptible pace of evolution led us to mistake continuity for finality, one consequence of this being that 'there is no wholeness in the universe', so that partiality is as real as totality – which is where the poet or artist comes in, creating 'small worlds of order'. A successful work of art inspires 'the force of faith without exacting belief'. A successful poem, for him, produces moments (moments, note) 'of infinite consequence', a separate reality from the biological world, spiritual but not theological. There is an overlap here with the views of Santayana.

Valéry was particularly concerned to show that there is a 'mutual irrelevance' of biological and spiritual values – for him that was the *point* of being human, that we had broken free of our biology. Biological life, as he characterized it, was 'ordinary' but though the soul was a partner to the body our most precious psychological experiences are those – such as delight in knowledge, or disinterested love – 'which envisage an end radically distinct from our involvement in life'. He thought that the Romantics' yearning after the unattainable stopped them – and many of us – from coming to terms with the fact that all stages in our quest for discovery 'are ineluctably provisional'.[30] Rather, he thought that man, 'a stranger on Earth', could not bend the world as it is to any purpose: we cannot modify the constitution of things, but we can modify their relation to one another.

Valéry felt that disappointment 'inevitably' arose in all earthly experiences because 'they are never quite adequate to what the self might hope to derive from them'. He applied this to works of art also: however significant the landmarks, they are never really definitive (this was summed up in his famous remark that a work of art is never finished, only abandoned at a certain stage). A poet should be easy to impress and impossible to convince; the spontaneous movements of the mind, especially our 'strange preoccupation' with immortality, must be verified and examined by a stricter second self.

'A work of art is always to some extent a disappointment to its author, but because it announces something less than the *intended discovery*, not because it is unequal to, or betrays, something already fully experienced and inadequately expressed. The perfection, to which the work is inadequate, lies beyond the work, not behind it; we are concerned with the falling short of a perfection whose complete conception – quite apart from concrete realizations – would itself be emergent, not with the imperfect expression of an ineffable but already known "profundity" [italics added].' And this argument applies equally to the self: the essential self, 'like the poetic reality which is one of its aspects', is something to be discovered by emergence which, even as it emerges, is never the end point. And '[t]he product of any . . . single act is to be regarded as contributing to the discovery, not as the imperfect announcement of a thing discovered in a more favoured state of consciousness . . . The discovery itself is a purpose.'

This is why, for Valéry, order, or form (the sonnet in poetry, for example), is not a limitation: the form is objective, not limited to an immediate occasion, and determines relationships recognized by author and beholder alike, both of whom can assess the success or otherwise of the realization, each having a more or less agreed idea of the form and how it affects expression. A work of art shows us what we are capable of and points to a perfection that will never exist except in the mind of either the artist, the beholder, or both. The perfection, however big or small, always remains ideal; we must accept our disappointment as we savour the ideal notion that the work of art has set before us.[31]

For Valéry as for Stefan George, poetry, the poetic use of language, even its artificiality – especially its artificiality – were spiritual, at least in intent: *'L'esprit est un souffle, la pensée un poids.'*[32] Our most intimate, our most profound thoughts, he said, come from the naivety and confusion of our ancestors, and no poetry worth the name can allow such thoughts to remain inexact – in that sense poetry has embodied progress, as a form of clarification (Thomas Nagel's definition of philosophy). The intellect is the real angel in our heads, it is the intellect that determines that the soul is an arbitrary construct, that art is the real spiritual construct, that spiritual life, seen in this way, is a proper part of nature. We are on the verge of the psychological age, he wrote.

Poetry was 'an absolute place', a voyage through 'the Netherlands of in-between existence', a way of thinking unlike any other, a way for thought and words to emerge, one result of Schopenhauer's 'will', which Valéry thought of as 'an urge without a goal', perhaps the most meaningless thing in the cosmos. A poem is not just a way of reli[e]ving an internal pressure in the poet, or of producing 'passive delight' in the reader or beholder, but an indispensable means of arriving at a unique state of aesthetic consciousness. It is not so much something divine, as Mallarmé had said, as 'the temporary depository of our intimations of divinity . . . the poem is, for the poet, at once an invitation to the reader, a stage in the realization of his own destiny, and no more than provisional in either of these functions'. In creating a poem, the poet becomes more than himself, a fuller form of himself; 'the real destiny of the universe is to be expressed by poets'. The self is inexhaustible.[33]

The very point of poetry, Valéry is saying, is for the human mind to approach asymptotically the experience which is as far from the materially real as it can be, and yet still means something: that is what spirituality *is*. Many have said that religions draw much of their lasting force in the world from the continued existence of suffering. Valéry saw that people are capable of far more than they will actually achieve in their lifetimes, and that this knowledge – derived from reading and sharing poetry – should strengthen them and help them prepare for, and respond to, suffering. In other words, we are bigger than traditional religions allow us to be.

It is this *ambition* that unites the figures in this chapter.

Evanescent Order

W.B. Yeats described himself as 'enthralled' by Nietzsche. In 1902 he wrote to his friend the American collector John Quinn, 'I have not read anything with so much excitement', and elsewhere he said that he found Nietzsche a 'joy'.[34] Otto Bohlmann finds many correspondences between the work of Nietzsche and that of Yeats, the latter distinguishing between a 'harsh' and a 'gentle' Nietzsche, and being drawn to the philosopher's 'darker' instincts and his ideas about man's 'frightful' inner nature. Yeats liked the fact that Nietzsche looked out on the world 'with unmoistened eyes', that he thought the 'total character' of the world was 'chaos', and that the fact that the world was 'rich in contradictions' was 'fruitful'. He was sympathetic to Nietzsche's opinion that love was 'a brief forgiveness between opponents'.[35]

For Yeats as for Nietzsche, personality 'is a constantly renewed choice', invariably giving life the qualities of a (Darwinian?) battle, which is nonetheless to be 'embraced as a joy'. Once we acknowledge life as a tragedy, and understand our limitations, he said, we open ourselves to the fact that 'even the shortest moments might contain something sacred, which outweigh [for that brief time] struggle and suffering'.

For Yeats, that's what the aim of poetry was: the creation of brief moments of 'ecstatic affirmation'. The world, as the phenomenologists say, is illogical, and reason, logic, poetic analogies and licence allow us to 'treat as equal what are merely similar', thereby creating order; and even evanescent order is better than none.

Like his fellow Irishman George Bernard Shaw, Yeats both was and was not religious. He thought that 'ultimate unity' can be achieved only beyond the physical world, but he also thought that subjectivity and objectivity need each other 'if wholeness is to be achieved'; and that is what poetry is, subjectivity and objectivity wrapped up into order. For him, 'all art is passion, the praise of life', and he shared with Shaw too the view that there is 'no final happy state except in so far as men may gradually grow better'. Great art – and great art always has tragic overtones – takes us 'beyond self-consciousness' into 'self-forgetfulness': this is what salvation *is*.

He too was influenced by Mallarmé and the Symbolists. When he read Villiers de l'Isle-Adam's occult drama *Axel*, he said, 'I could without much effort imagine that here at last was the Sacred Book I longed for.' He was drawn to the Symbolist technique of terse and open-ended communication 'that defies analytic attempts at exterior deciphering or decoding of ambiguities of meaning'. He liked the subtleties of poetry 'that have a new meaning every day'. For him this was 'the meaning of meaning in poetry'.

Nor was Yeats averse to regarding art as having a sacred function – the poet as secular priest. 'The arts in brooding on their own intensity have become religious and are seeking . . . to create a sacred book.' In 'The Autumn of the Body' he writes: 'The arts are, I believe, about to take upon their shoulders the burdens that have fallen from the shoulders of priests.' And, elsewhere: 'How can the arts overcome the slow dying of men's hearts that we call the progress of the world, and lay their words upon men's heartstrings again without becoming the garment of religion as in old times.'

His achievement in amalgamating metaphor and (Celtic) myth in noble, grandiose sweeps endowed poetry and poetry reading with a ritual, almost a ceremonial, quality, and that too suggests it was a secular replacement form of liturgy.

In many of his works the protagonists combat chance elements of an indifferent cosmos. However, unlike Mallarmé, Yeats never abandoned the possibility of spiritual transcendence, which is why his broader significance lies elsewhere. He was as much a child of his time as he was of his father. John Butler Yeats was a confirmed religious sceptic. A lawyer who abandoned the bar in Dublin to study painting in London, he was later described as a man 'who had an opinion about everything and information and eloquence to support it, and was always witty and intelligent even when inaccurate. Edward Dowden, G.K. Chesterton, Van Wyck Brooks, and others have testified to his personal charm.' Trained in law J.B. liked dichotomies, the social versus the individual, the intellect versus the emotions – in particular 'poetry is the Voice of the Solitary Spirit, prose the language of the sociable-minded'.[36] For him, Shakespeare's age was the ideal age, for then, 'everybody was happy'. Unhappiness came in with the French Revolution, 'which brought realism along with it'. And there were two kinds of belief, he maintained, the poetical and the religious, poetry expressing an absolute freedom, and religion embodying the denial of liberty.

W.B. Yeats was fortunate in having an educated and reflective father. In his early years he reacted against many of the elder Yeats's views, in particular his scepticism. But those views help partly to explain the poet, as does the general intellectual climate of the time. Because, as W.B. came on stream as a poet and as an individual, developments in Europe and America were influencing young men like him (see the following chapter for details). These events caused Yeats to react against his father's scepticism, but not to embrace what we might call the *status quo ante* – Christianity. Instead, like many others, in an attempt to combat the 'materialists', as he called them, he turned to semi-mystical thought, which refused to accept the universe identified by the scientists and the rationalists. He subscribed to a variety of occult theories, joined occult societies, and formulated a mystical nationalism which, while it resulted in some magnificent poetry, at this distance might seem embarrassing.

The point of Yeats is that the system he tried to adopt was far more all-embracing, far more ambitious, attempting to explain far more than anything that, say, Shaw or Valéry tried to do. *But Yeats ultimately failed.* In retrospect this was – and perhaps still is – his greatest significance, and it is the subject of the next chapter.

8

'The Wrong Supernatural World'

Yeats would probably not have turned to the occult sciences with such alacrity had not a movement in that direction already been well under way. As Richard Ellmann describes it: 'All over Europe and America young men dropped like him, and usually without his caution, into the treacherous currents of semi-mystical thought ... Since Christianity seemed to have been exploded, and since science offered to Western man little but proof of his own ignominiousness, a new doctrine purporting to be an ancient and non-European one was evolved by a strange Russian lady. The new movement called itself Theosophy and offered a "synthesis of science, religion, and philosophy" which opposed the contemporary developments of all three.'[1]

The 'strange Russian lady' was Madame Helen Blavatsky, born in 1831 in Yekaterinoslav, who advanced 'with certainty' her theories that 'man had never been an ape', that Herbert Spencer was in fundamental error, and accused in particular the Christian priesthood for modern materialism. Modern religion, she insisted, was but ancient thought *distorted*; and to uncover what such thought really was she turned to comparative mythology which, since about 1860, had been highly developed in books by such scholars as Max Müller, a German who taught at Oxford, and culminating in James Frazer's *The Golden Bough* (1890).

In an early work of her own Madame Blavatsky drew attention to what she saw as the similarity in the fundamental beliefs across all religions, and attributed this 'to the existence of a secret doctrine which was their common parent'. She claimed access to an oral tradition, for the true doctrine according to her had never been allowed to be set down. 'Now,' she said, 'an ancient brotherhood was keeping the secret wisdom high in the mountain fastnesses of Tibet.' The members of this brotherhood had no interest in spreading their wisdom, but should they choose to do so, she confided, they would 'astonish' the world. And they had at least shown certain things to Madame Blavatsky, for the onward transmission of their secret doctrine via the 'Theosophical Society'. 'As these mysteries were gradually revealed, the world would slowly progress towards the greater spirituality that had been prophesied for it.'[2]

One of the reasons the movement was popular – it was a 'magnet' for disaffected members of the educated public, says Yeats scholar Margaret Mills Harper – was because it was both anti-atheist and anticlerical. It attacked science but used scientific concepts where it suited the moment; it espoused fatalism, yet also offered hope of progress. 'Spiritual evolution restored the hope which natural evolution had removed.'

And it was Blavatsky's *The Secret Doctrine*, her chief work, that drew Yeats to theosophy, the first of several forms of occult reasoning that attracted him. Her doctrine proposed three main ideas. First, she said, there was an 'Omnipresent, Eternal, Boundless and Immutable Principle on which all speculation is impossible' – the theosophists paid little attention to deity. Second, the world is essentially a conflict of polar opposites, contraries without which life cannot exist. Third, she proclaimed the fundamental identity of all souls with the 'Universal Oversoul', which carried the implication that any soul might, under proper conditions, partake of the Oversoul's power, a heady possibility. The soul had seven elements, or principles, and it evolved through these elements over time. Heaven and Hell were to be considered as 'states', not actual places.

During this spiritual evolution humankind progressed from a more intuitive way of thinking to a more intellectual style, growing more conscious. This is where the world is at present, she said, in the fourth stage. In future stages – five, six and seven – intuition, intelligence and consciousness will fuse into an intense spirituality that, at present, we cannot imagine. When it suited them, the theosophists reinforced their arguments with examples from Eastern religions – for instance, they espoused the idea of Nirvana.

Several of Yeats's schoolfriends became interested in theosophy, which is how he learned of it. He met the woman herself in London, in 1887, and she persuaded him to join her 'lodge'. He was impressed by the fact that she was 'so fully herself'. Yeats was not altogether convinced of her occult powers (he was enough of his father's son) but he was impressed by the fact that, as he saw it, she 'held in her head all the folklore of the world and much of its wisdom'.³

Blavatsky warned her followers to beware of black magic, but not all of them went along with her, including Yeats, who took his friend Katharine Tynan to a spiritualist seance, 'where he was so upset by the supernatural phenomenon that he lost control of himself and beat his head on the table'. However, by that time the demand for 'magical instruction' was growing, and Blavatsky consented to form an 'esoteric section' of the society to accommodate it; Yeats joined enthusiastically. He hoped that it would prove to the satisfaction even of sceptics like his father that occult phenomena were possible.⁴ Several experiments were carried out, which sound ridiculous now but were taken seriously then. The esotericists tried (unsuccessfully) to raise the ghost of a flower, and to evoke certain kinds of dreams by sleeping with special symbols under their pillows. Madame Blavatsky took objection to these efforts, and Yeats was asked to resign from the theosophists, which he did.

But he had now been introduced to a system – and to other people who like him were opposed to scientific materialism and who accepted that there was a secret and ancient wisdom to be had. He hoped that he could bring into this wisdom all the fairy-tales and folklore he had heard in his childhood – for he regarded Ireland as a mystical land. In addition to Madame Blavatsky's doctrines, Yeats also subscribed to those of Jacob Boehme and Emanuel Swedenborg, and their concepts of cyclical history. Above all he was taken with the inherent secrecy of the movement and its idea that reality could not be 'facilely explained' as the perceptions of five senses; he felt sure that scientific rationalism had ignored or 'superficially dismissed' many important matters.

Some months before he left the theosophists he had joined the Hermetic Students of the Golden Dawn, a smaller organization with essentially similar beliefs, though they paid more attention to the European tradition of Kabbalistic magic than to the wisdom of the East. The aim of many members of the Golden Dawn was to show their power over the material universe.

France was especially susceptible to cults, where one sect gave degrees in Kabbalah. The Golden Dawn was run by a triumvirate of people, one of whom was married to the sister of Henri Bergson. Despite several factional disputes, Yeats joined the order in 1890 because the leaders' magical feats impressed him, some of which he was able to execute for himself. On one occasion, when he placed a death symbol on a fellow member's forehead, that individual, without knowing what the symbol was, immediately reported seeing an image of a hearse. Yeats later said that this kind of influence stayed with him until he was at least forty.

Some of his friends feared that he was veering 'far from life'.

In his first collected poems he stressed his intense concern with – and belief in – the occult, saying in a letter to Florence Farr (actress, mistress of George Bernard Shaw and a fellow member of the Golden Dawn) in 1901, 'All that we do with an intensity has an origin in the hidden world.'[5] He loved the rituals of the Golden Dawn and its central myth, the mystical death and resurrection of the adept. It was, as Ellmann says, a strange mixture of paganism and Christianity, and Yeats, dissatisfied with himself, as he arguably was throughout his life, was eager to be born anew.

The Castle of the Heroes

Alongside these activities went Yeats's involvement in nationalism. He was a romantic, largely ignorant – as many romantics were – of economics, history, politics and sociology; but he yearned for a heroic life, regarded Ireland as a 'mystical land', and saw his opportunity to help create an Irish literature that would define both what the country was and what it wanted to be, while serving as the best kind of propaganda. But it proved more difficult than he thought, because Irish nationalism was bred of seven hundred years of hatred of the occupying authority, and such well engrained attitudes were, as Ellmann nicely puts it, 'difficult to bridle'.

Yeats was in particular concerned that 'delicate qualities of mind' might be destroyed in a mob movement. There were many battles to be fought, but he gradually came to see that his own role was to set standards, to keep the movement intellectually respectable, while all the time exalting patriotism and heroism. He even argued at times that there were 'truths of passion that were intellectual falsehoods'.

His idea of the Ireland of the future was to recreate the Ireland of the past. 'Ireland . . . will be a country where not only will the wealth be well distributed but where there will be an imaginative culture and power to understand imaginative and spiritual things distributed among the people. We wish to preserve an ancient ideal of life. Wherever its customs prevail, there you will find the folk song, the folk tale, the proverb and the charming manners that come from ancient culture . . . In Ireland alone among the nations that I know [Britain, America, France] you will find, away on the Western seaboard, under broken roofs, a race of gentlemen who keep alive the ideals of a great time when men sang the heroic life with drawn swords in their hands . . . We must so live that we will make that old noble kind of life powerful among our people.'

What Yeats did was to mould both occultism and nationalism into his art. His father thought his interest in the occult was absurd and his patriotism a waste of energies that would have been better spent on his poetry; and certainly, as Ellmann observes, most of what Yeats wrote at that time was 'ostentatiously Irish and occult'. He even made speeches declaring his belief in fairies, though when pressed drew back and described them as 'dramatizations of our moods'. He considered combining Druidism with Christianity, as the Golden Dawn had comprised Rosicrucianism and Christianity, convinced that 'all lovely and loving places were crowded with invisible beings, and that it would be possible to communicate with them'.[6]

'The vague dream of an Irish cult slowly possessed Yeats's mind', and he thought of new forms of worship. It was against this background that he found an island with an unoccupied castle in Lough Key in the west of Ireland, and had the idea to turn it into the headquarters of a new cult 'through which the truths of the spirit might be disseminated to the materialistic nations. The doctrines would be the same as those of Theosophy and the Golden Dawn but associated specifically with Ireland. They would "unite the radical truths of Christianity to those of a more ancient world". To the "Castle of the Heroes" would come the finest men and women of Ireland for spiritual inspiration and teaching, and they would return, fortified by the supernatural powers which the Irish mystical order had concentrated, to act, in the words of Florence Farr, as living links "between the supernal and terrestrial natures".[7]

Yeats spent a great deal of time researching and developing a special rite for this new order, eventually deciding that the candidates must pass through the 'initiations of the cauldron, the stone, the sword and the spear', symbolizing the four elements and their spiritual equivalents.[8] Underneath it all, he was arguing that Irish life must have a basis in faith such as existing churches could not provide.

It was not dissimilar to his plan for a mystical theatre. The story of the founding of the Abbey is well known: a group of playwrights and actors wanted to establish a national theatre for the small nation that was Ireland, and they were phenomenally successful, in that the plays they produced have appeared all over the world. Yeats's goal was to show that Ireland was a holy land and one full of holy symbols, 'not in the orthodox clergyman's sense but in the poet's sense, which was also the mystic's sense; here alone in a degenerate Europe would spiritual realities be understood'.[9] Many of his early plays, *Countess Cathleen: A Miracle Play* (1899), *The Hour-Glass: A Morality* and *Where There Is Nothing* (both 1902), followed these ideas of fusing the occult and national interests.

He began to change again in the early years of the twentieth century, when his letters to friends begin to reflect his poetry and plays, when the language becomes less elaborate, more 'homely', more the idiom of common speech. 'All art is in the last analysis an endeavour to condense as out of the flying vapour of the world an image of human perfection, and for its own and not for art's sake.'[10] Here he had recourse to his famous notion of the mask: that the face we present to the world is designed to conceal as much as to reveal. He still maintained his obsession with spiritual struggle, that this was the way, eventually, to discover the meaning of life; and he was still conscious of the divisions within himself, as within people generally, getting in the way of any sense of unity – a sense that he badly wanted to achieve, that he thought was the very point of life.

In 1909, and especially from 1911, he began to take a serious interest in spiritualism, attending seances in an attempt, as he put it, to reunite the 'mind & soul & body'. Ellmann accepts that Yeats was more credulous than most, his investigations leading him to research alleged miracles; whether 'automatic [or 'free'] writers' could transcend the boundaries of their own minds and knowledge; the nature of spirits and of the afterlife.[11] (And he was not above 'less formal goals' such as the answer to the question, 'Am I to marry Maud Gonne?') There are countless examples of Yeats's collaboration, or attempted collaboration, with automatic writers, but despite this, Ellmann says, he did not see himself as 'particularly superstitious'. Rather, 'Unable to give full consent to the doctrines of psychical research, Yeats more and more inclined to the use of myth and metaphor which somersaulted over the question of literal belief.'[12]

'We sing amid our uncertainty,' Yeats had written in *Per Amica Silentia Lunae*, but Ellmann indicts him for at times, in his poetry, *pretending* to belief, for using artifice to evade direct questions, suggesting that Yeats was locked in 'an anxious struggle to escape from skepticism to direct belief'.[13] Yeats was, in other words, caught – as many were caught: he hated materialism but couldn't totally convince himself that there was another realm.

This attitude was reinforced by the behaviour and understanding of his father, who corresponded with the poet on many aesthetic issues, and at the same time made it clear, through his use of *psychological* terms, where he thought the future lay. J.B. Yeats was in some ways the antithesis of his son and, moreover, he seemed to be making a better fist of it – he was certainly more at peace with himself. Yeats wrote to his father at this time (1914–15) that he was trying to arrange his thought 'into a religious system', and in his diary noted that 'in the new Ireland a counter-religion would carry more weight than mere anti-clericalism'. At this time, too, he discovered (through Ezra Pound, who was the literary executor of Ernest Fenollosa, a scholar who had spent many years in Japan studying the Noh drama) that Japanese plays were full of spirits and masks and that their core drama was usually about the difference between mortality and the spirit.

Yeats thus threw himself into the development of a new form of drama, adapting Japanese ideas to the European context. The first play in this new form was *At the Hawk's Well*, terse, vivid, about the search for wisdom (the water in the well confers wisdom but, when the hero finally reaches it, the well has dried up). The play seemed to embody Yeats's deepest fears for himself.

Exalted Yeatsism

By this time he had met Georgie Hyde-Lees, a friend of Ezra Pound. She was interested in psychical research and in the Rudolf Steiner theosophists, and Yeats sponsored her for membership of the Golden Dawn. Then, after a short engagement, they were married in October 1917. And it was Georgie who amazed her husband by her abilities with 'automatic writing'. He gave up his obsession with seances, and he even gave up poetry for a time, until a message came from the automatic writing (a little too practical, perhaps): 'We have come to give you metaphors for poetry.'[14]

Mrs Yeats was blessed with a strong constitution and would work for hours to satisfy her husband's demands, all her effort contributing to Yeats's strange book, *A Vision*, in which he classified human personality into twenty-eight types, or phases, each phase being linked to one of twenty-eight phases of the moon, and each comprising one of the spokes of a Great Wheel. According to this system, any human 'soul' (he didn't really like that word, but found no alternative) passes through all twenty-eight phases. Later he paid more attention to the Four Faculties, which the 'soul' contains in varying proportions. These faculties were Will, Mask, Creative Mind and Body of Fate, the first two and the last two seen as pairs of contraries. Yeats had all sorts of geometric ideas about the shape of history and of character, and these, together with the twenty-eight phases and the four faculties – much of this based on research carried out through his wife's automatic writing – comprised what Ellmann calls 'esoteric Yeatsism', the development of which, he says, exalted the poet as never before.[15]

Yeats realized that his system brought with it problems. '[H]e saw clearly that by removing God from the universe and turning all life into cycles, he had deprived his system of any teleological basis for conduct except that, if one lived a harmonious life, one might expect more harmonious future lives . . . He could not define good and evil except in terms of complete or incomplete self-expression.' 'During the period said to commence in 1927 [as he had established in *A Vision*] . . . must arise a form of philosophy, which . . . will be concrete in expression, establish itself by immediate experience, seek no general agreement, make little of God or any exterior unity, and it will call that good which a man can contemplate himself as doing always [echoes of Nietzsche's 'external recurrence'] . . . Men will no longer separate the idea of God from that of human genius, human productivity in all its forms.'[16]

Later, Yeats emerged into what Ellmann calls a 'cantankerous acceptance of life' as a framework by which to live. This was the moment when in his poetry he acknowledged that life varied from 'The unfinished man and his pain' to 'The finished man among his enemies'.

He had not given up his nationalism. He now wanted to fuse life, work and country 'into one indissoluble whole'.[17] Later still, he discovered various Indian gurus (a final aspect of his occult search) but in his poem of this time, 'Byzantium', he extols the human imagination in a mighty imaginative work that doesn't evade the difficulties:

> A starlit or a moonlit dome disdains
> All that man is,
> All mere complexities,
> The fury and the mire of human veins.

Yeats's significance, for us, is well put by Ellmann: 'The war on God is the ultimate heroism, and like all heroism in Yeats ends in defeat.' But, in addition, in Yeats's case there was also the war with his father, as a result of which 'He went into manhood without religion, ethics or politics, but held together by a feeling of revolt against his father and his times'. That revolt meant that it was some time before he could take on board his father's almost throw-away remark that 'the poet's form of knowledge was different from that of a priest or scientist'.[18]

Yeats's finest achievement might be said to be in his nationalism. Passionate nationalism was good, he felt, maybe even necessary, but not if it degenerated into mere impotent Anglophobia. Yeats lived, as Dean Inge said in another context, 'between scepticism and superstition'. He never gave up hope of bringing together myth and fact into a new religion, or as he called it, 'a sacred drama'; but it is no more than the truth to say that, in old age, 'the answers came no more easily to him than when young'. The mood of his last poem, 'The Black Tower', is one of heroic despair.[19] And as he wrote in a letter two years before his death, 'There was no dominant opinion I could accept.'[20]

And so this is Yeats's significance for us. He hated the nineteenth-century material world, the world of particle physics, evolution and the deconstruction of the Bible; but try as he might, he could find no other realm, nowhere else to go; the supernatural world refused steadfastly to reveal itself to him, whatever occult practice he turned to. And W.H. Auden was harsh on him. 'How on earth, we may wonder, could a man of Yeats's gifts take such nonsense seriously?' T.S. Eliot was hardly kinder when he complained that Yeats's supernatural world was 'the wrong supernatural world ... It was not a world of spiritual significance ... but a highly sophisticated lower mythology summoned, like a physician, to supply a fading pulse of poetry with some transient stimulant so that the dying patient may utter his last words.'

Because his father had steered him towards psychology, he looked elsewhere for insight. He tried magnificently, heroically, to create another world with his poetry, and at times, as with his nationalist poems, he succeeded gloriously. But in Yeats's main aim – to explore, describe and communicate that other, non-materialistic realm – he failed, and his attempts to do so read, as Auden said, absurdly to us. *A Vision* spends a significant proportion of its pages 'preparing readers to encounter its strange explanation of the universe through geometric symbolism'.[21]

Unlike, say, Wallace Stevens, Yeats's own imagination was never enough; the real action was always going on somewhere else, somewhere he never found. He never escaped 'the fury and the mire of [mere] human veins'.

America's Shadow Culture

While none of the above is unfair to Yeats, he was far from being the only individual to adopt these beliefs that seemed so absurd to Auden. In fact, and so far as the United States is concerned, the Harvard historian of psychiatry Eugene Taylor has identified an entire culture, what he terms a 'shadow culture', of over two hundred years of alternative religions and 'pop-psych' movements. Standing outside mainstream psychiatry and the mainstream Churches, these movements comprised a variety of attempts to live in the post-Christian world, both before and after Nietzsche. Taylor calls it both a 'visionary' tradition and a 'crank literature', a 'folk psychology' and a 'psychospiritual tradition', focusing as it does on an 'experiential interpretation of higher consciousness'.[22] His survey is a clear account of an otherwise woolly world.

This shadow culture, Taylor said, comprised a vast unorganized array of discrete individuals 'who live and think differently from the mainstream but who participate in its daily activities'.[23] He traced this tradition back to the First Great Awakening in America in the first half of the eighteenth century, when an evangelical wave swept through the northeast and 250 new, emotionalist Churches were established outside the Calvinist faith. Such groups as that of Conrad Beissel and the Ephrata Mystics, the Shakers and other visionary communities, the Swedenborgians, with their concept of 'correspondence', that God speaks to man through Nature; and the Transcendentalists, who also believed that understanding could come through the contemplation of Nature – all of these shared the view that intuition was a higher faculty than reason.

The fashions and fads for homeopathy, phrenology, mesmerism, hydrotherapy, shamanism and Orientalism all came and went in the nineteenth century, some making bigger waves than others, but all leaving their mark. Figures like Emerson, Thoreau and Margaret Fuller were all regarded as inspirational leaders with spiritual qualities, together with John Muir, a vagabond from Scotland who arrived in the Unites States in 1849 and who, among his other achievements, deserves credit for saving the Grand Canyon in Nevada and the Petrified Forest in Arizona as Natural Parks.

Despite the rise and fall of many of these fads, Taylor argues, the last three decades of the nineteenth century 'produced full-fledged organizations devoted to spiritual therapeutics that were national, even international, in scope'.[24] One of the reasons for this, he says, was that the visionary tradition had been gradually suppressed within American high culture 'because of the rising tide of positivistic science'.

Utopian socialism was another part of the visionary tradition, Taylor says, and here he includes the Mormons, the Seventh-Day Adventists, charismatic religions aiming to change the experience of intimacy, and alternative forms of consciousness. Spiritualism, theosophy, New Thought and Christian Science drew their strengths from an interest in life after death, producing a parallel interest in 'automatic speech', table tipping, slate writing and 'rapping and knocking', as he put it. Books with titles such as *The Divine Law of Cure, Ideal Suggestion through Mental Photography* and *Esoteric Christianity and Mental Therapeutics* proliferated. In 1881 the Massachusetts Metaphysical College was formed by Mary Baker Eddy, the founder of Christian Science, which taught pathology, 'therapeutics', moral science and metaphysics. The American Society for Psychical Research was founded in 1885. Despite many experiments, Taylor reports drily, 'the psychical researchers were unable to discover any evidence for the reality of life after death'. But they did 'establish the reality of the unconscious'.

The impressive-sounding Boston School of Psychopathology comprised an informal knot of investigators including William James, the neurologist James Jackson Putnam, Richard Clarke Cabot and the neuropsychologist Morton Prince. Many of its members 'had direct ties either by birth or upbringing with the intuitive psychology of character formation bequeathed to them by Emerson and the Concord transcendentalists'. The Boston School was much more scientific than any of its predecessors, being much influenced by Darwin. Even so, James maintained, it was psychic phenomena that 'were destined to change the very shape of science in the future'.

There was, Taylor goes on, a dramatic expansion of psychotherapy in America after 1900, as people began to acknowledge that 'spirituality played a key role in a person's mental health'. Mystic states were key here, he said, but they were so different from 'the normal everyday waking state' that 'we don't know how to deal with them'. The Emmanuel movement was launched in 1906 at Emmanuel Church in Worcester, Massachusetts, 'to fuse modern scientific psychotherapy with the Christian teachings of moral character development'.[25] These meetings, which drew upwards of five hundred people twice a week, came to be called 'moral clinics'.

In addition, from 1893 when the World's Parliament of Religions met in America as part of the Columbian Exposition, marking the four-hundredth anniversary of the discovery of the New World, a number of Indian swamis and Japanese Zen spiritual elders, plus the White Russian mystic G.I. Gurdjieff, toured the United States to great acclaim, speaking at universities. These events resulted in the establishment, among other things, of Vedanta societies.

Taylor, alumnus of the fiercely positivist Harvard, nonetheless gave a sympathetic account of the visionary tradition, arguing that it was more open-minded than the more mainstream traditions, that it discovered the unconscious independently of, and maybe before, Freud; and that, at root, it conceded that mysticism is a genuine aspect of experience, not a pathology, and one that we need to take seriously and try to understand if we are ever to have a full life. The main thrust of his study, from our point of view, confirms that though Yeats embraced 'the wrong supernatural world', he was by no means alone in this. For twenty or thirty years either side of 1900, vast numbers on both sides of the Atlantic thought as Yeats did.

An Epidemic of the Occult

In Europe, many spiritualists were freethinkers who rejected mainstream religious practice and belief but were left cold by the certainties of positivism, the search for the laws of behaviour. 'One impulse was to turn to spiritualism as a means of reconciling science, deism and socialism. This utopian project took many forms, from an exploration of autokinesis [moving objects by thought] to automatic writing to séances.'

Quite a number of eminent writers, public figures, scholars and even scientists treated these matters as serious endeavours – Victor Hugo, Tennyson, Alfred Russel Wallace, Faraday. The Roman Catholic Church repeatedly anathematized the movement; spiritualist writings were placed on the Index and specifically denounced by the Holy See (in 1898 and 1917, for example). Jay Winter explains the rest of the intellectual background: 'In the early twentieth century those who entertained at least a suspension of disbelief about spiritualism did so for many different reasons. Some tried to translate traditional theology or the poetry of ancient metaphors about human survival into the language of experimental science. They point to magnetism, electricity, and radio waves as constituting unseen yet real phenomena of distant communication. Thought waves or other forms of human feeling or expression conceivably did the same.'[26]

This spiritualist approach, Winter says, was as remote as could be 'from the mental environment of fundamentalist Christianity. Observation, not Scripture, was the source of wisdom.' The pages of many journals – in France, Britain and America – were open to the possibility that spiritualist phenomena were worthy of investigation. Among those who shared these views were Sir Oliver Lodge, professor of physics at Liverpool University, later principal of Birmingham University and later still president of the Society for Psychical Research; the physicist Sir William Barrett; William McDougall, the Oxford and Harvard psychologist; Gilbert Murray, the Oxford classicist; William James; and Lord Rayleigh, Cavendish Professor of Physics at Cambridge and Nobel Prize winner in 1914. In Italy the criminologist Cesare Lombroso took part in seances, in Germany the Kaiser dabbled in spiritualism, while Thomas Mann provided an (admittedly ironic) account of seances in *The Magic Mountain* (1924). In Russia, the professors of zoology and chemistry at the University of St Petersburg joined the theosophical movement, and some published papers on spiritualism.[27]

Concerning the Spiritual in Art

Artists were not immune to these developments. Many, for instance, were drawn to theosophy: Mondrian joined the society in 1909, the composers Scriabin, Stravinsky and Schoenberg were all familiar with the work of Madame Blavatsky; and though Paul Klee adamantly denied he was a theosophist, he wrote 'My hand is wholly the instrument of some remote power. It is not my intellect that runs the show, but something different, something higher, more distant – somewhere else. I must have great friends there, bright ones but sombre ones too.'

Klee's interest in theosophy may have stemmed from his association with Wassily Kandinsky. Kandinsky adhered all his life to the Russian Orthodox beliefs he was born into, but he repeatedly meditated on theosophical themes, in particular the 'universal catastrophe' he believed was on the way, a belief he shared with his fellow Russian, the ballet impresario Sergei Diaghilev.[28]

Kandinsky's concern with theosophy is shown most in two written works, the *Blaue Reiter Almanac* of 1912 and *Concerning the Spiritual in Art*, written in 1909 and published two years later. The aim of the former, produced with his fellow artist the Bavarian Franz Marc, was to show what was happening in art all over Europe at any one time. Theosophy's shadow runs through many of the contributions. August Macke, the Expressionist painter from Westphalia, close to Marc and Klee, produced an essay on 'Masks' that Yeats would have found congenial. 'Form is a mystery to us,' Macke wrote, 'for it is the expression of mysterious powers. Only through it do we sense the secret powers, the "invisible God".' Franz Marc took up a similar theme in an essay on Cézanne and El Greco, which described them as masters of a 'mystical inner construction'. There was, he said, a 'secret connection of all new artistic production', awareness of which lay behind the ideas of the group known as Der Blaue Reiter. 'Its aim was to speak to the yet unknowing world of these spiritual developments.' The Russian artist David Burliuk wrote about his fellow countryman, the poet Andrei Bely, 'a follower of Rudolf Steiner's theosophy'.

Kandinsky was a fervent advocate for the spiritual in art. His essay in the *Almanac* explored the 'new value that lives within' man. This search, he said, leads to elevation, to a revelation that can be 'heard': 'The world sounds. It is a cosmos of spiritually effective beings. Even dead matter is living spirit.' Materialism, he insisted, has no capacity to hear, and must be replaced: 'The *final* goal (knowledge) is reached through delicate vibrations of the human soul.' These views, as Jay Winter emphasizes, are 'entirely consistent' with aspects of the theosophical systems of Steiner and Blavatsky.

In *Concerning the Spiritual in Art* Kandinsky said that the artist is at the pinnacle of a triangle, often alone, often scorned as a charlatan or a madman. Yet painting and art, he added, '[are] not vague production, transitory and isolated, but a power which must be directed to the improvement and refinement of the human soul – to, in fact, the raising of the spiritual triangle'. This too is consistent with theosophical elements, which see the clairvoyant, like the artist, as one who could discern the 'higher matter in which thoughts and feelings form patterns without any resemblance to the objects of the physical plane'.[29]

There is a good deal here that, to an outsider, is woolly, incoherent, even absurd. But none of these artists followed Yeats all the way to a belief in fairies, and Kandinsky was the man who invented – or discovered – abstraction in Western art. In this he was mixing the spiritual with the unconscious, or thought he was. Arguably, this was a more fruitful direction than the one Yeats took.

In a sense, Kandinsky discovered abstraction by accident, if we believe his story that he came home one day and saw a painting of 'real loveliness' in his studio, yet which had no identifiable shapes – until he realized that it was one of his own pictures lying on its side on an easel. However it happened, Kandinsky's abstractions conformed to the theosophical belief that the physical world – the world of objects, things – was losing its importance; indeed, it was preventing us from seeing the great spiritual world behind the world of objects and thus holding us back. It was central to theosophy that when the spirit was revealed there would be an end to history – the contingent pattern to human events – and a new order would be established or revealed.

Kandinsky's abstractions would help bring about this new state of affairs, by showing that beauty had no need of earthly forms, the recognizable shapes of things; that there was a reality underneath and elsewhere. Recent scholarship has shown that his painting *Little Pleasures* (1913), prefiguring Sartre's *Les petites heureuses*, is a theosophical reinterpretation of the Apocalypse of St John, in which the things of this world, the material reality whose small value is alluded to in the painting's title, are seen as passing away – disintegrating into abstractions before the new order arrives. Kandinsky cherished some elaborate ideas about the symbolism of colours and their synaesthetic qualities ('seeing' sounds and 'hearing' colours), all part of his conviction that there was a hidden reality behind the appearance of things that it was his responsibility to convey. For him, abstraction was a new way of understanding the world, a way of approaching the spirit: spiritual existence – ecstasy – was abstract, without shape as commonly understood.

The Romanian sculptor Constanin Brancusi, too, was a theosophist but he was also more of a phenomenologist than Kandinsky, exploring the structure and growth of real forms. To a degree he went in the opposite direction to the Russian. In works like *The Beginning of the World* (1924), which is a marble sculpture in the shape of an egg, Brancusi is attempting to give us a completely self-contained work, where the skin is part of the structure's expressive qualities but also inseparable from the rest. The theosophists thought that 'spirit' inhabited all matter, and so such a sculpture could be seen as liberating the spirit in marble. But we need not go that far. The simplicity and cleverness of Brancusi's perfect forms tell us in this case, for instance, that marble can be as full of meaning as anything it might be made to represent, that self-containment is the aim of life; that, in order to present a 'perfect skin' to the world, we need to live – to *be* – entirely within our nature, accepting its qualities *and* limitations; and that there is as much meaning in detail as there is in great abstractions. Brancusi emphasized this by making identical forms in different materials – *Bird in Space* (1925), for instance, exists in black marble, in white marble and in shiny metal. That the experience of each simple form is radically different shows how *detail* can be essence, can govern meaning. Meaning can be small as well as large.

The third of the important theosophical artists was Piet Mondrian, who was convinced that the purpose of art was 'spiritual clarification'. He was likewise convinced that matter was the enemy of spiritual enlightenment and that all forms of material existence were coming to an end – one of Helen Blavatsky's core ideas. 'Nothing but abstraction could do justice to the imminent dawn of the spirit.'[30]

Mondrian converted to theosophy in 1909, during the Cubist vogue and at the time when Kandinsky was edging towards abstraction. Classical, original cubism had been grounded in the city, in the metropolitan experience, but in his early grid paintings Mondrian explored nature – trees and oceans and skies – in which the main subject is *energy*, then a major concern of science (particles were forms of energy, and energy was locked up in matter as Einstein's $E=mc^2$ had shown); to theosophists, energy was a form of spirit, the ultimate basis of reality.

This is what Mondrian's grid paintings show: the energy of trees and the energy surrounding them, with the haphazard pattern of the branches incorporated into the sky that forms the background. The same is true of *Pier and Ocean* (1915) a decrepit pier in Scheveningen, on Holland's North Sea coast, is incorporated into the surrounding sea with only minimal transition. Thus, piers and oceans are different configurations of identical forces. Comparable with these two is Mondrian's best-known work, *Broadway Boogie-Woogie*, produced in 1942–3 after the Second World War had prompted his move to New York. His grid style suited the pattern of Manhattan's streets, but it is the movement – the energy – that is the most important element of this iconic painting.

Mondrian's images are as jerky, nervy and restless as Brancusi's are calm. In the 1920s as theosophy faded, the 'process philosophy' of Alfred North Whitehead took its place. By this account, the universe was and is a huge field of energy which takes different forms in a series of events. *Events* are the building blocks of nature – this is how the world is to be understood, as a series of manifestations, nodes of energy taking different forms. This had many ramifications, one of which was that actions could produce change in the world – events – just as much as thoughts could. This would give rise, in time, to the philosophy of existentialism. Mondrian was not an existentialist, not a classic one anyway, but his exploration of energy, restlessness beneath the surface, kept alive the essentially Platonic idea that there is a different realm, a superior realm, a more real realm, in existence somewhere.

PART TWO

One Abyss after Another

9

Redemption by War

In our own day the Great War stands alongside the Holocaust, Stalin's purges, Hiroshima and Nagasaki and the Killing Fields of East Asia as one of the defining horrors of the twentieth century. Let us remind ourselves of just one example of that conflict. The Battle of the Somme got under way at 7.30 a.m. on 1 July 1916; out of the 110,000 British troops who attacked that Saturday morning along the thirteen-mile Front, no fewer than 60,000 were killed or wounded on the first day – *still* a record. 'Over 20,000 lay dead between the lines, and it was days before the wounded in No Man's Land stopped crying out.'[1]

The Phenomenon of 1914

But that was 1916. The summer and autumn of 1914 were very different. Knowing what we know now, it is hard to credit the way people greeted war. There are two elements that concern us. One is illustrated by the fact that a London bookseller denounced the war as 'the Euro-Nietzschean war'. He was referring to the (for him) surprising fact that the outbreak of war saw a marked rise in the sale of works by Nietzsche. This was partly because many of Germany's enemies thought that the German philosopher was the chief villain, the man most to blame for the war in the first place, and the individual responsible, as time wore on, for its brutalities.

In his book *Nietzsche and the Ideals of Germany* H.L. Stewart, a Canadian professor of philosophy, describes the Great War as a battle between 'an unscrupulous Nietzschean immoralism' and the 'cherished principles of Christian restraint'. Thomas Hardy was similarly incensed, complaining to several British newspapers: 'I should think there is no instance since history began of a country being so demoralized by a single writer.' Germany was seen as a nation of would-be supermen who, in Romain Rolland's words, had become a 'scourge of God'.[2] To many it seemed as if the abyss had been plumbed, that the death of God, so loudly advertised by Nietzsche, had finally brought about the apocalypse many had predicted.

In Germany, the theologian and historian Theodor Kappstein admitted that Nietzsche *was* the philosopher of the world war because he had educated a whole generation towards 'a life-endangering honesty, towards a contempt for death ... to a sacrifice on the altar of the whole, towards heroism and quiet, joyful greatness'.[3] Even Max Scheler, a better-known philosopher (and later a favourite of Pope John Paul II), in *The Genius of War and the German War* (1915) praised the 'ennobling' aspects of conflict. He welcomed the war as a return to 'the organic roots of human existence ... We were no longer what we had been – alone! The sundered living contact between the series individual-people-nation-world-God was restored in an instant.'[4] The communal 'we', Scheler said, 'is in our consciousness before the individualized self', the latter being 'an artificial product of cultural tradition and a historic process'.[5]

Though the claims – both for and against Nietzsche's influence – may have been overblown, they were not without foundation. In Germany, together with Goethe's *Faust* and the New Testament, *Thus Spake Zarathustra* was the most popular work that literate soldiers took into battle, 'for inspiration and consolation'. More than that, according to Steven Aschheim, 150,000 copies of a specially durable wartime edition were distributed to the troops. Even one or two literate non-German soldiers took the book with them, notably Robert Graves and Gabriele d'Annunzio. Nor should we forget that the assassin of Archduke Franz Ferdinand, Gavrilo Princip, whose action precipitated the crisis of 1914, was fond of reciting Nietzsche's poem,

Ecce Homo: 'Insatiable as a flame, I burn and consume myself.'[6]

Whatever we make of all that, the second point still takes some getting used to. This is the fact that in 1914 so many people *welcomed* the war. This too had certain Nietzschean overtones, in that war was seen as the ultimate test of one's heroic qualities, a test of will, and an unrivalled opportunity for ecstatic experience. But it was more than that – far more. For many, the war was seen as *redemptive*.

But redemptive from what? one might ask. In fact, there was no shortage of candidates. Before 1914, the very appeal of Nietzsche lay in his widespread critique of the decadence people saw everywhere about them. Stefan George, as we have already seen, argued in *Der Stern des Bundes* that a war would 'purify' a spiritually moribund society, while the German dramaturge Erwin Piscator agreed, claiming that the generation that went to war was 'spiritually bankrupt'. Stefan Zweig saw the conflict as some kind of spiritual safety-valve, referring to Freud's argument that the release of 'the instinctual' could not be contained by reason alone. Typically, the Expressionists looked forward to the death of bourgeois society, 'from whose ashes a nobler world would arise'.[7]

In John Buchan's 1910 novel *Prester John* there is talk of wiping out the civilization of the West, which has lasted for more than a thousand years. One of the characters says: 'It is because I have sucked civilization dry that I know the bitterness of the fruit. I want a simpler and a better world.' In 1913 Gabriele d'Annunzio had told Maurice Barrès, the French novelist and anti-Dreyfusard, that 'a great national war is France's last chance of salvation' from a 'democratic degeneration, a plebeian inundation of her high culture'.[8] Barrès's countryman Henri Bergson thought that the war 'would bring about the moral regeneration of Europe', and accused the Germans of being 'mechanical men without soul'.[9] The French poet Charles Péguy, too, believed in 1913 that a war would be of value 'because it brings regeneration'. The Futurists in their manifesto released as early as 1909 had argued that war would be 'the only hygiene of the world'; and elsewhere: 'There is no beauty except in strife.'[10] And a yearning for some great redemptive cause that would satisfy desire is to be found in the pre-war poetry of Rupert Brooke:

To turn, as swimmers into clearness leaping,
Glad from a world grown old and cold and weary,
Leave the sick hearts that honour could not move,
And half-men, and their dirty songs and dreary,
And all the little emptiness of love.[11]

Alban Berg, Alexander Scriabin and Igor Stravinsky all subscribed to the view that war would 'shake the souls of people' and 'prepare them for spiritual things'. In Germany in particular it was felt that a commercial world 'had been swept aside for heroes'.[12] G.K. Chesterton was more prosaic but no less damning of the status quo, declaring that *both* religious and political ideals were in decay: 'Man's two great inspirations [have] failed him altogether.'

This is another of those issues that was much bigger, more divisive, then than now. Roland Stromberg in his *Redemption by War: The Intellectuals and 1914* notes that 'self-discovery through violence' was part of the intellectual furniture of those times, and that when war exploded in August 1914 it seemed to many 'a kind of triumph of spirit over matter'. Even such figures as Arnold Bennett, Sigmund Freud, Henry James and Marcel Proust were on record as saying they found life interesting again after the boredom before. 'War as restoration of community and as escape from a trashy and trivial way of life is probably more understandable today than war as salvation,' says Stromberg. 'Yet the commonest images aroused by the shock of August were the cleansing fire or flood, or "the blacksmith that will pound the world into a new shape",' as Ernst Jünger put it. 'Destruction and the right to realize oneself went together.' Or as Isaac Rosenberg, the British poet who would be killed in the war, wrote: the 'ancient crimson curse' would 'Give back the universe/ Its pristine bloom'.[13] Hans Rogger, the American historian of Russia, reported that many writers and intellectuals in Moscow and St Petersburg welcomed the war 'for having freed Russia of narrowness and pettiness and for opening new perspectives on greatness. Some viewed war as a spiritual awakening.'[14] Hugo von Hofmannsthal reported that in Austria 'the whole people is transformed, poured into a new mould'.

Sentiments like this reflected the general view, among intellectuals certainly, that the spirit was in an unhealthy state before the war; there was an obsession with materialism and a neglect of 'things of the mind'. Even during the war, when the scale of the carnage was already becoming apparent, these sentiments continued, up to a point. The great Danish composer, conductor and violinist Carl Nielsen, in his *Inextinguishable Symphony*, premiered in 1916 and featuring a 'battle' between two sets of tympani, paid tribute to the life force, constantly renewing itself even in death, 'and charg[ing] on again to a prodigal abundance'.[15]

Community: the Pervasive Theme of 1914

In tandem with all this went a rise in nationalism and patriotism, twin feelings that surprised many (especially socialists) who, before the war, had prided themselves on their cosmopolitanism and internationalism. Nationalism, says Roland Stromberg, was in some ways a substitute religion, quoting the potter and art historian Quentin Bell: 'Cambridge, like the great majority of the nation, had been converted to the religion of nationalism; it was a powerful, a terrible, at times a very beautiful magic.'[16] Nationalism, says Stromberg, 'coincided with the search for membership in a community, the pervasive theme of 1914'. 'One beautiful result of the war,' wrote Edmund Gosse, 'is the union of hearts.'[17] 'I don't want to die for my king and country,' Herbert Read, poet and art critic, wrote while he was in the trenches. 'If I do die, it's for the salvation of my own soul.' Elsewhere he wrote: 'During the war I used to feel that this comradeship which had developed among us would lead to some new social order when peace came. It was a human relationship and a reality that had not existed in time of peace. It overcame (or ignored) all distinctions of class, rank and education. We did not call it love; we did not acknowledge its existence; it was sacramental and therefore sacred.' As Stromberg confirms, sacrament hovers in the background of virtually every war novel, in this most literate of wars.[18]

Many intellectuals now felt that many non-intellectuals at last had a welcome chance to break out of their 'clipped and limited lives', which would help restore a sense of community. But the George circle in Germany had a different perspective: 'Tens of thousands must perish in the holy war,' George commented. Only in this way, said Gundolf, could the soul's sickness be cured, and the spiritual evolution of the German nation be enabled. The German historian Karl Lamprecht enthused about 'this marvellous upsurge of our national soul ... happy are those who have lived at a time like this'. Émile Durkheim thought the war would achieve his long-sought-after goal of 'reviving the sense of community'. The German theologian Ernst Troeltsch was convinced the war increased the feeling of *Deutschtum* – Germanness – among his fellow countrymen, which was 'equivalent to belief in God's divine power'. 'It is the tremendous significance of August,' he added, 'that under the impact of danger [the war] pressed the whole people together in an inner unity, such as never before had existed.'

Another effect of the war was that everywhere 'the religion of social services' propelled the conscience-stricken rich into the ghettoes to grapple – or at least familiarize themselves – with poverty. 'The urge to break away from a life-killing egoism often led to affirming one's organic connection with the great collectivity.'[19]

An underlying ingredient in all this talk of redemptive communities was the fact that many of the European states were ethnically and linguistically diverse.[20] They might live under a common law and a common government, but they did not necessarily speak the same language or inherit the same customs. This was especially true of Russia and Austria-Hungary, but it also applied to a lesser extent in Great Britain, Belgium, Germany and France. The newly sacred union spawned by danger overcame, for a time at least, all differences, though Hannah Arendt later dismissed these new communities as illusory (as indeed they proved).[21]

There was also the so-called elitist school of Max Weber, Gaetano Mosca and Vilfredo Pareto, who were sceptical of what the achievements of the war would be. Though Weber shared with many others what he called 'an almost unbearable nostalgia for the lost wholeness' in modern society, he also held to the view that 'the people can never rule, the state will never wither away, power will not be exorcised from the world by any poetic incantation. The realization of

Christian ethics,' he concluded, 'is not possible in human society.'[22]

Weariness set in eventually, of course, and disenchantment soon enough. The painter Lowes Dickinson decried the lack of diversity in discussion during the war. 'To win the war or to hide safely among the winners became the only preoccupation. Abroad was heard only the sound of guns, at home only the ceaseless patter of a propaganda utterly indifferent to the truth.' Quentin Bell said of the Bloomsbury Group that 'none of them, so to speak, "believed in" the war, and they refused, resolutely, to be religious about it'. D.H. Lawrence was ambivalent. He thought that 'humanity needs pruning', that 'the great adventure of death' was a suitable subject for a novel, and he had a thirst for a 'genuine community'. But there was no community in war for him: 'The War was not strife; it was murder.'

Gustave Le Bon had argued, as more than one sociologist after him had done, that 'war is an antidote to anomie or decadence, a restorer of solidarity'. Perhaps this explains why intellectuals were so much in favour of it to begin with: for people usually separated from the rest of the community by virtue of their education and interests, war perhaps had the advantage of 'reuniting' them with others.

The situation in 1914, Stromberg continues, had a unique quality about it that had never quite existed before and would not do so again: 'It was a moment in the growth of consciousness'; the most significant motif was the 'raw reality' of the reappearance of the sense of community. For many, he insisted, the war's psychological origins were not malevolent: they involved, rather, 'a powerful thirst for identity, community, purpose – positive and, in themselves, worthy goals, perverted and misdirected but not poisoned at the springs'.[23]

The spirit of the year 1914 was 'an antidote to anomie, which had resulted from the sweep of powerful forces of the recent past – urban, capitalistic, and technological forces tearing up primeval bonds and forcing people into a crisis of social relationship'.[24] But the antidote brought with it too high a price and so we are still searching for a viable alternative.

Given the importance of the themes of redemption and of restoration of community, and given the horrific nightmare that trench warfare quickly turned into, it is perhaps no surprise that two elements came to the fore in the Great War that particularly concern us here. One was poetry and the other was socialism. Socialism as a surrogate religion is considered in the next chapter. The extent to which poetry and war went together was extraordinary and revealing.

Irony and Innocence

'At no other time in the twentieth century has verse formed the dominant literary form' that it did during the First World War (at least in the English language), and there are those such as Bernard Bergonzi, whose words these are, who argue that English poetry 'never got over the Great War'. To quote Francis Hope, the British poet-critic, 'In a not altogether rhetorical sense, all poetry since 1918 is war poetry.' Again, in retrospect it is not difficult to see why this should have been so. Many of the young men who went to the Front were well educated, which in those days included being familiar with English literature. Life at the Front, intense and uncertain as it was, lent itself to a shorter, sharper, more compact verse structure, and provided arresting and vivid images in abundance. And in the unhappy event of the author's death, the elegiac nature of a slim volume had an undeniable romantic appeal. Many boys who went straight from the cricket field to the Somme or Passchendaele made poor poets, and the bookshops were crammed with verse that, in other circumstances, would never have been published. But among these a few stood out who are now household names.

Moreover, as Nicholas Murray has pointed out in *The Red Sweet Wine of Youth: The Brave and Brief Lives of the War Poets*, those poets have never been more popular than they are today, a hundred years on. 'War poetry is currently studied in every school in Britain. It has become part of the mythology of nationhood, and an expression of both historical consciousness and political conscience. The way we read – and perhaps revere – war poetry says something about what we are and want to be, as a nation.'[25] Websites are now dedicated to the war poets, and as the former Poet Laureate Andrew Motion has said, their work now comprises 'a sacred national text'.

Not that many of them confronted our subject directly. Siegfried Sassoon and Wilfred Owen were, by their own admission, anticlerical. Sassoon described himself as 'a very incomplete and unpractising Christian . . . the Churches seemed to me to offer no solution to the demented doings on the Western front . . . As far as I can remember, no one at the Front ever talked to me about religion at all. And the padres never came near us – except to bury someone.'[26] His poem 'Christ and the Soldier' was about a roadside Calvary in France 'which, for most soldiers, was merely a reminder of the inability of religion to cope with the carnage and catastrophe'. In 'February Afternoon' (1916) Edward Thomas found scant consolation in religion: in the poem, God looks down 'stone-deaf and stone-blind'. Owen said he had escaped from evangelical religion by mid-1912: 'All Theological lore is growing distasteful to me.'[27] Edmund Blunden's poem 'Report on Experience', one of his best, contains the lines:

> . . . I have seen the righteous forsaken,
> His health, his honour and his quality taken.

and culminates with an ironic 'God bless us all'.[28]

Irony. In his classic book *The Great War and Modern Memory* Paul Fussell argues: 'there seems to be one dominating form of modern understanding; that it is essentially ironic; and that it originates largely in the application of mind and memory to the events of the Great War'.[29] He gives examples of what he means. One reason the Great War can be seen as more ironic than any other is that its beginning was more innocent. Britain had not known a major war for a century. No man in the prime of his life knew what war was like. As Ernest Hemingway was to note, abstract words like 'glory', 'honour', 'courage' were hollow and obscene alongside 'the concrete names of villages, the numbers of roads, the names of rivers, the numbers of regiments and the dates'. Fussell lists propagandistic euphemisms that tried to lessen the impact of what was happening: a friend is a *comrade*; a horse is a *steed*; danger is *peril*; warfare is *strife*; not to complain is to be *manly*; the blood of young men is 'The red/ Sweet wine of youth' (Rupert Brooke). Apparently, war was at first regarded by some as a game, almost – at the

Battle of Loos in 1915 the 1st Battalion of the 18th London Regiment kicked a football towards the enemy lines while making their attack.

In many of the stories told about the war, the ending – and the nearest these stories come to a meaning – is ironic. Fussell quotes an episode from Edmund Blunden's *Undertones of War* in which the author came across a young lance corporal making tea in the trenches. Blunden wished him a good tea and moved on. Moments later a shell burst on the trench and the lance corporal was reduced to 'gobbets of blackening flesh'. While Blunden was taking this in, 'the lance-corporal's brother came round the traverse'.

The range of psychic phenomena reported at the Front itself was vast, Jay Winter reports, though the emergence of pagan or pre-rational modes of thought under the appalling stress of combat should surprise no one. Many soldiers carried cards bearing lucky emblems on their person, a different card carried in different pockets. Others carried soil from their home village or dust from their local church or chapel. One chaplain from Aberdeen remarked: 'The British soldier has certainly got religion; I am not so sure, however, that he has got Christianity.'[30] The problem was that 'the experience of the trenches could not easily be explained in conventional theological (or indeed any other rational) terms'.

Spiritualism proliferated most among those without strong ties to established Churches. The Frenchman Charles Richet conducted a remarkable piece of research at the Front, publishing his results in the *Bulletin des armées de la République* in January 1917. There had been many respondents – ordinary soldiers, doctors, officers – and they reported most commonly accurate premonitions of death, not just among the combatants themselves but among members of their families back home.

In Britain, Hereward Carrington produced a study entitled *Psychical Phenomena and the War*, which explored cases of dead soldiers apparently sending messages of hope and consolation to their grieving loved ones; and in both France and Britain there were many accounts of dead soldiers attending ceremonies of remembrance. Others saw angels on the battlefield, phantom cavalrymen, 'luminous mists'. Winter makes the point that proper burial was by no means guaranteed, or indeed the norm, which must help to account for many of these reports. It was this universality of bereavement that fed what Winter calls the 'spiritualist temptation'. This was all surely understandable, but no more than were the revulsion, disillusion and cynicism that came out of the four years of carnage, from which some sort of 'meaning' had to be extracted.

Fussell quotes Philip Larkin's poem, 'MCMXIV', written in the early 1960s, under the title 'Never Such Innocence Again'; and this is Fussell's main point, that irony then entered the world *as meaning*, even as redemption. But irony offers only small meanings, paradoxical meanings – you could say it is even *anti*-meaning and certainly *anti*-transcendental.

One can see what Fussell means. After the 'Great' War, the very concept of 'greatness' – great projects, great motives, great ideas – was under deep suspicion, if not dead in the water. This is perhaps why poetry was the dominant artistic wartime form: life – the good life, bad life, trench life, home life (when you are separated from your family) – is made up of the small things poets observe, the all-important details which, as often as not ironically, are made to seem meaningful. As the poets said, and as the phenomenologists and pragmatists had said before them, all the pleasure in life is in the small things. That is one meaning of the Great War. When irony enters the imagination, truth is not the first casualty of war: innocence is. This was an earthquake in the landscape of belief. After the Great War, people no longer trusted belief.

Theosophy and spiritualism may be thought of as having attempted to rescue religion by giving it a 'scientific' credibility that Christianity was seen to lack.[31] According to H.R. Rookmaaker in *Modern Art and the Death of a Culture*, 'Mondrian and others were building a beautiful fortress for spiritual humanity, very formal, very rational . . . they did so on the edge of a deep, deep abyss, one into which they did not dare to look.'[32] But, he said, another school emerged that did look into the abyss – Surrealism.

The immediate precursor to the Surrealists was Giorgio de Chirico, whose self-portait of 1913 was entitled *And What Shall I Worship Save the Enigma?*. Several of his other paintings continue the theme: *The Enigma of a Day* (1914), *The Mystery and Melancholy of a Street* (1914) and *The Disquieting Muse* (1916). All of these show his concern with the disturbingly strange in the midst of the ordinary, with strange lighting, long shadows where the source of the shadow is not shown.[33] His own comment on his work is that it seeks to identify a 'presentiment' that has existed since prehistory. 'We might consider it,' he says, 'as an eternal proof of the irrationality of the universe.' This uncanny feeling, by implication, is where the religious sentiment comes from.

André Breton picked up on this in his *Surrealist Manifesto* (1924), in which he stated that it was the Surrealists' aim to break free of the rational by such means as 'free' (or automatic) writing – of the kind Yeats had indulged in with his wife – in order to uncover the irrational forces of the unconscious. In this sense, Surrealism sought to self-consciously re-enchant a world that had been desacralized by science and, to that extent, it was essentially therapeutic.

Surrealism was different among modern art forms in being technically extremely accomplished (which helped make it popular), and different in that it was concerned with dreams, the possibility of their symbolism representing a 'deeper' reality below conscious life; and that order is merely on the surface and a different kind of meaning lies below. Breton stressed 'the omnipotence of the dream' in his manifesto, and also that there were 'certain superior forms' that remained to be discovered, the mark of them all being their irrationality. Surrealism sought to reveal these hidden forms, 'dictated by thought in the absence of any control exercised by reason, exempt from any aesthetic or moral concern'.[34]

This rejection of reason owed a lot, of course, to the ravages of the war and the sense that a new mode of living was now required. This was epitomized by Max Ernst, who wrote in his autobiography: 'Max Ernst died on 1 August 1914. He was resuscitated on 11 November 1918, as a young man aspiring to become a magician and to find the myths of his time.'[35] The new myths were intended to replace the old one, and this was shown most clearly in Ernst's painting *The Virgin Mary Spanking the Infant Jesus before Three Witnesses* (1926), the witnesses being Ernst himself, Breton and Paul Éluard. The painting parodies High Renaissance figures and pagan motifs. In several other paintings Ernst introduced non-Christian sources, as did Paul Delvaux and Joán Miró in their Surrealist work.[36]

But what strike us, above all, are the Surrealists' technical mastery and their compelling attempts to depict the disturbing world of the unconscious (though Freud observed that, however dreamlike Dalí's works were, for example, they were still the product of the conscious mind). The technical mastery was more than incidental. Méret Oppenheim has been described as a Surrealist – her *Fur Breakfast* comprises a standard cup, saucer and spoon made of fur. This is also pure phenomenology, drawing attention to the everyday qualities of cups and saucers and spoons by the simple expedient of interfering with that everydayness. The Surrealists aimed to show that there is more to reality than we think, that chaos and absurdity are as much a part of the human condition as reason, that irrationalism is a disturbing force, producing mystery, fear and wonder in equal measure, and that there is a difference between the surreal and the supernatural.

Perhaps the seminal Surrealist work is René Magritte's *The Human Condition*. This technically very accomplished picture shows a painting of sea and sand on an easel that is itself on a beach, so that the image on the canvas runs into the 'real' view beyond. It is disturbing, but conveys successfully the idea that being disturbed doesn't 'mean' anything. Religion is a response to a disturbing or fearful feeling that is just part of the human condition, a mystery that doesn't mean anything.

Surrealism was a much more serious – and more accomplished – art form than it is often given credit for.

10

The Bolshevik Crusade for Scientific Atheism

We saw in the previous chapter that the 'pervasive theme' of 1914, when so many people greeted the war so enthusiastically, was 'community', the wish to recover the community life that had existed before the forces of modernism destroyed it. In such an intellectual/ emotional climate, and with the social upheavals brought about by the conflict, one might have expected that socialism, one of the most vibrant surrogate religions of the time and perhaps of all times, would have been waiting in the wings, so to speak, ready to take advantage of the mayhem. In practice, it didn't work out like that.

Although Karl Marx and Friedrich Engels had written in *The Communist Manifesto* that 'the proletariat has no fatherland', although they were completely opposed to nationalism, viewed war as invariably inimical to the interests of the labouring masses ('injecting a shot of illicit profits to prolong capitalism's miserable life'), and although Marx had said that he saw war as the 'midwife to revolution', the Great War stimulated an outgrowth of nationalism which, in the main, the relatively new socialist parties embraced with as much gusto as anyone else. Nationalistic feelings, it would seem, outfaced international-socialist feelings everywhere. 'Socialist leaders felt a tide of spontaneous patriotism welling up from below, and responded to this.'[1]

Everywhere, that is, except in Russia, as all the world knows. There, as the Great War endured and losses mounted, revolution had been anticipated for months. In the new type of mass war the home front was not excluded, and the suffering intensified, not helped by one government scandal after another. All the same, the end of the tsarist regime came surprisingly quickly, with the February Revolution of 1917 (26–29 February, Old System/ 8–11 March, New System) resulting in a 'dual power'. Officially, a provisional government was now in place that would rule until elections could be held and a constituent assembly convened. But there was also an unofficial power centre, the Petrograd Soviet of Workers' and Soldiers' Deputies. This is where, for a time, the real power lay. Later in the year, soldiers began to desert from the Front en masse, peasants started seizing gentry land, and workers took control of the factories. The Bolshevik Revolution (26–27 October, OS/ 7–8 November, NS) established a 'dictatorship of the proletariat', whose immediate aims were the consolidation of Bolshevik power and getting the country out of the war.

This was not achieved without cost. In March 1918 the Russian government accepted German terms: the Treaty of Brest-Litovsk lost her the Baltic states, large areas of Ukraine (until then Russia's breadbasket), Bielorussia, Poland and swathes of Transcaucasia, not to mention an indemnity in gold. German troops did not withdraw until the following November (and only then as a result of the armistice on the Western front), and this left a power vacuum in which 'Red' and 'White' armies engaged in a bloody civil war.[2] By the time these hostilities were over, the economy was to all intents and purposes at a standstill and no fewer than thirteen million people were dead, most of them not as a result of war but from starvation and epidemics. Five million more were to die in the famine of 1921–2, as a result of which millions of orphaned or abandoned children roamed the countryside, forced to steal so as to survive.

The rest of the machinations and manoeuvrings via which the Great War led to the Russian Revolution need not concern us. What does concern us is the nature of Marxism, and for at least two reasons. One is that, in many ways, Marxism was conceived as an alternative religious structure; and the second, that it led to the most determined attempt yet made to eradicate God.

A New Stage in Mankind's Development

Marx, says Bruce Mazlish, was one of the Essenes of early socialism. This is meant to imply a certain religious and ascetic quality, but in fact Marx defies easy characterizations. At times he saw himself as a scientist, invoking the name of Darwin as analogous to his own role in discovering laws not of 'natural technology' but of 'human technology'. In the late 1830s, at the end of the Romantic period, Marx wrote poetry and forged friendships with Heinrich Heine, Ferdinand Freiligrath and Georg Herwegh. As Mazlish also points out, the spread of Marxism is analogous to the expansion of Christianity and Islam. So it should not be surprising to find that Marxism first succeeded in Russia, a backward and very religious country where capitalist industrialization did not yet exist.

Nor, says Mazlish, was Marx immune to the language of Luther in the latter's translation of the Bible. 'Some argue that Marx is heir of the tradition of the great Jewish prophets, thundering forth at mankind ... But Marx received that tradition in its Lutheran form, as a result of being raised a believing Christian. Marx, needless to say, did not remain a believing Christian, any more than Luther was a forerunner of communism ... What they do share ... is a rhetorical structure, namely the characteristic articulation of the apocalyptic tradition that moves step by step ... from the original condition of domination and oppression to the culmination of perfect community.'

Although he became a militant atheist, 'a scoffer at the "union with Christ"', the function of religion, its place in our psychology, remained of central importance to Marx.[3]

Marx was always a philosopher as much as an economist. His basic contention, culminating in *Das Kapital*, was that the worker becomes 'all the poorer the more wealth he produces'. He insists that the worker is poorer 'even if better paid', because of an increase in alienation – the worker has become impoverished *as a human being*. And so Marx developed the concept of alienation, arguing that it originated in labour and had four defining aspects: (1) labour is no longer the worker's own under capitalism – it is an alien entity, dominating him;

(2) the very act of production alienates the worker from his own nature – he becomes less than a man; (3) the needs of the market – and of the factory – estrange men from other men; and (4) from his surrounding culture. Marx believed these forces of alienation were producing a new psychology.

His first achievement was to write as if he had discovered a new science, one that revealed a new stage in mankind's development. He gives credit to the French and the English for first grasping that history is the history of industry and exchange, making economic history central. He dismisses political history; there is no social contract as such, à la Rousseau; only economic relations 'tie man to man'. Such a view marked a profound revolution in political science.[4]

Marx also argued that this financial division of labour underlies 'the emergence' of the state. The state offers what is in effect an illusory communal life. Families and classes exist, offering some identity, but 'it follows from this that all struggles within the State, the struggle between democracy, aristocracy, and monarchy, the struggle for the franchise, etc., etc., are merely the illusory forms in which the real struggles of the different classes are fought out among one another'. Political life is but a veil for the 'real struggles' based on the division of labour and private property, and this is a further cause of estrangement. This leads Marx to a famous passage addressing the 'ruling ideas' in a society: 'The ideas of the ruling class are in every epoch the ruling ideas: i.e., the class which is the ruling *material* force of society, is at the same time its ruling *intellectual* force.' Because of this, the alteration of men (for the better), 'on a mass scale', can be achieved only by an act, a *revolution*. 'Only in the activity of revolution itself [does] man make himself into a new man, cleansed and purified.'[5]

But is *Kapital* intended to be read as a dry textbook? Not really. 'Workers who never read *Capital* nevertheless could now trust that there was a scientific underpinning to their feeling of being exploited.'[6] The purpose of *Kapital* was, as Engels saw, to become the workers' Bible, part of a campaign to kindle revolution. In that, it eventually succeeded.

Steel, Hammer and Stone

Upon gaining power in 1918, the Bolshevik leaders moved swiftly to remove organized religion from Russian life. An early initiative was to alter the calendar from the Julian to the Gregorian system, aiming to confuse people about the holiday season of the Orthodox Church. They also created work schedules that invariably conflicted with religious holidays and, eventually, replaced the seven-day week with a six-day week – five days of work and the sixth off. In effect, they abolished Sunday so as to prevent believers from attending Sunday liturgy.[7]

In the 1920s the Communist Party created the League of Militant Atheists, designed to broadcast the doctrine of Marxism-Leninism, what came to be called 'scientific atheism'. 'In general, scientific atheism combined a belief in socialist utopianism with an ethical mandate to proselytize the message of atheism. The role of the League of Militant Atheists was to teach the ethics of scientific atheism as a replacement for the moral teachings of popular theologies. They argued that religious doctrines created, to use Nietzsche's term, a "slave morality" that fooled religious believers into mistaking passivity for moral goodness.'[8] To further their aims, the League set up atheist 'cells', or houses, a system by which the inhabitants of rural communities could learn about atheism and discuss the falsity of religion. An atheist newsletter, *Bezbozhnik*, was made available.

The Five-Year Plan of anti-religious propaganda adopted in 1932 envisioned eventually one million such cells, outnumbering the old parishes by sixty to one. The number of Russian Orthodox churches was reduced from 54,000 in 1914 to 39,000 in 1928 (and to 4,200 in 1941). And it wasn't only Christianity that was hit; the number of Islamic courts was reduced from 220 in 1922 to just seven five years later. The early communists particularly hated the supernatural element in religion. In its place, Marxism-Leninism was held to have exclusive access to the truth, through the 'sacred' writings of Marx and Engels, which for them had the status of divine revelation, placing economic relations, and exchange, at the centre of the belief system.

We shall come back to scientific atheism shortly, but first we need to return to Nietzsche because, as recent scholarship has shown, the early Soviet intellectual, social and political scene was almost as much influenced by the German philosopher as it was transformed by Marx, Engels and Lenin. The pre-eminent scholar in this field is Bernice Glazer Rosenthal, professor of history at Fordham University, who says that although for most of the Soviet period 'either [Nietzsche's] name was unmentionable, or it could be used only as a pejorative', and although from 1920 his books were removed from the People's Libraries, they were not removed from all of them and individually owned copies were passed from hand to hand, a practice that would become a tradition in Eastern Europe as the century wore on.[9]

Despite this, she says, the 'philosopher with a hammer', as Nietzsche was known in Russia, touched deep cultural chords. Dostoevsky had to an extent prepared Russia for Nietzsche, and in many respects the German's ideas were compatible with Marxism, or treated issues that Marx and Engels had neglected. Nietzsche's views on the malleability of language, his contempt for what he called 'old words' and his embrace of the 'new word', with its biblical undertones, impressed those whom Rosenthal calls the Nietzschean Marxists, people such as Aleksandr Bogdanov, Anatoly Lunacharsky and Maxim Gorky. Another area where Nietzsche and Marxism found themselves in tandem was the philosopher's decrying of individualism: the world was, as he put it, 'torn asunder and shattered into individuation', which was for him the source of all evil. Nietzsche championed a different form of individuality – 'self-realization within a community'.[10] The Bolsheviks also liked his view of the universe as an irrational place 'in which blind will is the only constant', and his notion that science diminishes man, especially Darwinism, because it stresses 'mere survival', not creativity.

Just as Dostoevsky had prepared Russia for Nietzsche, so too, Rosenthal says, had the Russian *intelligenty*, its intelligentsia. This was a movement born in the mid-nineteenth century, comprising mainly the sons and daughters of the nobility who were intent on transforming Russia, then a very backward country in terms of industrialization and urbanization. And although many of them were atheists, they accepted the kenotic values of self-sacrifice, humility and love, believing that ideas imported from more 'advanced' Western European countries could transform their land. This was, in effect, says Rosenthal, a surrogate religion, an ideology of salvation.[11] Nietzsche was even present, she suggests, in the pseudonyms that certain Bolsheviks adopted, in particular Stalin (born Josef Djugashvili), Molotov (Viacheslav Skriabin) and Kamenev (Lev Rozenfeld), names that stem from the Russian words for 'steel', 'hammer' and 'stone' respectively, and recall Nietzsche's injunction, 'Be hard!'[12]

In more narrowly cultural terms, which may be regarded as surrogate-religious and post-Christian in orientation, Rosenthal focuses on Russian Symbolism, Futurism and Proletkult, and particularly on Dmitry Merezhkovsky, Viacheslav Ivanov, Lev Shestov, Anatoly Lunacharsky, Maxim Gorky, Aleksandr Bogdanov and Sergei Eisenstein. 'Russian symbolism,' she writes, 'started out as a religion of art ... Aesthetic creativity gives life meaning ... art leads to high truths.'

Symbolism began in part as a rejection of vulgar mass culture. 'Symbolist works bypass the intellect to address the psyche directly and were crafted to evoke chains of subliminal associations and a mysterious, otherworldly mood. The poetry suggests rather than states, sometimes in arcane or vatic language.' Merezhkovsky thought that 'historical Christianity' was obsolete but argued that people need religious faith as much as they need food. He sought a 'new religious consciousness' through the example of such figures as Goethe, Pushkin and Tolstoy, with whom he disagreed on many details but with whom he aligned himself when Tolstoy was excommunicated by the Russian Church. Merezhkovsky helped to found the St Petersburg Religious-Philosophical Society, which was eventually closed down because the sight of clergymen and lay intellectuals debating on equal terms, as well as openly discussing the role of sex, was too intoxicating for the people, who attended the debates in capacity audiences.[13]

Sobornost and Creativity: 'Breaking Free of God'

Viacheslav Ivanov, described by Rosenthal as a 'Nietzschean Christian', was likewise to be understood as a Dionysian, a believer in the 'loss of self' that comes about in mystical ecstasy, and in the liberation of the 'passions and instincts' repressed by Christianity. Beauty and creativity were for him the dominant virtues, along with 'emotional liberation'. Ivanov also embraced what he called a 'mystical anarchism', a doctrine that purported to combine personal freedom with member-ship of a 'loving community'. He had a slogan, 'non-acceptance of the world', which entailed a refusal to accept the world God created, and chose instead to envision a 'new organic society' characterized by free-dom, beauty and love.

'Mystical anarchism' was in reality no more than a politicized Dionysianism that emphasized both destruction and creativity, and was therefore recognizably Nietzschean. But Ivanov repudiated Nietzsche's 'will to power', Rosenthal says; he emphasized instead powerlessness, a new society in which no human being would rule another and 'dominance and subordination would cease. The social cement would be the internal and invisible bonds of love, myth and sacrifice.' Ivanov didn't eschew Christianity entirely but thought it needed adding to and, in some areas, replacing. For example, Diony-sian theatre should replace the churches and 'inner experience' should replace dogma. In the original Dionysian theatre, he claimed, there were no spectators – each participant took part in the 'orgy of action', which became an 'orgy of purification'. 'The chorus was a mystical entity, an embodiment of *sobornost*, in which the participants shed their separateness, to achieve a "living union", which Ivanov hoped to extend to society at large. The chorus, not the newly created Duma, was the authentic voice of the people.' Ivanov contended that a theatre which directed itself at the unconscious and induced 'self-forgetting' in 'mystical ecstasy' would foster the 'non-egoistic, communitarian psyche required in a society without coercion'.

Dionysian theatre didn't catch on as much as it might have done, or as Ivanov and others hoped, though people did talk about the 'will to theatre' and Dionysian theatre-cafés were created, which abolished the stage and experimented with author–audience dialogue. Later still, Ivanov came round to the view that 'Dionysus in Russia is dangerous'.

Lev Shestov made his name with books offering new interpreta-tions of Dostoevsky, Tolstoy and Nietzsche. His core idea was that we must 'struggle with God', meaning dogma should never be accepted without being thoroughly examined, and sometimes it should not be accepted at all; likewise, he attacked philosophical systems (Christianity included) because, he said, they tried to impose a nonexistent unity on the world and, in the main, glossed over the horrors of life (which Dostoevsky and Nietzsche didn't do, but Tolstoy did). Shestov didn't believe in Utopia, or in community – suffering, he said, was always individual, and he therefore argued, scandalously for the time, that philosophy must abandon its search for eternal truths and instead 'teach people to live in uncertainty'.[14]

Nikolai Berdyaev proposed a religion of creativity, outlined first in *The Meaning of the Creative Act* (1916). In this work he explained that creative experience is a new kind of experience, and that 'creative ecstasy' is an 'out-breaking into another world'. Creativity was for him the ultimate free act and the act in which humans finally break free of God, or Christ. Creativity, freedom and individuality were one, a kind of post-Christian trinity, and all three involved sacrifice and suffering. 'Formal freedom', as he called it, political freedom, was empty and negative, unlike creativity, which was positive freedom. In the new world '"living dangerously" would be regarded as a virtue and living in beauty as a commandment . . . beauty is a great force and it will save the world'.[15]

The Nietzschean Marxists, a term coined by the American philosopher George Kline, despised both bourgeois and Christian morality. They also had what Kline called a 'voracious will to the future', which involved 'a readiness to reduce living individuals to instruments or means to a future goal, and to sacrifice their well-being and even their lives, for the sake of this goal'. Aleksandr Bogdanov believed that in a truly scientific society people would follow 'expediency norms' voluntarily, much as an engineer follows similar norms when designing a bridge. These norms would reflect the 'new society' values of labour, egalitarianism, collectivism and 'comradely cooperation'. Bogdanov listed his 'Ten Expediency Norms' to replace those other 'Thou shalts' and 'Thou shalt nots', among them:

1. There shall be no herd instinct.
5. There shall be no absolute norms.

6. There shall be no inertia.
7. There shall be no violation of the purity of purpose.

He contrasted 'creativity' with 'inertia' because he was worried by Nietzsche's criticism of socialism as being, like Christianity, a 'slave morality'.[16]

The Plan: the Ideal 'Ahead', not the Ideal 'Above'

Anatoly Lunacharsky, another of Kline's Nietzschean Marxists, argued that the idea of a just and harmonious society is an aesthetic ideal and that the *ideal ahead* was more of a motivating force than the *ideal above*, which only fosters 'passive mysticism and self-absorption . . . The task of the political activist is to develop people's confidence in their power to achieve a better future and seek a rational path to it. The task of the artist is to depict that future and to inspire people to struggle for it, to imbue them with the "feelings of tragedy, the joy of struggle and victory, with Promethean aspirations, stubborn pride, implacable courage, to unite hearts in a common rush of feeling for the Superman".' Lunacharsky even understood Wagner's operas in Nietzschean terms, believing 'that beautiful illusions are necessary now that "God is dead, and the universe is without meaning"'. In his essay *Art and Revolution* he endorsed Wagner's view that art and social movements have the same goal, 'the creation of a strong, beautiful [new] man, to whom revolution shall give his strength and art his beauty'.[17]

Fine-sounding words, but the Nietzschean Marxists also subscribed to the view that against the class enemy 'all will be permitted', even actions 'ordinarily considered criminal'. In Lunacharsky's book *Religion and Socialism* (two volumes, 1908 and 1911) one of the characters says: 'We have got to change our God . . . It is necessary . . . to invent a new faith; it is necessary to create a God for all.' That new faith, that new ideal, for Lunacharsky, was a *plan* by which man would reconstruct the world. 'In labour, in technology [the new man] found himself to be a god and dictated his will to the world.' Lunacharsky distinguished five stages of religion: cosmism (animism), Platonism,

Judaism, Christianity and socialism. Socialism was the 'religion of labour' and 'progress'.

Maxim Gorky, the third of the Nietzschean Marxists, 'Writer Number 1' in the Soviet Union and a great favourite of Stalin, distinguished himself by including the 'new woman' in all this. For him, she too could be heroic and independent, and in Bogdanov's utopian science-fiction novels *Red Star* (1908) and *Engineer Menni* (1913) the women are almost indistinguishable from the men, with equal access to employment, information and the pleasant suicide rooms where they can choose, as Nietzsche counselled, to 'die at the right time'.[18]

The futurists – the new man-artists – specifically affirmed life on this earth, concreteness, and an emphasis on the individual. They were famously obsessed by the new technology, not just in physics but in aircraft, which seemed to underlie the accelerated pace of change, which in turn fostered a belief in 'the transience of all things as a permanent condition'. The futurist opera *Victory over the Sun* (Pobeda nad solntsem, 1913) was both Wagnerian and Nietzschean in concept. 'The subtext of the opera, and of the futurist aesthetic in general, is Nietzsche's announcement of the death of God and its consequences – a world with no inherent order or meaning.' The sun of the title is Apollo, the god of rationality, clarity and logic, and consequently the arch-enemy, as Rosenthal puts it, of 'utopians and visionaries'. 'Its capture liberates humankind from the constraints of necessity. The chorus sings: "We are free/ broken sun . . . / Long live darkness!" The juxtaposition of discordant images underscores the lack of inherent meaning, order, or purpose in the world.'[19]

The futurists' 'new men', who capture the sun, are invariably variants of Nietzsche's 'barbarians', male or androgynous 'but definitely not female'. They are of enormous size, of great strength, robust, healthy and hard. Their names are generic ('aviator', 'sportsman') and their facial features never specified – a sharp break with Orthodox theology 'which regards the human face as the epitome of Christian personhood'.

Malevich thought that Cubism had freed humankind from being 'slavish' in its imitation of nature – the new world, he said, would be created out of new forms. With Suprematism (a Nietzschean coinage if ever there was one), his idea was to create in a way that was 'un-bounded' by nature, by reason, by content even, 'in order to depict a purely spiritual reality beyond the world of nature and objects, a break-through to the fourth dimension, a realm beyond death'. His *Black Square* (1915) symbolized 'formlessness, the abyss', whereas *White on White* (1918), in representing purity, was intended to herald the dawn of a new world 'to be constructed by artists'. He went so far as to call Suprematism a 'New Gospel'.[20]

Early Nietzschean alternatives to orthodox religion did not fulfil the promise. Mystical anarchism was a doctrine 'concocted' (says Rosenthal) by Georgy Chulkov (1879–1939) that sought to combine personal freedom within a loving community, but was in fact a 'mish-mash' of Nietzsche, Alexander Herzen, Bakunin and Merezhkovsky, Ibsen, Byron, utopian socialism, Tolstoy and Dostoevsky. It involved a refusal to accept the world God was held to have created, and was allied to a political Dionysianism that emphasized the link between destruction and creativity. All tradition had to be destroyed and a 'new organic society' created based on an idea of the 'mystical person' who seeks union with others, as opposed to the egoistic 'empirical person' who insists on his rights and interests. 'God-building' involved turning people from passive spectators into active participants in all matters. It embodied the idea that creativity was within everyone, that 'life-creation' was the purpose of existence and that, within a loving, democratic community, liberation for all would be possible.

God Defied

These tendencies were aided by the Great War, which seemed to in-dicate that the critics of the Enlightenment had been right – man is not naturally rational or good. In such a situation, material and spiritual revolution went together. In 1918 Lenin decreed a number of 'monumental propaganda' projects, including what were known as 'God-defying' towers and other structures (Tatlin's Tower was the most famous, although it only ever existed in model form and was never built). Lunacharsky and Ivanov regarded mass festivals as unions of the artist and the people, not only making the experience of living more vibrant but inculcating among them a 'will to power' without which the new society and the new spiritualism could not come into being. This particularly applied to the Communist Youth League (Komsomol). Hardness, daring and will became the watchwords in the fusion of Marxism and Nietzschean thought forged by Lenin, Bukharin and Trotsky. 'Cruelty to enemies became a sacred duty.'[21]

Was Lenin a closet Nietzschean? He was certainly a personification of the will to power, as Rosenthal says. He kept a copy of *Zarathustra* in his Kremlin office and *The Birth of Tragedy* in his personal library; and though Hegel, Clausewitz, Darwin and Machiavelli were more direct influences, his revolutionary immoralism, and his elitism, were classic Nietzschean positions.

In this he was supported by Nikolai Bukharin, the most erudite of the Bolsheviks, who had lived in Germany and Austria. Bukharin was enthusiastic about creating a new society and a new man; he thought that 'communist mankind' could be 'forged' out of the 'human material left from capitalism', reconceived the proletariat as the 'Promethean class', and the new culture as the 'proletarian avant-garde'. In particular, he endorsed Nietzsche's view that 'we should reconsider cruelty and open our eyes . . . Almost everything we call "higher culture" is based on the spiritualization of cruelty.' Communism, he was convinced, was going to lead to a higher culture than bourgeois culture. These were 'cruel times', and peace between the social classes was impossible. Trotsky was a more obvious post-Nietzschean, much influenced by the 'superman' idea, that the contemporary age was an age of chaos out of which the triumph of collectivism would reflect the 'will' of the people.

'A Higher Social-biologic Type'

We need now to discuss a number of rather distinct cultural developments that are also directly related to our theme. One was the emergence of the Scythians, followers of an ideology conceived by Ivanov-Razumnik (real name, Razumnik Vasilievich Ivanov,

1891–1981), essayist and poet, who helped to found the Free Philosophical Association of Petrograd (a successor to the St Petersburg Religious-Philosophical Society), which became home to many followers of the occult doctrine of anthroposophy, founded by Rudolf Steiner, a former theosophist.

The Scythian ideology distinguished between 'revolutionary socialism' and 'philistine socialism'. The Scythians thought of themselves as a new type, 'as man-artists who, like the original Scythians, would never settle down into some sort of bourgeois order' as had occurred in France after the Revolution. The Scythians, as envisaged by Ivanov-Razumnik, comprised a 'horde' galloping wildly across the steppes. These 'peasant-poets emphasized the dominance of the countryside over the city and were adamantly anti-intellectual'. They praised the 'barbaric potential of the people. 'They did not exalt cruelty, but they accepted it as part of a process of spiritual purification and cultural renewal. Their writings are studded with "will to" formulations such as the "will to cross the abyss".'[22]

Proletkult was a more general coalition of workers' clubs, factory committees, worker theatres and educational societies. Numbering half a million adherents at its peak in 1920, its mission was plainly to create a new man and a new culture. Its unofficial theoretician was Bogdanov, though Nadezhda Krupskaia (Lenin's wife) sat on the central committee. Pavel Kerzhentsev, a man of the theatre and a publisher, defined the 'task of the proletkults [as] the development of an independent proletarian spiritual culture, including all areas of the human spirit – science, art and everyday life'.[23]

Nietzsche imbued the Proletkult writers almost as much as did Marx, encouraging the proletariat to become supermen, capable of enormous feats, 'even miracles'. In a play by Pavel Bessalko (1887–1920) the workers are portrayed as not fearing God, because 'we are our own God, judge and law'. In Vladimir Kirillov's *The Iron Messiah* Jesus is an industrial worker. Various Proletkult poems were set to music 'and became revolutionary hymns'. Lunacharsky extolled Proletkult as a 'church militant' in a classless society, while others praised its attempts to escape from 'spiritual slavery' and 'spiritual subjugation'; this was to be achieved via the abolition of the difference between mental and physical work – 'even the most brilliant man of science must also be skilled in manual labour'.[24]

In summary, what we can say is that during the Russian Revolution the inherent Prometheanism of Marxism was aligned with Nietzschean ideas (and even some occult ideas), in which propagandists tried to replace faith in religion with faith in 'the wonder-working powers of science and technology. Cosmists, adherents of a quasi-occult doctrine at the margins of science, envisioned the abolition of death, space travel, and an immortal Superman capable of anything.'[25]

'The cumulative effect of Nietzschean ideas entering Soviet society through all these conduits was enormous,' concluded Bernice Glazer Rosenthal. The new Soviet man embodied the idea that people can be remade, 'that human perfection is possible . . . that the human species would (re)create itself according to its own specifications'. Trotsky expected (or said he expected) socialism to produce a 'higher social-biologic type', in effect, a superman who would 'learn to move rivers and mountains . . . The average human type will rise to the heights of an Aristotle, a Goethe or a Marx [imagine Goethe as the *average*!]. And above this ridge, new peaks will arise.'[26] This was, one might say, the essence of Eisenstein's films, so redolent of that era, in which a hero breaks out of the chorus (the ranks) to forge some great achievement but yet remains 'one of us'.

For the writer and artist Sergei Tretiakov, the futurist – the archetypal new man-artist – was an 'instigator-agitator . . . This new type of worker must feel a fundamental hatred toward all things unorganized, inert, chaotic, sedentary and provincially backward . . . He is repelled by thick pine forests, untilled steppes, unutilized waterfalls which tumble not according to our order . . . he finds greatness in every object of human production designed to overcome, subject, and master the elements and inert matter.'

The Church of Communism

Again, fine-sounding words, but . . . In the early years after the Revolution, Soviet leaders for the most part believed that religious faith was detrimental to society and could be expunged from the human psyche – all that was needed were the right incentives and education. Many appear to have thought that religion would simply 'evaporate' when the new, more egalitarian economic order emerged. In the early days, the 'renovationist' movement sought to recruit revolutionaries through religious channels but when this failed, and when the new economic order also failed to wash away religion, there emerged a growing antagonism towards both Christianity and Islam. And this led, eventually, to the deliberate creation of an atheist alternative to religion, which had three main elements. These were the Standing Commission on Religious Questions, which oversaw all religious policy matters, the League of Militant Atheists (mentioned earlier), to spread the message 'that religion was scientifically falsifiable', and a raft of atheistic universities to educate a new generation of intellectuals.

The League was the most active part of this set-up. It endured from 1925 to 1941, and after Leon Trotsky was replaced by Emelian Yaroslavsky, a close Stalin aide, a policy was followed whereby it was assumed that secularization could not occur unless religious cultural expression was abandoned. So began a series of crusade-like polemics to suppress religious expression and replace it with scientific atheism, under which, promoted by Stalin, 'a vast and intricate ceremonial system began to take shape that would grow throughout the Soviet era ... the creation of Soviet alternatives to baptisms, confirmations, religious marriages, funerals' and so on. In a Soviet ('Red') baptism, for example, the official recited the following invocation over the infant:

> Life becomes much brighter and more beautiful
> Much quicker is its wonderful course
> Suddenly here in our Soviet family
> A small person is born.
> Today we are celebrating in honour of him to whom
> Belongs the future, and we are saying to him
> 'Hail, new citizen of our great Soviet state.'[27]

Paul Froese, in his study of the Soviet secularization experiment, says that the Russians saw religious faith as a product of ignorance – as the fruit of ritual activity, as a collection of social institutions, as offering a set of social rewards, as offering salvation incentives, or as an aspect of the state. The 'ignorance' argument was strongly held, many Communist Party leaders feeling that, since the findings of science and the fruits of technology were wholly at odds with beliefs in the supernatural, once this knowledge spread, religious faith would fade.

Party intellectuals were well aware of the French sociologist Émile Durkheim's notion of religion: that its strength in part derives from the feeling of 'collective effervescence', from *participation in ritual* which generates emotion, and this they sought to counter, as we have seen, with new rituals of their own. But at the same time they realized they must destroy the Orthodox Church if the new rituals were to have any purchase. So began the massive – and ultimately brutal – attempts to destroy all traditional religious institutions – churches, monasteries, shariah courts, religious schools.

Yaroslavsky was certain – and told Stalin so – that too direct an assault would backfire, and so the brutality did not start immediately. In effect, the League of Militant Atheists served as a kind of church of Communism in the 1920s and early 1930s, distributing atheist newspapers, giving atheist lectures, preaching at meetings that people were compelled to attend, and mimicking religious institutions: theoretical Communist texts were treated like holy books, Soviet leaders were presented as saintlike, the doctrine of historical materialism was used to explain that paradise was now attainable here on earth, in this life. There was a concept of 'Soviet time', which held that future generations would remember this 'first generation' as pathbreakers in the new society, and so this first – in effect golden – generation would 'live for ever' in the collective memory of humanity: here was a secular form of immortality. In addition to which, religious believers were castigated as 'disbelievers' – disbelievers in the Soviet system, in effect non-combatants in the struggle for a 'higher' form of society.

Lenin in particular was vitriolic about religion. 'Every religious idea, every idea of God, even flirting with the idea of God, is unutterable vileness ... vileness of the most dangerous kind, "contagion" of the most abominable kind. Millions of sins, filthy deeds, acts of violence and physical contagion ... are far less dangerous than the subtle, spiritual idea of a God decked out in the smartest "ideological" costumes . . .' All the more ironic, then, that Lenin's embalming has to be seen in this light, since apart from anything else it was an intentional imitation of the way the bodies of saints were displayed in monasteries throughout Russia where, according to Orthodox belief, holy cadavers decompose at a slower rate than those of ordinary mortals.[28]

But it wasn't only Lenin – not by any means. Immediately following the 1917 revolution and in the civil war that ensued, the Bolsheviks were already targeting churches, monasteries and clerics as 'potential sources of antirevolutionary activity'. Church property was seized, and monks, priests and nuns were often killed in the process. In 1922 Patriarch Tikhon wrote a letter of protest to Lenin, complaining that thousands of clergy were being killed and that more than a hundred thousand believers had been shot. His protest was ignored, he was himself sent into exile, and a decade later he too was shot.

Other horrors followed. Metropolitan Vladimir of Kiev was castrated and shot, Veniamin of St Petersburg was doused with water in the freezing cold and turned into a pillar of ice, Bishop Germogen of Tobolsk was strapped to the paddle-wheel of a steamboat and mangled by the rotating blades, and Archbishop Andronnik of Perm was buried alive.[29] St Petersburg's Cathedral of Our Lady of Kazan was turned into the Museum of the History of Religion and Atheism, which, among other activities, held exhibitions illustrating 'the folly' of religion. The architecturally unique Cathedral of Christ the Saviour was blown up and set to be replaced with a shrine to Lenin, but in the end a swimming pool was put there instead. Church bells were melted down and icons stripped of their jewelled settings.[30]

In the many thousands of local 'cells' that were set up to replace the parish churches, discussions about atheism were held in which the main attraction was sometimes accounts by 'converts', people who had seen the light, abandoned their religious belief and embraced scientific atheism. 'Not less than one cell' was installed in each factory, government office or school; and in the countryside at each collective farm or machine tractor station. As we have seen, the League proposed one million cells throughout the country, though this total was never achieved.[31]

Prayers v. the Tractor

Since the factory was regarded by theorists as the proper substitute for churches 'as places of community, faith and purpose', urban factories were used as alternatives to churches. A large piece of machinery often served as the focus for communal gatherings, as a kind of secular altar serving 'the anti-God industry'. The common purpose of the factory was expected to replace the common purpose of worship. Workers were expected to show their new faith by adding the time they had formerly spent worshipping to the time they spent working. In the factories and in the countryside, technology was presented as a way to 'work miracles' – but demonstrating that miracles were the work not of God but of people. One propaganda poster read 'Prayers or the tractor' as alternative ways to produce change and improvement in the community.

Other scientific initiatives against religion included an examination of holy water under the microscope to show that it had no special properties. In the Museum of the History of Religion and Atheism, one exhibit showed that Noah's Ark could not have held all the animals then known to have existed on earth.[32] As homework, schoolchildren were sometimes given the task of converting fellow family members to scientific atheism. University courses carefully explained how physics, chemistry, mathematics and biology all showed that religion was wrong.

From the early 1920s, Trotsky realized that people do have a need for theatrical and emotional outlets at regular intervals and so, on gaining power, the Bolsheviks set about creating what was in effect a new liturgy. In addition to immediately changing the calendar from the Julian to the Gregorian, a new ceremonial year was introduced which celebrated such events as 18 March, 'The Day of the Paris Commune' (introduced in 1918); 5 May, 'The Day of the Press' (1922); the first Sunday in June, 'The Day of International Cooperation' (1923); and 7 November, 'Anniversary of the Great October Socialist Revolution' (1918).

The KGB insisted on vetting religious newspapers before publication and used bishops and clergy as informers against their colleagues.

These and other ploys compromised the Orthodox Church in the early years of Soviet control, but at the same time prolonged the life of the Church in a way that in the long run paid off. Nonetheless, the push–pull approach of the Soviet leadership also paid off to an extent in that, between the mid-1920s and the start of the Second World War, church attendance rates in Russia fell from more than 50 per cent to less than 20 per cent, while children throughout that same period were about 10 per cent less likely than their parents to go to church.[33] At the same time, there was a turn to smaller religious groupings, which would meet in secret.

It would be wrong, though, to give the impression that this change was uniform across the Soviet Union. Poland was exceptionally resilient in its religious beliefs, as was Lithuania, where microphones were forbidden in churches because they were felt to 'lure' people away from their work, and where the famous 'Hill of Crosses' took place after the Soviets had bulldozed a hill where locals had erected a number of crosses. Overnight, after the bulldozing, another array of crosses appeared, and this was repeated several times until the bulldozers gave up. But in central Asia it was a different story: there, the number of devout Muslims was reduced massively following Stalin's purges: both Lenin and Stalin regarded the central Asian Muslims as 'primitive' and, as Stalin said, Islam had to be destroyed. There was also a campaign, known as *hujum*, to force Muslim women to unveil. Though many women welcomed this, and complied with the campaign, the males did not accept the policy so equably and women were attacked and even raped for their actions.

The League of Militant Atheists claimed that its membership grew from 100,000 in 1926 to 5.5 million in 1932, impressive if true (some scholars have argued that its records were falsified). And here we encounter a genuine problem of interpretation. For Stalin's purges intensified during the 1930s, and by about 1937, when a census of religious faith was taken, it showed that 'religious belief and activity were still quite pervasive throughout the Soviet empire'. This was so unwelcome that 'religious persistence became the scapegoat of the Soviet ideological machine' and brutality was rained down on the offenders as never before. The latest investigations show that thousands of individuals were executed for religious crimes and hundreds of thousands were imprisoned in labour camps or psychiatric hospitals.[34] It was only on the eve of the Second World War that the killing of religious believers was halted, as the Soviet regime itself faced death from a foreign invader. For the duration of the war, atheist conversion was put on hold and the League was disbanded.

But it was not all over. After the war a new organization, the Knowledge Society, was created to carry on the work, and the greatest campaign in history to kill off God was resumed.

11

The Implicitness of Life
and the Rules of Existence

Early in 1919 the German sociologist Max Weber gave a lecture in Munich on 'the inner calling to science' (often translated into English as 'Science as a Vocation'). At the time, Munich, like many other large cities in Germany, was in a state of revolutionary upheaval; in fact, civil war was not far off and in Bavaria a Soviet Republic would be established as a result of which it was hoped to found a 'realm of light, beauty and reason'. Weber dismissed such ideas as 'irresponsible', on the grounds that 'politics is overtaxed when it is expected to establish sense and happiness'. But sense and happiness were his concern in his lecture.

The philosopher Karl Löwith, who had been injured in the war, had experienced its destructive power and had been captured by the Italians, was in the audience in Munich that day. He wrote later that Weber, who had only a year to live, 'strode through the overcrowded hall to the lectern, looking pale and tired. [His] face, surrounded by an unkempt beard, reminded me of the sombre glow of the prophetic figures of Bamberg Cathedral. The impact was stunning ... After the innumerable revolutionary speeches by the liberal activists, Weber's words were like a salvation.'

Weber's Uncertainty Principle

This speech, says the German historian Rüdiger Safranski, provoked a violent public controversy. 'On the surface it deals with the ethos of the sciences, but basically Weber addresses the question of how the yearnings for a meaningful life can still be fulfilled within the steel capsule of modern "rationalized" civilization.'[1] Weber argued that science can make a contribution to self-awareness but cannot relieve us of the decision on how to live our lives. Our civilization, he said, 'has so thoroughly and comprehensively moved into a belief in rationality that it undermines the individual's confidence in his own ability to make decisions'. Moreover, the certainty on technical matters that the sciences bring with them leads us to demand/expect the same certitude and objectivity in the life of values and ethics, and in the search for meaning. 'The result is a boom in ideologies wooing our trust by donning scientific garb.' This sees the emergence of what he called 'academic prophets' (*Kathederpropheten*), who 'react to the lost mystery of a world disenchanted by rationalism by wrongly rationalising the last magic that is left to it – the individual's personality and its freedom . . . Instead of leaving mystery where it still exists – in the soul of the individual – the "academic prophets" submerge the disenchanted world into the twilight of deliberate re-enchantment.'[2] Against this, Max Weber pleads for unmixing.

Weber was in no doubt that in the world created by science and technology God was dead. Either we must accept this, he insists, or become what he termed 'religious virtuosi', modelled on artistic virtuosi, sacrificing the intellect to living with faith in the way that artistic virtuosi live with their faith in their own abilities. The 'transcendental realm of the mystical life' can never be explained in scientific terms, he said, and we should never seek to amalgamate the two. Nor could there ever be the kind of certainty about mystical life that was available in science, but we might draw comfort from the 'brotherhood' of believers and the relationships available within that brotherhood.[3]

Safranski tells us that nearly every major town in Weimar Germany had at that time what he called the 'saints of inflation', eager to save Germany in its turmoil. 'In Karlsruhe there was one who called himself "Primal Vortex" and promised his followers a share in cosmic energy; in Stuttgart a "Son of Man" invited his followers to a redeeming vegetarian Last Supper; in Düsseldorf a new Christ preached the imminent end of the world and called for withdrawal into the Eifel mountains. In Berlin the great halls were filled by the "spiritual monarch", Ludwig Haeusser, who demanded "the most consistent Jesus ethics" in the sense of original communism, propagated free love, and offered himself as a "führer", as "the only hope of a higher development of the nation, the Reich, and mankind".'

Safranski puts these eccentrics down as 'aberrations' of the revolutionary excitement of those days in post-First World War Germany, 'decisionists of the renewal of the world, raving metaphysicians, and profiteers in the vanity fair of ideologies and surrogate religions'.[4]

Undisclosed Everyday Abundance

Amid this miasma of views and doctrines, one man (apart from Weber himself) stood out: Martin Heidegger, one of the most important, and controversial, philosophers of the modern period – and this would be true even without his Nazi affiliation. Born a Catholic in Messkirch in Baden-Württemberg, Heidegger was originally destined for the Church; but he converted to Protestantism before losing his faith entirely, then returned to Catholicism near the end of his life.

Heidegger is not an easy writer to paraphrase, as any number of scholars will confirm, and this has to do partly with his style, which is often turgid and opaque; but in fairness it has as much – if not more – to do with the fact that he was trying to put into words phenomena that he believed had not been put into words before in quite the way he had in mind. He was not a poet, but in effect he was trying to do what poets do – naming, identifying aspects of experience not identified before, in language appropriate to the new circumstances. In one of his writings he noted: 'Thoughts come to us; we do not think them up ... Thinking is a gift, or grace, an event that overtakes us.'[5] This links him with Rilke and his idea that poems 'came' to him (see

p. 232 ff.). Heidegger asks: 'How do we experience reality before we arrange it for ourselves in a scientific, or value-judging, or worldview approach?'[6]

For our purposes Heidegger's main ideas, as set out in his most important publications, *Being and Time* (1927), *What Is Metaphysics?* (1929), *The Origin of the Work of Art* and *Hölderlin and the Essence of Poetry* (both 1936), *The Question of Technology* (1953) and *Gelassenheit* (Composure, 1955), fall under the following headings: 'Being', 'Death', 'Caring' and 'Authenticity'.

According to Heidegger we are 'thrown' into the world, in circumstances not of our own choosing, a world which is already well under way, and we must adjust as best we can, learn the rules, the implicit ones as well as the explicit ones, while also acknowledging that the world is full of an 'undisclosed abundance' that we will never conquer totally. There is no inherent human nature, no essence to man, and as we confront this lack of essence, and are learning the rules – so far as they go – we also realize that we shall one day die. This set of circumstances means that one of the most important principles of life is decisiveness, that we are the product of our decisions and actions as much as (if not more than) our thoughts. Much of Heidegger's philosophy was given over to the idea of *intensification*, that to live life intensely – more intensely than we did, as intensely as possible – is as close to meaning as we will/can get.

This is where Heidegger's concept of Being comes in. This word is generally written with an initial capital in English, to draw attention to it (because in written German all nouns take a capital). The corresponding German word *Dasein* (composed of *da*, 'there' and *sein*, 'to be' ('being')) is now routinely used by English-language philosophers, mainly to emphasize that what Heidegger originally meant to stress was that Being is actually *Being-there* – that is, in some particular place and therefore at some particular time. Heidegger followed Husserl, to whom he was an assistant at the University of Freiburg between 1918 and 1923, in arguing against a theoretical approach to phenomena, stating that theory (a mainstay of science) involves abstractions that remove us from the everyday abundance of life.

The Gift of Surrender

Heidegger thought there were different forms of Being, different levels, of which some were much better than others. He thought that modern life, with its noise and bustle and speed, created an 'everydayness' in which there was no time for reflection and little opportunity for initiative or considered decision-making; that the science-led existence becomes the manipulation and control of the world rather than its enjoyment. This is what he meant by an 'inauthentic' life.

In contrast, he thought we should aim for an authentic life which accepted, with composure (the concept of *Gelassenheit*), our own finitude in the face of the insurmountable superabundant plurality of the world. Our stance towards the world, our heightened sense of Being, is to be achieved by 'dwelling' in the world, this world here and now, and by 'dwelling' he meant 'being at home' with our surroundings and our neighbours; the rapidly moving anonymous nature of modern city life was not Being in the fullest sense.

Heidegger thought that we should 'care' for the world – another aspect of *Gelassenheit*; that instead of trying to control and manipulate and exploit the environment we should 'let things be'. Here, he invoked poetry. He loved Hölderlin above all others, and believed that when we confront a poem (or 'board a poem', as Seamus Heaney once said), we have to 'surrender' to it; we cannot fight it, we cannot control it, we cannot exploit it. A poem is in some ways a gift to the world and we must receive it as such. Obviously we will enjoy some gifts more than others, but the world is full of such gifts – poems and a superabundance of other things.[7]

What We Know in Our Bones

More than this, Heidegger said he was only trying to bring into the light what we 'already know in our bones'; that there is an implicitness to life that is not the (Freudian or Jungian) unconscious but is shared by us all as a result of history, what has gone before and how people have evolved ways to live. His philosophy was to make what is implicit and important explicit.

For Heidegger, then, 'the meaning of Being' could not be, by definition, an abstraction. It was the practice of *Gelassenheit*, of caring for the world, submitting to its abundance, letting it be, 'willing not to will'; while at the same time acknowledging that there is no such thing as an 'I', if by that we mean an unchanging entity that meets each new day in the same manner. For Heidegger, 'to be' in 1927, when he wrote *Being and Time*, was not at all the same thing as 'to be' in 1933 when he joined the Nazi Party and made propaganda appearances in Leipzig, Heidelberg and Tübingen. Nor the same thing in 1936–40 when, in several lectures on Nietzsche, he criticized the 'power-thinking' of National Socialism and was put under surveillance by the Gestapo.

Heidegger, following on from Freud and Nietzsche and Weber, set this particular ball rolling. In particular he drew attention to what he called 'average everydayness' in which, he insisted, the self is not so much an object as an *unfolding event or happening*, a manifestation, the 'movement of a life course stretched out between life and death'. He also had a concept of the 'they', the backdrop of everydayness, what he called a primordial phenomenon of existence, not just other people but other people 'co-happening'. These manifestations bring with them two other aspects of being: first, 'being-toward', turning our face to the future, knowing it will be different, always changing; and that we must be *ready* for change, anticipate it, above all enjoy it. And second, 'being-toward-the-end' or 'being-toward-death', 'the realization of a final configuration of possibilities for . . . life overall'.

This brings to mind Rilke's idea of the 'good death', the 'individual death' (see p. 237), but Heidegger was also saying that, in order to feel fulfilled, to feel a sense of wholeness, we need to take on board very firmly the idea that death *is* the end, there is no afterlife; and we must develop some notion of what we would like our life-event, our life-manifestation, to look like, and then act on that decision, always realizing that we are finite individuals and that not all things are possible.

Radical Pastoralism

Heidegger also had the idea of 'marginal practices', what he called the 'saving power of insignificant things – practices such as friendship, backpacking in the wilderness, and drinking the local wine with friends'. This was his idea of 'radical pastoralism'.[8] All these things remain marginal, he maintained, 'precisely because they *resist efficiency*' (italics added). They remain outside – beyond – the reach of the modern attitude. This is not quite true, of course – backpacking can be harnessed to our concern with health and training, making us more efficient in that way. But Heidegger meant 'marginal practices' to be refuges from modern life, and used them as metaphors for his approach.

If we can sum up Heidegger's paradigm, it would be to experience the world *as* poetry, and *through* poetry. Poetry takes as its subject the inexhaustible abundance and plurality of the world, it does not reduce things to a single dimension (as science or the monotheisms attempt to do); the world comprises horizons that always recede before us as we approach; there is no 'regime of meaning'. To every poetic word, Heidegger claimed, belongs 'an inexhaustible range of complex spaces of [semantic] resonance'. This, for him, is the only transcendental phenomenon in the world. 'In poetic experience or in poetry-mediated experience, therefore, we "grasp" our lives as lived "in the face of the ungraspable", come face to face with the "mystery" of Being, with its "awesomeness".'[9] This is how to 'dwell' in the world, how to be 'at home' in it. Being at home in the world is the point of life.

Heidegger's poor writing style, his involvement with the Nazis, his disgraceful treatment of Edmund Husserl and Hannah Arendt, all make it difficult to judge him dispassionately. Part of the intellectual climate in the wake of 'the death of God' has been a parallel concern, a dissatisfaction with the explanations offered by science as somehow irrelevant to the concerns many have regarding how to live their lives, what values and moral attitudes to embrace, how to behave. Heidegger stands firmly in that strong strand of thought running through the twentieth century – the idea of phenomenology – leading from Husserl to the existentialists to the counterculture and to pragmatic philosophy (which we shall be exploring later). His ideas of *Gelassenheit*, of caring for the world – letting it be, submitting to its abundance, experiencing it poetically, breaking out of the everyday, being content to 'dwell' in the world, to be at home in it – have proved ever more prescient as the decades have passed.

The Central Sane Human Activity

Heidegger loved the poetry of Rilke, but it was also the *way* in which Rilke was a poet that mattered to the philosopher.

'Rilke was perhaps more exclusively a poet than anyone before him or since ... No other German author, Goethe included, began writing as trivially and ended writing as superbly as Rilke did.' This is Wolfgang Leppmann in his biography of Rilke, and it is no small thing to say. True as these remarks may be, and as appealing as Rilke's qualities were to Heidegger, we cannot nonetheless overlook the interesting and pertinent fact that Rilke was a much travelled man (about Europe, at least) who knew and befriended many contemporary luminaries: Gerhart Hauptmann, Hugo von Hofmannsthal, Stefan George, Paul Valéry, Paula Modersohn-Becker, Sergei Diaghilev. He visited Russia several times, where he met Leo Tolstoy; he spent several months in Paris, where he met and wrote about the same *saltimbanques* (travelling acrobats) that Picasso painted, and visited August Rodin before writing his biography.

And then there was his affair with Lou Andreas-Salomé, a beautiful Russian-born German writer and psychoanalyst, who had famously refused Nietzsche's proposal of marriage (Nietzsche said Wagner was the 'fullest' person he ever knew, but that Lou was the 'smartest'). She was the author of two novels, wrote the first biography of Nietzsche and, though married to Friedrich Carl Andreas, a lecturer in the Oriental Department at the University of Berlin, she refused to sleep with him, even on their wedding night; thereafter she took a series of lovers, always younger than herself, including Frank Wedekind who may have used her as the prototype for Lulu, the insatiable seductress in his *Earth-Spirit*.

In his biography of the poet, Leppmann chronicles Rilke's restless movements, year by year, showing that, from his early twenties on, he moved residence two or three times a year, sometimes more, sometimes much more. In saying that Rilke was *exclusively* a poet, Leppmann was using licence – or using the word in a very particular way. Rilke was a great letter-writer and always interested in the great issues of his day. He had many women friends and was popular among them – he was hardly a monk. Or at least, not to begin with. One of the notable transformations of Rilke's life was that he went from being a young man-about-town, who loved the company of beautiful women, the chatter of coffeehouses and the informed busy-ness of newspaper editorial offices, to someone who came to appreciate solitude and remote landscapes for their own sake.

But yes, he was an exceptional poet. He had a religious upbringing, and remained slightly mystical all his life, though he lost his faith under the influence of Hegel and Nietzsche, and wanted religious instruction removed from schools. He was, says Leppmann, a 'melancholy atheist, a nonbeliever with a guilty conscience'.[10] On his early trips to Russia he was impressed by the peasants (more so than Tolstoy was, who knew them better), in particular their concept of God, which he felt was much vaguer and less pretentious than the Western concept, 'in everything as yet unafflicted by the schism of consciousness'.

And original observation was Rilke's developed aim, as he matured, in both a poetic and a spiritual sense, which for him were much the same. 'What lends sense to life [i.e., the poet's life] is not transitory happiness but the acts of "saying",' Rilke stated, 'of internalizing and transforming into language all that is in danger of being made superfluous by a functional, machine-run civilization: "What is it you urgently ask for if not transformation? Earth, my love, I will do it."'[11] Rilke saw it as his self-imposed task in life to remove that schism between humans and nature that for him was the major crime of Christianity, because Jesus had created a kind of consciousness that has stopped us from experiencing the Earth as fully as we might, and it is the recovery of this experience that gives 'sense to life'. This was the idea of 'surrender' to nature, which Heidegger echoed in *Being and Time*.

Rilke's attempts to do this, his 'religion of aesthetic contemplation', as Michael Hamburger puts it, are revealed most clearly and most successfully in his major later works, in particular the *Sonnets to Orpheus* (1922) and the *Duino Elegies* (1923).[12] In a sense, what he was trying to do in poetry was not dissimilar to what Cézanne had sought to do in his painting, to approach nature in an unmediated way, trying to dispense with the accumulated practices of the past that hinder a true appreciation of what the Earth – which is all there is – has to offer. As part of this Rilke saw himself as a 'receiver' of his poems, rather than as the creator.

All prose talk of incandescent poetry such as Rilke's is bound to interfere with the experience, but we have to try. His most successful lines play with images of the Earth – the natural world – sewn seamlessly into our psychology, as when in the sonnet 'The Passing' he speaks of 'the boundless inner sky', or when, improbably but ambitiously, he brings the latest hard science to bear on intimate life:

> From star to star – such distances; and yet
> Those encountered here are harder reckoned.
> Someone – a child, say, and then a second . . .
> What dark matter holds them separate?

As that last line shows, Rilke could ask the most amazing questions, using them to locate all his spiritual wonder in the life we lead now. As Don Paterson argues in his examination of the sonnet sequence, Rilke refutes the two principal religious errors. 'The first is to think of truth as being in the possession of an inscrutable third party, whose knowledge and intentions can only be divined.' In fact, he says, the only thinking being done 'in this part of the universe' is by us; which means that 'truth' is not determined, but provisionally *decided*, in the manner of science. 'The Sonnets insist on sheer wondering enquiry as *the* central sane human activity, a way of configuring our most honest prepositional stance towards the universe.'[13]

> O happy Earth, O Earth on holiday,

> play with your children! Let us try
> to catch you . . .

'The second error is to think of any afterlife or any reincarnation we are bound for as more extraordinary than finding ourselves here in the first place.' By projecting ourselves into some future state, beyond our death, Rilke believed that we warp our behaviour in *this* life, and weaken our responsibility to the here and now, as well as our negotiations with those with whom we share the planet. Religion, Rilke thought, acted as though it held a copyright on the miraculous. But being here, he said,

> is a source
> with a thousand well
> heads; a net of pure force
> that no one can touch and not kneel down in awe.

He argued that 'we shouldn't know what to do with the consolation offered by a God'; for the most divine consolation 'inheres' in the human itself: 'our eye would have to grow just a little more seeing, our ear more receptive, the flavour of fruit would have to come home to us more completely, we should be able to bear more smell, and have more presence of mind' so as to derive more convincing consolations from our most immediate experiences.

Rilke thought that humans were probably unique among mammals in that they have conscious foreknowledge of their own death. And it is this end that imposes on us the idea of a narrative to a life, a narrative that has or will have meaning, a meaning that – because it comes to an end (and we know it, in advance) – has an overall shape: death drives the plot of life. It is this predicament that has to be overcome. It is a recognition that consciousness is, as some philosophers have described it, 'a crime against nature'.

This dual – or riven – state, this predicament, could best be dealt with – accommodated, enjoyed – by *singing*. Singing, Rilke said, is unique to humans. To sing as a human is not to sing as a bird; as birds sing, so humans talk. 'Music [in a song] weaves a line through the discontinuous present ... lyric unites the time-based events of our words by recalling them back into the presence of one another through the repetition of their sounds. By continually returning us to the previous moment, the lyre cheats that time which carries us to our deaths ... The endless river rolls on, but through song we can row against the current and arrest, for a little while, our own progress.'[14]

For Rilke, singing has another meaning too. Singing is what the Earth itself does and this meant that 'saying' and 'singing' overlapped. A good example here is the Tenth Duino elegy with its concept of 'Pain City', in which a young man follows a beckoning girl across the meadows. She is not just a girl, though, but an allegory – she is a young Lament, who soon passes him on to an older one, who explains: 'We were once a great race, we Laments.' She leads the man across a 'landscape of mourning', in which emotions have coalesced into geological and biological phenomena – here there is a 'polished lump of primeval pain', there a 'petrified slag of anger', elsewhere 'fields of sadness in bloom' and 'herds of grief'. These are attempts to reconfigure the Earth, to wonder at it and enjoy it in new ways, to surround ourselves with new experiences, new metaphors for expressing emotions, to realize 'unconceived spaces'.

In wonder we have to wrest from the Earth its ways of singing; Rilke's way was by naming new ways of seeing, new concepts, new juxtapositions, to suggest new ways of being. It was also a way to overcome what he felt was the illusory idea of a unitary self; he was convinced that the way to understand 'being' was 'as a flow', rather than something static and unchanging.[15]

Short-cuts to Life

He was also forever on the lookout for metaphors that provided short-cuts, as in his poem about a fig tree. Significantly, this tree goes straight to the fruit state without blossoming. Rilke is asking here whether we have to accept the familiar botanical metaphor in our own lives: blossoming may be a beautiful process and a lovely word, but isn't it at root an unproductive, ephemeral waiting period and in that sense a waste of time, the very opposite of a short-cut? Elsewhere he asks whether some people are '*Ganze geborne*', 'born into the whole', born with the knowledge of the total unity of experience? Is that where poetry comes from?

And all this led Rilke to argue that death ought to be the logical culmination of life, 'not something invading it with hostile step'.[16] Here he introduced his powerful image of a glass that shatters while it is ringing, that destroys itself by and in its own intensity, a poetic journey to nothingness.[17] To this he added his concept of death as 'uniquely one's own'.

> For we are only leaf and skin,
> The mighty death which each one bears within,
> That is the core around which all revolves.

A 'mighty death', an individual death (not just a slinking-away in what he called a 'ready-made' death) after a lifetime's singing about the Earth in new ways, approximates the rules of existence that Rilke sought. Aspire to make your death an event of consequence.

He died as a poet, Leppmann says, because 'even in the face of death his own imagination was more important and more real to him than reality . . . Just as he had closed himself off from whole areas of life – career, wealth, marriage – for the sake of the inner world that informed his poetry, so too did he refuse to acknowledge his imminent end.' According to his doctor, although he was in considerable pain he chose to get by without resorting to painkillers, and he never asked what the disease was that he suffered from.[18] A mighty death indeed.*

'Two Ways of Being in the World'

Despite its length, Robert Musil's four-volume unfinished *The Man without Qualities* does not take such a radical form as some other

---

* Rilke had leukaemia.

modernist novels, such as Kafka's *The Castle*, Proust's *À la recherche du temps perdu*, Virginia Woolf's *The Waves* or James Joyce's *Finnegans Wake*; but it did have, like some of those other works, a direct relationship with the author's life.

Musil was born in Klagenfurt in Austria in 1880. His father was an engineer from an old aristocratic family and he was himself ennobled in 1917, barely a year before the Austrian nobility was abolished. His family had hoped that Robert would embrace a military career, but despite serving with distinction in the war he chose to attend various technical universities, where he did a doctoral thesis on philosophy, natural science and mathematics, and wrote a treatise on the physicist and philosopher Ernst Mach. Early on he had a fascination with science, with what he called the 'sacred aura of exactness', the 'sobriety' of its techniques and the lack of illusion in scientific inquiry. But this enthusiasm passed: the routine nature of much experimentation, and the difference he observed between the professional and personal lives of the engineers and technicians – the way they failed to uphold at home the standards they employed at work – disillusioned him, and he turned to writing. At various times he was editor of the literary magazine *Die Neue Rundschau* and a theatre critic, and he won both the Kleist Prize and the Gerhart Hauptmann Prize for his play *Die Schwärmer*, about a professor of psychology who becomes disillusioned with both his marriage and his scientific study.

During the 1920s Musil began *The Man without Qualities*, and worked on it almost daily. Like Georg Lukács, Walter Benjamin and Virginia Woolf, he believed that the novel was the mode appropriate to the philosophical situation of his generation and that it embodied 'that terrible wonder in the face of an irrational world'. Novels – his novel, anyway – were a kind of thought experiment, on a par with Einstein's or Picasso's, where a figure might be seen in profile and in full face at the same time. J.M. Coetzee has described *The Man without Qualities* 'as a book overtaken by history during its writing'. This is surely true in one sense, at least: after the first three parts were published, in 1930 and 1933, Musil, whose wife Martha was Jewish, was forced into exile in Switzerland. He memorably described Hitler as 'the living unknown soldier'.

The book is set in 1913, on the eve of the Great War, in the mythical country of Kakania. Kakania is clearly Austria-Hungary, the name referring to *Kaiserlich und Königlich*, or K.u.K. standing for the kingdom of Hungary and the imperial-royal Austrian crown lands. Though daunting in length, it is for many the most brilliant literary response to the developments of the early twentieth century, one of a handful of works 'incapable of over-interpretation'. It has been described as post-Bergson, post-Einstein, post-Rutherford, post-Bohr, post-Freud, post-Husserl, post-Picasso, post-Proust, post-Gide, post-Joyce and post-Wittgenstein. And, it goes without saying, post-Christian.

There are three intertwined themes, which provide a loose narrative. First, there is the search by the main character, Ulrich von . . ., a Viennese soldier-turned-engineer-turned-mathematician-turned-intellectual who models himself on the 'hard spiritual courage' of Nietzsche. His search to penetrate the meaning of modern life involves him in a project to understand the mind of one Moosbrugger, the murderer of a young prostitute. Ulrich is in his early thirties and unmarried and has recently returned to Vienna after several years abroad. Though his mind still works like that of a scientist, he is (like Musil himself) no longer inspired by the scientific approach – in fact, passion has largely left his life and he joins the pre-war Viennese world, partly social, partly intellectual. Second, there is Ulrich's relationship (and love affair) with his sister, Agathe, whom he had lost contact with in childhood. Third, the book is a social satire on the Vienna of the time. Musil had not completed the fourth part of his massive work when he died, nearly destitute, in Switzerland, in 1942. (He never lost his acerbity: 'Today they ignore us,' he told a friend. 'But once we are dead they will boast that they gave us asylum.')

Musil researched the book in an almost scientific way, gaining access to a murderer in a Viennese jail. At one point he has Ulrich note that the murderer is tall, with broad shoulders, that 'his chest cavity bulged like a spreading sail on a mast', but that on occasion he feels small and soft, like a 'jelly-fish floating in the water', when he reads a book that moves him. No one description, no one characteristic or quality, fits him. It is in this sense that he is a man without qualities: 'We no longer have any inner voices; reason tyrannises our lives.' Moosbrugger, who does not believe in God, only in what he can figure out for himself, runs his life according to a deadly logic (other people are there 'only to get in his way') which leads him to murder.

Thus, the real theme of the book is what it means to be human in a scientific age. If all we can believe in are our senses, if we can know ourselves only as scientists know us, if all generalizations and talk of values, ethics and aesthetics are meaningless, as the philosophers of the Vienna Circle were saying (see chapter 14), how are we to live? The writing is a *tour de force*, full of acerbic, original and witty observations: 'In times to come, when more is known, the word "destiny" will probably have acquired a statistical meaning.' 'The difference between a normal person and an insane one is precisely that the normal person has all the diseases of the mind, while the madman has only one.' 'One should love an idea like a woman; be overjoyed to get back to it.'[19]

Nevertheless, Musil never quite gave up hope that some way might one day be found to bring the advances of science and technology, and even military precision, to the realm of the spirit, though he realized how elusive this hope was. 'It is not in someone's gift any more to interpret his or her experiences without doubt, hesitation and second-guessing – with all our knowledge now, explanations of phenomena have, as it were, the heart cut out of them: kindness is a special form of egotism; emotions are glandular secretions; eight or nine tenths of a human being consists of water; moral freedom is an automatic by-product of free trade; statistical graphs of births and suicides show that our most intimate personal decisions are programmed behaviour. [Ulrich] is always right, but never productive, never happy, and never, except momentarily, engaged.'[20]

Musil accepts that the old categories in which men thought – the 'halfway house' ideas of racialism, or religion – are of no use any more, but what are we to replace them with? Like Rilke he offers the notion of submission through one of his characters, here Clarisse, married to Ulrich's estranged childhood companion. She decides that 'one is obliged to surrender oneself to an illusion if one received the grace of having one'. (This would find an echo across the Atlantic in the plays of Eugene O'Neill (see the next chapter).) Nothing is straightforward in *The Man without Qualities*, but this idea – that being able to form a stable relationship with one great overriding idea, knowing it to be only one alternative among many, amounting to a secular form of grace in the modern world – may be taken as a kind of conclusion. It echoes the 'shared fictions' of Henry James.

The Other Condition

Musil also used a particular – secular – definition of the soul, as 'a certain state of excitement', which arose from his view that there are two ways of being in the world – and these two ways are explored throughout *The Man without Qualities* and provide an idea of how we are to live in a disenchanted world. The 'normal condition', as he called it, is the world of science, business, capitalism, 'the scientific attitude toward things, which amounts to seeing things without love'.[21] 'In contrast to facts, actions, business, the politics of force ... stand love and poetry. These are conditions that rise above the transactions of the world.'

David Luft tells us that, for Musil, Eros is like art 'because it focuses attention; it abstracts, hypnotizes, and changes states of being in an attempt to affect the world in magical ways'. Musil was convinced that an age of science and capitalism had lost track of this suppressed side of the self. 'The normal condition is keyed to what is useful, the other condition to what is enhancing.' His point was not that the everyday reality we know is unimportant but that it is enclosed in clichés and not 'imaginatively challenged'.[22] He argued that the lack of understanding in the realm of the soul was the source of contemporary suffering, although for him, as noted, the soul was a form of excitement, and the 'religious' and 'ethical' task of the artist was to free the human being from the rigidity of tradition, whether intellectual or emotional, so as to use experience to engender – and enhance – more motivation.[23]

The real challenge for Musil was for mankind to work out ways of maximizing the amount of time an individual could spend in the other condition (he called it 'the other condition' because it was so undefined he did not think it right to use a more specific term). The real goal of a novel, for him, was not to take part in philosophical debate but to help 'the founding of the realm of the spirit'. The language of feelings had not kept pace with modern developments.[24] He thought that the average person in the 1920s was 'a far more involved metaphysician than he is usually willing to concede ... A dull, persistent feeling of his strange cosmic situation seldom leaves him. Death, the tininess of the earth, the dubious illusion of the self, the senselessness of existence, which become more pressing with the years: these are questions at which the average person scoffs, but which he nonetheless feels surrounding him all his life like the walls of a dark room.'[25]

Musil believed that all the great religions were born of the 'other condition', but they had become clichéd, 'rigid, hard and corrupt' like skeletons, and it was the job of literature – of all art – to regain this other condition. This is what part three of *The Man without Qualities* faces up to, the 'condition' of love between Ulrich and Agathe.[26] Musil thought there was a need for more femininity in modern culture, that women were more open to the other condition, which he described as 'a condition of the undisturbed insideness of life ... [Ulrich] wants to live *in* something rather than *for* something, insideness often being "a world without words".'[27] In their intense love relationship, Ulrich and Agathe become sensitive to the other way of relating to the world, 'they experience a spiritual union. In this dissolution of the borderline between ego and non-ego ... [they] experience a sense of participation in the world, a supra-heightening ... This holiday experience, beyond the tyranny of churches and moralists, provides the sense of insideness that has been missing from their lives.'[28]

Musil was at pains to say that this state of grace, the other condition, can never be made into a norm, and we shouldn't try. 'The normal human pattern is to take a vacation from one condition of being into the other.' We will know when we are in this state of grace, he says, because we experience it as a rising feeling, rather than the normal condition, one of sinking. When it occurs, this makes us 'not so much Godless as much more God-free'.[29]

Each of the individuals in this chain – Heidegger, Rilke, Musil – was much more imaginative than Weber. Re-enchanting the world is a much more positive activity than merely mourning its disenchantment.

12

The Imperfect Paradise

It was the age of the flapper, of bathtub gin and raucous jazz bands, of 'The Charleston'. It was the age of the silent-screen movie star, no graduated income tax and some of the longest, sleekest automobiles ever built. Speaking of the few short years between the end of the First World War and the stock market crash of 1929, F. Scott Fitzgerald wrote: 'The Jazz Age now raced along under its own power, served by great filling stations of money.' Here is Amory Blaine, the young autobiographical hero of Fitzgerald's 1920 novel, *This Side of Paradise*: 'I'm rather pagan at present. It's just that religion doesn't seem to have the slightest bearing on life at my age.' And the novel concludes: 'Here was a new generation, shouting the old cries, learning the old creeds, through a revery of long days and nights; destined finally to go out into that dirty, gray turmoil to follow love and pride; a new generation dedicated more than the last to the fear of poverty and the worship of success; grown up to find all Gods dead, all wars fought, all faiths in man shaken.' Fitzgerald's capture of the mood of the era was so accurate that Gertrude Stein labelled *This Side of Paradise* the Bible for the younger generation.[1]

Money Replaces God

Henry Idema, the author of several of the above sentences, argues that secularization, in America certainly, accelerated in the 1920s. In 1933 at the height of the Great Depression the novelist Sherwood Anderson wrote to a friend: 'You know, my dear, it is not only the hunger and destitution – it's something gone out of America – an old faith lost and no new one got.' Van Wyck Brooks, the critic and historian, said that the postwar generation found themselves 'born into a race that has drained away all its spiritual resources in the struggle to survive and that continues to struggle in the midst of plenty because life itself no longer possesses any meaning'. Idema found three things happening simultaneously during that time: an increase in neurosis, due to the absence of the comfort people had traditionally enjoyed from the established Churches; the 'privatization' of religion; and a shift away from religious traditions towards affluence and materialism.[2]

Idema, an ordained Episcopalian clergyman with a PhD in religion and psychological studies from the University of Chicago (see chapter 18), thought that secularization had psychological roots. For him traditional religion derived its power, as Freud had said, from the family – the young child in its pre-oedipal state finding protection in the mother and later deriving discipline and respect for authority from the father. The two-parent family, in Idema's words, was a Freudian love triangle that the child learned to negotiate to achieve emotional maturity, and where many of the basic familial psychological functions, of protection and authority, were taken over by the churches. In the modern world, however, where, increasingly, mothers went out to work and were absent for long periods, and fathers might be even more absent, working unsocial hours in an often distant factory, the young child no longer interiorized parental values in the traditional way, and so no longer looked to the Church.

Idema found support for his arguments in the sociological landmark *Middletown* by Robert and Helen Lynd, a survey of what was later revealed as Muncie in Indiana, recording, among other things, the impact of new industries on a middle-American town – in particular the roles of the radio, the movie projector, the phonograph, the telephone, cosmetics and above all the automobile. In *Echoes of the Jazz Age* Scott Fitzgerald remembered exactly that: 'As far back as 1915 the unchaperoned young people of the smaller cities had discovered the mobile privacy of that automobile given to young Bill at sixteen to make him "self-reliant". At first petting was a desperate adventure even under such favourable conditions, but presently confidences were exchanged and the old commandment broke down.'[3] The automobile had become 'a house of prostitution on wheels', according to one Middletown judge, while 'Sunday driving' was denounced by the town's ministers.

Partly, the Great War was responsible. John Peale Bishop, a classmate of Fitzgerald's at Princeton, certainly thought so: 'The most tragic thing about the war was not that it made so many dead men, but that it destroyed the tragedy of death. Not only did the young suffer in the war, but so did every abstraction that would have sustained and given dignity to their suffering. The war made the traditional morality unacceptable; it did not annihilate it; it revealed its immediate inadequacy. So that at its end, the survivors were left to face, as best they could, a world without values.'

Disillusionment, in particular in regard to religion, stands out in the American novels of the period: in Hemingway's *The Sun Also Rises* and *A Farewell to Arms*, Sherwood Anderson's *Beyond Desire*, *Winesburg, Ohio*, *Dark Laughter* and *Windy McPherson's Son*, Fitzgerald's *The Great Gatsby* and *Tender Is the Night*. And, as Edmund Wilson noted about Fitzgerald's *The Beautiful and Damned*: 'The hero and heroine are strange creatures without purpose or method, who give themselves up to wild debaucheries and do not, from beginning to end of the book, perform a single serious act: but you somehow get the impression that, in spite of their madness, they are the most rational people . . . wherever they touch the common life, the institutions of men are made to appear a contemptible farce of the futile and the absurd . . . The inference is that, in such a civilization, the sanest and most credible thing is to live for the jazz of the moment and forget the activities of men.'

After the automobile, and perhaps even ahead of it, the expansion of education was regarded, by the Lynds at least, as the most secularizing force, in particular higher education. 'Education,' they wrote, 'is a faith, a religion.' It had the effects it did partly because, in taking them away to university, higher education helped young people break with home traditions. But it was not only that. 'Education appears to be desired frequently not for its specific content, but as a symbol.' It stood in many people's minds for an openness to alternatives to traditional (religious) values and in this way 'replaced religion as the most significant guide to life'. Fitzgerald captured some of this, too, in his story 'Benediction', where Lois explains to her brother, a Roman Catholic priest and monk, 'I don't want to shock you, Keith, but I can't tell you how – how *inconvenient* being a Catholic is. It doesn't seem to apply any more. As far as morals go, some of the wildest boys I know are Catholics. And the brightest boys – I mean the ones who think and read a lot, don't seem to believe in much of anything any more.'[4]

Science mattered too. The Lynds concurred with Fitzgerald on evolution. In *This Side of Paradise* Amory Blaine says of the older generation, 'They shuddered when they found out what Dr Darwin was about.' In Middletown, the Lynds discovered that '[t]he theory of evolution has shaken the theological cosmogony that had reigned for centuries'. Alongside this came the rise of modern psychology. In his book *Only Yesterday*, published in 1931, the American historian and editor of *Harper's* Frederick Lewis Allen put it this way: 'Of all the sciences it was the youngest and least scientific which most captivated the general public and had the most disintegrating effect upon religious faith. Psychology was king. Freud, Adler, Jung and Watson had their tens of thousands of votaries.'[5]

Idema went on to say that, despite the undoubted attractions of the changes overtaking America in the 1920s, a price was to be paid. There was, he said, an 'extraordinary increase' in neurosis, in divorce, in sexual and emotional conflict, which was reflected in both the literature of the time and in the personal lives of the authors. Sherwood Anderson's *Beyond Desire* was originally to be called 'No God'. One contemporary said of Fitzgerald, 'When Scott ceased to go to mass he began to drink.'[6]

Idema argues that Anderson's books mainly chronicle 'the American loneliness' that accompanied the weakening of traditional religious practices and that the same is true, to an extent, of Ernest Hemingway's. 'It was given to Hawthorne to dramatize the human soul,' wrote John Peale Bishop. 'In our time Hemingway wrote the drama of its disappearance.' More than that, though, Idema says Hemingway was especially concerned with the breakdown of religious communities and that the young replaced them with new communities that had their own secular rituals.

Idema shows, for instance, in *The Sun Also Rises* that the protagonist Jake Barnes finds in trout fishing and bullfighting 'the peace he does not find in the church'. 'In the novel,' he writes, 'religion no longer functions for Jake and his peers. Trout fishing and bullfighting become its secular substitutes. They function *like* church rituals and, thus, replace them. In an important sense, then, *The Sun Also Rises* depicts trout fishing and bullfighting as secular (even pagan), psychological, and private – not religious.'[7] Idema goes on: 'An efficacious ritual, whether sacred or secular, integrates thoughts with emotions. Second, ritual binds the anxiety of individuals.'

The critic Irving Howe had this to say about Anderson's Winesburg inhabitants: 'They are distraught communicants in search of a ceremony, a social value, a manner of living, a lost ritual that may, by some means, re-establish a flow and exchange of emotion.' In an early Hemingway story 'Big Two-Hearted River', the prolegomenon to *The Sun Also Rises*, the main character Nick Adams engages in a number of rituals in preparation for trout fishing – splitting off a slab of pine, putting up his tent, gathering grasshoppers *properly*. Carlos Baker, professor of literature at Princeton, says that one of Hemingway's father's favourite words was 'properly'. 'When in the outdoors with his son, everything had to be done in the proper way, whether building a fire, rigging a rod, baiting a hook, casting a fly, handling a gun, or roasting a duck or a haunch of venison.'

Henry Idema compares all this with what the Lynds observed in Middletown: 'When religion began to decline, people sought out secular "centres of 'spiritual' activity".' The Lynds mentioned the 'service' and 'civic loyalty' ethic of the Rotary Club and even the town's (very successful) basketball team. '"Rotary and its big ideal of Service is my religion," said one Sunday School worker in Middletown.

"I have gotten more out of it than I ever got out of the church.'"[8]

In *Death in the Afternoon* Hemingway was more specific in comparing bullfighting with Church ritual. He insisted on the ancient origins of both, compared matadors with altar boys and wrote that bullfighting 'takes a man out of himself and makes him feel immortal', 'gives him an ecstasy that is, while momentary, as profound as any religious ecstasy'. Bullfighting also creates a community, he said, a temporary community 'moving all the people in the ring together and increasing in emotional intensity as it proceeds'.[9]

But the most obvious effect of secularization from the 1920s to the 1980s, says Idema, is America's obsession with affluence and its symbols. Sherwood Anderson faced this issue in *Winesburg, Ohio*, where money replaces God as the unifying symbol in the life of Jesse, the main character, who nonetheless suffers a nervous breakdown. But it was Scott Fitzgerald above all who best described this new surrogate religion. Fitzgerald himself was raised a Catholic but came to regard money, not religion, as the source of security. In 'A Diamond as Big as the Ritz' one character says of his hometown: 'The simple piety prevalent in Hades has the earnest worship of and respect for riches as the first article of its creed – had John felt otherwise than radiantly humble before them, his parents would have turned away in horror at the blasphemy.'

Something Gorgeous that Has Nothing to Do with God

And then there was *Gatsby*. At one point a short story, 'Absolution' was going to form the first part of the book, a picture of Gatsby's early life. It was not, in the event, included in the final version, but tells the story of Rudolph Miller, a young boy growing up in the city of St Paul in Minnesota, forced by his strict Roman Catholic father to confess the sin of lying to the local parish priest. The boy is fearful of this encounter but finds to his amazement that the priest has the humanity to show him that he himself is in an even worse state, and rambles on about an amusement park with a big wheel 'made of lights turning in the air', urging the boy to go and see it. 'All this talking seemed particularly strange and awful to Rudolph, because this man was a priest. He sat there, half terrified, his beautiful eyes wide open and staring at Father Schwartz. But underneath his terror he felt that his own inner convictions were confirmed. There was something ineffably gorgeous somewhere that had nothing to do with God.'

Fitzgerald returned to this theme several times, once in 'A Diamond as Big as the Ritz' where a group of men in the fictional town of Fish gather each evening to watch the passing of the seven o'clock transcontinental express train from Chicago: 'The men of Fish were beyond all religion – the barest and most savage tenets of even Christianity could gain no foothold on that barren rock – so there was no altar, no priest, no sacrifice; only each night at seven at the silent concourse by the shanty depot, a congregation who lifted up a prayer of dim, anaemic wonder – here too was something gorgeous that had nothing to do with God.'[10]

The Next Greatest Power to Faith

At one point in his career Wallace Stevens broke his right hand in two places after provoking a drunken fight in Key West with Ernest Hemingway, cracking the other man's jaw and getting knocked to the floor himself. At another point, discouraged from drinking alcohol by his wife, he turned himself into a connoisseur of teas. This may make Stevens seem like a colourful bohemian, but this was a man who, from 1916 until his death nearly forty years later in 1955, was a three-piece-suit-and-tie businessman, head of the fidelity and surety claims department at the Accident and Indemnity Company in Hartford, Connecticut. Stevens is not easy to pigeon-hole, and that certainly applies to his artistic activities.

He was one of the finest exponents of an art form that blossomed throughout the twentieth century – a poet who wrote fascinating and exquisite prose. He used his prose above all to explain art and literature. One of his chief arguments was that in an age when God is dead, the arts in general, and poetry in particular, must take over – because God, like poetry, is an imaginary construct, and the greatest satisfactions to be had from life lie in the exploration and exploitation of the imagination. He also argued more clearly than most that the two rival phenomena that would replace God in the modern world were poetry and psychology. He was adamant that poetry was the better option.

Stevens was a slow starter. He and his siblings were read to from the Bible every night by their mother, who sat at the piano on Sunday evenings to play and sing hymns. At Reading Boys' School in the early 1890s, because of his poker and football activities he failed his exams. But he soon made up for lost time, winning prizes, delivering a prize-winning oration at school, entering Harvard in 1897 (where he met and was taught by George Santayana) and publishing his first poem a few months later, in January 1898. He would eventually win a Pulitzer Prize, the Bollingen Prize, a National Book Award and an honorary degree from Yale (the 'greatest prize for a Harvard man').

Stevens was exceptionally plain-speaking in his prose, and confidently advocated placing poetry at the centre of life. He considered Christianity 'an exhausted culture' and thought that 'loss of faith is growth'. As he freely admitted, he entertained a 'vast premise' that the world might be 'transformed in and through' a great work of art. 'God and the imagination are one. After one has abandoned belief in God, poetry is that essence which takes its place as life's redemption.'[11]

His work abounds in sentiments that directly address our theme:

> Poetry
> Exceeding music must take the place
> Of empty heaven and its hymns . . .

And:

> What is divinity if it can come
> Only in silent shadows and in dreams?
> Shall she not find in comforts of the sun,
> In pungent fruit and bright, green wings, or else

In any balm or beauty of the earth,
Things to be cherished like the thought of heaven?
. . .

Shall our blood fail? Or shall it come to be
The blood of paradise? And shall the earth
Seem all of paradise that we shall know?
The sky will be much friendlier then than now . . .[12]

'The paramount relation between painting and poetry today, between modern man and modern art, is simply this: that in an age in which disbelief is so profoundly prevalent or, if not disbelief, indifference to questions of belief, poetry and painting, and the arts in general, are, in their measure, a compensation for what has been lost. Men feel that the imagination is the next greatest power to faith: the reigning prince. Consequently their interest in the imagination and its work is to be regarded not as a phase of humanism but as a vital self-assertion in a world in which nothing but the self remains, if that remains . . . The extension of the mind beyond the range of the mind, the projection of reality beyond reality, the determination to cover the ground, whatever it may be, the determination not to be confined, the recapture of excitement and intensity of interest, the enlargement of the spirit at every time, in every way, these are the unities, the relations, to be summarized as paramount now.'[13]

'In an age of disbelief, in a time that is largely humanistic (much the same thing), in one sense or another, it is for the poet to supply the satisfactions of belief . . . I think of it as a role of the utmost seriousness. It is, for one thing, a spiritual role . . . To see the gods dispelled in mid-air and dissolve like clouds is one of the great human experiences. It is not as though they had gone over the horizon to disappear for a time; nor as if they had been overcome by other gods of greater power and profounder knowledge. It is simply that they came to nothing . . . What was most extraordinary is that they left no mementoes behind, no thrones, no mystic rings, no texts either of the soil or the soul. It was as if they had never inhabited the earth. There was no crying out for their return. They were not forgotten because they had been part of the glory of the earth. At the same time, no man ever muttered a petition in his heart for the restoration of those unreal shapes. There was always in every man the increasingly human self, which instead of remaining the observer, the non-participant, the delinquent, became constantly more and more all there was or so it seemed . . . Thinking about the end of the gods creates singular attitudes in the mind of the thinker. One attitude is that the gods of classical mythology were merely aesthetic projections. They were not the objects of belief. They were expressions of delight . . . It is one of the normal activities of humanity, in the solitude of reality and in the unworthy treatment of solitude, to create companions, a little colossal as I have said, who, if not superficially explicative, are, at least, assumed to be full of the secret of things . . . However all that may be, the celestial atmosphere of these deities, their ultimate remote celestial residences, are not matters of chance. Their fundamental glory is the fundamental glory of men and women, who being in need of it create it, elevate it, without too much searching of its identity. The people, not the priests, made the gods.'[14]

Later, Stevens said, during a lecture: 'My purpose this morning is to elevate the poem to the level of one of the major significances of life and to equate it, for the purpose of discussion, with gods and men . . . The gods are the creation of the imagination at its utmost . . . It comes to this, that we use the same faculties when we write poetry that we use when we create gods . . .'[15] In the absence of a belief in God, the mind turns to its own creations and examines them, not alone from the aesthetic point of view, but for what they reveal, for what they validate and invalidate, for the support that they give. God and the imagination are one.'[16]

This must be one of the most sustained attempts in modern literature to seek out a way to live without God. Stevens was not afraid to contemplate 'big' questions; he well realized that *appetite* is a crucial ingredient in the fulfilled life. And so, at the same time that he was making grand claims for the arts, embracing that 'vast premise' that he spoke about, he was equally ambitious in setting out what poetry is, its exact place in our lives, how it helps us, what it can achieve. 'A poet looks out at the world,' he said, 'somewhat as a man looks at a woman', a statement at once poetic and designed to get everyone's attention. He firmly insisted that poetry is

Sounds passing through sudden rightnesses
Containing the mind, below which it cannot descend.

The role of the poet, he insisted, 'is to help people live their lives . . . Poetry should provide the resistance to the pressure of reality through the activity of the imagination.' Nor was he afraid of any elitist implications. 'It is a world of fact given to us by someone with a range of sensibility greater than our own, a poetic sensibility. It is an *enlarged* world of fact, an "incandescence of the intelligence".' Like light, it adds nothing but itself. Close to the heat of that light, we can be said to live more intensely.[17] 'Enchanting should be understood literally, as singing the world into existence.' At its best, poetry 'offers an experience of the world as meditation, the mind slowing in front of things, the mind pushing back against the pressure of reality through the minimal transfigurations of the imagination.' There was, he thought, a kind of 'soul-peace' to be had through poetry.[18]

A poet writes about things, he said, and his words 'are of things that do not exist without words'. At the same time he was aware, as Valéry had been, that 'the mind's desire will always exceed the beauty that poetry can bring to reality'. He was drawn to poetry (rather than science, say) because in human nature 'one is better satisfied by particulars'. 'Poetic value is an intrinsic value. It is not the value of knowledge. It is not the value of faith. It is the value of the imagination.'[19]

In saying that God is a work of the imagination – as is poetry, or any successful artwork – Stevens also thought that many metaphysical and philosophical ideas are inherently poetic: that is to say, products of the imagination. The notion of 'infinity' was essentially poetic ('cosmic poetry', he called it), as were the idea of the Hegelian state, and, perhaps most pertinently for this book, the ideas of 'final cause' and 'wholeness', which people seem to find so important. (Does it make sense to speak of the 'final cause' of poetry? he asked.) The way in which a poem can suddenly 'enlarge' our lives, effect a change in us that is like going from winter straight into spring, is the creation of meaning; of approaching – however briefly – a feeling of wholeness. 'There is no wing like meaning,' he said. And we must hold within us the realization that '[i]t is not every day that the world arranges itself in a poem'.

'The poet is a stronger life . . . The poet feels *abundantly* the poetry of everything. The tongue is an eye but the eye sees less than the tongue says and the tongue says less than the mind thinks.' (Compare Valéry.) 'Poetry sometimes crowns the search for happiness. It is itself a search for happiness.' 'The purpose of poetry is to make life complete in itself.' 'Reality is a cliché/ From which we escape by metaphor.'[20]

There is nothing here that one would wish to fight with Stevens over. In making clear claims for the supremacy of poetry he manages to escape into metaphors that enlarge, reinforce and exemplify his arguments. And he chooses his moments to extend his claims to life in general and the role of the imagination in it. Here he brings a poet's command of language, and imagination, into observations, or *aperçus*, that are both general and specific and have almost a biblical quality: 'The imperfect is our only paradise.'[21] 'We receive but what we give/ And in our life alone does nature live.'[22] 'Things simply are, and are not molded to a human purpose.'

Elsewhere he speaks of 'the "neverthelessness" of nature'. 'The imagination is the power of the mind over the possibilities of things.' 'Life is a composite of the propositions about it.' 'Life lived on the basis of opinion is more nearly life than life lived without opinion.'

And perhaps this is Stevens's most significant observation, which coincides with and extends Valéry's main point: 'We never arrive intellectually. But emotionally we arrive constantly (as in poetry, happiness, high mountains, vistas).'[23] Once we understand this distinction, he is saying, once we accept that we will never feel whole intellectually or philosophically, we can get on and enjoy the emotional (artistic, imaginative) wholenesses, the 'sudden rightnesses', that *are* available to us.

So Happy for a Time

In the depths of the Depression, following the Wall Street crash of October 1929, only twenty-eight out of the eighty-six legitimate theatres on Broadway were still open, but Eugene O'Neill's *Mourning Becomes Electra* had sold out even its top-of-the-range six-dollar seats. O'Neill had been confirmed as 'the great US playwright, the man with whom true American theatre really begins', long before *Mourning*, which premiered on 26 October 1931.[24] Curiously, however, it was not until the other end of the decade, by which time O'Neill had turned fifty, that his two great masterpieces *The Iceman Cometh* and *Long Day's Journey into Night* were written. The intervening years have become known as 'the Silence'. We shall see how wrong this epithet is.

More than for most artists, certain biographical details are crucial to understanding his work. He had lost his faith in the summer of 1903 when he suddenly refused to go to mass with his father, and insisted on transferring from a Catholic school to a secular one.[25] Thereafter he always felt there was a 'spiritual vacancy' in his life and, as an adult, spoke of himself as a 'Black Irishman', one of the fallen, with a black soul.

When he was not yet fourteen, he found out that his own birth had precipitated a morphine addiction in his mother. He also discovered that his parents blamed their first son Jamie for infecting their second son Edmund with measles, from which he had died, aged eighteen months. When, in 1902, Ella O'Neill ran out of morphine, she attempted suicide; this set off in Eugene, then in adolescence, a period of binge drinking and self-destructive behaviour; he also began to hang around theatres (his father was an actor). After an unsuccessful marriage he attempted suicide himself, overdosing in a flophouse in 1911, after which he saw several psychiatrists; a year later his TB was diagnosed. In 1921 his father died tragically from cancer, his mother's death following in 1922; his brother Jamie died twelve months after that from a stroke, which followed an alcoholic psychosis – he was forty-five.

O'Neill had intended to study science at Princeton, but at university he was greatly influenced by his discovery of Nietzsche (his 'literary idol', as he put it), and adopted an approach to life that his biographer calls 'scientific mysticism'. He was eventually removed from the course because he attended so few classes. He began writing in 1912, as a journalist, but before long turned to plays. Autobiography apart, his dramatic philosophy may be inferred from his verdict on the United States: America, 'instead of being the most successful country in the world, it is the greatest failure. It's the greatest failure because it was given everything, more than any other country . . . its main idea is that everlasting game of trying to possess your own soul by the possession of something outside it.'

Politically, O'Neill was drawn to anarchism, and he always maintained a healthy disdain for capitalism, which promoted a 'vicious materialism', an acquisitiveness which invited people to 'clutch at everything but holding nothing fast', and 'put the mind to sleep'.[26] Nor was he totally sold on democracy which, he felt, when combined with capitalism, made America the land of desire, where people felt free to 'take what they want', where desire 'knows no bounds' (and therefore 'the soul knows no rest'); where, in fact, 'democracy is the expression of desire', in which man 'is one-tenth spirit and nine-tenths hog'. 'Success is still our only real living religion,' he wrote.[27]

But we are still only halfway there. As J.P. Diggins explains, 'For O'Neill, as for the modern philosopher, existence may have no meaning, yet the rage to live is stronger than the reason for life.' Desire can mean the need to avenge a wrong, the demand for social recognition, the greed for a piece of property, lust for another's body, but O'Neill saw power as the ultimate form of desire. Even so, and despite his political interests, he conceived power as the expression of the desire to control and dominate that has more to do with personal relations than with political activity.[28]

And that is why, probably, although he wrote three plays explicitly about religion – *Dynamo* (science versus religion), *Lazarus Laughed* (the dread of death) and *Days without End* (atheism, socialism, anarchism) – it is his two late masterpieces that most claim our attention (*The Iceman* has often been called a religious play). These works reflect his stated view that 'there are no values to live by today'. All the characters have seen better days, and all they have left is to fantasize about the future 'as the return of a past more imagined than true'. They need no guidance to recognize that 'one can be sentenced to life for simply living it'.

O'Neill shared with James Joyce a passion for finding larger meanings in small things, 'to make the rut of everyday life resound with meaning and significance'. And he shared with George Moore the conviction that 'all a man's interests are limited to those near him-self'.[29] He liked to say that theatre was a temple 'where the religion of poetic interpretation and symbolic celebration of life is communi-cated to human beings, starved in spirit by their soul-stifling struggle to exist as masks among the masks of the living'.

But above all – and this is where the drama in his plays chiefly lies – he knew that desire and its discontents can be a form of blindness. His plays show characters whose identities are *fixed* (unlike Shaw's, say), making difficult their attempts to clarify their own feelings and know their own reasons, as people who 'refuse to accept excuses as explanation'.

Both *The Iceman Cometh* and *Long Day's Journey* last several hours, and both are talking plays with little action. The characters, and the audience, are trapped in the same room, where conversation is unavoidable.

In *The Iceman* the characters are all assembled in the back room of Harry Hope's saloon, where they drink and tell each other the same stories day in, day out, stories that are in fact hopes and illusions that will never happen. One man wants to get back into the police force, another to be re-elected as a politician, a third simply wants to go home. As time goes by, from one thing and another that is said, the audience grasps that even these characters' far from exceptional aims are illusions – pipe dreams, in O'Neill's words. Later it becomes clear that they are waiting for Hickey, a travelling salesman who, they be-lieve, will make things happen, be their saviour (Hickey is the son of a preacher). But when Hickey finally appears, he punctures their dreams one by one.

O'Neill is not making the glib point that reality is invariably cold. What he is saying is that there *is* no reality; there are no firm values, no ultimate meanings, and so all of us need our pipe dreams and illusions (our fictions, if you like). Hickey leads an 'honest' life; he works and tells himself the truth, or what he thinks of as the truth. But it turns out that he has killed his wife because he could not bear the way she 'simply' accepted the fact of his numerous casual infidelities. We never know how she explained her life to herself (this is crucial, as we have seen, how we explain our lives to ourselves), what illusions she had and how she kept herself going. But, we realize, and this too is vital: they *did* keep her going.

The *Iceman*, of course, is death and it has often been remarked that the play could be called 'Waiting for Hickey', emphasizing the similarities to Samuel Beckett's *Waiting for Godot* (which we shall come to, as we shall also return to the concept of waiting and what it means).

Long Day's Journey is O'Neill's most autobiographical work, a 'play of old sorrow, written in tears and blood'. The action takes place in one room, in four acts, at four times of the day, at breakfast, lunch, dinner and bedtime, when the members of the Tyrone family gather together. As already mentioned, there are no great action scenes, but there are two events: Mary Tyrone returns to her dope addiction, and Edmund Tyrone (who is Eugene's brother, who died) discovers he has TB. As the day wears on, the weather outside turns darker and foggier, and the house seems more and more isolated. Various episodes are revisited time and again in the conversation, as characters reveal more about themselves and give their version of events recounted earlier by others.

At the play's core is O'Neill's pessimistic view of life's 'strange determinism'. 'None of us can help the things life has done to us,' says Mary. 'They're done before you realize it, and once they're done they make you do other things until at last everything comes between you and what you'd like to be, and you've lost your true self forever.' Elsewhere, one brother says to the other, 'I love you much more than I hate you.' And then, right at the end, the three Tyrone men, Mary's husband and two sons, watch her enter the room in a deep dream, her own fog. They watch as she laments, 'That was in the winter of senior year. Then in the spring something happened to me. Yes, I remember. I fell in love with James Tyrone and was so happy for a time.'

As Normand Berlin has written, it is those three final words of the play, 'for a time', that are so heartbreaking. O'Neill's relatives hated the play. For him, it was a mystery how one can be in love, and then not in love, and then be trapped for ever. In such devastating ways, he is saying, the past lives on in the present, and this is something science has nothing to say about.[30]

The Spiritual Middle Class and the Life-lie

We must allow for the fact that, as Berlin has also said, O'Neill was a 'gazer into abysses'. Like Nietzsche, he considered Greek tragedy the unsurpassed example of art *and* religion. Tragedy, he said, 'is the meaning of life – and the hope. The noblest is eternally the most tragic. The people who succeed and do not push on to a greater failure are the spiritual middle classes.' As Egil Törnqvist of the University of Amsterdam has put it, 'The struggle of Nietzsche's ideal man to turn himself into a superman (*Übermensch*) is the struggle also of the O'Neill protagonist. As the playwright himself said in an early interview: "A man wills his own defeat when he pursues the unattainable. But his *struggle* is his success!"' He goes on: 'For Nietzsche the tragic spirit equaled a religious faith . . . Out of the need to justify existence after the death of the old God was born the concept of the superman, the man who welcomes pain as a necessity for inner growth and who, like the protagonists in Greek tragedy, achieves spiritual attainment through suffering.'[31]

O'Neill accepted Nietzsche's argument, and in an often quoted statement commented: 'The playwright today must dig at the roots of the sickness of today as he feels it – the death of the old God and the failure of science and materialism to give any satisfying new one for the surviving primitive religious instinct to find a meaning for life in, and to comfort its fears of death with.'[32] Elsewhere, he said that the only cure for the sickness of today 'is through an exultant acceptance of life'.

For him that meant an acceptance of suffering, even within the family, *especially* within the family, and that brings with it the necessity of the 'life-lie', the idea that a man cannot live without illusions – about himself. For O'Neill the riddle of life is insoluble, whether we see our problems as psychological or metaphysical; essentially the search for the meaning of life is equivalent to finding a justification for suffering.[33] Simon Harford, in *More Stately Mansions* (written in the late 1930s but not produced until 1952), echoes Paul Valéry in asserting that men's lives 'are without any meaning whatever . . . human life is a silly disappointment, a liar's promise . . . a daily appointment with peace and happiness in which we wait day after day, hoping against hope.'[34]

Professor Berlin makes much of the fact that *The Iceman Cometh* was only tepidly received in New York on its first production in 1946, but was much more successful ten years later when it opened two weeks after Samuel Beckett's *Waiting for Godot*. As Berlin rightly says, the two plays occupy the same metaphysical ground. O'Neill himself felt that he had achieved a lot with *Iceman*. In a letter to Lawrence Langner he said: 'There are moments in it that suddenly strip the soul of a man stark naked, not in cruelty or moral superiority, but with an understanding compassion which sees him as a victim of the ironies of life and of himself. Those moments are for me the depth of tragedy, with nothing more that can possibly be said.'[35] Irony and tragedy: this was Paul Fussell's point in his book about the First World War (see chapter 9).

Forgiveness – and Faith – in the Family

O'Neill believed that illusions must be shared – and be sharable – if life is to be liveable; we all have them, and they are no disgrace (though he does refer to philosophers at one point as 'foolosophers').

At a time when, as we have noted, psychology came to replace – or attempted to replace – religion in people's lives, it is worth pointing out that, as much as anyone and far more than most, O'Neill homes in on the family as the locus – for most people – of the most 'significantly lived experience, complex and deep and passionate'. 'The love–hate within a family, the closeness–distance, the loneliness within a to-getherness, the guilt and need for forgiveness, the knowing and not knowing a loved one, the bewilderment in the face of a mysterious determinism – this is the human condition.' As *Long Day* draws to a close and Mary enters the room – the centre of the lives of her three men – they are sharing the death of hope; but they endure, and the human bond 'seems to transcend the stage'.[36]

O'Neill's late plays all show characters seeking a higher ground for human experience, hoping to endow that contemporary experience with transcendent meaning, highlighting the conflict – especially sharp in the United States, O'Neill felt – between materialistic greed and the desire for spiritual transcendence.[37] In *Dynamo* (1929) the search for 'God-replacements' (O'Neill's words) looked at Puritanism versus Science (electricity), which he regarded as no less futile. In America, he thought, even the arts had been taken over by a business ethic, and even the pursuit of knowledge for its own sake had been corrupted by the lure of grants for research. Money and wealth were false gods, and rather than 'waste time on the accumulation of material wealth or the illusion of power through the accumulation of knowledge', America should look to its spiritual health.

In truth O'Neill saw little hope that this search could be mounted, let alone succeed; but a starting point lay in the recognition that the human condition is 'innately contradictory', that suffering is a big part of it, and that there is no help for it, but we have a capacity for suffering and tragedy is, by its nature, 'both devastating and uplifting'.[38]

Again, this measure of self-understanding must be seen against the background of the family. Families, for O'Neill, are full of private spaces, secrets and concealments in which, despite all, understanding and forgiveness must be found. The importance of the family – unlike for Freud – lay not in the way it affected one's life in the early years, shaping character, but in its *continued* importance throughout life, as the site where our illusions cannot be maintained because fellow family members know too much, where excuses can never be offered or accepted as explanations. The family is where mutuality is to be achieved, despite everything and in the acknowledgement that intimacy can be as painful as it can be rewarding.

And happiness is no final state, any more than is fulfilment. The only 'final' state is self-understanding and, depending on what has gone before in a life, there is no saying what that may be. It may as easily be negative as positive. We should not expect anything else.

13

Living Down to Fact

One of Virginia Woolf's most famous statements, made in 'Mr Bennett and Mrs Brown' (1924), is that 'on or about December, 1910, human nature changed'.[1] The first version of this essay had been written in reply to an article by Arnold Bennett in which he argued that the foundation of good fiction 'is character-creating and nothing else', and asserted that Woolf's characters 'do not vitally survive in the mind because the author has been obsessed by details of originality and cleverness'. What Virginia Woolf meant by her remark was that there were so many cultural changes happening simultaneously that they were experienced as a change in nature. She added: 'All human relations have shifted – those between masters and servants, husbands and wives, parents and children. And when human relations change there is at the same time a change in religion, conduct, politics and literature.'

Her remarks arose partly out of her interest in painting, in how it differed from writing, and her interest in psychology, in particular psychoanalysis. The Hogarth Press, which she and her husband Leonard had founded in 1917, had begun publishing translations of Freud's work in the early 1920s. Virginia was impressed by painting's ability to present details simultaneously, whereas writing was linear, and she was impressed too by painting's other ability – explored in Cubism and Expressionism – to look at an object from different standpoints, often distorting images in the process. Recent science, too, she knew, had insisted on the distortions inherent in human perception.

Her interest in psychoanalysis (fuelled by her descents into madness throughout her life) also told her that people rarely *thought* in linear ways, as Arnold Bennett's stories implied. Rather, we think in 'splashes', as she put it, verbal splashes reflecting 'eddies of feeling' that are anything but linear. It was this, among other things, that she sought to express in her work.

Her awareness of the changes taking place around her was Woolf's chief strength in the long run – in fact, she never gave up her interest in change. Throughout the 1920s, arguably her most productive decade, one of her self-imposed tasks as a novelist, one of them anyway, was to describe God 'in the process of change'. She was very conscious of the nineteenth-century materialists, as she called them, and their concern with facts rather than with the souls of their characters. She praised James Joyce's *Ulysses* as an attempt 'to find an appropriate modern form of spiritual feeling' (see p. 270 for Joyce's attitude to fact).

Charisma and Everyday Life

Woolf was conscious, as Max Weber was conscious, of the 'disenchantment' of the modern world – what he called the 'routinization of charisma' – and she sought to bring about what he thought of as the greatest contemporary challenge, 'the return of charisma to everyday life'. One answer for Weber was the investment of charismatic authority, an emotional force, in gifted individuals (Hitler being one unfortunate example), but Woolf was much more concerned with the charisma that might be found in the ordinary. She developed a theory that, alongside the everyday – time spent enveloped by, as she put it, 'cotton wool' – there were 'moments of being', secular sacred moments 'in which experience enters the sublime, moments that transform and energise all the moments of non-being that surrounded them'. It was the business of art to identify these moments, describe them in as memorable a way as possible, and in that way preserve them.

By so doing, Woolf maintained, modern fiction could challenge modern civilization's preoccupation with material matters 'at the expense of other values'. In her books, different sets of values compete with each other and in this way she conceived the modern world as analogous to the pagan world, with many gods – not one – each representing some aspect of life but not the totality, and reconcilable only temporarily. 'The essential challenge for the modern novelist is to produce such moments of reconciliation without imposing a false harmony on the world of brute fact.'[2]

The change that Woolf identified meant that the world was no longer perceived by everyone in the same way, there were no longer fixed points of reference, no common grounds of agreement, no shared beliefs or communal experiences – the world was 'fragmented, unstable, asymmetrical'. Moreover, this put readers in an era of change, too: 'We, as readers, had to synthesise the broken pieces for ourselves. We had to make our own harmony, our own wholeness.'[3] This fitted with her remark about the change she perceived as having taken place in December 1910, in that for her (and, she believed, for others too) 'reality was no longer public' – it was private, personal, idiosyncratic, subjectively construed.

It followed from this that, as both Weber and Woolf recognized, spiritual experience in the modern world – without churches, still less cathedrals – could only be found in the intimate sphere; that since communion with God was no longer possible, communion with other people in an intimate embrace was its only replacement. 'Precisely the ultimate and most sublime values have retreated from public life either into the transcendental realm of mystic life or into the brotherliness of direct and personal human relations. It is not accidental that our greatest art is intimate and not monumental, nor is it accidental that today [1917] only within the smallest and intimate circles, in personal human situations, in *pianissimo*, something is pulsating that corresponds to the prophetic *pneuma* [spirit], which in former times swept through the great communities like a firebrand, welding them together.'[4]

Pianissimo is perhaps the crucial word here, for Woolf shared the view of many of her contemporaries that the Great War was the result of materialism and the aggressiveness of a male-dominated civilization. Her idea of a more intimate civilization, a more spiritual world, therefore included a change from what we might call male values to female ones: nurturing, caring, family life.

Weber had famously outlined an overlap between Calvinism and capitalism in his notion of 'the calling', the idea of 'vocation', which had moved out of the monasteries and into the classic Victorian idea of work as duty, a secularized form of asceticism. What he thought in particular had been lost in this process was the presence, authority and aura of sacred relics and the 'mediating fiction' of the priest. Woolf overlapped with Weber in that she thought the task of modern fiction was to reintroduce 'vision' into a genre that during the nineteenth century had come to be dominated by fact (itself, of course, an aspect of secularization). This was all the more important for Woolf because she also intuitively agreed with Weber that the advances in nineteenth-century and early-twentieth-century science, though remarkable, had actually done little to advance 'ultimate meaning'.

Woolf believed that literature had taken over some of the functions of religion, in that both were outside mainstream society and that in both it was the job of the cleric or writer to speak out truths, inconvenient or otherwise; to speak up for a set of 'spiritual' values that went against the prevailing 'materialism'.[5] She saw women as having a special place in this, and it is worth reminding ourselves once more that, alongside the more 'metaphysical' ideas of fulfilment and redemption considered in this book, many in the twentieth century – women, homosexuals, racial minorities – underwent a far more practical transformation in their sense of fulfilment as their material and psychological conditions improved. Woolf was alive to – and part of – these changes.

As noted above, both Weber and Woolf saw the modern world as not dissimilar to the pagan, pre-Christian world, in which there were many gods, representing many values, often competing and by no means always reconcilable. Furthermore, both saw that, in such a system, there was always the opportunity (and therefore the danger) for people to follow their own interests to the exclusion of almost everything else: this might well be fulfilling in personal terms but did little for the wider community. It was an individual, solitary – and possibly lonely – form of fulfilment.

A further parallel between Weber and Woolf lies in the former's argument that whatever advances science had made by then, none of its results had provided humanity 'with a sense of ultimate meaning'. Many of Woolf's characters (in *The Waves*, for instance, or *To the Lighthouse*) are continually searching for an answer to the meaning of existence but, for the most part, come up empty-handed. At the same time Woolf fills her books with what Lily Briscoe, the painter in *To the Lighthouse*, calls 'daily miracles, matches struck unexpectedly in the dark'; the characters, like Virginia Woolf herself, hoped to 'make of the moment something permanent' – an attitude which she says amounted to a manifesto that was 'of the nature of a revelation'. 'The quest for meaning will find resolution not in a grand gesture that encompasses everything, but in minor daily miracles.'[6]

With these concerns as her starting point and with Weber in the background, Woolf gradually came to focus on two aspects of experience that, for her, were of paramount importance and that became, again for her, what we might call a surrogate religion. These two elements were intimacy and 'moments of being'. She thought that the great philosophical/emotional/intellectual problem of her day, or any other, was how one mind could know another, how it is possible to *understand* another person's thoughts and values. 'For Woolf,' as Pericles Lewis says, 'no communion is possible with God or Christ, but she does seek some form of communion among selves.' For example, she asks herself how we can ever know what other minds think about God.

This leads on to the episode in 'An Unwritten Novel' (1920) where she is on a train sitting opposite a 'poor, unfortunate woman'. She gives the woman a fictitious – and somewhat mean – name, Minnie Marsh, and imagines her as an unhappy, childless spinster. She then tries to imagine what sort of God this other woman prays to: 'Who's the God of Minnie Marsh, the God of the back streets of Eastbourne, the God of three o'clock in the afternoon?' She can only imagine an old patriarch in a black frock-coat, a bullying parody of Jehovah, someone who resembles 'the leader of the Boers' – an old spinster like 'Minnie' would surely want 'a God with whiskers'. Her point is, of course, that she had absolutely no idea, and when 'Minnie' is met at Eastbourne station by her son, all Woolf's fantasies are exploded.

What is not exploded is her point that, if one person cannot begin to imagine what another person's idea of God is, or what their mental life is, how can we ever share anything? Is not the notion that all Christians, say, believe in the same God bound to be a fiction, an illusion?

As to the second aspect of experience that she regards as central, not all intimacies are the same, of course. Some people are proud, some spend their time brooding, others despise one another, making intimacy difficult, if not impossible. But in modern times, Woolf suggests, the only authentic spiritual experience is to be found in intense moments of vision, or ecstasy, that it is the specific business of art to identify, preserve and transmit. She contrasts these 'moments of being' with 'moments of non-being'. 'During moments of non-being', one is, as mentioned earlier, 'embedded in a kind of nondescript cotton-wool'. In her own case these moments all come from childhood: such as the sudden desire not to fight with her brother, or the vision of an apple tree as somehow connected with the suicide of a family acquaintance.

These moments usually contain a shock or even a blow, and usually promise 'a revelation of some order'.[7] They are similar to what James Joyce would call 'epiphanies'. And she went on to say something similar to what Rilke said about naming: 'From this I reach what I might call a philosophy; at any rate it is a constant idea of mine; that behind the cotton wool is hidden a pattern; that we – I mean all human beings – are connected with this ... a token of some real thing behind appearances; and I make it real by putting it into words.'

And somewhat like Rilke, too, Woolf saw herself as a receiver of observations rather than a God-substitute imposing patterns on her stories and characters. She was especially attuned, she felt, to observe moments of being, moments of ecstasy, involving 'the erasure of the boundaries that typically separate one self from another'.

These moments can be seen as a new form of the sublime, for which nineteenth-century realism had had little use. But in Woolf's hands the new sublime relates not so much to grand or extraordinary things as to modest, inconspicuous, everyday objects that turn out to open up unexpected worlds. She uses these moments – when someone sees a hatpin worn long ago, or remembers a kiss – to establish an intimate link (sometimes retrospective) between individuals, by means of an overwhelming 'oceanic' feeling traditionally associated with something altogether grander – mountains or cathedrals. For her, these episodes constitute the only really sacred moments available to us in a secular world, and it is the writer's job to draw attention to them, to highlight their value, and to preserve them for us in a permanent – immortal – form.

'The question that each of these ecstatic episodes poses is whether the meeting of minds that the sublime moment offers can lead to sustained communion. For Woolf, the "moment of being" . . . is a type of sacrament appropriate for a world in which no single measure of the sacred obtains, and in which community must result from the always temporary, ironic and visionary merging of competing value systems.'

As Freud's English-language publisher, Woolf embraced the psychoanalytic approach. She thought that the 'oceanic' feeling so sought after by religions and appropriated by them, and the 'intimate sublime moments of being' which so attracted her, had their origins in infancy, born of the time when the infant is separated from the mother, the warm embrace of first the womb and then the breast.

The nearest we can get to a spiritual feeling, Woolf is saying, is intense intimacy. By definition, therefore, we live most intensely in our families and with our friends. Indeed, this is the purpose of friendship, to search for, to create, intimate moments of being. The moments of bliss from our childhood create the benchmark; adult intimacy both recalls and overtakes that earlier experience. It is the purpose of art to identify these elements and preserve them, but the moments themselves are available to everyone.'

Idealism as Ruin

Virginia Woolf and James Joyce have often been compared – and as often contrasted – as experimental novelists, as explorers of the 'stream of consciousness' mode of writing. In her diary Woolf remarked that *Ulysses* was 'a misfire', 'pretentious' and 'underbred', though she thought it also had genius.

One big difference between them was that, unlike Woolf, Joyce thought of himself as a Nietzschean. In 1904, describing himself as 'James Overman', he was all for neopaganism, licentiousness and pitilessness. Nietzsche and others helped sustain his opposition to the totalizing religious and philosophical frameworks characteristic of the nineteenth-century bourgeoisie. Joyce wrote in a letter to his wife Nora: 'My mind rejects the whole present social order and Christianity.' Stephen Dedalus is fond of saying that 'the Absolute is dead'. *Portrait of the Artist* recounts Stephen's gradual rejection of his Catholicism. We feel the pull of religion as he accepts that his faith is 'logical and coherent'; but what he fears is 'the chemical reaction that would be set up in my soul by a false homage to a symbol behind which are amassed twenty centuries of authority and veneration'.[8] As Gordon Graham explains, 'the hope, in other words, is not theological truth but spiritual freedom'; Dedalus's aim is to discover 'the mode of life or of art whereby [the] spirit could express itself in unfettered freedom'. This is a vision of life as itself an aesthetic expression.[9]

But above all Joyce had an extraordinary attachment to fact, a 'scrupulous meanness', in Christopher Butler's words, to seeing things as they actually are. As he expressed himself to Arthur Power, an Irish friend who had lived in Paris before becoming art critic of the *Irish Times*: 'In realism you get down to facts on which the world is based; that sudden reality which smashes romanticism into a pulp. What makes most people's lives unhappy is some disappointed romanticism, some unrealizable misconceived ideal. In fact you may say that idealism is the ruin of man, and if we *lived down* to fact, as primitive man had to do, we would be better off. That is what we were made for. Nature is quite unromantic. It is we who put romance into her, which is a false attitude, an egotism, absurd like all egotism. In *Ulysses* I tried to keep close to fact [italics added].' So here Joyce is identifying a new form of false consciousness.

He also rejected any metaphysical order. Very possibly, he shared the views of his countryman Oscar Wilde, who said: 'It is enough that our fathers believed. They have exhausted the faith-faculty of the species. Their legacy to us is the scepticism of which they were afraid.' In *Stephen Hero*, Joyce the Catholic engineers Stephen Dedalus to confront loss of faith head on, at the same time retaining and secularizing whole swathes of the vocabulary of religion. This is shown most clearly in his interpretation of the notion of 'epiphany' as a secular spiritual moment when a collection of (usually ordinary) experiences, memories and ambitions coalesce in an intense, multi-layered explosion.[10]

This is seen in *Dubliners* when the boy narrator realizes, 'as the [Araby] bazaar is closing down around him, that he doesn't have enough money to buy a present for Mangan's sister [Mangan is one of his playmates]'. Elements of the episode – the shop girl's nationality (English), her flirtatious manner and his regret at not being able to reciprocate, the fact that he is in the bazaar at all, being there to escape his dismal home circumstances – comprise the Joycean epiphany, which does not so much confirm a truth 'as disrupt what one has grown comfortable in accepting as true'.[11] In other words, for Joyce, an epiphany is an inverted version of what it is in, say, the Christian world, producing a sinking feeling rather than a rising one. Living down to fact again.

As this suggests, Joyce, like other modernists (Chekhov, Proust, Gide, James, Mann, Woolf), is less a narrator in the traditional sense than an 'evoker' of a particular consciousness ('the transfiguration of the commonplace', in the critic Arthur Danto's words). His achievement in his three great works, *Portrait of the Artist as a Young Man* (1916), *Ulysses* (1922) and *Finnegans Wake* (1939), is best appreciated if they are seen as one collective enterprise, a portrait of the artist as a young man, as a middle-aged man and as an aged man. The fact that these works are long and difficult is part of the point. Joyce's view, which can scarcely be reduced to a few words without making him seem banal, entails offering a new golden rule or categorical imperative. Instead of 'Do unto others as you would be done by' he offers this: Lead your life so that, looking back on it when you are old, you will be able to say that you have become a person you would want to be, that you have actively chosen the self you are, without unreflectively acquiescing in the plans of others; life is to obtain its meaning by what we *do*, not what is demanded of us by some 'long-distance laird' (compare Gide, Rilke, Heidegger).

There should be a pattern to a life, Joyce says, one that we have woven ourselves and do not regret; it should contain intimate relationships, the desire to create, and an act of creation that has an effect on others; we should realize that there is a price to pay for conformity – that one becomes a sham – while the committed individualist risks becoming an outsider, 'locked into his or her narcissism' (compare Kafka below). These issues overlap and allow us during a lifetime to take on a number of identities, and it is important that we find one that makes life liveable. Furthermore, any acceptable narrative of a human life will have to come to terms with a fall from innocence, and will be judged by the actions that flow from that fall, by how we live down to fact (compare O'Neill). Ultimately, the great satisfaction – and significance – life has to offer is not just love (which many people have said) but, more precisely, *enduring love*.

When we have said this, though, we are only halfway there, at most. Joyce's language, famously, notoriously, was difficult but also musical, inventive and punning, designed to show the very great possibilities of human experience, the chaos and delicious contingency of who we are, as he sought to celebrate the delight we should take in everyday things. He shows that there is no significant difference between a life lived on a large scale and one lived on a small scale, that Christ's pain, as he puts it, was no more significant than is ALP's (one of the main figures in *Finnegans Wake*).

The celebrated puns and double-entendres are not intended merely as 'pun'ishments, but like Picasso's paintings they show us the units – here, the words – from different directions all at once, as devices to underline and celebrate the *joyful instability* of experience: an ageing woman is described as 'beautifell', the morning papers as 'moaning pipers' (as a Cockney might say), a fine backside as a 'beauhind'; à la Proust, the orchards of his youth are 'evremberried', a lover confesses he 'waged love' on a young girl, Shakespeare is variously Shopkeeper, Shapesphere and Shakhisbeard, a form of theatre is 'Ibscenest nansence', stories 'disselve', a prayer ends 'as it is uneven', a letter describes the writer's attendance at a grand 'funferall', and a question in a (Dublin) game is 'Was liffe worth leaving?'

But these puns and neologisms – call them what you will – are more than mere wordplay for the sake of it. Carefully chosen, based on close observation and reflection and rarely lacking in wit, they are in fact new names for the phenomena of the world, which invite and encourage us to notice, to recognize and to name new aspects of experience that we thought were familiar and settled. Moreover, out of all these at times hilarious, at times tedious, at times astonishing ambiguities and teases – a form of ordered and intended chaos – Joyce challenges us to forge a stable story; and this is how, ultimately, the dense form of his book shows us how to live. A successful achievement is a stable identity that has been *chosen and earned.*

A Comic Gospel and the Androgynous Man

Joyce said of *Ulysses* that it was an attempt to write a book 'from eighteen different points of view', and this certainly sums up Joycean criticism, which comfortably exceeds eighteen different points of view. From among this plethora two more are worth singling out.

Brett Bourbon makes the case that *Finnegans Wake* is in itself a spiritual exercise – that is, a modern form of *askesis*, the practice in ancient Greek philosophy that had as its goal 'the transformation of our vision of the world, and the metamorphosis of our being', a form of self-discipline. Bourbon argues that the *Wake* is ultimately nonsense, deliberate nonsense when conceived overall, but that it embodies an essentially comic stance towards the world – it is, in effect, a 'comic gospel'. He maintains that the *Wake* offers us an essentially theological lesson, exposing us to the 'entanglement' of our world, our way of thinking through words, which is designed to provoke self-reflection. 'What have replaced God in the *Wake* are particular kinds of nonsense . . . This nonsense, or rather the limit between nonsense and sense . . .'[12]

This lack of sense is designed to drive us back on ourselves in an examination of how we, individually and collectively, construct sense. Because the *Wake* as an entity has no meaning, we must do the work instead. In particular, there is no *intention* in the *Wake*, and showing what it is like to live in a world without intention is perhaps its most significant achievement. Intention is not God-given; it has to be conceived, then worked at. The lack – the absence – of intention is a form of salvation.

Declan Hibberd of University College, Dublin, introduces the idea that, in addition to all this, there was and is a specific point to the characterization in *Ulysses* (which originally had Homeric titles to all its chapters). Joyce thought that the search for heroics was vulgar, that man's littleness 'is the inevitable condition of his greatness'.[13] Likewise he disdained the 'muscular Christianity' preached in the schools of Ireland's occupying power, together with the 'redemptive violence' of the myths invented and reinvented by Irish authors such as W.B. Yeats. The central character of *Ulysses*, Hibberd reminds us, is an Irish Jew, who has no hankering to become a somebody, 'neither a Faust nor a Jesus'. (Jesus never lived with a woman; 'Surely living with a woman is one of the most difficult things a man has to do, and he never did it.')[14]

In *Ulysses* Joyce affords the body equal recognition to the mind, notes that real heroism is never conscious of itself, and indeed he redefines heroism as the capacity to endure rather than inflict suffering; he notes that a man requires great courage to enter 'the abyss of himself', that words as often conceal as they reveal, that language lags behind technical progress, that there are limits to communicability. But above all he wants (us) to go beyond what he saw as part of the ecclesiastical heritage – our false ideas of masculinity. The man of the future, for Joyce, the character type that gave hope to the world, would be the androgynous man – 'That's the new messiah for Ireland.'[15] Nothing was intrinsically masculine any more and he felt that many people knew this in their hearts without acknowledging it – it was implicit. Bloom, Hibberd says, never feels himself a freak in Dublin. 'On the contrary, his androgyny gives him a unique insight into womanhood.' In this he likens Bloom to 'that near-perfect androgyne', Shakespeare, and he finds a similar theme in Oscar Wilde, O'Casey, Shaw, Synge and even Yeats.

Joyce spoke of the 'plurability' of experience, of people having a multiple self, but above all Bloom represents 'a wholly new kind of male subject in world literature, a man whose womanly multiplicity is intended less to exact derision than to provoke admiration . . . Because the feeling of masculinity in males is less strong than that of femininity in females, there has been an ancient prejudice in most cultures against the womanly man ... it was Joyce who rendered the womanly man quotidian and changed forever the way in which writers treated sexuality.' It was this that provided the most original of the 'redemptive glimpses of a future world'.[16]

Biological Warmth and Warm Otherness

D.H. Lawrence had little time for Joyce. He rejected his work as 'too terribly would-be and done-on-purpose, utterly without spontaneity or real life'. The writer and critic Stephen Spender was in no doubt about the difference between the two men. In reviewing Joyce's letters, published in 1957, he said: 'In letters like those of the fathers of the early Christian Church there is interchange within God; in those of Keats and his friends there is interchange within poetry; in those of Vincent and Theo van Gogh, interchange within art; in those of D.H. Lawrence and Middleton Murry, interchange within wrath. In all these others there is agreement on both sides that the writer and the person written to share some overarching conception of life which is outside and beyond them both. With Joyce there is no sense of sharing at all ... His letters are, quite strictly, "hand-outs" ... what is lacking is love. In the acrimonious correspondence of Lawrence and Murry there is more love than in Joyce's most expensive bulletins.'

But there was this similarity, arguably more profound than the differences: 'David Herbert Lawrence spent much of his creative energies contriving a second faith, something to succeed what he considered false Christian philosophy and its successor, the sterile rationalism of science.' In *Psychoanalysis and the Unconscious* (1923), *The Plumed Serpent* (1926), *The Man Who Died* (1929) and *Fantasia of the Unconscious* (1930) Lawrence explored the post-Christian psychological world. He had several starting points. He had a mystical bent in which the oneness of all creation is the 'fundamental prehension', but he inveighed against all abstractions, including psychological ones. 'The original sin against life is abstract thought.'[17]

Lawrence believed, as Nietzsche believed before him, that life is erratic and irrational, and that we have a tendency to over-rationalize it. (Lawrence spent time in Germany, had a German wife, and was much influenced by German ideas, not only Nietzsche's.) But he also thought that life is fundamentally erotic. Freud was condemned in Lawrence's mind because psychoanalysis 'is out, under therapeutic disguise, to do away entirely with the moral faculty in man'. And he staked his case on a revival of 'the erotic mode as a therapeutic release from inwardness'.[18]

Lawrence equated mysticism with the unconscious – mystical knowledge, for him, is essentially unconscious self-knowledge, and is therefore non-rational. Science, in eschewing contact with the irrational, was for Lawrence distancing itself from 'life'. He thought the Christian God had died in 1914 and he disliked the religious conventions of the day, which were equally cold and automatic, and as distant from our experience as the Aztec gods he explored in *The Plumed Serpent*. He found humanism sentimental, he objected to science's way of assigning man a 'more modest' place in the scheme of things, and he saw the West's 'binge of inwardness' likewise as a diminishing of who we are. Our aim should be to lead an 'impassioned and yet social life'. He objected to science's 'machine metaphors' of the human passions which, he said, emptied passion of its social content.

The erotic aspect of life being so important to Lawrence, he was convinced that the relationship between men and women lay at the base of a happy and fulfilled life – at one stage he imagined an assembly of men and women who would form the 'nucleus of a new belief', an 'organic' society which would 'permit' communal passion.[19] The 'irrational power of love' was for him the antithesis of the coldly rational scientific world, and the freer expression of man's erotic behaviour was an expression of the divine.

The Plumed Serpent is a novel of pagan religiosity, its plot focusing on the conversion of a Western woman to a primitive Aztec cult. Lawrence invokes the ritual of sun dancing as a reflection of divine concern with the human being. The protagonist, Kate, is cultured, informed and educated and, moreover, not in thrall to any Western ideology. Moved by where she is, she accepts her religious duty, with its sexual implications, and consents willingly to marry the high priest of the cult. Lawrence's point is that she chooses to participate in a 'passional community', not simply remaining an observer, an outsider, as her European background would normally lead her to do. 'An embarrassment even to ardent exegetes of Lawrence, *The Plumed Serpent* runs together just these motifs – the sexual, the instinctual unconscious, and the religious – which in the European culture have strenuously been kept apart,' says Philip Rieff in his book *The Triumph of the Therapeutic*.[20]

In *The Man Who Died*, Lawrence contemplates the ending of the Christian passion, portraying Jesus as admitting the error of becoming Christ. Jesus is never named in the story, though he is clearly identified. We meet him as a confused and frightened man who was expecting to be rescued by his heavenly father before the time appointed for his crucifixion, and who therefore feels betrayed. He is also anxious that if the Romans find out that he has survived 'they will come for him and finish him off again'. He is now a far from spiritual figure – only too human; he travels to Egypt where he seduces one of the goddess Isis's Temple priestesses. When the Romans do catch up with him he escapes by boat, leaving a slave to be mistaken for him.

Baldly stated, the plot was probably at the time offensive to a great many people, as Lawrence intended. (Alternatively, it is another 'embarrassment'.) Upon his resurrection, Jesus realizes he cannot regain his moral edge; and he rediscovers what for Lawrence was his true divinity – his 'amatory humanity' – in a directly sexual way, via a blonde votary in the cult of another god. For Lawrence, this is a form of resurrection – Jesus, as a man now, has recovered his identity. Here one thinks of Joyce's assertion that the most difficult thing a man can do is live with a woman, which the biblical Jesus never did. Salvation, Lawrence's Jesus realizes, lies only in the intimate, private life – and that is his only lesson for others. Lawrence wrote to Bertrand Russell, the supreme intellectual of his day: 'For heaven's sake, don't think – be a baby, and not a savant any more. Don't *do* anything any more – but for heaven's sake begin to *be* – start at the very beginning and be a perfect baby: in the name of courage.' To Lawrence, thinking – the intellect – is not a virtue. We should stop thinking always of ourselves first; restraint and prudence are less needed than fortitude and justice.

Lawrence's two main criteria 'for the living of life' were, first, 'the need to unite with another in the alternately straining and easing relationship of love'; and second, the need for 'passionate purpose', quite separate from erotic engagement and its release, passionate purpose being about making 'something new and better in the world'. 'If passionate purposes are to be effective, they must be steady; and if they are steady, then they develop inevitably into "fixed ideals".' At the same time, he did believe that each self has one purpose only, namely to come into 'the fullness of its being', in which he thought that the 'fact of otherness', as experienced in the 'erotic crucible', could fuse together – if only for brief (sacred) moments – to 'proximate fulfilment'. The object of these experiences, Lawrence believed, was precisely what Freud meant by the 'oceanic feeling' – at one point Lawrence talks about the 'Oceanic God'. In *The Plumed Serpent*, when Kate decides to dance with one of the Quetzalcoatl men, looking to the primitive as a source of spiritual renewal for Europe as well as for herself, she slips into a trance-like 'second consciousness' and finds herself 'caught up and identified in the slowly revolving ocean of nascent life' around her.[21]

He thought that our aim should be 'biological warmth', in particular a biologically warm family; being a good parent was one way to preserve 'the human being [parent and child] all his life fresh and alive, a true individual'. The sense of otherness, which we gain in the crucible of the erotic, we must transfer to our relationships with our children, not in the same erotic sense but in the sense of 'warm otherness'. For Lawrence, love and otherness are the twin divinities: these are what we must show if we are to lead exemplary lives, always aware that this may reveal itself in 'patches of compromise', and that the desire for possession (of the loved other) is offset by the need to be free (of the other). (When he went to Mexico, he actually found the 'radical alterity' of the locals 'profoundly hostile'.)[22]

In all this, for Lawrence, the means are more important than the ends, our actions are what count – ecstatic, erotic action, an echo of Nietzsche in *The Birth of Tragedy*. For Lawrence, passion is holy: 'Screams of violence are more full of life than the hushed tones of tolerance.' (Owen, the American who travels with Kate in Mexico at the beginning of *The Plumed Serpent*, and refuses to leave the bullfight early because, he believes, 'Life means seeing anything ... on show', is condemned as having 'the insidious modern disease of tolerance'.) The core aspect of life is, after all, our encounter with instinct, and how we manage that encounter is all-important. God having died, we must learn to love ourselves as we 'collide' with our instincts, which means that the decisive factor in humankind is the will, or desire – not intellect.[23]

No less than Woolf or Joyce, Lawrence took risks with his writing – in style, in subject matter. But, like them, his aim was a larger, warmer life, living well among others close to him. Intimacy and accurate details are the key ingredients.

14

The Impossibility of Metaphysics,
a Reverence for Metapsychology

Towards the end of 1932, the British philosopher A.J. Ayer and his new wife Renée arrived in Vienna. He was there to work under Moritz Schlick, one of the leaders of the Vienna Circle, a group of radical philosopher-scientists, news of whose achievements was beginning to seep into the British and American consciousness.

The Vienna Ayer found was not so different, in many respects, from the city it had been before the Great War. It was busy and crowded, with two million inhabitants, still a wonderful architectural showcase, still home to a vibrant café culture where, for the price of a cup of coffee, 'one could spend a morning in an elegant salon reading newspapers in three or four languages'.[1] It was still famous for its music, its cheap dance halls and its anti-Semitism. Freud was still practising there.

The Vienna Circle was elaborating a tradition begun by such figures as Ernst Mach, Bertrand Russell, the Austrian physicist Ludwig Boltzmann and Ludwig Wittgenstein, and espoused a philosophy known to themselves as *Wissenschaftliche Weltauffassung*, 'the world scientifically conceived'. Its main members were Herbert Feigl, Otto Neurath and Friedrich Waismann, Austrian and Jewish, together with Moritz Schlick and Rudolf Carnap from Germany, and occasional members included Kurt Gödel and Karl Popper. Only two Anglo-Saxons were ever admitted, Ayer and the American, Willard Van Orman Quine, who was in Vienna at the same time as his British colleague. Several of the group had trained as scientists or as mathematicians before turning to philosophy, and such training clearly shaped their views.

The Circle had been launched in 1929 when Carnap and Neurath published *Wissenshaftliche Weltauffassung: Der Wiener Kreis* (The Scientific Conception of the World: The Vienna Circle): its main planks were empiricism and its commitment to logical analysis, and its distinguishing both of these from the belief – common since Kant's day, particularly among Hegelians – that there are certain metaphysical facts about the world (such as 'the Absolute') that we can know independently of experience.

The Circle saw itself as having two tasks. Negatively, as Ben Rogers put it in his biography of Ayer, its purpose was to 'warn people off' metaphysics, and particularly to counter the German fascination with Romanticism and idealism. At the same time, its more positive aim was to clarify the logic of science and commonsense observation. For Schlick, Neurath, Carnap and the others, science – to encompass commonsense observation as well – is the only source of real knowledge; everything is built up from sense experience and so any proposition which does not relate back to sense experience cannot lay claim to be knowledge. In Carnap's words: 'All knowledge stems from one source of knowledge: experience – the unmediated content of experience such as red, hard, toothache and joy.' This can be traced back to Wittgenstein's *Tractatus Logico-Philosophicus* and its claim that an utterance is meaningful if, and only if, it expresses a proposition whose truth or falsehood can be verified by empirical observation or solely by reference to the meaning of the terms it contains. If a statement could not be tested empirically, then according to the Vienna Circle it was meaningless. (Karl Popper would subsequently replace the notion of verifiability with that of falsification.)

What Can and Cannot Be Said

This had grave, even apocalyptic, consequences for metaphysics. 'The Vienna Circle no longer attacked propositions about the soul, God, the

Absolute, the after-life, historical destiny, national spirit, or transcendent values, as being false or unduly speculative. Instead it maintained that in so far as they were unverifiable, they were literally meaningless.'[2] Anything that could not be tested was out of court. The Circle's aim – as had been Wittgenstein's in the *Tractatus* – was to purify language, to make clear what can and cannot be said.

In a letter to friends in Britain at the time, Ayer wrote that the ultimate term of abuse among the members of the Circle was 'metaphysical'. Wittgenstein was treated, if not like a god (as that would have been metaphysical), 'as a second Pythagoras'.[3] All his life Ayer retained the view that there is no 'unknowable realm of hidden objects' or entities – such an idea was simply nonsensical, as it was to the members of the Vienna Circle. He started his famous book *Language, Truth and Knowledge*, which popularized the ideas of the Vienna Circle in the English-speaking world, in the summer of 1933, with the specific aim of 'demonstrating the impossibility of metaphysics'.

He began by criticizing the metaphysical thesis that philosophy affords us knowledge of a reality transcending the world of science and common sense.[4] Nothing concerning the properties, or even the existence, of anything super-empirical can legitimately be inferred. The impossibility of a transcendent metaphysic is a matter of logic. It was at the time impossible to verify, practically, that there were mountains on the far side of the moon, but it was verifiable in principle. On the other hand, 'the Absolute enters into, but is itself incapable of, evolution and progress', and is not verifiable even in principle. We cannot conceive of an observation that would verify this.[5] Most statements can never be more than highly probable – 'arsenic is poisonous', 'all men are mortal', cannot be established with certainty in an infinite number of cases. By the same token, statements about the past can never be more than highly probable.

There is a difference between being false and being nonsensical, and we are often confused by language. For example, the statements 'Unicorns are fictitious' and 'dogs are faithful' look similar, but fictitious objects like unicorns do not have some special form of existence, 'so as to be real in some non-empirical sense'. Just because something can be the subject of a sentence does not mean that it exists.

Ayer argues that fundamental ethical concepts are unanalysable because 'there is no criterion by which one can test the validity of the judgements in which they occur'. The reason is that they are pseudo-concepts. In saying 'You acted wrongly in stealing that money' I am saying nothing more than 'You stole that money'. No further statement is added other than moral disapproval. 'It is as if I had said "You stole that money" in a particular tone of voice ... Sentences which make moral judgements are pure expressions of feeling and do not come under the category of truth or falsehood.'[6]

Moreover, 'there cannot be such a thing as ethical science, if by ethical science one means the elaboration of a "true" system of morals'. One of the chief causes of moral behaviour, he says, is fear, both conscious and unconscious, of a God's displeasure, or fear of the enmity of society.[7] 'This is why [morals] present themselves as "categorical" commands. They are partly determined in turn by the society's condition of its own happiness. This is why altruism is preferred everywhere to egotism.'

Regarding the possibility of religious knowledge, Ayer says: 'If the conclusion that a god exists is to be demonstrably certain, then these premises must be certain. But we know that no empirical proposition can ever be anything more than probable. It is only a priori propositions that are logically certain. But we cannot judge the existence of a god from an a priori proposition ... It follows that there is no possibility of demonstrating the existence of a god.

'What is not so generally recognized is that there can be no way of proving that the existence of a god, such as the God of Christianity, is even probable. Yet this is also easily shown. For if the existence of such a god were probable, then the proposition that he existed would be an empirical hypothesis ... But in fact this is not possible. It is sometimes claimed that certain regularities in nature constitute sufficient evidence for the existence of a god. But if the sentence "God exists" entails no more than that certain types of phenomena occur in certain sequences, then to assert the existence of a god will be equivalent to asserting that there is the requisite regularity in nature; 'and no religious man would admit that this was all he intended'. He would say that in talking about God, he was talking about a transcendent being ... In that case "god" is a metaphysical term. And if "god" is a metphysical term, it cannot be even probable that a god exists. For to say that God exists is to make a metaphysical utterance that cannot be either true or false . . . This affects atheists and agnostics too. The atheist's assertion that there is no god is equally nonsensical.'

Thus the assertions of the theist cannot be valid, but they cannot be invalid either. As the theist says nothing about the world, he cannot be justly accused of saying anything false. 'It is only when the theist claims that in asserting the existence of a transcendent god he is expressing a genuine proposition,' says Ayer, 'that we are entitled to disagree with him.'

He goes on: 'Regarding the attributes of God . . . We may have a word which is used as if it names this "person" but unless the sentences in which it occurs express propositions which are empirically verifiable, it cannot be said to symbolise anything at all. And this is the case with regard to the word "god", in the usage in which it is intended to refer to a transcendent object. The mere existence of the noun is enough to foster an illusion that there is a real, or at any rate a possible entity corresponding to it. It is only when we enquire what God's attributes are that we discover that "God" in this usage, is not a genuine name. The same is true of soul and afterlife.[8] . . . We are often told that the nature of God is a mystery which transcends human understanding. But to say this is to say that it is unintelligible. And what is unintelligible cannot significantly be described. We are told that God is an object of faith and not an object of reason. This may be nothing more than an admission that the existence of God must be taken on trust, since it cannot be proved. If a mystic admits that the object of his vision is something that cannot be described, then he must admit that he is bound to talk nonsense when he describes it . . . The argument from religious experience is fallacious. The fact that people have religious experiences is interesting from the psychological point of view, but it does not in any way imply that there is such a thing as religious knowledge, any more than our having moral experiences implies that there is any such thing as moral knowledge. The theist, like the moralist, may believe that his experiences are cognitive experiences but unless he can formulate his "knowledge" in propositions that are empirically verifiable, we may be sure he is deceiving himself.'[9]

The logical positivists – as the followers of the Vienna Circle in the Anglo-Saxon world came to be called – all seemed to think, as Freud appears to have thought (see pp. 286 ff.), that simply by making their arguments available they would be accepted and eventually prevail. They saw no need to put anything 'in the place' of God. The major change that they sought to bring about was for philosophy to become a 'smaller' activity. Ayer argued that philosophy was nothing more than logical analysis, and in that case, he insisted, no sense could be made of a God who was held to have created the universe, on the grounds that no sense could be made of an entity existing outside space and time; and that 'in being made to transcend time, it loses all possibility of being, even in principle, accessible to our experience'.

Ayer became more and more convinced that philosophy was incapable of offering an authoritative answer to the question 'How should I live?' Put another way, he was saying that we can have knowledge of empirical truths and of the truisms of maths and logic, 'but not of values' – our morality is ultimately up to us. 'The purpose of man's existence is constituted by the ends to which he, consciously or unconsciously, devotes himself . . . In the last resort, each individual has the responsibility of choice; and it is a responsibility that is not to be escaped.'[10]

The Cruelties of Consolation

It is one of the sharper ironies of modern intellectual history that at exactly the time the logical positivists were focusing on 'the impossibility of metaphysics', Sigmund Freud and Carl Jung were introducing their own accounts as to how and why psychology 'explained' God. Each of them claimed he was an empiricist, that his theories were based on close observations of experience. Nonetheless several critics have described what they produced as 'metapsychologies'. Each constructed a very radical synthesis, each very different from the other, coming to diametrically opposed conclusions.

Freud was raised in a thoroughly secular household, as a 'Godless

Jew' in historian Peter Gay's words, in Vienna in the last half of the nineteenth century when the city, as we have seen, was one of the jewels of Europe in terms of its sophisticated secular culture: theatre, opera, architecture, science, sports, cuisine, leisure – a world, in Frederic Morton's account, of 'nervous splendor'. This may well have helped determine Freud's approach: that once the psychological basis of religion had been explained, and its 'errors' exploded, people would turn away, having no further need of religious psychological support. For Freud, as for the Vienna Circle, there was no 'need' for an alternative to religion. It was a shortcoming, a false path in human history, and it was time to move on.

Freud's first critiques of religion were, as we saw earlier, his 1907 paper 'Obsessive Actions and Religious Practices', and *Totem and Taboo* (1914). There, he had noted that several times in the past – in pre-exile Israel, for example, or classical Greece – gods had died or been killed off without too much fuss being made and without too many untoward effects being felt. In this sense, the death of god was nothing new. But now, as the Vienna positivists were circling their wagons, he produced three more books on religion, *The Future of an Illusion*, *Civilization and Its Discontents* and *Moses and Monotheism*. That number is a measure of the importance he attached to attacking/ explaining/explaining away belief in God.

The Future of an Illusion, published in 1927, was an all-out assault, a polemic of just ninety-eight pages in which Freud, then already seventy-one, dismissed outright the truth claims of religion and foresaw its continued demise. In the 1920s, psychoanalysis was becoming established internationally – the Vienna Psychoanalytic Institute was formed in 1924, the same year that the Institute of Psychoanalysis opened in London, while a Paris outfit was opened two years later. More personally, Freud had detected a benign growth in his mouth in 1923, a leukoplakia associated with smoking. But this would develop into a cancer, about which his doctor failed to inform him at first, worried that he might commit suicide. From the late 1920s, Freud was in almost constant pain.

In *The Future of an Illusion* he began by considering the cultural and psychological significance of religion. He said that the principal task of culture, 'its real *raison d'être*', was to defend mankind against nature. God, or the gods of the ancients, had the same threefold task: 'they must exorcise the terrors of nature, they must reconcile one to the cruelty of fate, particularly as shown in death, and they must make amends for the sufferings and privations that the communal life of culture has imposed on man'.[11] This is where Freud's idea of the soul comes in. Since it is obvious that man succumbs to fate, is often overwhelmed by nature, and invariably dies, only an element detached from the body – the soul – is capable of being perfected, and offers the chance of a new kind of existence after death. The soul is a psychological entity, not a theological one.

But Freud also claimed that 'society knows very well the uncertain basis of the claims it makes for its religious doctrines'. And here he begins his polemic: he was essentially arguing that there is something intellectually dishonest about the claims that religions make in modern society. He insists, for instance, that all the arguments for the authenticity of religious doctrines 'originate in the past' and that we should look to the present to see whether evidence is available. None of the 'spiritualists', as he calls them, referring implicitly to the contemporary doctrines of Madame Blavatsky, Rudolf Steiner and others, have 'succeeded in disproving the fact that the appearances and utterances of their spirits are merely the productions of their own mental activity' – in fact, he disparages them as 'foolish' and 'desperately insignificant'.

He is equally dismissive of arguments that claim truths must be 'inwardly felt', that 'one does not need to comprehend them'. This, he said starkly, is an attempt to 'evade' the problem. And the philosophy of 'as if' was an absurd evasion. Some people (he is referring here predominantly to the ideas of Hans Vaihinger) go so far as to say that, even if it could be proved that religion 'was not in the possession of the truth', we should believe 'as if' it were, in the interests of 'the preservation of everybody' and because countless people find consolation in the doctrines of religion. Freud contemptuously turns away from this, saying it is a purposeless cruelty; 'with the confession of absurdity, or illogicality, there is no more to be said'.[12]

This leads him to consider the psychical origins of religious ideas, and to this statement: 'These, which profess to be dogmas, are not the residue of experience or the final result of reflection; they are illusions, fulfilments of the oldest, strongest and most insistent wishes of mankind; the secret of their strength is the strength of these wishes.' Which in turn leads him to his famous distinction between errors and illusions. Aristotle's belief that vermin are evolved out of dung was an error, Columbus's belief that he had discovered a new sea route to India was an illusion, the difference being this: 'It is characteristic of an illusion that it is derived from men's wishes.' Illusions are not necessarily errors, he says. 'A poor girl may have an illusion that a prince will come and fetch her home. It is possible; some such cases have occurred.' Freud is very caustic about religious illusions: some of them are so improbable, so incompatible with the knowledge we have built up, he says, that they border on *de*lusions.[13] And then this: 'Where questions of religion are concerned people are guilty of every possible kind of insincerity and intellectual misdemeanour.' In particular, the meaning of the word 'God' has been stretched into 'vague abstractions'.

Warming to his theme, he asserts that culture incurs a great danger by maintaining its present attitude to religion, that religion has had quite long enough to show what it can achieve, and that if it were the success it claims to be, people would not be trying to change things. 'But instead what do we see? We see that an appallingly large number of men are discontented with civilization and unhappy in it, and feel it as a yoke that must be shaken off.'

To him the reason is clear. Religion no longer claims the support it once did, not because its promises have become smaller 'but because they appear less credible to people'. And this is so because of 'the increase of the scientific spirit in the higher strata of society'; science he describes, also in *The Future of an Illusion*, as offering 'opportunities for mental awakening'.[14] It would be an undoubted advantage, Freud says, to 'leave God out of the question altogether' and admit honestly the purely human origins of all cultural laws and institutions – then men would realize that the rigidity of many laws need not be immutable, which would be 'an important advance on the road which leads to reconciliation with the burden of culture'.[15] In fact, he thought that religious belief was on an inexorable decline and that, although in the past the consolations of religion had worked ('by accepting the universal neurosis [man] is spared the task of forming a personal neurosis'), the time had now come to replace the consequences of repression (required by culture) with 'the results of rational mental effort', a psychoanalytic treatment, as it were, of society as a whole. In any case, 'The truths contained in religious doctrines are ... so distorted and systematically disguised that the mass of mankind cannot recognize them as truth.'[16]

As one might expect, Freud was critical of the effects of a religious upbringing on children. He thought that the average child is not naturally interested in God, but is introduced to the idea by parents who, in doing so, transform the 'radiant intelligence of a healthy child' into the 'feeble mentality of the average adult'. 'So long as a man's early years are influenced by the religious thought-inhibition ... we cannot really say what he is actually like.'[17]

The Pleasure Principle

Freud had finished *The Future of an Illusion* in the autumn of 1927. During the following two years, no doubt on account of illness, he produced very little. But in the summer of 1929 he began another book, once more on a 'sociological subject'. The original title he chose was *Das Unglück in der Kultur* (Unhappiness in Civilization), but *Unglück* was later changed to *Unbehagen*, a word difficult to translate into English. Freud, who spoke English well, suggested 'Man's Discomfort in Civilization', but it was Joan Riviere, his translator, who came up with the form of words by which we know this work, *Civilization and Its Discontents*.

In some ways the original title would have been better, though since the book went to press in the immediate wake of the Wall Street crash which occurred at the end of October that year, it is easy to see why it quickly achieved the resonance it did. Its main theme is, in the words of its English editor, 'the irremediable antagonism between the demands of instinct and the restrictions of civilization'.[18]

It was in this book that Freud claimed that many people

acknowledged an 'oceanic feeling' as the basis of their religious belief, a feeling which, he said, he had never experienced himself. 'The "one-ness" with the universe which constitutes [the] ideational content [of the 'oceanic feeling'] sounds like a first attempt at a religious con-solation, as though it were another way of disclaiming the danger which the ego recognizes as threatening it from the external world.' The question of the purpose of human life 'has been raised countless times' but it had never yet received a satisfactory answer 'and perhaps does not admit of one'. He acknowledged that some had said that if life had no purpose, it would lose all value for them, but he dismissed this. 'Nobody talks about the purpose of life of animals, unless, per-haps, it may be supposed to lie in being of service to man . . . It looks, on the contrary, as though one had a right to dismiss the question, for it seems to derive from the human presumptuousness, many other manifestations of which are already familiar to us . . . the idea of life having a purpose stands and falls with the religious system.'

His own offering was much more down to earth: '[W]hat decides the purpose of life is simply the programme of the pleasure principle. This principle dominates the operation of the mental apparatus from the start.' Freud thinks that there can be no other purpose of life than 'happiness'. This was not the purpose of creation, he says, adopting a Darwinian view, and for that reason what we call happiness comes from the 'sudden satisfaction of needs which have been dammed up to a high degree in civilization', and thus by its nature it is 'only possible as an episodic phenomenon. When any situation that is desired by the pleasure principle is prolonged, it only produces a feeling of mild con-tentment. We are so made that we can derive intense enjoyment only from a contrast and very little from a state of things. Thus our possi-bilities of happiness are restricted by our constitution. Unhappiness is much less difficult to experience.'[19]

The Four Palliatives

For Freud, then, existence is something of a burden, and 'in order to bear it we cannot dispense with palliative measures' – analgesic, cultural and psychological tools and techniques – to help us get through. He specifically identifies four palliatives: religion, art, love and intoxication. Belief in a loving god and a blissful afterlife are 'wish-generated beliefs', illusions, which serve to soften the harsh realities of life. But, he said, 'Even religion cannot keep its promise. If the believer finally sees himself obliged to speak of God's "inscrutable decrees", he is admitting that all that is left to him as a last possible consolation and source of pleasure in his suffering is an unconditional submission. And if he is prepared for that, he could probably have spared himself the *détour* he has made.'[20]

Art, he thought, was a more respectable palliative, but not available to everyone; and even for those for whom it is, he didn't think it was anything other than a mild pleasure – it did not 'convulse our physical being'. Love, he thought, was the most sought-after palliative, which provided enormous comfort and, in sex, the most intense experiences. But it also carried enormous risks, since 'we are never so defenceless against suffering as when we love, never so helplessly unhappy as when we have lost our loved object or its love'. He thought that intoxication (and he himself took cocaine and tobacco) was the 'crudest but also most effective' method for ameliorating sensations of suffering. He added the important qualification that we should not look for the whole of our satisfaction from a single aspiration.

While Freud believed that a lot of our misery comes from the restrictions of civilization, he did not dismiss technological progress. On the contrary, he said that we ought not to infer that 'technical progress is without value for the economics of our happiness', that it was difficult to gauge how happy or otherwise people had been in the past, and that the values of cleanliness, order and justice, three of the most important features of civilization, stemmed from our early life in the family.

He cast doubt on what we might call the St Francis of Assisi doctrine, that universal love is the aim. Freud had two objections: 'A love that does not discriminate seems to me to forfeit a part of its own value, by doing an injustice to its object; and secondly, not all men are worthy of love.' He thought that, broadly speaking, Schiller had it right when he said that 'hunger and love are what move the world'. 'Hunger could be taken to represent the instincts which aim at preserving the individual; while love strives after objects, and its chief function, favoured in every way by nature, is the preservation of the species.'[21] He further felt that the education of the day concealed from children the part that sexuality would play in their lives, which hindered the integration into a human community, which community 'appears as a scarcely avoidable condition which must be fulfilled before the aim of happiness can be achieved'.

Freud concluded by reasserting that he had attempted to guard himself against 'the enthusiastic prejudice which holds that our civilization is the most precious thing we possess or could acquire and that its path will necessarily lead to heights of unimagined perfection'. Civilization is the work of man, not of God, and neither our future happiness, nor consolation, is guaranteed.

In *Moses and Monotheism* (1939) he argued that Moses was not Jewish but Egyptian. This theory was largely discredited before the ink was dry on the page but, as Michael Palmer says, that doesn't matter, in that the argument substantiates what Freud's other books on religion propose, that faith begins in the oedipal predicament, in each individual's need for a father figure. Jewish monotheism originated in a particular monotheistic episode of Egyptian history, in the course of which the people rose up against their father figure and killed him, as well as abandoning their new religion (symbolized by the story of the golden calf). They sought to forget this episode and fused Moses's identity with the Midianite Jethro, who was thus given the name Moses.[22] Elsewhere, Freud characterized Christianity as son worship replacing father worship (as in Judaism).

Freud never abandoned his view that religion was a form of infantilism, or rooted in infantile experience – the dependence of the child on the parent – and he believed that, just as in therapy when the patient is forced/invited to confront (unconscious) reality, so as society and civilization grew more 'mature', religion would wither away – much as Marx thought the state would wither away. Characterizing adherence to a religion as a form of unconscious mental illness, relegating it to that part of our nature that can usefully be discarded, was arguably the most frontal and offensive attack on God that a man could mount.

Viewed at this distance, we can see that Freud very much under-estimated the power of religion to endure in society. One might think that, as a specialist in the emotions, he should have realized this. In some ways – and this is a rare thing to say about Freud – he appears naive. But, as we have seen with the Vienna Circle and shall see again, he was not alone in his mistake.

No Refuge

By the time *Civilization and Its Discontents* appeared in 1929, Freud was well and truly estranged from Carl Jung, once his heir apparent and crown prince but now his most prominent rival. The rupture had begun as early as 1912 after they returned from their visit to America and Jung had published the second part of *Symbols of Transformation*, which aired for the first time his idea of the collective unconscious. In explaining religion, mythology and philosophy, he departed from – and threatened the status of – Freud's more scientific approach. The split became obvious a year later when *Symbols* was published in book form.

In *Totem and Taboo* Freud had taken on Jung on his own ground, so to speak, so it was perhaps no surprise that his rival should weigh in on much the same subject – the psychological plight of modern man – with an essay of his own.

Modern Man in Search of a Soul appeared in 1933. Although its title might seem to exactly address the matter we are considering here, in fact it ranged more widely. It was, for a start, an attack on Freud, one of its chapters airing the theoretical disagreements that Jung felt sep-arated them. The book was also a restatement, or an updating, of Jung's own psychoanalytical theories, in particular his theory of archetypes, which by then had reached as far as the notion of 'introverts' and 'extraverts', plus some thinking on the stages of life ('morning' and 'af-ternoon'), on psychology and literature and on 'archaic man'. The last two chapters only were given over to 'The spiritual problem of modern man' and 'Psychotherapists or the clergy'. He returned to the subject in his Terry Lectures, at Yale in 1937, and at other times after World War Two.

What particularly interested Jung was that twentieth-century man, in comparison with his forebears, was solitary, removed from the *participation mystique* and from 'submersion in a common unconsciousness'. Modern man no longer lives within the bounds of tradition and so has become 'unhistorical', discarding and outgrowing what went before. The new condition, Jung said, was a form of poverty and, in being unhistorical, a form of 'living in sin'. Modern individuals are aware of being 'the culmination of the history of mankind, the fulfilment and the end-product of countless centuries' and at the same time 'the disappointment of the hopes and expectations of the ages'. We have 'fallen into profound uncertainty', the Great War having shattered our faith in ourselves and in 'our own worth'. And that includes losing faith in the possibility of a rational organization of the world; 'that old dream of the millennium, in which peace and harmony should rule, has grown pale'.

Having lost all the metaphysical uncertainties of his medieval brother, modern man has set up in their place 'the ideals of material security, general welfare and humaneness'. But the very idea of 'progress', Jung said, had begun to 'terrorize' the imagination. 'Science has destroyed even the refuge of an inner life.' Thus had developed a widespread interest 'in all sorts of psychic phenomena as manifested in the growth of spiritualism, astrology, theosophy and so forth. The world has seen nothing like it since the end of the seventeenth century ... The modern movement which is numerically most impressive is undoubtedly Theosophy, together with its continental sister, Anthroposophy; these are pure Gnosticism in a Hindu dress. Compared with these movements the interest in scientific psychology is negligible.' The passionate interest in these movements arose from psychic energy which could no longer be invested in 'obsolete forms of religion ... For this reason such movements have a truly religious character, even when they pretend to be scientific.'[23]

Though Jung felt that this heightened concern with our psychic life was inevitable, he wasn't convinced that we should spend all our time dwelling on it. He thought that political internationalism, and sport, were antidotes to too great an obsession with psychic life, and that the political, social, artistic and psychological optimism of America had its place, too, in any future system.

Hitherto, only the more educated had sought psychological help, but in the future, he thought, this practice would spread to 'the masses'. Ever more clergymen were undergoing psychological training; indeed, only a method that comprised *both* psychology and religion could provide the enlightenment that most people sought from therapy – rather than, say, relief from neurotic symptoms. Jung states that people come to him to find meaning in their lives. And so what he sought, in effect, was to return them to religion (though not necessarily to any one particular confession). But that return would not be through faith per se so much as through psychological insight, the insight that religion performs various psychological functions in modern man and that only by explaining religion psychologically could many people be returned to the fold.

Unlike Freud, who grew up as a 'Godless Jew', Jung was the son of a pastor. Sons of pastors have played a significant role in Germanic philosophy and psychology – Gotthold Lessing, Johann Herder, Nietzsche himself, Wilhelm Dilthey, Jürgen Habermas were all sons of pastors. It is as if the son could not embrace the faith of the father and opted instead for a secular equivalent.

Jung entered university to study natural sciences, switched to medicine and then turned to psychiatry in his fourth year of study, when he attended a seance in which the subject was his fifteen-year-old cousin: in trance, she lost her Basel accent and spoke in High German, claiming she was controlled by spirits. An account of this episode formed the starting point of his first published work: his degree dissertation, *On the Psychology and Pathology of So-called Occult Phenomena* (1902). This neatly encapsulates his lively interest in both the occult and the unconscious.

His main disagreements with Freud lay in his rejection of the latter's insistence on the supreme importance of repressed sexuality in the aetiology of neurosis, and his conviction that beneath consciousness and the (personal) unconscious there is a third, deeper level, the collective unconscious. Jung's rival view, derived from his clinical experience and his researches among myths, ethnography and animal behaviour, he said, was based on observation, on the fact that, as he found it, 'psychic energy' was more significant as a source of neurosis than sexual repression. These researches showed, he claimed, that across the world – in myths, for example – there were many images and patterns that overlapped, causing him to conclude that they derive from very ancient experiences that have been incorporated into our nature 'at the deepest levels'.

To these patterns Jung attached the term 'archetype', of which he identified five as the most important: persona, anima and animus, extravert and introvert, shadow, and self.

Persona is the mask we present to the world, designed to mislead; anima is the female tendency in males and animus the male tendency in females; extravert and introvert are characteristic stances we have towards the world and represent perhaps Jung's most widely accepted innovation. What most concerns us here is his idea that God is an archetype. That is to say, it is a disposition within us, a disposition to believe in God, though at this point Jung gets very ambiguous.

An archetype cannot be known directly, he says, only inferred or intuited. Patterns observed – in mythology, for example – refer to 'archetype-contents', not to the actual 'archetype-form'. This is – or appears to be – a little like Moore's understanding of 'the good', which cannot be defined without corrupting and limiting the idea. Jung further complicates matters by arguing that the archetype of the self is very similar to – may even be identical with – the God-archetype. There are, within the collective unconscious, archetypes of 'wholeness' and 'perfection' (Jesus figures here); and the purpose of life, in the process of what he called 'individuation', is to bring the personal and collective unconscious into 'balance' so that the self-archetype and the God-archetype are in harmony.

This is certainly radical (insofar as it is understandable) – but is it friendly to religion, or blasphemous? This is the problem with Jung. He thought his concept of the collective unconscious was as important as quantum theory, but many people failed to grasp it. (No doubt many fail to follow quantum theory, but enough do to construct a technology based on it.) Critics point out that archetypes are as metaphysical as Plato's ideas and that although, after Jung, Claude Lévi-Strauss and Noam Chomsky found 'deep structures' in anthropology and linguistics, they have not produced a transformation in our understanding, as quantum theory has done.

Jung was convinced that the modern world is in a spiritual crisis brought about by secularization, materialism and extraversion. But he did not seek a return to the Church – he saw organized religion as 'spiritual death'. He thought we needed a 'massive reinvestment in spiritual life', to be achieved by reconnecting with the mythical world. 'Myths express life more precisely than science,' he said. 'Man cannot stand a meaningless life ... meaning comes from an unequivocal affirmation of the self ... The decisive question is: is man related to something infinite or not? ... The cosmic question is a fundamental requirement of the self.' As Anthony Stevens puts it, Jung himself had a reverence for the unconscious, the imagination, transcendence and gnosis (by which he meant knowledge through experience, not book-learning or belief) and he wanted others to experience the same. As Erich Fromm characterized it, Freud's unconscious contains mainly man's vices, Jung's contains mainly man's wisdom.[24]

At the same time, Jung insisted that the existence of a God-archetype was a psychological truth, not a theological one: it said nothing about the existence or otherwise of God or his/her/its form. This is why Jung has proved so controversial, and why his work so perplexes religious writers. His ideas are so ambiguous that we cannot be totally sure what he meant. At root he is saying – or seems to be saying – that man has an innate disposition to conceive of God (but not necessarily to believe in him), and that without coming to terms in some way with this disposition we can never feel whole or complete, or in balance; we cannot be spiritually healthy. We need to express the God-archetype to avoid neurosis.

Jung said that he 'abhorred metaphysics', yet his own thinking is even more metaphysical, less grounded in empiricism, than Freud's. And he finished by saying the exact opposite to Freud. Whereas Freud argued that religion was a form of collective neurosis, grounded in repressed sexual energy wrapped up in the oedipal dilemma, Jung said religious feelings helped cure neurosis. Whatever else it is, and however successful or unsuccessful his opaque theories may be, Jung's is the most elaborate attempt yet to marry theology and psychology.

The Myth of Wholeness

Were this book to follow a strictly chronological approach, this chapter would have begun with Franz Kafka. But there is a point in placing him here. His oeuvre is famously incomplete, his three more important books being unfinished when TB claimed him in 1924 at the age of forty; they were then published posthumously, having been put into order by his friend, the author and composer Max Brod. Any attempt at interpretation is, therefore, fraught with difficulty and to be treated with circumspection. That said, enough of his work remains in its original form for us to reconstruct at least some of Kafka's intentions; and from this we can see that those intentions were quite unlike those of any other author of modern times.

W.H. Auden said, 'Had one to name the author who comes nearest to bearing the same kind of relation to our age as Dante, Shakespeare and Goethe do to theirs, Kafka is the first one would think of.' Interpretation was the main concern of Kafka, in particular our search for wholeness which, he felt, was a legacy, an impossible legacy of traditional religion.

Each of his unfinished novels, *Amerika*, or *The Man Who Disappeared*, *The Trial* and *The Castle*, begins with the arrival of the main character in a complex social world where he is totally ignorant of the rules: America for Karl Rossmann, the law courts for Joseph K. and the village and castle for K. In each case, a variety of adventures follows but they notably fail to lead the protagonists to greater wisdom or understanding. These are not examples or symbols just of modern anomie, but more broadly of the human condition of 'natality', 'in which we all find ourselves confronted by [being born into] a world created by others according to a logic we do not intuitively understand'.[25] Karl Rossmann is seventeen, Joseph K. is thirty and K. is in his mid-thirties; none of them is a child but, equally, none of them has reached any kind of mature understanding of how the social world works. Nor will they make any progress in the course of the stories.

In these worlds of notable ambiguity, the most explicit of Kafka's stories is, perhaps (an inevitable qualifier), *The Castle*. To the main character K. the castle is less imposing than the church where he grew up, distant and inscrutable, just as the Judaeo-Christian God is distant and inscrutable. Even if we prefer the interpretation of *The Castle* as a parable of the modern phenomenon of bureaucracy, it too is often distant and inscrutable. This would appear to suggest that Kafka is describing the main problem of living in a secular world – people simply cannot believe or accept the faith of their childhood, when they thought the church magnificent (recalling Freud's arguments), but do not know what to replace it with. In the modern world we live without rules. We are forced to make interpretative judgements without sufficient information to base them on.

And this is the crux, the sediment left by the great monotheisms: that the mind of God can never be known, we shall never solve the mystery of God because God is the name we give to the mystery itself. Therefore, all we are left with in life is *interpretation*. We must construct our own interpretations of the world, and live with them. We never mature, as Freud anticipated, because we don't know the rules.

Any summary of a Kafka plot is, inevitably, more or less bloodless, for the point of his stories is to convey to the reader the unbalanced, uncomfortable, bewildering feeling that is the modern condition. Kafka exaggerates, but only in order to make his argument. And he lays before us his profound scepticism about interpretation itself. In 1970 Paul Ricoeur, the French Protestant professor of philosophy at the Sorbonne in Paris, identified what he called the 'hermeneutics of suspicion'. In *Freud and Philosophy* he said that Marx, Nietzsche and Freud were the 'masters of suspicion' because what they had in common was 'the decision to look upon the whole of consciousness primarily as "false" consciousness'. In particular, they were all suspicious, sceptical, of religious consciousness.

Each applied his theory to various aspects of contemporary life, including ideology, morality, art, literature and sexuality, but their core arguments were characterized by a suspicion of religion as myth – whether understood as 'an opiate that prevents the masses from awakening to their condition [Marx, whose ideas were at last being put into practice in the 1920s in Soviet Russia], a systematic form of *ressentiment* that subjects the great individual to a herd morality [Nietzsche], or a comforting illusion that allows civilized people to ignore their own repressed instincts [Freud]'. In rejecting religion as mere myth, if with a latent function, each of these masters had created his own alternative mythology, says Ricoeur, 'risking the accusation of having slain the Minotaur only to become himself the monster at the centre of the labyrinth'. They had, in effect, established their own new form of sacred myth, and this too was Kafka's point.[26]

Hermeneutics had developed in the late eighteenth and early nineteenth centuries in large part as an effort to understand Scripture as the word of God, whether in the Jewish tradition of the Talmud or the Christian tradition of allegorical interpretation. By this account, the all-important element in hermeneutics is that it is an outgrowth of monotheistic thought 'in which the apparent variety and heterogeneity of the world are understood to have a *unified*, underlying meaning, known only to God (or, in modern variants, to the skilled interpreter) [italics added]'.

And this is Kafka's ultimate concern, except that, like a good novelist, what he does is not *tell* us his argument but *show* us; he takes us into this new suspicious realm, he invites us to be suspicious of *all* interpretation, modern as much as traditional, by giving us a form of literature that *resists* interpretation.[27]

The Modern Trade-off

Some critics have seen *The Castle* as resembling the Bible, others have called it an allegory. K. is known only by his initial, other characters are known only by their professions or occupations; and the settings – the Castle, the Inn, the Schoolhouse – are drawn only in the most general terms, are given no proper names. This generality is broken from time to time by vivid detail. When K. sleeps on a straw mattress in the tap room of an inn, this echoes Christ's birth in the manger, but in the very next room the peasants are carousing – realistic details that strike a very different note. 'The effect is to leave the reader un-balanced,' says Lewis, 'threatening constantly to slip from one register to another, feeling increasingly as though some stabilizing level is just out of grasp.'

K.'s position as a secular outsider carries with it the task of bring-ing secular reason to his dealings with the sacred mystique of the Castle. The officials maintain this mystique in part through an elabo-rate hierarchy, in part through secrecy reminiscent of the bureaucrats in *The Trial*. In *The Castle* one figure in particular may be seen as close to being a God. This is Klamm, who seems on occasion to be an alter ego for K., whose initial he shares, at other times to be not dissimilar to Samuel Beckett's Godot. Klamm, in some ways, is 'God imagined as a senior bureaucrat'.[28]

What Kafka was most trying to do was to show his suspicion of hermeneutics. Indeed, as noted, his works *frustrate* attempts at in-terpretation. Invariably, they rebuff all attempts to give them a single meaning. Harold Bloom here expresses the opinion of many critics: '[W]hat most needs and demands interpretation in Kafka's writing is its perversely deliberate evasion of interpretation.' His recourse to multiple meanings 'challenges attempts to find a single latent truth but leaves open the (never confirmed) possibility of a higher revelation standing behind his texts. It is this quality that gives many of Kafka's texts the air of scriptural authority.'[29]

Moreover, interpretation for Kafka, as for Freud, offered op-portunities for belonging to a community. Neither writer was fully assimilated, and Kafka in particular was aware that he would always find it difficult to be anything other than 'a community of one'. But he seems to have felt that the way to a 'balanced' life – one without bewil-derment, comfortable rather than uncomfortable – was to become a member of an 'interpretative community'. This coincides, to an extent, with Henry James's idea of 'shared fictions'.

For Kafka, then, the modern condition is a trade-off. The most au-thentic course is to live as an outsider. Otherwise, one is a member of an interpretative community in which one finds the comfort of num-bers and the illusion of certainty but at the cost of hostility towards – and from – others who do not share the community's beliefs: there is no happy medium. Culture wars will replace – or add to – religious wars (how right he was about that).

What Kafka is showing us, then, is that religious belief is itself an interpretation, one centred on the idea of unity and latency, the idea that there *is* an ultimate meaning. And this is a notion that no longer suffices, not because it is wrong in its details (if God could ever be called a detail) but because our basic predicament is 'natality', profound ignorance. We don't know the rules of existence, we don't even know if there *are* any. All we can do is make the most of it. Other interpretations of life – Marxism, Nietzscheanism, Freudianism, for example – may seem to have a handle on reality, for a time at least; but the real legacy of the great monotheisms is to leave us with the *conviction* that there is an underlying unity to reality. Kafka's stories *show* us that we have no way of knowing whether that is true, not even in principle. There is no such thing as wholeness, because wholeness, too, is an interpretation. Kafka seemed to take delight in creating disturbing societies where the rules of existence are unfathomable.

15

The Faiths of the Philosophers

As has often been pointed out, the God of the philosophers of the past – Boethius, Hume, Spinoza – differed in the glosses placed on his divinity, as to whether and to what extent he (usually 'he') was omniscient, omnipresent and all-powerful, or co-ruled with nature. This book has already explored what such figures as Edmund Husserl, the American pragmatists and Martin Heidegger thought should be the main philosophical concerns in the post-Nietzschean, post-Christian world, but in the interwar years – with the painful memories of the Great War still so vivid, with Russia and Germany in thrall to totalitarianism and with the West disfigured by depression – philosophers on both sides of the Atlantic regrouped, to assess recent political and scientific developments, and to offer their thoughts on the way forward.

Dewey's Common Faith

The American philosopher and psychologist John Dewey, born in Burlington, Vermont, held that 'democracy begins in conversation'. 'Conversation' is a gentle word, but then Dewey was a gentle man for whom democracy, what it meant, how it might be better achieved, was all-consuming. And it naturally affected his thinking about God.

For him it was possible to experience religious feelings without metaphysical commitments to anything supernatural. Born in 1859, by the time he was thirty-five he had dispensed with much of the doctrine unique to Christianity, though he kept to Christianity's ethical concerns. He never gave up entirely on the idea of God, though he abandoned it in its traditional theological form. For Dewey, in *A Common Faith* (1934), there is no privileged standpoint (such as science or theology) from which the fundamental metaphysical structure of nature 'in itself' can be determined. Such entities as 'values', 'freedom', 'purposiveness', which distinguish us from other animals, 'belong to our human nature'.[1]

For Dewey, 'Any activity pursued on behalf of an ideal and against obstacles and in spite of threats of personal loss because of conviction of its general and enduring value is religious in quality.' The religious must be liberated from the supernatural commitments of actual historical religions, from dogmas and doctrines that are, pragmatically, unnecessary. The values and ideals belonging to the religious attitude are not imaginary but real; they are "made out of the hard stuff of the world of physical and social experience".' The religious feeling is, by this account, a natural part of nature. The problems arise when we become entangled in the supernatural. 'Religion must be brought down to Earth, to what is "common" between us. Supernaturalism – especially the claim that religions have a monopoly of supernatural means to further human ideals – is an obstacle in pursuing the natural changes that are in our power to bring about; hence religious values need emancipation.'

For Dewey the crux of the matter lies in the distinction between religion and 'religious'. A religion is 'a special body of beliefs and practices having some kind of institutional organization', whereas 'religious', an adjective, 'does not denote any specific entity but "attitudes that may be taken toward every object and every proposed end or ideal"'.

Dewey is focusing on religious experience as a common faith or attitude rather than an individual one. 'Religious' can be connected with aesthetic, scientific, moral or political experience, as well as companionship and friendship. Whenever we experience the plenitude of life, a religious attitude, outlook or function is in play. And 'the paradigmatic case of a social enterprise carrying religious qualities is science', whose methods he actively sought to introduce into political society. 'Faith in the continued disclosing of truth through directed cooperative human endeavor is more religious in quality than is any faith in a completed revelation.'

He insists there can be no return to pre-scientific revealed religion. Rather, we must understand faith as 'the unification of the self through allegiance to inclusive ideal ends, which imagination presents to us and to which the human will responds as worthy of controlling our desires and choices'. Again, he underlines that these ideal ends are not supernatural. 'The assumption that the objects of religion exist already in some realm of Being seems to add nothing to their force, while it weakens their claim over us as ideals, in so far as it bases that claim upon matters that are intellectually dubious.' The aims and ideals that move us are generated through imagination. 'But they are not made out of imaginary stuff. They are made out of the hard stuff of the world of physical and social experience.'[2]

'Use of the words "God" or "divine" to convey the union of actual with the ideal may protect man from a sense of isolation and from consequent despair or defiance.' In other words, if people want to use the word 'God' for this feeling they have, that is OK by Dewey; but he himself has no need of it – it is a psychological matter, not a supernatural one.

More important, this way of conceptualizing God enables him to promote his view of *continuous growth* as our highest goal. The growth of knowledge stemming from scientific inquiry, or 'growth in understanding of nature', may be regarded as religious, and insofar as it liberates religious ideas from narrow supernaturalism it is ethically, socially and politically relevant: 'I cannot understand how any realization of the democratic ideal as a vital moral and spiritual ideal in human affairs is possible without surrender of the concept of the basic division to which supernatural Christianity is committed. Whether or not we are, save in some metaphorical sense, all brothers, we are at least all in the same boat traversing the same turbulent ocean. The potential religious significance of this fact is infinite.'[3]

His point here is this: 'We have the potential to grow, struggling together toward the actualization of ideals, instead of assuming that

our ideals are "already embodied in some supernatural or metaphysical sense in the very framework of existence".' For Dewey there can
be no such thing as 'the very framework of existence' – that is woolly
metaphysics. Religious feeling, when it occurs, stems from 'the sense
of awe we have at being part of the immense (but entirely natural)
cosmos'.

There is no ready-made divine reality 'out there', in a transcendent
world order, which we will one day penetrate through either religious
experience, dogmatic revelation or theological sophistry. There is,
rather, the human pursuit of religiously conceptualizable ideals, 'an
ongoing struggle for the good in the natural world of material and
social existence', an entirely human achievement – crucially, more
than the sum of its parts – produced by our own intelligence and imagination. If we want to call the harmony we achieve when the ideal
and the actual meet, divine, then so be it, but we shouldn't take it for
something it is not.[4]

His crucial point was that religion should 'return to an intimate
connection with our other social pursuits'. In *The Quest for Certainty*
(1929) Dewey characterized the religious attitude as 'a sense of the
possibilities of existence and as devotion to the cause of these possibilities, as distinct from acceptance of what is given at the time'. As
Sami Pihlström says, Dewey's 'God' is something like a combination
of social intelligence, democracy and science. Dewey was not a theist,
and he dismissed any idea of a transcendent God. 'God' for him was at
most 'a poetic symbol to identify those forces and values in experience
that are of ultimate concern to a people in their quest for well-being'.[5]
Like poetry, religious feeling should be one of the 'unforced flowers of
life'. He was criticized by theologians for devising what they considered 'a watered-down version of faith', as well as by atheists who didn't
see why he needed to use words like 'God' or 'divine' at all.

What is most valuable in Dewey's work is his rigorous attempt to
reconcile scientific and religious thinking. He sums up: 'Ours is the
responsibility of conserving, transmitting, rectifying and expanding
the heritage of values we have received, that those who come after us
may receive it more solid and secure, more widely accessible and more
generously shared than we have received it. Here are all the elements

for a religious faith that shall not be confined to sect, class or race. Such a faith has always been implicitly the common faith of mankind. It remains to make it explicit and militant.[6]

Wittgenstein's Wordless Faith

Ludwig Wittgenstein's views on religion are generally less well known than the picture theory of language that he sets out in the *Tractatus Logico-Philosophicus*. He wrote no books on the subject, but he gave a series of lectures on religious belief in Cambridge in 1938. What we know about these lectures stems from a curious publishing venture carried out by Cyril Barrett, who compiled a volume, not published until 1966, entitled *Lectures and Conversations on Aesthetics, Psychology and Religious Belief*. Barrett's book is based not on Wittgenstein's own lecture notes, but on those of the students who attended the lectures. He points out that since these students were among the most ardent followers of the master, 'we may safely assume that they have provided a faithful record of his teaching'.[7]

In these lectures, Wittgenstein explores two areas that especially interest us. First, in characteristic Wittgensteinian style he analyses the language of belief to show how misunderstandings arise, how believers and non-believers 'talk past' each other. And second, he explores the idea of the mystical – this too, he says, is related to the use and misuse of language.

He starts from the premise, familiar from the *Tractatus*, that there are limits to language, that language is, in effect, the limit of our world, and that the idiosyncrasies of language have 'bewitched the intelligence'. In the realm of ethics, for example, the sentence 'He is a good man' looks like the sentence 'He is a good tennis player' but it is not. A man or a woman might or might not want to be a good tennis player, and that would not necessarily be of interest to a third party. But if someone were to say, 'I don't want to be good', this would seem shocking to most people. The imperative to be good in this latter sense is something we should care about for its own sake, 'irrespective of any end to which it may be the means'. Similarly, when we use the term 'eternity', whether we are religious or not, we do not mean by that 'infinite temporal duration', we mean 'timelessness'.

This is more than splitting hairs, because he thinks that the limits of language are really at the basis of what we mean when we say we have a mystical experience. Wittgenstein did not accept that there is any such thing as metaphysics or transcendence in the supernatural sense. Rather, he thought that the mystical arises from the fact that some things can be 'shown but not said'. In a vivid example, he identifies how impossible it would be for an artist to paint us a picture of his *way* of painting. Every artist has his or her own distinctive mode (think of how a Renoir is different from a Degas or a Van Gogh), such that no signature is ever needed. 'But what could we be asking for, if we said to one such artist, "We don't want a picture of anything which you see in the world around you. What we want is simply a picture of your way of painting things. Not an example of that way, mark you! A picture of that way itself!"? Patently, this is a request which no artist could fulfil ... An artist's way of painting is manifest in his [or her] every picture, but it cannot (logically) be the subject matter of any of his [her] pictures.'[8]

In other words, there are certain aspects of experience/the world that cannot be put into words, or painted. He went on to say, more generally: 'The propositions of philosophy and logic are not themselves logical pictures of possible states of affairs. They show what the structure of language is, although this cannot be said.' Wittgenstein came to the conclusion that language gives us a feeling of the world as a whole, but a limited whole, and it is this sense of limits, and that there is something beyond those limits, that constitutes the mystical. 'Answers to questions concerning the sense of the world must necessarily take us beyond the world (i.e., "all that is the case").' And '[T]he sense or value of what is the case cannot (logically) be answered. . . . To view or feel the world as a limited whole is to be aware of the limits which meaning-rules impose on what can be said.'[9]

Wittgenstein thought that mysticism stems, at least in part, from 'wondering' at the world, that it should exist at all. This, too, he felt, was a misuse of language, because we can't really *imagine* what it would be like for the world not to exist. We can imagine a house that we know not to exist – and we can imagine what that plot of land would look like without the house on it – but we can't even begin to imagine what the universe or the world would look like without the universe in the universe: it doesn't make sense, we have come up against the limits of language, and it is at these logical/semantic limits that the sense of the mystical is grounded.

And this is where Wittgenstein is at his most distant from the logical positivists, in particular in his remark quoted at the start of this book: 'We feel that even when *all possible* scientific questions have been answered, the problems of life remain completely untouched [italics in original].' (*Tractatus*, 6.52.)

Wittgenstein, like Schopenhauer, believed that morality is a sphere for the exercise of the will rather than reason. 'It is the will alone that can break out from the limits imposed by language . . . If the good or bad exercise of the will does alter the world, it can alter only the limits of the world, not the facts – not what can be expressed by means of language . . . The world of the happy man is a different one from that of the unhappy man.'[10]

He further felt that the mystical shows itself in both art and action. He discussed with his friend Paul Engelmann the way the mystical could manifest itself in poetry: the sense of a poem going 'beyond' words, breaking the limits of language, is shared by many. He thought, too, that the mystical showed itself in the schoolteaching that he undertook between his various spells at Cambridge, but Wittgenstein also believed that there are aspects of schoolteaching that also go beyond words, beyond the facts of the case, and that too may be regarded as a mystical experience.

Engelmann says that Wittgenstein had a concept that he called 'wordless faith', a conscious effort to live out the implications of the *Tractatus* – that is, to *do* what could not be said but could be shown. In regard to ethics, Wittgenstein believed that any attempt to put them into words, to make of them a doctrine, was invariably a corruption. 'The thing to do is to *say* nothing about ethics or religion but simply to act.' (This coincides with Moore's idea that 'good' cannot be defined.) We must remember that it is logically impossible for the sense of the world to be itself part of the world, 'since the meaning of anything cannot be part of that of which it is the meaning'.[11]

A concern with the mystical understood in this way could make someone religious in a Wittgensteinian sense, but it would be a religion, as he asserted, without a doctrine, even without doctrinal principles. He saw certain similarities between being religious – in the mystical sense he described – and being in love. No one who has been in love asks the purpose of it, or thinks that it can be put into words without losing some of its experiential quality. This links with Robert Musil's 'other condition'.

So, always acknowledging that any attempt to put Wittgenstein's idea of the mystical into words is by definition self-defeating, his ideal type of the mystical/religious individual, who did not embrace supernatural doctrines, would be someone who so loved poetry or paintings or teaching that he or she devoted a lifetime to creating, or intimating – in their art or actions – what could not be said. Living at the limits of language, and being aware of those limits, is to live on the edge of a mystical life. At certain points in his career Wittgenstein seems to have felt the urge to live in this way, that it was somehow a special form of intensity, a life that was somehow 'higher': 'The highest cannot be spoken; it can only be done.'[12]

He also tackled the question of the soul. He thought that religious forces had taken over two psychological phenomena and amalgamated them. One is the fact that we know we understand ourselves very differently from the way we understand others. We are 'inside' ourselves in a way that we can never be inside anyone else. At the same time, explaining the second phenomenon: 'When we are grief-stricken, where do we feel our grief?' We could say we feel it more over our right eye than over our left ear, he suggests, but we don't say it because it's not what we feel. His point is that we don't have a language to talk about many aspects of experience, not even after all these years of evolution. This is where areas of ambiguity arise, and 'soul' is the name we give to this gap in our self-understanding.

The concept of the soul is thus one aspect of the mysticism he identified, perhaps the most personal aspect of his wordless faith. Using his illustration – we feel grief in our soul because we have no other way to describe it, there is nowhere else to place it.[13]

Whitehead's Faith in Process

The meeting and subsequent friendship between Wittgenstein and Bertrand Russell has become famous. The former turned up unannounced in the latter's room in Cambridge while Russell was having tea. Wittgenstein spoke little English, but refused to converse in German. Despite this unpropitious beginning, Russell quickly determined that Wittgenstein was a genius, and the Austrian was invited to join the Apostles (see p. 79).

Like Wittgenstein, Russell was an aristocrat. The godson of the philosopher John Stuart Mill, he was born halfway through the reign of Queen Victoria, in 1872, and died nearly a century later, by which time he, like many others, saw nuclear weapons as the greatest threat to mankind. Once described as 'an aristocratic sparrow', he is shown in Augustus John's portrait to have had 'piercingly sceptical eyes, quizzical eyebrows, and a fastidious mouth'.[14] He once wrote that 'the search for knowledge, unbearable pity for suffering and a longing for love' were the three passions that governed his long life. 'I have found [life] worth living,' he concluded, 'and would gladly live it again if the chance were offered.'

One can see why. John Stuart Mill was not his only eminent connection – T.S. Eliot, Lytton Strachey, G.E. Moore, Joseph Conrad, D.H. Lawrence, Ludwig Wittgenstein and Katherine Mansfield were just some of his circle. He championed the Soviet Union, won the Nobel Prize for Literature (in 1950), and appeared (sometimes to his irritation) as a character in at least six works of fiction, including books by Roy Campbell, T.S. Eliot, Aldous Huxley, D.H. Lawrence and Siegfried Sassoon. When Russell died in 1970 at the age of ninety-seven, there were more than sixty of his books still in print.

Of all his publications the most original was the massive tome that appeared first in 1910, entitled, after a work by Isaac Newton, *Principia Mathematica*. This book is one of the least read of modern times. In the first place it is about mathematics, not everyone's favourite reading. Second, it is inordinately long – three volumes running to more than two thousand pages. But it was the third reason which ensured that this book – which indirectly led to the birth of the computer

– was read by only a few: it consists mostly of a tightly knit argument conducted by means of specially invented symbols. Thus 'not' is represented by a curved bar; a bold-face **v** stands for 'or'; a square dot means 'and'. The book was ten years in the making, and its aim was nothing less than to explain the logical foundation of mathematics.

In December 1889 Russell went up to Cambridge – an obvious choice since the only passion that had been observed in the young man was for mathematics, and Cambridge excelled in that discipline. Russell loved the clarity and certainty of maths, and found it, he said, as moving as poetry, romantic love or the glories of nature. He particularly liked the fact that the subject was 'totally uncontaminated by human feelings'.

At Cambridge he attended Trinity College, where he sat for a scholarship, and here he enjoyed good fortune, for his examiner was Alfred North Whitehead. Then barely twenty-nine, Whitehead was a kindly man (he was known in Cambridge as 'cherub'), already showing signs of the forgetfulness for which he later became notorious. No less passionate about mathematics than was Russell, he exercised that passion in an irregular way. In the scholarship examination Russell came second – a young man named Bushell gained higher marks. However, Whitehead convinced himself that Russell was the abler man and so burned all the examination answers, and his own markings, before recommending Russell for the scholarship.

Russell did not disappoint, and graduated as a 'wrangler', as first-class mathematics graduates are known at Cambridge. But if this makes his success sound effortless, it is misleading. Russell's finals so exhausted him (the same happened with Einstein) that afterwards he sold all his maths books and turned with relief to philosophy. He said later that he saw philosophy as a sort of no-man's-land between science and theology. By then he was aware that Whitehead, now a good friend, was working on many of the same problems, and they decided to collaborate.

The collaboration was a monumental affair, with a few side issues (there are grounds for believing that Russell fell in love with Whitehead's wife). For a decade the book dominated both men's lives, and when it appeared in December 1910 it was clear that Russell and

Whitehead had discovered something important – that most mathematics, if not all, could be derived from a number of axioms logically related to one another. In the *Spectator*, the reviewer concluded that the book 'marked an epoch in the history of speculative thought' in its attempt 'to make mathematics more solid than the universe itself'.

After *Principia*, the two men began to go their separate ways. (They would remain friends for the rest of their lives but Russell's anti-war activities during 1914–18 did not sit well with Whitehead, who lost his son during the hostilities.)

Both now embraced philosophy more fully. Whitehead left Cambridge, after twenty-five years, and moved to University College, London; then, four years later, he was appointed professor of applied mathematics at Imperial College. He stayed there for ten years, producing *The Concept of Nature* and a book on relativity, among other works. In 1924 he moved to Harvard as professor of philosophy, sparking the quip that the first philosophy lectures he ever attended were those he delivered himself.

While he was in London, Whitehead had turned his attention to the philosophy of science, and it was this that led him to reconfigure ideas about God. His knowledge of mathematics, and physics too, led him to reject the traditional view that each object has a simple temporal and spatial location. Instead, he proposed that all objects should be understood as fields having both spatial and temporal extensions. He illustrated his argument by asserting that there is no such thing as a point, an entity without mass. Nor can there be a line, understood as something with length but no breadth. These are abstractions, not concrete entities. This led him to the view that objects, things, are events, the result of (essentially ongoing) processes, and that this, *process*, is the 'fundamental metaphysical constituent' of the world, rather than substance. The basic fact of life is flux: even stones or pebbles, which appear to lie in just one place for years on end, are changing slowly – the whole world is forever 'becoming'. This is the essence of Whitehead's *Process and Reality*, published in 1929 (which started life as a series of Gifford Lectures in 1927/28).[15]

The 1920s were a decade of remarkable progress in quantum physics: wave-particle duality was discovered, Einstein's theory of relativity had been empirically confirmed, the uncertainty principle had been demonstrated, and Newton's fixed mechanical universe was exploded once and for all. It was Whitehead's view, in response to these latest discoveries, that energy was the underlying principle of reality, that it was constantly forming and reforming; and this had two consequences of particular interest here. First, that this process, flux, becoming – call it what you will – is in fact the only divine entity that exists, that God in effect set the world in motion; he is the flux that brings everything into actuality, but he doesn't directly govern the form the process takes – there is freedom in the processes by which energy takes its various forms. And second, that the main concern of traditional religions has been to find some order in the flux of process, in an attempt to make sense of what has gone before, in order to anticipate what lies ahead.

Whitehead's writing style leaves a lot to be desired, his arguments are not always easy to follow, but it would seem that he advocated a form of post-Nietzschean deism in which there is a God who creates energy but little more, and in which there is certainly no role for Abraham, Isaiah, Jesus or Mohammed. Perhaps because of his poor style, perhaps because deism is too abstract for many would-be believers, his attempt to marry science and religion has never proved very attractive.

Russell's Faith in Knowledge and Love

Russell's message was very different. In books and essays, *Why I am not a Christian*, *The Conquest of Happiness*, *Satan in the Suburbs*, *Behaviourism and Values*, *Eastern and Western Ideals of Happiness*, *The Danger of Creed Wars*, Russell faced the problems and opportunities of secular society head on, in much plainer language than Whitehead seemed capable of. Described by Paul Edwards as 'one of the great heretics in morals and religion', Russell was never a purely technical philosopher. He had, said Edwards, 'always been deeply concerned with the fundamental questions to which religions have given their respective answers – questions about man's place in the universe and the nature of the good life'.[16]

Russell's style was uncompromising and combative. 'I think all the great religions of the world – Buddhism, Hinduism, Christianity, Islam, and Communism – both untrue and harmful.' After noting that a belief in hell was no longer necessary among Christians (their beliefs were getting 'smaller'), he dismissed the reasons people have for believing in God. 'What really moves people to believe in God is not any intellectual argument at all. Most people believe in God because they have been taught from an early infancy to do it, and that is the main reason.' He thought it doubtful that Christ ever existed, and declared that Christianity was a doctrine that 'put cruelty into the world and gave the world generations of cruel torture'. He saw no evidence that religion made people virtuous – in fact, 'every moral progress that there has been in the world, has been consistently opposed by the organized Churches of the world'.[17]

Furthermore, neither experience nor observation had led him to think that believers were either happier or unhappier, on average, than unbelievers.[18] 'The whole conception of God is a conception derived from the ancient Oriental despotisms ... it seems contemptible and not worthy of self-respecting human beings ... A good world needs knowledge, kindliness, and courage.' All of what he called the great cosmic philosophies showed, he said, a naive humanism: '[T]he great world, so far as we know it from the philosophy of nature, is neither good nor bad, and is not concerned to make us happy or unhappy. All such philosophies spring from self-importance and are best corrected by a little astronomy ... We are ourselves the ultimate and irrefutable arbiters of value, and in the world of value Nature is only a part. Thus in this world we are greater than Nature.'[19]

The First World War 'was wholly Christian in origin'. All the politicians involved in it were 'applauded as earnest Christians'. He also held that the dangerous features of communism were 'reminiscent of the medieval Church. They consist of fanatical acceptance of doctrines embodied in a Sacred Book, unwillingness to examine these doctrines uncritically, and savage persecution of those who reject them.'[20]

But Russell wasn't merely a negative heretic, pointing out the falsehoods and harmful effects of religions. 'Knowledge and love are both indefinitely extensible,' he said, 'therefore, however good a life may be, a better life can be imagined. Neither love without knowledge, nor knowledge without love, can produce a good life.' Love was more fundamental, 'since it will lead intelligent people to seek knowledge, in order to find out how to benefit those whom they love'.

'In all descriptions of the good life here on earth we must assume a certain basis of animal vitality and animal instinct; without this, life becomes tame and uninteresting. Civilization should be something added to this, not substituted for it; the ascetic saint and the detached sage fail in this respect to be complete human beings. A small number of them may enrich a community; but a world composed of them would die of boredom.' Love at its fullest, he said, 'is an indissoluble combination of the two elements, delight and well-wishing . . . Delight without well-wishing may be cruel; well-wishing without delight easily tends to become cold and a little superior . . . Delight, in this actual world, is unavoidably selective and prevents us from having the same feelings toward all mankind.'

He had no doubt that all human behaviour springs from desire, and therefore ethical notions can have no importance except as they influence desire. 'Outside human desires there is no moral standard.' 'The whole effectiveness of any ethical argument lies in the scientific part, i.e. in the proof that one kind of conduct, rather than some other, is a means to an end which is widely desired.'[21]

He had several interesting 'smaller' ideas along the way – for example, that children should be taught about sex before puberty, 'when it is not exciting'; that conscience is a 'fallacious' guide, 'since it consists of vague reminiscences of precepts heard in early youth, so that it is never wiser than its possessor's nurse or mother'; and that the Christian idea of conversion was dangerous to the extent that it encouraged the notion that salvation can be suddenly brought about. On the contrary, 'there is no short cut to the good life, whether individual or social'. This is why, he believed, personal salvation 'cannot serve for the definition of the good life'.[22]

To live the good life in the fullest sense, 'a man must have a good education, friends, love children (if he desires them), a sufficient income to keep him from want and anxiety, good health and work which is not uninteresting. All these things, in varying degrees, depend upon the community, and are helped or hindered by political events. The good life must be lived in a good society, and is not fully possible otherwise.'[23] He wasn't convinced by Moore's arguments. 'It is no use to give men something abstractedly considered "good"; we must give them something desired or needed if we are to add to their happiness. Science may learn in time to mould our desires so that they shall not conflict with those of other people to the same extent as they do now; then we shall be able to satisfy a larger proportion of our desires than at present. In that sense, but in that sense only, our desires will then have become "better". A single desire is no better and no worse, considered in isolation, than any other; but a group of desires is better than another group if all of the first group can be satisfied simultaneously, while in the second group some are inconsistent with others. That is why love is better than hatred.'[24]

He agreed with William James that the test of a belief is not its conformity to some 'fact', 'since we can never reach the facts concerned; the test is its success in promoting life and the achievement of our desires'. He agreed with Whitehead's views on matter, that substance is a series of events, but disagreed fundamentally on the question of order and God's role, or non-role, in that: 'There is no reason to deny the apparently piecemeal and higgledy-piggledy nature of the world.' Knowledge, to which he attached the highest importance, alongside love, nonetheless is 'a natural fact like another, with no mystic significance and no cosmic importance'.[25]

He concluded that the main difference between the West and the East, in the realm of religion/philosophy, was that in the East there was no doctrine of original sin. Confucius, for instance, believed that men are born good. This made a profound difference, because it meant that, in the East, men were 'more apt to submit to reason'.[26]

Would each of these men – all noble and original in their aims – have had more of an impact had not events in Germany in the 1930s claimed more of everyone's attention?

16

Nazi Religions of the Blood

When he was a boy of six, Adolf Hitler was for a short time a choirboy at the Benedictine monastery at Lambach in Austria. What he loved most, he said later, was 'the solemn splendour of church festivals'. By the time he reached Munich in 1919 as a thirty-year-old ex-soldier, such religious feelings as he still had were far removed from Catholicism. By now Hitler was caught up with the *völkisch* movement, shaped by such individuals as Paul de Lagarde, who held that Christianity was a bastardization of faith in that both Catholicism and Protestantism were 'distortions' of the Bible, brought about mainly by St Paul who, Lagarde insisted, had 'Judaized' Christianity.[1]

Many crude publications circulated in the Vienna of Hitler's day, one entitled *Forward to Christ! Away with Paul! German Religion!* Here too the argument was that the 'poisoner Paul and his *Volk*' were the 'arch-enemies of Jesus', who 'had to be removed from the entrance to the kingdom of God' before 'a true German church can open its doors'. The difficulty of Jesus being Jewish was circumvented in various ways, either by making him 'Aryan' or, in the case of Theodor Fritsch, an anti-Semitic engineer-turned-publisher, by arguing that Galileans were in fact Gauls, who in turn were German. (He claimed to have demonstrated this philologically.) All of which became a central element in Hitler's own view of Christianity, but in addition he claimed to see in Jesus a mirror image of himself, 'a brave and persecuted struggler against the Jews'.

Nonetheless, Hitler was not anxious for the fledgling Nazi movement to antagonize established religion. Dr Artur Dinter, a former scientist and dramatist who had lost his young daughter tragically, called for 'a German national Church' that would counter modernism, materialism and the Jews, 'much as Jesus had done' (his *Richtrunen* were intended to replace the Ten Commandments). Hitler dismissed him, telling Dinter, who had joined the National Socialists before Hitler himself and held Party card no. 5, that he would waste no time on a 'religious reformation'; he would steer clear of religious issues 'for all time to come'.[2]

The German Theological Renaissance

He didn't stick to his word. When the Nazis did achieve power, their relationship with religion would remain troublesome. In some ways their views were simplistic, in other ways cynical and manipulative. Hitler himself seems to have a had a vague notion of a 'sacred universe', but in purely intellectual terms the Nazis largely ignored the fact that Germany was just then undergoing a renaissance in religious thought.[3] It is a fact largely overlooked that, just as the Germans had produced a 'golden generation' in physics, philosophy, history and film as the 1920s turned into the 1930s, so in theology there was a parallel cohort of very creative individuals. According to Alister McGrath, writing in 1986, modern German theology has an 'inherent brilliance', but since the Second World War 'the equivalent of a theological iron curtain appears to have descended upon Europe, excluding ideas of German origin from the theological fora of the English-speaking world'.[4]

This German theological renaissance – comprising Albert Schweitzer, Rudolf Steiner, Karl Barth, Rudolf Bultmann, Martin Buber and Dietrich Bonhoeffer – and the world's ignorance about it, are interesting enough phenomena in themselves, but they concern us for three reasons. First, their scholarship gave a more prominent role to Paul in the creation of early Christianity, and this in turn gave a certain credibility to later Nazi claims that Paul had somehow perverted

Jesus's message. Second, several of these men (Barth, Bonhoeffer and Buber in particular) were very brave in standing up to the Nazis and between them suggest, along with other evidence, that the Nazis' chief worry in the early stages of the Third Reich was that organized Christianity was the main threat to their authority. The fact that this threat never materialized is outside the scope of this book, but it is a major unanswered conundrum of twentieth-century history and conceivably a terrible indictment of the religious stance. The third issue that concerns us is embodied in the work of Karl Barth.

Barth (1886–1968) is widely regarded as the greatest Protestant theologian of his century, and possibly the greatest since Luther.[5] Born in Basel where his father Fritz was a minister and professor of New Testament and early Church history, Barth studied at Bern, Berlin, Tübingen and Marburg Universities. At Berlin he attended the seminars of Adolf von Harnack, professor of church history at Giessen, whose book *The Essence of Christianity* (1900) tried to go beyond all the historical criticisms of the Bible that had accreted during the nineteenth century. And it was there that Barth first encountered the ideas of liberal theology (mainly the search for the historical Jesus) that he would eventually rebel against. After his studies he returned to Switzerland as a pastor.[6]

He came to believe that the 'higher criticism' in Germany, although largely responsible for the new scholarly techniques, nevertheless missed the point. The concern with Jesus as a historical figure obscured Jesus as the revealed word of God. Mankind no longer consulted the Bible in the way that its compilers intended it to be read. In the midst of war, Barth re-examined the scriptures and, in particular, in 1916 began a careful examination of Paul's Letter to the Romans. This proved of great significance for him, and in 1922 he published *The Epistle to the Romans*, the main message of which was, as Paul himself had said, that God saves only those who 'trust not in themselves but solely in God'.[7] This led to Barth's seminal view, what he called 'the Godness of God': that God 'is wholly other', totally different from humans.[8]

It was this idea, that God is 'wholly other', that brought him to the attention of other theologians and many of the faithful. In the year he published *The Epistle*, together with a number of other theologians, including Rudolf Bultmann, he started a journal, *Zwischen den Zeiten* (Between the Times), which formed the main outlet for what became known as 'Crisis Theology' (the 'crisis' being the First World War and the 'sinfulness', the great distance from God, that it was deemed to be evidence of). *Zwischen* remained a powerful force until it was closed down in 1933.[9]

Barth was therefore responsible for a completely new understanding of God, a God more abstract and, in a sense, less knowable than ever before. It was an idea that probably opened up an even wider gap between believers and unbelievers than had ever existed before, in the sense that Barth's God was *defined* by his unknowability (Freud in particular was dismissive). In addition, Barth's idea of 'otherness' was to prove very influential later in the century, when the 'Postmodernist Turn' took place and a focus on the 'other' (not just in a theological sense) became a central concern (see chapter 26).

Such was the impact of Barth's theology, in Germany in particular at first, that by the time the Nazis came to power in 1933 he was a public figure. He then emerged as one of the leaders – if not *the* leader – of church opposition to the National Socialists, expressed in the Barmen Declaration of 1934.[10] In the previous April the 'Evangelical Church of the German Nation' had been created under Nazi influence and had published its guiding principles, which made anti-Semitism a central plank of this new religion and forbade marriage between 'Germans and Jews', concluding: 'We want an Evangelical Church that is rooted in our nationhood.'[11]

In response, Barth was one of those founding the so-called 'Confessing Church' which rejected the attempt to set up a German Church, and in particular the Nazi concept of 'blood and soil' as a basis for it. In May 1934 representatives of the Confessing Church met at Barmen and delivered their declaration, based on a draft that Barth had prepared, in which they rejected the 'false doctrine' that 'there could be areas of our life in which we would belong not to Jesus Christ but to other lords'. Barth himself refused to take the oath of unconditional allegiance to Hitler, was dismissed and returned to Basel, where he continued to speak out in support of the Jews.[12]

The Nazi Form of Christianity

For a while after taking office, Hitler was careful to offer some comfort to the Churches. He confided to Goebbels that the best way to treat them was to 'hold back for the present and coolly strangle any attempts at impudence or interference in the affairs of state'. In reality the Führer was contemptuous of the Lutheran clergy, as 'insignificant little people . . . They have neither a religion they can take seriously nor a great position to defend, like Rome.'[13]

Hitler recognized the Catholic Church's institutional force, and even though the Pope had condemned Mussolini's species of fascism in 1931 as 'pagan worship of the state', the Führer signed a concordat with the Vatican two years later. On the Vatican side, the agreement was chiefly the work of Cardinal Eugenio Pacelli, the Vatican secretary of state and the future Pius XII, who had been nuncio in Munich in the 1920s and had lived in Berlin. Pacelli managed to retain autonomy for the German *see* and some control over education, at the price of diplomatic recognition for the new regime.*

The Nazis moved swiftly in religious education. New regulations stipulated that all parents must enrol their children in religious instruction. Seven Catholic feast days were sanctioned as public holidays, and Nazi Party members who had left the Church were ordered to rejoin. Until 1936 the German army stipulated that every serving soldier must belong to either the Catholic or one of the evangelical denominations.

But a lot of this, in retrospect, can be seen as tactical manoeuvring. Many thought that the real founding moment of Nazism was the Nietzschean 'death of God'. More recently, however, Richard Steigmann Gall has shown how the National Socialists – Hitler as much as anyone – never really followed through on their earlier intentions, in particular the much advertised attempt to introduce, or reintroduce, 'pagan' ideas. Instead, the Nazis' original plan was for a concept expressed as 'Positive Christianity', which had three key ideas: 'the spiritual struggle against the Jews, the promulgation of a new social

---

* His controversial career falls outside the scope of this book.

ethic, and a syncretism designed to bridge the confessional divide between Protestant and Catholic'.

Positive Christians conceived of Nazism as a struggle not unlike Christ's own, in particular his campaign against the Jews. Hitler, like many leading Nazis, held to the view that Jesus was not a Jew and that the Old Testament should be discarded from Christian teaching.[14] The second aspect of Positive Christianity, its social ethic, was embodied in the phrase 'public need before private greed'. This perhaps glib slogan enabled the Nazis to present themselves in an ethical-moral light in regard to their supervision of the economy. They could advertise as one of their main aims the desire to end class strife in Germany and to create, or more properly recreate, a 'People's Community', an organic, harmonious whole.

The final element of Positive Christianity, the attempt to create a 'new syncretism', was in some ways the most important, because many leading Nazis viewed the divide between Catholics and Protestants as the greatest stumbling block to the national unity that they would need if they were to force the changes in society that they were intent upon. Himmler expressed this most clearly: 'We have to be on our guard against a world power which makes use of Christianity and its organisation to oppose our own national resurrection by methods of which we're everywhere conscious.' He was anticlerical but not anti-Christian, he added. The elevation of the *Volk*, the community, as a mystical, almost divine entity, was the main device for overcoming the sectarian divide, and at the same time a political manoeuvre to combat the rival analyses of Marx and the materialist economists of the West.[15]

More than theology, or paganism (which many Nazis, despite Himmler, thought was laughable), Positive Christianity stressed *active* Christianity – helping the *Volk*, preserving the sanctity of the family, keeping healthy, practising anti-Semitism, getting involved in the winter-relief programme to feed the poor – rather than reflection. Indeed, these activities seemed designed to *prevent* contemplation, and again this suggests that the Nazis' real concern over Christianity was that it represented potentially the most powerful force against them.

'Races Are God's Thoughts'

During the Weimar years there was a continual battle between the rationalists – the scientists and academics – and the nationalists, the pan-Germans, who remained convinced there was something special about Germany, her history, the instinctive superiority of her heroes. In *The Decline of the West* Oswald Spengler had stressed how Germany was different from France, the United States and Britain, and this view, which appealed to Hitler, gained ground among the Nazis as they edged closer to power. From time to time Hitler attacked modern art and modern artists. Like other prominent Nazis, he was by temperament anti-intellectual; for him, most great men of history had been doers, not thinkers. There was, however, one exception to this mould, a would-be intellectual who was even more of an outsider in German society than the other top men.

Alfred Rosenberg's family came from Estonia, which until 1918 was one of Russia's Baltic provinces. As a boy he was fascinated by history, especially after he encountered Houston Stewart Chamberlain's *Foundations of the Nineteenth Century* on a family holiday in 1909. He now felt he had a reason to hate the Jews every bit as much as his experiences in Estonia gave him reason to hate the Russians. Moving to Munich after the Armistice in 1918, he quickly joined the fledgling NSDAP (Nationalsozialistische Deutsche Arbeiter-partei, the German National Socialist Workers' Party) and began writing vicious anti-Semitic pamphlets. His writing ability, his knowledge of Russia and his facility with the Russian language all helped to make him the Party's expert on the 'East'; he also became editor of the *Völkischer Beobachter* (the People's Observer), the Nazi Party's newspaper. During the 1920s, together with Martin Bormann and Heinrich Himmler, he began to see the need for an ideology that went beyond *Mein Kampf*, and in 1930 he published what he believed would provide the intellectual basis for National Socialism. In German its title was *Der Mythus des 20. Jahrhunderts*, usually translated as *The Myth of the Twentieth Century*.[16]

Mythus is a rambling and inconsistent book. It conducts a massive assault on Roman Catholicism as the main threat to German civilization – the text stretches to more than seven hundred pages. The third section is entitled 'The Coming Reich'; other parts deal with 'racial hygiene', education, religion and international affairs. Rosenberg was another of those who argued that Jesus was not Jewish, that his message had been perverted by St Paul, and that it was the Pauline/Roman version that had forged Christianity into its familiar mould by ignoring ideas of aristocracy and race and creating the 'fake' doctrines of original sin, the afterlife, and hell as an inferno – all of which beliefs, Rosenberg insisted, were 'unhealthy'.*

His aim – and at this distance his audacity is breathtaking – was to create a substitute faith for Germany. He advocated a 'religion of the blood' which, in effect, told Germans that they were members of a master race, with a 'race-soul'. He quoted the works of the Nazis' chief academic racialist, the anthropologist H.F.K. Günther, who claimed to have 'established on a scientific basis the defining characteristics of the so-called Nordic-Aryan race'. Like Hitler and others before him, Rosenberg did his best to establish a connection with the ancient inhabitants of India, Greece and Germany, and to do so he brought in Rembrandt, Herder, Wagner, Frederick the Great and Henry the Lion to produce an entirely spurious but nonetheless heroic history specifically intended to root the NSDAP in the German past.

For Rosenberg, race – the religion of the blood – was the only force that could combat what he saw as the main engines of disintegration – individualism and universalism. 'The individualism of economic man', in effect the American ideal, he dismissed as 'a figment of the Jewish mind to lure men to their doom'.

Hitler seems to have had mixed feelings about *Mythus*. He held on to the manuscript for six months after Rosenberg submitted it, publication not being sanctioned until 15 September 1930, *after* the

---

*Mussolini declared: 'Fascism is a religious conception in which man's immanent relationship with a superior law, and with an objective Will that transcends that particular individual, raises him to conscious membership of a spiritual society.' Gordon Lynch says that the cult of personality established around Mussolini became an idealized embodiment of this sacred national community and even led to the creation of a new School of Fascist Mysticism, led by Mussolini's brother, which devoted itself to the study of the dictator's thought.[17]

Nazi Party's sensational victory at the polls. Probably Hitler put off approving the book until the Party was strong enough to risk losing the support of Roman Catholics, which would surely follow publication. If so, he was being no more than realistic – the Vatican was incensed by Rosenberg's argument and in 1934 placed *Mythus* on the index of prohibited books. Cardinal Schulte, archbishop of Cologne, set up a 'defence staff' of seven young priests who worked round the clock to list the many 'errors' in the text, the corrections being published as anonymous pamphlets printed simultaneously in five different cities so as to evade the Gestapo. Rosenberg nonetheless remained popular with Hitler, and when the war began he was given his own unit, the Einsatzstab Reichsleiter Rosenberg, or ERR, charged with looting art.

Mythus left no doubt as to what the Nazis thought was wrong with German civilization – and this despite the book that was to achieve such notoriety being hardly coherent.[18] In terms of both organization and style it left a great deal to be desired, to the extent that one of Rosenberg's Munich colleagues felt the need to publish a glossary of no fewer than 850 obscure words and phrases to be found in it. One German theologian dismissed it as 'stark dementia'. Yet after Hitler had finally approved its publication, all schools in the Reich were forced to order copies, ensuring that Rosenberg became a rich man.

One of the incoherences in the book is that although Rosenberg identified Christianity as part of the intellectual problem facing the Nazis in regenerating Germany, he also veiled his ideas in what has been called a 'Nordic mist'. He attacked the growth of astrology and other superstitions in Germany, and he opposed Steiner's anthroposophy, which he dismissed as a parallel to the precepts of the Masonic lodges. In declaring that the cult of Wotan was dead, though, he was no orthodox heathen, as some early Nazis were. But he did not count himself an atheist. The loathing that the Nazis had for the Churches was based largely on political grounds, because Hitler's acolytes realized that, should they have chosen to (which they mainly did not), the Churches could have mounted the most forceful opposition to Nazi ideology. Officially, and on the surface, everyone was free to believe what they wanted, provided those beliefs did not interfere with the aims of the state (as did the beliefs of Jehovah's Witnesses, who rejected military service).

Although Rosenberg wrote respectfully about Jesus Christ as a heroic historical figure, he also wrote approvingly of the Arian heresy, which denies Christ's divinity (a view popular among early Lombards and Goths). Robert Cecil says that Rosenberg, like Himmler, 'delighted in all expressions of religious heresy'. He also rejected the doctrine of original sin – at least insofar as it applied to Germans – and the idea of the afterlife and the 'dismal pictures of the pains of hell'. He made his views plain in the memoir he wrote in Nuremberg jail: 'Man's existence is perpetuated only in his children or his work.' He refused all religious paraphernalia before his execution.

On the other hand, he deplored the decline of Christianity because it left, he thought, an intellectual/emotional gap that would be filled either by the Jews or the Marxists. He based his substitute faith in *Mythus* on one of Paul de Lagarde's aphorisms: 'Races are God's thoughts.' This led directly to 'the religion of the blood', in which (as noted earlier) each race evolved its own religion and had its own 'race-soul' – 'race is the external form of soul'.[19] Only through the survival of the race could the individual soul survive the death of the physical body. In one of his speeches he said, 'From this secret core ... there develops what we call racial characteristic [*Volkstum*] and race culture.'

Rosenberg was much influenced by his discovery of the medieval Dominican friar Meister Eckhart, who as long ago as 1327 had been obliged to appear in front of the Pope and Curia to answer accusations of heresy. Rosenberg persuaded himself that Meister Eckhart had been defending a German form of faith against the arid scholasticism of Rome and its priestly tyranny. In this way, he managed to find (a German) historical precedent for what he himself was doing. The clear line from Eckhart to Luther to the race theorist H.S. Chamberlain proved to Rosenberg that Germany had continually sought to distance herself from Rome, that she was in some way special, theologically speaking.

Of the precursors it was Chamberlain who was of most use – not surprisingly, since he was still alive at the time and very much part of the same intellectual tradition as the Nazis. Chamberlain in his books had recognized what he regarded as the Aryan race. He knew that outside the realm of language this was a fiction, having nothing to do with anatomy. He got round this by saying that an individual was Aryan if he or she felt him- or herself to be Aryan; if he or she had the experience of *being* Aryan, then he or she was. This conveniently allowed Rosenberg to include many impressive figures from the past as Aryan achievers, further solidifying what was an entirely artificial concept. A final plank in this construction was the work of H.F.K. Günther (already introduced), who claimed to have identified on a scientific basis the racial characteristics of Nordic–Aryan man, in a line that stretched from India to Greece to Germany, a northern trajectory to compare with the 'classical' version that went up through Greece and Italy to France.

Historically, Rosenberg purported to show that nations, cultures and civilizations rise and fall according to their racial purity, and that implied – more than implied – that the racial inclusivity of Christianity could not be successful and could not apply in Germany. 'For example, the Germanic ideal of living in conformity with nature and esteeming fine physique and manly beauty has been undermined by Christian antagonism to "the flesh" and by sentimental ideas about preserving the lives of defective children and allowing criminals and those with hereditary illness to propagate their defects.' As he put it, the 'feebler' nations became, through absorbing the Christian doctrines of individualism and love of humanity, the more easily could they be ruled, or dominated, by Rome. This is why the doctrine of original sin was eschewed. Rosenberg told people at a Nuremberg rally: 'The German people is not born in sin, but born in nobility.'[20]

A later enemy was Freemasonry which, Rosenberg said, had its origins in England, France and Italy, promoting individualism and then the 'atomization' of democracy. In this way a German tradition of honour and aristocracy was pitched against the more 'Western' notions of equality, not just of all Europeans but of all races. But Rosenberg was not content with this: most abhorrent to him were the Jews and the Marxists (often the same people), through which we arrive at economic man as 'a figment of the Jewish mind'.

Against all these forces the only salvation, for Rosenberg, was a new faith. 'Within the bond of race man can escape "the throttling of individual life under the materialistic pressure of the age". Without this faith he is condemned to frustration and despair.'[21]

And this was the underlying appeal of Nazism: 'to stand together, to feel strong, to act heroically'. People were able to feel chosen, potential heroes, simply by virtue of being born Germans, 'predestined to greatness', while all opponents were 'flying in the face of the laws of Nature'. Each German was, in effect (and this was a Nietzschean idea), a 'superman'. The 'blood' was the divine essence which had to be defended against all others.

Why was this idea so powerful? A lot had to do with the political atmosphere in Germany after the Great War, with the fact that, intellectually speaking – in science, in philosophy, in music, in theatre and other forms of literature – Germany had led the way and was now brought low. There was such a feeling of resentment for this somersault in her status (as Nietzsche had also foreseen, long before the war) that the inconsistencies, non sequiturs and errors in *Mythus* were allowed to pass without significant comment. Nor did it matter that many of Rosenberg's main ideas were in fact Christian, so long as the Christian symbols were changed (as they were). 'The men of the coming age will transform the heroes' war memorials and glades of remembrance into the places of pilgrimage of a new religion; there the hearts of Germans will be constantly shaped afresh in pursuit of a new myth.'

The new religion needed a tradition, but one in which the Second Reich was felt to be inadequate. So Rosenberg and Himmler looked back to Saxon times. At Verden in Lower Saxony, where Charlemagne had defeated heathendom, Rosenberg called for a memorial consisting of 4,500 stones, one for each Saxon slain. In May 1934 he organized the commemoration of the seven-hundredth anniversary of the battle of Altenesch, in which a whole community, condemned as heretics by a Catholic bishop, had been put to death. In front of a crowd that Rosenberg later claimed was forty thousand-strong, consisting predominantly of peasants and farmers, he asserted 'to great applause': 'The Holy Land for Germans is not Palestine . . . Our Holy Places are certain castles on the Rhine, the good earth of Lower Saxony and the Prussian fortress of Marienburg.'[22]

Rosenberg's job was to an extent made easier by the fanatical following achieved by Hitler – many Germans simply saw him as a Messiah, ascribing to him supernatural powers. But other traditions were fabricated. One of these was the 'blood flag', said to be stained with the blood of sixteen Nazis killed before the Feldherrnhalle in the Munich putsch of November 1923. This flag was henceforth used to dedicate other flags, echoing the apostolic succession. In 1934 the remains of the dead putschists were removed without the permission of their families and placed in a new 'Temple of Honour' in Munich. Hitler called out the name as each coffin was brought in and a detachment of the Hitler Youth replied 'Here!' From now on, the Nazi dead were referred to as 'summoned to Horst Wessel's standard', in honour of the 'least savoury of all the Nazi heroes', Horst Wessel, the author of the lyrics to the Party anthem.

The traditional Churches in Germany were somewhat compromised by the fact that in the nineteenth century they had become tainted with nationalism, anti-socialism and anti-Semitism and so found it difficult to oppose the NSDAP, though the Catholics made more of a stand than the Protestants did, at least until Hitler came to power. The abdication of the Kaiser in November 1918 meant that the evangelical Churches had lost their secular head, and they 'relapsed into a loose association of twenty-eight Land Churches'. More than that, Lutherans who believed that God manifested himself in history not once, in the person of Christ, but repeatedly, were, as one critic put it, 'painfully exposed to the euphoria of the hour'. 'Christ has come to us through Adolf Hitler,' said one.[23]

But Rosenberg did not want too much religious organization. Along with Hitler and Himmler he recognized that, if it chose to do so (which it did not, as mentioned earlier), the organized Church could become the only real threat to National Socialism. As far as Rosenberg was concerned, as Lagarde had said, 'the state cannot create a religion', for religion was something between a man and his own soul or, 'if he had the good fortune to be a German, between himself and the folk-soul'.

The Myth of the Twentieth Century found a huge readership. A protestant pastor, one Heinrich Hueffmeier, who published his own refutation of *Mythus* in 1935, nonetheless admitted that the book was read 'by all those who made the least pretensions to intellectual development'.[24] Which may explain why none of Rosenberg's fellow defendants at Nuremberg would confess to having read it.

The 'Undeniable Hardness' of the World

The theologian who had the greatest ambitions, after Rosenberg, was Jakob Wilhelm Hauer (1881–1962), founder of the German Faith Movement. He had millions of followers, according to the historian and anthropologist Karla Poewe, including luminaries such as Mathilde Ludendorff, Dietrich Klagges, the best-selling novelist Hans Grimm and the popular writer on anthropolgy, H.F.K. Günther.[25]

According to some scholars, Hauer had it in mind to create a political religion in that, like Rosenberg, he wanted his ideas to be the ideological basis for National Socialism – though he never had the ear of senior Nazi figures as the latter did. Much impressed by Rudolf Steiner and his anthroposophy movement, which he thought heralded a new era of spiritual creativity, Hauer inhabited the same intellectual and cultural milieu as Rosenberg. He held mystic notions of the *Volk* and medievalism, and of the Indo-Germanic tradition that saw a line of influence stretching from Buddhism and Hinduism through Greece to medieval Germany, then on into the Nordic realm as far as the Eddas and sagas and the Icelandic myths.

In addition, he had three interdependent concepts: being 'grasped' by the sacred, being led by a powerful personality, and understanding the needs of the time. These should come together, he thought, or hoped, in a religious/political genius who related instinctively to his time and place – that is, to an ethnically specific predicament. To this was added a social Darwinism (and a Nietzscheanism) in which the 'undeniable hardness' of the world was to be appreciated – the need for conflict and its associated sense of heroism 'with which we can enjoy life's battle, where we win and lose, have joy and suffering, pain and delight, the will to live and preparedness to die'. By means of a religion of the blood and soil (a wearily familiar German concept), a *Volk* could not renew itself through a Christian idea of salvation. Rather, it must realize its renewal as coming from its own psychological centre.[26]

Apart from the notion that only a politico-religious leader could help Germans find the truth, Hauer laid down several specific aspects of 'concrete content' for his German Faith: namely, that the great figures of German history were prophets, that the German domain was where the revelations took place, that God favoured the Germans and the German way, that the German will was a specific form of revealed divinity, that battle and tragedy were the eternal law of human beings, making the German homeland 'nearer to heaven than any paradise'. 'Obedience to the leader is the highest fortune and the most blissful peace.'[27] His faith, essentially pagan, evolved its own symbols, and its main cohesive force was an unremitting war of attrition against Christianity.[28] Hauer wanted to destroy what he called 'secularized Christianity' and replace it with faith in the Third Reich.

Around him were a number of other neopagan sects, including Mathilde Ludendorff's Society for God Knowledge, an extreme form of nationalism, whose aim was the 'immortality of the race or nation' via sticking closely to certain precepts – notably, that since death is inevitable, not a day must be wasted in working for the benefit of the *Volk*. Another such sect was Sigrid Hunke's Unitarians, who maintained that everyone differs in their spirituality but that, even so, people should live in communities that constantly challenge their beliefs, which may thus go on changing throughout life.

At the root of all these manifestations is Nietzsche's idea of a 'will to a stronger and higher existence'.[29]

Despite such eloquent and (often pseudo-sophisticated) ideas and rationalizations for Nazi practices from the Protestant theologians and would-be theologians, assaults on Christianity in the Third Reich grew in intensity as Nazi confidence solidified. Although religious instruction was at first compulsory, attendance at school prayers was later made optional and religion was dropped as a subject from school-leaving examinations. Then, priests were forbidden to teach religious classes. In 1935, by Bryan Moynahan's count, the Gestapo arrested seven hundred Protestant pastors for condemning Nazi neopaganism from the pulpit. In 1937 the Gestapo declared that the education of candidates for the Confessional Church was illegal, and Martin Niemöller, its leading light, was condemned to a concentration camp, refusing the offer of release because it required his collaboration.[30] (The medical orderly in Sachsenhausen found him to be 'a man of iron'.)

In 1936 the assault on Catholic monasteries and convents began: they were accused of illegal currency trading and sexual offences. In that year too, the Nuremberg rallies bore an aura of paganism – the songs, or hymns, were pastiches redolent of traditional Christian worship:

> Führer my Führer
> Thou hast rescued Germany from deepest distress
> I thank thee for my daily bread
> Abide thou long with me, forsake me not
> Führer my Führer, my faith and light.

All this was part of the initiative to 'dechristianize' rituals and festivals. At weddings, for instance, bride and groom would be blessed by 'Mother Earth, Father Sky and all the beneficent powers of the air', and extracts from Nordic sagas would be read out. At 'christenings' the infant was cradled on a Teutonic shield, swaddled in a blanket adorned with oak leaves and swastikas. The celebration of Christmas – the word itself was replaced by 'Yuletide' – was exchanged for a 'festival of the winter solstice', held on 21 December. The cross was never abolished; attempts *were* made in 1937 to take it out of school classrooms, but the measure had to be rescinded (perhaps confirming that Himmler did see Christianity as the paramount threat). The Vatican complained formally to Berlin almost monthly, but the regime took next to no notice. Some of the Nazi innovations eerily echoed what had already been tried in Stalinist Russia.

From Hitler's point of view, probably his greatest achievement was in nullifying the oppositional potential that the Church – had it so minded – could have mustered. This is worth underlining: at a time when religious faith was most needed, it failed to rise to the challenge. Too little is made of this.

PART THREE

Humanity at and after Zero Hour

17

The Aftermath of the Aftermath

'We were born at the beginning of the First World War. As adolescents we had the crisis of 1929; at twenty, Hitler. Then came the Ethiopian War, the Civil War in Spain, and Munich. These were the foundations of our education. Next came the Second World War, the defeat, and Hitler in our homes and cities. Born and bred in such a world, what did we believe in? Nothing. Nothing except the obstinate negation in which we were forced to clothe ourselves from the very beginning. The world in which we were called to exist was an absurd world, and there was no other in which we could take refuge ... If the problem had been the bankruptcy of a political ideology or a system of government, it would have been simple enough. But what happened came from the very root of man and society. There was no doubt about this, and it was confirmed day after day not so much by the behavior of the criminals but by that of the average man ... Now that Hitler has gone, we know a certain number of things. The first is that the poison which impregnated Hitlerism has not been eliminated; it is present in each of us ... Another thing we have learned is that we cannot accept any optimistic conception of existence, any happy ending whatsoever. But if we believe that optimism is silly, we also know that pessimism about the action of man among his fellows is cowardly.'[1]

Albert Camus delivered these words in 1946 at Columbia University in New York. An Algerian-born French journalist and philosopher whose father had been killed in the First World War, a one-time communist and anarchist, Camus had worked for the Resistance newspaper *Combat* during the second war. In his first novel *The Outsider* (*L'Étranger*, 1942) the main character, Meursault, has killed a man and is scheduled to be executed; he is pondering Camus's central concern, the 'absurdist' position that a life so important to him (his own) can have so little meaning, if any, in the wider scheme of things.

Though his talk at Columbia was clearly personal it reflects European and French experience and exemplifies a generation of intellectuals. Trapped in an untidy and unpredictable chain of bloody events catalysed by 1914–18, Camus and his generation were subjected to what Jeffrey Isaac has called 'a particularly brutal form of intellectual shock therapy'. As Nicola Chiaromonte recalled, 'I remember being totally obsessed by a single thought: we had arrived at humanity's zero hour and history was senseless.' Even the more conservative and religious thinkers, who for years had drawn attention to what they saw as the threat of modern secularism and the original and unremitting sinfulness of human impulses, could not escape the feeling that 'all bets were off', that traditional ways of understanding ourselves – via class, community, nation, church, God – were now simply inadequate to the problems facing the postwar world.[2]

Chicago was no different from Paris or New York. When the American philosopher Allan Bloom first attended university in Chicago just after World War Two, one of the things he soon noticed was that 'American university life was being revolutionized by German thought'. At that time, in Chicago anyway, Marx was revered, he said, but the two thinkers who generated most enthusiasm were the sociologist Max Weber and the psychoanalyst Sigmund Freud, who in turn had both been profoundly influenced by Friedrich Nietzsche.

It is not hard to see why such pessimism – even nihilism – should prevail. Soviet troops had reached Auschwitz on 27 January the year before; the Soviet news agency Tass had published a special bulletin, an interview with two hundred survivors, on 7 May, twenty-four hours before VE Day in Europe. The atomic bomb had been dropped on Hiroshima on 6 August, and on Nagasaki three days later. Pierre Laval, who had served twice as head of the Vichy regime, had been shot for collaboration on 15 October, and Vidkun Quisling, who had seized power in Norway in 1940 in a Nazi-backed coup, had been executed in the same way and for the same offence nine days later. Civil war had broken out in China at the beginning of 1946; Winston Churchill had drawn attention to the existence of the Iron Curtain at much the same time; war crimes trials were being held in Nuremberg (ten had already been sentenced to death) and Tokyo; an anti-Jewish pogrom had taken place in Kielce in Poland, despite the Auschwitz revelations; and French troops had bombarded Haiphong in northeast Vietnam, killing twenty thousand.

In the immediate aftermath of the Second World War, as Camus said, this was itself an aftermath of sorts, following on from so many catastrophic and bloody events that had occurred since 1914. However, it is three longer-term consequences of the war that are our focus here.

The first was the germination, predominantly in France, of the existential philosophy that had begun with the phenomenological ideas of Edmund Husserl but had come to fruition in the cauldron of war and Occupation. Second was a broad change that had been registered in American society, a change that might well have happened anyway but was certainly accelerated by the war. This has been called 'the permissive turn', the development of much more liberal attitudes and practices, a lurch forward in secularization that resulted in the fairly rapid replacement of religious understandings of society and people by a psychological understanding. And the third consequence was the effect that the Holocaust had on Jewish thinking. How could a God who loved his people have allowed such terrible things to happen? How could Jews be Jews after the death camps? Was the Holocaust the greatest nihilistic act of all time? What were the causes and the implications?

These three consequences of the Second World War were big events, concerns that reached well beyond the end of hostilities and shaped thinking and culture – and continue to shape thinking and culture today – in both the religious and the secular context.

18

The Warmth of Acts

The response to the outbreak of the Second World War was nothing like the reponse to that of the Great War. There was no euphoria, no aggressive manifestos produced by scores of intellectuals, no rush of poets to enlist, certainly no feeling among the general public that more fighting would bring about spiritual renewal. But there was the 'phoney war', as it came to be called, when after the blitzkrieg on Poland in September 1939 nothing much of military significance occurred until April 1940, and many of the children evacuated from Britain's major cities had begun to drift back home again. Winston Churchill called it the Twilight War, while the Germans called it *Sitzkrieg*, the sitting war.

But the second war did produce some major changes in the way people thought, which rivalled the transformations in sensibility wrought by the earlier conflict.

Some of the ideas that emerged are less surprising in retrospect than they seemed at the time. They were encapsulated in a series of works reassessing the way humans can live together to the benefit of all – war is, perhaps, exactly the time when such reassessments take place. These were Joseph Schumpeter's *Capitalism, Socialism and Democracy* (1942), in which the author argued that entrepreneurs, not capitalists as such, are the motivating force of capitalism; and Karl Mannheim's *Diagnosis of Our Time* which came out a year later, in which he advocated a new 'planned order'; there could be 'no way back' to the old laissez-faire capitalism that had produced the Crash and the Depression. Then in 1944 Friedrich von Hayek produced *The Road to Serfdom* which opposed planning: we should put our faith in 'the invisible hand' and look to 'the spontaneous social order' for guidance, because it had evolved by itself to safeguard internal peace and individual freedom, without which no satisfying life is possible. And Karl Popper wrote *The Open Society and Its Enemies*, which argued that political solutions are like scientific ones in that they 'can never be more than provisional and are always open to improvements'; life has to move forward by trial and error, there is no 'iron law' of history.

These four authors, all Austro-Hungarian, produced short books (owing to paper rationing) that were hard-hitting in a down-to-earth, practical sense. Neither religion nor salvation featured. Here is another occasion when we do well to remind ourselves that the everyday practicalities of life are, for many people, far more pressing than metaphysical matters.

This was underlined by William Temple's *Christianity and the Social Order*. Temple, Archbishop of Canterbury, argued for the Church's right to 'interfere' (his word) in social issues that could not help but have political consequences. In the body of the book he kept his remarks general (about fellowship in the workplace, the nature of freedom, and so on), but in an appendix he firmly aligned himself with Mannheim on planning; he argued for a Royal Commission on housing that would decide how everyone could be properly housed, giving commissioners draconian powers to avoid land speculation; he wanted the school-leaving age raised from fourteen to eighteen; the return of the guilds, with all three parties – workers, management and capital – represented; and a five-day week, so everyone would have enough leisure.

Many of these recommendations were incorporated, to a degree, in *Social Insurance and Allied Services*, better known as the Beveridge Report; published in November 1942, it became the basis of Britain's modern welfare state. The idea would spread and solidify after the war (Bismarck had originally introduced it in late-nineteenth-century Germany).

Across the ocean a rather different report appeared just as the war was turning in the Allies' favour, in January 1944. This was *An American Dilemma: The Negro Problem and Modern Democracy* by the

Swedish social scientist, Gunnar Myrdal. Well aware, as others were, that many blacks were fighting in Europe and the Pacific, Myrdal was asking: '[If] they were expected to risk their lives equally with whites, why shouldn't they enjoy equality afterward?' This was not the only spur to the civil rights movement, but it was an early indication of an awareness of the imbalance in American society; and concerns over race would, in a relatively short time, incorporate demands for equality among other minority groups, women and homosexuals in particular.

So the Second World War was a seed ground for many of the social advances that would be made, on either side of the Atlantic, in the second half of the twentieth century – purely secular manoeuvres enabling many more than ever before to lead fulfilling lives in all realms of activity. This should never be lost sight of. Everyday practicalities are no small thing.[1]

Resistance and Ritzkrieg

One of the curious paradoxes at the end of World War Two was that Paris, which had been occupied for so long, was perceived as a livelier city than London, which had never suffered such indignity. (The French capital, after all, had been spared the Blitz.) Visiting London, the American writer Edmund Wilson said that he found there 'a sense of depression and anti-climax'. Graham Greene even admitted he felt 'a nostalgia for the hum of a robot bomb'. Though Paris – indeed, the whole of France – was bankrupt, the Liberation was a powerful symbol of hope. 'It was an article of faith that ideas would triumph over "filthy money".'

The French were naturally relieved to see the back of the Germans, and Paris in particular was inundated with sophisticated Anglophone visitors who had been starved of Paris culture for too long. Jean Cocteau held court at the Hôtel Saint-Yves in the rue Jacob, where he was famous for his monologues ('the spoken word was his language and he used it with the virtuosity of an acrobat'). Picasso and Dora Maar could be found in the rue des Grands Augustins at Le Catalan, virtually an extension of his studio. Jean-Paul Sartre and his companion Simone de Beauvoir wrote for six hours a day at the Café Flore, or the Deux Magots, though Brasserie Lipp on the Boulevard St-Germain was out of favour for a time because its Alsatian dishes had proved popular with German officers.

The autumn of 1945 saw what Antony Beevor and Artemis Cooper called 'the great existentialist boom', though it was in truth a time of general cultural innovation. An astonishing number of newspapers and literary magazines were launched (despite the paper shortage being so acute that *Le Monde* was reduced from a broadsheet to tabloid size, becoming known as '*Le Demi-Monde*'). Theatres proliferated, so did jazz and cabaret: Juliette Gréco and Marlene Dietrich had stayed at the Ritz – 'Ritzkrieg', it came to be called – in between entertaining the troops at the Front. And there was a vogue for American novels, now that they could be freely obtained. All this was happening in an atmosphere of such penury that people took to using 1920s-style cigarette holders, so they could smoke their Gauloises and Gitanes down to the very end. (When she was introduced to Sartre by Maurice Merleau-Ponty, Juliette Gréco was amused to see that he left his silver cigarette case with the management at the Flore as a deposit against settling his bill.)[2]

Sartre was to be a central figure in the 'existentialist boom', which began – in the popular mind at least – with a lecture he gave at the Club Maintenant in Paris in the autumn of 1945. It came to be regarded as a seminal event, one of the best accounts being that by the French writer and journalist Michel Tournier in his autobiography: 'On October 28, 1945, Sartre called us together. It was a mob scene. An enormous crowd pressed against the walls of the tiny hall. The exits were blocked by those who had not managed to gain entry to the sanctuary, and women who fainted had to be piled on a convenient grand piano. The wildly acclaimed lecturer was lifted bodily over the crowd and on to the podium. Such popularity should have alerted us. Already the suspect tag "existentialism" had been attached to the new system. Having tumbled into the darkened nightclubs of Paris, the new star attracted a grotesque fauna of singers, jazz musicians, soldiers of the Resistance, drunkards, and Stalinists. So what was existentialism? We were soon to find out. Sartre's message could be stated in six words: existential-ism is a form of humanism . . . We were floored. Our master had gone and fished up that worn-out old duffer Humanism, still stinking with sweat and "inner life", from the trash heap where we had left him, and now he trotted him out along with the absurd idea of existentialism as if he had invented both. And everyone applauded.'[3]

How very French: an enjoyable account that also manages to be a stylish put-down. But Tournier's observations were true enough in that, although for many people Sartre's lecture had kick-started a new philosophy – and a new way to attempt to live without God – in practice the ideas he made use of had been germinating in France and Germany all through the 1930s and even during the war, with the not necessarily paradoxical result that several leading Resistance figures continued to read and follow the teachings of the German philoso-pher, and notorious Nazi-sympathizer, Martin Heidegger.

This way of thinking began, as perhaps it was bound to, with the successive disasters and catastrophes of the First World War, the terror and purges in Stalin's Russia, the stock market crash and the ensuing Depression, the Spanish Civil War and its horrors, such as the bomb-ing of Guernica. Against this background such figures as Alexandre Kojève, Alexandre Koyré and Georges Bataille, following Heidegger, found traditional atheism – replacing God with man, history, nations and states – a 'sinister impoverishment'. They were also at pains to point out that their ideas were an 'anti-humanism'. Humanism, they went so far as to say, had led to fascism. What they meant by this was that humanism, even atheistic humanism, carried with it the idea that man was an end, a *fixed* end, a form of unchanging perfection already created. For them, this manifestly wasn't true – man is still in the process of being formed, and it was the very idea that we un-derstand what man *is* that had led to the catastrophes, as the dictators and other politicians tried to force man into a set mould. 'Neither Marxists nor Capitalists nor humanists . . . can fully explain mankind, they are incomplete (and possibly erroneous) ways to understand ourselves.'[4]

Kojève et al. were much influenced by science, especially by what was then recent science, advances in physics, mathematics and anthropology in particular. Science in general they thought had impoverished us because 'completeness' is inherent in scientific and mathematical thought; this was not only itself a limiting factor and/or metaphor, but was where the idea of 'perfection' had come from in the first place. But the findings of physics and mathematics – in particular, Heisenberg's uncertainty principle – had shown that we are not separate from nature, that the very measurement of the 'outside' world is affected by our presence; and in any case, as Kurt Gödel had shown, there are logical limits to what we can know. Moreover, there is no such thing as Nature with a capital N, there is no *fixed* nature because science is always advancing our grasp of what nature consists of.

The discoveries of anthropology had shown furthermore that there are very great differences between peoples, not least in their understanding of God. Therefore, there is no such thing as *being* in the abstract; to *be* exists only at a specific time and a specific location, we can only understand ourselves via the immediacy of the concrete, meaning there is no 'pure', privileged perspective on life, we cannot avoid having a central standpoint. This was all derived, ultimately, from Heidegger, Husserl and the phenomenologists.

The Battle over Transcendence

And what follows from this, they deduced, is that we can have no access to transcendence. We cannot step back from the world, as Heidegger said, with Kojève and the others following; there is no 'nature' prior to its interaction with man, man cannot be 'outside' the world in some way, meaning that transcendence is simply not possible, not available. There is no teleology, no direction to the world. One aim of life is to surpass oneself; but even here no generalizations are possible because no generally agreed *direction* can exist, *even in principle*, since man cannot transcend his subjectivity.

All we can hope for, as Emmanuel Lévinas put it in a useful neologism, is 'excendence', a striving to escape from our condition. But even this is at least partially doomed – Lévinas also espoused the concept of 'subjective insufficiency' – meaning is not controlled by man, by the subject, and so, as Valéry said, we are condemned to live within limits and with disappointment.[5]

All this amounted to a re-proportioning of man, and here violence played a crucial role. Before the disasters of the twentieth century, violence had been regarded as what the historian Stefanos Geroulanos of New York University has called, in a nice phrase, 'the left-over darkness' of the Enlightenment, occurring in places 'where the light of reason had not yet reached'. But violence – the violence of the Gulag and the Holocaust death camps, for example – was no longer just that. Violence, by this account, was inescapable in modern society, because reason isn't something that exists prior to man, but has to be *constructed*. We are, in effect, 'emptied out', there is no stability in human nature, there are no absolutes, no idealized understanding of humanity. We must seek what satisfaction we can here on earth, within the state and with all the shortcomings that carries with it, implying that our existence is invariably and always one of struggle and, if we are not to descend into further catastrophe, *constant criticism*.[6]

And it was this set of ideas, sometimes called proto-existentialism, that concerned the Resistance during the war. In addition to Sartre, other figures active here included Jean Beaufret, Gaston Fessard and Joseph Rovan. Beaufret first encountered the ideas of Heidegger while in the Resistance network 'Pericles' in the mountains around Lyon, when he was given a copy of *Being and Time* by Rovan, who had translated part of the book into French (Rovan was an important *résistant* himself, a talented forger of identity papers). Beaufret published his own writings on Heidegger in *Confluences* and *Fontaine*, both of which, like Sartre's *Les Temps modernes*, were journals inspired by the Resistance. So integral was his 'resistantialism' to his reading of Heidegger that, on the very day the Allies launched the Normandy invasion, 6 June 1944, Beaufret claimed that 'he reproached himself for rejoicing more for realizing some of what Heidegger was all about than about being told about the invasion itself'. Again, how very French. Fessard, Jesuit theologian and philosopher, taught Heidegger throughout the occupation. As Geroulanos sums up: 'Not only did these figures relegitimate the study of Heidegger's thought during and after the occupation, they also helped make Heidegger . . . a cornerstone of *Résistance* morality.'[7]

We can now see the significance of Michel Tournier's comments in regard to Sartre's lecture 'Existentialism Is a Humanism' of 28 October 1945. In France at least, humanism had lost its lustre.

Sartre, though, had not lost *his*. This was due to his ability to express his philosophy not just in academic journals, the normal outlet for philosophical writings. His talents ranged much wider – to novels and plays, and to the popular *Temps modernes*. The journal's title was partly inspired by Chaplin's film *Modern Times*, but its editorial committee, led by Sartre, was impressive enough in itself to attract attention. It included de Beauvoir, Albert Camus, Maurice Merleau-Ponty as philosophy editor, Michel Leiris and Raymond Queneau for poetry and literature, as well as Raymond Aron and Jean Paulhan. André Malraux was invited to take part, but declined. Other existential ventures of the time included plays such as Jean Giraudoux's *Sodome et Gomorrhe*, Jean Anouilh's *Antigone* and Camus's *Caligula*.

The 'existentialist boom' in Paris did not last long. By the end of 1949 the heyday of Saint-Germain-des-Prés was over. 'In Paris, perhaps one needs a war to launch a *quartier*,' quipped the poet and screenwriter Jacques Prévert. But existentialism's legacy was more enduring.[8]

Intensity as Meaning

Though he shared many of their ideas, André Malraux did not really belong in this intellectual circuit comprising men like Kojève and Koyré, spiritual heirs of Heidegger. He was much more a man of action, travelling to Cambodia and China in his twenties. While in Cambodia he had been arrested for removing some antiquities; his sentence was later revoked but that didn't stop him being critical of the French colonial authorities. In 1930 his father, a banker, committed suicide after the stock market crash. In the mid-1930s Malraux fought in the Spanish Civil War; during the Second World War he was captured in 1940, escaped and joined the Resistance, being later decorated by both the French and British governments. He also found time to write; his 1933 book *La Condition humaine* won the Prix Goncourt.

His background was important for his philosophy which, despite reflecting a lifestyle different from those of the other Paris intellectuals of the 1930s and during the Resistance, nonetheless formed part of the canon of existentialism. He accepted that we can have no preconceived idea of man, that 'existence precedes essence' – the founding mantra of existentialism – and that therefore there is no 'model existence' we can aspire to. Instead, he said, we must aspire to two things: that our lives 'leave a scar on the face of the earth'; and that our actions be conducted with other men – 'common action is a common bond'. Life is not sacred, he argued, it is not a possession, but 'an instrument of value only to the extent that it is utilized'.[9] Malraux thought that the obsession with an 'inner world, the inner life', was a red herring. He had discovered a different mentality in China, so different in fact that he wondered whether it is even possible to speak of the 'human mind' in the abstract. 'The Chinaman, for example, does not conceive of himself as an individual, the notion of "personality" is foreign to him. The Chinese feel themselves far less distinct from others and from things than does the Westerner.' To an extent he shared that view.

If there is no direction to life, Malraux decided, then its only meaning 'must lie in its intensity'. 'I can no longer conceive of man apart from his intensity,' he said. And intensity is determined by action, from which it follows that the only plan the world will ever have for us is the one 'we temporarily force upon it'. He could not just *accept* that our condition is absurd, as Gide and Valéry did, but argued that we must *revolt* against that idea – nothing must be accepted without a fight, the 'constant criticism' of the proto-existentialists. This also meant refusing to accept all forms of order, such as one's position in society; and the apparent order in personality – never accept that you are one type of person or another, everything is always changing. He agreed with Gide that there is nothing beyond the immediate, no understanding apart from experience; that what is not available to sensation does not exist and that therefore nothing can be known beyond *action*.[10] This is what his novel, *La Condition humaine*, is about.

The focus on action among the existentialists stemmed partly from the philosophy of Maurice Merleau-Ponty and his idea that consciousness is not a function just of the brain but of the entire body. Merleau-Ponty, who as a student attended lectures alongside Sartre, de Beauvoir and Simone Weil, subsequently became a child psychologist and a phenomenologist, teaching at the Sorbonne and the Collège de France. He argued that the body sets limits to experience and that style in art, the physical movements that create distinctive styles, cannot be put into words, much as Wittgenstein had said (see chapter 15). Style, he maintained, is a fruit of the body as much as of the mind, and if we are to feel fulfilled we must satisfy the body as much as the mind. Acts do that; that is why they are fulfilling.

Love as Refuge

Returning for a moment to Malraux, his real dilemma was this: if our action – the decisions we take and the movements we make – is to remain 'pure', pristine, then how can we account for other people? Action and solitude go together: the immediate experience of action – its very intensity – distances us from others. And this gives rise to the statement: 'Love is not a solution to human solitude; it is a refuge from it.'[11] This may be extended, to say that there are no solutions to the mysteries of life, only (temporary) refuges from the constant struggle. Indeed, Malraux goes so far as to suggest that intercourse with other people can never satisfactorily cure solitude – only feeling that we have a reason for being on earth can do that; but metaphysics and religion he dismisses as no more than irrelevant 'half-way houses'. If we are to lead an intense life through action, solitude is the inevitable price we pay – this is one of our dilemmas. The other dilemma arises when we consider whether or not action should sacrifice its 'purity' in an attempt to achieve something that is beyond the immediate. In living for others, however worthwhile that is from their point of view, we sacrifice intensity.

Living as we do with these dilemmas, which constitute our 'existential anguish', means we are often ready to give up our individuality in order to conform to some model that we imagine will enable us to have 'perfect communication' with our fellow men and women. But this is an illusion, Malraux says, and he repeats: 'Love is not a solution to human solitude; it is a refuge from it.'

It is a phrase worth repeating because Malraux was convinced that communication between individuals, to the extent believed possible in the old days of religion and metaphysics, when people believed in 'transcendence', for example, is no longer on the cards. This is shown clearly, he said, in the phenomenon of modern art, which has a sacred quality, in that it is dedicated not to God but to itself. '[Modern] art is a "closed system", without indebtedness to the exterior world whose domination it is the very meaning of art to contest . . . Human freedom could hardly be carried further. But the liberation has been effected at the cost of introducing a new kind of separation between man and his world; not that of an attempt on the part of the mind to gain perspective on matter, but that of a withdrawal into a *different* world.'[12]

In other words, the artist is constructing something that 'resists' the outside world. He or she has shown us his or her product. We, as spectators, recognize what he or she is trying to do but we can never understand totally. Art before the death of God, a painting by Raphael, say, or da Vinci, contained transcendental subjects to which there was a 'common', shared, reaction. But that was illusory too. That was our choice, and another dilemma: an illusory commonality, or our cold appreciation of what is *not* common.

Malraux thought – and acted – according to his belief that the universe is not a riddle to which we must find the key, but that in fact the universe has nothing to conceal from us. We must explore it as intensely as we can, trying as best we can to both enjoy the experience and *observe ourselves experiencing it*. To a degree, inevitably, we will fail in this; but we must make the most of it all the same, for that is all there is. Since the universe has nothing to conceal from us, life is its own answer and we must ensure that we live it as intensely as we can. If we need a metaphor by which to live, we should be like modern artists, creating something which is its own justification and which others will understand only incompletely.

Inspiration, before Persuasion

Though he is best known for being a pioneer aviator and for his novella *The Little Prince* (translated into no fewer than 250 languages), Antoine de Saint-Exupéry won several literary prizes, in France and the United States, and fought as a member of the Free French Air Force in North Africa in the Second World War (despite being wildly over age). His books earned the distinction of being banned in both occupied France and free France (he was very suspicious of de Gaulle). He disappeared on a reconnaissance flight over the Mediterranean in July 1944.

Despite his literary talent, Saint-Exupéry had no special fondness for men of letters. Like Malraux, he believed in action. 'The role of spectator has always been my bugbear. What am I if I do not take part? If I am to be, I must take part.' Because the universe is not rational, he said, 'it reveals itself to action and not to thought'. He believed that 'man has no "interior" considered either as a depository of "innate" truths, as a receptacle for facts acquired by perception and reason or as a set of clearly defined characteristics'. He agreed with Malraux, and as he showed via his character Robineau in *Vol de nuit*, that 'neither action nor individual happiness allow of being shared'. For him, throughout history there have been two means of responding to the 'spiritual dry-rot' of bourgeois society – love and religion. But both responses are alien. 'To love, to love and nothing else – what a dead end!'[13]

Contemporary religion, Saint-Exupéry claimed, is unsure of itself, of the message it brings, or the light it offers, and so is unbelief too. '[Jacques] Bernis [a character in *The Aviator*] enters a church to listen to a sermon which seems to him a cry that has long since ceased to expect an answer.' To expect an answer to a question is the wrong way to look at the world. Life is not what we possess, he is saying, but what we *win*, and he means this literally. In *Pilot de Guerre* (Flight to Arras) he says: 'Anguish is due to the loss of a real identity, and it is only through action that identity may be regained.' And he admits this is based on his own experience. In the lull before his sortie to Arras, he felt he was awaiting an 'unknown self' which he sensed was 'coming towards him from outside, like a phantom'. By the time his mission was completed, his 'unknown self' was no longer unknown, he had discovered a little more of who he was through his deeds. 'Humanism,' he liked to say, 'has taken too little notice of deeds.' Being cultured is not to be achieved by contemplation, but by being enriched by action, doing. 'There is no existence that is not contact with things.'[14]

And 'life', moreover, is not just one thing. We are constantly *redefining* what it is by our actions. Saint-Exupéry's ideal – his model – was not that of a great writer or philosopher, but that of Hochedé, an ordinary man, a fellow pilot during the war. Hochedé had no real inner life, Saint-Exupéry tells us, he was 'pure existence' in that his acts and his identity were one. He writes about having experienced this himself just once, briefly, when he was over Arras: there, in the thick of enemy fire '[y]ou are lodged in your act . . . Your act is you . . . You no longer find anything else in you.' This for him was sheer being, completeness, transcendence, a concept that is quite new to our civilization, according to Everett Knight. 'Hochedé . . . would not know how to throw any light upon himself. But he is constructed, he is complete . . . We usually think of an "accomplished" man as one who has somehow found time to bring to perfection both his mental and physical activities, who is both philosopher and peasant, or statesman and soldier. Hochedé, however, has no "inner" life, yet he lacks for nothing; for what really exists, exists in things exterior to us and comprehensible in themselves.'[15]

As Malraux said – and Saint-Exupéry would have agreed – the universe holds no secrets from us, it conceals nothing, there is no mystery to be 'rescued' by thought. This is why we gain fulfilment by doing rather than by thinking.

But Saint-Exupéry took this further, arguing that, because there are no absolutes, we must replace the idea of *duty towards* by *responsibility for*. This is not just splitting hairs. Duty implies teleological ends, obligations laid down by others – by ancestors or by God, for example – and therefore negates freedom. Responsibility, on the other hand, implies freedom – we *choose* whom and what we wish to be responsible for. This is what Saint-Exupéry learned in the course of his mission to Arras, the consequences of which he develops in the final pages of *Pilote de guerre*. 'The fraternity which made his flight group a single organism must be extended to ever larger groups. The fraternity that men once enjoyed in God, they would now have to reconstitute in man himself; the fraternity of action must replace that of common origin; sacrifice must replace possession.'

This is the philosophy that his book *Citadelle* addresses. The mind is not a 'container', a receptacle of fact and memories, but *an act*; the world is not rational but inexhaustible, making acquisition pointless, another red herring. *Citadelle* shows 'the fallacies inherent in "the great longing to possess", whether it be goods for the body or principles for the mind. Life is "movement towards" and not material possession. Happiness is the "warmth of acts"; a civilization rests upon what it exacts from its people, not what it furnishes them; life is a permanent creation.'[16]

Saint-Exupéry, like Kojève and Koyré before him in the 1930s, was much influenced by the advances in physical science between the wars. 'Anyone who proposes to comprehend life by trying to penetrate beyond what is immediately given, is in somewhat the predicament of the physicist who studies phenomena so minute that any attempt to observe them causes a change in their comportment . . . No useful purpose is served by making of life an object of study, for there is nothing "behind" or "beyond" it . . . The attempt to "possess" life in the capsule form of principles assimilable to the intelligence must therefore be as unsuccessful as that of the petit bourgeois to possess it in the form of the goods it offers . . . Life is not a sphinx's question with our salvation hanging in the balance . . . Language does not resolve the ambiguity of life, it is part of it.'

One of the characters in *Citadelle* is content that God should remain inaccessible, for otherwise 'I have finished my becoming . . . Men cease to become when they find a solution.'[17]

The 'broken world' we are born into must somehow be put back together, always remembering that there are no 'eternal principles' on which we can base our work. Throughout *Citadelle* there are references to the 'cathedral', the 'Empire', the 'domain', which, in addition to the sum of their parts, contain something that Saint-Exupéry calls 'the divine knot', or 'the meaning of things', an intangible entity which transforms otherwise everyday things or words. He likens poetry, and the ordinary words of which it is composed, to a cathedral and the common-or-garden stones of which it is built. And he approaches poetry and cathedrals as the phenomenologists do, not as examples of some theory or other, but as events, the magnificent result of acts, *efforts* intended 'to inspire and not to persuade'.

Life without Alibis

As Walter Kaufmann has said, Sartre's writings bear the stamp of his experience from the outset. He was very much affected by the events of the 1930s – the mass unemployment and the Depression, the rise of fascism in Germany and Italy, the purges and terror in Stalin's Russia – and in the Second World War as a soldier he fought against Hitler. He was captured, returned to Paris and became a member of the Resistance.

These events shaped his thinking, but he was criticized by several of his fellow countrymen who said that his philosophy was second-hand, a pale imitation of Martin Heidegger's. Though it is true that Heidegger's views preceded and overlapped with Sartre's, it is also true that for many Sartre was by far the clearer exponent of existentialism, not just in his essays but in his novels and plays, which attracted a far greater audience than Heidegger's dense – indeed, often impenetrable – prose. Far more than Heidegger, Sartre came within the excellent tradition that recognizes certain writers as straddling philosophy and literature – Montaigne, Pascal, Voltaire, Rousseau.[18]

That clarity of Sartre's began with his saying that a man is not a homosexual, or a waiter, or a coward in the same way that he is six feet tall or blond. 'The crux of the matter is suggested by such words as possibility, choice and decision. If I am six feet tall, that is that. It is a fact no less than that the table is, say, two feet high. Being a waiter or a coward, however, is different: it depends on ever new decisions.' In his essay 'Portrait of the Anti-Semite' he again shows that a man is not an anti-Semite in the way that he is blond: he chooses to be an anti-Semite 'because he is afraid of freedom, openness and change and longs to be as solid as a thing. He wants an identity, he wants to be something in the manner in which a table is something, or a rock.'[19] This has strong echoes of Gide (see chapter 3).

Sartre's choice of illustrative examples in his work is instructive, showing how the war affected his thinking: his choice of cowardice, for instance, or the example he gives in his lecture entitled 'Existentialism Is a Humanism', referred to earlier. Here, he considers the young Frenchman who, at a certain point in the war, cannot decide whether to stay at home in occupied France and become a collaborator, looking after his ailing mother who badly needs him, or leave for England and join the Free French, who will one day – he hopes, he assumes – help in the liberation of his country. The young man had sought Sartre's advice, and although Sartre does not actually say what advice he gave, he rehearses the arguments for both sides in such a way that we pretty much understand what it was.

In that lecture he begins with the main doctrine of existentialism, encapsulated in the phrase we have already met: 'existence precedes essence'. For Sartre, at bottom there always remains 'a possibility of choice', and this is crucial. When we see a paperknife, he said, we know that it had a maker and that the artisan who made it had an idea of a paperknife before he set out to create it. 'One cannot suppose that a man would create a paperknife without knowing what it was for.' On this basis, God – for believers – is a kind of 'supern[atur]al artisan'; when God creates, 'he knows precisely what he is creating'.[20] Even after the death of God, in the philosophic atheism of the eighteenth century, Sartre goes on, the notion of God is suppressed, but not that of 'human nature' – human nature as something fixed, universal, found in every man. It was this conception of a fixed human nature, he says, agreeing here with the proto-existentialists, that led to fascism. Like Gide, like Malraux, like Saint-Exupéry, he rejected this idea.

If God does not exist, 'it is necessary to draw the consequences of his absence right to the end'. And there is one place, at least, where it leads: 'It is nowhere written that "the good" exists, that one must be honest or must not lie, since we are now upon the plain where there are only men ... For if indeed existence precedes essence, one will never be able to explain one's actions by reference to a given and specific human nature; in other words, there is no determinism – man is free, man *is* freedom.'

In the case of the boy torn between staying with his mother and risking the tag of 'collaborator', and leaving for Britain to join the Free French, Sartre had two things to say. He allied with the pragmatists in arguing that the boy would not stay with his mother because of some 'mother love' deep within him, but that he would show his 'mother love' by staying: he had a choice, and by exercising that choice he *behaved* his values – 'feeling is formed by the deeds that one does . . . I can neither seek within myself for an authentic impulse to action, nor can I expect, from some ethic, formulae that will enable me to act . . . if you seek counsel – from a priest, for example – you have selected the priest; and at bottom you already knew, more or less, what he would advise . . . You are free, therefore choose – that is to say, *invent*. No rule of general morality can show you what you ought to do [italics added].'[21] The young man's values did not effectively exist until he acted.

But Sartre also said that, when we act, when we *choose*, we must do so knowing that we are, and are not, alone. 'In reality, things will be such as men have decided they shall be . . . Man is nothing else than what he purposes, he exists only in so far as he realizes himself, he is therefore nothing else but the sum of his actions . . . there remains within me a wide range of abilities, inclinations and potentialities, unused but viable, which endow me with a worthiness that could never be inferred from the mere history of my actions . . . But for the existentialist, there is no love apart from the deeds of love; no potentiality of love other than that which is manifested in loving; there is no genius other than that which is expressed in works of art . . . reality alone is reliable . . . the coward makes himself cowardly, the hero makes himself heroic.'

There *is* a human universality, he goes on, 'but it is not something given; it is being perpetually made'; and that is because we are all aware of purposes, that other people exist who may have identical, similar, or quite different purposes, and we are aware of them. Sartre called this 'intersubjectivity', and it affects our moral choices. These moral choices are comparable to the construction of works of art, in that works of art are the product of actions, and when we construct a work of art no one questions why we produced *this* work and not another. This is why existentialism is a humanism, he says: it allows that freedom is to be willed *in community*, it is to be achieved, acted upon. If my purposes are to be absolutely free, if my decisions, my choices, are to be absolutely my own, then it follows that everyone else must be free. Otherwise, freedom is a contradiction in terms.

Therefore – and this goes back to the young man in occupied France – the decisions we take, while not forced in any way, must be made in the awareness of how society, community, would be if everyone made that same decision. If the young man *acted* his love for his mother, as he is free to do – if he chose to – what would be the consequences of that action if universally applied? Are we free to make these choices? Yes, but there will be consequences that we cannot necessarily foresee.

Many people, then and now, have regarded existentialism as a tragic and pessimistic doctrine. The first charge is true, but not the second. 'Life,' Sartre liked to say, 'begins on the far side of despair ... Work out your own salvation with diligence', *diligence* being the crucial word. Life is serious and our decisions matter, not always immediately, but eventually. 'All man's alibis are unacceptable; no gods are responsible for his condition; no original sin; no heredity and no environment; no race, no caste, no father, and no mother; no wrongheaded education, no governess, no teachers; not even an impulse or a disposition, a complex or a childhood trauma. Man is free; but his freedom does not look like the glorious liberty of the Enlightenment; it is no longer the gift of God. Once again, man stands alone in the universe, responsible for his condition, likely to remain in a lowly state, but free to reach above the stars.'[22]

Absurd and tragic as man's situation is, that does not rule out integrity, nobility, valour or effort. These are the ways of *defying* the world, of being in it and knowing and relishing that we are in it. There are no alibis.

Scorn, and the Breathing Spaces in Life

The last word in this chapter returns us to Albert Camus, who in his book of reflections *The Myth of Sisyphus* (1942) considers the figure who Homer thought was the wisest and most prudent of mortals but who to others was no more than a highwayman and who, by various misfortunes, was condemned in perpetuity to push a huge stone to the top of a slope, at which point the stone rolled back down to the bottom, where Sisyphus had to start all over again.

This is in itself a pretty obvious metaphor for the ordeals of life, but what interested Camus were the brief interludes when Sisyphus was free of his burden and what he thought about during the stone's descent; how his life – the decisions he had taken – had brought him to this point. Camus saw that the answer was scorn. That however bleak the fate, however eternal the burden, however dreadful the ordeal, there will always be breathing spaces; and that is what happiness is, this is what freedom is – essentially, a series of decisions and acts that lead to consequences. Not all the consequences will be good or fulfilling but we must scorn those that are not and dwell on those that are, creating for ourselves brief moments of respite.

Live with the consequences of your deeds and enjoy the warmth they create. The only warmth in the cold, indifferent universe is that which we create ourselves. And that is what a work of art is, it is what a constructed life is, a fulfilled life, the warmth of acts.

19

War, the American Way
and the Decline of Original Sin

The wartime successes that had produced the atomic bomb, radar and penicillin promised much for peacetime, and engendered a sense of optimism that the applications of science would make possible improvements across a wide range of activities. The prestige of science rubbed off on the social sciences, psychology in particular, and on expertise generally, but change was happening anyway. It was Alan Petigny who identified 'the permissive turn' in American society in the 1940s, which was essentially a challenge to traditional and religious views of the way life should be ordered.

Although we shall be making the case for a 'psychological turn' happening in America especially, in the wake of the war, it would be wrong to ignore earlier moves in that direction. Tufts Medical School had established the first American course on psychotherapy as early as 1909, the year that saw the foundation of the National Committee for Mental Hygiene. In 1908 the Episcopalian Emmanuel Movement, based on the Emmanuel Church in Boston, had founded a journal, *Psychotherapy*, which carried articles by theologians, neuroscientists, Freudians and philosophers. Some people were already talking of 'self-realization' rather than 'self-mastery'. In 1924 *Atlantic Monthly* identified what it called 'a psychological revival', listing a raft of books on psychology and sex life, psychology and business efficiency, psychology and the Christian religion, psychology and parenthood, psychology and preaching, and even psychology and insurance and psychology and golf.[1]

The sociological study *Middletown* (mentioned earlier) found, among many other things, that the residents of the town took out twenty-six times as many books on psychology and philosophy in 1923 as they had done twenty years earlier, while at much the same time at Riverside Church in New York, Harry Emerson Fosdick wrote that counselling, not preaching, was his main interest; and his favourite sermon subjects were 'the mastery of depression, the conquest of fear, the overcoming of anxiety, and the joys of self-realization'. The goal of pastoral care was changing, he said, from 'adjustment' to 'self-realization', and 'a new era in the history of the care of souls' had arrived.

A further change occurred in 1939 when Rollo May published *The Art of Counseling*, grounded not in the usual American traditions but in the work of European analysts – Freud, Jung, Rank and Adler. May was a young pastor who had studied at both Adler's Vienna clinic and New York's Union Theological Seminary. He believed that men and women were 'finite, imperfect and limited', that counselling was as much a moral as a psychological encounter, and that counselling that did not take account of 'subconscious impulses' was 'superficial'.[2]

Self-understanding, not Self-condemnation

Joshua Loth Liebman may not be remembered today as much as other contemporary writers (he died young, in 1948), but in his day he was every bit as widely read. His *Peace of Mind*, published in 1946, was top of the *New York Times* best-seller list for fifty-eight consecutive weeks, a record until it was overtaken by Norman Vincent Peale's *Power of Positive Thinking* (see p. 368). Liebman, a Boston-based rabbi, began by drawing attention to the shortcomings of both religion and psychology. Many religious books, he wrote, succeeded only in making people feel more guilty and sinful, while many psychology books, although seeking to reassure, in fact made people feel abnormal, regarding themselves as 'case histories'. His aim in *Peace of Mind*, he said, was to explain what modern psychology had discovered about human nature, over and above what religion said, including why people lose their faith.

Everyone wanted salvation, he argued, but it was no easy matter to 'look within'. Traditionally, religion had had a monopoly on the ways of doing this but, in the half century up until the Second World War 'and rapidly within the last decade, there has been developed a new method of gaining insight into the deepest emotional and psychologic disturbances that threaten man's peace of mind'. The Freudian technique, he said, was so shocking, so unflattering, that many people were frightened of using it. Like other sciences, psychology had no moral goal, it was not a philosophy of life; and therefore, as he put it, it was only a key to the temple, not the temple itself. It must be supplemented by religion.[3]

But religion was wanting too, he admitted, and that was because religion was pre-scientific, and in particular was formulated before the psychological revolution. He agreed that many people thought religion had shrunk in the wake of the scientific onslaught, and that they worried it might shrink further after the psychological revolution. But, he pointed out, 'Wiser religious leaders today are coming to see the fallacy of identifying truth with the frozen concepts of the past . . . Religion must not hesitate to use the microscope of psychology, with its depth analysis of the human mind.' He did not think there was the gulf between psychology and religion that some claimed, because Freud really had a spiritual purpose, 'even though he may not have been aware of it'. In fact, in psychotherapy man and God become one, and for that reason there was 'no danger' that psychiatry could ever displace religion, just as it was no longer possible for religion 'to sweep back the rising tide of psychological knowledge'.[4]

Religion, he said, for all its wonderful achievements, has been responsible 'for many morbid consciences, infinite confusions, and painful distortions in the psychic life of people'. Religion – not God – was to blame for this: the likes of Paul, Augustine, Calvin and Luther had all been obsessed with the notion of wickedness. (It is worth remembering that this is a Jewish author writing of Christianity.) He drew attention to the fact that the overall strategy employed by the

Church to cope with wickedness has been repression. With few exceptions, Western religions have insisted that people can be good only through the stern repression of sensual thoughts and impulses; and, most importantly, he concluded, that strategy has not worked. 'Religion too frequently has encouraged men to make a complete detour of their un-angelic nature.' Psychotherapy, on the other hand, 'has been able to evolve a reassuring approach to the problem of evil'.

As many others had done before him, Liebman compared psychoanalysis with the confessional, but he made the important distinction that whereas atonement is the aim of the confessional, psychotherapy does not require someone to feel sorry for their 'sins' as they *outgrow* them. Liebman acknowledged that there is little growth available via the ecclesiastical route of confession, reproof and penance. Indeed, he went so far as to say that 'the confessional only touches the surface of a man's life', the spiritual advice of the Church throwing no light on the *causes* that lead someone to the confessional in the first place. Moreover, priestly strictures about people needing to show more 'willpower' were ineffective.[5]

Psychotherapy, on the other hand, is designed to help the individual work on his or her own problems without 'borrowing' the conscience of a priest or pastor, and 'it offers change through self-understanding, not self-condemnation'. And this, said Liebman, was the way to inner peace. The human self, he maintained, was not a gift from God but *an achievement*, and this was how we should regard it. The religion of the future must take a leaf out of the psychiatrist's notebook. Emerson had it right when he wrote that there is 'a crack in everything God has made', and this changes things, even the Commandments. In the style of the Book of Exodus, he told his readers: 'Thou shalt not be afraid of thy hidden impulses.' And henceforth it is not 'Thou shalt love thy neighbor as thyself' but 'Thou shalt love thyself properly and then thou wilt be able to love thy neighbor'. We must accept our imperfections, we must learn to accept the pluralism in ourselves, as well as the notion that failure is as much one of 'the great human experiences' as is success – all of which we encounter in the heroic battle for self-discovery.

'The primary joy of life is acceptance, approval, the sense of appreciation and companionship of our human comrades. Many men do not understand that the need for fellowship is really as deep as the need for food.'

Liebman thought that atheism has psychological causes, too, that it stems from a 'distrust' of the universe brought about by early childhood events, when parents let their children down 'catastrophically'. He maintained that the emotions generated by these experiences are more powerful than any rational arguments, leaving the victims unable and/or unwilling to believe in man or God. 'The *inconsistent* home breeds a spiritual schizophrenia; parents are warm in their actions but embrace a God that is stern and avenging.'[6]

A 'Shrunken' God

Furthermore, we have to realize, said Liebman – and this was new for many of his readers – that God is not omnipotent but *limited* (in other words, religion *has* shrunk in some way); and this implies that we have to be *partners* with God, co-workers, aided by the truths that psychiatry adds to religion. He accepted that religion could be 'a kind of poison', stressing man's evil proclivities, and so it had become essential that theology 'don the more tolerant robes of psychiatric wisdom if it is to be a true ministry to our civilization and its discontents'. Religion, he insisted, must be brave enough to admit its errors and, guided by psychology, 'must now recognize how profoundly it has gone astray in its attitude toward emotion'. Dynamic psychotherapy in a religious context 'can make life whole again . . . We now know enough to liberate man.'

Liebman's close comparison of religion with psychotherapy – his admission that in many respects they perform the same function, fill the same gap – said plainly what many individuals were already concluding for themselves. The book was a holding action for religious souls but its arguments that religion could be improved by psychotherapy only underlined, for those who had left the church, or who were considering doing so, that a modern technology was available in place of an outmoded, and in some cases, unnecessarily cruel tradition in which, as Alan Petigny has put it, 'religion as a relationship to the supernatural was replaced by religion as therapy'. (Liebman himself held to his faith; when he died tragically young in 1948 Boston's schools closed early as a sign of respect.)

Liebman had tackled the parallels between religion and psychology head on. Others had as big an effect but in an indirect or unexpected way. They were part of the context rather than the narrow focus, but nonetheless exerted a profound influence. One crucial figure here, who helped to spawn the 'permissive turn', was Dr Benjamin Spock, who became interested in methods of child-rearing and in Freud at much the same time. As with the very different attitudes to art at the turn of the twentieth century, so child-rearing practices then were very different from now, and that difference is largely due to Dr Spock.

Until the early 1940s many parents – especially first-time parents – sought advice on child-rearing from the Bible or their local preacher, many of whom, it has to be said, regarded children 'as the tainted product of original sin'. Indeed, the grandfather of Spock's own wife had written a book about child-rearing called *Christian Nurture*, published in 1847. Others had thought that children's characters were the product of heredity and evolution as much as anything, and therefore not readily susceptible to alteration or modification. Such practices as tying children's wrists in such a way as to prevent them sucking their thumbs were widespread.

Spock trained as a paediatrician, and was drawn to psychoanalysis partly by nature but also because his wife Jane had undergone it (she was later admitted to an asylum, suffering from alcohol dependency, among other things). Psychoanalysis was still on the fringes of American medicine when Spock signed up for twice-weekly seminars at the New York Psychoanalytic Institute and entered analysis himself. In analysis, and in the seminars, he was introduced to what he felt were the 'deep' reasons behind such processes as breast-feeding, weaning and toilet-training. Gradually he came to the view that there were no bad children, as the advocates of original sin said, but only badly handled children. He discovered the work of Erik Erikson and Margaret Mead, who showed how children were raised differently in other cultures, some less strictly, more relaxedly, than in America. This triggered in Spock a search for a practical way to adapt Freud's ideas to child-rearing – at that time, Freud himself was not popular, in particular his notion of childhood sexuality. Spock first applied Freudian concepts in 1938.[7]

The invitation to write a childcare book came from the publishers Doubleday, with the rather odd stipulation that it should cover the psychological development of the child but that that section 'does not need to be very good'. What Spock brought to the book was a thoroughgoing common sense. Children shouldn't be intimidating, he said; unlike the Calvinist view, children are good at heart, not little villains; parents should trust themselves; they should calm their fears about budding childhood sexuality in the context of the oedipal situation. Spock had a sense of humour and a practical streak. Parents need not have an answer for everything; they should not spend their time telling their child 'thou shalt not', but aim to produce 'a democratic person at home with him- or herself'. They should be flexible.

One of the reasons for the phenomenal success of Spock's book was that it gave many parents who had themselves had a strict or unhappy upbringing the chance to do better by their own children, to break with their own past and be more loving than their own parents had been. And America embraced Spock. America loved his new rules, about discipline, self-demand feeding, about cuddling being more important than cleanliness, about avoiding spanking and other physical punishment (but not feeling guilty about it, either, when they felt it was necessary).

Spock has been compared to Locke and Rousseau in the effect he had on our thinking, and his book was translated into three dozen languages. Published in 1946, it sold a million copies in its first year, four million by 1952, then went on selling a million a year throughout the 1950s. Two-thirds of American mothers read it, and surveys showed that although in the early 1940s only 4 per cent of families fed their babies when they were hungry, by the end of the decade that figure had risen to 65 per cent. At the same time, children were spanked and scolded less often.

Spock's importance from our point of view is that from Freud he developed a moral base that sprang from human experience rather than from a deity. His 'rules' fostered a belief in the human individual, in dignity and even nobility.[8]

The Origins of Self-help

There were other important knock-on effects too. Spock's book, or rather its success, invited a revision of Freudian ideas, and in emphasizing the emotional satisfaction of being a good mother, it helped to kick-start an explosion of self-help books, some better than others. This was the beginning of what Philip Rieff would soon call 'the Triumph of the Therapeutic', and it helped establish the therapy boom that we shall be exploring later.

The new ethic, as spawned by Spock, and the new understanding of the overlap between religion and psychotherapy as outlined by Liebman, coincided with a growing criticism of mass culture and the bureaucracy that sustained it while at the same time impoverishing many aspects of life. Here, two European expatriate psychoanalysts were especially influential.

The first was Erich Fromm, a German refugee who had worked for the Frankfurt Institute in Weimar Germany and one of whose projects was an attempt to reconcile Marx and Freud in a critique of modern capitalism. Fromm's books, *Escape from Freedom* (1941), *Man for Himself* (1947) and *The Sane Society* (1955), caught the mood of the moment perfectly. His work described the antagonism between the aims of modern society and the full development of individuals, and the emergence within capitalism of a distinctive form of human character, one with 'a "marketing" orientation that compelled people to "sell" their personalities in a social market which rewarded charmers and back-slappers'.

Fromm argued that human nature was, in essence, a cultural product, that the religious quest was basic, and that in modern society the central problem was that real freedom was isolating, making people lonely in a way that they found difficult to manage. 'The ambiguity of autonomy had become, for many people, simply unbearable.' For Fromm the modern world encouraged certain reactions in people that were 'non-productive': people were either 'receptive' (dependent on outside sources for support and reward), 'exploitative' (determined to take what they wanted), 'hoarding' (stingy with their goods and feelings), or 'marketing' (eager to sell themselves in a personality market).[9]

Karen Horney was another German refugee, from Berlin. In *The Neurotic Personality of Our Time* and *New Ways in Psychoanalysis* she argued that aggressive, competitive Western society had produced neurosis in 'practically everyone': this distorted the growth of the personality, fostering cravings for 'affection, power, and status', where conformity was the least common denominator of society.

Both Fromm and Horney therefore embraced self-realization as the goal of life. 'Growth' was to be achieved, first, by distinguishing the 'real' self from the 'public' self, which was in part a 'pseudo' self. Underneath the pseudo self and the public self was an original self, a deeper self, which was capable of self-realization. For Fromm this is what virtue was – the expression of one's 'unique individuality' – and it was the job of therapy to realize this unique individuality, the basic currency of which was love. He was highly critical of the Calvinists and of Kant, who deprecated self-love. Only those who truly loved themselves, Fromm said, could truly love others, and this was the basis for living together in society. In *The Art of Loving* (1956), the 'spontaneous affirmation of others' in a form of union that would maintain one's integrity and one's individuality was identified as the way to realize one's potential.

Karen Horney was even more explicit in arguing that moral problems 'were involved in every neurosis'. She thought that both children and adults, overwhelmed by a threatening world, 'compensated for their anxiety by creating an ideal image of themselves – the "idealized self" – which gradually constituted their sense of who they were'. The result was 'their self-imposed subjection to "the tyranny of the should"'. The unending hunt to realize the perfectionist image inevitably trapped them within 'a pride system, which veiled a hidden self-contempt and alienation. Life became a series of hostile inward encounters, with the "actual" self living in a constant tension, torn between the tyrannical demands of the "ideal" self and the insistent efforts of the submerged "real" self to express its need for spontaneous growth.' This meant that, for her, self-realization, the move towards autonomy and fulfilment, was as much *moral* progress as anything else. Here too, then, the overlap between religious and psychological concerns was evident.

All this reflection and analysis came at a good time. Thanks to the GI Bill there was an explosion of returning soldiers only too keen to go to college, spreading higher education more widely than ever before. The same people contributed to the postwar baby boom, which created more parents than ever before. Many of the GIs had been stationed abroad where norms were different, and where the danger they had been in had been accompanied by a charged sexual atmosphere (who knew what would happen next?), from which there was no going back. All this had ramifications for psychological and religious change. In 1951 the psychologist Carl Rogers claimed that 'professional interest in psychotherapy was in all likelihood the most rapidly growing area in the social sciences today'. 'Psychology, like God,' said E. Brooks Holifield in his *History of Pastoral Care in America*, 'seemed omnipresent, if not omnipotent.' In 1957 *Life* magazine announced: 'This is the Age of Psychology.'[10]

But the change that was being brought about, in America at any rate, was to an extent camouflaged by the fact that various forms of 'liberal' behaviour were taking place at a very conservative time.

No one illustrates this more clearly than Norman Vincent Peale. Peale was close to the Republicans, to the Eisenhower administration, and to Billy Graham's National Association for Evangelicals. He was a conservative on racial issues, notoriously advising a young African-American woman not 'to provoke matters' by marrying the white man she was in love with. At the same time, and importantly from our point of view, in his landmark work *The Power of Positive Thinking*, alongside chapters entitled 'Try Prayer Power' and 'How to Use Faith in Healing', Peale was paralleling Spock in advocating far more liberal patterns of parenting, and establishing himself as one of the country's leading proponents of psychological counselling. While he may be best known for his book having occupied the top slot in the *New York Times* best-seller lists for a record-breaking ninety-eight weeks, his more important contribution was his establishment in 1953 of a new type of hybrid organization, the American Foundation of Religion and Psychiatry (AFRP). This had two primary tasks – the provision of psychological training for clerics and the offer of counselling to the public.

A Warmer God: Pastoral Psychology

By the time the AFRP was formed, in fact, psychology had invaded pastoral counselling to the extent that Brooks Holifield could announce 'the Renaissance of Pastoral Psychology'. In 1939, pastoral psychology courses in seminaries were rare. But by 1950 four out of five theology schools had one or more people listed as 'psychologists' on their faculty. In 1947 the *Journal for Clinical Pastoral Work* and the *Journal of Pastoral Care* were founded; *Pastoral Psychology* appeared three years later. The latter soon had sixteen thousand subscribers, seven-eighths of them ministers. By 1955, three out of four American seminaries either had their own clinical training programmes or were sending their students to approved clinical courses elsewhere, and seven universities, including the University of Chicago, had established advanced graduate programmes in pastoral psychology, pastoral counselling or pastoral theology. By the end of the decade, 117 centres for clinical pastoral education had been established.

This was something of a turning point. Freud, though radical in so many ways, had always insisted that humans had limits, and that there were restrictions to what theory could achieve, and in this sense (if in no other) he came close, in mood at least, to traditional religion. But that went against the optimism of the postwar years. What was wanted now was what came to be called 'humanistic psychology', in which the emphasis was on a person's ability to persevere, to overcome, to triumph; it is now that the words 'potential' and 'growth' begin to appear and reappear, and this was reflected not just in therapy but in religion too. About now, in sermons and in theological works, God becomes warmer, less forbidding, less judgemental.[11]

Alongside the professional journals in pastoral counselling came the textbooks, and here two stood out. The first was Seward Hiltner's

Pastoral Counseling and the second was Carl Rogers's *Counseling and Psychotherapy*. Between them, these faced head-on the central dilemma posed when psychology was set alongside religion. Humanistic psychology, especially of the non-directive type proposed by Carl Rogers, was democratic and anti-authoritarian. Doris Mode, of the Institute for Rankian Psychoanalysis, objected: 'A permissive atmosphere where nothing occurs but an echo of the clients' own attitudes would indeed be empty of all value and judgment, and thereby of all therapy also.' She did not see how Rogerian therapy could work. Under his system the therapist was so passive and non-judgemental, expressing no blame at any point, that she felt the therapist had abandoned all values of his own, the end result, she said, being a spiritual vacuum that prevented the patient (client) from ever becoming whole. 'If God were not judgmental,' wrote Mode, 'there would be no meaning to life, and if he were not loving, there would be no fulfilment. Both of these concepts must flow through the therapist to the client if he is to become whole again.' Is the concept of wholeness here being used in a psychological or a theological way?

The fuzziness at the heart of the enterprise was shown by the fact that many of the mental health professionals in the American Foundation of Religion and Psychiatry were themselves reluctant to subscribe to any body of religious dogma or doctrine. In 1956 Iago Gladston, chairman of the research committee, admitted that he 'dreaded to commit himself to another man's concept of God' and refused to accept the 'propriety' of spiritual counselling, preferring to await further research which would 'give the answer as to whether spiritual therapy is a pious hope or an actuality'. In the AFRP, psychology took precedence over prayer and scripture reading.[12]

The Church showed some resistance to certain of these developments, in particular psychoanalysis. Monsignor Fulton Sheen condemned psychoanalysis as a form of escapism, no more than an 'unsatisfactory mix of materialism, hedonism, infantilism and eroticism'; and, in contrast to the confessional, therapy offered no norms or standards. 'There are no more disintegrated people in the world than the patients of Freudian analysis.' This intransigence didn't last, however, because in February 1954 Pope Pius XII gave a tentative go-ahead for pastoral psychology, after which more than 2,500 ministers took advantage of a summer course on the subject, held at St John's University of Minnesota.

As a result of these various changes, one can say that in America by the mid-1950s Carl Rogers (and to a lesser extent Abraham Maslow and Rollo May) was more important than Sigmund Freud, and this marks the maturation of the 'psychological turn', the point at which a psychological model of 'fulfilment' and 'wholeness' began to outweigh the religious concept of 'salvation'. This was true not least because of the media's burgeoning interest in 'personal fulfilment', an obsession that would last for many years and has recently seen a resurgence. Alongside this, less emphasis was now placed on self-mastery than on self-expression.

'Oozing' into the Future

All these matters came to a head in the late 1950s when both Maslow and Rogers attempted to explain and clarify what was happening. At a psychology conference in Cincinnati in the autumn of 1959, Maslow spoke of what he called the 'total collapse of all sources of values outside the individual'. He argued that there had been a breakdown of authority, a realization (even then) that neither economic prosperity nor political democracy was able to provide life with value and meaning, and that 'there is no place else to turn but inward, to the self, as the locus of values'. Rogers was equally forthright. His main interest was what he called 'the self-actualized' individual, by which he meant 'the person who is living the process of the good life'. He had found, he said, that such individuals did not depend on the judgement of others or on their own past behaviour, nor did they have any need for guiding principles. Instead, he said in his book *On Becoming a Person*, they looked within. 'I find that increasingly such individuals are able to trust their total organismic reaction to a new situation because they discover to an ever-increasing degree that if they are open to their experience, doing what "feels right" proves to be a competent and trustworthy guide to behaviour which is truly satisfying.'[13]

There was a growing awareness also, says Alan Petigny, that truth could not be accessed through sacred texts, Sunday School, or an amorphous set of norms commonly known as 'the American way'. Nor, for that matter, could science provide the answer, despite its enormous prestige in answering questions of fact. This is where the self-actualizing theories of Carl Rogers came in.

One basic difference between Rogers and Freud lay in the fact that Rogers did not believe, as Freudians did, that therapy needed to be a five-day-a-week affair, lasting for months or years on end before it was effective. Humanistic psychologists thought that situational factors were as important – if not more so – as the early years and the subject's relationship with his or her parents. The 'self-actualizing tendency', popularized by Rogers, was specifically designed to be political in the widest sense, encouraging people to develop 'an optimistic, self-determined, positive philosophy about human existence rather than one that is cynical, negative, and externally determined'. As he himself put it, 'it is the *client* [not the patient, note] who knows what hurts, what directions to go, what problems are crucial, what experiences have been deeply buried. It began to occur to me that unless I had a need to demonstrate my own cleverness and learning, I would do better to rely upon the client for the direction of movement in the process.' The therapist, he said elsewhere, should 'prize' the client and 'demystify' the practice of therapy.

His theories took no account of possible disease processes, unconscious motivation or developmental history. Rogers saw people as being on an endless growth journey, 'a journey which is sometimes blocked by negative or incongruent images of oneself'; and freeing them so that they might accelerate the journey became the great challenge of humanistic psychology. This is what came to be called the Human Potential Movement, expressed through more than three hundred 'growth centers' in the United States.

At the same time, as Richard Evans points out in his biography, Rogers was responsible for a new level of discontent. 'The discrepancy between what people are ordinarily *able* to make happen in their relationships and what they have come to believe is *possible* to make happen . . . is the cause of much disruption in their lives.' Essentially, the Rogers view is 'the more the better ... Rogers would have you believe that the more congruence, the more honesty, the more intimacy, the more closeness, the more empathy, the better.' He concedes that Rogers has changed the way we all think about human relationships, and given us a new way to be with one another, 'an ethical basis for human interaction'; but his methods allow little role for power, status, culture, history, technology or politics, and this is why, perhaps, they have not always brought the lasting change that is promised.

Rogers's most characteristic idea, self-actualization, 'implies that the person is acceptantly aware of what's going on within and is consequently changing practically every moment and is moving on in complexity'. 'I *ooze* toward my future,' he famously said. Rogers saw a division between the ideal self and the real self, his research showing, he believed, that people did not value all aspects of their self equally, and that what was important for therapy was the picture of the self that they would like to be, as compared with the self as they currently perceived it.[14]

A Higher Humanism: the New Intimacy

In his 'client-centred' therapy Rogers concentrated on the present, accepted the client as a separate person without judging him or her, as an equal, rather than perceiving the relationship as one of the doctor 'above' the client. It was this attitude as much as anything that led him to create what came to be called 'encounter groups', which he thought were 'one of the most significant social inventions of this century because it is a way of eliminating alienation and loneliness, of getting people into better communication with one another, of helping them develop fresh insights into themselves, and helping them get feedback from others so that they perceive how they are received by others'. He thought that it would not be a bad idea if universities allowed students time to participate in client-centred therapy, which might help towards the full development of their personality 'and provide for an opportunity to become more self-actualized'. (He noted that the universities had never taken to psychoanalysis.)

One of the results of his therapeutic technique, he said, in which the therapist was more a 'skill facilitator' than a therapist in the conventional way, was that self-hatred decreased, people became more accepting of themselves, more confident, more constructive. They were moving, he said, from a preoccupation with guilt (the religious imperative) to a preoccupation with identity, shifting from a political view of life to a more philosophical one. There was, however, a danger that the preoccupation with identity was taking the spontaneity out of life. Part of the success of his approach, he said, was down to the fact that '[t]he churches ceased some time ago to have a significant societal influence'.[15]

Rogers concluded that men and women are 'incurably social' animals and that 'a new configuration' was emerging, 'a higher humanism', in which people had a desire for authenticity, eschewed the old acceptance of authority for authority's sake, whether in government, the military, the Church, corporation or school; there was abroad a new wish for intimacy, a distrust of the abstractions of science, and a conviction that 'within ourselves lie undiscovered worlds'. This 'new configuration', he concluded, engenders 'almost the antithesis of Puritan man, with his strict beliefs and strong controls over behavior, who founded our country. [The new man] is very different from the person who brought about the Industrial Revolution, with his ambition, productivity and greed, and competitiveness. He is deeply opposed to the Communist culture with its controls on individual thought and behavior in the interest of the state. His characteristics and his behavior run strongly counter to the orthodoxies and dogmas of the major Western religions – Catholicism, Protestantism, and Judaism.' In a way, he said, we were seeing a return to the situation of classical Greece or the Renaissance. Given all this, in the modern world what he called 'situation ethics' were better than 'some absolute ethic', as for instance laid down by religion.[16]

Situation Ethics

This phrase 'situation ethics' refers to a movement within religious circles that ran parallel to what was happening in psychology.

Traditionally, religious ethics took their colour from the Bible or the Ten Commandments, and were held to apply everywhere and in all situations – to be 'universal'. In 1954 the Reverend Ernest Bruder, a prominent figure in the pastoral care movement, wrote a highly critical review of Monsignor Fulton Sheen's *Peace of Soul*, which as we have seen was a response to Liebman's *Peace of Mind* (see p. 360).

Bruder pilloried Sheen for giving the impression that 'peace of soul' was a state which could only be reached by accepting the thinking and dictates of others. This was not 'peace', claimed Bruder, but an 'unhealthy resignation to authority'. Religious doctrine encouraged an unhealthy state of affairs, he went on, and many agreed. Paul Tillich, H. Richard Niebuhr and Joseph Fletcher all advocated that their fellow Americans oppose 'legalism', as the Sheen approach was called, and cultivate a non-authoritarian moral code 'by looking inward and submitting to God's love', thereby challenging the universality of moral principles. Tillich put the new approach well: 'Let us suppose that a student comes to me faced with a difficult moral decision. In counseling him I don't quote the Ten Commandments, or the words of Jesus in the Sermon on the Mount, or any humanistic ethics. Instead, I tell him to find out what the commandment of *agape* in his situation is, and then decide for it even if traditions and conventions stand against his decision.'

In other words, the one axiom to follow was the commandment of *agape*, or the law of love.

In the 1950s religious leaders began promoting 'situation ethics', and in 1966 Joseph Fletcher's *Situation Ethics: The New Morality* was published, selling 150,000 copies in the first two years. Fletcher became an intellectual celebrity. Vatican II (1962–5) went so far as to consider what is changeable and what is universal in a moral context.[17]

The Apotheosis of Optimism

Arguably, the people who benefited most from these changes, albeit not for a decade or more, were women. The United Methodist Church, the second-largest Protestant denomination, opened up its clergy to women in 1956. The Presbyterians and Episcopalians followed suit in relatively short order. The late 1940s had seen the publication of Simone de Beauvoir's *The Second Sex* (1949) and Ferdinand Lundberg and Marynia Farnham's *Modern Woman: The Lost Sex* (1947). Particularly among those educated to university level, attitudes towards women working, having careers and even becoming President, changed markedly. In the late 40s several states repealed laws preventing women serving on juries, more women were going to college (37.1 per cent as against 31.6 per cent), Equal Opportunity Day was instituted in 1956, and within two years thirty state governors had given it their public support. More women were willing to abandon their virginity before marriage, and more men agreed that it did not matter if their bride was not a virgin on their wedding day. The availability of the contraceptive pill in 1960 naturally had a big effect on behaviour, and gradually on attitudes too.

The 1950s saw much less disparaging of women though many still felt that their biological imperative was still motherhood and the kitchen. Abraham Maslow applied his understanding of humanistic psychology to women as much as to men, and in the late 1960s women would find his and Carl Rogers's theories very helpful in what became known as consciousness-raising groups. Betty Friedan, in her highly successful *The Feminine Mystique* (1963), used many Maslovian and Rogerian concepts such as self-actualization.

One last, and rather different, factor that came into play was, paradoxically enough, science. By the end of the 1950s it was being increasingly recognized that science, however successful it was in solving questions of fact and in producing new technologies that made life more agreeable, did not solve the enduring questions relating, for instance, to beauty, courage, loyalty – the 'realities by which men live in the fullest sense', as Howard Keniston of the University of Michigan put it. Intuitive understanding, he said, 'is the only access we have to the deepest and highest aspects of our individual and collective lives'. Not everyone would have agreed with his words, or their implications, but even Albert Einstein had said that 'objective knowledge provides us with powerful instruments for the achievement of certain ends, but the ultimate goal itself and the longing to reach it must come from another source'.[18]

America's great turn inward during the 1940s and 50s, to be followed, to an extent, by other Western nations, marked, in one observer's words, 'the apotheosis of the optimistic portrayal of the self'. It embodied above all the decline of the doctrine of original sin: the individual was no longer seen as 'inherently depraved' – instead, the self became what one made of it. This freed people, in the words of Norman Mailer, in *The White Negro*, 'to set out on that uncharted journey into the rebellious imperatives of the self'.

Thus as postwar prosperity established itself, for the growing numbers who had left the Church the goal of salvation was replaced by that of self-realization. It was conceivably the biggest acceleration in secularization there has ever been, and it laid the intellectual and emotional groundwork for the therapy boom that took place from the 1960s on.

Height Psychology

The work of the Viennese psychiatrist Viktor Frankl provides an apt link between this chapter and the next, on the Holocaust and its effect on religious understanding and secularization.

Frankl decided to be a doctor very early on, and was fascinated by psychoanalysis. He wrote to Freud while still at school, as a result of which the master submitted one of Frankl's essays to the *International Journal of Psychoanalysis*. Under Freud's influence Frankl turned to psychiatry, and by 1939 he was head of the neurology department at the Rothschild Hospital, the only Jewish hospital in Vienna. This gave him and his family some protection against deportation, but in 1942, when the American consulate in Vienna told him he was eligible for a visa that would guarantee his survival, he decided to stay, probably because his parents were aged. In September that year Viktor and his family were arrested and deported, Frankl spending the next three years in four concentration camps – Theresienstadt, Auschwitz-Birkenau, Kaufering and Türkheim, part of the Dachau complex. He and his father had been separated from the rest of the family, and he watched his father die in the camp where they were then incarcerated.

When Viktor returned home, he found that his mother, brother and wife had also perished.

Before he went to the camps he had begun a book on a new form of psychotherapy (which we shall come to), but it was confiscated and he never saw it again. His experiences during those years, however, reinforced his beliefs, and when he returned to Vienna he wrote a new book, in nine days. It was published in 1946 in German as *A Psychologist Experiences the Concentration Camp*, the title later changed to *Say Yes to Life in Spite of Everything*; and in 1959 it appeared in English as *Man's Search for Meaning*. It has since sold more than twelve million copies in twenty-four languages, and has been voted among the ten most influential books in America.[19]

Frankl evolved 'logotherapy', by which he meant a system of psychiatric treatment for what he called the 'meta-clinical problem of our day' – namely, the 'mass neurosis' concerning the meaning of life. His most vivid insight, he said, had come to him in the camps with his identification of what someone else had called 'give-up-itis'. One day an individual in the camps would simply refuse to get out of bed in the morning, dig deep into a secret pocket, to find one remaining cigarette, and start to smoke. Inevitably, within forty-eight hours they were dead.

Frankl's main argument is that we have a choice of how we will respond to suffering. We all suffer – not to the same extent, of course – and for most of us nowhere near as much as people suffered in the camps. But we are free to respond to that suffering, to make it an achievement, even to make it ennobling. 'We give suffering a meaning by our response.' He disagreed with Freud that the aim of life is pleasure, and with Adler that the aim is power. For Frankl the main aim of life is the discovery of meaning, and he quoted various polls, in Europe and America, which showed that at the time more people were concerned about meaning in their lives than, say, money. He referred to Irvin Yalom's book, *Existential Psychotherapy* (1980), which said that 30 per cent of the people who came to him for help were searching for meaning in their lives, and that 90 per cent of alcoholics said they found their lives meaningless.

For Frankl modern life is lived in an existential vacuum, where we have been estranged from our instincts and have lost our traditions; we live within a 'tragic triad' of pain, guilt and death. The way out of this triad, he insisted, was 'out there' in the world, not within us, and meaning was to be found in one of three ways – by deed, actions in the world; by someone, love; or by turning our inevitable suffering into something ennobling. We must not fear death, but use its inevitability to underscore the transitoriness of the world so that we act now rather than later. He agreed with Carl Rogers that self-actualization was the aim, but that it could only be achieved as a side-effect of self-transcendence – surpassing ourselves – in which the conquest of suffering offers the most widely available possibility. We must lead our lives constantly imagining we are on our deathbed looking back, and asking ourselves whether we have lived a life we can be at peace with.

Frankl lived a long life (dying at ninety-two in 1997), and he practised into old age his twin passions of flying and mountaineering. He liked to say that whereas Freud, Adler and Jung have given us 'depth psychology', he had given us 'height psychology', 'helping people to reach new heights of personal meaning through self-transcendence'. He was once asked to express in one sentence the meaning of his own life. His reply was: 'The meaning of your life is to help others find the meaning of theirs.'[20] Is that a too-easy answer?

20

Auschwitz, Apocalypse, Absence

The murder of six million Jews by the Nazis and their collaborators during the Second World War, its systematic and arbitrary nature, was destined to eclipse all other calamities of the twentieth century, including the carnage of the first war, and the millions of Russians killed in both wars and in Stalin's purges in between. The Holocaust brought cruelty to a new level. 'The great psychological fact of our time which we all observe with baffled wonder and shame is that there is no possible way of responding to Belsen and Buchenwald. The activity of mind fails before the incommunicability of man's suffering.' This is Lionel Trilling in *The Liberal Imagination*, published in 1950. Better known, perhaps, is Theodor Adorno's remark, that '[t]o write poetry after Auschwitz is barbaric'. But Adorno changed his mind after encountering Paul Célan's poem 'Death Fugue', and although many people shared Trilling's bafflement there were those who sought to confront the horror head-on.

From our point of view, the question that emerges as the most insistent is this: how could people who had perhaps not agreed with Nietzsche before and continued to believe in God, still carry on believing when evil, cruelty and suffering had reached such epic proportions? How could an omnipotent, benevolent God allow such calamities? Where was God in Auschwitz?

Some statistics first. Before the genocide, most people who would survive the camps had believed in the existence of God; afterwards, only 38 per cent did. The belief that Jews were a chosen people also suffered: 41 per cent held this view before the war, one third afterwards. Only 6 per cent of the survivors thought that the creation of Israel, in the wake of the war, had been worth the sacrifice of six million lives.[1]

In her book *Suffering as Identity*, Esther Benbassa argues that suffering is a part of Jewish identity, that the trials and tribulations undergone by the Jews throughout their history have become part of who they are and that, for many people, for many Jews, the Holocaust fitted into this paradigm. She referred back to the work of Hermann Cohen (died 1918), who argued that 'misery and pain are needed in order to awaken the conscience of men and thereby to advance the cause of ethical progress'.

In Nazi Germany that attitude continued, for the ultra-Orthodox produced ready theological responses to anti-Semitism. Ahiezer de Vilna and Elchonon Wasserman, who lived through Kristallnacht (9–10 November 1938) but died before the death camps, argued that 'the whole of history unfolds under God's aegis', meaning that even the Nazis were his instruments. De Vilna thought that the Reformed Jews were responsible for what was happening; Wasserman blamed the abandonment of the Torah, assimilation and Zionism, which he regarded as a lack of trust in religion and in God. Both maintained that what was required of the Jews was a turning *to* God, by way of the Torah. 'The more the apparent increase in the power of evil and the sterner the chastisement, the closer one was to redemption. Thus Nazis, Zionists, heretics, the assimilated and Reformed Jews were all instruments of the divine plan of salvation.'[2]

Aharon Rokeach, leader of the Hasidic community in Belz in western Ukraine, whose eldest son was burned alive in a synagogue that the Germans had torched, said: 'It is indeed a kindness of the Almighty that I also offered a personal sacrifice.' Suffering, for him, was a form of God's 'hidden grace' that prayer and study of the Torah could 'transform into revealed goodness'. Several Hasidic teachers, such as Shem Klingberg when he was in the Plaszow death camp (in a suburb of Krakow), urged the faithful to accept suffering and death 'with love, even during the Final Solution'. Even Hasidic rabbis in the Warsaw ghetto argued that suffering came from God: 'It had not been caused by their sins, but was part of his plan for humanity.' Yitshak Weiss, the spiritual head of the Spinka dynasty, in the Maramures region of Romania near the Hungarian border, danced and sang on the train that took him to Auschwitz. 'Purify our hearts,' he prayed, 'and we shall serve you in truth.'

Many other examples of this kind of reasoning, having its origin in the Jewish notion of 'sanctification of the Name of God', could be given. Traditionally in the Talmud such sanctification can occur only when, by not denying their faith, Jews attain a choice in the manner of their death. This doctrine was amended during the Holocaust. Although Jews scarcely had a choice in their death, it was deemed by Orthodox leaders that they had a choice in the *way* that they died – a choice between death amid degradation, and death 'with inner peace, nobility of soul, and self-respect'.

To avoid being intimidated into prostitution, which the German military were intent on, ninety-three young women of the Orthodox Bais Yaakov school in Krakow committed suicide by taking poison after reciting one last prayer. Their sacrifice was immortalized by the Hebrew poet Hillel Bavli in a poem that has been incorporated into the liturgy of Yom Kippur, the Jewish Day of Atonement, 'in a spirit reminiscent of the medieval custom of liturgizing catastrophes and acts of martyrdom for the instruction of future generations'.[3]

Hitler the New Nebuchadnezzar

Ultra-Orthodox arguments went so far as to say that 'Hitler was the new Nebuchadnezzar sent by God to chastise his people'. Yoel Teitelbaum cursed the Zionists for behaving in such a way as to precipitate and legitimize the Final Solution – 'just punishment for an act of blasphemy, that of initiating a return to Zion on their own and, thereby, acting as substitutes for the awaited Messiah'. Some Hasidic thinkers even saw the mass murder 'as "the labour pains" that are to precede the coming of the Messiah'. The movement known as Chabad considered the entire modern age as the dawn of the messianic era, 'which could only be preceded by cataclysmic events'.

On this reasoning the genocide was 'thought to have saved the people of Israel by amputating one of its gangrenous members ... the suffering endured by pure, holy beings in this period had been merely temporal. What did it matter when measured against eternal life? ... To suffer for the love of God – therein lay the significance of being chosen.' Chabad's charismatic leader Menachem Mendel Schneerson went furthest, arguing that the genocide had been the work of a 'just God' and had been caused by the sins of the Jews, and that God carried out his work 'with the help of Hitler, his messenger'.

By no means everyone accepted such reasoning, and in practice there were three alternatives. One had it that God had been *hidden* during the genocide. The second said that God had to be redefined – he was no longer omnipotent or benevolent, or even a 'he'; while the third alternative proclaimed that God had been *absent* from Auschwitz and elsewhere 'because God was dead'.[4]

The first argument was put forcibly by the Orthodox rabbi Eliezer Berkovits. His view was that Auschwitz was not unique because there had been similar disasters in the past that put the Jews' faith to the test. However, he did not attribute the death camps to Israel's sins, as did Schneerson and some others. Berkovits accepted that the Final Solution was 'an absolute injustice', but turned to the concept, contained in the Bible, that God had 'veiled his face'. On this reasoning, from time to time in history God withdraws, 'thereby allowing certain events that he could have prevented to take place'. This withdrawal by God does not mean – or even imply – that he *wanted* these (often terrible) events to occur, but rather it reflects his desire to grant humans greater spiritual freedom.

'Such "veiling" is the price to be paid for the emergence of a moral humanity ... It would be impossible to be humane if God were rigorously just.' For Berkovits the 'absence of God' is nothing new – every generation has had its Masada or Auschwitz – suffering is a consequence of free will. As a creator, God is 'obliged' to create an imperfect world, while at a personal level 'suffering is positive', it 'purifies and deepens the personality'. For Berkovits the Final Solution was 'an attempt to dethrone God', but the fact that Israel was (re)-born on its territory so soon afterwards 'proves that God is not absent from history'. Many others share Berkovits's view that Israel, despite its avowedly secular character, is in fact a religious institution: one role of the Jews, and of Jewish suffering, was to lead the Gentiles to God.[5]

For Irving Greenberg, 'all the old truths and certainties, all the old commitments and obligations, have been destroyed by the Holocaust' and any 'simple faith' is now impossible. The Holocaust ended the old era of Jewish covenantal existence and brought in a new one. He terms this 'the third great cycle of Jewish history', after the biblical age and the rabbinic age. In the new dispensation, the Jewish covenant with God is voluntary. On this analysis the building of Israel is not the work of God but of the Jewish people. For Greenberg this meant that God still existed but the understanding of him could no longer owe anything to rabbinic teaching: the people must set the agenda, creating a modern, post-Holocaust religion in which all the old prejudices and oppressions must be dispensed with.

Three theologians – Arthur A. Cohen, Hans Jonas and Melissa Raphael – chose instead to *redefine* God in the wake of the Holocaust. In *The Tremendum: A Theological Interpretation of the Holocaust* Cohen argued that traditional notions of a beneficent and providential God could no longer be entertained. For him, God could no longer be understood as a direct causal agent in human affairs. He is a mystery, and it is that mystery that provokes our searching, and that searching which, ultimately, brings about our moral development, because we can no longer ask anything of God.

Hans Jonas, in a work that he admitted was purely speculative, also argued that God can no longer be understood as omnipotent, but rather, that he suffers alongside humankind and 'becomes', just as people do, implying that he needs the actions of people 'to perfect the world'. Melissa Raphael suggests that, after the Holocaust, the patriarchal notion of God as almighty and omniscient is simply incompatible with what happened in the death camps, and should be understood rather as 'God the mother', caring, suffering, loving, but not omnipotent. She 'secretly sustains the world by her care'.[6]

A New Meaning for Prayer

For many people, it should be said, and as the statistics mentioned at the beginning of this chapter showed, these arguments took some swallowing. That was certainly so for Richard Rubenstein, who in *After Auschwitz* (1966) roundly broke with the classical idea of an omnipotent, benevolent God, and, echoing Nietzsche, declared that God is dead, that Auschwitz had made any theology espousing Judaism's traditional providential God 'intellectually untenable'. Rubenstein called for traditional theology to be replaced; instead, there should be a positive affirmation of the value of human life 'for its own sake, with no theological references. Joy and personal fulfilment have from now on to be sought in this world, rather than in a mystical eschatological future. There is no hope of human salvation for the human race, whose ultimate fate is to return to nothingness.'[7] We are finite beings, he insisted, with finite selves. Self-discovery in this world should be our aim. Prayer should no longer be understood as attempts at a dialogue with God but as expressions of our aspirations. If God is to be understood in any way at all it is as a focus, an aide in concentrating 'on what is of genuine significance in the business of life'. Rubenstein's theories upset many in the Jewish community, and he was 'exiled'.[8]

Amos Funkenstein, professor of Jewish studies at the University of California at Berkeley, also criticized the view that the Holocaust was incomprehensible. He thought that historians, psychologists, sociologists and philosophers 'ought to make every effort to comprehend the catastrophe and ought to be guided by reasonable expectation that they can comprehend it'. To understand the Holocaust, he insisted, we have to turn 'from God to man'.[9]

Emil Fackenheim, a German refugee who escaped the Nazis and eventually took Canadian nationality, coincided with Rubenstein in his reasoning. In two books, *The Human Condition after Auschwitz* (1971) and *God's Presence in History* (1970), Fackenheim found the idea of a redemptive God after Auschwitz to be untenable. The imperative now, he said, had to be Jewish *survival*, to remain 'alive, resistant and united as a distinct, identifiable people': 'After the death camps, there remains only one supreme value: existence.' In fact Fackenheim made survival a commandment – the 614th. (Rabbinical Judaism maintains that there are 613 commandments in the Torah.) For him, too, the state of Israel is 'a riposte' to Auschwitz, and in that sense redemptive.[10]

Being Jewish without God: the Religion of the Holocaust

The uniqueness – or otherwise – of the Holocaust has become an important distinguishing factor as between religious Jews, especially Orthodox, and secular Jews. For the Orthodox and for practising Jews the Final Solution has been incorporated into a long line of Jewish misfortunes and previous ordeals which are part of Jewish history and identity. For many secular Jews, however, who may sympathize with – and approve of – the existence of Israel but have no wish to live there, the Holocaust, Esther Benbassa suggests, has *itself* become the core idea of a new religion, a secular surrogate equivalent but without a God, 'a self-sufficient religion with its rites, ceremonies, priests, places of pilgrimage, modern martyrs, rhetoric, and one supreme commandment: the obligation to remember. At the centre of this religion stands Auschwitz.'

The adoption of Auschwitz is curious, in the sense that the overwhelming majority of the seventy thousand prisoners there were Russian or Polish prisoners of war, whereas at nearby Birkenau between 1.1 and 1.6 million people were gassed, 90 per cent of them Jews. The new religion, Benbassa says, took shape following the Eichmann trial in 1961 and gained strength during the 1967 Six Day War, when it seemed possible that yet another genocide might occur. 'Auschwitz was eventually transformed into a new Sinai: the place where a new Judaism, a Judaism made to order – less constraining, without the onus of Jewish religious practices or Jewish culture – was revealed to man. Jewishness was thus no longer a religious category, properly speaking, but, rather, an ethics adapted to the demands of a modern society in which mixed identities co-exist without discomfiture.' This new Judaism is called the Judaism 'of the Holocaust and Redemption', raising the destruction of the Jews 'to the level of an event possessing intense transcendental meaning, while conferring qualities of the same order, redemptive in this case, on the creation of the state of Israel'.

On this basis, the Holocaust was unique, incapable of being explained or historicized. Isaac Deutscher and Elie Wiesel (and Adorno, to begin with) advocated silence, on the grounds that the genocide 'would forever remain beyond the grasp of the human mind'. But the Holocaust as a religion of suffering has been adopted by the Jewish masses, 'who remain deaf to historicization, which has essentially been restricted to scholarly circles'. All the talk about the 'impossibility of representation' after Auschwitz contributes to the mythologization of the event. 'In traditional Jewish theology, the ways of god are inscrutable. The ways of Auschwitz now become inscrutable as well.'

But Benbassa has her doubts: 'One may wonder, indeed, how long this secular religion can provide the grounds for a viable Jewish identity, when one considers that it has been erected mainly on a foundation of suffering and victimhood and makes its followers eternally vigilant Jews plunged into a permanent state of insecurity.'[11]

The genocide has become an essentially religious mystery. 'It was also an election, a self-election, of the human, by the human, and for the human: without God.' It was a new religion of the 'absolute exception', with the result that some individuals, like Alvin Rosenfeld, insist that the memoirs, the prose and poetry of the genocide be regarded as 'holy' texts. Arnost Lustin maintains that some of the works written about the catastrophe 'can stand comparison with the best written parts of the bible'.

Another aspect of this new religion is that for several Jewish generations the memory of the catastrophe has been bequeathed to them by the media's treatment of it, and this has served to construct a 'transnational community' made up of Sephardim and Ashkenazim alike – in effect, Israel and the Diaspora have found themselves united in a new shared religion 'that outsiders could immediately recognize and was easy to practice. It was a religion of those chosen by suffering, an ersatz for Judaism that protected them from anti-Semitism, at least for a time, and acted as a brake on assimilation.'[12]

These developments have not been without their critics: 'The uses to which memory has been put [in the various museums of the Holocaust in the United States, for example] border on expropriation.

In fact, the religion of the Holocaust that was put in place after the Six Day War rang in the era of being Jewish without Judaism and, of course, without God . . . In the process of being converted into a universal religion with a message that is easy to understand, the memory of the genocide contributed, paradoxically, to de-universalizing the Jews, distancing them from others who suffered and gradually shutting them inside their own pain.'[13]

Apocalyptic Fulfilment

The events at Hiroshima and Nagasaki on 6 and 9 August 1945 that killed upwards of 250,000 people, injured far more, and brought the Second World War to an end in Asia, also required some theological adjustment on the part of the many who, notwithstanding Nietzsche and all that had happened in the previous years and decades, had remained religious. In particular, it became necessary to redefine God.

One of the most considered responses came from Jim Garrison, theologian and president of Wisdom University (in Oakland, California dedicated to the study of the world's wisdom traditions), who used the 'process' philosophy of Alfred Whitehead and the psychoanalysis of Carl Jung to adapt traditional images of God to the modern world, some of his ideas overlapping with Jewish theologians of the Holocaust. It was Jung's argument, Garrison said, that 'God' was an 'archetype', synonymous with the unconscious; that the religious impulse stemmed from the unconscious (see chapter 14). Archetypes, according to Jung, are ancient ways in which our psychology is organized, aspects of the collective unconscious that lie at the root of human nature. These usually take the form of pairs of opposites (introvert/extravert, anima/animus, for example), and shape our psychology accordingly. Reconciling these opposites, he said, comprises the 'burden of completeness' which is our essential existential predicament. Garrison argued that the religious archetype within us also had a dual nature, that there is – to resort to traditional terminology – a God of lightness within us and a God of darkness.

He gave the God of darkness the archetypal name of 'Wotan',

thinking that darkness was an especially German trait; all the horrors of the 1939–45 war, including the Holocaust, were merely 'a curtain raiser' to Hiroshima and Nagasaki. 'The fanaticism of the Germans against the Jews has been replaced by the anti-communism of the West in general.'[14] Jung had said that we have within us a 'hungering for the infinite', an 'eschatological expectation of the Great Fulfilment', and that one way to achieve this was to generate our own apocalypse. This is where Garrison brought in Whitehead's process philosophy as well as something the former called 'panentheism', the notion that *creation, evolution, progress, process* and *change* are identical with divinity, so that if these bombs were invented they served a divine purpose.

To a non-believer this too sounds like a 'just-so' story, but what Garrison meant was that in bringing us to the point where we can actually destroy the earth and everyone alive on it, the divine process was bringing itself not just to an end but to an apocalyptic fulfilment. And in doing so it was forcing man – who had removed his gaze from the heavens ever since the Renaissance and had looked ever more 'horizontally', towards other men – to look again upwards, to the heavens. The threat of Hiroshima and Nagasaki, therefore, raised the possibility of us killing mankind *and* God – the creative principle – at one and the same time.

Garrison thought the Christian Church had been particularly lame in its responses to the 'God is dead' debate, and that it had also been blind to the fact that 'the hand of God' could be discerned at Hiroshima. But for him the idea that supreme creativity (conceiving and building the atomic bomb) should also be the instrument by which all creativity, all life, could be annihilated, that the forces of the unconscious could eliminate all consciousness, was not so much a bitter irony as one way for mankind to experience apocalyptic fulfilment. Its attainment, if it occured (and in the Cold War it never seemed far away), would be, so to speak, a negative goal of wholeness, a dark form of completeness but, he said, this was the situation we were faced with in a post-Hiroshima world.

As with some of the post-Holocaust theories, this amounted to saying that God – viewed as creativity, process – is neither wholly beneficent nor omnipotent.

Theothanatology

While the Holocaust may have had a more powerful effect on Jewish thought than on most, it did not concern Jews exclusively. Moreover, the atomic bombings in Japan clearly showed what else was at stake, for everyone, and the growing awareness of Stalin's Great Terror was another factor in the equation. These events gave rise among some Christians to what John Warwick Montgomery called 'the new theological science of Theothanatology, wherein God's mortal illness or demise serves as the starting point for a radically secular approach to the modern world'.[15]

The movement received widespread publicity – for example in *Time*, the *New Yorker* and the *New York Times* – and was a wholly Protestant initiative. Its half-dozen or so proponents could be divided into 'hard' radicals and 'soft' radicals, according to how fervently they argued that God was now dead all over again.

The first name among these theothanatologists was Gabriel Vahanian. Born in Marseilles, he studied under Karl Barth, then taught for twenty-five years in the United States before retiring to Strasbourg. Vahanian's argument was that God had become irrelevant in cultural terms, that the levelling down of 'transcendent values' to 'immanental ones' was bound to result in the demise of God because he became just another 'cultural accessory', no different really from other cultural ideas. Vahanian thought that we must wait for this view to pass, for people to realize that 'the finite cannot comprehend the infinite', that until we acknowledge the total 'otherness' of God (Barth's seminal idea), God will remain to all intents and purposes dead.

Harvey Cox of the Harvard Divinity School, second among the Death of God theologians, wrote *The Secular City* in 1965 after he had lived in Berlin for a year, where he taught in a Church-sponsored education programme that had branches on both sides of the barbed wire. Since the Berlin wall had just been erected, he was forced to commute back and forth through Checkpoint Charlie. In Berlin he came under the intellectual influence of Karl Barth, as well as of Dietrich Bonhoeffer, who espoused an idea concerning what he called the 'defining edge of evil', positing that to do good we must always act immediately, before our self-regarding conscience intervenes. Cox adapted some of these thinkers' ideas, arguing in his book that secularization occurred most often and most easily in the city environment, and that it was a positive phenomenon 'whereby "society and culture are delivered from tutelage to religious control and closed metaphysical world views"'.[16]

Echoing the views of Jonathan Raban in *Soft City: The Art of Cosmopolitan Living*, where it was argued that there is no single point of view from which we can grasp the city, Cox said the same is true of religion. Secularization raises the stakes, increasing the range both of freedom and of responsibility. Cox argued that art, social change and the fleeting I–you relationships of city life could breed a new spiritual atmosphere, very different from the traditional ideas of God. 'This may mean that we shall have to stop talking about "God" for a while, take a moratorium on speech until the new name emerges.' In other words, here too, as with Vahanian, 'waiting' is recommended; but this should not necessarily strike us as strange, Cox says, because 'hiddenness stands at the very center of the doctrine of God'.

What he meant by there being no single viewpoint from which to grasp religion was that, as Garrison had intimated, not all of religion is good – that it is in part inflexible and intolerant; but secularism too has its faults. John Paul II, he said, was good on a united Europe, but not on contraception. The Church embraced both the achievements of Mother Teresa and the corruptions of Jim and Tammy Bakker. These ideas, which gave rise among other things to liberation theology, started from the postmodern viewpoint that we 'cramp' the divine presence by confining it to some specially delineated spiritual or ecclesial sector, whereas in the city there are all sorts of perspectives – not just 'the classical God of metaphysical theism'. In the city, where there are so many 'others', we may find God in Someone Else.

Cox reflected his debt to Bonhoeffer in saying that theology comes after the commitment to action. Religion shouldn't stifle thought, it is not necessarily, or first and foremost, a worldview – it is action. By the same token, his time in Berlin had taught him that communism needed secularizing – it also was too confined to ersatz customs. Cox took action himself and joined the civil rights activities at Selma, Alabama, in 1965 and was jailed briefly. He insisted the believer must engage in justice in the world, not pause for theological reflection.

Much influenced by Mircea Eliade, Carl Jung, Søren Kierkegaard, Nietzsche and Tillich, Thomas Altizer (born 1927) is one of the most radical of the radicals in the Death of God movement. In his view God is wholly dead, and the Church – especially the Christian Church – is moribund; all traditional teaching has to be discarded (it was always provisional), even Jesus as traditionally understood. The deadest idea is that of metaphysical transcendence, so that all we are left with, says Altizer, is the idea of resurrection. We don't know what form this will take, when or even if it will occur; nothing that happens in the future can be identified with anything that happened in the past; but we must hold ourselves ready for a new epiphany that may be so unlike the old ones that we will never be sure that it *is* one. This is the apotheosis of the idea of kenosis, emptying oneself of will, to make oneself available for God to take over. Here too we find the idea of waiting.

Another of the radicals is William Hamilton. In his seminal essay 'Thursday's Child' he depicts the theologians of today and tomorrow as 'men without faith, without hope, with only the present and therefore only love to guide them' – 'a waiting man and a praying man'. At the same time he affirms the literal death of God. All that was left was to discover Jesus in the world – he argued that Jesus may be concealed in the world, engaged in the struggle for justice. In the secular world man becomes the focus, 'while we wait prayerfully for the epiphany of a God of delight' – we must try to enjoy (the idea of) God, says Hamilton, even if we cannot use him.

For Hamilton, God is in some sense still there, 'waiting as we wait, the recipient of our prayers'. For Paul van Buren, however, even this no longer applied: 'I don't pray. I just reflect on these things.'[17] Like the others he was influenced by Barth, under whom he took a doctorate in Basel. But van Buren also came under the influence of Wittgenstein, and this led to his *Secular Meaning of the Gospel*. His version of 'Christian atheism' argued that God had died, in part, from 'a thousand qualifications'; that attempts like Whitehead's to define God as process philosophy had been one such qualification; and that such modifications had killed God partly because their multifarious nature had removed the possibility of epiphany.

Van Buren was one of those who thought that the modern world was much too pluralistic ever to be defined by one theological idea, and that in any case a theology that is only about God has no place in the modern world, where human life and human history are what count. If theology can't address this, he said, it has no use. This means that Jesus is to be understood as a man, not as God, and Easter is to be understood metaphorically, as an aspect of one man's freedom. 'So let us frankly embrace the secular world of which we are a part. Religious thought is "responsible to human society, not to the church. Its orientation is humanistic, not divine. Its norms must lie in the role it performs in human life ... Any insights into the "human situation" which our religious past may provide us, therefore, can be helpful only insofar as we bring them into a dynamic conversation with and allow them to be influenced by our rapidly changing technological culture.'[18]

Vahanian was French, and all the other theothanatologists but one were or are American. The last to add to the mix is John Robinson, Bishop of Woolwich in South London, whose *Honest to God* (1963) was a publishing sensation.[19] It argued that secularized man, having rejected the idea of 'God up there', also needs to recognize that the idea of 'God out there' is an outdated simplification of the nature of divinity. Instead, he said, we should take our cue from the existentialist theology of Paul Tillich and regard God as 'the ground of our being'. He also embraced Bonhoeffer's idea of a religionless Christianity: that God's continuing revelation to humanity is brought about in the culture at large, not just in the confines of 'religion' or 'Church'. Robinson argued that God as somehow 'above the universe' is still part of our mental furniture, although we no longer think of reality in that way. He embraced some aspects of postmodernism (see chapter 26), in which God is increasingly thought of as *our creation*.

Perhaps his most original idea, for most people, was the notion that God is 'the ground of our being', meaning that we give special *attention* to what we think is the ultimate in our lives – when we pray we are identifying the most important, intimate thing, and whatever that is, it is God. This too, of course, can be seen as a human creation, and it partly coincides with Nietzsche's notion of 'eternal recurrence' – that we should live for those moments we would like to live over and over again. By this account, God is a way of attaching importance to the world, or part of the world; of being serious about life, of recognizing what is important to us. Robinson did not believe in supernatural entities, but opted for 'naturalism', which 'identifies God, not indeed with the totality of things, the universe, per se, but with what gives meaning and direction to nature'. The supernatural, he said, was 'the greatest obstacle to an intelligent faith'.

His view of Jesus was the same as Bonhoeffer's, that he was 'a man for others'. Robinson insisted Jesus was not a God–Man, did not have a dual nature, was not a God incarnate walking about on earth; rather, he was a man who never claimed anything special for himself, but so loved others that he always put them first (and that, Bonhoeffer said, was what Christians should seek to do). One of Bonhoeffer's main points, which Robinson followed, was that to lead a moral life one should not wait when confronted with evil; that to wait always means we begin to put our own interests before others', which are the urgent ones.

Most theothanatologists did not appear to think that God would remain dead. The traditional idea of God was dead, yes, but after a period of waiting, a new pattern, a new idea of what used to be called God, would come into view. Meanwhile, we should wait and hope. They did not turn to the other figures discussed in this book. To that extent, their minds were closed.

21

'Quit Thinking!'

In the lengthening wake of World War Two, with more and more people turning away from God, three movements in the arts sought to show how we might make sense of – and address – the changes that were occurring, and how we might seek new ways of fulfilment. The first of these was minimalism; then the 'culture of spontaneity'; and third, one that concerned a new understanding of the body's role in the search for meaning, the culture of 'kinetic knowledge'. What they had in common was what the jazz musician Charlie Parker ('Bird') advised his disciples: that in expressing themselves they should – as D.H. Lawrence had advised Bertrand Russell in an earlier time – 'Quit thinking!'

The Ablation of Desire

As the 1950s gave way to the 60s, art less and less referred to anything outside itself, and there was a refusal to find patterns of any kind, either among objects or events. Rather, there was an insistence on the absence of order, the random quality, of experience. This was, many felt, the death of God followed to its logical conclusion.

Such thinking certainly applies to that foundational work of minimalism, Samuel Beckett's *Waiting for Godot*. Beckett is famous for his bleak view of life, his obsession with suffering, his preoccupation, as his friend and publisher John Calder summed him up, with 'the search for meaning in the world ... [he was] unable to come to any conclusion about purpose, unable to believe in any creed or even any personal philosophy other than maintaining a dogged stoicism'. Or, as Beckett himself put it in a discussion with Georges Duthuit, an art critic with whom he played chess in Paris, 'there is nothing to express, nothing with which to express, no power to express, no desire to express, together with the obligation to express'.[1]

Born in 1906 near Dublin, Beckett was the son of well-to-do Protestants. After Trinity College, Dublin, and a spell of teaching, he travelled across Europe, meeting his fellow Irishman James Joyce in Paris. They became friends. Beckett then settled for a while in London, and in 1934 began psychoanalysis with Wilfred Bion at the Tavistock Clinic. Bion was a colleague of the paediatrician and psychoanalyst D.W. Winnicott, who had brought to the fore his concept of the 'transitional object'. Many babies, as they are weaned from the breast and come to face the beginnings of independence, make use of a 'transitional object' such as a soft cuddly toy or a small blanket, from which they cannot be separated. Winnicott thought this phenomenon entirely healthy (provided it didn't last too long).

It is certainly possible, according to some psychoanalytical critics of Beckett's work, that it influenced the playwright's view of God as a sort of transitional object in the lives of many adults, a purely psychological entity but one that wasn't temporary. Though Christian symbolism peppers his works, as it peppered Joyce's, Beckett dismissed the God that is worshipped in churches as 'a very small God' – one who is portrayed like a king, a man, who apparently enjoys being worshipped and taking the credit for the 'accidental good things around us', and who is 'never blamed for the multiple evils of the world'.[2]

Waiting for Godot was written in four months, starting in early October 1948, a time when Hiroshima and Nagasaki were fresh in the mind, when the full horror of the Holocaust was still emerging, as were the details of Stalin's Great Terror. Beckett also had horrors of his own: the play was written during the two years when, fearful that a growth found in his cheek was signalling his end, he squirrelled himself away to write. In that time he produced *Godot* and what is often referred to as the 'trilogy' – *Molloy, Malone Dies* and *The Unnamable*. *Godot* was not produced until 1953. Despite mixed reviews, his friends having to 'corral' people into attending, it turned out to have been worth the wait.

It is a spare, sparse play; its two main characters (there are five in all) occupy a stage that is bare save for a solitary tree. The play is notable for its long periods of silence, its repetitions of dialogue (when dialogue occurs), its lurches between often witty metaphysical speculation and banal cliché, the near-repetition of the action, such as it is, in the two halves of the play, and the nonappearance of the eponymous Godot. Despite all of this, it is wonderfully entertaining.

Godot was cleverly summed up by one critic: 'Nothing happens, twice!' The two tramps are waiting for Godot: we don't know why they are waiting, where they are waiting, how long they have been waiting, or how long they expect to wait. Beckett stated more than once that Godot is not God, but in his apparent remoteness, it must be said, he is very like God; and the two tramps need a saviour to help them out of their dilemma. Of course, if God does not exist, as Beckett held, there was no 'him' or 'it' for Godot to be like in the first place.

In personal terms, Beckett was a mild and courteous man, but his view of our predicament was extreme. He spent several years in the French Resistance during the war (a war in which Ireland was never a combatant), which forced him to spend months in hiding. This gave him, as many have remarked, an intense and dangerous experience of waiting. He concluded that the speculations of Sartre and the other existentialists were pointless. For Beckett, science had produced a cold, empty, dark world in which, as more details emerged, the bigger picture drained away, if only because words were no longer enough to account for what we know, or think we know. In a letter to his fellow playwright Harold Pinter he said, 'If you insist on finding form [for my play] I'll describe it for you. I was in hospital once. There was a man in another ward, dying of throat cancer. In the silences I could hear his screams continually. That's the kind of form my work has.'[3]

Beckett was convinced that man is unimprovable and that evil exists. The first step was to recognize it in oneself; second, even life's victims are often evil themselves – evil is all around. His view was that the original sin lies in being born at all – Beckett at his most extreme. Birth, he maintained, is foisted on us by our parents, and life is the punishment for it. This led him to the view that the only antidote to the continuance of human suffering 'must lie in an awareness of consequence, so those responsible enough to realize what the consequences are likely to be, can develop the discipline to overcome nature's compulsion to procreate'. John Calder tells us that the sight of children saddened Beckett. 'He thought there should be children's lanes on streets' – for prams and nannies and pushchairs – so the rest of us, Beckett in particular, could avoid them.

Women, he said, are more endowed by nature with the desire to procreate than are men, and so he often cast women in highly stylized roles, as temptress, whore, the destroyer of peace, 'forcing her physical demands on man, who becomes torn between his natural lust and his desire for freedom'. It follows from this that companionship and friendship among males are what he highlighted in his most moving works: 'It is the antidote to loneliness, and without the complications of sex.' Beckett also pinpointed the difference between friendship and comradeship. Comradeship is love created by need and experience – with comrades there is a degree of tension 'because the goal is not arrival but the journey'. *Waiting for Godot* contains a realistic version of love as comradeship, a bonding that will surely last so long as the protagonists survive. In the play, Vladimir and Estragon agree and disagree without rancour. This too may have been a lesson learned amid the hardships and dangers of the wartime Resistance.

There are elements, almost, of Buddhism in some of Beckett's views. He was fond of quoting the Italian poet Giacomo Leopardi, who said that 'wisdom consists not in the satisfaction but in the ablation of desire'. For him, as for the Buddha, the pain of living cannot be avoided; it can at best be reduced, partly by the reduction of desire.[4]

His view of happiness and its attainment was also very much his own. Happiness is possible in the course of a life, but, if we examine it closely, only when it is already in the past. 'Present happiness, if one is aware of it, is really a celebration of some event that has just been accomplished: this could be some career triumph or a successful sexual coupling, but as soon as one is aware of being happy the reason for it has ended.'[5]

For Beckett even art was no real help. It was a kind of trap to divert our eyes from the dreadful realities of life and the true horror of our predicament. We must turn back again so as to starkly face the horror, which was for him the only way to be truly alive.[6]

Life is like picking at a wound; we have a strange love–hate relationship with the sore. He thought that modern ideas about God had become increasingly abstract, like paintings, and, 'like paintings, abstract Gods fail to convince anyone other than those who conceive them'.[7] One of the primary purposes of all religions has been to solemnize respect for authority and instil obedience through habit and fear. Part of living, therefore, entailed for him a constant attack on Christianity, and he did this by having his characters pick at the absurdities of belief and ritual, raising the questions the priests never raise, gradually removing the Church's vestments until it was embarrassingly naked.[8] Picking away at the sores of life, and at a Church that didn't focus on these sores, that ignored the malignity all around, was for him a way to live; a suitably small repertoire of actions that reflects our minimal stature and effectiveness. To get through life we need two things: the courage of the Stoics and the 'wisdom to discard' – another ablation – not only possessions but what he called the mythology of success and the sense of our own personal value and our desires, which are the fuel of ambition. Only if we do that can we enjoy the wait.

Doubts over Depth

Artists such as Robert Rauschenberg, Andy Warhol, Roy Lichtenstein, Kenneth Noland and Jasper Johns took Beckett's minimalism further, adopting styles that were deliberately neutral, carefully devoid of affect, their objective being to blur the boundary between illusion and reality, between art and everyday life, between being extremely serious and being bland. Creativity would no longer be the private monopoly of 'creative' people. This went totally against the high ideals of modernism, the minimalist sensibility embracing the elimination of craftsmanship, even of the artist himself, or at least 'a drastic reduction of his role as an interpreter of experience'. Artists such as Donald Judd, Carl Andre, Frank Stella and Robert Morris openly removed from their art all metaphorical allusiveness and meaning. And pop art had much the same intention: one favoured technique was to use facsimiles of industrially produced artifacts *without commentary or attitude* – the central aesthetic was Let things be, let them be themselves. It was, in a way, a form of phenomenology.

Ad Reinhardt was a perfect example. He specialized in monochromatic canvases that were intended to defy interpretation or analysis. By the same token, the minimalists stuck to the surface of things and steadfastly refused to look beneath. 'It is part of the vulgarism of our culture,' said Carl Andre, 'to ask "What does it mean?" A work of art means what it appears to mean and nothing more. Art should make no attempt to refer to anything outside itself, that we can experience more authentically elsewhere ... Urban experience emphasizes the superficial, and denies interiority. Our culture contains too many objects already. We now require a significant blankness.'[9] Together with Andre the minimalists and the pop artists repudiated uniqueness and objected to permanence, adopting what one critic called 'a self-protective silence', refusing the pains of self-revelation.

These artists were very serious about what they saw as the lack of a need for depth, about the fact that 'depth' was for them a false metaphor, that it somehow put off living until later (because 'depth' is itself a metaphysical mystery that requires time to explore). They were keen to show that we are too concerned with thinking and attach too much meaning to the very concept of meaning.

The arch-advocate of this view is Thomas Pynchon, whose 'ambitious but intentionally inconclusive' novels dramatize the sheer difficulty of holding oneself together in a world without meaning or coherent patterns. His books work by exploring what we might call the pathology of the quest for meaning. His characters suspect 'plots' everywhere, but there is never any clear sight of the 'Ultimate Plot that has no name'. And this, as several observers have pointed out, leads to paranoia, 'which serves as a substitute for religion because it provides the illusion that history obeys some inner principle of rationality, one that is hardly comforting but that is preferable to the terrors of anti-paranoia'. The point of Pynchon's books is that they manufacture an illusion of meaning, a plot where everything fits – 'Paranoia is the *discovery* that everything fits.' But since Pynchon's plots lead nowhere, his work becomes a parody of the romantic chase after meaning and the selfhood that goes with it.

In the many shadows of Auschwitz, Hiroshima, the Great Terror, the Berlin Wall and so much else, the minimal sensibility cast doubt not just on the existence of God, but on the very possibility of deep spiritual life, even an artistic life. Indeed, at times it mocked such an aspiration.

The Restrictions of the Ego

One rainy night in 1953 on the Lower East Side of New York City, Rob Reisner, a budding writer and impresario, came across the jazz legend Charlie Parker, all alone in the street. Reisner couldn't believe his luck and immediately engaged 'Bird' in conversation.* It turned out that Parker, then at the height of his fame as one of the most innovative jazz musicians of all time, was pacing the night-time streets, alone, because his wife was in the course of giving birth and he was trying to manage his anxiety.

Within two years of this encounter Parker was dead, at the tragically young age of thirty-five. He had had a legendary capacity for drugs and alcohol, which had led to his arrest, incarceration in a psychiatric hospital and the need to carry a pistol in his pocket, alongside the precious mouthpiece of his saxophone, just in case he should get 'jumped' by one or other of the unstable characters that peopled the drugs underworld.

Reisner, who later became curator-librarian of the Institute of Jazz Studies at Rutgers University in Newark, New Jersey, was interested

---

* 'Bird' was short for 'Yardbird', the nickname given to the saxophonist after the young Parker found a couple of dead chickens on the road on his way to a performance. He had scooped them up and asked the landlady where he was boarding to cook them. No one ever forgot the incident.

in the wider significance of Parker, and of jazz itself. In the definitive biography *Bird: The Legend of Charlie Parker* that he edited in 1962, comprising interviews with eighty-one contemporaries and assessing Parker's cultural importance, Reisner identified 'the hipster' as being 'to the Second World War what the Dadaist was to the First. He is amoral, anarchistic, gentle, and over-civilised to the point of decadence ... He knows the hypocrisy of bureaucracy, the hatred implicit in religions – so what values are left for him? – except to go through life avoiding pain, keep his emotions in check, and after that "be cool", and look for kicks.'[10]

To be 'cool' sounds like a minimalist ideal, and so it was. But Reisner was identifying a different, though no less influential trait: spontaneity, improvisation. The art forms of jazz (bebop, in particular), the works of the Abstract Expressionists and action (or 'gesture') painters, the writings of 'beat' novelists and poets such as Jack Kerouac and Charles Olson, the dance styles of Merce Cunningham and Twyla Tharp, the Zen potters like Mary Caroline Richards – all these employed spontaneity in much the same way as the Dadaists did, as Reisner foresaw. Its use aimed to avoid the constricting and restricting influence of the ego, to unleash what were felt to be the far healthier forces of the unconscious. And this applied to drugs too, which were also felt to liberate inner impulses kept in check by our conscious minds.

The 'spontaneous gesture', says Daniel Belgrad in his study of the culture of spontaneity, was 'a sign of the times'.[11] Science, corporate liberalism, the mass media were between them *reducing* American life (and by implication Western life) in its aims and enjoyments. This was seen as a form of oppression and alienation not anticipated by Marx – amid material abundance here was spiritual poverty. Against this, Belgrad identified various enclaves around the country dedicated to resisting this ideology: Black Mountain College in North Carolina, the 'bohemias' of North Beach, San Francisco, and Greenwich Village in New York. At the San Remo bar in Greenwich Village in the early 1950s, a visitor would soon have run into scores of people engaged in some aspect of the postwar aesthetic of spontaneity ... Paul Goodman, John Cage, Merce Cunningham,

Miles Davis, Jackson Pollock, Allen Ginsberg, Jack Kerouac.

The culture of spontaneity developed an alternative metaphysics that can be summarized as 'intersubjectivity and mind–body holism'. Corporate liberalism embraced objectivity, which was the basis of its advanced technological mastery over nature. Spontaneity countered this with intersubjectivity, 'in which "reality" was understood to emerge through a conversational dynamic. Objectivity understood "rationality" to be defined exclusively by an intellect that separated objective truths from subjective perceptions; thus it posited a dichotomy of mind and body. By contrast, the [American-led] avant-garde defined "rational" as a viewpoint determined by the interaction of body, emotions, and intellect.'[12]

We have been here before, in the works of the Dadaists, when the aim was much the same, to access the subconscious directly, bypassing the forces of the conscious ego in an effort to unlock and liberate the hidden – and theoretically more fundamental – aspects of our nature. Only by liberating the unconscious mind can we live more fully, allow all aspects of our being full expression; only in this way can we experience 'wholeness'. This called into question Thomas Mann's statement that 'In our time the destiny of man presents its meaning in political terms.' But by now there were more traditions to build on. As a cultural movement, spontaneity boasted a formidable intellectual heritage, 'including the works of John Dewey, Alfred North Whitehead and Carl Jung, in addition to existentialism, surrealism, Gestalt psychology and Zen Buddhism'.[13]

A final characteristic of this new aesthetic (new in American terms, certainly) was the notion that the body, as much as the brain or mind, was the 'locus of unconscious knowing', which 'tangibly links internal experience to external reality'. The body is 'a complex of occasions', and art and life proceed by 'plastic dialogue', by the interaction of the body (as much as the mind) in an *encounter*, even a struggle, with the world. This is recognizably Expressionism as much as it is Dada or Surrealism, and it explains the art forms to which the culture of spontaneity gave rise: bebop, scat singing, Abstract Expressionist (or action, or gesture) painting, dance, beat writing and Zen pottery (a term that will be explained shortly).[14]

Improvisation and the Body

Perhaps the most obvious cultural manifestation of this new aesthetic came in bebop, which grew out of the very different genre of 'big band' swing. The big-band swing era (roughly speaking, the mid-1930s to the mid-1940s) was itself a racy legacy of turn-of-the-century New Orleans jazz, as adapted in a cross-over form to the traditional high-culture orchestral concert – highly disciplined, highly syncopated, and playing to both black and white audiences as well as servicemen overseas.

Bebop began at the start of the Second World War during after-hours jam sessions after the swing gigs had finished, in the nightclubs of Harlem – in particular, Monroe's Uptown House and Minton's Playhouse, above 110th Street on the West Side. Although the elements of bebop have been identified as polyrhythm and prosodic tone, it was really the third quality, antiphony, or 'call and response', that determined its development and character.

Call and response, or 'cutting', had been a part of black music for some time, as one player (the saxophonist, say) would let rip with an improvised burst, and was then 'answered' by another musician (on the piano, perhaps). These exchanges had the quality of both conversation – call and response – and competition. They were virtuoso displays of individual skill, in both a technical and an imaginative sense – it was music shared, an encounter. Most of the body could be called into play, in addition to fingering, blowing and drumming.

As the war ended, the small bebop ensembles began to spread out from Harlem, further downtown into Manhattan and out to St Louis, Chicago and Los Angeles. There, the music quickly began to be associated with the new urban black consciousness demanding greater recognition for the African-American contribution to American society. The performers saw themselves less as entertainers and more as musicians and intellectuals – there was an unwritten rule, according to Belgrad, that they would avoid the traditional 'clowning' or 'showboating' image of the 'Negro' entertainer in a predominantly white world. Formally, their music often blurred the line between harmony and dissonance, sometimes building on the innovations of Bartók and Stravinsky earlier in the century and creating 'polytonality'. But that may mislead – Parker advised others to follow their intuitions when playing, to 'quit thinking!'.

Most of the musicians learned their craft by listening to others rather than in more formal ways; and that was important too, for the tone, rhythm and attack that they brought to their performances could not be caught on traditional notation techniques. Improvisation was key. One other way in which bebop jazz differed from swing was the phenomenon of scat singing, in which prosody – the rhythm and tone and timbre of words – takes precedence over the traditional meaning. 'It was nonverbal communication grounded in sensual perceptions and intended to appeal to unconscious emotions rather than to the intellect.'[15]

Bebop was a catalyst. In the jazz clubs of New York City – the Five Spot, the Café Bohemia, Arthur's Tavern and the Village Vanguard – the musical experimenting of Charlie Parker, Thelonious Monk, Charles Mingus, Sonny Rollins and Ornette Coleman was enjoyed by artists such as, among many others, Willem de Kooning, Franz Kline, Jack Tworkov, Grace Hartigan, and the writer Frank O'Hara. The painter Larry Rivers, also a saxophonist, played bebop, and Lee Krasner has described the profound influence of bebop on her husband Jackson Pollock when he was developing his 'gesture-field' style of painting. The beat poets took bebop prosody as the basis of their spontaneous poetics.

Plastic Dialogue: the Revelation in the Act

Painting in postwar America overlapped with bebop in that it explored spontaneity and mind–body holism as a way to artistic fulfilment, though there were many other influences at work as well.

Two of these were Alfred North Whitehead and his 'process philoso-phy', and Carl Jung's idea of the collective unconscious. Whitehead's philosophy, it will be recalled, proposed that the universe is basically a domain of energy in its various forms, and this energy is the common unifying feature. According to Whitehead all objects, whether ani-mate or not, are nodes of energy, surrounded by fields of lesser force but which connect us all. Jung's notion of the collective unconscious also connects us all, and it proved popular.

The defining moment, or at least the defining criticism, so far as postwar painting in America was concerned, was contained in Harold Rosenberg's essay 'The American Action Painters', published in *Art News* in December 1952. Rosenberg was the first to draw attention to what Robert Motherwell called the 'plastic automatism' of Abstract Expressionism.

According to Rosenberg, what distinguished Abstract Expressionism, what set it apart from other art styles, in particular Surrealism and Cubism, was 'its intense dramatization of the *process* of painting, as if to imbue each gesture of the painter with the quality of a different moral decision [italics added]'. And he didn't stop there: 'At a certain moment the canvas began to appear to one American painter after another as an arena in which to act – rather than as a space in which to reproduce . . . [H]e went up to it with material in his hand to do something to that other piece of material in front of him. The image would be the result of this encounter . . . What matters always is the revelation contained in the act.'[16] Appreciation of the new painting, Rosenberg insisted, required a new attention to the artist's gestures, each stroke to be examined for its 'inception, duration, direction', for what that revealed about the 'psychological dynamics' of the painter, in particular his 'concentration and relaxation of the will', his passivity, his 'alert waiting'.

Arguably the best exponent of this approach was Willem de Kooning, in particular in his *Woman* series produced between 1948 and 1955. '[The paintings] depict the human body not as the container of an ideal essence, but as organic matter that confronts the mind of the painter: these are messy bodies, spilling outside projected boundaries, leaking into their surroundings, leeringly imposing their presence . . . Their almost obsessive reworking implies that the artist conceived of the task as impossible or never-ending, a version of the mind's struggle to impose order on existence.'[17] This recalls the struggles of Van Gogh and the German Expressionists, and there is also something existential about the paintings as they confront the sheer physicality of the world and of experience, as they fight the 'tyranny of concepts', as Sartre put it. What, who exactly, *are* de Kooning's women? Rosenberg compared de Kooning's struggle with paint with 'crossing an ocean or fighting a battle', and the artist himself said he was at times desperate and lost, that painting often seemed to him an absurd activity, 'an arbitrary leap toward meaning'.

While de Kooning's paintings, then, are laden with existential elements – not least, the notion that conscious choice is the only source of freedom in a meaningless universe – this should not blind us to the fact that most of the other action painters were more concerned with what came to be called 'field theories' and with the continuum between mind and body that provided 'a common foundation for conscious and unconscious thought'. [18]

Here the best – or the clearest – exponent was Jackson Pollock, who in 1946 created a series of paintings, *Sounds in the Grass*, in which he put the unstretched canvases on the floor and applied – even poured – the paint while walking around, or on them. He felt in that way he could be more a part of the painting, even be *in* it. In these and subsequent 'all-over palimpsest', 'gesture-field' paintings, no single figure emerges from an undifferentiated ground but there is a multitude of figures which cumulatively form the 'ground', made up of entwined gestural strokes. There is a constant shift in attention as one part of the painting is foregrounded by the viewer, then recedes as another takes over, as if challenging him to constantly reorient himself towards the work. As Lee Krasner put it, 'It breaks once and for all the concept that was more or less present in the Cubist-derived paintings, that one sits and observes nature . . . out there. Rather it claims a oneness.'

Such paintings exist on several levels. By their very nature, they represent the painter's struggle with his or her materials. Their visual ambiguity challenges the viewer to conduct his or her own dialogue with the work, and underlying it all is the notion of what came to be called 'radical subjectivity', that there is no ultimate truth to be arrived at, only different perspectives that can, perhaps, be synthesized. The basis of reality is, therefore, *dialogue*. (This is not quite call and response, as in bebop, but close.)

And this was all built on by the concept of *plastic* dialogue. Pollock's paintings are all about the relation between the painter – a holistic mind *and* a body – and his materials, a synecdoche for the reality and resistance of the world and, in its automatism, a release of unconscious forces. This is what plastic dialogue *is*; and, it was felt, no one is or can be external to this process. Pollock's paint-pouring technique emphasized that the body is as important as the mind in determining the image, and that a painting is as much the product of an action as of thought. This links directly with André Malraux and Saint-Exupéry's concept of the 'warmth of acts', that the reality we create is the result of actions that exert some change on the world, on reality, rather than mere thoughts.

In a symposium on 'all-over' painting in the early 1960s, Martin James identified another trend: namely, that the new painting did not lay claim to any *fixed* truth, but that through its intersubjectivity it carried validity and conviction *in the context of its time*. And this was perhaps the most radical notion of all, that the most socially signifi-cant art may be the most ephemeral precisely because it speaks to the moment and the situation for which it is created. It is, in short, art with no afterlife, a new form of minimalism. Art, like life, is an experience, an 'intersubjective' experience, not a monument.[19] Like life, art is an encounter with the *resistance* of the world, and this is what the mean-ing of life *is*: an encounter with the resistance of the world in which we produce change through action rather than, as much as, thought.

Kinetic Knowledge

The boundaries between the plastic and the performing arts were the subject of experiments carried out at Black Mountain College in the early 1950s. Located in North Carolina, the college operated on Deweyan principles, in which art played a key role in education. Al-though it closed in 1957 after only twenty-four years, its roster of staff and alumni was impressive: Buckminster Fuller, Merce Cunningham, John Cage, Willem and Elaine de Kooning, Walter Gropius, Alfred Kazin, Robert Motherwell, Robert de Niro Sr, Kenneth Noland, Robert Rauschenberg and Cy Twombly.

The dance critic Roger Copeland has called Hans Namuth's

portrayal of Jackson Pollock painting 'one of the world's most significant dance films'. It showed, he said, that 'the fundamental impulse behind abstract expressionism was *the desire to transform painting into dancing*'. This may be going a bit far, but there is no doubt that modern dancers and choreographers like Martha Graham used Jungian psychology and its concept of the unconscious store of symbols, as the basis for their work, and that Merce Cunningham and Katherine Litz (also a choreographer), for instance, abandoned narrative dancing for plastic dialogue, investigating the body as an instrument, dance as an experience rather than a story, emphasizing what body parts could do.

The 'kinetics of the body' became central to the art form.[20] Another idea was that of 'body armour', that every person, in seeking survival and fulfilment, organizes an outlook on the world. This outlook eventually becomes 'routinized', then recedes from awareness but remains active in governing the outlook, including the 'physical attitude of the body'.[21] Muscular tensions and blind spots in proprioception 'represented learned inhibitions and self-aggressions, the physical counterparts to rigidities in mental attitude'. Our bodies come to reflect our attitude to life.

Charles Olson, one-time head of Black Mountain College, proposed that kinetic knowledge of the body was superior to knowledge that was merely descriptive; that for a full life, use of the body was as essential as use of the mind; and that such usage was simply beyond the reach of science. According to Olson, the body offers resistance: overcoming this resistance, as achieved by the best modern dance, can take us a good part of the way towards fulfilment. Early religions appreciated this (as did the Nietzsche cults in Ascona), but the main monotheisms have not.

Merce Cunningham, who studied with Martha Graham in the early 1940s, then taught dance at Black Mountain College during the 1950s, left to start on his own because he wanted to present movement 'in itself' and not as 'an allegory of "inner" emotions'.[22] He worked hard to free dance from its dependence on both music and narrative, so as to explore the subjectivity of the human body and its range of expression. In particular, he developed what came to be called 'all-over' dances; as in all-over gesture-painting, there was no centre-stage or hierarchy of position. Cunningham and his long-time partner the composer John Cage called this 'polyattentiveness'. No less than Jackson Pollock, Cunningham was relying on an energy field. As he himself put it, 'The logic of one event coming as responsive to another seems inadequate now. We look and listen to several at once.'

This, then, is also plastic automatism, the kinetic impulse originating in the body and not in the mind. Cunningham's dances stemmed not from an idea about character or story, but from *movement*. The dance proceeds according to the dancers' bodies, their movements, the space and time available. 'It is not,' he said, 'subject to a pre-arranged [intellectual] idea as to how it should go any more than a conversation you might have with a friend.' His dances do not have a chorus with soloists, but individuals with their different voices, all 'intersubjective', all aware at any one time of what the others are doing, and fitting in. This, by common consent, creates a high-energy field of great intensity – so that his dances are like a moving Pollock painting.

Conversations with Clay

The aesthetic of spontaneity and plasticity led artists to choose (and respond to) materials that lent themselves to bodily impulses, most particularly clay. In the 1950s, under the influence of Abstract Expressionism, 'the craft of clay pottery was lifted to the status of a high art'. Plastic and malleable, clay offered excellent possibilities for 'dialogue'. Manipulating clay requires a high degree of bodily movement as well as sensitivity, since the material cannot be 'forced' beyond a certain point. As Peter Voulkos, the most famous of the abstract expressionist potters said, it is a spontaneous art form since there is not much time before the clay dries out and this made clay the ideal material for a 'conversation' between the artist's unconscious and the environment, moreover a conversation mediated through the body.[23]

This was another area where Black Mountain College shone, attracting potters from the British Arts and Crafts movement – Bernard Leach in particular – and several Japanese potters influenced by Zen Buddhism. Mary Caroline Richards, who also learned her skill at the

College, described the experience of pottery: 'Potter and clay press against each other. The firm, tender, sensitive pressure which yields as much as it asserts. It is like a handclasp between two living hands, receiving the greeting at the very moment that they give it. It is this speech between the hand and the clay that makes me think of dialogue. It is a language far more interesting than the spoken vocabulary which tries to describe it, for it is spoken not by the tongue and the lips but by the whole body, the whole person, speaking and listening.'[24] Other potters, such as Toshiko Takaezu, compared plastic dialogue to 'dancing with the clay'.

Other metaphysical aspects of pottery were developed by Peter Voulkos. He rejoiced in making huge pots – some eight feet high – because these involved 'wrestling' with the clay, struggling with the resistance it offered. This all recalls Martin Heidegger's idea that we ourselves are 'thrown' into the world and formed, as we age, by means of the resistances we meet. By this account, pottery was the perfect synecdoche for existence.

Prosody as Meaning

The final aspect of the culture of spontaneity comprises what became known as the 'beat' writers, a phenomenon that encompassed poetry, novels and travel writing. Most people think of beat writing as beginning with the famous reading of 'Howl', Allen Ginsberg's poem of 1955, in San Francisco. But here too we find the background was more interesting, again featuring Black Mountain College, and the jazz clubs of Harlem and Greenwich Village. 'Howl' was modelled on the tenor saxophone playing of Lester Young. As Ginsberg commented, 'The ideal . . . was the legend of Lester Young playing through something like sixty-nine to seventy choruses of "Lady Be Good", you know, mounting and mounting and building and building more and more intelligence into the improvisation as chorus after chorus went on.'

Ginsberg and Jack Kerouac, another leading beat writer, had met at Columbia University in 1944, when the former was eighteen and the latter four years older. Kerouac had already quit college and Ginsberg would later be suspended. It was wartime and Columbia, like many other universities, had embraced the military-industrial complex, an approach that would continue and intensify during the Cold War. Intellectually, as Ginsberg characterized it, life was narrowed and reduced by the 'anxieties and rigidities of war corporatism', in response to which the beats regarded their marginal status not as a failing but as an asset.

When Black Mountain College began to disintegrate in 1956 several of the faculty there, notably the poets, transferred to San Francisco, as did Ginsberg. The last issue of *Black Mountain Review*, in which Kerouac's essay 'Essentials of Spontaneous Prose' was published, was put together in San Francisco. Other San Francisco poets – Kenneth Patchen, William Everson, Philip Lamantia, Jack Spicer – formed a particularly cohesive group, having spent the war years in a work camp for conscientious objectors in Waldport, Oregon.

Ginsberg was the most aware of the beats, in terms of the traditions and figures who would give rise to its approach, quite apart from his own debts to Lester Young and the jazz clubs of New York. He initiated correspondence with Ezra Pound, William Carlos Williams and Charles Olson. Olson's seminal idea, published in an essay in 1950, was 'projective verse', a new kind of poetry, he said, 'rooted in spontaneity'. It was '(projectile (percussive (prospective', the unusual punctuation being part of his innovation. He intended a poem to be a projectile, something thrown by the poet (like the potter throws clay) in a transfer of energy to the reader-listener; it was percussive in being about sound, and prospective in the sense of the prospector or archaeologist unearthing he knew not what when he first set out.

A convinced follower of Jung, Olson believed that the conscious mind was a gatekeeper that stopped many basic ideas from surfacing, or else falsified them; they could only be released through spontaneity, which offered unmediated access. He insisted that this poetic approach should be incorporated into everyday life, that we should lead speeded-up lives, without reflection, and just 'get on with it'. He argued that logic forced a structure on syntax and that it was poetry's duty to escape this. Form was ephemeral. Experimental forms communicated new visions of reality, and the best source of new visions was spontaneous verse 'unfettered' by rules. As he put it: 'Write carelessly so that nothing that is not green will survive.'[25]

He also had the idea of what he called 'proprioceptive immanence', in which the body was the unifying locus of experience, which the art form must make use of. Ginsberg agreed and showed this in the famous first rendering of 'Howl', which he didn't 'read' or 'speak' so much as intone. The occasion was a *performance* in which his whole body took part. Ginsberg also saw his poems as collages with the mind–body communicating spontaneous ideas through an energy field – it was the transfer of energy that counted rather than any specific idea, energy being the fundamental ingredient of a full life. 'The first rule of the writer was, as in projective verse, to write only what created an empathic flow of energy in the reader.'[26] Excitement, for the beats, equalled authenticity. It was the meaning of both art and life.

Aside from 'Howl', the most famous of the beat writings is *On the Road*, Jack Kerouac's novel. It began to take shape in April 1951 when, high on Benzedrine, he inserted a roll of paper into his typewriter, and over three weeks produced a 120-foot scroll of single-spaced typescript which became the raw material for his novel. He later explained his technique: the key was to avoid searching for words or imposing structure, but to let them emerge as one struggled 'to keep in time with one's thoughts . . . Not selectivity of expression but following free deviation (association) of mind into limitless blow-on-subject seas of thought, swimming in seas of English with no discipline other than rhythms of rhetorical exhalation.' And he too compared the process to an improvised jazz solo.[27] Kerouac also warned of the perils of 'afterthought', in which one might try to improve the original images. In so doing, '[y]ou think what you're *supposed* to be thinking [italics added],' said Kerouac, and the point of beat writing – one point, anyway – was to circumvent that.

Performance was an important element of beat poetry. In a sense, performance is an element in all poetry, but it was especially true of the beats with their concept of energy exchange. Readings circumvented the time lag involved in printing and publishing, and contributed to the idea that culture was *happening* – as Whitehead had said, the basic unit of the energy-field universe was the *event*. Readings also, of course, maximized spontaneity. Poems could be amended, or even created 'on the hoof'. But the actual reading, the sounds, the body movements of the poet, the energy contained in those movements and sounds, were part of the *exchange*, part of what made it more like jazz.

Finally, in a reading, the public were *there*, face to face with the poet, in the room, responding. This was intersubjectivity at its rawest. Performance both magnifies the indeterminacy of a poem and, paradoxically, at the same time adds meaning.

There was no shortage of critics of the culture of spontaneity, from Norman Mailer to Norman Podhoretz to Diana Trilling. People criticized the writers and painters for being educated beyond their intellectual level, for being charlatans, for being affected, for being pretentious. Nonetheless, by 1959 there were estimated to be more than three thousand Americans in the 'bohemian enclaves' of Venice West, North Beach and Greenwich Village, all pursuing their own versions of the spontaneous lifestyle. Francis Rigney, a social psychologist who studied the North Beach community, concluded they were not as different from mainstream communities as the mainstream thought. But he also found that it was hard, for many, to maintain such a lifestyle – it was often possible only in fits and starts. This is one reason why, as the 1950s gave way to the 1960s, it fragmented and disintegrated.

Negative Exuberance: the Intensity of the Inverted Life

Philip Roth's novels are in almost every way as bleak as Samuel Beckett's novels and plays. They pick at the sores of life, especially as those sores concern American Jews living in the shadow of the Holocaust. First and foremost, however, Roth's work is about intensity, intensity as the only form of meaning in an otherwise meaningless world.

Roth, Jewish himself, argues that Jews in America have the best and the worst of worlds. In *The Ghost Writer* he castigates his fellow Jews who have embraced the Holocaust as an aspect of their identity, when in reality many of them have led comfortable lives in leafy suburbs well away from the horrors of that episode. As may be imagined, it was not a popular message. Closer to our theme, in such books as *Goodbye Columbus* and *The Plot Against America* he shows how assimilation of the Jews in those same leafy suburbs has entailed the abandonment of large parts of their religious identity. Assimilated Jews don't give up a belief in their God entirely, perhaps, but they give up much of the ritual life entailed in being the observant faithful – and that poses risks.

In identifying American Jews as what the sociologists call 'marginal' figures in a modern democratic society, Roth spotlights assimilation not as a form of spiritual death, exactly, but as a diminution of identity. Thus, in most of his books the only pleasure in life lies in the realm of sin, and in a secular democracy the only way to be sinful is to go against the majority in the matter of agreed manners, and give offence – what the critic Harold Bloom called 'negative exuberance'. Like Beckett, Roth thinks one should continually approach life in attack mode.

In *Sabbath's Theater*, for example, the main character Morris 'Mickey' Sabbath is, as one critic put it, 'a walking insult'.[28] 'Despite all my troubles,' he says, 'I continue to know what matters in life . . . All I know how to do is antagonize.' And he lives for sex. 'You must devote yourself to fucking the way a monk devotes himself to God. Most men have to fit fucking in around the edge of what they define as more pressing concerns . . . But Sabbath had simplified his life and fit the other concerns in around fucking.' Sabbath delights in *inverting* life. Sex, for him, is innocent of higher meaning. This is so because 'Anyone with any brain understands that he is destined to lead a stupid life *because there is no other kind* . . . A world without adultery is unthinkable.'

Sabbath is minimalist enough not to expect any great lucidity from his behaviour, nor a return to 'the warm nervous conspiracy of family life'. He is defined by what he has been but no longer is: an ex-son, ex-husband, ex-puppet artist, and the only way he knows how to be alive is 'to affront and affront and affront till there is no one on earth unaffronted'. He knows himself 'well enough for judgment but not well enough for correction'.[29] He is limned by his defeats; his blasphemy, his promiscuity, his effrontery are all designed to create an anti-theology theology, with the aim of spoiling life, to overturn it, to create a 'counter-life' (the title of one of his books), but in an orgy of intensity (all Roth's books are 'noisy', as one critic said, and all the sex is raucous). For Nathan Zuckerman too, Roth's other creation, and 'the American authority on Jewish demons', it is not easy to discern 'between the heroic and the perverse'.[30]

For Roth, for Roth's characters like Mickey Sabbath and Nathan Zuckerman, all coherence in life is imaginary, and to achieve coherence we must violate the division of, say, life and art in ways that will offend the self-appointed arbiters of both.[31] Like Beckett, Roth worried that art was a trap, a too neat rejection of the messiness of life – there are always competing claims on our identity, and they remain so.

In *The Anatomy Lesson* Nathan Zuckerman gives himself over to unrestrained sensual pleasure, to escape the clutches of self-justification so as to lead a wholly indefensible, unjustified life – 'and to learn to like it'.[32] For Zuckerman, Sabbath and Roth himself life is full of deadly toxins, and in a novel like *American Pastoral* (1997) and *The Dying Animal* (2001) as well as those already mentioned, there is a 'clamorous bleakness'. Here too the only way to avoid spiritual meltdown is rebellion, noise, blasphemy. In *I Married a Communist*, Roth cannot refrain from drawing attention to 'a spiritual woman's decolletage'; in another novel 'infidelity comes with the marriage vows'; in another, 'self-immolation is undertaken with gusto'. Life must press on with 'a tincture of rancor', 'with the illicit pleasures of exposure and revenge'.[33] Overscale eroticism is Roth's trademark, and his characters' way out.

Whereas Beckett gives us silence, Roth gives us noise; whereas Beckett gives us the last hope of comradeship, Roth gives us the self-loathing promiscuity of the solitary offender; whereas Beckett gives us waiting, Roth gives us hyperactivity. In a world without God, we have to make the most of our doubt, and we can best do that by committing blasphemy, sleeping with our friends' wives, giving offence. Because nobody knows anything, we can never know when we are right; we can never know, therefore, what is good. Only by being in the wrong can we know anything of ourselves, and that is the most intense way to be.

And this too he shares with Beckett: he enjoys the same level of popularity and significance, but most people could no more live up (or down) to Roth's philosophy than they could to Beckett's. Its very extremeness, though, gives us pause, makes us reflect. Does knowing what is wrong help? The fact that his bleak message is laced with humour also links him to Beckett and makes what he has to say somewhat more palatable. Because of this, and despite all, we give him a hearing. As Harold Bloom put it, they both offer us 'ordeal by laughter'.

22

A Visionary Commonwealth
and the Size of Life

In September 1989 Boris Yeltsin, at that stage a member of the Russian parliament but not yet the country's President, made a much publicized visit to the United States. The visit was noteworthy for at least two reasons. One was Yeltsin's drinking – he was drunk at a number of important engagements, not least on a visit to the White House. And second, for his astonishment at the abundance of America – especially in food and housing – which he said had been hidden from him and his fellow Russians by Soviet propaganda. It was partly as a result of what he saw in America that he returned home a rebel against the Soviet system and successfully challenged Mikhail Gorbachev for the presidency just over a year later.

But there was a third noteworthy aspect of Yeltsin's visit, which has normally attracted little comment. This was the fact that the visit was sponsored by the Esalen Institute of Big Sur in California. Esalen had been chosen in preference to fifteen other possible organizations, including the Rockefeller and Ford Foundations and the Council on Foreign Relations. The prior negotiations had been carried out on behalf of Esalen by Jim Garrison, the administrative director of the institute's Soviet–American Exchange Program (Garrison's book *The Darkness of God: Theology after Hiroshima* is discussed on p. 388).

The prestige of Esalen, as revealed in this set of events, was all the more remarkable for the fact that, strictly speaking, its golden age was well over by then. In his book *Esalen: America and the Religion of No*

Religion (2007–8) Jeffrey J. Kripal says that the late 1960s and the early 70s were the golden age of Esalen. They were also the golden age of the counterculture.

At its height the counterculture was probably the most sustained attempt there has ever been to fashion a way of living not just without traditional Western ideas of God, but outside science, capitalism and conventional morality. And Esalen was arguably the quintessence of the counterculture, the fullest and most perfect realization of its values and aspirations. Named after a Native American tribe, it exists to this day, on its original site.

'We will never know how many people belonged to the counterculture,' says Theodore Roszak, the man who coined the phrase and wrote its definitive history. 'It may be wrong to speak of it having a membership at all. Rather, it was a vision that, to one degree or another, drew the attention and fascination of passing many. More important than the size of the dissent was its depth. Never before had protest raised issues that went so philosophically deep, delving into the very meaning of reality, sanity, and human purpose.'[1]

Three elements comprised the backbone of the countercultural approach. These were, first, new techniques of therapy, what Roszak called 'techniques of inner manipulation', often organized via therapeutic communities; second, drugs, as the source of alternative forms of consciousness; and third, music, rock and roll. The only reason all this amounted to a *counterculture*, he said, was because 'the culture it opposed – that of reductionist science, ecocidal industrialism, and corporate regimentation – was too small a vision of life to lift the spirit'.[2]

The therapeutic approach was probably the most basic of the three. It was founded on the idea that 'until the advent of psychoanalysis, the vocabulary of our society was woefully impoverished'. In the 1960s, President Lyndon Johnson had installed – or hoped he had – what he called the Great Society. Basing itself on the civil rights movement but also incorporating several other social issues (feminism, poverty, the environment), it was essentially sociopolitical and designed to help the participants in its programmes lead better lives. Many of those who advocated the counterculture, however, saw that building the good

society 'is not primarily a social, but a psychological task'. The therapeutic approach 'strikes beyond ideology to the level of consciousness,
seeking to transform our deepest sense of the self, the other, the
environment'.[3]

Political and social consciousness, as the Harvard psychologist
Timothy Leary put it, gave way to *consciousness* consciousness', the
overall aim being to discover new types of community, new family
patterns, new sexual mores, new kinds of livelihood, new aesthetic
forms, new personal identities that would bring new meanings to
lives.[4] It was essentially an anti-rational, anti-science stance, promoting a meaningful life of feeling.

There was at that time, says Roszak, a sense in the air, especially
among the young, that Marxism and liberalism had largely ceased to
provide explanations of the world; that they were as much a part of
the problem as of the solution. Also, survey figures showing that some
38 per cent of Americans were unchurched suggested that the mainline Churches had lost touch with the experiential basis of spirituality.[5]
Popular here was the German philosopher Herbert Marcuse's notion
of 'surplus repression'. *Some* repression, basic repression, is normal, not
unhealthy; it is bound to occur in any society, Marcuse said, simply as
a consequence of people living together. Surplus repression, however,
is that 'which the invidious logic of domination demands'. Surplus repression 'is what "a particular group or individual" imposes on others
"in order to maintain and enhance itself in a privileged position"'.
From this it followed, for Marcuse as for Marx, that 'the shortening
of the working day' was the fundamental premise out of which everything else flowed. We must set aside the 'rationality of domination' in
favour of 'libidinal rationality, which takes the possibility of freedom
and joy as axiomatic'.[6]

Marcuse also had an idea of transcendence, though by this he
meant historical transcendence, not in any way religious, in that he
thought domination, exploitation and repression transcended historical periods, so that we take the status quo for granted. And it was his
aim to overcome this state of affairs by showing the basically political nature of existence, which could only be overcome by the Great
Refusal, the rejection of social domination 'in the name of joy and

freedom' – the 'Enormous Yes' – using the 'transcendental wisdom' of poetry.[7]

A second aspect to the psychological changes sought by the counterculture was, as Roszak put it, 'the journey to the East'. This leads, he says, to such figures as Alan Watts, originally a British philosopher and theologian, who had studied at the School of Asian Studies in San Francisco after leaving his position as an Anglican counsellor at Northwestern University in Evanston, Illinois. Watts wrote books on Zen and Taoism, in an attempt to translate their insights into the language of Western science and technology, perhaps the best-known being *The Way of Zen*, *The Joyous Cosmology* and *Psychotherapy East and West*. In the latter Watts proposed that Buddhism could be thought of as a form of psychotherapy and not just as a religion. Neither Hinduism nor Buddhism, he says, can be classified as religions, philosophies, sciences or mythologies, or even as amalgamations of all four, 'because departmentalization is foreign to them, even in so basic a form as the separation of the spiritual and the material'.[8]

What the counterculture offers us, then, 'is a remarkable defection from the long-standing tradition of sceptical, secular intellectuality, which has served as the prime vehicle for three hundred years of scientific and technical work in the West. Almost overnight (and astonishingly, with no great debate on the point) a significant portion of the younger generation has opted out of that tradition.'[9] Roszak acknowledged that there were 'manifestations' around the edges of the counterculture that were 'worrisomely unhealthy' – pornographic grotesquery, blood-curdling sadomasochism, mock-Dionysian frenzy – but held that the exploration of 'non-intellective powers' was its greatest achievement.[10]

Roszak asks if we can blame the young for getting involved in an 'occult Jungian stew', when the life of Reason has too obviously failed to bring us the agenda of civilized improvements 'that Voltaire and Condorcet once foresaw' and shown itself to be merely a 'Higher Superstition'. He says it is impossible any longer to ignore the fact that 'our conception of intellect has been narrowed disastrously by the prevailing assumption' that the life of the spirit is '(1) a lunatic fringe best left to artists and marginal visionaries; (2) an historical bone yard for antiquarian scholarship; (3) a highly specialized adjunct of professional anthropology; (4) an antiquated vocabulary still used by the clergy, but intelligently soft-pedalled by its more enlightened members'. The end result, as Michael Novak has put it, is a middle-class secular humanism which 'eschews the "mystic flights" of metaphysicians, theologians and dreamers; it is cautious and remote in dealing with heightened and passionate experiences that are the stuff of great literature and philosophy, limiting itself to this world and its concerns, concerns which fortunately turn out to be largely subject to precise formulations, and hence have a limited but comforting certainty'.

And just look at the new rituals of the young, he says. 'They gather in gay costume on a high hill in the public park to salute the midsummer sun in its rising and setting. They dance, they sing, they make love as each feels moved, without order or plan ... All have equal access to the event; no one is misled or manipulated. Neither kingdom, nor power, nor glory is desperately at stake.'[11]

The Religion of No Religion

This approach, these values, were reflected above all at Esalen. Jeffrey Kripal subtitled his book *America and the Religion of No Religion* because it was designed, he said, as a utopian experiment 'creatively suspended between the revelations of the religions and the democratic, pluralistic, and scientific revolutions of modernity'. It was a place where the therapeutic encounter was the core principle, 'a spiritual space where almost any religious form can flourish, provided – and this is crucial – that it does not attempt to impose itself on the entire community or claim to speak for everyone. As an early Esalen motto put it, "No one captures the flag."' At Esalen they hold their dogmas lightly, they describe themselves as 'spiritual but not religious... Mysticism here is not some transcendent abstraction without political or moral content. Another way of putting the Esalen ethic is that ... the humanist is after the openness of *wonder*, whereas the scientist is after the closure of *explanation*.'[12]

Esalen came out of the tradition of Aldous Huxley, who had

explored ideas of utopia and dystopia, and the 'precognitive' writings of Henry Miller who had lived in Big Sur. The early figures at Esalen were Michael Murphy and Frederic Spiegelberg, the latter an exile from Germany where he had been friendly with Paul Tillich and Carl Jung. Also influenced by Rilke, it was Spiegelberg who conceived the phrase, and wrote a book called, *The Religion of No Religion*. For him, historical religions have made two major mistakes. They have consistently misread their own symbolic statements as literal truths, and they have traditionally devalued one side of reality (the natural world) for the sake of the other (the transcendent divine).

Spiegelberg thought that the paradoxes at the heart of these two mistakes were what, for most people, made traditional religions unthinkable; and at the same time he adopted an essentially Heideggerian approach, a sense of the astonishment of being. This, he found, could be enhanced by Zen Buddhism and Indian yoga, which recognizes, particularly in its Tantric form, that 'the final temple of the divine is, again, the human body'.[13] Moreover, he saw art and psychoanalysis as two Western ways of thinking by which the 'higher gnosis' could be achieved.

These ideas of Spiegelberg's set the scene at Esalen, but were built on by many others – and this variety was key to the institute's early success. Innovations included the Buddhism taught by Dick Price with its idea of *anatman*, no-self, 'no special status for anything', in which the 'unfolding' of life was regarded as the only divine force; physical movement and nonverbal experience, body awareness and sensory reawakening; J.B. Rhine's notions of parapsychology and the nature of man; Alan Watts's ideas as expounded in *Joyous Cosmology*; Timothy Leary and 'psychedelic Orientalism'; and the 'third force psychology' of Abraham Maslow with its 'self-actualizing' 'peak experiences'. Sex was never far away. In fact, says Kripal: 'Central to Esalen's enlightenment of the body is a kind of mystical psychoanalysis that is as comfortable with "sex" as it is with "peak experience" . . . that sees the peak spiritual experience as orgasmic and the orgasm as potentially spiritual.'[14]

Abraham Maslow, the central figure in 'third force' psychology, had been active in the field for some time before he went to Esalen:

he had helped Alfred Kinsey with his sex research in New York while teaching at Brooklyn College. He invoked the orgasm as an appropriate metaphor or analogy for his concept of a 'peak experience', which for him was 'an extraordinary state of personal history' that 'fundamentally alters the individual's worldview through an overwhelming explosion of meaning, creativity, love and Being'.[15]

Maslow described peak experiences as very like orgasms: 'the peak experience is temporary, essentially delightful, potentially creative, and imbued with profound metaphysical possibilities'. One cannot live on such peaks but, he insisted, a life without them is unhealthy, nihilistic and potentially violent. The peak experience sat at the summit of a pyramid built on a hierarchy of psychological and physiological needs. At the base of the pyramid was food, shelter, sleep; above that came sexuality, safety and security; above that, love, belonging, self-esteem; and finally, at the peak itself, self-actualization. This last state was regarded as spiritual but in no way religious. One of the achievements of a peak experience, Maslow thought, was that people became more democratic, more generous, more open, less closed and selfish, achieving what he called a 'transpersonal' or 'transhuman' realm of consciousness. He had the idea of a 'non-institutionalized personal religion' that 'would obliterate the distinction between the sacred and the profane' – rather like the meditation exercises of Zen monks, whom he compared to humanistic psychologists. Maslow's idols in this were William James and Walt Whitman.

Encounter groups and 'T-groups' were part of life at Esalen, drawing on the work of Carl Rogers (discussed in chapter 19). The aim was ultimate honesty: 'Under the Encounter Contract I say how I feel about you. My obligation to be polite, kind or considerate is, for the time being, set aside.' And in another, more startling, innovation people were invited to expose their genitals and discuss the fears and desires aroused by such exposure in a world where those organs were so central. These encounters, obviously enough, could be very intense, creating 'transcendent spaces', new experiences in which people forgot who and where they were, and all feelings of time.[16]

Arica Awareness Training, Rolfing, Orgone Therapy, Full-body Contemplative Massage, biofeedback, hypnosis, the Spiritual

Emergency Network, the Spiritual Tyranny Conference, the Tao of Physics, Sufism, the Spiritual Art and Intuitive Business of Managing Emptiness – all these therapies, experiences and events, and more, have characterized Esalen from the start. Some observers have dismissed it as a 'spiritual supermarket'. It still exists, as a nonprofit organization providing a 'decent but quite humble' livelihood for 150 individuals who between them manage four hundred seminars a year. Their aim is to continue to imagine a new 'spiritual' America, to embrace a 'democratic mysticism, a religion of no religion', a spiritual utopia that still embodies the values and aspirations of the counterculture.

Better Living through Chemistry

The second core element of the counterculture was drugs. The fascination with hallucinogenics underlies much of post-Second World War counterculture. For many people through the ages, plants known as 'entheogens' (generators of the divine or spirit within) have offered an 'alternative spirituality'.[17]

This aspect of the counterculture has been examined by Martin Torgoff in *Can't Find My Way Home: America in the Great Stoned Age, 1945–2000*. Stating that roughly one in four Americans has used illegal drugs – so it is hardly a fringe activity – Torgoff made the point that getting high wasn't just about fun – 'it was about rebellion and bohemia and utopia and mysticism . . . [about] refusing to accept or even acknowledge limits of any kind'.[18]

Dope was a whole way of life: 'it was like living in a walled city with your own kind, where you could make up your own language and create your own set of rules, it was a badge which made people different from the rest of the world'. In one sense, jazz was about the profound isolation and pathos of the life around heroin – the cravings, the desolate loneliness of the search, the blissful relief of the shot. In theory at least, a new kind of existence was available, an unselfconscious 'radiant burning', living for kicks, tasting the pure ecstasy of life. The fact that it didn't last didn't matter: 'all the philosophies tell us that nothing does, but while it did last everything was experienced as holy'. It was 'the sacralization of the mundane'.[19]

Many at the time saw parallels with what they were doing and the ancient Indian shamans' experience of 'peyote vision'. Here too drugs brought salvation. In the Native American tradition known as the 'vision quest' people would be required to survive in the wilderness, procuring a guardian spirit, often by means of the New World 'narcotic complex' comprising the Americas' eighty to a hundred mind-altering plants (about which there is copious documentation), compared with the Old World's half-dozen. These and other Native American traditions were introduced to mainstream America by Carlos Castaneda, who in 1968 published *The Teachings of Don Juan: A Yaqui Way of Knowledge*. Originally a university-press book, this purported to be based on Castaneda's field notes taken during his four years as a participant-observer researching into Yaqui beliefs and practices. But his book became a phenomenal best-seller and led to six titles in total, with *A Separate Reality*, 1971, becoming most well-known, the books selling in all some eight million copies. What Americans learned from Castaneda's books was that Native American culture was intimately bound up with hallucinogenic drugs, used to gain 'insight into a world not merely other than our own, but an entirely different order of reality'.[20]

It was this that interested Timothy Leary, who in 1960 first ingested *Psilocybe mexicana*, the mysterious magical mushroom of Mexico, in a house he had rented in Cuernavaca. Torgoff tells us that 'During the experience his mind had completely deliquesced, opening to the most enthralling visions: "Nile palaces, Hindu temples, Babylonian boudoirs, Bedouin pleasure tents."' He slipped further and further back in time, 'so far back that he became the first living being'. Leary came to the view that mushrooms could 'revolutionize' psychology and carried with them the possibility of 'instantaneous self-insight'.

Leary felt that psychology had become too involved with the study of behaviour and had neglected the phenomenon of consciousness. In the first experiment, to test 'the potential of psilocybin for social re-engineering', it was used in Concord State Prison in New Hampshire, where the changes brought about in the inmates were said to be dramatic: '[F]riction and tension were lowered, and there was talk in the sessions about "love" and "God" and "sharing".' Leary thought he had discovered a method of 'imprinting' new behaviour patterns on adults: psychedelic imprinting, he claimed, would rank with DNA deciphering as 'one of the most significant discoveries of the century'.

Over about four years, Leary and his assistants managed, as they put it, to 'arrange transcendental experiences' for more than one thousand persons, including Aldous Huxley, Allen Ginsberg and Alan Watts. Their studies showed that 'when the setting was supportive but not explicitly spiritual, between 40 and 75 per cent of their subjects . . . reported life-changing religious experiences. Yet when the set and setting emphasized spiritual themes, up to 90 per cent reported having mystical or illuminating experiences.'[21]

When the news leaked out that scientists at President Kennedy's old university were using mind-altering drugs in a social-engineering project, there was an almighty fuss. But Leary himself was taking more interest in spiritual, religious and mystical matters, as was a Harvard doctoral candidate, Walter Pahnke, who sought to determine empirically whether the so-called transcendental component of psychedelic experience was truly the equal of those reported by saints and mystics. With the support of a university professor he gathered a score of divinity students from a seminary and divided them into two groups. The experiment took place on Good Friday, 1962, after a service in the chapel. Some of the students were given psilocybin, others a placebo of nicotinic acid, which should have produced only hot and cold flushes.

After thirty minutes, 'it was very apparent who had taken the psychedelic and who had not. The ten who had ingested the nicotinic acid were sitting there facing the altar; the others were lying on the floors and pews, wandering round in rapt wonderment, murmuring prayers as one of them played "weird, exciting, chords" on the church's pipe organ. Another . . . clambered across the pews and stood facing the crucifix, transfixed, arms outstretched as if somehow trying to identify physically with Christ and his suffering on the cross.'[22] To Leary and his aides, the experiment proved that 'spiritual ecstasy, religious revelation, and union with God were now directly accessible'.

When *Time* got hold of the story, however, Harvard Divinity

School took a very different view: follow-up studies were cancelled, while a medical administrator from the FDA described the psychological benefits of the study as 'pure bunk'.

Leary, however, stuck to his guns and began to think of different ways to pursue his interests. Other observers were becoming interested in LSD (lysergic acid diethylamide), which now acquired some revealingly colourful names, Pearly Gates, Heavenly Blue. What Leary had in mind was what he called 'a new frontier of expanded consciousness', and in a speech to the Harvard Humanists (a group dedicated to ethical development based on reason, not religious dogma) he announced the formation of the International Foundation for Internal Freedom (IFIF) – freedom in particular, he said, from 'the learned, cultural mind'. He even foresaw a change in the US constitution to guarantee an individual's right to seek an expanded consciousness. But while he was in Mexico on IFIF business, Harvard officials found that he had given drugs to an undergraduate, and used this as a pretext to get rid of him.

It was not the personal disaster it might have been, had it happened earlier in his career, because he was becoming less and less interested in Harvard. After a period of exile, therefore, he moved to the Hudson Valley and continued what was to become his next project. 'Everything we did in the 1960s was designed to fission, to weaken faith and conformity to the 1950s social order. Our precise surgical target was the Judeo-Christian power monolith, which had imposed a guilty, inhibited, grim, anti-body, anti-life repression on Western civilization. Our assignment was to topple this prudish, judgmental civilization.' And, as he famously wrote, 'The paradox must be stated as follows: it becomes necessary for us to go out of our minds in order to use our heads . . . The game is about to change, ladies and gentlemen . . . Drugs are the religion of the twenty-first century . . . Turn on. Tune in. Drop out.'

When R.E. Masters and Jean Houston wrote their much quoted book, *The Varieties of Psychedelic Experience*, they took it for granted that 'psychedelic (mind manifesting) drugs afforded the best access yet to the contents and processes of the human mind'. They argued that there are four distinct levels of psychedelic experience, each successively 'deeper' than its predecessor. The first level is that of enhanced sensory awareness; the second is reflective-analytic; the third, attained by fewer subjects, they called the symbolic level, at which the subject 'experiences primal, universal, and recurring themes of human experience' (in a Jungian archetypal sense); the fourth, and deepest, is the integral level. 'The integral level is mystical in nature. It affords individuals a vivid sensation of being "one" with the deeper level of reality.' Only 11 per cent of subjects reached this level, but those that did reported a feeling of 'oneness with God'. Masters and Houston note, however, that their subjects' descriptions of God did not match conventional religious language. Rather than describing God in biblical terms, they said, they used words more reminiscent of Paul Tillich's definition of God as 'the Ground of being' (see above, p.393).[23]

For a time, 'dropping out' became an act of religious affirmation, Robert Fuller says in his history of drug use in American religious life. Several short-lived churches emerged that used drugs as the focus of their otherwise indeterminate theologies, such as the Shiva Fellowship Church, the Psychedelic Venus Church, the Fellowship of the Clear Light and the American Council of Internal Divinity. One follow-up study found that only about half a dozen of these lasted into the 1990s, with a minuscule attendance.

Leary, meanwhile, made a case for not needing to be attached to any kind of formal religion at all. A real religious experience, he maintained, is 'the ecstatic, incontrovertibly certain, subjective discovery of answers to four basic spiritual questions: What is the ultimate power of the universe? What is life – why and where did it start? Whence did humans come and where are we going? What am I – what is my place in the grander plan?'

And for a time at least, it appeared that a 'fourth great awakening', as the historian William McLoughlin termed it, had occurred in American religious life. The four major themes of this spiritual reorientation were: (1) a shift from mainline to nonconformist churches; (2) a rediscovery of natural rather than revealed religion; (3) a new appreciation of Eastern religious thought; and (4) a new Romanticism that accords spiritual importance to certain non-rational modes of thought and perception. 'In general, this represented a shift from seeking God in the church to seeking God in the depths of nature (including the depths of our own psychological nature) ... And although this new mode of awareness gave rise to insights that were ineffable upon return to the normal waking state, it nonetheless left the lasting impression that the world is surrounded by a higher order of being.'[24]

'Rock and Drugs Work Wonders'

Although at times it might have seemed that LSD was the only game in town, that was far from being so. In the mid-sixties, says Torgoff, 'there seemed to be more potential pot smokers on American campuses than ever before. They were easy to identify – rebels, diehard nonconformists, egghead intellectuals, abstract painters, blue-jeaned folk musicians, jazz disciples, leotarded modern dancers, vegetarians. "You wore sandals," said one, "you went to poetry readings . . . We got stoned on the peace march. You were *chosen*, man!"'

But the defining moment, the transitional moment in American history, was the emergence of the civil rights movement. 'By and large, white people felt completely trumped by black people at the time, who went out and set this incredibly courageous moral example by putting their lives on the line. And I think that those of us who were not actively involved with freedom marches in the South were pressed to come up with an identity and self-image of equal integrity or at the very least didn't want to participate in a culture which produced that kind of racism . . . [T]here was this growing desire to create this other realm, imagine yourself into it and act it out – and one of the tools that would soon materialize to prize yourself out of that box was psychedelics.'[25]

It was about this time that Ken Kesey, author of *One Flew Over the Cuckoo's Nest* (in which the patients really do take over the asylum, if only for a day), got together with Hunter S. Thompson and Hells Angels, 'the rottenest motor cycle gang in the history of Christendom', to conceive the first psychedelic bus; the time when Tom Wolfe wrote his perceptive *Electric Kool-Aid Acid Test* (without ever attending a session of acid-taking, or taking it himself), and when Augustus Owsley Stanley III (Owsley to most, Bear to a few) manufactured four kinds of LSD.

No one knows how much LSD Owsley produced before the Bureau of Narcotics and Dangerous Drugs arrested him in 1969, but he was famous for 'never raising the price of a hit above two dollars because he believed that acid for the masses would be the engine that would save the world'.[26] (Leary called him 'God's secret agent'.) Partly because LSD could be obtained so cheaply, a number of 'acid tests', or rock-and-drug events, took place, with bands such as the Grateful Dead and performers like B.B. King taking part. There, 'religious' experiences and epiphanies continued to occur. Tom Wolfe covered much of this in *The Electric Kool-Aid Acid Test*. At that point, the drug was still legal.

In Los Angeles, Paul Rothchild, a record producer, was supervising Jim Morrison and the Doors in one of the first, if not *the* first, album to be produced either on or about LSD. Rothchild thought that one particular session was 'one of the most important moments in recorded rock and roll'. Morrison had 'imbibed' the influences of Blake, Rimbaud, Poe, Joyce, Brecht, Weil, Artaud and Nietzsche, plus notions of shamanism and Dionysus, '[o]nly here it was being filtered through a new LSD-enhanced state of reality – or non-reality, however you looked at it'.

Rothchild himself was no stranger to drugs. He had smoked marijuana since he was seventeen, then graduated to peyote. He considered that the drug experience had taught him new ways of 'talking, thinking, being', and 'the landscape of drugs' had shaped his creativity as a record producer. Marijuana, he believed, had allowed him to 'crawl deeply' inside the music of Bach, for example, and understand the composer's love of Christ – 'an experience I might never have allowed myself as a Jew unless I had gotten high and opened my synapses enough to truly experience the gestalt of the music'. Then came peyote and, he said, all his thoughts turned to 'the oneness of mankind . . . From that moment on I believed it was possible to find your way to God through psychedelics! . . . At that time getting high was never just about getting high. It was about our willingness to accept change and visualize another world – what later became known as "grokking" ... To deepen understanding.' Rothchild had cut his teeth in the music world at the Kettle of Fish Bar and the Gaslight Café in Greenwich Village, smoking pot. When acid began to 'trickle in', he says, he witnessed an immediate impact on music.

For him, it happened one night when he visited the Woodstock home of Albert Grossman when Bob Dylan was there after a tour of New England colleges. They opened the refrigerator to find sugar cubes with little gold dots on them, wrapped in aluminium foil. They took the acid and from that moment, Rothchild remembers, Dylan's music changed '[f]rom simple but powerful songs of social observation and protest and moral conscience to those elusive compositions of no single message or ultimate meaning ... The experience of drugs seemed to splinter Dylan's mind into brilliant kaleidoscopic flashes of poetry; the result was strange, mystical, beautiful compositions like "Mr Tambourine Man".'

In the early weeks of 1967, Rothchild adds, something seemed to give way, and the Beatles personified it. *Sgt Pepper's Lonely Hearts Club Band*, released in May, was everywhere, and more than anything else it validated the new culture: it was regarded as 'a masterpiece' of the psychedelic age, thereby confirming that the Beatles had 'incorporated the sensibility of consciousness-altering substances into every aspect of its creation'. At the Monterey pop festival John Philips of the Mamas and the Papas would remark, 'Now there was an album that proved to the masses what musicians had believed for years: that music and drugs work wonders together.'

'Our Godless Civilization Approaching Zero Point'

The psychedelic spring was followed by the summer of love.

Amphetamine was the perfect ego drug for the 1960s: Torgoff depicts it as having to do with being bigger, better, stronger, smarter and quicker. Or, as Andy Warhol observed, 'Amphetamine doesn't give you peace of mind, but it makes not having it very amusing.' The people who used the drug as a way of life 'believed in throwing themselves into every extreme – sing until you choke, dance until you drop, brush your hair till you sprain your arm'.[27]

'The whole Catholic church is *gone*, and Greenwich Village is in its place,' said Pope Ondine, actually Robert Olivo, an actor who appeared in several films by Warhol. In *Chelsea Girls*, in what he called his papal bull, he said: 'My flock consists of homosexuals, perverts of any kind, thieves, criminals of any sort – the rejected by society, that's who I'm pope for.' *Chelsea Girls*, put together in 1966, showed shooting up on screen, more than a little violence, and was described in a review as portraying 'Our Godless Civilization approaching the zero point'. The *New York Times* called it 'a travelogue of hell, a grotesque menagerie of lost souls whimpering in a psychedelic moonscape'. Despite its commercial and cult success, conjuring up perverse images of peace and love, it famously concluded with the shooting of Warhol by Valerie Solanas, in June 1968.[28] Vietnam was hallucinogenic for many, who got their hands on drugs during Rest and Recreation in Australia.

Peter Coyote, sometime actor, founder of the Diggers, an anarchist group who supplied free food, housing and medical aid to runaways turning up to sample San Francisco, wrote: 'Drugs became the experiment to extend the edges of the envelope to find the limits in the personality, what had really been ground into you by social conditioning before you had the opportunity really to question it . . . Everywhere the sacrament of LSD was being consumed.' There was a new generation of seekers willing to proclaim the holiness of everything and elevate the whole planet with their vibrations. Leary urged people to start their own religions based on the sacramental use of marijuana and psychedelics.[29]

On 15 August 1969 roughly half a million people gathered in Bethel, New York, for 'the greatest party of the twentieth century'. The Woodstock Festival was the ultimate be-in of the era. 'Psychedelic drugs not only turned Woodstock into an acid-drenched holy quagmire but also shaped its soundtrack.' Woodstock quickly passed into myth and became the ultimate affirmation of the alternative values of a generation – peace, love, freedom, spirituality, sex, drugs and rock and roll – all of which had fused into an entity called the counter-culture. 'Before long it was being considered in religious terms – the people were seekers, the rock stars their prophets and drugs pretty much their staff of life', as a reporter wrote in *Life* magazine.[30]

The 1970s would become the golden age of marijuana, which was for many a benign substance with great spiritual, medicinal as well as commercial potential. Cocaine was another hidden secret thing. 'Most of the San Francisco bands sailed headlong into cocaine' – Johnny Cash had recorded 'Cocaine Blues' in 1969. But it was primarily a sexual stimulant and rarely brought with it any notion of metaphys-ical properties.

The passing of the psychedelic era came with Hunter S. Thomp-son's 'Gonzo epic', *Fear and Loathing in Las Vegas* (1971). Far from stressing the metaphysical qualities of drugs, Thompson saw them as the 'pharmacological equivalent of nitroglycerin'. As one observer wrote, '[*Fear and Loathing*] sounded the death knell for the whole self-conscious, pious Timothy Leary approach to psychedelics, of sit-ting on a Persian rug and listening to Indian music. There was nothing about taking LSD and seeing God here; it was a matter of survival, dealing with madness, about how sometimes you took drugs and you were hopeless, dangerously fucked up – the dark side of psychedelics that people did not want to talk about.'[31]

The last decades of the twentieth century saw a further change in drug use among the predominantly young – towards drugs that promote collective intimacy. These included Prozac and empathogens such as MDMA (Ecstasy), evocatively described as 'penicillin for the soul', creating not so much a sense of 'oneness' as of connection with nature and with other people, including complete strangers. Fuelled by MDMA, people went to mass 'raves' and reported being changed by the experience, described as equal parts therapy, mass catharsis and tribal bonding. 'Ecstasy had become the vehicle for a generation's at-tempt to set itself apart from the world and find its own place where it could Let Love Rule.' Or, as Terence McKenna put it, 'there *is* better living through chemistry'.[32]

Aesthetics and Morals

Theodore Roszak remained throughout an acerbic observer, and the problem for him was that psychedelics did not remain a mere attempt to access new forms of knowledge and experience. Rather, drugs became an end in themselves, an obsession that took people *away* from the search. They may have offered a new way of life – 'Ecstatic Living', in Timothy Leary's words – but that life was too often unreflective. Nor should we entirely overlook Nicholas von Hoffman's remark that psychedelics were 'the biggest crime story since prohibition'.

In rounding out his analysis of the counterculture Roszak referred to the 'visionary sociology' of Paul Goodman, in particular his idea that the criterion of psychological health is a moral–aesthetic one, that the aim of a life should be to achieve a 'moral–aesthetic comfortable-ness' similar to that natural aptitude in children, primitives, artists and lovers, 'those who can lose themselves in the splendor of the moment'. Goodman imagined a kind of utopian communitarianism in which communities are 'decentralized and elastic' to allow for the inevitable fallibilities of men and women, but in which we can each share in the beautiful achievements of others, the objective being to remove 'mass or collective loneliness'.

A last element in the countercultural way forward lay in what Roszak called 'the myth of objective consciousness', or the exploration of 'non-intellective consciousness'. This idea drew support from recent ('postmodern') developments in science and philosophy, which argued that there is no such thing as objectivity, because no one – not even scientists or philosophers – can step outside the human condition. Even in hard science we move ahead by *agreement* rather than by some 'outside' or 'superior' knowledge. By the same token, consciousness is not an objective entity but an arbitrarily agreed construct 'in which a given society in a given historical situation has invested its sense of meaningfulness and value'.[33]

Here, Roszak is moving towards a more phenomenological way of approaching the world. He quotes Maslow: 'Organizing experience into meaningful patterns implies that experience itself has no mean-ingfulness . . . that it is a gift from the knower to the known. In other words, "meaningfulness" of this kind is of the realm of classification and abstraction rather than of experience.' He refers back to Bergson's understanding of time as a 'vital flow' that has been 'arbitrarily segmented', so that 'to experience time in any other way becomes "mystical" or "mad"'.

To question this scientific way is, says Roszak, to insist that the primary purpose of human existence is not to devise ways of piling up ever greater heaps of knowledge, 'but to discover ways to live from day to day that integrate the whole of our nature . . . What is important, therefore, is that our lives should be as *big* as possible, capable of embracing the vastness of those experiences which, though yielding no articulate, demonstrable propositions, nevertheless awaken in us a sense of the world's majesty . . . What is at issue is the size of a man's life. We must insist that a culture which negates or subordinates or degrades visionary experience commits the sin of diminishing our existence.'

The scientific consciousness, Roszac claims, depreciates our capacity for wonder 'by progressively estranging us from the magic of the environment . . . The scientist studies, sums up, and has done with his puzzle; the painter paints the same landscape, the same vase of flowers, the same person over and over again, content to re-experience the inexhaustible power of his presence interminably . . . What he has seen . . . is not improved upon by being pressed into the form of knowledge.'[34]

His point, ultimately, is that there are *no experts* in life (much as G.E. Moore said (see chapter 2)), that literature – both sacred and secular – is full of individuals undergoing 'turning points' in their lives. 'What befalls us then is an experience of the personality suddenly swelling beyond all that we had once thought to be "real", swelling to become a greater and nobler identity than we have previously believed possible.'[35]

Encounter Groups in the White House

Roszak returned to the matter a few years later in *Where the Wasteland Ends: Politics and Transcendence in Postindustrial Society*. Here he argued that the religious sensibilities in our culture had been systematically repressed 'over the past few centuries', but that the loss of 'transcendent energies' had not been *felt* as a loss but as a 'gain in maturity'. By then, however, there was a new radicalism abroad, 'which refuses to respect the conventions of secular thought and value, which insists on making the visionary powers a central point of political reference. This book is written against a background of significant, if as yet amorphous, religious renewal in the western world.' And here the crucial element was the idea of transcendence, or rather its absence: this was the 'negative achievement' of the scientific approach.

In this new world, he imagined: 'Encounter grouping will become a national ritual practiced from the White House on down as a means of fulfilling the existential vacuum with instant intimacy and push-button friendship – on conveniently short-term arrangements. Sexual gratification, once ideally inseparable from love and a personal commitment to the beloved, will be available in a variety of erotic participations by way of the avant-garde theater, the mate swap, the group grope party, the weekly love-in at the local park.'[36]

He argued that the 'privations required by our culture's orthodox consciousness' constituted a 'psychic wasteland' that we carry within us as we make our way through the real world of 'the artificial environment'; people had begun to feel 'restive' with the 'diminished self we have become'. But there was a minority, what he referred to as a 'eupsychian network' of 'human potential movements', yogic, Taoist and Tantric sources which sought to propagate 'a variety of techniques for expanding personality'. He thought there was great potential for these movements, but until that point there had been a 'haunting ambiguity' about their intentions. For many, he said, the therapy offered was 'like mysticism with all the metaphysical commitments drained off; it can end in a kind of splendid psychosensory athleticism, with all the emotional knots untied and the kinks carefully smoothed away. One meets people like this in the movement. They tune their psyches with marvelous self-indulgence until there is not an inhibition, not a frustration left to ruffle their calm. They are much like the body-builders who fastidiously train every last little muscle and tendon to perfection.'[37]

Roszac was not embarrassed to mention mysticism: 'The mystic quest very likely begins no further off than just the other side of the commonplace, daily repressions.' The artificial environment of science had closed the mystical doors, all alternative ways of seeing the world. Science has become our religion because most of us cannot 'see around' it. He quoted with approval José Ortega y Gasset: 'Life cannot wait until the sciences have explained the universe scientifically. We cannot put off living until we are ready.'

Roszak thought there were six basic ways in which society had changed in the modern era – invariably for the worse. In the first instance, 'the big sciences' had brought about the undoing of the human scale. What humans have done to the earth had brought about the undoing of progress. Technocracy had helped to destroy the open society, while the new ways in which people could be categorized – as consumers, customers, tourists – had caused the undoing of the political community. Overall, the reductionist assault – the achievement of the hard sciences, again – had resulted in the dissolution of the mysteries; and the exploration of esotericism, not least with the aid of mind-altering drugs, had caused the undoing of shared culture.[38]

In many ways, Roszak thought the change was more than an unravelling, or undoing, a subtraction story as Charles Taylor would say. He felt that as the baffling subtleties of contemporary science drift further away from the understanding of the lay citizen, 'the resulting spiritual strain will be much greater than most people can live with gracefully . . . one cannot go on indefinitely in this way without being eaten alive by self-loathing . . . An intellectual enterprise grounded in depersonalized specialization and aimed at the boundless proliferation of knowledge for its own sake is inherently non-participative. It deserves its place in the world, but its place is not at the top. It cannot sustain a democratic culture; it cannot generate a shared reality – other than the alienated existence of the artificial environment.'[39]

One of the effects of this sixfold dissolution, Roszak said, was the loss of the richness of 'transcendent symbols'.[40] He thought that the basic task of human culture 'is the elaboration of root meanings in the form of ritual or art, philosophy or myth, science or technology – and especially in the form of language generally, by way of progressively more attenuated metaphors drawn from the original symbol . . . They cannot be explained but are what we use to give meaning to lesser levels of experience.[41] Symbols for us, he said, have been densified and lose their subtlety. They harden into purely secular things. For him, 'Mother Earth' is not a superstitious mistake but a brilliant and beneficial insight. Ours is a culture alienated in fact and *on principle*.

Salvation, he insisted, was to be found nowhere but in the collective, historical process – 'in making, doing and improving'.[42] He praised the fact that the counterculture had spawned what he called a 'visionary commonwealth', a thousand fragile experiments of communes, organic homesteading, extended families, free schools, free clinics, Gandhian ashrams, neighbourhood rap centres, labour gift exchanges. Only in these ways, he thought, could the peaceful personal intimacy be created which alone allows for spiritual growth. He called for an awakening from the 'single vision and Newton's sleep', where we have dreamt that only matter and history are real.

'More and more . . . psychotherapists find that what their patients suffer from is the existential void they feel at the bottom of their lives.' 'Is it merely coincidence that, in the midst of so much technological mastery and economic abundance, our art and thought continue to project a nihilistic imagery unparalleled in human history?' 'Are not our technological achievements *meaningless* in the absence of a transcendent correspondence?' 'How can we help but to be creatures in search of value and meaning?'

The answer for Roszak was what he called the 'rhapsodic intellect', in which the chief ingredient was not calculation, or control of the world, but its enjoyment through *resonance*. By this he meant a search for enhanced meaning 'in the feel of words', which aims to reclaim transcendent symbols – the resonance of root meaning – as a result of which 'we are left knowing more than we can say'.[43] Roszak himself does not have the same resonance as, say, Beckett, or Roth, or even Charley Parker. But he should.

23

The Luxury and Limits of Happiness

We might do well to stop for a moment to ask ourselves once more whether happiness and fulfilment and the search for meaning are, in a sense, luxuries. While this book mainly concerns itself with meaning in its broadest sense – the sense in which most educated Westerners think of it, as a metaphysical, religious, post-religious or psychological conundrum – for many the purpose of life is, as noted earlier, far more down-to-earth, bordering on the naked struggle for survival.

While this must always have been true, the problem of existential security has become much more visible since the Second World War, and especially since the establishment of the United Nations in 1945. The various subsidiary organizations of the UN such as the Food and Agriculture Organization, UNESCO and UNICEF have drawn attention to the uneven economic picture across the world, and programmes designed to offset or alleviate areas of poverty and underdevelopment have become a major activity of these outfits.

The broad thrust of these programmes has been to redefine the problem from one that is, generally speaking, economic, to one that encompasses a wider understanding of what it means to be poor – what the cultural and psychological consequences are, including the impact on access to natural resources, to education and to medical facilities, political representation and civil liberties. This has led to a shift in emphasis, from GNP to the UN Human Development Index, introduced in 1990. Partly as a result of this change we now hear more talk of 'human well-being' and 'human flourishing', even 'happiness', rather than narrowly economic terms like 'wealth' or 'productive base'. These concerns are not ignored, but they are subsumed into the wider understanding of what determines the quality of life and a more complex and inclusive concept of personhood.[1]

This has given rise, among other things, to a new term to set alongside 'Utopia': 'Agathotopia', meaning 'a good enough society', the kind that economists and UN officials will settle for as an attainable goal in the foreseeable future, developing out of the present Kakotopia, the imperfect society.

Professor Partha Dasgupta of Cambridge University has said that an adequate supply of commodities and an absence of coercion 'are the means by which people can pursue their own conception of the good'.[2] The notion of well-being is pluralist 'in the sense that well-being isn't taken to be a single measure (e.g. happiness), but embodies the idea that we face trade-offs between a plurality of goods (e.g. health, happiness, the ability to be and to do)'.[3] Recall the quote by Robert Musil in chapter eleven, to the effect that people may 'scoff' at metaphysical preoccupations but privately we all have such concerns at heart. Well-being, flourishing and happiness are entirely secular ideas. We might say that they are the secular equivalents of what 'salvation' is to a religious person, though many would reject that idea. We shall discuss this issue later, but the point here is that concern with well-being and related concepts came to the fore in the last decades of the twentieth century; indeed, a whole area of scholarship arose to consider them.

As Dasgupta says, the word 'happiness' 'doesn't even appear in textbooks on modern welfare economics', a state of affairs that he finds 'repugnant'. Happiness is not the same as well-being, he points out. It is notoriously difficult to measure and varies over time; and in any case many people do not see it as the state's job to be concerned with their citizens' happiness. 'Rather, they see the business of the state as making sure that basic liberties are enjoyed, so that citizens are able to protect and promote their own projects and purposes.'[4] The evidence, such as it is, suggests that what is conducive to happiness is strikingly different as between the very poor and the rich. In poor countries, indices of consumption, health and civic and political liberties reveal the main determinants of happiness. In rich countries, health is an important determinant, as are educational attainment and associational life: people who are more engaged in civic activities are happier; unemployment, not surprisingly, contributes significantly to unhappiness.

For the Canadian philosopher Charles Taylor happiness is a 'thin' idea, at least compared with fulfilment, or the gift of 'wholeness' offered by religion. But it does no harm to make what sense we can of it, the more so as a number of governments (such as the UK's coalition government) have recently begun to show interest in how, exactly, and if at all, our happiness can be measured, sustained and augmented.

Happiness is the core concern of another Canadian philosopher, Mark Kingwell, in that he went in search of it. In his book *In Pursuit of Happiness* (1998), he begins by acknowledging that in general the inhabitants of rich countries are happier than those of poorer ones. (As the famous Ukraine-born American actress and singer Sophie Tucker (1886–1966) said, 'I've been rich and I've been poor – believe me, honey, rich is better.') But at the same time, Kingwell argued, consumerism, one of the predominant achievements of capitalist culture, is based on envy; and advertising, the main capitalist means of 'selling' consumerism, works by 'creating unhappiness'. In such an environment, he says, happiness is treated as a 'good' in a consumerist sense, as the attainment of a (static) final state, a possession and an achievement.[5]

The attraction of Kingwell's survey (a professor of philosophy at the University of Toronto) was that he was himself ready to sample various methods of attaining happiness – taking Prozac, for example, and enrolling in the Option Institute and Fellowship, an outfit (happiness@option.org) that focuses exclusively on 'the elusive condition of happiness'. He reviewed courses that promised people they could lose weight and increase their happiness at the same time; others that promised happiness in eight minutes by changing the way we breathe, or that taught people to see themselves 'as God sees us'. He reports how the BBC commissioned programmes on 'how to be happy', run by a self-described 'professor of fun'. (The TV critic of the *Scotsman* described the show thus: 'Tonight's fascinating documentary follows three misery-guts as they go on an eight-week course in how to be happy, and sees whether they end up feeling ripped-off as well as sad.')

Kingwell considered the idea that happy people are those with 'normal' levels of serotonin in their brains, and how that level could be manipulated. He surveyed Abraham Maslow's ideas (see chapter 21), concluding that there was more than a whiff of self-congratulation and elitism about them; he noted that Maslow himself, ironically, became more embittered and disillusioned as he grew older, as well as 'increasingly dismissive of those who sold their psychotherapeutic wares by claiming that self-actualization was available to everyone'.[6]

The Art of Diminished Expectations

Kingwell began by considering some authors, such as John Ralston Saul, who suggested we stop using the word 'happiness' altogether, since it has lost the ancient philosophical robustness it once had and has come to mean mere material comfort, or simply 'pursuit of personal pleasure or an obscure sense of inner contentment'.[7] For his part, Kingwell thought that we must understand the modern search for happiness as part of 'a story of growing human self-interpretation in the modern world, the creation of a self-consciousness that goes beyond the limits of earlier worlds ruled by ignorance, church authority, or other traditional forces'. It is about more than material comfort: 'Of equal, if not greater, significance is the general movement of Western culture in the last two centuries toward ever greater degrees of individuation.'[8]

One of his conclusions was that material reality has lost its role 'as the fount of all fulfilment' (at least in rich countries), to be replaced by psychological well-being.[9] He quoted Bill Bryson, the American writer who, having lived in Britain for a while, concluded that the English are the happiest people on earth 'because they have mastered [the] art of cheerfully diminished expectations, the sort of thing embodied in catch phrases like "Well, it makes a change", "Mustn't grumble", "You could do worse."'

Kingwell noted that there has been an 'implicit psychologization of happiness in our culture', that we have – as Freud intimated – exchanged 'a portion of happiness for a portion of security', that the rhetoric of achievement, so redolent of American culture, reinforces the 'machine imperatives' of pleasure, the idea that happiness is 'essentially a problem to be solved, a psychological portfolio to be managed'. And we are caught up in an endless round of 'buying and selling ourselves': is there anywhere else to go, he asks, any identity to adopt 'that is not already encapsulated by the forces of the market'? Americans in particular have allowed their expectations of leisure and comfort to rise so high that almost anything that falls below utter luxury 'begins to seem inadequate'. This is why people feel less happy now, and more deprived (this was in the late 1990s), than in the 1950s when real incomes were much lower.[10]

Kingwell goes on to note the rise, beginning in Paris and Amsterdam in the early 1990s, of philosophical cafés and philosophical therapists, followed by their swift rise in Germany and elsewhere, so that now tens of thousands of people avail themselves of such innovations. For him this suggests that 'there is a hunger out there' for philosophical thinking. But he notes that this trend has not spread to North America.[11] Americans, he says, get some of their best philosophy, about how to live the good life, from self-help manuals, which make it feel not like philosophy but plain common sense.

He explores the old idea that happiness is a state that exists only in recollection when, looking back, we realize that, fleetingly, 'for a time' (as O'Neill has Mary Tyrone say in Long Day's Journey), we were happiest when we lost our sense of self, that 'self-forgetting' which, as several philosophers have said, is part of the experience of happiness. In like vein he refers with approval to Bertrand Russell's view that it has become common in our day to suppose that 'those among us who are wise have seen through all the enthusiasms of earlier times and have become aware that there is nothing left to live for. The men who hold this view are genuinely unhappy, but they are proud of their unhappiness, which they attribute to the nature of the universe and consider it to be the only rational attitude for an enlightened man.' Kingwell thinks this attitude is both cheap and paradoxical, in that such people are actually happy in their unhappiness. He quotes the Scottish philosopher Alasdair MacIntyre in After Virtue: 'The good life is the life spent seeking the good life.'[12]

Upgrade Anxiety

One other aspect of modern capitalism that contributes to *un*happiness is the amount of information we are inundated with, which gives many people a feeling of being left behind – what Kingwell calls 'upgrade anxiety', the endless feeling that we have to 'catch up', which is energy-sapping. We are simply overwhelmed by cultural content with little chance to make sense of the context. And naturally this interferes with – sabotages – our desire for completeness.

Then there are the paradoxical elements in our lives themselves. For example, as the psychiatrist Anthony Storr said, 'It is widely believed that interpersonal relationships of an intimate kind are the chief, if not the only, source of human happiness . . . Yet the lives of creative individuals often seem to run counter to this assumption.' This echoes what Rilke had to say about Rodin and Picasso (see chapter 11). Kingwell says the evidence for this is overwhelming and calls on Thomas De Quincey for confirmation: 'No man will ever unfold the capacities of his own intellect who does not at least checker his life with solitude.' He identifies Descartes, Newton, Locke, Pascal, Spinoza, Kant, Leibniz, Schopenhauer, Nietzsche, Kierkegaard and Wittgenstein as great figures who never married (though we know Nietzsche proposed to Lou Andrea-Salomé but was turned down).[13] This reflects evidence that adults without children are happier than those with them, and are more likely to achieve greatness.

Kingwell reports a variety of definitions of, and comments on, happiness: 'Happiness is not about feeling good all the time. It is, rather, about the ability to reflect on one's life and find it worthwhile . . . Happiness is not simply a feeling or emotion; it is a connection to the world, a realization of one's place within it.' He ends with a return to Bertrand Russell: '[G]etting everything you want is not the source of happiness but of unhappiness, for when striving ceases so does life.' '[T]o be without some of the things you want is an indispensable part of happiness.'[14]

One can see why some sixty of Russell's books were still in print when he died, aged ninety-seven, in 1970. Happiness may be a 'thin' idea to

Charles Taylor – and Terry Eagleton, the British philosopher, called it a 'holiday-camp type of word' – but thin or not, Russell realized that its pursuit and possession are far from straightforward. This became even clearer towards the end of the twentieth century as it emerged that the 'psychologization' of life, the replacement of religion with psychology, had thrown up unforeseen problems and paradoxes.

In August 2000 the Archbishop of Canterbury remarked: 'Christ the Saviour is becoming Christ the Counsellor.' It was no more than the truth, up to a point, but still a remarkable statement from such a source. However, as perhaps befits the holder of a traditional Church position, the archbishop was somewhat out of date when he made his remark. In fact, by the turn of the twenty-first century the counterculture, the 'better living through chemistry' culture, the therapy culture, as it also came to be called, had already come under sustained attack.

None was more acerbic than Christopher Lasch. Lasch (1932–94) came from a highly political family; he was the son of a Pulitzer Prize-winning journalist of St Louis, Missouri. Educated at Harvard and Columbia, he became a professor at the University of Rochester. Always sceptical of liberalism, in the 1970s he developed a form of cultural criticism that was an amalgam of conservatism, Marxism and Freud-influenced critical theory. In *Haven in a Heartless World* (1977), *The Minimal Self* (1984) and, most famously, *The Culture of Narcissism* (1979) he tore into the forces to which he attributed a decline in the quality of life in America and, by implication, throughout the West, in particular our moral and spiritual life. These forces were consumerism, proletarianization and the therapeutic sensibility. It was his assault on the latter that made Lasch famous.[15]

As he presented it, the world of the counterculture effectively embodied a change in sensibility from a way of life that was dying – the culture of competitive individualism and the 'pursuit of happiness' – to 'the dead end of narcissistic preoccupation with the self'. 'To live for the moment is the prevailing passion – to live for yourself, not for your predecessors or posterity.' Our eyes, he said, are fixed on our own 'private performances', we cultivate a 'transcendental self-attention'. The contemporary climate 'is therapeutic, not religious. People today hunger not for personal salvation . . . but for the feeling, the momentary illusion, of personal well-being, health and psychic security. Even the radicalism of the sixties served, for many of those who embraced it for personal rather than political reasons, not as a substitute religion but as a form of therapy. Radical politics filled empty lives, provided a sense of meaning and purpose.' This was secular salvation, defined as establishing an identity rather than submerging oneself in a larger cause.[16]

Because of this inner emptiness, said Lasch, the psychological man of the twentieth century sought neither individual self-aggrandizement, nor spiritual transcendence, but peace of mind, though conditions have increasingly militated against it. 'Therapists, not priests or popular preachers of self-help or models of success like the captains of industry, become his principal allies in the struggle for composure; he turns to them in the hope of achieving the modern equivalent of salvation, "mental health".' This, he thought, made therapy an anti-religion, because 'love' as self-sacrifice or, as 'submission' to a higher loyalty, is regarded as intolerably oppressive. Mental health means – or has come to mean – the overthrow of inhibitions and the immediate gratification of every impulse.[17]

He reminded us that Freud had said that all psychoanalysis could hope to do was to substitute 'everyday unhappiness' for debilitating neurosis, making the sacrifices exacted by civilized life easier to bear. 'But psychoanalysis held out no cure for injustice or unhappiness; nor could it satisfy the growing demand, in a world without religion, for meaning, faith and emotional security.' But, he went on, it was *exactly* belief and personal power that Americans hoped to find in therapy. These ideas had begun in Europe, in particular with the work of Adler and Jung. Adler's notion of the inferiority complex, reinterpreting the 'will to power' in a therapeutic context, had appealed to Americans even more than had Freud's ideas. Jung addressed himself to a disease no less pervasive in modern society than the sense of personal inadequacy – the impoverishment of the spiritual imagination. He sought to restore the illusion of faith, if not its reality, by enabling the patient to construct a private religion made up of the decomposing remnants of former religions, all of them equally valid in Jung's eyes and therefore 'equally serviceable in the modern crisis of unbelief'.

And so both systems – Adler's and Jung's – replaced self-insight with ethical teaching, thereby transforming therapy into, as Freud foresaw, a 'new ethico-religious system'. One result of this, Lasch said, is narcissism, in which an ethic of pleasure replaces an ethic of achievement.

Narcissists divide society into two groups: the rich, great and famous on the one hand and the common herd on the other, and they themselves are afraid of being 'mediocre'. The narcissist also creates an ironic distance from everyday life, and is forever outside himself, watching himself, and in that sense never has an authentic experience. Both sexes cultivate a protective shallowness but at the same time demand from personal relationships the richness and intensity of a religious experience.[18] 'In a dying culture, narcissism appears to embody – in the guise of "personal growth" and "awareness" – the highest attainment of spiritual enlightenment.' But they do not involve themselves in making a better society; they have no vision of a new society, a decent society. 'The old order took matters more seriously than the narcissists do, who take them for granted.'[19]

Modern (late 1970s) man, Lasch said, had became imprisoned in his self-awareness; he 'longs for the lost innocence of spontaneous feeling. Unable to express emotion without calculating its effects on others, he doubts the authenticity of its expression in others and therefore derives little comfort from audience reactions to his own performance.' The consequences of this were profound, as we shall see.[20]

Another light is shed on the 1960s and 70s by Louis Malle's 1981 film, *My Dinner with André*. Two old friends meet up at a restaurant in New York after many years, and defend the choices they have made in their lives. André has travelled across the world in search of 'spiritual enlightenment', while Wally stayed put in New York 'grubbing' for work as a writer/actor, sharing what he admits has been a fairly humdrum existence with the same girlfriend throughout. What to Wally are everyday comforts and conveniences are for André (with his exotic-sounding foreign name) merely attributes of a mindless material culture. Wally's approach has been to content himself with 'small pleasures' and 'small, attainable goals'; André has sought spiritual transcendence, 'higher states of consciousness'. He has tried Eastern religions, mind-altering spiritual exercises, communal retreats.

Returning to New York after a long absence, what he finds is for him little short of a concentration camp, but one populated by 'robots and lobotomized individuals'. He and his wife, he tells Wally, feel like the Jews in Germany in the late 1930s, and they want to escape.

Malle is not in a hurry to take sides. Both strategies are means of survival, different but perhaps equivalent responses to an uncertain world of impermanence. If anything, Malle makes Wally look like 'a model of common sense and democratic decency'. In his loyalty to familiar surroundings he retains some of what Hannah Arendt called 'a love of the world – the world of human associations and human works, which give solidity and continuity to our lives'. At the same time, it has to be admitted that Wally has lowered his sights, he takes one day at a time, and pays a price for the radical restriction of perspective that he has embraced, which precludes intelligent political activity, a larger role in life – a larger life, in fact – that many would find fulfilling. 'It allows him to remain human – no small accomplishment in these times. But it prevents him from exercising any influence over the course of public events.'[21]

In the end, neither André nor Wally has confidence in the possibility of cooperative political action, which for Hannah Arendt, Christopher Lasch and, perhaps, Louis Malle, is the real purpose of life, the only way out that truly enlarges us.

A Legitimate Palliative?

Just as the therapy culture came under fire from Lasch and others, so too was the drug culture attacked by all sorts of people. G.T. Roche begins his examination of the effects of the drug experience on knowledge: 'If any intoxicating substances induce experiences that are similar to religious ecstasies, suggests Bertrand Russell, so much for religious ecstasies: we "can make no distinction between the man who eats little and sees heaven and the man who drinks much and sees snakes". Each is in an abnormal physical condition, and therefore has abnormal perceptions.' Given the widely reported relationship between abnormal states and religious ecstasy, this objection is not easily dismissed. Conversely and controversially, Theodore Schick claims that the need to alter consciousness 'is just as basic as the need to eat and sleep'.

While conceding that it is possible that a 'handful of philosophers' have been imaginatively inspired by drugs (William James thought that inhalation of nitrous oxide gave him a new appreciation of Hegel), and although other philosophers and scientists have used meditation to enhance their thinking (William Harvey would meditate in a coal mine), Roche remains deeply sceptical of claims such as Timothy Leary's that he could directly experience DNA under the influence of LSD, or the assertion of Rick Strassman, a Los Angeles psychiatrist specialising in psychopharmacology, that another hallucinogenic, DMT (dimethyltryptamine), 'allows one to see dark matter'. Roche also points out that reports of experiencing 'cosmic oneness' or a 'real loss of ego' are problematic, as there is always still an ego – an experiencing subject – that observes the event. And he questions claims of 'moral or existential enlightenment', partly because others (such as Huxley and Leary) maintain that drugs actually seem to *suspend* the moral sense. This undermines any 'straightforward case' for drug-inspired moral wisdom.[22]

We are therefore left in a paradoxical situation: the extravagant claims for the drug experience – that it produces a 'multidimensional super-consciousness, new categories of knowledge, a better guide to reality' – are challenged, Roche says, by evidence of the 'well-researched capacity of the psychedelic drugs to *impair* cognition, perception and concentration'. He concludes that the drugs' 'revelatory powers are clearly exaggerated' and so the real question becomes: '[W]hat knowledge is only acceptable to the individual through chemically degrading one's capacity for rational thought? ... Watts, Leary and Huxley all write of the insight acquired through the psychedelic experience as a *direct apprehension* of some deep truth, rather than through *intellectual* insight. Without an argument as to how such a direct, drug-induced experience can warrant such certainty, Watts, Leary and Huxley are essentially appealing to their own authority [italics in original].'

There remains the issue of 'psychedelic spirituality'. But psychedelic experience hardly fits with the religious view that God is unknowable and therefore cannot be perceived or even sensed. The God of the Torah never appears to humans directly, so, says Roche, what are we to make of claims by schizophrenics, epileptics and people on drugs that they have had direct encounters with God or seen angels face to face? Then there is the simple argument that no omniscient or omnipotent being, by definition, could be summoned by whatever worldly means against his or her will.[23]

Furthermore, unpleasant psychedelic experiences are by no means unknown, as are experiences where faith is *reduced*. And some cult leaders have used drugs as a means of control over their members (such as Shoko Asahara, responsible for the 1995 sarin gas attack on the Tokyo subway).

Maybe the proof of this particular pudding is in the eating. LSD use dropped off markedly in the late 1970s. There was a return to it in the 90s and the early 2000s, but to nowhere near the levels of the 60s and early 70s. On the other hand, the use of cannabis, whose history goes back several thousand years, continues strong (according to the World Health Organization, in 2010 more than 147 million people worldwide consumed cannabis regularly). Its effects are much milder than LSD's, and no great metaphysical claims are made for it in regard to 'visions' it might induce, though its effects vary with strength. Rather, as Mark Thorsby says, it offers a temporary alleviation of the strains of living in the world, 'a momentary escape from the desert of alienation'. Insofar as cannabis increases our capability to enrich our lives, and makes us more creative, as some artists and musicians assert, and so long as *they* make our lives *feel* more fulfilling, is there any harm in that? As Professor Brian Clack puts it, following on from Freud's claims about palliatives, 'Existence might just require this sort of augmentation.'[24]

Solace by Diagnosis

Criticisms of the drug aspect of the counterculture are real enough, and they sit neatly with the fact that drug use, though it has by no means disappeared, has declined as a means of accessing what we might call an alternative spiritual realm. There are still advocates of marijuana use as a 'spiritual facilitator' and as a palliative, but the use of LSD, as just noted, has greatly declined.*

The same cannot be said about therapy. In a wide-ranging critique of what he calls the 'therapy culture', Frank Furedi, professor of sociology at the University of Kent in the UK, has argued that, by the beginning of the twenty-first century, the legacy of the therapeutic revolution is that 'society is in the process of drawing up a radically new definition of what constitutes the human condition'.[25] He has found that therapy, happiness and fulfilment can be damagingly intertwined.

The core element in this new condition, he says, is that many experiences that have hitherto been interpreted as a normal part of everyday life have been redefined as injurious to people's emotions. He quotes a wealth of figures to substantiate this, including the fact that children are far unhappier these days than ever before, that children as young as four are 'legitimate targets for therapeutic intervention', that there has been a 'massive increase' in depression 'due to the difficulty that people have in dealing with disappointment and failure'.[26]

The number of mental health counsellors has snowballed, in both the UK and the USA. In Furedi's critique, 53 per cent of British students had 'anxiety at pathological levels', and a host of new 'illnesses' have been conceived, or created, by new professions who 'invent the needs they claim to satisfy'.[27] He explores many aspects of this 'medicalization', or 'psychologicalization' or 'pathologicalization' of life, arguing that there has been a 'promiscuity' in therapeutic diagnosis: counselling for redundancy, for people who are 'exercise addicts' or 'sex addicts', for the recently divorced, for women who have just given birth or who are depressed by having to do housework, for athletes who retire from competition and face 'the onset of post-sporting depression'. He describes self-help books to help people survive their twenties, claims that office politics has been redefined as 'bullying',

---

* In the US general election of 2012, two states voted to legalize cannabis. It is too soon to say where this will lead.

caution as 'inhibition' and diffidence as 'withholding'. In a survey carried out in 1985 and again in the same place in 1996, he reports, there was found to have been an increase of 155 per cent among 16–19-year-olds who considered themselves disabled.

His point is that, from birth to education to marriage and parenting, all the way through to bereavement, 'people's experience is interpreted through the medium of the therapeutic ethos'. Among all this, religion has been subordinated to therapy.[28] 'This subordination of religious doctrine to concern with people's existential quest reflects a wider shift towards an orientation towards a preoccupation with the self. A study of "seeker churches" in the US argues that their ability to attract new recruits is based on their ability to tap into the therapeutic understanding of Americans.'[29]

Furedi believes, as Christopher Lasch does, that there has been a powerful shift away from the more traditional affirmation of communal purpose towards encouraging people to find 'meaning through their individual selves'. And this is where the fundamental problem lies. It is a problem because it exaggerates people's vulnerability. Some accounts of therapeutic culture associate it with the 'selfish or at least self-centred' quest for fulfilment, but, he argues, in fact therapy culture promotes self-*limitation*. 'It posits the self in distinctly fragile and feeble form and insists that the management of life requires the continuous intervention of therapeutic expertise.'[30] He finds that in therapy culture many emotions are depicted negatively 'precisely because they disorient the individual from the search for self-fulfilment'.

Even love, though portrayed as the supreme source of self-fulfilment, is depicted as potentially harmful 'because it threatens to subordinate the self to another'. In books such as Anne Wilson Schaef's *Escape from Intimacy* and *Women Who Love Too Much* by Robin Norwood, 'Intense love towards another is regularly criticised for distracting individuals from fulfilling their own needs and from pursuing self-interest.' In a similar vein, 'It has been suggested that people who have too much faith may be suffering from religious addiction.' Father Leo Booth in his *When God Becomes a Drug* warns of becoming 'addicted to the certainty, sureness or sense of security that our faith provides'.[31]

The rise of confessional novels and television programmes, what Joyce Carol Oates has described as 'pathography', has eroded the sphere of private life, with the result that no shame now attaches to negative events and 'mere survival is presented as a triumph', as we sacralize self-absorption. From this it follows that we have redefined the meaning of responsibility: 'This redefinition of responsibility as responsibility to oneself helps provide emotionalism with moral meaning.'[32]

What has happened, says Furedi, following Ernest Gellner, is that in our risky modern society the spiritual struggle of former times has been replaced by a personal struggle for 'attention and acceptance'. The decline of tradition helps situate the demand for new ways of making sense of the world. The weakening of shared values fragments this quest for meaning, privatizes it and lends it an individual character. 'Therapeutics promises to provide answers to the individual's quest for the meaning of life.' But this gives rise, he says, to a therapeutic ethos in which there are no values higher than the self. Therapy attempts to avoid the problem of how people can be bound to a shared view of the world (as with religions) by offering individuated solace.[33]

Furedi argues that the invasion of the therapeutic ethos into life has reached such proportions that '[b]eing ill can now constitute a defining feature of an individual's identity' (not a million miles from Esther Benbassa's notion of suffering as identity – see pp.386–8) Self-esteem has become paramount in our psychological lives: almost any action or policy can be justified by its effect on our self-esteem, almost any behavioural wrong or dereliction can be put down to lack of self-esteem. He scoffs at the absurdities it can lead to, such as the case of Jennifer Hoes, a Dutch artist who was so much in love with herself, she said, that she decided to marry herself. 'Self-esteem has acquired a free-floating character that can attach itself to any issue.'[34]

For the psychiatrist Patrick Bracken, the continuous search for a diagnosis 'represents an attempt to find meaning in confusion'. The sociologist Peter Berger thinks that our 'cultural fixation with trauma', with pathologizing so many experiences once regarded as unexceptional, can be linked to a 'dread brought on by a struggle with meaning'. This has led us to the 'age of values', he says, values in the sense of 'truths that have been deprived of their commanding character' and which are oriented towards the individual self. And when so much is directed towards the self, in a confusing and risky world, this leads to a need for recognition. It is this which accounts for the rise of identity politics, he says, for the obsession with fame, with the idea of the 'equality of esteem', in which all sectors of society must be esteemed.

But Furedi's overriding point is that therapeutic culture *holds people back*. He can find no evidence that, despite decades of therapeutic culture, self-knowledge is on the increase. Therapy has not 'realized' personal growth to any appreciable degree – on the contrary, it has been 'much more an instrument of survival than a means through which enlightenment can be gained'. People undergoing therapies are told they 'will never be completely cured'. Furthermore, therapeutics have transformed 'the experience of estrangement from a problem into an object of veneration'. Therapeutic culture, as Kenneth Gergen, professor of psychology at Swarthmore College in Pennsylvania, has noted, offers 'invitations to infirmity' in which suffering is a 'social virtue' and people's identity depends on professionals and institutions.[35]

Furedi's conclusion directly addresses our subject: 'Contemporary society lacks certainty about its beliefs. It finds it difficult to transmit a clear vision of a just world. In particular, there seems to be great hesitancy about offering people a clear system of meaning. It is this confusion about providing people with meaning that provides the therapeutic world-view with considerable opportunity to spread its influence. Today's cultural elite may lack confidence in telling people what to believe but it feels quite comfortable about instructing people how and what to feel.'[36]

Another important 'achievement' of therapeutics has been to distract people from engaging with wider social issues in favour of this inward turn to the self. '[Therapy culture] seeks to exercise control not through a system of punishments, but through cultivating a sense of vulnerability, powerlessness and dependence. Through normalizing the sick role and help-seeking, therapeutic culture promotes the virtue of dependence on professional authority. At the same time it discourages dependence on intimate and informal relations – an act which weakens the sense of belonging in the individual . . . most important of all it indicates that a regime of self-limitation has become institutionalized ... the passive sense of self projected today does not so much take risks, as is at risk. In this scenario, the experimenting and transformative role of the individual is all but extinguished ... This static conservative view of the self represents a rejection of previous more ambitious calls for "changing yourself", "improving yourself" or for "transcending yourself". The call for self-acceptance represents a roundabout way of avoiding change.'[37]

Is this an indictment of mere happiness?

If Furedi and the other authors are right – and between them they have amassed copious supporting evidence – then the therapeutic movement has come full circle, to stand for the opposite of what it began as. Instead of offering an expansion of experience, instead of helping people create a fuller life, a larger life, a richer life – as Theodore Roszak envisaged – it has become, in the perhaps laudable interest of a more 'sensitive' society, a holding action and one which, moreover, helps diminish life rather than enhancing it, by viewing many people, to begin with, as less than full, as vulnerable victims, whose only opportunity is to recover some of their 'lost' abilities, as if they were half-empty vessels whose best hope is to be slightly less empty. And, since they can never be 'cured' completely, they can never move on, to explore new ways of enlargement.

It is easy to go along with Furedi and the others, and decry what therapy has become, to lament its diminishing of life. Or, is this no more than realistic? Maybe it is partly what writers like Philip Roth are getting at. It may be a terrible thing to say, but perhaps consolation by diagnosis is a reminder that that is what – for many people, in a fast-changing and risky world – a fuller life *is*.

24

Faith in Detail

One evening in Belfast in 1972, the poet Seamus Heaney had arranged to meet his friend, the singer David Hammond. They were to rendezvous in a BBC studio to put together a tape of songs and poems for a mutual friend in Michigan. The idea of the tape was to commemorate an earlier celebration, when the American had been in Belfast and an 'expansive' evening had been enjoyed by all. In the event, the tape was never made. On their way to the studio 'a number of explosions occurred in the city and the air was full of the sirens of ambulances and fire engines. There was news of casualties.' Both men felt that 'to sing at that moment when others were beginning to suffer seemed like an offence against their suffering'. Hammond packed up his guitar, and 'we both drove off into the destroyed evening'.

Heaney tells this story at the beginning of his book of essays on poetry, *The Government of the Tongue* (1988), and he began in this way, he said, because the episode dramatized a tension that underlay the poetry – and perhaps all the art – of the twentieth century. This tension, which the Polish poet Czeslaw Milosz also observed, began for Heaney with the horrors of the First World War. '[I]t is from this moment in our century that radiant and unperturbed certitudes about the consonance between the true and the beautiful become suspect.'[1] Heaney fastened on Wilfred Owen: 'Owen so stood by what he wrote that he seemed almost to obliterate the line between art and life ... His poems have the potency of human testimony, of martyr's

relics, so that any intrusion of the aesthetic can feel like impropriety
... the First World War was a wonderful example of a moment when
poets functioned as effective and heroic figures in the life of their
times.'

Owen and the others like him in the trenches of Flanders, Heaney
argues, were among the first of 'a type of poet who increasingly appears
in the annals of twentieth-century literature, and who looms as a kind
of shadowy judging figure ... the shorthand name we have evolved for
this figure is "The poet as witness"'.[2]

The Witness of Poetry was published by Czeslaw Milosz in 1983,
when he no longer lived in Poland but was professor of poetry at
Harvard. These prose books, along with others by poets (Michael
Hamburger's *The Truth of Poetry* (1982), Joseph Brodsky's *Less Than
One* (1986) and Kathleen Raine's *The Underlying Order* (2008)), suggest Heaney and Milosz were on to something, something that was in
the air. This something may have had to do, as Milosz said, with the
fact that 'poetry is a more reliable witness than journalism'.[3] Witness
to what? And what, in any case, does that have to do with the theme
of this book? There are two related answers, which keep us close to
Heaney's opening story.

First, much of the poetry of the twentieth century, again in
Milosz's words, 'comes from a blank spot on the map'. He is referring here to his native Poland and also to the Lithuanian poet Adam
Mickiewicz who 'is virtually unknown in the West'. This is his point
– that the political and self-inflicted humanitarian disasters of the
twentieth century created many intellectual and artistic 'blank' spots
on the map: in Eastern Europe, Soviet Russia, and in ex-colonial ter-
ritories in Latin America, the Caribbean, Africa and Asia. Given this,
should it come as a surprise that some of the great poets of modern
times have emerged from the blank spots? Poets such as Witold Gombrowicz, Zbigniew Herbert, Tadeusz Rozewicz, Anna Swir, Anna
Akhmatova and Osip Mandelstam, whose work Heaney too explores in his book, adding for good measure Pablo Neruda and Derek
Walcott.

Recognizing Our True Desires

We see, then, that poets have indeed been witness to the omnipresent gloom of the twentieth century. 'How did it happen,' Milosz asks, 'that to be a poet of the twentieth century means to receive training in every kind of pessimism, sarcasm, bitterness, doubt?' This gloom, he says, answering his own question, owed something to 'the victorious scientific *Weltanschauung*' and to the nihilism resulting from religion having been 'hollowed out from inside', the idea being that art would replace it as 'the only dwelling place of the sacred'.[4]

Elsewhere in his book Milosz draws on the sentiments of a distant relative, Oscar Milosz (1877–1939), who defined poetry as 'a companion of man since his beginnings', '[a] passionate pursuit of the Real ... bound more rigorously than any other mode of expression to the spiritual and physical Movement of which it is the generator and a guide ... fully aware of its terrible responsibilities, the mysterious movements of the great soul of the people ... the incessant transformations of religious, political and social thought'.[5]

Czeslaw Milosz makes a rather different second point: that modern poetry, as well as serving as a witness (and therefore as a warning), builds on that fact – partly by means of its continued existence – to offer what the pragmatists also argue is the greatest virtue we can display in these troubled times: hope. That beauty continues to be made is a form of hope, Milosz says. He surveys briefly the more negative aspects of modern culture, from Dostoevsky forward, to the dystopian science fiction of H.G. Wells, the totalitarian dystopias of Yevgeny Zamyatin and Aldous Huxley, the decadence of the various bohemias, existentialism, above all perhaps the cruelties of the First World War.

And he does this in order to make a point not often made: 'It should be remembered,' he writes, that after the disasters of the Great War 'the next war was envisioned as a poison-gas war, and the Yperite, or mustard gas, employed at the end of World War I at Ypres, became a symbol like the atomic bomb later on. Here ... the prophecies proved not quite correct. When the next world war broke out, its horrors were of a sort unforeseen by anyone, and neither side made use of gas on the battlefield.'

Introducing this idea of failed prophecies leads him to what he sees as an even bigger failure, that of democracy itself, which he characterizes as 'a model taken by Rousseau from the assemblies of the entire population of a small Swiss canton'. His real point is that democracy 'has shown little ability to expand beyond its area of origin' (he was writing in 1983). No less important, more often than not its rulers 'appear as an incarnation of a general will that, if left to itself, would not know its own true desires'. And this, it would appear, is Milosz's overriding point: that the more reliable witness of poetry offers the best hope for recognizing our true desires.

Here he is on his friend the Polish writer Witold Gombrowicz, who died in 1969. Amid all the misery of the twentieth century, Gombrowicz declared himself to be like the baritone in Beethoven's 'Choral Symphony' who says: 'Friends, enough of this song. Let more joyous melodies be heard.' He plays down alienation: 'Alienation? No, let us try to admit that this alienation is not so bad, that we have it in our fingers, as pianists say . . . [to] give the workers almost as many free and marvellous holidays a year as work days.' Then the other nightmares of the modern condition: 'Emptiness? The absurdity of existence? Nothingness? Don't let's exaggerate. A god or ideals are not necessary to discover supreme values. We only have to go for three days without eating anything for a crumb to become our supreme god: it is needs that are at the basis of our values, of the sense and order of our lives.' And 'Atomic bombs? Some centuries ago, we died before we were thirty – plagues, poverty, witches, Hell, Purgatory, tortures . . . Haven't your conquests gone to your head? Have you forgotten what we were yesterday?'

Yesterday is important to Milosz. For him, the poet was and is set apart in that poets presuppose the existence of an ideal reader, 'and the poetic act both anticipates the future and speeds its coming'. In that future, he thought, we would see a return to history as a source of identity and transcendence, using that word in a specific sense. 'Daring to make a prediction, I expect, perhaps quite soon, in the twenty-first century, a radical turning away from the *Weltanschauung* marked principally by biology, and this will result from a newly acquired historical consciousness. Instead of presenting man through those traits that link him to higher forms of the evolutionary chain, other of his aspects will be stressed: the exceptionality, strangeness, and loneliness of that creature mysterious to itself, a being incessantly transcending its own limits. Humanity will be increasingly turning back to itself, increasingly contemplating its entire past, searching for a key to its own enigma . . . A one-dimensional man wants to acquire new dimensions by putting on the masks and dress, the manners of feeling and thinking of other epochs.'[6]

At pains to show that poetry is at the forefront (another reason for hope, another *form* of hope), he asserts that what is new is that our future will not be determined by jets as the means of transport, or by a decrease in infant mortality, important as those things may be. 'It is determined by humanity's emergence as a new elemental force; until now humanity had been divided into castes distinguished by dress, mentality, and mores.' This transformation is causing the disappearance of certain mythic notions, 'widespread in the last century, about the specific and presumably eternal features of the peasant, worker and intellectual. Humanity as an elemental force, the result of technology and mass education, means that man is opening up to science and art on an unprecedented scale.'[7] Is the disappearance of religion in our lives any different from the disappearance of some of those other nineteenth-century myths, embodied in imperialism, racial superiority and colonialism? he asks. No one mourns *their* passing and no one foresees their return.

Our Achievements and Our Limits

Milosz is saying that the best way to understand humanity is historically, that the way man has historically transcended his limitations is the only form of transcendence available, and that we should not ignore the many ways in which, throughout history, life has got better – more fulfilling and, yes, more meaningful – for countless ordinary people, in more or less ordinary ways. Only by understanding humanity's historical achievements and limits can we hope to extend – transcend – those limits in our lifetime by our own achievements.

And it is in the nature of things, he insists, that 'reflection by a well-stocked mind' offers the best hope of recording and describing those limits and achievements – 'the poetic act both anticipates the future and speeds its coming'.

We are fortunate in having at least two sets of reflections by well-stocked minds that address our subject. These are Iris Murdoch's *Metaphysics as a Guide to Morals* (1992) and George Steiner's *Real Presences* (1989) and *Grammars of Creation* (2001).

Murdoch trained as a philosopher, and as a novelist she was particularly 'exercised' by art. These two she brought together in *Metaphysics*, arguing that 'moral philosophy should attempt to retain a central concept' – the concept of transcendence. She was convinced that transcendence, 'in some form or other', belongs with morality, adding that we need to retain 'a metaphysical position but no metaphysical form'. Above all, 'the Good is certainly transcendent'.

Looking around her, she felt compelled to say that 'there is more than this', and went on to plead that philosophers 'try to invent a terminology which shows our natural psychology can be altered by conceptions which lie beyond its range ... the Platonic metaphor of the Good provides a suitable picture here'. 'God does not and cannot exist. But what led us to conceive him does exist and is constantly experienced and pictured. That is, it is real as an idea, and also incarnate in knowledge and work and love.' We can all receive moral help 'by focusing our attention on things which are valuable: virtuous people, great art ... the idea of Good itself'. Moreover, 'Beauty is the visible and accessible aspect of the Good. The Good is not itself visible.'

She is convinced that the Good finds 'empirically discoverable' incarnation in great works of art. This contemplation, she says, is 'an entry into (and not just an analogy of) the good life', since it involves 'the checking of selfishness in the interests of the real.' When we read Shakespeare or Tolstoy, two of her perennial favourites, 'we learn something of the real quality of human nature ... with a clarity which does not belong to the self-centred rush of ordinary life'. Murdoch says that art cannot be altered or possessed by us, and that in itself is liberating. And it is important because '[e]thics means the annihilation of self before the irreducibility of other people'. It is the serious and successful novel that can 'deliver us from the tyranny of ourselves', and this informs her criticism, too. T.S. Eliot, she says, doesn't want us 'to attend to other people' – he wishes us to attend to God.[8] In successful art we contemplate in quietness something whose authority makes us unaware of ourselves. An artist is someone who lets others *be* through him.

George Steiner's well stocked mind is everywhere evident in his work. He is a passionate worshipper of high art, in an old-fashioned way, as if from a time when high art really mattered. High-art names teem across his pages – Van Gogh and King Lear, Mondrian and Chartres Cathedral, Paul Valéry and Henry Moore – corralled passionately into the 'speculative ordering' Steiner gives them. Though his books are ostensibly arguments or theories, as one critic said they are essentially statements of faith – Steiner wants high art to reclaim 'its primary importance and its primal power'.[9] His essential argument is that the special place high art should have in the hierarchy of human activities is religious in nature: 'great literature or painting or music are spiritual in their impulses, transcendent in their meanings, mysterious in their force'.

In Steiner's view we are living, metaphorically, in the Saturday between Good Friday and Easter Sunday, in effect a period of waiting between the death of God and his resurrection. Waiting and patience are part of the human condition, he says, for we have been waiting for centuries – for aeons – for signs of God's existence, and it is this waiting, this theological understanding of ourselves, without any certainty, that has given rise to our culture and is responsible for what we have achieved.

Since Nietzsche announced the death of God we have been living in a secondary world where art, with a few exceptions, has been taken over by journalism, by critics and the academy rather than by the artists themselves – worlds that are either trivial, consumer-driven, in too much of a hurry ('Fashion is the motor of death'), or scholastic in the medieval sense of arguing over minute issues that scarcely matter. During that time, he says, art has moved from mimesis to abstraction, and in doing so has lost its language. With the added impact of science and technology, literacy has been replaced by numeracy; a passion for words has been undone by an obsession with numbers.

For Steiner this is a major break, a fall, and a catastrophe. Our world is impoverished because we have lost the ability to 'respond responsibly' to art, the task having been taken over by secondary critics, so that the narrative of one art responding to another has been lost – 'The best readings of art are art.'[10] The process of artistic insight is not cumulative and self-corrective as the sciences are; art does not supersede art the way later science supersedes earlier science, and as such it is unsuited to the academy. Art is 'immediate' and 'free' in a way that science is not, one artwork does not necessarily 'verify' another; as William Blake put it, 'it is of the minute particular', its purpose is often intuitively self-evident but difficult – even impossible – to articulate. Art cannot be paraphrased, and there is no boundary to language.[11]

For this reason Steiner proposes that *poiesis*, the act and experienced act of creation, is the fundamental aspect of being and of meaning. Moreover, the concept of transcendence brings us up against the even more fundamental concept of the 'other', and this is what God is, above everything else. It is this radical difference of God, and the uncertainty surrounding 'him', that inclines us to make intuitive leaps, to search for forms of words that can nevertheless only approximate the 'other', that make indeterminacy 'pivotal': part of the point of *poiesis* is mystery.

Steiner's point is that, rather than criticism, whether academic or journalistic, the spiritual in art can best – and perhaps only – be had from studying the *chain* of artworks; that watching the response of one great figure in the modern world to another in the ancient (that is, the religious world) is the closest we can come to the spiritual and the sacred: Nietzsche on and 'against' Wagner, Proust face to face with Vermeer, Mandelstam reading Dante, Karl Barth labouring after Mozart. These transformations as between successive figures – secular artists responding to religious ones – are the greatest opportunity we have to see how a secular world can flourish. The *bond* between the former and the latter is what we should seek to identify, describe and understand. It is the best way to assimilate what has been lost and to see how it might be recovered.

For Steiner the problem with science is that it is not disinterested;

as Heidegger said, it aims at mastery, whereas art does not. There may be eternal truths in science; but though we ourselves will not live for ever, an aesthetic truth that quickens 'into lit presence the continuum between temporality and eternity' has a metaphysical resonance even if it isn't purely religious. An aesthetic observation that will be good for all time gives us a warm feeling of completion that science, for all its strength, does not.

Despite this, and perhaps a little regretfully, Steiner notes that, although religion may have informed art in the past with what was felt to be a 'real presence', this can no longer suffice. Not just because God is dead, but because, throughout history, art has been a form of *dialogue*, a much more practical and immediate and even productive form of dialogue than, say, prayer is. He shows, by his many references to the ways in which different artists pay homage to one another in their work, by his assertion that no work of art is autonomous and that that realization is one of the secrets – perhaps *the* secret – of art appreciation, that the conversation of mankind through its major works of art is the path to truth and beauty. And the way later works of art build on earlier works – with courtesy, hospitality and even love – is a model of interaction for the rest of us in a secular world. By studying this progression, by immersing ourselves in high art, we can achieve a 'transformative intensity' in our lives that is available nowhere else.

A Premonition of Harmonies Desired

As Steiner would readily concede, both religion and science are great universal enterprises. Science seeks understanding via laws that apply at all times and everywhere. Religion seeks and offers a metaphysical unity on the grounds that this is what people want, that the certainty of an underlying unifying idea – the Absolute – is the most satisfying and rewarding experience of 'Reality' that is available for many. We find that Czeslaw Milosz's perspective is a valuable corrective to both these statements: that the value of science, for most people, lies in its specific technological achievements rather than its universal laws; and that what we might call metaphysical fulfilment is for many a luxury, and comes a distant second in the scheme of things compared with the everyday requirements of living.

Milosz, in fact, is saying something not dissimilar to what James Joyce said: '[I]f we lived down to fact, as primitive man had to do, we would be better off. That is what we were made for. Nature is quite unromantic. It is we who put romance into her, which is a false attitude, an egotism.' Heaney concurs, except that he is also saying, as are Milosz and Joyce, that living down to fact is not, in any way, as Charles Taylor might be tempted to observe, a 'subtraction story'. Quite the contrary: the *authority* of poetry, the conviction with which it speaks, the unflinching accuracy with which it addresses the world, are part – even a large part – of the joy of living. It is part of the point of poetry to explore the limits of our world, and part of its achievement to transcend those limits. This is the best – and maybe the only – form of transcendence available.

As a preparation and explanation of what poetry is, and seeks to be, and how it brings meaning to our lives, and what *type* of meaning, Heaney can hardly be bettered: '[A poem] begins in delight, it inclines to the impulse, it assumes direction with the first line laid down, it runs a course of lucky events and ends in a clarification of life – not necessarily a great clarification, such as sects and cults are founded on, but in a momentary stay against confusion ... in its repose the poem gives us a premonition of harmonies desired and not inexpensively achieved. In this way, the order of art becomes an achievement intimating a possible order beyond itself, although its relation to that further order remains promissory rather than obligatory. Art is not an inferior reflection of some ordained heavenly system but a rehearsal of it in earthly terms; art does not trace the given map of a better reality but improvises an inspired sketch of it.'[12]

There are two points here that relate directly to our theme. One, that poetry offers clarification that is 'not necessarily great', and two, that art intimates a possible order beyond itself.

First, Heaney is considering the *size* of poetry and its relation to the size of life, both the size of an individual life and the size of 'life' in general. This is important because even a short poem can have a 'big' subject and because, as James Wood has said, the idea of 'one overbearing truth' is exhausted in our time, meaning that poetry, the poetic approach, is, at least in theory, more relevant and important than ever before. And although Heaney is admirably ambitious for poetry, he is also quite content for its concerns and abilities to be on the small side, the human scale, not the superhuman. He speaks of poets providing us with 'the shimmer of reality', 'cadences that drink at spots of time'. Osip Mandelstam's poems are represented as nuggets of harmony, the details 'clear as rivets brightened by the punch'. Heaney quotes the Polish poet Anna Swir: 'For one moment [the poet] possesses wealth usually inaccessible to him, and he loses it when that moment is over.' Elsewhere, he likens poetry to the clapper in a bell. Poetry is the experience of being 'at the same time summoned and released'. He praises Auden for his 'defamiliarizing abruptness', and early Auden he likens to the shock of bare wire.[13]

He quotes Robert Lowell in his epoch-making *Life Studies*: 'A poem is an event, not the record of an event'; the language of a poem should be 'a bolt of clarification', 'a "momentary stay against confusion" in the discovery of a firmly verified outline'. Speaking of Lowell's mature works: 'A sense of something utterly completed vied with a sense of something startled into scope and freedom. The reader was permitted the sensation of a whole meaning simultaneously clicking shut and breaking open, a momentary illusion that the fulfilments which were being experienced in the ear spelled out meanings and fulfilments available in the world.' In Sylvia Plath's verses, he says, there is a sense of 'surprised arrival'; in her later poems, a 'sudden in-placeness about the words and all that they stand for', which recalls Wallace Stevens's definition of poetry as 'sounds passing through sudden rightnesses'. Elsewhere, Heaney says, Plath's work had 'unprecedented pitch and scald'.[14]

Heaney says of Philip Larkin's *The Whitsun Weddings*: '[T]he concluding lines constitute an epiphany, an escape from the "scrupulous meanness" of the disillusioned intelligence.' Yet while Larkin is exemplary in the way he sifts the conditions of contemporary life, refuses alibis and pushes consciousness towards an exposure that is neither cynicism nor despair, 'there survives in him a repining love for a more crystalline reality to which he might give allegiance. When that repining finds expression, something opens and moments occur which deserve to be called visionary.'[15]

It is in the nature of poetry to be short. If we agree with James Wood that a poem is 'the most realised form of intention', then brevity becomes an important part of the point. Heaney's claims for poetry, for the government of the tongue (and other poets have made equivalent claims), become in this way also a claim for the poetic aesthetic, for the fact and promise of brevity. In this way poetry does not become the only way to regard life, but it does become the pithiest and *richest* way to marry experience, language and meaning. It highlights the point that new experience, the experience of new knowledge, is, by definition, invariably brief. The knowledge stays with us, but the first encounter with – and the apprehension of – such knowledge happens immediately. Immediacy is the point of phenomenology. Immediacy equals intensity. Intensity is one of the purposes of life.

Auden's Quarrel with Meaning

All this has important consequences for the very nature of meaning: namely, that there is no single 'big' answer to the meaning of all life, but only a series of 'small' answers to parts of it, and that over time we may accumulate them, to form our own well stocked minds.

The fulfilments of poetry *are* its meanings (plural). In *The Government of the Tongue*, Heaney devotes many pages to W.H. Auden whom, he reminds us, the Nobel Prize-winning Russian poet Joseph Brodsky described as 'the greatest intelligence of the twentieth century'. For Auden, Heaney says, 'poetry could be regarded as magical incantation, fundamentally a matter of sound and the power of sound to bind our minds' and bodies' apprehensions within an acoustic complex; on the other hand, poetry is a matter of making wise and true meanings, of commanding our emotional assent by the intelligent disposition and inquisition of human experience. In fact, most poems – including Auden's – constitute temporary stays against the confusion [a phrase Heaney uses several times] ... We want a poem to be beautiful, that is to say, a verbal earthly paradise, a timeless world of pure play which

gives us delight precisely because of its contrast to our historical existence . . . and a poet cannot bring us any truth without introducing into
his poetry the problematic, the painful, the disorderly, the ugly.'[16]

All this, says Heaney, applies to other poets also, but where Auden
stood out was in his quarrel with meaning. 'To avoid the consensus
and settlement of a meaning which the audience fastens on like a security blanket, to be antic, mettlesome, contrary, to retain the right to
impudence, to raise hackles, to harry the audience into wakefulness –
to do all this may not only be permissible but necessary if poetry is to
keep on coming into a fuller life.'[17]

What this all implies, first, is that a fuller life is to be had not from
one portmanteau idea, as religions typically offer, as the idea of one
God offers, and the idea of therapy often implies, but from a collection of altogether smaller ideas achieved piecemeal, by poems or other
works of art, or conversations with others. It recalls George Steiner's
arguments.

A Holiday from Rationality

To take up the second point: what order (if any) does poetry intimate
beyond itself? Not one single overriding order, of course, and any selection risks distortion. But a beginning can be made.

Perhaps the first thing to say is to underline what Michael Hamburger says in *his* prose book about poetry, repeating Baudelaire's
comment that poetry 'marches fraternally' between science and philosophy, and that the best way to embrace life and enjoy it, and to find
fulfilment within it, is via the process of what Jean-Paul Sartre called
'lyrical phenomenology'.[18] Science and philosophy are essentially
about what rational generalizations we can *agree* upon after observing
the world about us; and agreement, clearly, is something we enjoy and
which we find convincing; both agreement and being convinced are
rewarding pleasures and contribute to meaning.

Poetry explores the world piecemeal, *detail by detail*, as the poet
finds a form of words – what Heaney calls the 'jurisdiction of achieved
form' (itself a pleasure) – that marries observation *and emotion* in an

intuitive order that can be had in no other way, in which there is as much feeling as understanding. In doing so, poetry provides, as perhaps all art provides, what James Wood has called 'a holiday from rationality'. It follows from this that much of what poetry has to offer is what Hamburger refers to as 'minute realities', which echoes with Sartre's *petites heureuses* and with the idea of it being but a momentary stay against confusion.[19]

The Italian poet Eugenio Montale conveyed something of this in these lines:

> *Non sono*
> *che favilla d'un tirso. Bene lo so: bruciare,*
> *questio, non altro, è il mio significato.*

> I am no more
> than a spark from a beacon. Well do I know it: to burn,
> this, nothing else, is my meaning.

Is this as much as we can hope for? Poetry seeks to convince, by the accuracy of its form, but at its best it does much more. Here, perhaps the most fundamental experience that poetry has to offer, the order that it intimates, is in fact the *lack* of order, not only in the world but even in the individual, which may be the beginning of the real road to fulfilment.

Hamburger reminds us that W.B. Yeats strove to render 'the multiplicity of the self without loss of intensity'. Pablo Neruda begins his poem, 'Muchos somos' (We Are Many):

> Of the many men who I am, who we are,
> I cannot settle on a single one.

Ezra Pound put it this way: 'In the search for oneself, in the search for "sincere self-expression", one gropes, one finds some seeming verity. One says "I am this, that, or the other", and with the words scarcely uttered one ceases to be that thing.'[20]

In *The Elder Statesman*, T.S. Eliot has a character say:

I've been freed from the self that pretends to be someone
And in becoming no one, I begin to live.

All this recalls Keats's discovery of the 'negative capability' of poets, 'their chameleon mutability', one's need 'to make up one's mind about nothing, to let the mind be a thoroughfare for all thought not a select party', to have 'no identity', no fixed character, no fixed opinions.[21] And Faust: 'Two souls, alas, dwell in my breast apart.'

In *The Estate of Poetry* Milosz says:

The purpose of poetry is to remind us
how difficult it is to remain just one person.

Naming

Still sticking with Milosz, 'No science or philosophy can change the fact that a poet stands before reality that is every day new, miraculously complex, inexhaustible, and tries to enclose as much of it as possible in words. That elementary contact, verifiable by the five senses, is more important than any mental construction. The never-fulfilled desire to achieve a mimesis, to be faithful to a detail, makes for the health of poetry and gives it a chance to survive periods unpropitious to it. The very act of naming things presupposes a faith in their existence and thus in a true world, whatever Nietzsche might say.'[22]

And how creative naming can be. 'Objects, landscapes, events and people give me much pleasure,' says the French poet Francis Ponge, who died in 1988. 'They convince me completely. For the simple reason that they don't have to. Their presence, their concrete evidence, the solidity, their three dimensions, their palpable, not-to-be-doubted look . . . it is beautiful.'[23] Zbigniew Herbert agrees when he writes:

The pebble
is a perfect creature
equal to itself
mindful of its limits

filled exactly
with pebbly meaning

with a scent which does not remind one of anything
does not frighten anything away does not arouse desire . . .

Pebbles cannot be tamed
to the end they will look at us
with a calm and very clear eye

But naming means much more than this. It means recognizing phenomena in the world, not only pebbles and landscapes, but feelings, attitudes, emotions, relationships, that we have almost but not quite put into words. In such circumstances, naming *enlarges and warms* the world and our experience of it. Auden again:

If equal affection cannot be,
Let the more loving one be me.

Here we have a part of life named and, as Heaney said, clicking shut and breaking open at the same time.

Heaney informs us that Patrick Kavanagh's work has 'a direction rather than any sense of anxiety about the need for a destination'; it is not a response to 'some stimulus in the world out there' but, in a happy phrase, 'a spurt of abundance from a source within' that 'spills over to irrigate the world beyond the self'. Heaney compares the following poem to one of those Chagall paintings in which the characters are airborne in the midst of their own dream:

But satire is unfruitful prayer.
Only wild shoots of pity there,
And you must go inland and be
Lost in compassion's ecstasy,
Where suffering soars in a summer air –
The millstone has become a star.

The idea of suffering soaring, and in a summer air, is thoroughly counterintuitive, and yet when we encounter it we experience a sense, as in Plath's poetry, of surprised arrival.

We can find in definitions of poetry good and big things that have been said and which make us feel warm. Song and poetry 'have added to the volume of good in the world', poems are 'examples of self-conquest' and 'self-cleansing', they are 'experimental acts'; poetry is a repository of 'stored goodness' or, alternatively, 'stored pity'.

For Philip Larkin it is 'unfenced existence'. For Heaney poetry is more a threshold than a path, 'a break with the usual life but not an absconding from it'. For Auden it is something that makes us 'Taller Today' and can bring a peace which 'No bird can contradict'. For Wislawa Szymborska, Milosz tells us, poetry 'is no more than a broken whisper, quickly dying laughter'. For himself, Milosz says, one purpose of poetry is 'to give purer meaning to the words of the tribe', and in writing poetry, one 'bets everything one has'. The French poet Yves Bonnefoy is convinced that 'poetry has to do with truth and salvation', while for Robert Duncan it brings poets 'up against the limits of their own consciousness'. 'Poetry is the breath and finer spirit of all knowledge,' says Elizabeth Sewell. For Wallace Stevens, 'The poet is the priest of the invisible.'[24]

Poetry is all of these things and more, but let us concentrate here on the *activity* of poetry, rather than any individual poems, poetry as a way of approaching the world, as a form of knowledge, even as a form of living. By doing so we find four elements that together add up to the activity of poetry and help us understand its meaning. Three of these we have already met. The act of naming the inexhaustible features of the world about us is, as Milosz puts it, the 'eternally insatiable' appetite of poetry and those three elements – the activity of naming, the inexhaustibility of the features/facts of the world, and the insatiable appetite of poetry (Larkin's 'Enormous Yes') – together comprise a meaning, to which we need to add one other element: that poetry, like all art, is 'disinterested'.

The Spanish poet Juan Ramón Jiménez emphasized the special place of poetry. 'Literature is a state of culture,' he wrote, 'poetry a state of grace, before and after culture.' He thought that the primacy of the imagination in poetry 'forbids the total integration and assimilation of poetic values into any social or cultural order that exists in the modern world'. Gottfried Benn insisted that poetry is 'addressed to no one', and denied that it can have any public function. 'Works of art,' he wrote in 1930, 'are phenomena, historically ineffective, without practical consequences. That is their greatness.'[25] 'Works of art endanger no one,' says Seamus Heaney, 'they are benign', and we all 'have rights-of-way' in published poems. One of the points of art, says Iris Murdoch, is its independence of us, an independence 'that cannot be altered or possessed by us'. Part of the attraction of art, says James Wood, is that it 'is not in any racket'.[26]

Naming the world means describing it in ever more accurate detail, so that we know more of it today than yesterday and can hope to know more tomorrow, always appreciating that there is no 'agenda' to discover, no specific destination to aim for, that pleasure lies in the *inexhaustibility* of the details of the world, and that very inexhaustibility fuels our appetite for more. On this account, both phenomenology and poetry mean 'more'.

'There Is More to Life than We Ever Imagined'

In 1998, in an article called 'Pragmatism and Romanticism', the American philosopher Richard Rorty tried to restate the argument of Shelley's 'Defence of Poetry': 'At the heart of Romanticism . . . was the claim that reason can only follow paths that the imagination has first broken. No words, no reasoning. No imagination, no new words. No such words, no moral or intellectual progress.' Rorty contrasted the poet's ability to give us a richer language with the philosopher's attempt to acquire non-linguistic access to the 'really real'. He described Plato's dream of such access as itself an act of great poetic achievement but, he said, by Shelley's time 'it was dreamt out'. He went on, 'We are now more able than Plato was to acknowledge our finitude – to admit that we shall never be in touch with something greater than ourselves. We hope instead that human life here on earth will become richer as the centuries go by because the language used by our remote descendants will have more resources than ours did. Our vocabulary will stand to theirs as that of our primitive ancestors stands to ours.'

He was using 'poetry', Rorty said, in 'an extended sense'. 'I stretched Harold Bloom's term "strong poet" to cover prose writers who had invented new language games for us to play – people like Plato, Newton, Marx, Darwin and Freud, as well as versifiers like Milton and Blake. These games might involve mathematical equations, or inductive arguments, or dramatic narratives, or (in the case of the versifiers) prosodic innovation. But the distinction between prose and verse was irrelevant to my philosophical purposes.'

In an earlier essay, 'The Inspirational Value of Great Works of Literature', Rorty presented a polemic against the postmodern approach to literature (see chapter 26), which he felt was transforming the study of great literature into 'cultural studies' – 'one more dismal social science' in which context was all and such concepts as 'charisma' and 'genius' no longer have any place. He quoted with distaste from Fredric Jameson's *Postmodernism, or The Cultural Logic of Late Capitalism*: '[The] new order no longer needs prophets and seers of the high modernist and charismatic type, whether among its cultural products or its politicians. Such figures no longer hold any charm or magic . . . woe to the country that needs geniuses, prophets, Great Writers, or demiurges!'

Rorty flatly disagreed with this view. He believed that there is such a thing as Great Literature and its role is to be 'inspirational'. He quoted from an essay by the writer Dorothy Allison, 'Believing in Literature', in which she referred to her 'atheist's religion', a religion shaped by literature and 'her own dream of writing': 'There is a place where we are always alone with our mortality, where we must simply have something greater than ourselves to hold on to – God or history or politics or literature or a belief in the healing power of love, or even righteous anger. Sometimes I think they are all the same. A reason to believe, a way to take the world by the throat and insist that there is more to this life than we have ever imagined.'[27]

And this is what Rorty meant by inspirational literature, that which makes people 'think there is more to life than they ever imagined'. 'Inspirational value is typically *not* produced by the operations of a method, a science, a discipline, or a profession . . . If it is to have inspirational value, a work must be allowed to recontextualise much of what you previously thought you knew . . . Just as you cannot be swept off your feet by another human being at the same time that you recognize him or her as a good specimen of a certain type, so you cannot be simultaneously be inspired by a work and be knowing about it.' He believed that people have been 'saved' by books: 'They are people whose motto is Wordsworth's "What we have loved/ Others will love, and we will teach them how."'

He shared an aspiration, he said, with Matthew Arnold: 'the hope for a religion of literature, in which works of the secular imagination replace Scripture as the principal source of inspiration and hope for each new generation. We should cheerfully admit that canons are temporary, and touchstones replaceable. But this should not lead us to discard the idea of greatness. We should see great works of literature as great because they have inspired many readers, not as having inspired many readers because they are great.'[28]

Not long after he had completed his essay on 'Pragmatism and Romanticism', Party received the devastating news that he had inoperable pancreatic cancer. Not long after that, he was drinking coffee with one of his sons and a visiting cousin. The cousin, a Baptist minister, was prompted to ask him if he had found his thoughts drifting to religious topics. No, said Rorty. 'Well, what about philosophy?' his son asked. No, he said. His son persisted: 'Hasn't *anything* you've read been of use?' And then Rorty blurted out that, yes, poetry had been of use. When asked which poems in particular, he quoted two old 'chestnuts' that he had 'dredged up' from memory and been 'oddly cheered by'. One, from Swinburne's 'Garden of Proserpine':

> We thank with brief thanksgiving
> Whatever gods may be
> That no life lives for ever;
> That dead men rise up never;
> That even the weariest river
> Winds somewhere safe to sea.

and the other, from Landor's 'On His Seventy-Fifth Birthday':

> Nature I loved, and next to nature, Art;
> I warmed both hands before the fire of life,
> It sinks, and I am ready to depart.

Rorty said he found comfort 'in those slow meanders and those stuttering embers', and added, 'I suspect that no comparable effect could have been produced by prose. Not just imagery, but also rhyme and rhythm were needed to do the job. In lines such as these, all three conspire to produce a degree of compression, and thus of impact, that only verse can achieve. Compared to the shaped charges contrived by versifiers, even the best prose is scattershot.'

Rorty confessed that he wished he had spent more of his life with verse. 'This is not because I fear having missed out on truths that are incapable of statement in prose. There are no such truths; there is nothing about death that Swinburne and Landor knew but Epicurus and Heidegger failed to grasp. Rather, it is because I would have lived life more fully if I had been able to rattle off more old chestnuts – just as I would have if I had made more close friends. [Remember Oscar Milosz described poetry as 'a companion of man since his beginnings'.] Cultures with richer vocabularies are more fully human – farther removed from the beasts – than those with poorer ones; individual men and women are more fully human when their memories are amply stocked with verse.'[29]

25

'Our Spiritual Goal Is the Enrichment
of the Evolutionary Epic'

In the Preface to *Unweaving the Rainbow: Science, Delusion and the Appetite for Wonder* (1998) Richard Dawkins, then Oxford's Professor for the Public Understanding of Science, recounted two incidents that in part prompted him to write his new book. One concerned an unnamed foreign publisher who had told him that, after reading his first book *The Selfish Gene* (1976), he could not sleep for three nights, so troubled was he by its 'cold, bleak message'. The other story concerned a teacher 'from a distant country' who had written to him reproachfully that a pupil had come to him in tears after reading the same book 'because it had persuaded her that life was empty and purposeless. He advised her not to show the book to any of her friends, for fear of contaminating them with the same nihilistic pessimism.'

Dawkins then went on to quote from his colleague Peter Atkins's book, *The Second Law* (1984): 'We are the children of chaos, and the deep structure of change is decay. At root, there is only corruption, and the unstemmable tide of chaos. Gone is purpose; all that is left is direction. This is the bleakness we have to accept as we peer deeply and dispassionately into the heart of the Universe.'[1]

Dawkins comments: '[S]uch very proper purging of saccharine false purpose; such laudable tough-mindedness in the debunking of cosmic sentimentality must not be confused with the loss of personal hope. Presumably there is indeed no purpose in the ultimate fate of the cosmos, but do any of us really tie our life's hopes to the ultimate fate of the cosmos anyway? Of course we don't; not if we are sane. Our lives are ruled by all sorts of closer, warmer, human ambitions and perceptions. To accuse science of robbing life of the warmth that makes it worth living is so preposterously mistaken, so diametrically opposite to my own feelings and those of most working scientists, I am almost driven to the despair of which I am wrongly suspected.'

On the contrary, he wanted to convey the sense of awed wonder that science can give us and which makes it 'one of the highest experiences of which the human psyche is capable'.[2]

The title of Dawkins's book comes from a poem by Keats, who believed that Isaac Newton had destroyed all the poetry of the rainbow by reducing it to the prismatic colours. Dawkins did not accept this argument. He insisted that scientists and scientifically literate people everywhere who can read Keats as well as Newton have two ways of experiencing and understanding rainbows, not one, and that must be an advance.

He then set about demonstrating his own wonder at the natural world and the cosmos, ranging from bacteria, insect ears, birdsong, the rings in the trunks of sequoias, cuckoos and their habits with eggs, to snail polymorphism and much else. Along the way he dismissed paranormal activities, astrology, all forms of superstition and gullibility. He peppered his text with poems – some good, some indifferent – in a fulsome attempt to show that an appreciation of science in no way compromises enjoyment of poetry, not least because '[s]cience allows mystery but not magic'.[3] That, in fact, an awareness of scientific inaccuracies in literature was and is another form of poetic appreciation.

At the end he made a claim for what he calls 'poetic science': the notion that a Keats and a Newton, listening to each other, 'might hear the galaxies sing'. Thanks to language, which separates us from the other animals, '[w]e can get outside the universe . . . in the sense of putting a model of the universe inside our skulls. Not a superstitious, small-minded, parochial model filled with spirits and hobgoblins, astrology and magic, glittering with fake crocks of gold where the rainbow ends. A big model, worthy of the reality that regulates, updates and tempers it; a model of stars and great distances, where Einstein's noble spacetime curve upstages the curve of Yahweh's covenantal bow and cuts it down to size ... The spotlight passes but, exhilaratingly, before it does so it gives us time to comprehend something of this place in which we fleetingly find ourselves and the reason that we do so. We are alone among the animals in foreseeing our end. We are also alone among animals in being able to say before we die: Yes, this is why it was worth coming to life in the first place.[4]

In the past few decades, both evolutionary biologists like Dawkins and cosmologists – physicists and astronomers – have mounted a spirited attack on the basic dimensions of religion, in particular the main monotheisms, and in doing so have tried hard to reshape what – for the sake of a better phrase – we may call our spiritual predicament.

The collective achievements of these two sciences have been three-fold. First, they have sought to show that religions are themselves entirely natural phenomena; they have evolved, like so much else, and from this it follows that our *moral* life is also a natural (evolved) phenomenon, not rooted in any divine realm or mind. In this sense, the details of evolution teach us how to live together without any reference to God. Nothing is put in his place, because nothing is needed. Second, science has discovered – or reconfigured – some new aspects of the human condition, which provide us with principles for arranging our affairs for the greater benefit of the greatest number. Again, there is no need of God. Third, evolutionary biology and cosmology have given us some radically new ideas as to what the organizing principle(s) underpinning the universe are. Some have gone so far as to call these new principles divine in themselves, but many others see them as entirely natural features of the natural world.

Some of these innovations are controversial, some are fantastical (part of their point being to gain our attention), and some are contradictory. They bring us up to date.

The Concept of Cultural Health

Richard Dawkins is probably the most controversial figure in the current debate between science and religion. In *Unweaving the Rainbow* he sought to show that a scientific approach to creation can be just as 'awesome' and fulfilling as religious belief. In *The Blind Watchmaker* (1986) he set himself two more objectives. First, to explain in the only way possible – as the result of thousands and thousands of incremental evolutionary advances – the great biological complexity we see around us. And second, to argue that, if complexity can arise only in this way, there is no need of a complex God in the first place – in fact, it is a contradiction in terms. He insists that 'Darwin made it possible to be an intellectually fulfilled atheist'.[5]

He returned to the attack in 2006 with *The God Delusion*. Here he repeated some of his arguments against God – for example, that God would have to be complex to create the evolutionary mechanism, so why would he need to create evolution to manufacture complexity all over again? He looked at the several projects that have subjected prayer to experimental verification – and found them severely wanting. He looked at the roots of morality and examined a number of religious stances, which he found suspect. For instance, he believed that hardly anyone any longer 'looked forward' (if they ever did) to the afterlife. So religion for him was a sham.

Dawkins didn't have much to say about how we should live without religion – he took it for granted that his own lifestyle as perceived via his writings was evidence enough – but in typically combative fashion he described several instances of individuals 'escaping' (his word) from their faith, to show that it could and can be done, and he published as an appendix a list of 'friendly addresses', mainly of humanist associations around the world, where people escaping from their Church could find refuge and intellectual support.[6]

In *Breaking the Spell: Religion as a Natural Phenomenon* (2006) Daniel Dennett, a philosopher at Tufts University and a colleague of Dawkins, argued that it was now time for religion 'as a global phenomenon' to be subject to multidisciplinary research, 'because religion is too important for us to remain ignorant about'.[7] Until now, he said, there has been a tacit agreement that scientists will leave religion alone, but with fundamentalist terrorism so widespread 'we are paying a terrible price for our ignorance'.[8] He pointed out that two or three religions come into existence *every day* and that their typical lifespan is less than a decade, with even the great monotheisms not being that long-lived by the standard of other human institutions – writing, say, which has been around for five thousand years, or agriculture, ten thousand, or language, hundreds of thousands of years.[9] By examining humans' need for intensity, for ritual, for attributing agency to anything that puzzles them, for finding patterns almost everywhere, for some people to assume the role of steward and others to cede it, he showed how folk religions evolved seamlessly into organized religions.

It is 'belief in belief' that really matters, Dennett asserted; many people don't actually believe many of the tenets of their religion (a belief in hell, say, or in the Golden Calf), but they do believe in the *concept* of God. Belief in belief is an elusive matter, but it has played an important role in the development, in the twentieth century in particular, of the concept of God as 'apophatic' – meaning that God is 'ineffable, unknowable, something beyond all human ken'.[10] He was particularly dismissive of this concept (made popular by Karl Barth in the 1920s).

He concluded by asking if people are right in thinking that the best way to live a good life is through religion; the world is 'sick and tired', he said, of the demonstrations of devotion by one fundamentalist terrorist or another.[11] The political agendas of fundamentalists and fanatics often exploit the organizational infrastructure of the religion they profess to belong to and their traditions of unquestioning loyalty. Al Qaeda and Hamas terrorism are Islam's responsibility.

In writing his book, he said, he had come across one widespread opinion, albeit expressed in a variety of ways: in essence, this was that 'man' has a 'deep need' for spirituality. 'What fascinates me about this delightfully versatile craving for "spirituality" is that people think they know what they are talking about, even though – or perhaps because – nobody bothers to explain what they mean.'

Dennett had three things to say about how we should live. The secret to spirituality had nothing to do with the soul, or anything supernatural – it was this: let your *self* go. 'If you can approach the world's complexities, both its glories and its horrors, with an attitude of humble curiosity, acknowledging that however deeply you have seen, you have only just scratched the surface, you will find worlds within worlds, beauties you could not heretofore imagine, and your own mundane preoccupations will shrink to *proper* size, not all that important in the great scheme of things. Keeping that awestruck vision of the world ready to hand while dealing with the demands of daily living is no easy exercise, but it is definitely worth the effort, for if you can stay *centred*, and *engaged*, you will find the hard choices easier, the right words will come to you when you need them, and you will indeed be a better person [italics in the original].'[12]

It was a matter of urgency, he thought, that people understand and accept evolutionary theory. 'I believe that their salvation may depend on it! How so? By opening their eyes to the dangers of pandemics, degradation of the environment, and loss of biodiversity, and by informing them about some of the foibles of human nature. So isn't my belief that belief in evolution is the path to salvation a religion? No . . . We who love evolution do not honor those whose love of evolution prevents them from thinking clearly and rationally about it! . . . In our view there is no safe haven for mystery or incomprehensibility . . . I feel a moral imperative to spread the word of evolution, but evolution is not my religion. I don't have a religion.'[13]

As indicative of another way forward, Dennett recommended the work of the British psychologist Nicholas Humphrey, who has pioneered, he said, the consideration of the ethical issues involved in deciding how to decide 'when and whether the teaching of a belief system to children is morally defensible'. Humphrey advocates teaching them about *all* the world's religions, 'in a matter-of-fact, historically and biologically informed way', just as we teach them about geography, history and mathematics. 'Let's get *more* education about religion in our schools, not less.' We should teach rituals and customs and the positive and negative aspects of religious history – the role of the Churches in the civil rights movement *and* the Inquisition. No religion should be favoured, and none ignored. And as we learn more about the psychological and biological basis of religion, this should be included too. 'The field of public health expanded to include cultural health will be the greatest challenge of the next century.'

In fact, Dennett's call for more research into religion overlooks the fact that this is already under way, most notably as recorded in David Sloan Wilson's *Darwin's Cathedral* (2002) which looks at a variety of religions – those of the Nuer, Dagara and Mbuti, of John Calvin's Geneva and of the Christian Koreans in Texas. He concludes that religions are adaptive units that form in order to access resources (often, material resources) that can only be obtained through coordinated group action. Catechisms and the concept of forgiveness can also be regarded as evolved phenomena, he claims.[14]

New Rules to Live By: Trust, Trade and a Tragic Vision

Sam Harris, in *The End of Faith: Religion, Terror, and the Future of Reason* (2004), mounted a coruscating attack on all religions, stating that both the Bible and the Koran contain 'mountains' of life-destroying gibberish; that the 'land' most terrorists are fighting over is not to be found in this world; and asking why God would make Shakespeare a better writer than himself. Science, he said, is gradually encompassing life's deepest questions and we are beginning to understand why humans flourish. We are beginning to understand, for instance, the role of the hormone oxytocin in the brain and its link with human well-being.

Thanks to such discoveries we will be able eventually to say, objectively, that there are right and wrong answers to moral questions, because once we put religion in its place, '[w]ell-being captures all that we can intelligibly value'.[15] Harris argued from the failures of the kibbutzim in Israel that some forms of social life are less moral than others; that conservative societies have higher rates of divorce, teenage pregnancy and pornography; that it is societies whose members are allowed to maximize themselves and others that are the most successful. We *are* changing morally, and improving, he emphasized – for instance, we are less prepared than we used to be to accept collateral damage in conflict situations. One of his prime conclusions was that 'There may be nothing more important than human cooperation.'

This was the conclusion, also, of Matt Ridley, a British polymath who combines being a scientist with a number of other roles, including chairman of a bank. In his book *The Origins of Virtue* (1996) he argued that 'moral sentiments are problem-solving devices to make highly social creatures [us] effective at using social relations to ensure their genes' long-term survival'. Moral life, he concluded, is based on the fact that 'selfish genes make us social, trustworthy and cooperative'. There was morality before the Church, trade before the state, exchange before money, social contracts before Hobbes, welfare before the rights of man, culture before Babylon, self-interest before Adam Smith, and greed before capitalism. The main element in cooperation, he said, is trust, 'a vital form of social capital'. Where authority replaces reciprocity, the sense of community fades. For trust to grow, we must reduce the power of the state and devolve our lives into parishes, computer networks, clubs and teams, self-help groups and small businesses – 'everything small and local'.

In *The Rational Optimist* (2010) Ridley argues that, in contrast to what many people think, in the last thousand years life expectancy has increased dramatically, indicators show a decrease in violence, and average income has increased exponentially. Humans are the only living beings, he points out, to have been able to continuously increase their quality of life. No other species with a prominent brain, such as dolphins, chimpanzees, octopuses and parakeets, have achieved this, so it cannot be simply a matter of brain size. His answer is trade. It is trade between *unrelated* parties that has increased our collective intelligence, to the benefit of all.[16] More open trade should be the faith of the future.

Steven Pinker, the Harvard psychologist, very largely agrees. In *The Blank Slate: The Modern Denial of Human Nature* (2002) he explored what he thought were humanity's greatest fears so far as human nature is concerned – the fear of inequality, the fear of imperfectibility, the fear of determinism and the fear of nihilism. Against this, religions have traditionally provided 'comfort, community and moral guidance' to countless people, and according to some biologists the sophisticated deism towards which many religions are evolving 'can be made compatible with an evolutionary understanding of mind and nature'.

Furthermore, with increasing knowledge our moral circle has in fact been expanding. Instead of religions focusing on their own kind, greater biological understanding has led to the entities worthy of moral consideration being 'poked outward' from the family and the village towards the clan, the tribe, the nation, the race and, most recently (as in the Universal Declaration of Human Rights), towards all of humanity. Nor will it stop there, as some seek to include within their orbit certain animals, zygotes, fetuses and the brain-dead. The latest cognitive science has agreed upon a list of 'core intuitions', he reports, on which we base our understanding, such as an intuitive physics, intuitive engineering and psychology, spatial and number sense, sense of probability and intuitive economics. We once had an intuitive sense of the soul, which it is no longer possible to reconcile with biology, and that means we now need to reconfigure our moral understanding, which is better understood as a system of trade-offs according to circumstances. This is, in effect, a return to situation ethics, first encountered in chapter 19.

Pinker himself tends towards a 'tragic' intuition of life, rather than a 'Utopian' one, which contains these elements at least: the primacy of family ties; the limited scope of sharing and reciprocity which leads to 'social loafing'; the universality of dominance, violence and ethnocentrism; the partial heritability of intelligence, conscientiousness and antisocial tendencies; the prevalence of defence mechanisms; biases in the moral sense towards preference of kin and friends; and a tendency to confuse morality with conformity, rank, cleanliness and beauty. In *The Better Angels of Our Nature: Why Violence Has Declined* (2011) Pinker identifies six periods in which violence decreased significantly, proving, he argues, that we *are* getting more moral.[17]

Though Pinker has been widely criticized, as was Ridley, for his Panglossian tendencies, and though Pinker thinks that the advent of a strong state has a lot to do with the decline in violence, he also believes that another major factor has been commerce, 'a game which everyone can win'. 'As technological progress allows the exchange of goods and ideas over longer distances and among larger groups of trading partners, other people become more valuable alive than dead. They switch from being targets of demonization and dehumanization to potential partners in reciprocal altruism.'

For Harris, Ridley and Pinker, then, moral progress has been and is being made, and it has nothing to do with religion and never has had. Trade is perhaps not usually pitched against religious values as much as science has been; but the effect is much the same. Trade is a horizontal activity, carried out between people on the same level, and by definition it is a this-worldly activity. Like most other human activities, it has evolved.

George Levine's aim is different, but not unrelated. In *Darwin Loves You* (2006) he aims to introduce us to a 'kinder, gentler' Darwin, a man who was a romantic at heart, a nature lover, a man who helps us understand the world as a more – not less – enchanted place. Through Darwin, he says, we get a deep sense of the power of nature, which he equates to a religious feeling, going so far as to say that evolutionary theory is a form of nature worship – and a 'more effective' one because it embodies a different *relation* to nature, one of which humans are a part rather than being somehow separate from it and receiving it as a gift from God, as Christianity has it.

He sees Darwin's attention to minutiae as a moral act, and a model, because 'this is where non-theistic enchantment begins'. He argues that Darwin's inspection of the 'lower' animals was important, for understanding hierarchy and the human place in nature.[18] Darwin's contribution was as both participant and observer – again, an excellent model. 'Darwin offers us no mysteries, no transcendence, but an earth that is room enough. We have been misled by 2,500 years of monotheism into expecting some larger meaning, meaning that is not material. That is too bad.'

Each of these biologists writes combative prose, born of a conviction that evolution is, as Dennett puts it, 'the most important idea, ever'. Indeed, they have been accused, as we shall see presently, of being the new dogmatists. But that hardly applies to the doyen of evolutionary biologists, the Harvard entomologist E.O. Wilson, who has been by far the most inventive and positive evolutionist of modern times and also the most stylish writer.

Raised as a Southern Baptist in Alabama (where he read the Bible from cover to cover, twice), he lost his faith suddenly on being introduced as a young man to evolution. ('It seemed to me that the Book of Revelation might be black magic hallucinated by an ancient primitive.')

It also seemed to him that the biblical authors had missed the most important revelation of all – they had made no provision for evolution. 'Could it be,' he asked himself, 'that they were not really privy to the thoughts of God? Might the pastors of my childhood, good and loving men though they were, be mistaken?' It was all too much, and he was a Baptist no more.

Even so, he had no immediate desire to purge himself totally of his religious feelings. 'I also retained a small measure of common sense. To wit, people must belong to a tribe; they yearn to have a purpose larger than themselves. We are obliged by the deepest drives of the human spirit to make ourselves more than animated dust, and we must have a story to tell about where we came from, and why we are here. Could Holy Writ be just the first literate attempt to explain the universe and make ourselves significant within it? Perhaps science is a continuation on new and better-tested ground to attain the same end.'[19]

Viewed in one way, Wilson is as uncompromising as his biologist colleagues, but he also has the distinction of coining three words that were to prove influential, and which address our subject. These were 'sociobiology', 'biophilia' and 'consilience'. 'In *Sociobiology* (1975) he proposed that the biological principles which we now know govern animal life could be profitably applied to human societies. But if these premises were correct, he insisted, then humans were presented with two great spiritual dilemmas. 'The first is that no species, ours included, possesses a purpose beyond the imperatives created by its genetic history. [Everything,] even the capacities to select particular aesthetic judgements and religious beliefs[,] must have arisen by the same mechanistic approaches [that is, according to biological principles] . . . The first dilemma, in a word, is that we have no particular place to go. The species lacks any goal external to its own biological nature . . . Educated people everywhere like to believe that beyond material needs lie fulfilment and the realization of individual potential. But what is fulfilment, and to what ends may potential be realized? Traditional religious beliefs have been eroded, not so much by humiliating disproofs of their mythologies as by the growing awareness that beliefs are really enabling mechanisms for survival. Religions, like other human institutions, evolve so as to enhance the persistence and influence of their practitioners.'

The similarities between the early civilizations of Egypt, Mesopotamia, India, China, Mexico and Central and Southern America, he said, cannot be explained away as the products of chance or cross-fertilization. The way that chronic meat shortages in history have (allegedly) shaped religious beliefs, why certain animals are treated as sacred, the way that inmates in prisons organize themselves into extended 'families', with surrogate mothers, fathers, aunts and uncles – all this suggests, he says, a 'stubborn core of biological urgency'. Although, as he puts it, God's immanence has been pushed to somewhere below the subatomic particles or beyond the furthest visible galaxy, thanks to the relentless advances of science new theories of what God is still keep coming. But, Wilson adds, mankind has produced, according to one authoritative account, in the order of a hundred thousand religions, a statistic that depresses him: 'Men, it appears, would rather believe than know.'[20]

The practice of religion, he acknowledges, is one of the major categories of human behaviour that is unique to the human species and constitutes a major challenge to sociobiology, because religion requires individuals to subordinate immediate self-interest to the interests of the group, meaning that they operate by motivations that are partly rational and partly emotional. 'When the Gods are served, the Darwinian fitness of the members of the tribe is the ultimate if unrecognized beneficiary.' Wilson suggests that there is a genetic predisposition to conformity and consecration because the highest forms of religious practice 'can be seen to confer biological advantage', not least in the sacralization of identity, in which myths of origin 'explain a little bit of how nature works and why the tribe has a favoured position on earth'. He goes on to note, what other scholars have noted since, that belief in high gods is not universal, that the concept of a high god most commonly arises with a pastoral way of life: '[T]he greater the dependence on herding, the more likely the belief in a shepherd God of the Judeo-Christian type.'

Religion is a sociobiological/anthropological category, not a theological one. This is our second great spiritual dilemma.

Religion without Theology

This biological explanation of faith in God, says Wilson, leads to the crux: the role of mythology in modern life. We now live with three great myths: Marxism, traditional religion and scientific materialism (he was writing in 1979).

The mythology of scientific materialism was for Wilson the most powerful. Until now it 'has always, point for point in zones of conflict, defeated traditional religion. Its narrative form is the epic: the evolution of the universe from the Big Bang of fifteen million years ago through the origin of the elements and celestial bodies to the beginnings of life on earth ... Most importantly, we have come to the crucial stage in the history of biology when religion itself is subject to explanations of the natural sciences.' As a result, he says, 'theology is not likely to survive as an independent intellectual discipline. But religion itself will endure for a long time as a vital force in society.'

Because the evolutionary epic denies both immortality to the individual and divine privilege to the society, he thought that humanists could never enjoy 'the hot pleasures of spiritual conversion and self surrender'. Therefore, he asked, '[D]oes a way exist to divert the power of religion into the services of the great new enterprise that lays bare the source of that power?'

His answer: hope. The hope of the future resided in the laying of a proper foundation for the social sciences so that they would be consistent with the findings of biology. Although natural selection has been the prime mover, it works through a cascade of decisions based on secondary values that have historically served as enabling mechanisms for survival and reproductive success. 'These values are defined to a large extent by our most intense emotions: enthusiasm and a sharpening of the senses from exploration; exaltation from discovery; triumph in battle and competitive sports; the restful satisfaction from an altruistic act well and truly placed; the stirring of ethnic and national pride; the strength from family ties; and the secure biophilic pleasure from the nearness of animals and growing plants.'

The mind will always create morality, religion and mythology, he believed. Science is a myth because its truths can never be proved conclusively. Nonetheless, the scientific ethos is superior to religion: its repeated triumphs in 'explaining and controlling' the physical world, its self-correcting nature, and the possibility of explaining religion in an evolutionary sense, all means that 'the evolutionary epic is probably the best myth we will ever have ... Our spiritual goal is the enrichment of the evolutionary epic.'[21]

The Biophilia Revolution

In 1984 Wilson coined 'biophilia', an idea that grew out of his conviction as a biologist that the most important issue facing mankind – as the population increases, as technology proliferates, as more and more urban environments are created – is the loss of biodiversity. In his book of that title, published in 1988, he described many of the ecosystems of the world, in particular the rainforests, showing that many different species of animals and plants inhabit even relatively small areas, that they are interdependent, that it takes a long time for even a simple ecosystem to emerge and, most importantly, that once an ecosystem is destroyed it is almost impossible for it to recover. Wilson thought that we were destroying the natural world at a more catastrophic rate than we know, with consequences that we cannot predict. He calculated that we may be making extinct as many as six species an hour, one thousand to ten thousand times more than in prehistoric times. Yet he characterized biodiversity as the modern creation story, which was now at risk, following the five previous mass extinctions of the past 550 million years. 'More organization and complexity exist in a handful of soil than on the surface of all the other planets combined.'

But he did not feel that all was lost, thanks to biophilia, which he regarded as a basic aspect of our own human nature that is not fully acknowledged and which he defined as the 'tendency to focus on life and life-like processes'. Our human inclination to affiliate with life is innate, part of the evolutionary story, and it is 'likely to increase the possibility for achieving individual meaning and personal fulfilment'.[22]

Wilson's ideas struck a chord with many biologists. A number of experiments were carried out to test them, and reported on at a conference held in 1992 at the Woods Hole Oceanographic Institution in Massachusetts. Studies showed, for example, that not only did hospital patients prefer wards with a view of trees and parkland, rather than buildings or brick walls, but they needed fewer treatments and got better faster in those conditions. Much the same applied to inmates in prisons. Research also showed that young children appear to have a natural preference for landscapes and water scenes, and almost everyone prefers an urban landscape where trees are present to those where trees are absent.

David Orr, editor of the journal *Conservation Biology*, went so far as to say that a 'biophilia revolution' is under way; he perceived 'a love of life based on a knowledge and conviction that in our deepest affiliation with nature is the key to our species' most fundamental yearnings for a meaningful life and fulfilling existence'. Michael E. Soulé, one-time president of the Society for Conservation Biology, added that the psychological benefits of outdoor activity 'appear to be a sense of well-being' not far removed from religious experience – grace, connectedness with nature. He concluded: 'If biophilia is destined to become a powerful force for conservation, then it must become a religion-like movement. The social womb for such "biophilism" could be bioregional communities that recapture tribal-hunter-gatherer-pagan wisdom, integrating it with relevant science, appropriate technology, family planning, and sustainable land-use practices. Such communities already exist in the foothills of the Sierra Nevada.'[23]

Not content with giving us 'sociobiology', 'biodiversity' and 'biophilia', in 1998 Wilson came up with 'consilience'. In *Consilience: The Unity of Knowledge* he tells us: 'The greatest enterprise of the mind has always been and will always be the attempted linkage of the sciences and the humanities.' This is the definition of 'consilience', the aim of which, in this new age of synthesis, is agreement on a common body of abstract principles that bring together four all-important strands of thought – ethics, social science, environmental policy and biology. Signs are beginning to appear, he argues, of a fundamental order in the natural world, as different spheres are found to conform to similar algorithms – so that, for example, archaeology, genetics and linguistics are starting to overlap, to the extent that they tell the same story viewed from different vantage points, as do plate tectonics, evolutionary history and climate research.[24]

And this leads him to believe that an important convergence is now going on between cognitive neuroscience, human behavioural genetics, evolutionary biology and environmental science, which will expand our understanding of the social sciences and the humanities in ways not envisaged before. The biological origin of the arts shows itself, he says, in the fact that Hollywood plays well in Singapore and that the Nobel Prize for Literature is given to Africans and Asians as well as Europeans. But, he says, the arts also nourish our cravings for the mystical, which is a subconscious hangover from the Palaeolithic environment in which the brain evolved. 'In our emotions, I believe, we are still there.'[25]

Which brings him to moral behaviour, which he says is everywhere 'consilient' with natural science. And here he too eschews the 'transcendental' position, that moral values exist in some independent, metaphysical realm; instead, they are empirically grounded in our evolutionary history – they are adaptations. 'On religion I lean towards deism but consider the proof largely a problem in astrophysics. The existence of a cosmological God who created the universe (as envisioned by deism) is possible, and may eventually be settled, perhaps by forms of material evidence not yet imagined. Or the matter may be forever beyond human reach. In contrast, and of far greater importance to humanity, the existence of a biological God, who directs organic evolution and intervenes in human affairs (as envisioned by theism), is increasingly contravened by biology and the brain sciences. The same evidence, I believe, favours a purely material origin of ethics.'

He goes on to point out that, out of the estimated 100,000 belief systems that have existed in history, many have fostered ethnic and tribal conflict, which means that every major religion today is a winner in the Darwinian struggle waged among cultures – 'none ever flourished by tolerating its rivals'. He notes that the most dangerous of beliefs is the one endemic in Christianity: I was not born to be of this world. 'With a second life waiting, suffering can be endured – especially in other people. The natural environment can be used up. Enemies of the faith can be savaged.' Ethical and religious beliefs are created from the bottom up, from people to their culture, not from the top down.

We are still easily God-struck, says Wilson, and that is because, although our ethics are practical adaptations to the everyday world we live in, we also need something more, something he describes as 'the poetry of affirmation', and the craving for authority. And this is one of the reasons religions work: 'Recognize that when introits and invocations prickle the skin we are in the presence of poetry, and the soul of the tribe.'

But that is as far as it goes. 'We can be proud as a species because, having discovered that we are alone, we owe the gods very little. Humility is better shown to our fellow humans and the rest of life on this planet, on whom all hope really depends.' Communion is the key, and the idea of mystical union, either with nature or with the cosmos, 'is an authentic part of the human spirit'.[26]

People need a sacred narrative, he says, but it cannot be in the form of a religious cosmology: '[I]t will be taken from the material history of the universe and the human species. That trend is in no way debasing. The true evolutionary epic, retold as poetry, is as intrinsically ennobling as any religious epic ... The eventual result of the competition between the two world views, I believe, will be the secularization of the human spirit and of religion itself.'[27]

A Modern Science of the Soul

Although, as mentioned above, Theodore Roszak became famous for coining the term 'counterculture' and for writing its history, he preferred to be known for inventing what he described as a new speciality that met the needs of the time. This speciality, which he named 'ecopsychology', was in a sense another form of biophilia. Ecology had been gathering momentum as a major concern – ever since Rachel Carson's *Silent Spring* in 1962 and the first intimations of global warming, which had pinpointed for many the all too finite quality of the earth's resources. Roszak, always alert to our spiritual travails, saw early on that our responsibility to 'the nonhuman world' offered a morally acceptable way to 'span the gap between the personal and the planetary', giving a sense of purpose and wholeness not available elsewhere.

Roszak saw ecopsychology as a healthy way of leading people out of the 'self-cloistering' of the therapeutic ethic, a step forward from the counterculture, a way in which people might capture the sense of 'oceanic unity' that Freud had spoken of in relation to religion. Roszak went so far as to suggest that it could become a modern science of the soul, but based on more than sex, family and social bonds. He found some sense in Jung's writings, feeling that the Swiss had in effect collected together from among the myths and religious symbols of other cultures across the world a 'reservoir of salvation teachings'. These showed that there had been four elements integral to, or relating to, the psyche that had been repressed in modern man – nature, animals, primitive man and creative fantasy. 'Underlying, or cradling the mind, he envisioned a nonmaterial collective unconscious that contains the compounded wisdom of the human race.' Roszak saw Jung's work as 'an effort to heal the urban neurosis of atheism', agreeing with him that in our time the natural world had been surrendered to 'desacralized science . . . deepening the rift between the physical and the spiritual'.[28]

Here, then, was the beginning of an ethic, of a transactional bond between the human and the natural, founded in a belief that something has been lost in our separation from the natural world – 'a loss of experience, a loss of sensibility, a loss of communion, above all perhaps a loss of harmony that once existed between precivilized people and their habitat'. In helping this distance between nature and humans to grow, Roszak argued, science has left us 'underdimensioned'. And, he thought, a mutual concern for the environment had the best chance of uniting us – both as one people with one overriding common problem, and as our individual selves, each playing our part in an environmental campaign, giving us a feeling of wholeness.

The Plenitude Aesthetic

The next step was Gaia. The Gaia theory is the work of the British scientist James Lovelock and the American microbiologist Lynn Margulis.

The theory holds that all species in the planetary biomass act symbiotically to enhance the total life-giving potential of the planet. For example, the earth has remained a comfortable place to live for the entire 3.5 billion years since life began, despite, as Lovelock puts it, a 25 per cent increase in the output of heat from the sun. Somehow, living organisms have kept their planet 'fit for life'. The importance of this view is that it relegates natural selection – Darwin's overriding principle – to a position less important than the overall integration of living things within a symbiotic global network. 'The basic unit of evolutionary survival becomes the biomass as a whole, which may select species for their capacity to enhance the liveability of the planet.'[29]

There have been many arguments as to whether Gaia is a metaphor, or something more. Lovelock, though he does not see Gaia as 'sentient', does admit to finding it 'satisfying' that his theory has found a spiritual as well as a scientific reading.[30] The very latest research casts doubt on the phenomenon itself.

Whether or not we accept Gaia as something more than a metaphor, Roszak's main point is that the ordered complexity that it and chaos theory and the ubiquitous success of mathematics are examples of, are essentially a new form of Deism, that we are witnessing the birth of a form of scientific aesthetics, a plenitude feeling that is as close to a spiritual experience as we are presently capable of. Roszak proposed that the 'core of the mind is the ecological unconscious': thus, the essential purpose of life is to 'awaken the inherent sense of environmental reciprocity' – in some ways a reprise of Heidegger's plea for us to care for the planet (see chapter 11).

Evolution as a Religion, Science as Salvation

The meaning offered by evolutionary science has been roundly attacked by Mary Midgley, former senior philosophy lecturer at the University of Newcastle. She has taken on the subject of evolution as a religion, and science as salvation.

In *Evolution as a Religion* she proposes that Marxism and evolution are the two great secular faiths of our day. Each displays several features reminiscent of religion: they are large-scale ideologies with ambitious systems of thought designed to articulate, defend and justify their ideas; both aim essentially at the spiritual nourishment and salvation of the human race.[31] And they raise – and seek to answer – questions of human purpose. They do this, she says, by creating, as did traditional religions, a sense of 'having one's place within a whole greater than oneself' – a whole 'whose larger aims so enclose one's own and give them point that sacrifice for it may be entirely proper'. Both Marxism and evolution, she says, call for a new set of expectations about the future.

The theory of evolution is her main target. It is ironic, she says, that while for many people one of the prime aims of science is to get rid of religion, evolution has many features suggesting it is itself such an entity.

Not unlike a religion, evolution makes prophecies, in particular that mankind is on an 'upward escalator' as a result of which individuals of the future will be more intelligent and in other ways more complete and talented. In wide-ranging references to the works of the psychologist B.F. Skinner, the biologists Jacques Monod, Richard Dawkins, Francis Crick, James Lovelock, Lynn Margulis, E.O. Wilson and the theoretical physicist Steven Weinberg, she focuses first on genetic engineering as a way of achieving human salvation, contrasting that with 'the incoherence of supposing that we understand our own nature well enough to get it right'. (She particularly contrasts the 'thinness' of social scientists' descriptions of man with those of novelists.) She looked at books such as the philosopher Jonathan Glover's *What Sort of People Should There Be?*, where she says, DNA is considered 'as a sort of film strip'.

What direction should we go in? – do we know enough? Human nature, she tells us, is not a machine to be built after a model. She notes Skinner appeals for a technology of human behaviour that will free us, make us happy and give us greater dignity, but adds that nothing like such technology is remotely available – certainly not in biology and not even in physics.

Figures like Francis Crick, she says, are always predicting – 'nay, demanding' – the continued upward development of the human species. But this is not a scientific approach – science offers no mandate for it. The scientists' faith, as she calls it, is placed in 'three concentric entities – the scientific profession, the human race, and life or evolution. The direction of all three is the same. Evolution, they argue, "is the enterprise of the universe, into which we are born".' This 'religion' lacks a sense of reverence, awe or goodness, but retains 'some sense of vastness and majesty . . . [and is] intense and evangelical'.[32]

The New Dogma and the New Metaphysics

Midgley notes that to apply the word 'selfish' to the word 'gene' is not a conventional use of that adjective. There has always been something unpleasant about it – indeed, to be described as selfish was and is an insult. But the new selfishness, the new 'ego-charged approach to evolution', particularly in its sociobiological or social-Darwinist context, gives an allegedly biological underpinning to crass individualism, 'which manifestly goes against the tenets and experience of our own civilization'. In *The Solitary Self: Darwin and the Selfish Gene* she says it is absurd to say we are always ruled by self-interest – if it were so, the word 'selfish' would never have been invented.

The main fault of evolution, and science in general, she felt, was to keep us detached from our world picture, as if we can do nothing about the 'fact' of evolution, the 'fact' of the gene, the 'fact' of natural selection. 'The impersonality required [which this approach appears to dictate] is not total detachment, because this is impossible. It is responsible objectivity – the far more difficult task of becoming more aware of one's own world-picture, doing all one can to correct its more obvious faults.' But in fact she thinks that social Darwinism, or Spencerism, is 'the unofficial religion of the west . . . People want a religion for this world as well. They find it in the worship of individual success . . . Mystical reverence for such deities as progress, nature and the lifeforce is then invoked to explain and justify cut-throat competition.'[33]

She returned to the attack in *Science as Salvation* (1992). Here she argued that the need for salvation is universal, 'urgent and drastic', that 'faith' is a kind of map, a way of organizing a vast jumble of data, which does not necessarily need a God (as in Marxism and Taoism); but 'looking outwards with reverence' is part of all serious endeavours, 'an unavoidable part of any serious pursuit of knowledge'. Mere intellectual predation – fact-swallowing – is not enough for effective thought. Jacques Monod is a particular target of hers. She says that he wants us to get rid of all belief in something greater than ourselves, he invites us to see the universe as something to be conquered, something beneath us. But she insists that the cult of fact is, actually, a new faith, and that big conceptual scientific schemes like the Big Bang are not really science, but metaphysics.

She returns to the certainty that the world is ordered and accessible to us – and asks: What is the implication of that? Could it be that there is someone who knows better than us? 'It is better to look upon the universe as a Thou than an It.' She notes that the idea of an ordered world may be an important element in our salvation – it controls confusion and is sustaining. We *trust* the physical world – this is what makes knowledge possible, to assume it has an underlying order.[34]

Moreover, she says, scientists have made the meaninglessness of the universe into a new dogma. This has arisen from their own modes of study, culminating in a heat death, centring the meaninglessness of the creation and destruction of the universe. Dawkins, Wilson et al., she concludes, display a 'remarkable faith in unknown future science'.[35]

God and the Cosmologists

Midgley was equally dismissive of the interventions of physicists in religion, finding their contributions less than useful. That might be true of Fritjof Capra's *The Tao of Physics* (1976), which claimed to find significance in the parallels between relativity theory and quantum theory on the one hand, and Eastern mysticism on the other. Many particle physicists found the parallels that he highlighted questionable. Quantum theory, he said, 'forces us to see the universe not as a collection of physical objects, but rather as a complicated web of relations between the various parts of a unified whole. This ... is the way in which Eastern mystics have experienced the world.' The symmetries of quarks, in their properties of spin and 'upness' or 'downness', he added, recall many Eastern symmetrical diagrams ('koans'), the yin–yang motif perhaps being the best-known. Critics pointed out sharply that the existence of 'parallels', as Capra called them, didn't prove anything, that we can find parallels galore in all walks of life without that being a sign of anything fundamentally similar between them.

In 1993 Theodore Roszak published a list of no fewer than 188 titles, all released in the previous decade and a half, on the subject of God and modern cosmology. The main point of his list was to show that, with more and more being discovered about the heavens and the way the universe worked, in both infinitely large and infinitely minute ways, it was a natural area for synthesis to be attempted.

Two further ideas, despite Midgley's general scepticism, had at least the merit of being extremely imaginative. In *The Mind of God: Science and the Search for Ultimate Meaning* (1992) Paul Davies, professor of natural philosophy at the University of Adelaide, advanced the view that, given that modern physics has now explained how the universe began – not so much in a big bang as in a gradual separation out of time and space, an entirely natural process – there is no need of a God hypothesis for its creation. Davies's main concern was the examination of the relationship between the laws of physics and mathematics. For him, this was and is the central mystery – and the main joy – of life: that scientific laws exist that may be encoded in mathematical formulae. These mathematical laws are 'eternal', 'omnipotent', 'transcendent' – all words used about God. Davies is convinced there must be some 'deep reason' for the accord between physics and mathematics; and, moreover, 'It is very hard to see how abstract mathematics has any survival value. Similar comments apply to musical ability.'

Darwinian evolution has equipped us, he says, to know the world by direct perception, and in this there are clear evolutionary advantages. But there is no obvious connection between this sort of sensorial knowledge and what he calls intellectual knowledge.[36]

The crucial point for him is that the world is both rational and intelligible – there is a graspable logic behind physics: 'existence . . . can be compressed into a compelling and succinct form'. It is the so-far mysterious 'bond' between contingency and order that leads him to think 'we have no choice but to seek [an] explanation in something beyond or outside the physical world – in something metaphysical – because ... a contingent universe cannot carry within itself an explanation for itself'. At the same time, the new mathematical science of chaos theory shows that a few simple rules can lead to chaos and then on to 'self-organization', which may be a model for how the universe developed, since it cannot have 'evolved' in a true Darwinian sense, having no reproductive capacity.

Davies therefore leans towards a form of process philosophy not so different from Alfred North Whitehead's (see chapter 15), in which 'it is simpler to posit the existence of an infinite mind than to accept, as a brute fact, the existence of this contingent universe'. So, Davies concludes, 'belief in God is largely a matter of taste'. However, this 'postulated being who underpins the rationality of the world' bears little relation to the personal God of the familiar religions, 'to the God of the bible or the Koran'.

Davies is saying that the transcendent reality is mathematics, that the fact that mathematics and physics coincide so closely is the all-important fact in the world; and that the practice of science, and the philosophy of science, are the closest we can get to the truth and/or truths. In this sense, he says, science offers the greatest opportunity for spiritual satisfaction. 'Even the most hard-nosed sceptic must surely be tempted to conclude that there [is] "something going on"', that there is an 'elegant and powerful unity' beneath mathematics, that the beauty of mathematics is evidence for 'a genuine transcendent reality'.[37]

The Physics of Immortality

If science as a form of worship, and mathematics as a transcendent entity, seem strange, physics as a form of theology will feel even more so. But that is what is proposed by the Oxford physicist David Deutsch in his 1997 book *The Fabric of Reality* (incorporating the work of other scientists such as Frank Tipler, Roger Penrose, Alan Turing and Kurt Gödel).[38]

Deutsch's fundamental point is that we all inhabit 'parallel universes', that there is a 'multiverse' made up of many universes and that we – or copies of us – inhabit many of these universes, of which we are only intermittently and dimly aware. He bases his argument on a series of patterns thrown by light on to a screen after it has passed through a number of slits. Depending on the number of slits, some areas on the screen are now white and some dark. This pattern can only be explained, he says, if we assume that, besides the photons that we *can* see – that are 'tangible' – there are also 'shadow' photons that are dark and intangible and 'interfere' with the patterns on occasions. This leads him to the idea of parallel universes – and it is a profound idea, he says, because it explains so much that is otherwise incomprehensible.

His other main theory, building on Davies, is that computation, mathematics, accords with physics – this is what makes the world comprehensible – and, moreover, and most importantly, it is the only form of knowledge. The increase of such computational knowledge, he says, is the purpose of life. He entertains the idea that in a universe made according to the laws of physics and patterned on mathematics, at some point in the future all of this mathematical, computational knowledge will be known, and 'life will have conquered'.

Along with Frank Tipler of Tulane University in New Orleans, he looks forward to a future billions of years ahead when computational knowledge will have expanded immeasurably from where it is now. It will have reached the point where not only space travel will be familiar, but possibly time travel too, and where we may be able to avert the final phase of our universe which, according to current knowledge, will end in a cataclysmic 'big crunch'. This, roughly speaking, is what Frank Tipler explores in his book *The Physics of Immortality*, in which his concept of the 'omega point' is fleshed out.

As the big crunch approaches and the universe contracts, more and more energy will be concentrated in less and less space-time, which will mean that 'people's minds will be running as computer programs in computers whose physical speed is increasing without limit'. By this point, billions of years ahead, with the computing power then available, experience will be determined not by elapsed time 'but by the computations that are performed *in* that time [italics added]'. 'In an infinite number of computational steps there is time for an infinite number of thoughts – plenty of time for the thinkers to place themselves into any virtual-reality environment they like . . . They will be in no hurry for subjectively they will live forever. Within one second, or one microsecond, they will have "all the time in the world" to do more, experience more, create more – infinitely more – than anyone in the multiverse will ever have done before then.'

There are preparations that will have to be made, Deutsch says, but again – and the point is crucial to this theory – the physical knowledge we have today means that all this reasoning is exactly that, reasoning based on current knowledge, not speculation. We shall need to 'steer' the universe to the omega point, and along the way several deadlines will need to be negotiated. One is about five billion years from now, when the sun, if left to its own devices, will become a giant red star and wipe us out. He continues – insouciantly, you might think – 'We must learn to control or abandon the Sun before then.' The omega point theory 'deserves to become the prevailing theory of the future', Deutsch says – it is only Tipler's 'quasi-religious' interpretation of that future that has prevented it from being taken more seriously.

At the omega point, Tipler insists, everything about the universe will be known; whatever and whoever exists then will, therefore, be omniscient, from which it follows they will be omnipotent and omnipresent. 'And so [Tipler] claims that at the omega point limit there is an omniscient, omnipotent, omnipresent society of people. This society, Tipler identifies as God.'

Deutsch emphasizes that there are great differences between Tipler's idea of God and what most religious people believe in today. The people near the omega point would be so different from us that they couldn't communicate with us. And they couldn't work miracles; they did not create the universe or the laws of physics, so they could never violate those laws. They would be opposed to religious faith and have no wish to be worshipped (who would do the worshipping?). Technology would be so advanced at that point, he thinks, that they could resurrect the dead. This would be possible because by then computers would be so infinitely powerful that they could create any virtual world that ever existed, including our world in which humans have evolved. All this, in an infinite system, would enable computers to improve our world materially, to become one in which people will not die. This, Tipler says, is a form of heaven.[39]

What people would actually *do* at the omega point (people very different from us, beyond what we can imagine) is a matter of informed speculation, say both Tipler and Deutsch, because the omega point is a singularity, in which the laws of physics break down. But they insist that present-day physics and mathematics support the narrative up to the omega point.

This is all very heady – in fact, way over the heads of most of us – but what Deutsch and Tipler give us, they believe, is a glimpse of an ideal world, or universe, which science is inexorably leading us to.

Does all this teach us how to live? In the immediate and near future, it tells us an education in physics and mathematics is likely to help us understand the future better. It seeks to give us some idea of the changes that are coming our way, it gives us an idea above all of how knowledge might change – computation has no need of a God or gods – and it offers an ideal end-point to history, which subjectively will last for ever (a form of mathematical immortality), with the prospect of a (sort of) resurrection for, in theory, anyone who has ever lived.

It is a breathtaking vision and, needless to say, both Deutsch and Tipler have been heavily criticized (not just by Midgley) for 'unwarranted speculation' about events so far in the future as to be meaningless to most people. But they insist their theories are based on today's real knowledge of physics and computation. Evolution has shown us that life has proliferated on earth for roughly 3.5 billion years and it has taken that time for us to become aware, for example, of the future demise of the sun. We must learn to think in such timeframes.

Evolution brings us back to earth, though it was no less imaginative or controversial than the omega point when it was first conceived. But as more and more has become known (and it is one of the great episodes of intellectual heroism in the twentieth century, along with modern physics), evolution has provided us with an alternative vision and one which, moreover, has had a distinct impact on our moral views, which religions claimed as their special territory for so many centuries. Our post-Darwin, post-Nietzsche, post-Christian moral life is the subject of the next chapter.

The one puzzle that remains with evolution is why, although most scientists are so enthusiastic about it for the understanding it gives us in so many realms, very many others remain unconvinced. Even Richard Dawkins, one of evolution's staunchest advocates, admitted in *The Blind Watchmaker* that Darwinism 'seems more in need of advocacy than many other similarly established truths in other branches of science . . . Many of us have no grasp of quantum theory, or Einstein's theories of special and general relativity, but this does not in itself lead us to oppose these theories.' There are two reasons why evolution is in need of such advocacy, and they go to the heart of this book. They will be discussed in the Conclusion.

26

'The Good Life Is the Life Spent Seeking the Good Life'

In 1948 T.S. Eliot published a short, sharp book entitled *Notes Towards the Definition of Culture*. He had done so, he said, because he felt that anxiety had been growing over the previous six or seven years about the word (and the notion of) 'culture'.

He worried that no culture had ever appeared or developed 'except together with a religion' – they are 'different aspects of the same thing' – and that the artistic sensibility is impoverished by any divorce from the religious sensibility. 'We can assert with some confidence that our own period is one of decline; that the standards of culture are lower than they were fifty years ago; and that the evidence of this decline is visible in every department of human activity.' He saw this against the background of Christian culture in Europe, which he regarded as 'the highest culture that the world has ever known'. Religion, while it lasts, he wrote, provides the framework for culture, protects the mass of humanity from boredom and despair, and gives meaning to life.[1]

As this shows, Eliot had an elitist view of progress. It is the function of the superior members of a society, and superior families (his words), to preserve the culture, and it is the function of the producers of culture to change it. High culture, he said, is more 'conscious' than lower culture, and this is its function. There was no distinction, he thought, between religion and culture in primitive societies, but in modern times there had been a movement towards 'aggressive unbelief', producing a culture severed from religion – a process that 'might well' confirm the general lowering of culture. Without a common faith the search for unity – in a community, a nation, or a people – can only be an illusion, and a country like Britain had become 'unconscious' of the importance of religion. In our modern culture, he said, we need fewer books and more conversations; life is about manageability; about the passions of individuals rather than the huge impersonal forces that affect the masses, which are just necessary conveniences of thought.[2]

One of the outcomes of these modern trends, he thought, was the belief that superiority always means superiority of intellect and that education should be devised to 'infallibly nourish it'. This led, he felt, to the most dogmatic of modern beliefs, that *equality of opportunity* is what counts, which for him could only be achieved if 'the institution of the family is no longer respected'. Thus were ruled out self-sacrifice on the part of parents, ambition, foresight, parental control and responsibility. Education in the modern sense, he claimed, implies a disintegrated society in which it has come to be assumed that there is one measure of education according to which everyone is educated more or less.[3] Eliot thought that in this matter society had become unidimensional, and that by educating everyone we cannot help but lower standards, from which we will all, eventually suffer.

This went right against the grain of much that was in train in many areas of the world at the time, but especially in Western Europe and North America. In the wake of Eliot's book, the West – the highest culture, the most advanced, as he insisted – entered on the most secular period there has ever been; and the widespread popularity of film and radio, of the gramophone and then television, brought about a flourishing of popular culture that was also unparalleled.

By Eliot's lights, culture should have collapsed, and many fellow thinkers who outlived him (he died in 1965) no doubt agreed. But as this book has tried to show, there was no shortage of attempts to find meaning, ways to live, in the wake of World War, the Holocaust, the Gulag, Hiroshima, Nagasaki, Mao and his wife and the Cultural Revolution. Earlier chapters have explored how painters, poets, psychologists, biologists and other scientists have confronted and constructed the post-religious secular world that Eliot so feared. There remains one realm unexplored, a form of intellectual activity less concentrated than science, less suited to the visual images that so dominate our lives these days, and much harder to distil within the short-term attention span of our very diverse late-capitalist popular culture. This is the realm of contemporary moral philosophy, a totally secular activity.

The End of Meta-narrative

We begin with a transformation that, as transformations are apt to do, turned Eliot's approach on its head. It was a transformation described as the 'apotheosis of secularization'.

At 3.32 p.m. on Saturday, 15 July 1972, the Pruitt-Igoe housing development in St Louis, Missouri, was dynamited. A one-time prize-winning version of Le Corbusier's 'machine for modern living', designed by Minoru Yamasaki, it was now deemed an uninhabitable environment for its low-income residents. This moment, says the architectural historian Charles Jencks, was the symbolic end of modernism and marked the passage to the postmodern. It signalled the end of abstract, theoretical and doctrinaire ideals – in architecture in this case – but postmodernism was at much the same time invading all areas of life.

In literature, in film, in art and philosophy as well as architecture, a new ethic and a new aesthetics came into play. As the cultural historian David Harvey has put it, the most startling fact about postmodernism was its total acceptance of the ephemerality, fragmentation, discontinuity and chaos of modern life. Universal and eternal truths, 'if they exist at all, cannot be specified'. All 'meta-narratives' which seek to explain the broad sweep of history – Marxism, Freudianism, Christianity, the secularizing influence of modernism, for example – are eschewed. Despite postmodernism itself being a feature of a Western way of life, the Western way of life was now criticized for its long-term neglect of the 'other'. Other worlds, and the inexhaustibility of this world, were what counted now – heterotopia, not utopia.

We cannot aspire to any unified representation of the world, 'or picture it as a totality full of connections and differentiations rather than as perpetually shifting fragments'. The individual could no longer be understood as 'alienated', because that presupposes a coherent centre from which to be alienated.[4] Alienation is replaced by fragmentation.

Fredric Jameson said that all this was nothing more than the cultural logic of late capitalism – postmodern pluralism fuelling an ever more frenetic pursuit of this-worldly pleasures (increasingly varied and increasingly available), consumption in this world replacing otherworldly forms of comfort and salvation.

True enough, but not the whole picture. What Karl Marx and Friedrich Engels astutely anticipated was the 'everlasting uncertainty and agitation' of late capitalism, driven ceaselessly by technological advances 'in which the desire for the new is so intense that new fashions and new ideas "become antiquated before they can ossify into custom"'. The never-ending carnival of consumerism, where information, or 'facts', are as plentiful (and ever-changing) as objects, where the half-truths and half-lies of advertising set a cynical standard for public discourse, where in any case facts and events in the news change so quickly that no one can absorb anything into any kind of totality – in such circumstances ready-made belief systems have an undeniable attraction.

These ready-made belief systems are not necessarily traditional religions but what Philippa Berry, paraphrasing Jacques Derrida, calls 'a numinous and nonhuman force loosely called "spirit"'. In part, this overall stance was a reflection of the digital world then emerging in computer science, where 'bits' of information came in one of two types, 1 and 0. Postmodernism turned its back on this, arguing that polarizations in politics (left–right), in philosophy (reason–emotion), in history (classicism–Romanticism), in literature and art (narrative–discursive), in science (progress–retribalization) and in everyday life were over-simple and misleading.[5]

'Bricolage' Beliefs

In religion it has been slightly more complicated. At one level the polarization between faith and doubt has come under attack, at another the focus has been on the concept of the 'other', as originally envisaged by Karl Barth (see chapter 16). New modes of spirituality have been explored that have been described as post-religious, post-sceptical or post-dualistic (all together, described as 'quasi-religious'). These typically draw on pre-Christian and non-Christian sources and, as Clifford Longley wrote in the *Daily Telegraph*, 'People have moved away from "religion" as something anchored in organized worship and systematic beliefs within an institution, to a self-made "spirituality", outside formal structures, which is based on experience, has no doctrine and makes no claim to philosophical coherence.'[6] Opinion polls show that one in four Americans believes in astrology, one in five in reincarnation; in Britain, as we saw earlier, more people believe in UFOs than in God. The New Age fits in here too, combining high consumerism and belief in all manner of things.

These phenomena are characterized, Berry says, by their 'bricolage' quality – bits and pieces, picked up as we go along – by the fact that they are both like and unlike traditional religions, and it is not yet clear whether they are quasi-religious or post-religious. David Barrett in his 544-page survey *The New Believers*, an account of sixty-nine contemporary religions, cults and sects, found that there were a lot of 'counterfeit Christianity' movements among them, and that the most postmodern of the cults were the 'New Age' variety whose adherents claim that the previous age was dominated by male characteristics, 'leading to aggression and obsession with power'. 'The New Age concept is based on a balance of male and female qualities.'

New Age has been described as a smorgasbord of spiritual substitutes for Christianity. It is essentially an astrological idea, the basic belief being that sometime in the 1970s we passed from the astrological age of Pisces, the fish, into the age of Aquarius, the water-bearer. The age of Pisces stretched back to the beginning of Christianity and took in the Renaissance, the Reformation and the rise of humanism. It was the age of authority, when Judaeo-Christianity was dominant and controlled man's thinking. The age of Aquarius, beginning around the turn of the twenty-first century, would herald a new spirit, leading to 'consciousness expansion', to man's wholeness. The New Age consistently teaches that a personal God does not exist. It is intended to fill the post-Christian spiritual vacuum.[7]

What Is Missing Is 'Practice'

Although postmodernism made the intellectual running for several decades in the late twentieth century, the bricolage ethic it fostered created an ideal environment for philosophical figures who offered clarity and – though against the tide – a coherence that postmodernism denied. Alasdair MacIntyre was one who seemed to be more systematic than most about these matters.

A Scotsman and a Marxist, who emigrated from Britain to the USA in 1970 and later became a Catholic, MacIntyre set out his views in an important series of books on moral philosophy: *After Virtue* (1981), mentioned earlier, *Whose Justice? Which Rationality?* (1988), *Three Rival Versions of Moral Enquiry* (1990) and *Dependent Rational Animals* (1999). To see how we should live in a world without God, he had the idea of going back, ideologically, to ancient Greece, to the time of Aristotle, to a time before the great monotheisms evolved. He saw the current situation as pretty dire, because in this world of corporate liberalism there is not only no agreement on God, but we cannot even agree on what would count as a reasoned argument for or against him. The individualistic ethic by which we live now amounts to people advocating 'whatever they think will give them control', or will achieve the outcome they prefer (another postmodern claim was that power was and is all-important). Moral principles are chosen today on the grounds of their effectiveness. We live, said MacIntyre, in a world of 'emotivism', the doctrine that 'all evaluative judgments and more specifically all moral judgments are *nothing but* expressions of preference, expressions of attitude or feeling'.

MacIntyre believed this to be wrong because 'we can in fact rationally determine the best possible life for human beings and therefore can have moral judgments that are more than mere preferences'.

What is missing from modern life, he said, is the concept of 'practice', and here he used the example of playing chess. In any practice there are two kinds of 'good' attaching. There are the external 'goods' – money, power and fame, derived from being good at the game and reaching the top. And there are internal 'goods', achieved by participating in the practice itself. These provide an education in the virtues – the virtues of honesty (no cheating), courage (keeping going when you are losing), generosity towards others (who may be better than you), magnanimity (to those less good than yourself). You must also rely on others to judge you – you cannot be a chess grand master just because you say so.

Societies, MacIntyre says, in order to *be* societies and offer the best chances to the greatest number, need the practice of certain virtues – honesty, courage, justice, as in the example given above. Good societies should be made up of people who know each other and can practise and polish the virtues. The fault with liberal democracies, he says, is that they are really disguised oligarchies, where corporate liberalism (or capitalism) derives its power from fragmentation: typically, individuals have no chance to come together to pursue the common good and therefore no chance to develop the virtues. Liberalism, he goes on, claims to be neutral about what constitutes the best way forward, but this very neutrality is also a disguise designed to maintain corporate liberalism's control over the manufacture of goods, with the overall effect of keeping the experience of virtue in society to a minimum. And it is virtue that people find satisfying and fulfilling. Even tradition, which once provided a framework for virtue, is being eroded.

MacIntyre was well aware, of course, that the modern world was nothing like Aristotle's Athens, and could never be. He used St Benedict as his model, not so much because he was religious as because he started some small communities – monasteries – in which everyone knew each other, everyone depended on each other, everyone could freely practise the virtues. The spread and duration of the Benedictine jurisdiction show that, given the right circumstances, it can thrive. MacIntyre thought that in the current climate the teaching and organization of modern universities could be modified to create the sort of small community that could kick-start a new way of living together.[8]

Another ideal society was suggested by John Rawls, whose totally secular model for arriving at a way to live together attracted a great deal of attention. Robert Nozick, whose own work we will consider presently, called Rawls's *A Theory of Justice* (1971) the most significant work of political philosophy since John Stuart Mill. Rawls argued that a just society – which Christianity had hardly advanced in its two thousand years – is one that will guarantee the most liberties for the greatest number of its members, and that therefore it is crucial to know what justice is and how it might be attained. Arguing against the utilitarian tradition (holding that actions are right because they are useful), he tried to replace the social contracts of Locke, Rousseau and Kant with something 'more rational'. This led him to his view that justice is best understood as 'fairness', and it was Rawls's way of achieving fairness that was to bring him so much attention. To do this, he proposed an 'original position' and a 'veil of ignorance'.

In the original position the individuals drawing up the social contract – the rules by which they will live – are assumed to be rational but ignorant. They do not know whether they are rich or poor, old or young, healthy or infirm; they do not know which god they follow, if any; they have no idea what race they are, how intelligent or stupid, or whatever other gifts they may have or lack. In the original position, no one knows his or her place in society, and so the principles by which they elect to live must be chosen from 'behind a veil of ignorance'. For Rawls, whatever social institutions are chosen in this way, those engaged in the choosing 'can say to one another that they are co-operating on terms to which they would agree if they were free and equal persons whose relations with one another were fair'.[9]

Rawls was criticized for assuming an ideal original position when in real life no such state of affairs can exist, and for the fact that, unlike in his scheme of things, if someone has a higher than average intelligence (say), this does not *deprive* anyone else. Rawls's system, his critics said, was too simple.

Art as Escape from Time

A very different ideal was proposed by the German philosopher, Hans-Georg Gadamer (1900–2002). For him the purpose and meaning of life were to be found in art, and in poetry in particular. For him art and philosophy overlapped more or less totally. His essay 'Philosophy and Poetry' was published in 1986.

Born in Marburg, the son of a pharmacology professor, Gadamer worked as Heidegger's assistant. 'I always had the damned feeling that Heidegger was looking over my shoulder,' he said later. He did not become known outside his own professional circle until the publication in 1960 of *Truth and Method*. This established him, in the eyes of many, as one of the most important thinkers of the twentieth century.

From our point of view, Gadamer's most important contribution lay in his exploration of culture, in particular his essay 'The Relevance of the Beautiful', in which he considered 'art as play, symbol and festival'. He thought that the meaning, or role, or function of art often got lost in the modern world, and that play – the activity of disinterested pleasure – was also overlooked. For him art had an important symbolic role, to open up for us 'a space in which both the world, and our own place in the world, are brought to light as a single, but inexhaustibly rich totality', where we can 'dwell' out of ordinary time. The disinterested pleasure we take in art is an aid to escaping from ordinary time into 'autonomous time'. The other quality of the successful artwork – art as festival, as he put it – also takes us out of ordinary time and opens us up 'to the true possibility of community'.[10]

Above all, Gadamer thought there is something unique about poetry, that there is, as he put it, a special relationship between poetic discourse – above all the lyric – and speculative philosophy, that there is a peculiar *completeness* of the poetic word, that it is made in such a way that it has no other meaning 'beyond letting something be there'.[11] Poetic language, he said elsewhere, is 'always bestowing a certain intimacy with the world of meaning'. Poetry is always 'a thinking word on the horizon of the unsaid'.

Gadamer insisted that art in the modern age has been 'definitively shorn' of its traditional relationship to Graeco-Christian religion and mythology and is wholly thrown back on the resources of the word, becoming a self-sufficient *auto-telic* activity. Poetry since Hegel, Gadamer thought, has become more inward precisely because it has severed its connection with religion and is now 'more modest'; though that has, paradoxically, resulted in a poetry that is more radical in its 'purchase' on the world. 'Poetry is a making oneself at home in the world, of showing how we share the world.' Poetry is a 'finality without purpose', since it shares with speculative discourse – philosophy – an existence at the limits of verification. The religious element in life, in our minds, has found a new home in the 'inward dimension of poetic speech'.[12]

Many of these observations coincide more or less with those made in chapter 23, on poetry. And that is Gadamer's point, that poetry is a form of philosophy, especially where it relates to the horizon of language (and therefore meaning); and that, as Sartre said, the dimension of lyricism is something over and above philosophy. In order to live well, we must be able to *sing*.

Meaning as Oppressive Illusion

Music – or at least harmony – is one of life's chief assets, according to the British philosopher A.C. Grayling and as expounded in his book *The Choice of Hercules: Pleasure, Duty and the Good Life in the Twenty-First Century* (2007). Grayling is a brisk thinker and a brisk writer. Here, he sees no need to go back to basics – some basics are self-evident – 'The case for the humanist outlook is overwhelming.' He goes straight to the point, as he sees it. The average human lifespan is fewer than 1,000 months long (it sounds shorter when laid out as numerals), so we need to make the most of it. Good lives must be lived in the appropriate social and political setting. To live well and enjoy a good life, we don't need religion: we must have an ideal and work towards it.

He proposes that there are seven 'notes', in a musical sense, that can produce a harmonious existence. These seven notes are: meaning, intimacy, endeavour, truth, freedom, beauty and fulfilment. Fulfilment, he says, means integrating the other six into one's own chosen project. To these he adds the arguments that we should all have a life-long commitment to education – one never stops learning – and that, regarding the question of meaning, unity of purpose is what counts, for 'unity of purpose is often exactly what is missing' when people are unfulfilled.

Also, we must be aware of the successes of science, for 'eventually we will all use a biological, or even a physical language' (much as David Deutsch and Frank Tipler have said – see chapter 25). And he thinks we cannot live a good life without an involvement of some sort in politics, because nothing can take the place of the individual – liberty, equality and community all depend on each other. And the 'sovereign virtue' of the political community should be a concern equal to the concern we feel for our own well-being, because this safeguards the well-being of others. To achieve this we must look forward to a global ethics, the idea of a good world, as the ultimate ideal and the backbone of meaning.[13]

Terry Eagleton, another British philosopher, is equally brisk – brusque, even. A hundred-page book on *The Meaning of Life* (2007) is no mean feat, the more so as he dedicates it to his son, 'who found the whole project embarrassing'. He leaps straight in: What is the cause you would be prepared to die for? He observes that during the twentieth century, perhaps because life was so cheap, spirituality became 'rock hard or soggy' – unshakeable fundamentalisms on the one hand, gurus and spiritual masseurs, the 'chiropractors of piped contentment', on the other.

The fact that there may be many meanings to life, he thinks, is perhaps the most precious meaning of all: 'The din of conversation is as much meaning as we shall ever have.' He doesn't think that God is the answer – 'he tends to thicken things rather than make them self-evident'. And Eagleton asks whether the whole question isn't overblown. 'Many people have led superlative lives without apparently knowing the meaning of life.' Desire is eternal, while fulfilment is sporadic, so that intensity counts in a fulfilled life. Meaning, he thinks, is an oppressive illusion. 'To live without the need for such a guarantee is to be free ... To keep faith with what is most animal about us is to live authentically' (as James Joyce also said). Helping others is a 'little death', a *petite mort*; it helps us to live well but is not the real deal. The meaning of life is less a proposition than a practice – it is not an esoteric truth but a certain *form* of life. Happiness, as we noted earlier,

Eagleton describes as a 'feeble, holiday-camp sort of word', maintaining, as others have, that it is a by-product of a practical way of life, not some private inner contentment.[14]

The Impossibility of Transcendence

The American philosopher Thomas Nagel concurs with Bertrand Russell: he does not believe that we can ever be fully content, because there is an inherent paradox or dual aspect to our existence which just cannot be overcome, and we need to learn to live with it if we are to have satisfaction. A religious solution, he says, gives us a 'borrowed centrality' in the paradox through the intervention of a supreme being.

Professor of philosophy and law at New York University, Nagel likes to give his books arresting titles: *Mortal Questions*, *What Does It All Mean?*, *The View from Nowhere*, *The Last Word*. In *The View from Nowhere* and *Mortal Questions* he tackles the problem of meaning in our lives, which he believes stems from this basic, unavoidable predicament – namely, that we inhabit both a subjective world and an objective world. We all face the predicament, he says, of looking at the world from our own point of view, while at the same time realizing that we are but an insignificant part of that world, looking down on ourselves as if from a great height. We are ambitious to get outside ourselves, but can't quite manage it. It is this 'dual vision', he says, which accounts for our bewilderment and our wish for – and failure to find – transcendence.

He is particularly critical of what he calls 'scientism' which 'puts one type of human understanding in charge of the universe and what can be said about it'. But scientism is myopic when it assumes that everything must be understandable by the employment of scientific theories, 'as if the present age were not just another in the series' of theories that have been generated to date. Set against this, philosophy has the difficult task of seeking to express 'unformed but intuitively felt problems in language without losing them'. At every point, he says, philosophy faces us with the question of how far beyond the relative safety of our present language we can afford to go without risking completely losing touch with reality.[15] Religion does the opposite, in that it places the supernatural beyond the limits, so that those limits are never extended here on earth.

Nagel is at pains to show that we don't really possess the language to describe our experience. Realism is most compelling when we are forced to recognize the existence of something that we cannot describe or know fully, because it lies beyond the reach of language, proof, evidence or empirical understanding. '*Something* must be true with respect to the 7s in the expansion of π, even if we can't establish it.' The world of reasons, including 'my' reasons, does not exist only from my own point of view.[16] A further problem as between subjectivity and objectivity is that we have an enormous mental capacity that is not explicable by natural selection. In an important way, natural selection does not explain everything.

In *Mind & Cosmos: Why the Materialist Neo-Darwinian Conception of Nature Is Almost Certainly False* (2012) Nagel takes this argument daringly – some would say recklessly – further. While he robustly declares himself an atheist, he argues that the reductive account of evolution – that life has evolved accidentally by purely physical and then chemical and biological principles – goes against common sense, and moreover that 'almost everyone in our secular culture' has been 'browbeaten' into regarding the reductive research programme as 'sacrosanct', on the grounds that anything else 'would not be science'.[17] It is 'an open question' as to whether there has been enough time for evolution to have produced the teeming life we see around us, having begun as a 'chemical accident'. Though he distances himself from the advocates of 'intelligent design', he insists they do not deserve the scorn that has been directed at them, because some of their objections to classical evolutionary theory have been well made.

He is careful not to invoke any 'transcendental being', but feels justified in speculating about an alternative to reductive physics as the basis for a theory of everything. Instead, as he puts it, there might be 'complications to the immanent nature of the natural order'. What he means by this – and it is his guiding conviction and his main complaint against reductive physics – is that 'mind' is not just an afterthought, or an accident of evolution, or a simple add-on. It is 'a basic aspect of nature'.

In particular, he does not think that the three aspects of mind – consciousness, reason and value – could result from natural selection because they do not obviously confer selective advantage. Evolutionary naturalism, for instance, is indifferent to morality (value), as is higher mathematics (reason, logic). Why should evolution prefer the perception of moral truth to whatever happens to be immediately advantageous for reproduction? For that matter, what is evolutionarily advantageous about knowing the theory of evolution? For Nagel this is no more than commonsensical, but it is these matters, he says, that we have been browbeaten over.

It is also obvious to him that we find it impossible to abandon the search for a transcendent view of our place in the universe. Although he continues to reject any notion of a transcendent being, he sees this as further underlining the fact that any explanation of the universe as just 'a physical process' cannot be justified: it has to include teleological elements.[18] Teleology is the nub of the argument in *Mind & Cosmos*.

This vacancy in our understanding, as he puts it – that physics and evolution are inadequate – he addresses by speculating about the 'possibility of a principle of change over time tending toward certain types of outcome'. This is a coherent view, he maintains, which implies that the physical laws we are familiar with are not fully deterministic. Moreover, consciousness is permeated with intentionality, intentions based on capacities that were unimaginable in the remote past. And he repeats: there is no adaptive need for many mental capacities, and it is not easy to see how they have survival value.

But, he goes on, if we believe in a natural order (an order we recognize), 'then something about the world that eventually gave rise to rational beings must explain this possibility'. Natural teleology is the answer, he says, and is distinct from the other alternatives – chance, creationism, and disinterested physical law. Seeing the world in teleological terms means that in addition to physical laws of the familiar kind we have to accommodate other laws of nature that are 'biased toward the marvelous'. There is, in other words, 'a cosmic predisposition to the formation of life, consciousness and the value that is inseparable from them'. 'The process seems to be one of the Universe gradually waking up.' He found all this entirely congruent with his atheism, but 'I conclude that something is missing from Darwinism'.[19]

Nagel offers the view that there is a 'cosmic predisposition' over and above the laws of physics, 'without positive conviction'. He is simply trying to extend the boundaries of 'what is not regarded as thinkable', but adds that he is willing to bet 'that the present and right-thinking consensus will come to be seen as laughable in a generation or two'.

Mind & Cosmos is a short but breathtakingly ambitious work. Despite his avowed atheism, Nagel's book received a warm reception from creationists and believers in the concept of intelligent design; the Discovery Institute, advocates of intelligent design, have approved his supposed 'deconversion from Darwinism'. Orthodox scientists have been less appreciative, arguing that he has confused the fact that evolutionary theory is incomplete with the idea that it is false. Others point out that 'epistemic humility' – the recognition that one could be wrong – is a hallmark of science; no one has been 'browbeaten' into any sacrosanct view – it is simply that, so far, Darwinism has had the better of the argument.

Yet others have confessed to being confused by Nagel's notion of natural teleology in view of the fact, for example, that there are so many different forms of life on earth, and so many instances of extinction. Also, mindless creatures far outnumber sentient ones. Several evolved eyes and then lost them as they adapted to dark environments; several parasites, having begun their evolutionary careers as complex organisms, became simpler after taking up their parasitic lifestyles. How, these scientists have asked, can teleology account for any of this?

Steven Pinker, the Harvard experimental psychologist and author of *The Blank Slate: The Modern Denial of Human Nature*, has described Nagel's book as a piece of 'shoddy reasoning by a once-great thinker'. Others have argued that Nagel makes no attempt to back up empirically what is in effect an intuitive argument, and in that sense has contravened simple scientific (not to mention commonsensical) principles. They say that recent research, with which Nagel appears unfamiliar, points towards an 'RNA world', a simple ribonucleic acid, where self-replicating molecules may have emerged – still accidentally, but much less accidentally than previously thought. And philosophers point out that values – ethics and morals, for example – are *guides* to behaviour, not explanations for it. We should give up the idea (as other philosophers have done) that there are objective moral truths, applicable everywhere and in all circumstances.

It is much too early to gauge the impact of Nagel's *Mind & Cosmos*, but it is nonetheless notable – together with Paul Davies's *The Goldilocks Enigma*, which argues for a 'life principle' in the universe – as yet another example of what we might call the 'what is missing?' genre in recent philosophy.

The Unsatisfiability of Life

Imaginative and provocative as *Mind & Cosmos* is, however, from our point of view it is more instructive to return for a moment to *The View from Nowhere*, where Nagel says that we have to live not just within the predicament of being on the edge of language, but with the realization that natural selection does not explain everything.

There are three possible routes out of the impasse he identifies. Rather, what he actually says is that there is *no* way out but there are 'adjustments' we can make 'to live with the conflict'. One, tried in the past, is to withdraw from the specifics of human life as much as possible, 'minimize the area of one's local contact with the world and concentrate on the universal' – contemplation, meditation, abandonment of worldly ambition, so that we achieve 'a withering away of the ego'. He suggests this is a high price to pay for spiritual harmony. 'The amputation of so much of oneself to secure the unequivocal affirmation of the rest seems a waste of consciousness.'

The second adjustment is the opposite of the first: 'a denial of the objective unimportance of our lives, which will justify full engagement from the objective standpoint'. This is in many ways the narcissist's view; the extent to which it can fail was discussed earlier, when it was suggested that narcissists sometimes have an unrealistic appreciation of their own abilities. The objective world is there, and always will be, whether we like it or not.

Nagel's third adjustment is to accept that the dual vision – the co-existence of a subjective and an objective world – is part of our humanity, which means accepting that we cannot break free of the predicament – that's what being human, with consciousness and language, *means*. Objectivity *transcends* us, has a life of its own, is always changing, with implications for our subjective identity, including its limits.

One of the ways this predicament can be eased, if not escaped entirely, says Nagel, is to live a moral life. In so doing we seek to live as an individual who affirms the equal worth of other individuals. 'The most general effect of the objective stance ought to be a form of humility; the recognition that you are no more important than you are, and the fact that something is of importance to you, or that it would be good or bad if you did or suffered something, is a fact of purely local significance.' We don't have to be pious about it, he says: humility falls between nihilistic detachment and blind self-importance. We must try to avoid the familiar excesses of envy, vanity, conceit, competitiveness and pride. 'It is possible to live a complete life of the kind one has been given without overvaluing it hopelessly.'

To this he adds what he calls the 'non-egocentric respect for the particular'. He is alluding here not just to the aesthetic response (though that is included too): 'Particular things can have a noncompetitive completeness which is transparent to all aspects of the self. This also helps explain why the experience of great beauty tends to unify the self: the object engages us immediately and totally in a way that makes distinctions among points of view irrelevant . . . It is hard to know whether one could sustain such an attitude consistently towards the elements of everyday life.'

To repress either side – the subjective or the objective – impoverishes life, he concludes. 'It is better to be simultaneously engaged and detached, and therefore absurd, for this is the opposite of self-denial and the result of full awareness.'[20]

Believing Is Public

Richard Rorty, who in chapter 24 was extolling the merits of 'old chestnut' poetry, agreed with Nagel that the aim of life is full awareness, but he was convinced that it can only be achieved via our relations with other people. 'The candidate for the most praiseworthy human capacity,' he said, prefiguring Sam Harris and Matt Ridley, 'is the ability to trust and co-operate with others.' We must abandon the search for something stable outside of us (such as deities or universal human nature) and that we think provides us with an independent criterion for judging. On the contrary, there are no unconditional, transcultural moral obligations, rooted in an unchanging, ahistorical human nature. Being Darwinian, he said, means accepting a world where the aim is to devise tools that help us have less pain and more pleasure. By this account, the benefits of space travel and modern astronomy 'outweigh the advantages of Christian fundamentalism'.[21]

Truth is not the goal of inquiry, whatever the Churches or secular scholarship tell us. 'The purpose of inquiry is to achieve agreement among human beings about what to do. All areas of culture are parts of the same endeavour to make life better.' The Enlightenment was mistaken when it replaced the idea of supernatural guidance with the idea of a 'quasi-divine' faculty called 'reason'. Reason involves choice and choice is invariably a compromise between competing goods, not between absolute right and absolute wrong; and the same applies to moral struggle. Likewise, the struggle for existence – there is no invisible tribunal of reason, just as there is no God. In this way we must hope that the human race will gradually come together as a community – this will be an evolutionary achievement, with consequences. We like to talk about our responsibility to truth or reason, but this must now be replaced by our responsibility to our fellow human beings.

Rorty believed that there has been, or is, or ought to be a paradigm shift from metaphysics to what he called 'weak thought'. Whereas the metaphysical tradition has been dominated by the idea that there is something nonhuman that human beings should try to live up to, something grand and all-encompassing that provides the largest possible framework for discourse, 'weak thought' acknowledges its limitations and 'just wants to make finite little changes', piecemeal re-formulations rather than intellectual revolutions. Instead of claiming that their ideas stem from something profound, advocates of 'weak thought' 'put forward their ideas as suggestions that might be of use for certain particular purposes'.

The way to regard religion is as a 'habit of action', from which it follows that our principal concern must always be the extent to which the actions of religious believers frustrate the needs of others – this is what matters, rather than the extent to which religion gets something right. 'Our obligation to be rational is exhausted by our obligation to take account of other people's doubts and objections to our beliefs.' The truth is not some absolute but, rather, 'what would be better for us to believe'. The religious believer has a right to his or her faith only insofar as it does not conflict with his or her intellectual responsibilities. Believers' need to justify their beliefs arises only when their habits of action interfere with the fulfilment of others' needs. This means that religion is inevitably privatized. If a private relationship with God is not accompanied by claims to knowledge of the divine will, there may be no conflict between religion and utilitarian ethics. But there is a duty not to believe without evidence: 'A belief accepted without evidence is a stolen pleasure.'[22]

That said, there is no way that a religious person can claim the right to believe as part of an overall right to privacy – because believing is inherently a public project: 'All language-users are in it together.' We all have the responsibility, Rorty says, not to believe anything that cannot be justified to the rest of us. 'To be rational is to submit one's beliefs – all one's beliefs – to one's peers.' Other, non-cognitive, states – such as desires and hopes – can be held without evidence, but belief cannot.

Whereas science gives us the ability to predict and control, religion holds up before us a larger hope, something to live for (Rorty's words). 'To ask which of the two accounts of the universe is true may be as pointless as asking: Is the carpenter's or the particle physicist's account of tables the true one? Neither needs to be answered if they can keep out of each other's way.' Moreover, people have a right to faith, just as they have a right to fall in love, to marry in haste, and to persist in love despite endless sorrow and disappointment.

Scientific realism and religious fundamentalism, Rorty contends, are products of the same 'urge', the attempt to convince people that they have a duty to develop what Bernard Williams calls 'an absolute conception of reality'. But, claims Rorty, both scientific realism and religious fundamentalism are 'private projects which have got out of hand', having become attempts to make one's own private way of giving meaning to one's own life obligatory for the general public.

The contemporary pragmatist philosophy of religion, therefore, must make a sharp distinction between faith and belief. Rorty argues that Tillichians strive not towards some elaborate creed or doctrine, not to produce any *specific* habit of action, but rather 'to make the sort of difference to a human life which is made by the presence or absence of love'. (Echoes here of Robert Musil's 'other condition'.) He draws a parallel between Tillich's religion and being in love with someone the rest of us can't love. 'We do not mock a mother who loves her psychopathic child. [William] James said, on the same basis we should not mock people who say "the best things are the more eternal things".'[23]

Rorty ends up with a 'faith' in the future possibilities of moral humans. 'I shall call this fuzzy overlap of faith, hope and love "romance".' Our insistence that some or all mortal humans can be far more than they have yet become is what counts; what matters is the insistence itself, the romance, 'the ability to experience overpowering hope, or faith, or love etc.'. What is distinctive about this 'overpowering' state is that it 'carries us beyond argument, because beyond presently used language. It thereby carries us beyond the imagination of the present age of the world.' At one point in our history, he says, to be religious and to be imaginative were the same thing. But things are different now, because of human beings' success (however slow at times) in making their lives and their world less wretched. It is non-religious forms of inspiration that have brought us to this point.

In the end, Rorty feels, democracy has had more to do with the demise of religion than has science (though the way science operates is of course itself a form of democracy). 'Democracies contain people who retain radically diverse ideas about the point and meaning of life, about the path to private perfection.' And he returns to his hero, John

Dewey. 'The core of Dewey's thought was an insistence that nothing – not the Will of God, not the Intrinsic Nature of Reality, not the Moral Law – can take precedence over the result of agreement freely reached by members of a democratic community.'

Rorty says that Habermas's idea of communicative reason – that reason emerges from communication between people and is like a conversation, not something laid down logically 'out there' somewhere – rightly, lowers our sights from the 'unconditional above' to the communities around us. Once that happens, other things come into view – progress, for instance. Progress, as Rorty defines it, is in fact nothing more than an idea absurd to one generation that becomes common sense to the next. In any case, we shall never be 'purified' or perfected because we can never do more than tinker with ourselves. Which in turn sabotages the idea of redemption and redemptive truth, the need to fit everything into a single context, the true realm beyond appearances. For there *is* no one true realm – as Harold Bloom said, the point of reading a great many books is to realize that there is an infinity of viewpoints, all more or less equally valid.[24]

Rorty observed that the question 'is it true?' was being replaced by 'what's new?', and that worked for him because 'A life not lived close to these limits is not worth living.' The aim of life is the enlargement of the self; by our joint efforts more and more ways of being human are becoming available. 'Intellectual and moral progress is not a matter of getting closer to an antecedent goal, but of surpassing the past. Increased knowledge is not an increased access to the Real, but an increased ability to *do* things, to make possible richer and fuller lives ... We shall never find descriptions so perfect that imaginative re-description will become pointless ... Men should walk as prophecies of the next age, rather than in the fear of God or in the light of reason.'[25]

Why Do What Is Right?

The Harvard philosopher Robert Nozick, who died in 2002, believed that philosophy needed to take account of recent scientific developments. In the three books he was most proud of – *Anarchy, State and Utopia* (1974), *The Examined Life* (1989) and *Invariances* (2001) – he drew on relativity, quantum mechanics, evolutionary theory and game theory to arrive at his own ethical system. He thought that ethics had been generated by evolution, the 'core' of ethical belief being the coordination of activity for mutual benefit. But unlike other evolutionary ethicists, if we can call them that, he believed there are four layers of ethics.

The first layer is the level of *respect*: that is, the rules and principles respecting another person's life and autonomy and restricting interference with another person's domain of choice. The second level is the ethic of *responsiveness*, which 'mandates acting in a way that is responsive to people's value, enhancing and supporting it, and enabling it to flourish'. Next comes the ethic of *caring*, which mandates 'non-harm, *ahimsa* and love to all people, perhaps to all living creatures'. The last he terms the ethic of *light*, which encompasses the dimensions of truth, beauty, goodness and holiness: 'Socrates, Buddha, and Jesus, along with various less-known *rishis*, *tzaddiks*, saints and sages point the way.' His view was that only the first level is mandatory, the only one that societies should compel, and that the others are a matter of choice and personal development.[26]

He also tackled another question that has taxed scientists and others: namely, why has it been so difficult for psychologists to formulate an accurate predictive theory of human behaviour? Why have psychologists been unable to account for more than 50 per cent of the variance in human behaviour?

His answer lies in the fact that a major cause of the explosion in the size of the human brain 'was the need of our ancestors to anticipate and counter the actions of reasonably intelligent conspecifics in situations of conflict of interest, when those others were also trying to anticipate and counter actions . . . Survival of the fittest led to survival of the brainiest.' In such circumstances violence would sometimes have been needed, but – surprisingly – unpredictability, even irrationality, would have paid off at other times. We would have learned to veil our behaviour, to behave in nonlinear ways, so as to disguise our motives. By this account, unpredictability would have had a biological function and would have led to more complex behaviour. Breaking from the norm can sometimes be exactly what is needed. Self-awareness is necessary for ethical behaviour, but from time to time non-ethical behaviour is a successful adaptive strategy.

Why this is of particular interest to us is that such behaviour, unpredictable and complex, may well be where our ability to do higher mathematics and abstract cosmology comes from. The argument of biologists such as E.O. Wilson and philosophers like Thomas Nagel – that this kind of behaviour cannot have evolved because it confers no evolutionary advantage – begins to be addressed by these arguments of Nozick.[27] As we saw, Nagel thought it was at the root of the dilemma we feel about our position in the cosmos.

In *The Examined Life* Nozick makes a partial return to Socrates, who according to Plato made the well known statement 'The examined life isn't worth living' at his trial for impiety and corrupting the youth of Athens in 399 BC. And Nozick had the interesting idea of considering what an examined life would be now (1989). He wrote as a philosopher but in everyday, non-technical language – in the form of 'meditations' – tackling the questions that he thought every reader would want to ask: What would immortality be like and what would be its point? Why isn't happiness the only thing that matters? Are Eastern doctrines of Enlightenment valid? What has gone askew when a person cares mainly about personal wealth and power? Can a religious person explain why God allows evil to exist? What is especially valuable in the way romantic love alters a person?[28]

His choice of questions he thought important, as a philosopher and as an individual, is perhaps as interesting as the answers, together with the aspects of life he thought worth meditating about: dying; parents and children; creating; the nature of God and the nature of faith; the holiness of everyday life; sexuality; being in love; happiness; focus; when do we feel most real? when do you feel most yourself? our stance towards life; what is importance and what is important? theological explanations.

He points out that to live an examined life is to make a self-portrait, that the activities of a life are 'infused' with examination,

not just affected by it, and their character is also different when permeated by the results of concentrated reflection. There are three types
of happiness: being happy that something or other is the case; feeling
that your life is good now; being satisfied with your life as a whole. But
happiness is only a small part of the interesting story, and there is no
benchmark out there – we have to set one for ourselves.

He agrees with Nagel that we all have two viewpoints, our own
and 'that of the universe', but that neither is more real. 'The realm of
reality is not the same as what exists. The greater the reality a feature
has, the more weight it has in our identity.' He argues that a properly
lived life involves giving everything its proper due, and he invites us
to think of reality as a score where the maximum is 1. 'This is what
poets and artists bring us – the immense and unsuspected reality of
a small thing. *Everything has its "own patient entityhood".*' We should
live proportionally and give everything its due.[29]

To seek to give life meaning, he said, is to seek to transcend the
limits of one's individual life, achieving an enlarged identity. 'If we
go beyond our boundaries a regress is launched. Religion used to be a
stopping place for this regress, for questions about meaning, by speaking of an infinite being, which was not properly seen as limited.' The
question of limits is all-important, for us and for God. For Nozick the
central problem is the question of the existence of evil and whether
God can be omniscient, omnipotent and good. As he puts it, God
cannot proceed 'merrily' along – this question must be answered,
and is all the more urgent now because the Holocaust was 'a rift' in
the universe. With the Holocaust, humanity has desanctified itself.
God, he says, cannot be detached; we must have a two-way relation
with him, whatever the Jewish philosophers say. For him, the Holocaust 'shut the door that Christ opened. In this sense the Christian era
has closed.'

His final word: 'We must become a vehicle for truth, beauty, goodness and holiness, adding our own characteristic bit to reality's eternal
processes. The wanting of nothing else, along with its attendant emotion, is . . . what constitutes happiness and joy.'[30]

The Duty to Live Responsibly

The philosopher whom many other philosophers defer to, or refer to most, or whose ideas they take as their starting-off point, is Ronald Dworkin, Sommer Professor of Law and Philosophy at New York University and Jeremy Bentham Professor of Jurisprudence at University College, London until his death in 2013. Dworkin was at one stage clerk to the exotically named Judge Learned Hand, the most quoted judge in US legal history, so he had an excellent pedigree to justify his eminence, as well as a number of books on the evolving law of human rights. In *Justice for Hedgehogs* (2011) his argument culminated in a magisterial account of how we are to live now. In *Religion without God* (2013) he advanced the argument that the term 'religious atheist' is not an oxymoron.

His basic premise in *Justice for Hedgehogs* was that ethical value and moral value depend on each other, and he offered this as a creed – they support a consistent way to live. But this depends on two things that come first: we must cherish both our dignity and our self-respect. 'The only value we can find living in the foothills of death is adverbial value. We must find the value of living – the meaning of life – in living *well*, just as we find value in loving or painting or writing or singing or diving well . . . There is no other enduring value or meaning in our lives, but that is value and meaning enough. Dignity and self-respect are indispensable conditions of living well [italics added].'[31]

He accepted what the ancients said when they commanded us to seek 'happiness' not as episodic glows of pleasure, but as the fulfilment of a successful life conceived as a whole. 'Our existence precedes essence [as the existentialists said] because we are responsible for the latter'; and he deferred to Nietzsche as the most influential figure in this tradition, who said, 'The only real imperative of life is *living* – the creation and affirmation of a human life as a singular and wonderful creative act.'

Dworkin thought that one of the boons of science has been that the widespread agreement over phenomena has given us confidence that there is truth to be had. The linearity of science is also a comfort in the sense that new ideas are built on firm ground. But once we accept the crucial distinction between ethics and morals, he thought, truth is as possible in law as it is in science. Moral standards prescribe how we ought to treat others; ethical standards how we ought to live ourselves. We must distinguish between living well and having a good life. 'Living well means striving to create a good life, but only subject to certain constraints essential to human dignity . . . Living well means creating a life that is not simply pleasurable but good in that critical way.'

Responsibility to whom? he asks. His answer: We are charged to live well by the bare fact of our existence as self-conscious creatures with lives to lead. 'It is *important* that we live well; not important just to us or to anyone else, but just important.' An illustration: a person who leads a fairly humdrum conventional life without close friendships or challenges or achievements, who is merely 'marking time' until he goes to his grave, has not had a good life, 'even if he thinks he has' and even if he has thoroughly enjoyed the life he has had. For Dworkin, 'He has failed in his *responsibility* for living.'

Living, we should never forget, involves a performance that can be better, or worse. We value great art not just because the end product enhances our lives but because the whole enterprise embodies a performance, 'a rising to artistic challenge'. A human life well lived also embodies a performance, 'a rising to the challenge of having a life to lead'. The final value of our lives is adverbial, not adjectival. It is the value of the performance, not anything that is left when the performance is subtracted. It is the value of a brilliant dance or dive when the memories have faded and the ripples died away. 'Performance value is the value of a life.'[32]

Value is not entirely about consequence. As Dworkin puts it, 'Philosophers used to speculate about what they called the meaning of life. (That is now the job of mystics and comedians.)' If we did measure the value of life by its consequence, 'all but a few lives would have no value and the great value of many others would have only accidental value (like carpenters who worked on Shakespeare's Globe)'.

There are two principles governing the fundamental requirements of living well. The first is self-respect. 'Each person must take his own life seriously; he must accept that it is a matter of importance that his life be a successful performance rather than a wasted opportunity.' Collecting matchbook covers is not just wrong but silly – the choice of something trivial is not ethically reasonable. The second is the principle of opportunity. Every individual is responsible for identifying those opportunities that count as success in his own life through 'a coherent narrative or style that he himself endorses'. Together the two principles offer a conception of human dignity: dignity requires self-respect and authenticity. Acts are wrong if they insult the dignity of others.

Living well means not just designing a life as if any design will do, but 'designing it in response to a judgment of ethical value'.[33] Enjoyment is in most cases an epiphenomenon of the conviction that we are living as we should.

All this poses problems for theocratic communities that impose their own closed ethical regime by coercion, which compromises their subjects' authenticity. On the other hand, in liberal political communities, individuals who subject themselves to the ethical authority of their Church do so voluntarily, unless their adherence is mechanical and plays no part in the rest of their lives.

The idea that the universe houses some force 'bigger than we are' is held by us all, Nagel included. Dworkin admits that even atheists may have some cosmic notion. But he says that the main ethical import of the 'force larger than we are' idea, in a secular world, is not to provide a distinctive (religious) way of living but rather 'to provide a defence against the frightening thought that *any* way we live is arbitrary'. This is of course the basis of the whole notion of the 'absurd' that so taxed the existentialists and others. But Dworkin challenges this. Why, he asks, is it not as valuable to live up to the pointlessness of eternity, if the universe is pointless, as to live up to its purpose if it has one? For even if there is no eternal planner, '*we* are planners – mortal planners with a vivid sense of our own dignity and of good and bad lives, that we can create or endure. Why can we not find value in what we create? Why must value depend on physics?'[34]

The wholly unexamined life, as the ancient philosophers warned us, is also a bad one. Some effective ethical conviction, 'at least [being] sometimes engaged', is essential to responsible living. You live badly if you do not try hard enough to make your life good. Just government is drawn from dignity and aims at dignity. We make our lives tiny diamonds in the cosmic sands. The meaning of life is dignity.

The Beauty of Mystery and the Mystery of Beauty

In *Religion without God** Dworkin argues that the familiar stark divide between people of religion and people without it is too crude. This distinction leaves many people out in the cold, he says, but many who do not believe in a personal God or who reject the 'inanity' of the biblical account of creation, for instance, nonetheless believe in a 'force' in the universe 'greater than we are'. It is this, he says, that leads them to 'an inescapable responsibility' to live their lives well, with due respect for the lives of others; and if they feel their life is wasted they suffer inconsolable regret. Religious atheism is not a contradiction in terms because even atheists can feel 'a sense of fundamentality', that there are things in the universe that, as William James put it, 'throw the last stone'.

Life's intrinsic meaning and nature's intrinsic beauty, Dworkin says, are the main ingredients of a religious attitude, irrespective of whether people believe in a personal God. When scientists confront the unimaginable vastness of space and the astounding complexity of atomic particles they find the universe awe-inspiring and deserving 'of a kind of emotional response that at least borders on trembling'. This recalls Nagel's comment that 'existence is something tremendous'. Moreover, Dworkin adds, these are convictions that one cannot isolate from the rest of life.

He suggests that some of the confusion we experience arises from the fact that the Abrahamic religions in particular have a 'scientific' part (the creation, the afterlife, the dialogue of prayer and judgement) and a 'value' part, whereas the religious attitude depends on the full independence of value – the world of value is self-contained and

---

*This had not appeared in book form as *The Age of Nothing* went to press, but several long extracts had appeared, on which this discussion is based.[35]

self-certifying and quite distinct from the 'scientific' part of the traditional monotheisms. He argues that we find it impossible not to believe the elementary truths of mathematics and, when we understand them, even the complex equations, we do not need any independent corroboration. We have this capacity but we do not know how we have it, and the religious attitude insists that we embrace our values in the same way. 'I do not mean that value judgments are in the end only subjective. Our felt conviction that cruelty is wrong is a conviction that cruelty is really wrong: we cannot have that conviction without thinking that it is objectively true.' The fact that theodicy has produced no answers to evil that are even 'remotely satisfying' is perhaps the strongest argument against the existence of a personal God (in this he agrees with Robert Nozick).

And Dworkin believes that what he calls the 'scientific' part of theistic religions – their claims about historical events, about causes and effects (miracles, for example), about how people should live, via ritual duties of worship, prayer, turning to Mecca and so on – can be discarded by non-believers without damaging the value part of religion, which determines ethics and morals. Whether traditionally religious or not, people 'accept that nature is not just a matter of particles thrown together in a very long history but something of intrinsic wonder and beauty'.

The 'science' part of the traditional monotheisms cannot ground the value part, he insists, because they are conceptually independent. 'Human life cannot have any kind of meaning or value just because a loving god exists. The universe cannot be intrinsically beautiful just because it was created to be beautiful. There is no direct bridge from any story about the creation of the firmament, or the heavens and earth, or the animals of the sea and the land, or the delights of Heaven, or the fires of Hell, or the parting of any sea or the raising of any dead, to the enduring value of friendship and family or the importance of charity or the sublimity of a sunset or the appropriateness of awe in the face of the universe or even a duty of reverence for a creator god.'

The principle is this: one cannot support a value judgement – an ethical or moral or aesthetic claim – just by establishing some 'scientific' fact about how the world was, is or will be. What divides godly and godless religion, he says, is the 'science' of godly religion, but that is not as important as the faith in value that unites the two.

What finally creates the religious attitude, Dworkin says, is aesthetic – that we find the universe beautiful – but how we can do so (because we have no extracosmic standards with which to compare it) is a mystery; and he agrees with Einstein (and, it should be said, with Wallace Stevens) that mystery is the greatest beauty.

We feel that the explanation (of what is) has to end somewhere more fundamental, in a cascade of ever deeper reasons, but is this really the case? There is a beauty in the inevitability of mathematics, but mathematical solutions just end, without the need to go anywhere else, anywhere more fundamental. Is there a lesson in that? On this analogy, any activity in life – aesthetic, moral, ethical, scientific – can be an end in itself, with nothing further to be said. Liberty is one's right to define one's life and its end. There need be no more fundamental answer.

In this argument, taken in conjunction with those in *Justice for Hedgehogs*, Dworkin is articulating an aesthetic meaning to life, that it should be beautiful morally and ethically and above all not trivial. His concern with the centrality of value overlaps with Thomas Nagel's, but that is as far as the overlap goes. As indicated, on this Dworkin has more in common with Nozick.

A Synthetic Unity Has Held Us Back

Jürgen Habermas has led the way in a new kind of thinking. He coincides with Rorty, Dworkin and Hilary Putnam in arguing that we now inhabit a world of 'intersubjective acceptability' so far as what we know is concerned – what Putnam calls 'warranted assertability', derived from science. Habermas says it is not that the multiplication of roles in modern life has increased our autonomy, but that we simply have more socially binding roles, and what is needed, if we are to lead fulfilling lives, is a concept of individuation 'that captures the missing dimension of autonomy and the capacity to be oneself'. He identifies the crucial change as coming not with Nietzsche but with Rousseau, who said that we should not appeal to God for truth, but instead to the 'unrestricted universal public'. There is no transcendental perspective, he asserted, but a plurality of perspectives. Progress comes from 'unforced agreement in dialogue', what Dewey called 'the unforced flowers of life'.[36]

But Habermas goes on to say two things more. First, that we should think of ourselves as a 'me' rather than an 'I'. This captures the – what is for him – social and reflexive nature of individuality: that, whether or not we know it, or like it, we live surrounded by norms. Only by being aware of norms can we break out of them and achieve autonomy.

Second, he argues that the fallibilism of science has been as important as its technological successes and its theoretical breakthroughs. It is the 'procedural reasoning' of science that counts, the process by which understanding is built up by trial and error. This goes counter to the previous (religious) manner of living, which 'crystallised around the theoretical attitude of one who immerses himself in the intuition of the cosmos'. The same question is posed again and again: 'how are the one and the many, the infinite and the finite, related to each other?' The answer: 'The cosmological idea plays the role of a methodological principle of completeness; it points to the goal of the systematic unity of all knowledge.'[37] The triumph of the one over the many is, for Habermas, the most important aspect of metaphysical thinking, underpinning much of religion as well.

Even idealism traced everything back to 'the one', he says, with the consequence that the metaphysical mind regarded 'mere phenomena' as secondary. 'Transcendental singulars introduced a synthetic unity into the pluralities of history, cultures and language': that, he feels, held us back. Post-metaphysical thinking is an important step forward.[38]

The Rationality of Religion: a Post-secular Society?

In *Between Naturalism and Religion* Habermas tackled the problems of what he called a 'post-secular world'. He thought that archaic religious doctrines had been overtaken but that ideological polarization threatened to undermine civic cohesion across the globe, as the use of religion for political ends increases. He observed that religious traditions and faith communities have become more important since the fall of the Berlin Wall and the concomitant changes of 1989–90, and that it is around religious family law in particular that the problems congregate. He therefore felt that some plain speaking was needed in regard to relations between the religious and secular sectors in the modern state.

On the one hand, reason must be detranscendentalized and the self-understanding of the constitutional state must rely on public natural reason, arguments equally accessible to all. Church and state must be separated, religious traditions must accept the neutrality of the state vis-à-vis religious questions and practices; we must accept that we have a duty of civility. More controversially, he stated that 'people must not be allowed to express and justify their convictions in a religious language (even when they cannot find "secular translations" of them)'; and, no less controversial, that faith and reason are 'two forms of dogmatism'.[39]

Habermas then considered what most people found his most original argument: namely that, although the disagreements between secularists and religious believers 'can never be solved at the cognitive level', religions are far more rational than atheists think, and it is the responsibility of secularists *to accept this* (his emphasis). 'Today religious traditions perform the function of articulating an awareness of what is lacking or absent [in our lives]. They keep alive a sensitivity to failure and suffering. They rescue from oblivion the dimensions of our social and personal relations in which advances in cultural and social rationalization have caused utter devastation.'

He then elaborated, arguing that concepts like autonomy and individuality, emancipation, solidarity and inspiration all developed under religious systems; that the deeds and words of prophets and saints are to be understood as edifying narratives to help us overcome the weaknesses of human nature; that revelation is to be understood merely as a concept that 'shortens the route to the dissemination of rational truths'; that piety has the rational function of sustaining the conduct of the believer. Moreover, he believed that transcendence is a way of transposing the divine standpoint into a functionally equivalent inner-worldly perspective; that religions make truths accessible in doctrinal form that human beings *could and ought to have arrived at* [his italics]; that modernity and science should be understood as the outcome of a history of reason 'of which the world religions are an integral part'.[40]

He thought it worth making these points for two reasons. First, if different religions were to recognize that they had the same origin, it would make tolerance much easier. Second, because of the adjustments religious people have to make in a secular state, they bear 'cognitive burdens' that secular citizens do not. So to even up the score, so to speak, he proposed that if secularists accept that we *are* in a post-secular society, then they too must accept some cognitive burdens: 'In line with the standards of an enlightenment endowed with a critical awareness of its own limits, the secular citizens [must come to] understand their non-agreement with religious conceptions as a *disagreement* that it is *reasonable* to expect [his italics].' Religious and secular citizens must undergo complementary learning processes.

Habermas wasn't so unworldly as to think that all this would come about easily. He noted – as Dworkin noted, as Freud devoted a career to noting – that 'the sources of sensuousness escape the understanding', and that the secular consciousness would always find it easier to be neutral. 'For the religious, other ways of life are not merely different but mistaken. To be made to understand is felt as an imposition.' Therefore, there will always be an asymmetry as regards the burdens borne by believers and by unbelievers. We should seek to minimize them in the knowledge they can't be removed entirely.[41]*

---

* In 2012 the British writer Alain de Botton published a popular version of this argument in *Religion for Atheists*, where he accepted the proposition that religious practices are grounded in reason and speculated on how some of these practices might be 'updated'. For example, he thought we might have 'Agape' restaurants, where guests could not sit with their friends but would be made to meet new people. Taking their seats, they would find a guidebook in front of them, 'laying out the rules for how to behave at meals'. 'The Book of Agape would direct diners to speak to one another for prescribed lengths of time on predefined topics . . . Thanks to the Agape restaurant our fear of strangers would recede.' Another suggestion was for quarterly 'Days of Atonement', on which it would become institutionalized for people to apologize for their mistakes over the previous weeks, and scores would be settled and not allowed to fester. A third idea was an annual night off from our spouses, when everyone would be allowed 'to party and copulate

*

Finally, we return to where we came in, to Habermas's *An Awareness of What Is Missing*. This book was a collaboration with Jesuits from German universities, who were responding to the essay from which the book took its title. In it, Habermas repeated many of his views, concluding – more vigorously than before – that what is missing now is 'solidarity'. We have not mastered the dynamics of modernity, he insisted, and most of us feel that it is 'spinning out of control'. Religion cannot be characterized simply as irrational; reason has its limits; and the 'scientistic' belief that science will give us a new self-understanding is, moreover, bad philosophy. The modern world encourages a retreat into the private domain but this is, for the most part, 'awkward and prickly'. Secular morality is not embedded in communal practices, and we lack any 'impulse to solidarity'.[42]

Is there something disappointing in this conclusion? Is it true that secular morality is not embedded in communal practices? Certainly, such contemporary minds as Rorty, Hilary Putnam, Nozick and Dworkin agree in foregrounding ever more inclusive communities. Recent developments in the law – which are practices of a sort – reflect this impulse. The cognitive divisions, as Habermas or Dworkin would put it, between secular and religious people are here to stay, and are conceivably ineradicable. Those differences have not as yet led to conflicts of the kind that we see routinely between religious groups across the world.

And maybe there is a lesson here, one that Habermas has not written about. He is probably right in saying that the secular bear less of a cognitive burden in living in modern society than do the religious. And that shows in their tolerance. In modern societies, it is easier to be secular – less of a burden – than to be religious.

Among other things, it is the collective achievement of the figures introduced in this book. What does that tell us?

------

randomly and joyfully with strangers, and then return next morning to our partners, who will themselves have been doing something similar, both sides knowing that it was nothing personal'. De Botton's ideas were either, as one critic put it, just plain 'silly', or else heroic. Possibly both.[43]

CONCLUSION

The Central Sane Activity

Shortly before Christmas 1996 the author Salman Rushdie was still in hiding, driving south from Sydney with his girlfriend and son to spend the holiday with the novelist Rodney Hall. Rushdie had been in Australia, under guard, to publicize a book and had decided to stay on. His police protection team had said it was safe because no one would know he was staying on. So they withdrew, though by then, despite the hit squads not having found Rushdie, they had found his Italian translator and his Norwegian publisher, who had been attacked and injured, and his Japanese translator, who had been murdered.

About halfway through their journey, as Rushdie and his party were passing through the small town of Milton, the tape they had been listening to (Homer's *Iliad*) came to an end and Rushdie, who was at the wheel of the rental car, took his eye off the road for a 'fraction' of a second to press the eject button. At that very moment an enormous articulated truck swung out of a side road. There was an equally enormous tearing sound, 'the horrible death-noise of metal on metal', as the truck's cab hit the driver's door, crumpling it inwards. The car wasn't dragged under the truck, as it might well have been, but bounced off a wheel and across the road, hard against a tree. The windscreen was smashed and the driver's door wedged shut, but the three occupants were largely unhurt – Rushdie himself the most badly, with a fractured arm.

Milton had a small medical facility and an ambulance was quickly brought. When the ambulance men arrived, they stopped and stared. One of them said, 'Excuse me, mate, but are you Salman Rushdie?' Right then he didn't want to be – he wanted to be an anonymous person receiving medical treatment – but he admitted that, yes, he was. 'Oh, OK, mate, now this is probably a terrible time to ask, but could I get an autograph?'

Across the road the shocked truck driver wasn't getting any better treatment. The police had arrived, they too had recognized Rushdie and so wanted to know what the driver's religion was. The driver was bewildered. 'What's my religion got to do with anything?' Was he trying to carry out the fatwa? he was asked. The driver didn't know what a fatwa was.

He was let go, but that still wasn't the end of it. The truck turned out to have been carrying fertilizer. 'Having eluded professional assassins for almost seven years, [Rushdie] and his loved ones had almost met their end under a mighty avalanche of dung.'[1]

It is a good story, but it reminds us of the sheer monstrosity of the fatwa's continued existence. The horrors perpetrated against Rushdie, in the name of Islam, may not have matched the scale of the attacks on the Manhattan World Trade Center of 11 September 2001, in terms of lives lost, but the very fact that it was to be more than twenty years before he felt safe enough to publish his memoir carries its own intimate level of horror. Rushdie is an atheist and the book that sparked the fatwa, *The Satanic Verses*, is in part an ironic discussion of certain verses in the Koran – the off-message message of which, some Koranic scholars have suggested, can only be explained if the prophet was at the time accidentally taking dictation not from God but from Satan. The ludicrous improbability of such an interpretation makes the ensuing deadly events all the more absurd and criminal.

This book began by showing how the infinity of horrors committed in the name of religion has driven many people away from belief in God, and to look elsewhere for satisfaction, fulfilment and meaning in their lives. Now, toward the end of our journey, we can see that this search constitutes a major plank of modernity, and has been a preoccupation of many serious and creative minds in the past 130 or so years since Nietzsche's madman made his fateful pronouncement.

We need to remind ourselves one last time that many people – and perhaps the quieter souls among us – see no problem in God being dead. For them his death is no source of anxiety or perplexity. Such individuals may call into question Robert Musil's claim that even people who scoff at metaphysics feel a strange cosmic presence, or Thomas Nagel's comment that we all have a sense of looking down on ourselves as if from a great height. But such individuals are not 'metaphysical types' and seek no 'deep' meaning in existence. They just get on with their lives, making ends meet, living from day to day and season to season, enjoying themselves where they can, untroubled by matters that so perplex their neighbours. They have no great expectations that 'big' questions will ever be settled, so devote no time to their elucidation. In some ways, they are the most secular people of all and perhaps the most content.

Countless others live in circumstances so meagre, so minimal, so fraught with everyday material difficulties that there is no time for reflection; circumstances where such an activity is beyond their means. By such people's standards a concern with meaning, a preoccupation with the difference between how to live a good life and how to live well, is something of a *luxury*, itself the achievement of a certain kind of civilization. We must accept that the search for meaning is, by this account, a privilege.

This has been an eventful journey, but it cannot claim to exhaust its subject. Though there are good reasons for having begun with Nietzsche (not least because the late nineteenth century was the time when most prominent scientists stopped believing in God), we could have started earlier, with Søren Kierkegaard or Arthur Schopenhauer. Among more recent figures we might have considered Harold Bloom's ideas about literature as a way of life, his worship of Shakespeare and Whitman ('For me, Shakespeare is God'); his idea that informed *appreciation* is a pleasure and that though poems are 'sacred vessels', even poetry is a Darwinian exercise of insidious competition; and his suggestion that a great writer's aim is to create 'heterocosms', alternative but accessible worlds, open to us all.

We might have considered the sociologist Robert Bellah's notion (echoing Descartes) of 'civil religion': that citizens, whatever their confession, venerate in a secular way such entities as national anthems, national flags, war victims, foundation myths, inaugurations and coronations, the funerals of great political figures; and espouse such unifying concepts as, in America, for example, the constitution (and its various amendments) and what he calls 'manifest destiny'. Or we might have considered Richard Sennett, who as a one-time musical prodigy-turned-sociologist has brought a kind of poetry into his discipline by examining aspects of the secular world that stand outside most traditional sociological categories: respect, craftsmanship, the rituals and pleasures of cooperation – and above all the way we get on with fellow citizens who are 'alien' to us. He has examined, in secular detail, how we confront Karl Barth's abstract idea of the 'other', and in doing so identifies this as a major predicament of our time and seeks practical ways to confront it.

Or again, we might have looked at the American lawyer Alan Dershowitz's secular theory of the origins of rights: namely, that rights do not come from God, or nature, or logic but from our piecemeal experience of injustice – rights come from wrongs; we are always more likely to agree on what wrongs exist than what a perfect system of justice would be.[2] Or Mihaly Csikszentmihalyi's idea of *Flow: The Psychology of Optimal Experience*, where he identifies the aim of life as a tussle between anxiety and boredom, the way out being autotelic activities, activities that are enjoyable in themselves, not for any larger purpose, because there *is* no larger purpose. On this account, there are four kinds of pleasurable activity – *agon*, where competition is the main dimension, *alea*, activities of chance, *ilix*, activities that alter normal perception, and *mimicry*, dance, theatre, the arts in general. When you close in on 'flow', however, it appears as yet another word for happiness-fulfilment (though perhaps more precise than other accounts), echoing phenomenology above all other approaches, and indeed the author does refer back to Heidegger, Sartre and Merleau-Ponty. Bergson, Rilke and Whitehead all had an understanding of life as 'flow'.

All these and more could have been added to the mix. But if this exercise has been worth doing, one reason is that it has revealed overlaps as between the ideas of many of the figures discussed. Some overlaps have been more obvious than others, but the very fact that they exist surely tells us something, gives us a starting point when trying to work things out for ourselves.

One place to start is with James Wood's paraphrase of Thomas Mann, that 'the idea of one overbearing truth is exhausted'. Mann and Wood meant these words in a special way, but they apply more generally too. The overall intellectual trajectory of the long twentieth century, of modernism and postmodernism, has been to reinforce the argument that there is not – there cannot be – any privileged viewpoint from which to look out upon the world. This has serious consequences for religion, and it doesn't stop there. During the past 130 years many of the dominant political ideas (colonialism, imperialism, communism, fascism), the great psychological ideas (the unconscious, personality), and the great philosophical ideas (Hegelianism, positivism, Marxism), have been exploded too, to be replaced not by other grand 'isms' but by much smaller, less ambitious, more pragmatic notions.

We are concentrating on religion because God has been – and for many still is – the greatest and most overbearing idea there is or has ever been. But in fact the death of God, our subject here, is only one death among many. In that sense he was not singled out.

It is difficult to exaggerate the effects of this change. As we have observed, Virginia Woolf was so taken by the changes taking place in the 1920s that she felt human nature itself was being transformed. We don't need to go that far. In the last thirty or forty years we have grown used to the geneticists telling us that certain aspects of our nature are so fixed that there will always be a 'stubborn biological core', a limit to what we can improve on, unless we are willing to embark on a radical interference with our genetic code.

As we have noted, religion has not been immune to this generally evolving intellectual climate, which has taken place among some of the worst atrocities ever inflicted by human beings on other human beings, and on many other forms of life too. As a result, even among believers ideas about God have changed – to the point where he may not be omniscient after all, or all-powerful, or always wholly good, or wholly perfect; where he sometimes veils his face from humankind (turning his back on us); and, most profoundly or oddly, depending on your viewpoint, where he is completely 'other', a different kind of phenomenon altogether (except that the word phenomenon, by definition, can't apply in this case); where he is defined by what he is not, where his existence is asserted precisely on the grounds that there cannot be any evidence – evidence that we wouldn't understand even if it did exist.

This seems to be the end point of a certain kind of reasoning – an overbearing idea that lacks any attributes by which it might 'overbear', a breathtakingly insouciant endpoint in an infinite regression of what a God might be.* Add to this Olivier Roy's analysis, referred to in the Introduction, that globalized, deterritorialized religions now risk being decultured and therefore 'purified', becoming more fundamental and ideologically 'thinner'. Far from being 'timeless', religions are still evolving.

Against all this it is surely a relief to turn to ideas that we can recognize as manageable, modest, reasonable, which are based on observation and evidence, and are mutable. Once we accept that the age of overbearing ideas is over, we are free to move on, to examine the 'lesser' ideas that have been found serviceable, since Nietzsche slipped into a coma in that Turin street in 1889.

Meaning Is Not a Security Blanket

Science and psychoanalysis apart, the most profound development in thought since Nietzsche, as far as we are concerned, is the phenomenological approach to the world. Mallarmé sought 'words without wrinkles', Baudelaire cherished his *minutes heureuses* and Valéry his 'small worlds of order', as we have seen; Chekhov concentrated on the 'concrete individual' and preferred 'small-scale and practical answers', Gide thought that 'systematizing is denaturing, distorting and

---

* Although many people find the concept of the 'other' new, St Augustine, sixteen hundred years ago, defined God as a phenomenon that couldn't be known.

impoverishing'. For Oliver Wendell Holmes, 'all the pleasure of life is in general ideas, but all the use of life is in specific solutions'. Wallace Stevens considered that we are 'better satisfied by particulars'. Thomas Nagel put it this way: 'Particular things can have a noncompetitive completeness which is transparent to all aspects of the self. This also helps explain why the experience of great beauty tends to unify the self: the object engages us immediately and totally in a way that makes distinctions among points of view irrelevant.' Or as Robert Nozick, who counselled us to make ourselves 'vehicles' for beauty, said: 'This is what poets and artists bring us – the immense and unsuspected reality of a small thing. Everything has "its own patient entityhood".' George Levine calls for a 'profound attention to the details of this world'.[3] (And chapter 24 was entirely given over to poetry's faith in – and affirmation of – detail.)

In turn, this coincides with the idea of the episodic in life, Proust's *moments bienheureux*, Ibsen's 'flashes of spiritual value', Shaw's 'infinitesimal increments' and 'moments of infinite consequence'. Kandinsky spoke of 'little pleasures', Malraux of 'temporary refuges', Yeats referred to 'brief moments of ecstatic affirmation' and Joyce to his 'epiphanies'. Abraham Maslow had his 'peak experiences', modelled on the orgasm, and Freud thought that happiness was invariably episodic. Impressionist art was in reality not so much impressionistic as painstakingly given over to capturing the evanescent nature of experience – here, Monet's Rouen Cathedral, his haystacks and water lilies are archetypal examples. Again, in chapter 24, we learned of Seamus Heaney's 'shimmer of reality' and 'momentary stays against confusion', of Mandelstam's 'nuggets of harmony', Lowell's 'bolts of clarification', experiences of life 'clicking shut and breaking open', of Sylvia Plath's poems of 'surprised arrival', and Eugenio Montale's

> I am no more
> than a spark from a beacon

Virginia Woolf, Robert Musil, Eugene O'Neill and Samuel Beckett too have noted that moments of 'being' can only ever be just that – moments. That the most we can hope for are brief experiences of heightened intensity. It is as if there are two realms of existence (as expressed by both Woolf and Musil, but also Rilke and Wittgenstein); to live a full life we must be alive to these two realms but not expect more than is there. There is no supernatural realm, only, as Woolf put it, brief holidays from our 'cotton wool days'. George Santayana and Philip Roth shared this view. Santayana thought that well-being occurred in 'reflective episodes of consummate joy that gave *point* to things'; that we need a 'holiday life', a time and place where we can get away from the workaday world and play, that the aim of life should be 'spontaneous affirmation' of what is lovely and lovable. Philip Roth's 'Mickey' Sabbath delighted in his 'holiday' from rationality. Jonathan Lear, professor of philosophy at Chicago, says that life without the idea of the irrational 'is incomplete'.

What is central to all this is the *size* of life, the parameters of living, and, as Joyce said, 'living down to fact'. It is the very opposite of what we might call 'cosmic consciousness', which fuels so many religious feelings and it is reinforced by the ideas of such figures as George Moore, Virginia Woolf and David Sloan Wilson, who suggest we 'act locally', intimately, with those closest to us. Moore thought that our most vivid experiences would be with close relations and friends; for Woolf intimacy was as close to spiritual feeling as we are capable of, while Wilson thinks we are most likely to encounter enchantment in local activities. Here too it is the size of life that is being emphasized.

One reason for the episodic nature of experience is the allied idea that the personality is not fixed, that none of us is just one person. Richard Rorty reminds us that several philosophers have concluded 'there is no structure of human existence'. For Santayana there was no core human nature, 'which is merely a name for a group of qualities found by chance in certain tribes of animals, artificially foregrounded by us'. Gide thought he had a new self every day and Czeslaw Milosz wrote about how difficult it was 'just to remain one person'. Yeats thought that 'personality is a constantly renewed choice', and Pound and Eliot said much the same. Goronwy Rees wrote '[A]t no time in my life have I had the enviable sensation of constituting a continuous personality.' While for the British philosopher John Gray, 'We cannot shake off the sense that we are enduring selves and yet we know we are not.' (He remarks of Rees's life that it was not a novel but a series of short stories.)[4] Eugene Goodheart of Brandeis University summed up this view: 'The coherent person is not a seamless unity, but the representative of the will to self-mastery.'

In turn, unity has come under scrutiny – not just the lack of unity of the individual but of the universe, the cosmos – for what effect its breakdown has had on our thinking, in terms of metaphysics, transcendence and the very image of what God might be.

The one form of unity that holds fast is narrative, the narrative of a life, made up of discrete episodes. Alasdair MacIntyre argues that action – behaviour – becomes intelligible only within a narrative. As Gordon Graham puts it, 'The key to living a life as opposed to merely existing . . . lies in an acquired, and increasingly sophisticated, ability to see and act in accordance with the requirements of narrative intelligibility.' He adds: 'We learn to do this in part by imitation, but we are also enabled to forge such connections by the opportunities for understanding that fiction provides.' Life, by this account, is 'a constant hermeneutic movement' guided by the 'anticipation of the [narrative] whole'. Bruce Robbins, professor in the humanities at Columbia, says that secularism is itself a narrative of progress; and, in that, an improvement over religious belief.

This brings us back to there being no overbearing idea. One of the achievements, perhaps, of the twentieth century was the retreat from the idea of 'wholeness', 'oneness', the search for one all-encompassing meaning; the idea that meaning is a big thing, a security blanket, as Auden intimated. Which returns us to Wittgenstein, who believed that there are certain aspects of experience/the world that cannot be put into words, or be painted; that language gives us a feeling of the world as a whole, but a limited whole; and it is this sense of limits, and that there is something 'beyond' those limits, that constitutes the mystical, the idea that there is something missing. There is an overlap here with Paul Valéry's idea that the poet approaches the world 'asymptotically', that we get closer and closer to meaning without ever quite reaching it. There may be no boundary to language, George Steiner says, but – again – let us not expect more than there is. The Cambridge philosopher, Simon Blackburn, catches something of the same sense when he writes, 'There always seem to be better words, if only we could find them, just over the horizon'. And goes on to echo Alasdair MacIntyre, 'I believe the process of understanding the problems [of life] is itself a good.'[5]

Secularization, then, goes well beyond unbelief towards a new, and more or less coherent, way of approaching life. It teaches us how to look out upon the world, appreciating it detail by detail. We can't all be artists, but we can all use the artistic approach; as Santayana said, art shows us 'finite perfection' without a deity. Or, as summed up by Wallace Stevens: 'We never arrive intellectually. But emotionally we arrive constantly (as in poetry, happiness, high mountains, vistas).' There is in the world a superabundance of meaning, not just one security blanket.

There remains one major issue to consider. The approach followed here has identified a strong secondary side to secularization. In Stefan George's opinion, science has not improved the world, but impoverished it. Eugene O'Neill believed science had been co-opted by capitalism, and so was diverted from more charitable aims. Virginia Woolf, though interested in psychology, thought that the other sciences had no part to play in our moral or aesthetic lives. For D.H. Lawrence, science, in eschewing contact with the irrational, was distancing itself from 'life'. For George Steiner science was and is contaminated because, as Heidegger said before him, it aims at mastery. Gordon Graham has said that 'science does not produce the sort of truths that one can live by. What it can do, and manifestly has done, is generate techniques for desire-satisfaction.' For Thomas Nagel, in his latest book, the reductive evolutionary narrative is 'almost certainly' wrong.

Some of these arguments cannot be sustained. Their interest lies in their being evidence for the fact that the great rival 'magisterium' to religion, as Stephen Jay Gould described the scientific world view, has not found quite the universal acceptance that many of its adherents would wish. As we have seen, there is no shortage of people who do find science a perfectly adequate alternative to religion, who clearly *do* see in the details and processes of nature enough awe, beauty, enchantment and elevation to last a lifetime. And they are also finding science a help in understanding our moral lives, how we can live together for the greatest benefit of all.

And yet, there is no denying, either, that many other people do not share their view quite so enthusiastically. It is important to say that these other individuals are not necessarily 'anti-science', and they are often well informed. But they are not *moved* by science as, for instance, Dawkins, Dennett and Levine so clearly are. For those others, science is not enough. Freud had a word for this – 'intellection'. Early on, he believed that once his patients had 'proper information' about their condition they would be cured; later he realized that they had to 'work through' it and come to terms with the 'affective' elements.

Is something similar at work in the general response to science?*

'A Want of Living Glow'

There are at least two possibilities. One is that the whole approach of science – its aim being not just ever more accurate descriptions of nature, but ever more abstract theories *about* nature, explaining more and more with fewer and fewer formulae – is too far removed from everyday life. It is *too* abstract, even too constricting. Abstraction, though exciting for many, may be just too dry, too uninvolving as an experience if you are not a direct participant. (Scientists are constantly telling us that more children should be persuaded to study science, that it offers an exciting, rewarding life. The fact that they keep doing it seems to suggest that their exhortations rarely work.)

Walt Whitman said evolution betrayed 'a want of living glow, fondness, warmth'. Could this be why the phenomenological approach to life has been so successful in the time since Nietzsche had his say? Is it more than coincidence that Edmund Husserl set down his views at more or less the time Nietzsche did? The phenomenological approach, understanding life as an inexhaustible number of individual

---

* The Bolsheviks made the same mistake in Russia, thinking that once the errors of religion were explained to the people, faith would drain away.

experiences, appreciating the individuality, concreteness and voluptuousness of objects, events and experiences, has remained strong
and constant. Jean-Paul Sartre's 'lyrical phenomenology' catches it –
singing about the sheer multiplicity of experience as the joy of being
alive.

Dennett, Dawkins, Levine and the other evolutionary biologists
would object to this way of seeing things and, to an extent, they would
be right. Darwin himself was a great observer of detail; evolutionary
theory depends on adaptation and variation, which are specific ways
of showing how detail has profoundly affected our long-term history.
As Dawkins has said, we now have two ways of appreciating rainbows,
poetically and scientifically.

Consider Mallarmé's desire to name flowers 'absent from all bouquets', or these lines describing Stefan George:

> The pain from some old cruelty
> Etched in his cheeks

These lines may be saying no more than that poetry is different from
science, though they may help explain why poetry appeals in a different way. *Engagement* with poetry is more immediate than engagement
with science; the sharing that a poet offers is different from the sharing a scientist offers. Reading a poem, we enter more into the life of
the poet than, when reading a scientific report, into the life of a scientist. We can follow Darwin on the *Beagle*, and the reasoning that
led him to imagine natural selection, which we easily concede is an
awesome achievement. Biologists say it moves them. (And Dawkins
said Darwin made it possible to be an intellectually fulfilled atheist.)
We can also agree that when Niels Bohr realized that the outer orbits
of the electrons in the atom explained chemical reactions – thereby
linking physics and chemistry – something inside him and us clicked
shut and broke open, as Seamus Heaney wrote of good poetry.

With poetry, *verification* becomes a pleasure for the reader, there
is no need for a third party; and this is a crucial difference – the poet
leaves something for the reader to discover for him- or herself, *about*
him- or herself. Phenomenology offers a way of being in the world, at

home in the world, as Heidegger said, that science, for all its successes, does not.

The second reason why science has not had quite the impact some of its adherents anticipated is that, although the fundamental process of evolution and natural selection has to do with sexual reproduction, evolutionary biology is rather dry – bloodless, one might say – when it comes to the subject of desire. Eugene O'Neill wrote a lot about desire – the desire to avenge a wrong, the desire for social recognition, the greed for a piece of property, for power, the lust for another's body. But desire for most people refers to this last: sexual desire, the most interesting, forceful and – well – desirable form of desire there is. Anna Clark's book *Desire* is subtitled 'A History of European Sexuality'. Henry James, the Utopians, Sherwood Anderson in *Beyond Desire*, Tennessee Williams in *A Streetcar Named Desire*, all considered desire to be the greatest source of satisfaction *and* therefore the most disruptive element in life. So too did Stefan George, James Joyce and Philip Roth. Henry James thought that desire is at the root of all evil. Christopher Hitchens reminds us that the divorce of sex from fear and from religious tyranny was one of the great events of the twentieth century. Wilhelm Reich was convinced that 'the ecstatic attitude is preferable to the analytic'.[6]

Valentine de Saint-Point had her 'Manifesto of Lust' in 1913, Léger spoke of 'the binding energy of desire transformed into rhythms of shape'. Milan Kundera wrote about the 'tyranny' of desire, Michel Foucault about power and desire. Jacques Lacan said, accurately enough, that 'desire repeats itself until it is recognized', Jean-François Lyotard that 'western man wants to conquer, not love' and that men feel 'undone' when they love. The novel, as one critic put it, is 'the repetitious discovery of sexual motive'. All religions have at their heart the control of desire, which, as often as not, the Churches see as the pre-eminent basis of sin.

But Roth's Nathan Zuckerman had it right, as the writers of another genre we might have included – utopian fiction – had it right when, to a man (Wells, Zamyatin, Hauptmann, Huxley), they saw desire as above all a *disruption* in life, the source of unruliness and subversion (Zuckerman abandons himself to uncensored desire). This is because, as John Gray – the Nietzsche of our day for his pithy and aphoristic style – says, 'Sexual passion enables the species to reproduce; it cares nothing for individual well-being or personal autonomy.'[7] Desire is without question the most important *irrational* aspect of life; as Eugene Goodheart states in *Desire and Its Discontents*, desire is a destabilizing force, disintegrating; it leads to extravagance and excesses of the will. All desires have a right to be fulfilled, but to experience desire, says Jonathan Lear, denotes a kind of lack in life. Ideals, he adds, give shape to desire, though at the same time 'The pleasure principle is at loggerheads with the whole world.'[8] Desire, too, of course, links to intimacy, mentioned earlier.

And here again we see a temporal coincidence, except that perhaps again it wasn't really a coincidence. As religion declined, as Nietzsche announced the death of God, so arrived more or less on cue the theories and practices of Sigmund Freud, whose psychoanalysis was based largely on a recognition of the disruptive fires of desire in the form of the libido, a sexual force of great power, infinitely malleable but ineradicable. Freud's influence was second to none in the twentieth century.

To what extent are these temporal coincidences, if such they are, related, and to what extent do they account for the fact that science, despite its undoubted successes both intellectual and moral, has not engaged the imaginations of as many people as might have been expected? In fact, the impact of detail and desire go together – they both speak to an *immediacy* that the abstractions of science do not. Relevant here is Habermas's theory that the idea of the cosmos brings with it the concept of unity, which has proved so influential in religion, metaphysics and other forms of philosophy. But if we accept David Deutsch's idea that there are in fact a number of cosmoses, parallel universes, in a multiverse (a concept easier to accept than Tipler's omega point), then the idea of cosmic unity goes out of the window too. We may still view the totality of the multiverse as a single entity, perhaps, but that is a much less overbearing idea than that of one single cosmos. In the modern world, in modern science, the idea of unity as a basic concept is under threat, as much as is the idea of one overbearing truth. The theory of everything, so sought after by physicists, which aims/hopes to find a common thread between the four main forces of the physical world – electromagnetism, the strong and weak nuclear forces, and gravity – will not, even if discovered, affect the idea of parallel universes. The very fact that unity is proving so hard to demonstrate is itself important – it may never regain the overriding force it once had.

So we are thrown back again on to a phenomenological approach, to find solace and meaning away from the 'grandeur' of the universe(s) and stick to what we know intimately and immediately. As Ortega y Gasset said, we cannot put off living until the scientists say we are ready.

This matter of size – of grandeur or its opposite – may be all-important. To what extent has religion, especially the great monotheisms, given us a false sense of the size of life? The very concepts of salvation, redemption, transcendence, eternity and infinity, in which monotheisms routinely deal, invite us – like science, in this respect – to contemplate the grandeur of abstract notions, into which fits quite seamlessly what Cynthia Ozick calls our 'haunted desire for human completion' – desire again.[9] Is the very idea of completion, wholeness, perfectibility, oneness, misleading, even diverting? Does the *longing* for completion imply a completion that isn't in fact available? Is this our predicament?

This in turn leads us to ask whether, just as the religious idea of the 'whole' has been punctured, other religious notions have been similarly mistaken? For example, has life really become less enchanting because Max Weber said so? Could it be that Weber was seriously wrong in telling us that the post-religious world is disenchanted?

Let us look at the timing of his statement. Weber made his remarks in 1918 when the ravages of the First World War were fresh in the mind, before the blood of millions of dead had congealed, when the world was anything but enchanting. And this was a war, moreover, that in many people's eyes owed a lot to the nihilistic writings of Friedrich Nietzsche. But in May 1919 Arthur Eddington confirmed the existence of relativity, an experimental observation soon followed by others that led on to quantum mechanics and such extraordinary ideas as the wave–particle duality and the exclusion principle. Other discoveries, such as dendrochronology, carbon valency, the Big Bang theory and the evolutionary synthesis, followed.

To say that such notions are not enchanting is to bend the meaning of enchantment. To many people they were certainly weird ('quantum weirdness', in particular), equivalent to the magic on which religions relied in an earlier age. But the new enchantment was and is explicable – an advance, surely. Weber died in June 1920, soon after his pronouncement. Had he lived on through the 1920s, he would surely have changed his mind. Had he fully engaged with Darwinian variation, becoming ever clearer in the early years of the century due to burgeoning research in the new field of genetics, and had he come fully to terms with the clinical nature of psychoanalysis in which interpretation was always made on an individual basis; had he encountered Niels Bohr's linking of physics and chemistry in the structure of the atom, or Linus Pauling's explanation as to why some substances are yellow liquids and others black solids – he would surely have concluded that the world was now more engrossingly enchanting than ever. Similarly, had he lived to witness the rise of film, with silent movies giving way to sound, he would surely have seen this as an even more accessible source of enchantment – for most people, no doubt, much more so than quantum weirdness.

As Bruce Robbins says, the disenchantment narrative ignores a great deal about the pre-modern world that was far from enchanting (brought home recently in the German film *White Ribbon*). It needs repeating that the world is vastly more enchanted now than it was before the death of God.

By the same token, is redemption any longer a useful concept? Richard Rorty didn't think so because, as he put it, we are not degraded. Roger Scruton, though religious, half-agrees when he argues that modern art is a 'redemption of the commonplace' (this we might characterize as a 'small' form of redemption). Transcendence has been dismissed time and again by modern philosophers (Bernard Williams, Thomas Nagel, Ronald Dworkin, Jürgen Habermas) as a non-phenomenon. For Rorty, again, neither the word nor the concept of the 'sacred' is any longer of use, because 'everything is up for grabs'. And as already mentioned, if we accept Olivier Roy's account of the globalization, deculturation and deterritorialization of religion, it is faith that is changing its contours, becoming 'thinner', not the secular life. Terry

Eagleton said mischievously that he thought happiness was a 'holiday-camp' sort of word. And as for happiness (or self-actualization), there seems to be general agreement that one can't go looking for it, that it is the by-product of other, more worthwhile activities, and this may be why it is most often encountered in recollection.

The two big ideas that everyone seems to agree about, as regards our subject, are hope and the need for a more inclusive community – this is where we are to find meaning. George Santayana, Scott Fitzgerald, E.O. Wilson, Richard Rorty, Czeslaw Milosz, Charles Taylor and Pope Benedict XVI all introduce the matter of hope into their writings. (Nietzsche, of course, regarded hope as a trick played on mankind, causing us to be more optimistic about progress than it really merited, especially since the 'false dawn' of the Enlightenment.)

The Meta-narrative of Emancipation

For many people, too, hope is engendered by the expansion of the moral community which, despite all, is happening, if fitfully. Gianni Vattimo and Richard Rorty insist that 'no experience of truth can exist without some participation in a community'. Minority ethnic groups, women, homosexuals, the disabled, religious sects and many others are now being accorded greater equality and respect; we are becoming less tolerant of such matters as 'collateral damage' in wars, while at the same time more tolerant in any number of ways – this is the process known as 'social hope' (something John Gray has dismissed as 'shallow'). Being more tolerant may not feel like meaning, but it is to those who are the recipients of the new tolerance, allowing them to live fuller lives.

Of all these minorities, no doubt the most important politically are the ethnic groups. In terms of numbers – and often because of their religious identities – this means that in the foreseeable future they will be the world's major concern and remain the bitterest sources of conflict. In terms of psychological and philosophical adjustment, on the other hand, the most important development in the future may be what some have called a switch to female values. Nietzsche called truth a woman; James Joyce foresaw, with pleasure and optimism, a world where hope lay with the female side of men. Andrea Dworkin has emphasized that the world we have now is 'man-made', a term by no means complimentary. Wallace Stevens admonished us to 'embrace an idea like a woman'. Politically, too, this is a highly relevant issue; who can doubt that one of the ways in which Islam is most backward is in its (often disgraceful) treatment of women.

Triviality and Consequentiality

These issues are not unimportant and are part of a larger picture, but in a sense they skirt around the main concern of this book.

On this issue, how we are to live without God, it seems clear that the crux is the moral life. Philosophers of all stripes (except Thomas Nagel, especially lately) are in agreement with the evolutionary biologists that morality has evolved, along good Darwinian principles. (David Sloan Wilson's recent exploration of the evolution of catechisms and forgiveness is a tantalizing step forward.) Not only is God not needed to explain this, but evolution is a better *authority* so far as morals are concerned. It is experimentally confirmed that evolution shows rationally why morality is justified, identifies the benefits, and highlights what is lost when the rules aren't adhered to. In particular – and this may be the most important point of all – the studies show how the requirements of the 'selfish gene' lead to the need for, and justification of, cooperation. Biology links ethics to morals.

Ronald Dworkin writes most clearly about the distinction between ethics and morals. Ethics refers to the way we lead our own lives, reflects our responsibility to ourselves, not in a narcissistic way, but by understanding life as a *performance* which we can carry through either well or not so well. He invites us to reflect on our lives – conceivably along the lines that Robert Nozick exemplified in his book *The Examined Life* – to construct a narrative that is coherent, moral and non-trivial. The idea that there is a narrative to a life is very powerful for many people. Dworkin thinks our aim should be a narrative that allows us to marvel at the universe and gives us dignity and self-respect. For him, this *is* being religious without God. There is nothing deeper, or grander.

If that is our first duty, our second is to other people, to accord them respect so as to preserve *their* dignity, and the people we should show respect to include an ever-expanding group until, eventually, it will include everyone. This is one aim of life, what Bruce Robbins calls the 'metanarrative of emancipation'.

The need to be 'consequential' is more controversial, given that not everyone can be equally consequential, and if we judged a life solely by its consequences most people would be found to lead inconsequential lives, or lives that are only accidentally consequential. Dworkin's point about life being a performance, which can be carried out either well or not so well, is surely another aspect of consequence: we construct the performance of our own lives to have a coherence, a coherence that is in some sense non-trivial and truthful – those two qualities together giving us self-respect and dignity – and allows us, as Nozick said, to become a vehicle for beauty as well as truth, coherence itself being a form of beauty.

Secular Revelation: What We Didn't Know We Had within Us

To this we can add an idea of Seamus Heaney's. Heaney is endlessly quotable: poetry adds to the volume of good in the world; a new rhythm is a new life given to the world; poetry produces a sense of at-homeness and trust in the world; poetry is a natural process, simultaneously proffered by the phenomena of the world and engendered by the frolic of language; it is the transmission of intuited knowledge; poetry is to keep on coming into a fuller life, it is an experience of enlargement; poems stand like cathedrals in the wilderness; they offer an infrangible dignity, unconsoled clarity, unfenced existence, they are the outward sign of an inner grace; they are examples of self-conquest; they show that the reality of the world should not be underprized; they offer a sense of sufficiency, and a spurt of abundance from a source within.

It is this last that we focus on here. In one of his essays Heaney quotes from Czeslaw Milosz's *The Estate of Poetry*:

> In the very essence of poetry there is something indecent:
> A thing is brought forth which we didn't know we had within us[10]

Isn't that second line a secular equivalent of a revelation and a profound guide to leading a life? To keep on coming into a fuller life, to not underprize the reality of the world, to explore our unfenced existence, don't we have to bring forth something that 'we didn't know we had within us'? And how are we to do that? What criteria can we use by which we will know that we have achieved that aim, that our activities – like those of Dworkin's matchbook-cover collector – are not trivial?

There is almost certainly no one criterion that would fit the bill to everyone's satisfaction, but there is one poet who has influenced many philosophers and other writers precisely because he made a determined and imaginative stab at it, and whose life certainly had a distinctive narrative.

Naming the World

Rainer Maria Rilke thought that what lends sense to life is the act of 'saying', of transforming into language all that is in danger of being lost in our hurry to move ahead. In particular he felt that the details and glories of nature were under threat and that Christianity's emphasis on the afterlife had prevented us from experiencing this Earth – which is all there is – as fully as we might, and that it is the post-Christian recovery of this experience that gives 'sense to life', making sheer wondering enquiry the 'central sane activity'.

> O happy earth, O Earth on holiday,
> Play with your children! Let us try
> To catch you . . .

In one sonnet he spoke of a 'boundless inner sky' – words that sit happily on a page with Seamus Heaney. What Rilke was trying to do in his poetry was not dissimilar to what Cézanne had sought to do in his painting, to approach nature – the Earth – in an unmediated way, trying to dispense with the accumulated practices of the past, notably Christianity, which have hindered a true appreciation of the Earth and the sheer joyfulness of existence. Rilke also thought that the Earth could be best enjoyed by singing, singing being unique to humans, and with music weaving a line through the present, 'lyrics uniting the time-based events of our words by recalling them back into the presence of one another through the repetition of their sounds'. For him, saying and singing overlapped.

And that is the point. In his *Sources of the Self: The Making of the Modern Identity* Charles Taylor says that we have lost the power to name things. Taylor is surely as way off the mark here as Weber was earlier. For with the advent of science, our ability to name things has increased exponentially. And this too is the point, or a large part of it, because naming, saying, singing the world constitute the very criterion by which, it is being suggested here, we may judge whether that something we have within us which we bring forth is to be assessed as a success, even consequential. And along the way, of course, singing the world is – literally – enchantment.

Identifying the electron, the double-helix structure of DNA, the process of natural selection or cosmic background radiation – all this is naming the world. So is identifying viruses and the identification of the ice ages, the Stone Age, the Bronze Age. So is the identification of the formula $E=mc^2$, or the principle of flight, or the phenomena of sea-floor spreading and tectonic plates. But so too are these lines of the American poet Elizabeth Bishop:

> The five fishhouses have steeply peaked roofs
> and narrow, cleated gangplanks slant up
> to storerooms in the gables
> for the wheelbarrows to be pushed up and down on.
> All is silver: the heavy surface of the sea,
> swelling slowly as if considering spilling over

Bishop, who described herself in childhood as 'full of hymns', was a fervent admirer of Darwin. She thought he had built up a 'solid case' based on 'heroic observations', and on her visit to Britain in the 1960s she journeyed by Green Line bus to Darwin's house. She continued to return to his 'beautiful books' because she was convinced, as she knew he was, that, as he confided to his notebooks, 'the sublime is reached through the commonplace', the 'slow accretion of facts'. This made her, according to Guy Rotella, 'a religious poet without religious faith'.

Rebecca Stott highlights these lines of Bishop's about a meandering bus journey along the Nova Scotia coastline:

> A moose has come out of
> the impenetrable wood
> and stands there, looms, rather,
> in the middle of the road.

Stott describes this episode as a collective epiphany of the bus passengers, 'locked in the otherworldly stare of the moose who is "high as a church"'. It is a Darwinian sublime, a secular enchantment, but it is not an apotheosis – 'the bus departs, leaving only the smell of gasoline behind'. In Bishop's work, Stott says, the sublime moment is 'giddying' but there is no transcendence, no significance that is *above*; it is instead a fall, a falling back into the smell of the gasoline, or the memory of the smell, an *immersion* (Stott's preferred word) in *this* world.[11]

Or consider 'beautifell', 'As it is uneven', 'beauhind' from *Finnegans Wake*: seemingly inconsequential, but they are not just puns – clever or irritating or juvenile as the case may be: they enable and encourage us to see the world in new ways; or they clarify and crystallize thoughts we have *almost* had, that we wish we had had, or would have had, had we slowed down enough and honed our own observations a bit more. At the same time, and ironically and paradoxically, they recall George Steiner's words, that aesthetic truths quicken our life, linking temporality and eternity in a way unavailable elsewhere. And remind us of Dworkin's claim that performance itself has value, is part of the point. Throughout this book, it has been not just what has been said, but the style and force with which it has been said that counts equally.

That phrase of Elizabeth Bishop's about the sea 'considering spilling over' is also a thought we have all almost had, that we grasp immediately and silently thank her for, with a nod of the head – silver words that extend our world, underlining our uncertain and unfinished relationship with the sea and its unfathomable behaviour. Zbigniew Herbert's poem about a pebble, cited earlier, could be set alongside Brancusi's sculpture of an egg, which, as Robert Hughes said, draws much of its expressive power from its 'eloquent material presence' and resists analysis because 'it does not seem to be put together'. It has a patient entityhood.

These words may not have changed the world as much as, say, the quantum, the electron or the gene (who was it who said no poem ever stopped a tank?). But they don't need to, to be consequential, if they enlarge the experience of other people, and enchant us. If there is one thing that the thinkers discussed in this book are agreed upon it is that there is no one, overbearing benchmark by which the world may be judged, so let us relish that truth, not continually try to deny it. Observation of the world can be heroic. That is what the people in this book have taught us. Observation can be liberating, enlarging – that is what we thank them for.

'We Shall Grieve Not. Rather Find/Strength in What Remains Behind'

Which brings us back again to that most underrated movement of the twentieth century, the philosophy of phenomenology, the idea that life is made up of *les minutes heureuses*. And the notion that in a world no longer illumined by God or reason, all attempts to reduce its infinite variety (the universe, experience) to concepts, ideas or essences – whether religious or scientific, whether they involve the 'soul', or 'nature', or 'particles' or the 'afterlife' – *diminish* the actual variety of reality which is part, and maybe the biggest part, or even the whole, of its meaning.

Religious people can approach the world as phenomenologists every bit as much as the secular can. But how, exactly, are they to calibrate their response? In his *Proof of Heaven: A Neurologist's Journey to the Afterlife*, referred to in the Introduction, Eben Alexander describes the heaven he visited during his coma as containing butterflies and flowers. Were these more beautiful than the butterflies and flowers on earth? If so, how are we to regard the ones we see in this life? – as inferior? If the flowers and butterflies in heaven are not more beautiful, does that not take away part of the purpose of heaven? Alexander also said that heaven was 'populated' by angels and souls and that the whole experience was blissful. Does this mean that the people we see on earth are, again, in some way inferior, imperfect? If so, how can we fully enjoy what we have on earth, knowing something better is to come? No wonder John Gray snorts: 'What could be more dreary than the perfection of mankind?'[12]

With a little effort, armed only with imagination, the great majority of us can surely 'name' the world in some fashion, or try to. Rilke, Santayana, Stevens, Lawrence, Steiner, Rorty, Scruton and many others have extolled the unrivalled importance of imagination. The beauty of naming lies in the fact that we need no great undertaking – like a war, the Large Hadron Collider built by the European Organization for Nuclear Research (CERN) in Switzerland, or a politico-social project like building a new town or a nuclear submarine – to achieve something consequential, in the sense that naming the world extends it and fulfils us and helps engender a greater sense of community. That is, in other words, a success both ethically and morally.

And this is perhaps the greatest achievement of contemporary moral philosophers. Probably, everyone of a secular inclination has always known, deep within themselves, that the aim to bring about a wider, more inclusive sense of community – as a reflection of greater equality, liberty and fairness – is the best and, indeed, the only way forward. But that this cannot be achieved without a sense of responsibility *to ourselves*, without dignity, without a sense of life as a *performance*, without avoiding *triviality*, without a personal narrative, needed clarifying. This puts into context Thomas Nagel's admonition that we cannot find meaning by helping others. That is, not *only* by helping others.

The central role of ethics and morals leads us to divide life into three realms: the realm of science, which most of us can't escape and which has brought us so many advances, technological, intellectual and in terms of expanded *understanding*; the phenomenological world, the world of Sartre's *petites heureuses*, of art and poetry, the world of small, patient, non-competitive entityhood, which is its own form of understanding and so complements science. And the world of desire.

Not enough has been made of desire, perhaps, since Nietzsche made his pronouncement, though he was himself very much alive to the difference between the Dionysian and the Apollonian. Advances have been made in this realm to widen the acceptable arenas of desire: for instance, homosexuals and women have had their lives, if not transformed, at least eased.

But there have been losses, setbacks and stalemates too, one being in the matter of female circumcision, barbarically still practised in several regions of the world.

James Joyce, back in the 1920s and 30s, identified losses too (in *Ulysses* and *Finnegans Wake*). Joyce saw that with all the changes taking place around him, in Europe in particular, in terms of the family, living conditions, education, contraception, greater mobility and in the mass media, the great casualty in life would be *enduring love*; that this intimate form of fulfilment, available to everyone, would be much harder to achieve.

As the latest divorce figures would seem to show, not only do most people not achieve enduring love, they don't *expect* it any more; many may not think it worth achieving, or even be aware that it is an available goal. The recent French film *L'Amour* tells the story of an old couple who have experienced an enduring love and a life rich in music, but now in old age the wife has a stroke, then a second, and eventually becomes incapable of anything at all, let alone love. For her husband there is nothing left *to* love. Music is no consolation. He smothers her, out of enduring love, and commits suicide.

In this one sense, then, modern life is impoverished, is harder for us to find meaning within. Religious people might claim that they experience an enduring love for the Church, or their God, but can a Church or a God *reciprocate* like a wife, a husband or a partner? Is reciprocity not the essence, the pleasure of desire, the heart of its desirability? Is there anything more consoling, satisfying, fulfilling than to be desired, and to go on being desired? The many child abuse scandals involving priests would seem to suggest that even a life spent in the Church does not offer the kind of fulfilment of desire that adult human reciprocity bestows.

But the religious life also suffers greatly by comparison when it comes to naming. Religions – at least the great monotheisms – look back, by definition. Habermas is right, that many aspects of religious doctrine and ritual are rational, designed to ease the human condition; and this is the aim, too, of the new rituals Alain de Botton has suggested for atheists. But the greatest advance, if it can be called that, made by religion since Nietzsche is the idea that God is totally 'other', defined by . . . well, by being unnameable. By being, in a sense, nothing.

But where does that get us? In his recent book *Anatheism* (meaning 'the return to God') Richard Kearney states that, after the disasters of the twentieth century, traditional ideas of God can no longer be entertained. He discusses the work of such figures as Paul Ricoeur, Emmanuel Lévinas, Jacques Derrida and Julia Kristeva and their views about what form religious belief can take now. But the opacity of both his own and their prose, the density of the lockjaw syntax, the difficulty they all experience in trying to name what Kearney concedes is the unnameable, makes his book the very opposite of poetry – rather than being a stay against confusion, his words at times are that confusion.[13] He appears to be saying that some people just like being in a 'faith-state', prefer having faith to not having faith, and so will always be on the lookout for something to have faith *in*. Is this evidence for whatever is the object of their faith? No, but then faith doesn't require evidence, and we are back where we started.

By this account, then, the latest developments in religion cannot give us meaning, or sensible purpose, *by definition*, because they define God as unnameable; they have no part to play in the ever expanding, forward-looking naming of the world. The lines from Wordsworth that grace the heading of this section have his unmistakable – and magnificent – stamp. But if one criticism may be levelled, they imply that what is left behind is static, whereas the world has moved on, in so many ways; and as the French philosopher and theologian Nicolas Malebranche said over three hundred years ago, 'The world is unfinished.'

So let us end by repeating the wise words of that great lover of poetic chestnuts, the philosopher Richard Rorty, referring to those who have named more of the world: 'Cultures with richer vocabularies are more fully human – farther removed from the beasts – than those with poorer ones.'

NOTES AND REFERENCES

Introduction: Is There Something Missing in our Lives? Is Nietzsche to Blame?

1 Salman Rushdie, *Joseph Anton*, London: Jonathan Cape, 2012, pp. 236–7.

2 Thomas Nagel, *Secular Philosophy and the Religious Temperament: Essays*, New York and Oxford: Oxford University Press, 2010, pp. 8–9.

3 Thomas Nagel, *Mind & Cosmos: Why the Materialist Neo-Darwinian Conception of Nature Is Almost Certainly False*, Oxford and New York: Oxford University Press, 2012. Ronald Dworkin, 'Religion without God', *The New York Review of Books*, 4 April, 2013. See also the three Einstein lectures Dworkin delivered at the University of Bern on 12–14 December 2011, at: http://www.law.nyu,edu/news: Ronald Dworkin. And see, for example, Mary Jo Nye, *Michael Polanyi and His Generation: Origins of the Social Construction of Science*, Chicago and London: University of Chicago Press, 2011, pp. 289–94.

4 Charles Taylor, *A Secular Age*, Cambridge, Mass.: Belknap Press/ Harvard University Press, 2007, pp. 20, 44.

5 Taylor, *op. cit.*

6 Richard Kearney, *Anatheism (Returning to God after God)*, New York: Columbia University Press, 2010.

7 London *Times*, 5 January 2011, p. 1. For the Lee Enfield motor cycle worshipped in India, see 'Travellers flock to find roadside comfort at the shrine where Royal Enfield is God', London *Times*, 5 February 2011.

8 Peter L. Berger (ed.), *The Desecularisation of the World, Resurgent Religion and World Politics*, Washington DC: Ethics and Public Policy Center/William B. Eerdmans Publishing Company, Grand Rapids, Michigan, 1999, p. 2.

9 Berger, *op. cit.*

10 Eben Alexander, *Proof of Heaven: A Neurologist's Journey to the Afterlife*, New York: Piatkus, 2012, *passim*.

11 Pippa Norris and Ronald Inglehart, *Sacred and Secular: Religion and Politics Worldwide*, Cambridge UK: Cambridge University Press, 2004, p. 3.

12 Norris and Inglehart, *op. cit.*, p. 13.
13 *Ibid.*, p. 14.
14 *Ibid.*, p. 221.
15 *Ibid.*, p. 16.
16 *Ibid.*, p. 23.
17 John Micklethwait and Adrian Wooldridge, *God Is Back: How the Global Revival of Faith Is Changing the World*, London: Allen Lane, 2009. Rodney Stark and Roger Finke, *Acts of Faith*, Los Angeles, Berkeley and London: University of California Press, 2000, pp. 4, 79. London *Times*, 2 May 2009, pp. 58–9.
18 Micklethwait and Wooldridge, *op. cit.*, p. 58 and quoted in London *Times*, 2 May 2009.
19 Norris and Inglehart, *op. cit.*, p. 231. Jonathan Haidt, *The Righteous Mind: Why Good People are Divided by Politics and Religion*, New York and London, 2013, pp. 311–13.
20 Norris and Inglehart, *ibid.*
21 Nigel Biggar, 'What's it all for?' *Financial Times*, 24 December 2008.
22 'God eclipsed by ghost believers', London *Daily Mail*, 24 November 2008. Thomas Dumm, *Loneliness as a Way of Life*, Cambridge, Mass.: Harvard University Press, 2010.
23 Michael Foley, *The Age of Absurdity*, New York: Simon & Schuster, 2011. Ben Okri, 'Our false oracles have failed. We need a new vision to live by', London *Times*, 30 October 2009. Jeanette Winterson, 'In a crisis art still asks simply that we rename what is important', London *Times*, 1 November 2008.
24 London *Times*, 4 September 2009, p. 15. Betsey Stevenson and Justin Wolfers, 'The Paradox of Declining Female Happiness', *American Economic Journal*, vol. 1 (2), pp. 190–225, August 2009.
25 *New York Times*, 20 January 2013, p. A3.
26 Curtis Cate, *Friedrich Nietzsche*, London: Hutchinson, 2002, p. 395.
27 Cate, *op. cit.*, p. 395.
28 Luc Ferry, *L'Homme-Dieu ou le sens de la vie*, Paris: Grasset, 1996. *Man Made God: the Meaning of Life*, trans. David Pellauer, Chicago: Chicago University Press, 1995. See also Ferry, *What Is the Good Life?*, Chicago University Press, 2009.
29 Ferry, *Man Made God*, p. 153.
30 *Ibid.*, p. 180.
31 *Ibid.*, p. 183.
32 *Ibid.*, pp. 167, 181.
33 Jennifer Michael Hecht, *Doubt as History: the Great Doubters and Their Legacy of Innovation, from Socrates and Jesus to Jefferson and Emily Dickinson*, San Francisco: HarperSan Francisco, 2004, p. 371.
34 Owen Chadwick, *The Secularisation of Europe in the Nineteenth Century*, Cambridge UK: Cambridge University Press, 1975, p. 89 and *passim*. See also James Thrower, *The Alternative Tradition: Religion and the Rejection of Religion in the Ancient World*, The Hague and New York: Mouton, 1980.
35 Larry Witham, *The Measure of God: History's Greatest Minds Wrestle with Reconciling Science and Religion*, San Francisco, Harper, 2005, *passim*.
36 Callum Brown, *The Death of Christian Britain, Understanding Secularisation 1800–2000*, 2nd edn, London and New York: Routledge, 2009; see especially ch. 6. And Olivier Roy, *Holy Ignorance: When Religion and Culture Part Ways*, trans. Roy Schwartz, London: Hurst, 2010, especially chs 4, 7.
37 Chadwick, *op. cit.*, p. 133.

1: The Nietzsche Generation: Eros, Ecstasy, Excess

1 Steven Aschheim, *The Nietzsche Legacy in Germany*, Ca. and Oxford, England: University of California Press, 1992, p. 17.
2 Aschheim, *op. cit.*, p. 19.
3 *Ibid.*, p. 20.
4 *Ibid.*, p. 22.
5 *Ibid.*, p. 25.
6 Seth Taylor, *Left-wing Nietzscheans: The Politics of German Expressionism*, Berlin: Walter de Gruyter, 1990. Richard Schacht (ed.), *Nietzsche, Genealogy and Morality: Essays in Nietzsche's Genealogy of Morals*, Berkeley and London: University of California Press, 1994, p. 460.
7 Aschheim, *op. cit.*, p. 31.
8 *Ibid.*, p. 33.
9 *Ibid.*, p. 39.
10 *Ibid.*
11 For an idiosyncratic view see Bernard Shaw, *The Sanity of Art: An Exposure of the Current Nonsense about Artists Being Degenerate*, London: New Age Press, 1908.
12 Joachim Köhler, *Nietzsche and Wagner: A Study in Subjugation*, trans. Ronald Taylor, New Haven and London: Yale University Press, 1998, chapters 4 and 9.
13 Aschheim, *op. cit.*, p. 40.
14 *Ibid.*, p. 43.
15 *Ibid.*, p. 45.
16 *Ibid.*, p. 49.
17 Paul Bishop (ed.), *A Companion to Nietzsche: Life and Works*, Rochester, NY: Camden House, 2012, pp. 51-7.
18 Aschheim, *op. cit.*, p. 51.
19 *Ibid.*, p. 52.
20 *Ibid.*, p. 57.
21 Martin Green, *Mountain of Truth: The Counterculture Begins: Ascona, 1900-1920*, Hanover and London: Tufts University Press, New England, 1986, p. 185.
22 Green, *op. cit.*, p. 186.
23 *Ibid.*, p. 56.
24 *Ibid.*, p. 68.
25 *Ibid.*, p. 71.
26 Joachim Köhler, *Zarathustra's Secret: The Interior Life of Friedrich Nietzsche*, trans. Ronald Taylor, New Haven and London: Yale University Press, 2002, especially chapter 10.
27 Aschheim, *op. cit.*, p. 221.
28 *Ibid.*, p. 70.
29 *Ibid.*, p. 102.
30 Eugene L. Stelzig, *Hermann Hesse's Fictions of the Self: Autobiography and the Confessional Imagination*, Princeton and Oxford: Princeton University Press, 1988, pp. 117-18.
31 Aschheim, *op. cit.*, p. 64.
32 *Ibid.*, p. 60.
33 Green, *op. cit.*, p. 95.
34 *Ibid.*, p. 96.
35 *Ibid.*, pp. 99–100.
36 Susan A. Manning, *Ecstasy and the Demon: Feminism and Nationalism in the Dances of Mary Wigman*, Los Angeles, Berkeley and London: University of California Press, 1993, p. 127.
37 Aschheim, *op. cit.*, p. 102.
38 *Ibid.*, p. 103.
39 *Ibid.*, p. 106.
40 *Ibid.*, p. 107.
41 Rudolf Laban, *The Mastery of Movement*, Plymouth: Northcote House, 1988. John Hodgson, *Mastering Movement: The Life and Work of Rudolf Laban*, London: Methuen, 2001, pp. 72, 82-3.
42 Aschheim, *op. cit.*, p. 143.
43 *Ibid.*, pp. 143-4.
44 Tom Sandqvist, *Dada East: The Romanians of Cabaret Voltaire*, Cambridge, Mass.: MIT Press, 2006, pp. 87, 188.
45 Aschheim, *op. cit.*, p. 61.
46 *Ibid.*, pp. 62-3.
47 Manning, *op. cit.*, pp. 160-1.
48 *Ibid.*, p. 115.
49 Neil Donohue (ed.), *A Companion to the Literature of German Expressionism*, Rochester, NY,

Woodbridge: Camden House,
2005, pp. 175–6.
50 Aschheim, *op. cit.*, p. 65.
51 J.M. Ritchie, *Gottfried Benn: The Unreconstructed Expressionist*, London: Wolff, 1972.
52 Aschheim, *op. cit.*, p. 68.
53 *Ibid.*, p. 112.
54 *Ibid.*, p. 117.
55 *Ibid.*, p. 124.
56 Adian Del Caro, *Nietzsche contra Nietzsche: Creativity and the Anti-Romantic*, Baton Rouge: Louisiana State University Press, 1989.

2: No One Way that Life Must Be
1 Louis Menand, *The Metaphysical Club*, Cambridge UK: Cambridge University Press, 2001, pp. x–xii.
2 Peter Watson, *Ideas: A History from Fire to Freud*, London: Weidenfeld & Nicolson, 2005, p. 936.
3 *Ibid.*, p. 935.
4 Edward Lurie, *Louis Agassiz: a Life in Science*, Chicago: Chicago University Press, 1960, pp. 346–7.
5 Watson, *op. cit*, p. 944.
6 Richard Rorty, *Philosophy and Social Hope*, London: Penguin, 1999, p. 77.
7 Menand, *op. cit.*, pp. 357–8.
8 Rorty, *op. cit.*, p. xviii.
9 *Ibid.*, p. 30.
10 *Ibid.*, p. 31.
11 *Ibid.*, p. 33.
12 *Ibid.*, p. 34.
13 *Ibid.*, p. 36.
14 Geoffrey Hodgson and Thorbjørn Knudsen, *Darwin's Conjecture: The Search for General Principles of Social and Economic Evolution*, Chicago and London: Chicago University Press, 2010, pp. 229–32.
15 *Ibid.*, p. 50.
16 John J. Stuhr, *100 Years of Pragmatism: William James's Revolutionary Philosophy*, Bloomington, Ind.: Indiana University Press, 2010, chapters 1 and 10.

17 Rorty, *op. cit.*, p. 57.
18 *Ibid.*, p. 77.
19 *Ibid.*, p. 78.
20 Jay Martin, *The Education of John Dewey: A Biography*, New York: Columbia University Press, 2002, pp. 439ff and 502.
21 Rorty, *op. cit.*, p. 83.
22 *Ibid.*, p. 87.
23 Henry Samuel Levinson, *Santayana, Pragmatism and the Spiritual Life*, Chapel Hill and London: University of North Carolina Press, 1992, p. 174.
24 Levinson, *op. cit.*, p. 155.
25 *Ibid.*, p. 148.
26 *Ibid.*, p. 90.
27 *Ibid.*, p. 248.
28 Marianne S. Wokeck and Martin A. Coleman (co-eds), *The Life of Reason, or, The Phases of Human Progress*, by George Santayana, Introduction by James Gouinlock, Cambridge, Mass.: MIT Press, 2011, pp. 81, 118–19, 183–4.
29 Rorty, *op. cit.*, p. 178.
30 *Ibid.*, pp. 124, 131.
31 *Ibid.*, p. 51.
32 *Ibid.*, p. 138.
33 *Ibid.*, p. 36.
34 *Ibid.*, p. 234.
35 Wokeck and Coleman, *op. cit.*, pp. 150–1, 188.
36 Rorty, *op. cit.*, p. 177.

3: The Voluptuousness of Objects
1 Everett W. Knight, *Literature Considered as Philosophy: The French Example*, London: Routledge & Kegan Paul, 1957, p. 19.
2 Knight, *op. cit.*, pp. 21–4.
3 *Ibid.*, p. 36.
4 *Ibid.*, p. 43.
5 *Ibid.*, p. 45.
6 *Ibid.*, p. 54.
7 *Ibid.*, p. 77.
8 Michael Roberts, *T.E. Hulme*, London: Faber, 1938, p. 83.
9 Roberts, *op. cit.*, p. 248.
10 Karen Csengeri (ed.), *The Collected*

Writings of T.E. Hulme, Oxford: Clarendon Press, 1994, p. 140.

11 Tom Regan, *Bloomsbury's Prophet: G.E. Moore and the Development of His Moral Philosophy*, Philadelphia: Temple University Press, 1986, p. 35.

12 Regan, *op. cit.*, p. 8.

13 *Ibid.*, p. 23.

14 *Ibid.*, p. 28.

15 *Ibid.*, p. 169.

16 Thomas Baldwin, *G.E. Moore*, London: Routledge, 1990, part III. See also Paul Levy, *G.E. Moore and the Cambridge Apostles*, London: Weidenfeld & Nicolson, 1979.

17 Regan, *op. cit.*, p. 202.

18 *Ibid.*, pp. 209–10.

19 *Ibid.*, p. 240.

20 *Ibid.*, p. 265.

21 Ronald W. Clark, *Freud: The Man and the Cause*, New York: Random House, 1980, p. 349.

22 Clark, *op. cit.*, p. 350.

23 Penguin Freud Library, Sigmund Freud, *The Origins of Religion*, London: 1985, p. 40 (vol. 31 of Freud's *Collected Works*, p. 13).

24 *Ibid.*

25 Quoted in Henry Idema III, *Religion and the Roaring Twenties, A Psychoanalytic Theory of Secularization in Three Novelists: Anderson, Hemingway and Fitzgerald*, Savage, Maryland: Rowman & Littlefield, 1990, pp. 5–6.

26 Penguin Freud Library, *op. cit.*, p. 40.

27 Clark, *op. cit.*, p. 352.

28 *Ibid.*, p. 355.

29 Peter Gay, *A Godless Jew: Freud, Atheism and the Making of Psychoanalysis*, New Haven and London: Yale University Press, 1987, p. 147.

4: Heaven: Not a Location but a Direction

1 Robert Hughes, *The Shock of the New*, London and New York: Thames & Hudson, 1980 and 1991, p. 9.

2 Hughes, *op. cit.*, p. 10.

3 *Ibid.*, p. 36.

4 Otto Reinert (ed.), *Strindberg: A Collection of Critical Essays*, Englewood Cliffs, New Jersey: Prentice-Hall Inc., 1971, p. 16.

5 Malcolm Bradbury and James McFarlane (eds), *Modernism: A Guide to European Literature 1890–1930*, London: Penguin Books, 1976, 1991, p. 499.

6 *Ibid.*

7 Errol Durbach, *Ibsen the Romantic: Analogues of Paradise in the Later Plays*, London: Macmillan, 1982, pp. 4–5.

8 Durbach, *op. cit.*, p. 6.

9 *Ibid.*, p. 7.

10 Bradbury and McFarlane, *op. cit.*, p. 501.

11 Durbach, *op. cit.*, p. 15.

12 *Ibid.*, p. 9.

13 *Ibid.*, p. 26.

14 Toril Moi, *Henrik Ibsen and the Birth of Modernism: Art, Theater, Philosophy*, New York and Oxford: Oxford University Press, 2008. John Northam, *Ibsen: A Cultural Study*, Cambridge, UK: Cambridge University Press, 1973, pp. 222–3.

15 Durbach, *op. cit.*, p. 129.

16 *Ibid.*, pp. 177–9.

17 Naomi Lebowitz, *Ibsen and the Great World*, Baton Rouge: Louisiana State University Press, 1990, pp. 82, 95, 100, 107.

18 Durbach, *op. cit.*, p. 192.

19 Reinert, *op. cit.*, p. 8.

20 *Ibid.*, p. 33.

21 John Ward, *The Social and Religious Plays of Strindberg*, London: Athlone Press; Atlantic Highland, NJ: Humanities Press, 1980.

22 Reinert, *op. cit.*, p. 81.

23 J.L. Wisenthal (ed.), *Shaw and Ibsen: Bernard Shaw's The Quintessence of Ibsenism and Related Writings*, Toronto:

University of Toronto Press, 1979, pp. 30–51.

24 Robert F. Whitman, *Shaw and the Play of Ideas*, Ithaca, New York: Cornell University Press, 1977, p. 23.

25 Whitman, *op. cit.*, p. 36.

26 *Ibid.*, p. 37.

27 *Ibid.*, p. 41.

28 *Ibid.*, p. 42.

29 Sally Peters, *Bernard Shaw: The Ascent of the Superman*, New Haven and London: Yale University Press, 1996, p. 95.

30 Whitman, *op. cit.*, p. 98.

31 *Ibid.*, p. 109.

32 A.M. Gibbs, *The Art and Mind of Shaw*, Basingstoke: Macmillan, 1983, pp. 32ff.

33 Whitman, *op. cit.*, p. 131.

34 *Ibid.*, p. 139.

35 Gareth Griffith, *Socialism and Superior Brains: the Political Thought of Bernard Shaw*, London: Routledge, 1993, p. 159.

36 Whitman, *op. cit.*, p. 201.

37 *Ibid.*, pp. 208–9.

38 *Ibid.*, p. 226.

39 Bernard Shaw, *John Bull's Other Island; and Major Barbara; also How He Lied to Her Husband*, London: Constable, 1911.

40 Whitman, *op. cit.*, p. 236.

41 *Ibid.*, p. 242.

42 J.L. Wisenthal, *Shaw's Sense of History*, Oxford: Clarendon Press, 1988, pp. 121ff.

43 Whitman, *op. cit.*, p. 278.

44 *Ibid.*, p. 286.

45 Joe Andrew, *Russian Writers and Society in the Second Half of the Nineteenth Century*, London: Macmillan, 1982, p. 152.

46 Andrew, *op. cit.*, p. 153.

47 *Ibid.*, p. 163.

48 *Ibid.*, p. 168.

49 Philip Callo, *Chekhov: The Hidden Ground: A Biography*, London: Constable, 1998, p. 296.

50 Andrew, *op. cit.*, p. 184.

51 *Ibid.*, p. 189.

5: Visions of Eden: the Worship of Colour, Metal, Speed and the Moment

1 Robert Hughes, *The Shock of the New: Art and the Century of Change*, London and New York: Thames & Hudson, 1980, 1991, p. 9.

2 Hughes, *op. cit.*, pp. 118–21.

3 *Ibid.*, p. 124.

4 *Ibid.*, p. 114.

5 Delmore Schwartz, *Seurat's Sunday Afternoon along the Seine* [a pamphlet], Warwick: Greville Press, 2011.

6 Hughes, *op. cit.*, p. 139.

7 *Ibid.*, p. 141.

8 Christine Poggi, *Inventing Futurism: the Art and Politics of Artificial Optimism*, Princeton and Oxford: Princeton University Press, 2009, pp. 1–16.

9 Hughes, *op. cit.*, p. 61.

10 *Ibid.*, p. 273.

11 *Ibid.*, p. 277.

12 *Ibid.*

13 Roger Shattuck, *The Banquet Years: The Origins of the Avant-Garde in France 1885 to World War 1*, London and New York: Vintage, 1968, p. 40. It is from this book that I have taken the term 'avant-guerre' for Part One's title.

14 Shattuck, *op. cit.*, p. 32.

15 *Ibid.*, p. 33.

16 Hanna Segal, *Dreams, Phantasy and Art*, Hove: Brunner–Routledge, 1991, pp. 86–7.

17 Hughes, *op. cit.*, p. 41.

18 *Ibid.*, p. 331.

19 David A. Wragg, *Wyndham Lewis and the Philosophy of Art in Early Modernist Britain: Creating a Political Aesthetic*, Lewiston, NY: Lampeter: Edwin Mellen Press, 2005, p. 336.

20 Hughes, *op. cit.*, p. 345.

21 *Ibid.*, p. 348.

6: The Insistence of Desire

1 Everett Knight, *Literature*

Considered as Philosophy:
The French Example, London:
Routledge & Kegan Paul, 1957,
p. 97.

2 Harold March, Gide and the
Hound of Heaven, Philadelphia:
University of Pennsylvania Press,
1952, p. 312.

3 March, op. cit., p. 231.

4 Knight, op. cit., p. 81.

5 March, op. cit., pp. 262, 362.

6 Ibid., p. 385.

7 Knight, op. cit., p. 98.

8 March, op. cit., p. 298.

9 Knight, op. cit., p. 99.

10 Ibid., p. 105.

11 Ibid., p. 112.

12 Roger Kempf, Avec André Gide,
Paris: Grasset, 2000, p. 45.

13 Knight, op. cit., p. 123.

14 Pericles Lewis, Religious
Experience and the Modernist
Novel, Cambridge, UK: Cambridge
University Press, 2010, p. 57.

15 Ross Posnock, The Trial of
Curiosity: Henry and William
James and the Challenge of
Modernity, New York and Oxford:
Oxford University Press, 1991,
pp. 29–34.

16 Lewis, op. cit., p. 55.

17 Ibid., p. 57.

18 Ibid., p. 60.

19 Ibid., p. 61.

20 William James, The Varieties of
Religious Experience, New York:
Longmans Green, 1925 (35th
imp.). See also Michael Ferrari
(ed.), The Varieties: Centenary
Essays, Exeter: Imprint Academic,
2002.

21 Lewis, op. cit., p. 78.

22 Rosalynn D. Haynes, H.G. Wells:
Discoverer of the Future, London
and Basingstoke: Macmillan, 1980,
p. 242.

23 Haynes, op. cit., p. 86.

24 Ibid., p. 96.

25 Ibid., p. 124.

26 Ibid., pp. 125–7.

27 Michael Sherborne, H.G. Wells:

Another Kind of Life, London:
Peter Owen, 2010, p. 239.

28 Haynes, op. cit., p. 95.

29 W. Warren Wagar, H.G. Wells:
Traversing Time, Middletown,
Connecticut: Wesleyan University
Press, 2004, chapters 3, 6, 9 and 11.

30 Haynes, op. cit., pp. 148–50.

31 Ibid., p. 151.

32 See: John Partington, Building
Cosmopolis: The Political Thought
of H.G. Wells, Aldershot: Ashgate,
2003, chapter 3 for general context.

33 See also: Roger Shattuck, Proust's
Way: A Fieldguide to In Search of
Lost Time, London: Allen Lane,
2000, p. 212.

34 Lewis, op. cit., p. 86.

35 Ibid.

36 Margaret Topping, Proust's Gods:
Christian and Mythological Figures
of Speech in the Works of Marcel
Proust, Oxford: Oxford University
Press, 2000.

37 Lewis, op. cit., p. 83.

38 Ibid., p. 92.

39 Ibid., pp. 97–8.

40 Ibid., p. 109.

7: The Angel in Our Cheek

1 Jean-Paul Sartre, Mallarmé, or
the Poet of Nothingness, trans.
Ernest Sturm, University Park
and London: Pennsylvania State
University Press, 1988, p. 4.

2 Sartre, op. cit., p. 94.

3 Ibid., p. 145.

4 Anna Balakian, The Fiction of
the Poet: From Mallarmé to the
Post-Symbolist Mode, Princeton
and Oxford: Princeton University
Press, 1992, p. 4.

5 Balakian, op. cit., p. 7.

6 Ibid., p. 16.

7 Ibid., p. 17.

8 Sartre, op. cit., p. 188.

9 Balakian, op. cit., p. 42.

10 Robert E. Norton, Secret Germany:
Stefan George and His Circle,
Ithaca and London: Cornell
University Press, 2002, p. 504.

11 Norton, *op. cit.*, p. xii.
12 *Ibid.*, p. 74.
13 *Ibid.*, p. 135.
14 *Ibid.*, p. 225.
15 Melissa Lane and Martin A. Ruehl, *A Poet's Reich: Politics and Culture in the George Circle*, Rochester, NY; Woodbridge: Camden House, 2001, pp. 91ff.
16 Norton, *op. cit.*, p. 230.
17 *Ibid.*, p. 267.
18 *Ibid.*, p. 286.
19 Jens Rieckmann (ed.), *A Companion to the Works of Stefan George*, Rochester, NY: Camden House, 2005, pp. 145ff, 189ff.
20 Norton, *op. cit.*, p. 410.
21 *Ibid.*, pp. 412–13.
22 *Ibid.*, p. 429.
23 Lane and Ruehl, *op. cit.*, pp. 56 ff and 91 ff.
24 *Ibid.*, p. 437.
25 *Ibid.*, p. 486.
26 *Ibid.*, p. 492.
27 *Ibid.*, pp. 480–1.
28 Rieckmann, *op. cit.*, pp. 161ff.
29 Norman Suckling, *Paul Valéry and the Civilized Mind*, Oxford: Oxford University Press, 1954, pp. 161ff.
30 Suckling, *op. cit.*, p. 17.
31 *Ibid.*, p. 19.
32 *Ibid.*, p. 31.
33 *Ibid.*, pp. 46, 94.
34 Otto Bohlmann, *Yeats and Nietzsche: An Exploration of Major Nietzschean Echoes in the Writing of William Butler Yeats*, London and Basingstoke: Macmillan, 1982, p. xi.
35 Bohlmann, *op. cit.*, p. 26.
36 Richard Ellmann, *The Identity of Yeats*, London: Macmillan, 1957, pp. 214, 231ff.

8: 'The Wrong Supernatural World'

1 Richard Ellmann, *The Identity of Yeats*, London: Macmillan, 1957, p. 58.
2 Ellmann, *Ibid.*, p. 60.
3 *Ibid.*, p. 65.
4 *Ibid.*, p. 66.
5 Ann Saddlemyer, *Becoming George: The Life of Mrs W.B. Yeats*, Oxford: Oxford University Press, 2002. See also: Ann Saddlemyer (ed.), *W. B. Yeats and George Yeats: The Letters*, Oxford and New York: Oxford University Press, 2011, pp. 400–1.
6 Ellmann, *op. cit.*, p. 107.
7 *Ibid.*, p. 125.
8 *Ibid.*, p. 129.
9 Terence Brown, *The Life of W.B. Yeats: A Critical Biography*, Oxford: Blackwell, 1999, p. 134.
10 Ellmann, *op. cit.*, p. 189.
11 *Ibid.*, p. 197.
12 *Ibid.*, p. 205.
13 *Ibid.* See also: Keith Alldritt, *W.B. Yeats: The Man and the Milieu*, London: John Murray, 1997, p. 177.
14 Ellmann, *op. cit.*, p. 225.
15 *Ibid.*, p. 239.
16 *Ibid.*, p. 252.
17 *Ibid.*, p. 269.
18 *Ibid.* See also: David Dwan, *The Great Community: Culture and Nationalism in Ireland*, Dublin: Institute for Irish Studies, University of Notre Dame, 2008, p. 84 for other advice to the son from his father.
19 *Ibid.*, p. 295.
20 *Ibid.*, p. 278.
21 Marjorie Howes and John Kelly (eds), *The Cambridge Companion to Yeats*, Cambridge UK: Cambridge University Press, 2006, p. 147.
22 Eugene Taylor, *Shadow Culture, Psychology and Spirituality in America*, Washington DC: Counterpoint, 1999, p. x.
23 Taylor, *op. cit.*, p. 9.
24 *Ibid.*, p. 113.
25 *Ibid.*, p. 177.
26 Jay Winter, *Sites of Memory, Sites of Mourning: The Great War in European Cultural History*, Cambridge UK: Cambridge University Press, 1995, 1998, p. 56.

27 Winter, *op. cit.*, p. 57.
28 *Ibid.*, p. 147.
29 Helmut Friedel and Annegret
    Hoberg, with contributions by
    Evelyn Benesch et al., *Vasily
    Kandinsky*, Munich and London:
    Prestel, 2008. See also Hedwig
    Fischer and Sean Rainbird
    (eds), *Kandinsky: The Path to
    Abstraction*, London: Tate Gallery
    Publishing, 2006.
30 Robert Hughes, *The Shock of the
    New*, London and New York:
    Thames & Hudson, 1980, 1991,
    p. 202.

9: Redemption by War

1 Peter Watson, *A Terrible Beauty:
   The People and Ideas That Shaped
   the Modern Mind*, London:
   Weidenfeld & Nicolson, 2001,
   p. 146.
2 Steven Aschheim, *The Nietzsche
   Legacy in Germany*, p. 132.
3 *Ibid.*, p. 143.
4 Max Scheler, *On the Eternal
   in Man*, London: SCM, 1960.
   Max Scheler, *On the Nature of
   Sympathy*, trans. Peter Heath, with
   an Introduction to the general
   works of Max Scheler by W. Stark,
   London: Routledge & Kegan Paul,
   1954.
5 Aschheim, *op. cit.*, p. 146.
6 *Ibid.*, p. 134.
7 Judith Malina, *The Piscator
   Notebook*, London: Routledge,
   2012, p. 4 says Piscator was
   'ashamed' in the war.
8 *Ibid.*, p. 102.
9 *Ibid.*
10 Roland N. Stromberg, *Redemption
   by War*, Kansas City: Regents
   Press of Kansas, 1982, p. 28. It is
   from Professor Stromberg's book
   that I have taken the title for this
   chapter.
11 Stromberg, *op. cit.*, p. 34.
12 *Ibid.*, p. 23.
13 *Ibid.*, p. 12.
14 *Ibid.*, p. 40.

15 *Ibid.*, p. 13.
16 *Quentin Bell: A Man of Many Arts*
   (exhibition catalogue), foreword by
   Norbert Lynton, Charleston Trust,
   University of London, 1999.
17 Stromberg, *op. cit.*, p. 43.
18 Nicholas Murray, *The Red Sweet
   Wine of Youth: The Brave and Brief
   Lives of the War Poets*. London:
   Little, Brown, 2010, Prologue,
   pp. 1-10.
19 Stromberg, *op. cit.*, p. 103.
20 *Ibid.*, p. 90.
21 Hannah Arendt, *Reflections on
   Literature and Culture*, ed. and
   with an Introduction by Susannah
   Young-ah Gottlieb, Stanford,
   Calif.: Stanford University Press,
   2007.
22 Stromberg, *op. cit.*, pp. 98-9.
23 *Ibid.*, p. 191.
24 *Ibid.*, p. 198.
25 Murray, *op. cit.*, p. 8.
26 Paul Fussell, *The Great War and
   Modern Memory*, Oxford: Oxford
   University Press, 1975, p. 134.
27 Fussell, *op. cit.*, p. 139.
28 *Ibid.*, p. 255.
29 *Ibid.*, p. 29.
30 Jay Winter, *Sites of Memory, Sites
   of Mourning: The Great War
   in European Cultural History*,
   Cambridge UK: Cambridge
   University Press, 1995, 1998, p. 64.
31 Gordon Graham, *The Re-
   enchantment of the World: Art
   versus Religion*, Oxford: Oxford
   University Press, 2004, p. 58.
32 Graham, *op. cit.*, p. 59.
33 *Ibid.*, pp. 59-60.
34 David Lomas, *The Haunted
   Self: Surrealism, Psychoanalysis,
   Subjectivity*, New Haven and
   London: Yale University Press,
   2000, p.74.
35 *Max Ernst: A Retrospective*, ed.
   and with an Introduction by
   Werner Spies, London: Tate/
   Prestel, 1991.
36 Patrick Elliott, *Another World:
   Dalí, Magritte, Miró and the*

Surrealists, Edinburgh: National Galleries of Scotland, 2010, pp. 1–5.

10: The Bolshevik Crusade for Scientific Atheism

1 Roland N. Stromberg, *Redemption by War*, Kansas City: Regents Press of Kansas, 1982, p. 130.
2 Bernice Glazer Rosenthal, *New Myth, New World: From Nietzsche to Stalinism*, University Park, Pennsylvania: Pennsylvania State University Press, 2002, p. 117.
3 Peter Watson, *A Terrible Beauty: The People and Ideas That Shaped the Modern Mind*, London: Weidenfeld & Nicolson, 2001, p. 345.
4 Watson, *Ideas*, op. cit. p. 768.
5 *Ibid.*, p. 769.
6 Watson, A Terrible Beauty, op. cit. 293.
7 Paul Froese, *The Plot to Kill God: Findings from the Soviet Experiment in Secularization*, Los Angeles, Berkeley, London: University of California Press, 2008, p. 60.
8 Froese, *op. cit.*, p. 55.
9 Rosenthal, *op. cit.*, pp. 2, 173, 179.
10 *Ibid.*, p. 15.
11 *Ibid.*, p. 9.
12 *Ibid.*, pp. 126–7.
13 See: A.G. Bulakh, N.B. Abakumova, J.V. Romanovsky, *St Petersburg: A History in Stone*, St Petersburg: St Petersburg University Press, 2010, chapter 17, pp. 139ff for an outline of St Petersburg architecture in 1917.
14 Rosenthal, *op. cit.*, p. 56.
15 *Ibid.*, p. 61.
16 *Ibid.*, p. 74.
17 See also: A.L. Tait, *Lunacharsky, Poet of the Revolution (1875–1907)*, Birmingham: University of Birmingham Department of Russian Language and Literature, 1984, p. 91 for Lunacharsky's views of the amateurs in the arts.

18 Rosenthal, *op. cit.*, p. 83.
19 *Ibid.*, p. 98.
20 *Ibid.*, p. 109.
21 Alexander Rabinowitch, *The Bolsheviks Come to Power*, Bloomington, Ind.: Indiana University Press, 2008 p. 150.
22 *Ibid.*, p. 152.
23 The classic account is Robert H. McNeal, *Bride of the Revolution: Krupskaya and Lenin*, London: Gollancz, 1973, p. 157.
24 Frank Westerman, *Engineers of the Soul: In the Footsteps of Stalin's Writers*, trans. Sam Garrett, London: Harvill Secker, 2010, p. 140p–3.
25 Rosenthal, *op. cit.*, p. 178.
26 *Ibid.*, pp. 201–2.
27 Froese, *op. cit.*, p. 7.
28 *Ibid.*, p. 40.
29 *Ibid.*, p. 49.
30 Bulakh et al., *op. cit.*, p. 52.
31 Rosenthal, *op. cit.*, p. 56.
32 *Ibid.*, p. 58.
33 Joshua Rubinstein, *Leon Trotsky: A Revolutionary's Life*, New Haven and London: Yale University Press, 2011, pp. 115–6
34 Rosenthal, *op. cit.*, p. 122.

11: The Implicitness of Life and the Rules of Existence

1 Rüdiger Safranski, *Martin Heidegger: Between Good and Evil*, trans. Ewald Osters, Cambridge, Mass.: Harvard University Press, 1998, p. 89. Max Weber, 'Der Beruf zur Politik', in Weber, *Soziologie, Weltgeschichtliche Analysen, Politik*, Stuttgart: Kröner, 1964, p. 322.
2 Safranski, *op. cit.*, p. 91.
3 *Ibid.*
4 *Ibid.*, p. 92.
5 *Ibid.*, pp. 337–8.
6 *Ibid.*, p. 93.
7 Charles B. Guignon (ed.), *The Cambridge Companion to Heidegger*, Cambridge UK: Cambridge University Press, 2006,

pp. 268–9.

8 Safranski, *op. cit.*, p. 366.

9 *Ibid.*, p. 377.

10 Wolfgang Leppmann: *Rilke: A Life*, trans. Russell M. Stockman, New York: Fromm, 1984, p. 361.

11 *Ibid.*

12 Michael Hamburger, *The Truth of Poetry: Tension in Modern Poetry from Baudelaire to the 1960s*, Manchester: Carcanet New Press, 1982, p. 27.

13 Don Paterson, *Orpheus: A Version of Rilke's 'Die Sonette an Orpheus'*, London: Faber and Faber, 2006, pp. 66–7.

14 *An Unofficial Rilke: Poems: 1912–1926*, selected and trans. Michael Hamburger, London: Anvil Poetry Press, 1981, p. 69.

15 Leppmann, *op. cit.*, p. 184.

16 *Ibid.*

17 *Ibid.*

18 *Ibid.*, p. 386.

19 David S. Luft, *Robert Musil and the Crisis of European Culture 1880-1942*, Los Angeles, Berkeley and London: University of California Press, 1980, *passim*; and David S. Luft, *Eros and Inwardness: Weininger, Musil, Doderer*, Chicago: University of Chicago Press, 2003, p. 121.

20 Jane Smiley, *Guardian*, 17 June 2006.

21 Luft, *Crisis of European Culture*, p. 252.

22 Luft, *Eros and Inwardness*, p. 124.

23 Luft, *Crisis of European Culture*, p. 219.

24 Luft, *Eros and Inwardness*, pp. 120–1.

25 *Ibid.*

26 Luft, *Crisis of European Culture*, p. 255.

27 *Ibid.*, p. 201.

28 *Ibid.*, p. 255.

29 *Ibid.*, p. 260.

12: The Imperfect Paradise

1 Henry Idema III, *Freud, Religion and the Roaring Twenties: A Psychoanalytic Theory of Secularisation in Three Novelists: Anderson, Hemingway, and Fitzgerald*, Savage, Maryland: Rowman & Littlefield, 1990, p. 1.

2 Idema, *op. cit.*, p. 6.

3 Robert S. Lynd and Helen Merrell Lynd, *Middletown: A Study in Contemporary American Culture*, London: Constable, 1929, pp. 245ff.

4 Idema, *op. cit.*, p. 44.

5 *Ibid.*, p. 47.

6 *Ibid.*, p. 73.

7 *Ibid.*, p. 171.

8 Lynd and Lynd, *op. cit.*, pp. 275ff.

9 Idema, *op. cit.*, p. 174.

10 *Ibid.*, p. 204.

11 Wallace Stevens, *Collected Poems and Prose*, New York: Literary Classics of the United States, 1997, p. 20.

12 Stevens, *op. cit.*, pp. 53–4.

13 *Ibid.*, p. 748.

14 Leon Surette, *The Modern Dilemma: Wallace Stevens, T.S. Eliot and Humanism*, McGill: Queen's University Press, 2008, pp. 199ff.

15 Stevens, *op. cit.*, p. 845.

16 *Ibid.*, p. 914.

17 *Ibid.*, p. 55.

18 Simon Critchley, *Things Merely Are: Philosophy in the Poetry of Wallace Stevens*, London: Routledge, 2005, pp. 73–4.

19 Idema, *op. cit.*, p. 92.

20 *Ibid.*, p. 13.

21 Bart Eeckhout, *Wallace Stevens and the Limits of Reading and Writing*, Columbia and London: University of Missouri Press, 2002, pp. 226–7.

22 *Ibid.*, pp. 9–11.

23 *Ibid.*

24 Peter Watson, *A Terrible Beauty: The People and Ideas That Shaped the Modern Mind*, London: Weidenfeld & Nicolson, 2001, New York: HarperCollins, 2002, p. 345.

25 John Patrick Diggins, *Eugene*

O'Neill's America: Desire under Democracy, Chicago: University of Chicago Press, 2007, pp. 183–4.

26 Diggins, *op. cit.*, p. 65.

27 *Ibid.*, pp. 186, 259–60.

28 *Ibid.*, p. 37.

29 *Ibid.*, p. 47.

30 Michael Manheim (ed.), *The Cambridge Companion to Eugene O'Neill*, Cambridge UK: Cambridge University Press, 1998, p. 19.

31 Manheim, *op. cit.*, p. 20.

32 See: Bennett Simon, *Tragic Drama and the Family: Psychoanalytic Studies from Aeschylus to Beckett*, New Haven and London: Yale University Press, 1988, pp. 180ff, for a discussion on psychodynamic themes in O'Neill.

33 Manheim, *op. cit.*, p. 30.

34 *Ibid.*, p. 84.

35 *Ibid.*, p. 86.

36 Normand Berlin, *Eugene O'Neill*, London: Macmillan, 1982, pp. 128ff for a chapter on 'Endings'.

37 Manheim, *op. cit.*, p. 139.

38 Berlin, *op. cit.*, p. 216.

13: Living Down to Fact

1 Pericles Lewis, *Religious Experience and the Modernist Novel*, Cambridge UK: Cambridge University Press, 2010, p. 144.

2 *Ibid.*, p. 146.

3 Mitchell Leaska, *Granite and Rainbow: The Hidden Life of Virginia Woolf*, London: Picador, 1998, p. 235.

4 Leaska, *op. cit.*, p. 146.

5 *Ibid.*, p. 147.

6 *Ibid.*, p. 152.

7 Lewis, *op. cit.*, p. 155.

8 Gordon Graham, *The Re-enchantment of the World: Art versus Religion*, Oxford: Oxford University Press, 2004, p. 95 (*Portrait of the Artist*, 1992 edition, p. 265).

9 *Ibid.*, p. 96.

10 Derek Attridge (ed.), *The Cambridge Companion to James Joyce*, Cambridge UK: Cambridge University Press, 2004, p. 91.

11 *Ibid.*

12 Brett Bourbon, *Finding a Replacement for the Soul: Mind and Meaning in Literature and Philosophy*, Cambridge, Mass. and London: Harvard University Press, 2004, p. 145.

13 Declan Hibberd, Introduction to the Penguin edition of *Ulysses*, 1922, 1992, p. x.

14 Hibberd, *op. cit.*, p. xv.

15 *Ibid.*, p. lvii.

16 *Ibid.*, p. lxxviii.

17 Philip Rieff, *The Triumph of the Therapeutic*, London: Chatto & Windus, 1966, p. 194.

18 Rieff, *op. cit.*, p. 196.

19 *Ibid.*, p. 208.

20 *Ibid.*, pp. 211–13.

21 Jad Smith, '*Völkisch* Organicism and the Use of Primitivism in Lawrence's *The Plumed Serpent*', *D.H. Lawrence Review*, 2002, vol. 30, p. 3 (*The Plumed Serpent*, 1998 edition, pp. 129–31).

22 Smith, *op. cit.*, p. 11.

23 Rieff, *op. cit.*, pp. 228–31.

14: The Impossibility of Metaphysics, a Reverence for Metapsychology

1 Ben Rogers, *A.J. Ayer: A Life*, London: Verso, 2000, p. 82.

2 Rogers, *op. cit.*, p. 89.

3 *Ibid.*, p. 95.

4 A.J. Ayer, *Language, Truth and Logic*, London: Gollancz, 1936, p. 33.

5 Ayer, *op. cit.*, p. 36.

6 *Ibid.*, p. 108.

7 *Ibid.*, p. 113.

8 *Ibid.*, p. 116. See also A.J. Ayer, *The Meaning of Life and Other Essays*, Introduction by Ted Honderich, London: Weidenfeld & Nicolson, 1990.

9 Ayer, *Language, Truth and Logic*, p. 120.

10 *Ibid.*, pp. 200–1.
11 Sigmund Freud, *The Future of an Illusion*, publ. 1927; vol. 21 of the Standard Edition of the Complete Psychological Works of Sigmund Freud, London: Hogarth Press and the Institute of Psychoanalysis, 1968.
12 Freud, *Illusion*, p. 50.
13 *Ibid.*, p. 55.
14 *Ibid.*, p. 67.
15 *Ibid.*, p. 73.
16 *Ibid.*, p. 78.
17 *Ibid.*, p. 83.
18 Sigmund Freud, *Civilization and Its Discontents*, trans. Joan Riviere, revised and ed. James Strachey, London: Hogarth Press and the Institute of Psychoanalysis, 1979, p. x.
19 Freud, *Civilization*, pp. 13–14.
20 *Ibid.*, p. 22.
21 *Ibid.*, p. 54.
22 Michael Palmer, *Freud and Jung on Religion*, London and New York: Routledge, 1997, *passim*.
23 Carl Gustav Jung, *Modern Man in Search of a Soul*, London: Kegan Paul, Trench and Trübner, 1933, p. 239.
24 Erich Fromm, *Psychoanalysis and Zen Buddhism*, London: Unwin Paperbacks, 1960, p. 43.
25 Pericles Lewis, *Religious Experience and the Modernist Novel*, Cambridge UK: Cambridge University Press, 2010, p. 134.
26 *Ibid.*, p. 114.
27 *Ibid.*, p. 134.
28 *Ibid.*, p. 135.
29 June O. Leavitt, *The Mystical Life of Franz Kafka: Theosophy, Cabala, and the Modern Spiritual Revival*, Oxford: Oxford University Press, 2012, pp. 122–3, 137–9 for a discussion on Kafka and the Bible.

15: The Faiths of the Philosophers
1 Molly Cochran (ed.), *The Cambridge Companion to Dewey*, Cambridge UK: Cambridge University Press, 2010, especially ch. 10: Sami Pihlström, 'Dewey and Pragmatic Religious Naturalism', p. 213.
2 Pihlström, *op. cit.*, p. 215.
3 *Ibid.*, p. 218.
4 *Ibid.*, p. 226.
5 *Ibid.*, p. 220.
6 *Ibid.*, p. 232.
7 W. Donald Hudson, *Wittgenstein and Religious Belief*, London: Macmillan, 1975, p. 114.
8 Hudson, *op. cit.*, pp. 70–1.
9 *Ibid.*, p. 79.
10 *Ibid.*, p. 92.
11 *Ibid.*, p. 106.
12 *Ibid.*
13 *Ibid.*
14 Quoted in Peter Watson, *A Terrible Beauty: The People and Ideas That Shaped the Modern Mind*, London: Weidenfeld & Nicolson, 2001, p. 99.
15 *Stanford Encyclopedia of Philosophy*, Internet entry on Whitehead, p. 5 of 9.
16 Bertrand Russell, *Why I Am Not a Christian and Other Essays on Religion and Related Subjects*, London: George Allen & Unwin, 1954, p. v ('Why I Am Not a Christian' was given as a lecture in 1927).
17 Russell, *op. cit.*, p. 15.
18 *Ibid.*, p. 179.
19 *Ibid.*, pp. 43–4.
20 *Ibid.*, p. 177.
21 See: Ray Monk, *Bertrand Russell: 1921–1970: The Ghost of Madness* (vol. 2), London: Jonathan Cape, 2000, p. 36 for his relationship with Dora. See also: Nicholas Griffin (ed.), *The Cambridge Companion to Bertrand Russell*, Cambridge UK: Cambridge University Press, 2003, especially ch. 15.
22 *Ibid.*, p. 60.
23 *Ibid.*, p. 59.
24 Bertrand Russell, *Sceptical Essays*,

London: George Allen & Unwin, 1929, p. 68.
25 Russell, *Sceptical Essays*, p. 70.
26 *Ibid.*, pp. 116–17.

16: Nazi Religions of the Blood

1 I have used Brian Moynahan, *The Faith*, London: Aurum, 2002, p. 675.
2 Moynahan, *op. cit.*, p. 675.
3 F.X.J. Homer, 'The Führer's Faith: Hitler's Sacred Cosmos', in F.X.J. Homer and Larry D. Wilcox (eds), *Germany and Europe in the Era of Two World Wars: Essays in Honour of Oron James Hale*, Charlottesville: University Press of Virginia, 1986, pp. 61–78.
4 Alister McGrath, *The Making of Modern German Christology: from the Enlightenment to Pannenberg*, Oxford: Blackwell, 1986, p. 5.
5 Bruce L. McCormack, *Karl Barth's Critically Dialectical Theology: Its Genesis and Development, 1909–1936*, Oxford: Clarendon Press, 1995, pp. 38ff for 'The theological situation at the turn of the century'.
6 Eberhard Busch, *Karl Barth: His Life from Letters and Autobiographical Texts*, trans. John Bowden, London: SCM Press, 1976, pp. 38ff.
7 Busch, *op. cit.*, pp. 92ff, 117ff.
8 Zdravko Kujundzija, *Boston Collaborative Encyclopedia of Western Theology*, entry on Barth, p. 16.
9 Busch, *op. cit.*, pp. 120ff. McCormack, *op. cit.*, pp. 209ff.
10 Busch, *op. cit.*, p. 245.
11 Kujundzija, *op. cit.*, p. 17.
12 McCormack, *op. cit.*, p. 449.
13 Moynahan, *op. cit.*, p. 678. Ernst Christian Helmreich, *The German Churches under Hitler: Background, Struggle and Epilogue*, Detroit, Ill.: Wayne State University Press, 1979, p. 123. J.S. Conway, *The Nazi Persecution of*

the Churches, 1933–1945, London: Weidenfeld & Nicolson, 1968, p. 2.
14 Richard Steigmann-Gall, *The Holy Reich*, Cambridge UK: Cambridge University Press, 2003, p. 1.
15 *Ibid.*, p. 42.
16 James R. Dow and Hannjost Lixfeld (eds), *The Nazification of an Academic Discipline: Folklore in the Third Reich*, Bloomington, Ind.: Indiana University Press, 1994, p. 21.
17 Robert Cecil, *The Myth of the Master Race: Alfred Rosenberg and Nazi Ideology*, London: B.T. Batsford, 1972, p. 82.
18 Gordon Lynch, *The Sacred in the Modern World: A Cultural Sociological Approach*, Oxford: Oxford University Press, 2012, p. 117.
19 Cecil, *op. cit.*, p. 85.
20 *Ibid.*, p. 92.
21 *Ibid.*, p. 93.
22 *Ibid.*, p. 96.
23 *Ibid.*, p. 99.
24 *Ibid.*, p. 103.
25 Karla Poewe, *New Religions and the Nazis*, London: Routledge, 2006, p. 1.
26 Poewe, *op. cit.*, p. 73.
27 *Ibid.*, p. 76.
28 *Ibid.*, p. 111.
29 *Ibid.*, p. 165.
30 James Bentley, *Martin Niemöller*, Oxford: Oxford University Press, 1984, pp. 81ff, 143ff.

17: The Aftermath of the Aftermath

1 Jeffrey C. Isaac, *Arendt, Camus and Modern Rebellion*, London and New Haven: Yale University Press, 1992, p. 21.
2 Isaac, *op. cit.*, p. 22.

18: The Warmth of Acts

1 Joseph Schumpeter, *Capitalism, Socialism and Democracy*, publ. 1942, 2003 edition: London: Taylor & Francis; Karl Mannheim, *Diagnosis of Our Time: Wartime*

Essays, London: Routledge, 1943; Friedrich Hayek, *The Road to Serfdom*, London: Routledge & Kegan Paul, 1944; Karl Popper, *The Open Society and Its Enemies*, London: Routledge & Kegan Paul, 1962; William Temple, *Christianity and the Social Order*, London: Shepheard-Walwyn, 1976; Gunnar Myrdal, *An American Dilemma: The Negro Problem and Modern Democracy*, London: Harper Brothers, 1944.

2 Antony Beevor and Artemis Cooper, *Paris after the Liberation: 1944–1949*, London: Penguin Books, 1994, 1995, p. 214.

3 Stefanos Geroulanos, *An Atheism that is Not Humanist Emerges in French Thought*, Stanford, Calif.: Stanford University Press, 2010, p. 227.

4 Geroulanos, *op. cit.*, p. 242.

5 *Ibid.*, p. 271.

6 *Ibid.*, p. 307.

7 *Ibid.*, p. 230.

8 *Ibid.*, p. 387.

9 Everett Knight, *Literature Considered as Philosophy: The French Example*, London: Routledge & Kegan Paul, 1957, p. 132.

10 Olivier Todd, *Malraux: A Life*, New York: Knopf, 2005, pp. 108–13.

11 Geroulanos, *op. cit.*, p. 151.

12 *Ibid.*, p. 159.

13 See: Stacey Schiff, *Saint-Exupéry: A Biography*, London: Chatto & Windus, 1994, pp. 105 and 197 for Saint-Exupéry and Malraux.

14 Geroulanos, *op. cit.*, p. 170.

15 *Ibid.*, p. 171.

16 *Ibid.*, p. 174.

17 *Ibid.*, p. 179.

18 Walter Kaufmann (ed.), *Existentialism: From Dostoevsky to Sartre*, New York and London: Penguin Books, 1956, 1975, p. 43.

19 Kaufmann, *op. cit.*, p. 44.

20 *Ibid.*, p. 348.

21 *Ibid.*, p. 356.

22 Knight, *op. cit.*, pp. 42–3.

19: War, the American Way and the Decline of Original Sin

1 Alan Petigny, *The Permissive Society: America, 1941–1965*, Cambridge UK: Cambridge University Press, 2009. E. Brooks Holifield, *A History of Pastoral Care in America: From Salvation to Self-Realization*, Nashville: Abingdon Press, 1983, pp. 201–2.

2 Holifield, *op. cit.*, p. 213.

3 Joshua Loth Liebman, *Peace of Mind*, London and Toronto: William Heinemann, 1946, p. 12.

4 Liebman, *op. cit.*, p. 20.

5 *Ibid.*, p. 31.

6 *Ibid.*, p. 154.

7 Thomas Maier, *Dr Spock: An American Life*, New York, San Diego, London: Harcourt Brace & Co., 1998, p. 114. Petigny, *op. cit.*, pp. 37–41.

8 Maier, *op. cit.*, p. 283.

9 Petigny, *op. cit.*, p. 285.

10 *Ibid.*, p. 50.

11 *Ibid.*, p. 79.

12 *Ibid.*, p. 81.

13 *Ibid.*, p. 239.

14 Richard I. Evans, *Carl Rogers: The Man and His Ideas*, New York: Dutton, 1975, p. xxiii.

15 Evans, *op. cit.*, p. 151.

16 *Ibid.*, p. 165.

17 Petigny, *op. cit.*, p. 276. Joseph Fletcher, *Situation Ethics: The New Morality*, London: SCM, 1966, *passim*.

18 Petigny, *op. cit.*, p. 246.

19 Viktor Frankl, *Man's Quest for Meaning*, Boston: Beacon Books, 1962, 1984, 2006, Afterword by William J. Winslade, p. 155.

20 Frankl, *op. cit.*, p. 164.

20: Auschwitz, Apocalypse, Absence

1 Esther Benbassa, *Suffering as Identity: The Jewish Paradigm*, London and New York: Verso,

2010, pp. 92–3.
2 Benbassa, *op. cit.*, p. 94.
3 *Ibid.*, p. 97.
4 *Ibid.*, p. 99.
5 *Ibid.*, p. 101.
6 See: Imre Kertész, *The Holocaust as Culture*, trans. Thomas Cooper, London: Seagull Books, 2011, p. 62 for people who explicitly rejected religion *and* culture as plans to fall back on.
7 Benbassa, *op. cit.*, p. 103.
8 *Ibid.*, p. 409.
9 Steven T. Katz et al. (eds), *Wrestling with God: Jewish Theological Responses During and After the Holocaust*, Oxford: Oxford University Press, 2007, pp. 639ff.
10 Benbassa, *op. cit.*, p. 104.
11 *Ibid.*, p. 108.
12 Norman G. Finkelstein, *The Holocaust Industry: Reflections on the Exploitation of Jewish Suffering*, London: Verso, pp. 79ff.
13 Benbassa, *op. cit.*, p. 114.
14 Jim Garrison, *The Darkness of God: Theology after Hiroshima*, London: SCM Press, 1982, p. 159.
15 Bernard Murchland (ed. and with an Introduction by), *The Meaning of the Death of God*, New York: Random House, 1967, p. 25.
16 Murchland, *op. cit.*, p. 30.
17 *Ibid.*, p. 37.
18 *Ibid.*, p. 40.
19 J.A.T. Robinson, *Honest to God*, London: SCM Press, 1963, *passim*.

21: 'Quit Thinking!'
1 John Calder, *The Philosophy of Samuel Beckett*, London: Calder Publications, 2001, p. 41.
2 Calder, *op. cit.*, p. 79.
3 Peter Watson, *A Terrible Beauty: The People and Ideas That Shaped the Modern Mind*, London: Weidenfeld & Nicolson, 2001, p. 418.
4 Calder, *op. cit.*, p. 65.
5 *Ibid.*, p. 70.

6 *Ibid.*, p. 74.
7 *Ibid.*, p. 83.
8 *Ibid.*, p. 92.
9 Raymond Yasmil, *Carl Andre: Sculpture as Place: 1958–2010*, New Haven and London, Yale University Press, 2013.
10 Martin Torgoff, *Can't Find My Way Home: America in the Great Stoned Age: 1945–2004*, New York: Simon & Schuster, 2004, p. 27.
11 Daniel Belgrad, *The Culture of Spontaneity: Improvisation and the Arts in Postwar America*, Chicago: Chicago University Press, 1998, p. 1.
12 Belgrad, *op. cit.*, pp. 5–6.
13 *Ibid.*, p. 10.
14 *Ibid.*, p. 27.
15 *Ibid.*, p. 112.
16 See: Carl Woideck, *Charlie Parker: His Music and Life*, Ann Arbor: University of Michigan Press, 1996, p. 23 for music and the speed of playing as an aspect of *acting*.
17 Belgrad, *op. cit.*, p. 108.
18 *Ibid.*, p. 110.
19 Geoffrey Rayner, Richard Chamberlain, Annemarie Stapleton, *Pop! Design, Culture, Fashion, 1965–1976*, Woodbridge: ACC Editions, 2012, p. 119.
20 Belgrad, *op. cit.*, p. 158.
21 *Ibid.*, p. 151.
22 *Ibid.*, p. 162.
23 Geoffrey Beard, *Modern Ceramics*, London: Studio Vista, 1969, p. 165.
24 Belgrad, *op. cit.*, p. 170.
25 *Ibid.*, p. 31.
26 See: Bill Morgan, *I Celebrate Myself: The Somewhat Private Life of Allen Ginsberg*, New York: Viking, 2006, pp. 516–7 for John Lennon's reaction to Ginsberg reading 'Howl'. See also: James Campbell, *This Is the Beat Generation*, New York; San Francisco; Paris, London: Secker & Warburg, 1999.
27 Belgrad, *op. cit.*, p. 205.
28 James Wood, *The Broken Estate:*

Essays on Literature and Belief, Jonathan Cape, 1999, p. 217.

29 Wood, *op. cit.*, p. 222.

30 Harold Bloom, 'His Long Ordeal by Laughter', *New York Times Book Review*, 19 May 1985.

31 Timothy Parrish (ed.), *The Cambridge Companion to Philip Roth*, Cambridge UK: Cambridge University Press, 2007, p. 35.

32 Parrish, *op.cit.*, p. 45.

33 *Ibid.*, p. 150.

22: A Visionary Commonwealth and the Size of Life

1 Theodore Roszak, *The Making of a Counter Culture: Reflections on the Technocratic Society and Its Youthful Opposition*, London: Faber, 1970, p. xxvi.

2 Roszak, *op. cit.*, p. xxxiv.

3 *Ibid.*, p. 49.

4 *Ibid.*, pp. 64–6.

5 Herbert Marcuse, *Counter Revolution and Revolt*, London: Allen Lane, 1972, chapter 2, pp. 59ff.

6 Roszak, *op. cit.*, p. 109.

7 *Ibid.*, pp. 119–20.

8 *Ibid.*, p. 14.

9 See also Alan Watts, *Does It Matter? Essays on Man's Relationship to Materiality*, New York: Pantheon, 1970.

10 Roszak, *op. cit.*, p. 83.

11 *Ibid.*, p. 149.

12 Jeffrey J. Kripal, *Esalen: America and the Religion of No Religion*, Chicago: University of Chicago Press, 2007, 2008, p. 213

13 Kripal, *op. cit.*, p. 11.

14 *Ibid.*, p. 139.

15 *Ibid.*, p. 149.

16 *Ibid.*, p. 170.

17 Martin Torgoff, *Can't Find My Way Home: America in the Great Stoned Age, 1945-2000*, New York: Simon & Schuster, 2004, 2005, p. 123.

18 Torgoff, *op. cit.*, pp. 8, 11.

19 *Ibid.*, p. 44.

20 *Ibid.*, p. 271.

21 Robert C. Fuller, *Stairways to Heaven, Drugs in American Religious History*, Boulder, Colorado: Westview Press, 2000, p. 67.

22 Torgoff, *op. cit.*, p. 85.

23 Fuller, *op. cit.*, pp. 72–4.

24 *Ibid.*, p. 85.

25 Torgoff, *op. cit.*, p. 111.

26 *Ibid.*, p. 123.

27 Tony Scherma and David Dalton, *Andy Warhol: His Controversial Life, Art and Colourful Times*, London: J.R. Books, 2010. See also Victor Bokris, *Warhol*, London: F. Muller, 1989, p. 193.

28 Torgoff, *op. cit.*, p. 179.

29 *Ibid.*, p. 209.

30 Carl Belz, *The Story of Rock*, Oxford: Oxford University Press, 1969, does not mention drugs or psychedelic events.

31 Torgoff, *op. cit.*, pp. 256–7. See also Hunter S. Thompson, *Fear and Loathing in Las Vegas: A Savage Journey to the Heart of the American Dream*, London: Flamingo, 1993, *passim*.

32 Roszak, *op. cit.*, p. 410.

33 *Ibid.*, p. 215.

34 *Ibid.*, p. 254.

35 *Ibid.*, p. 236.

36 Theodore Roszak, *Where the Wasteland Ends: Politics and Transcendence in Postindustrial Society*, London: Faber and Faber, 1973, p. 71.

37 Roszak, *Where the Wasteland Ends*, p. 101.

38 *Ibid.*, p. 254.

39 *Ibid.*, pp. 260–1.

40 *Ibid.*, p. 346.

41 *Ibid.*, p. 356.

42 *Ibid.*, p. 450.

43 See: Joel Parris, *Psychotherapy in an Age of Narcissism: Modernity, Science and Society*, Basingstoke: Palgrave Macmillan, 2013, p. 97 for a sceptical discussion on therapeutic language.

23: The Luxury of Happiness

1 Partha Dasgupta, *Human Well-Being and the Natural Environment*, Oxford: Oxford University Press, 2001, p. xxii.

2 Dasgupta, *op. cit.*, p. 13.

3 *Ibid.*, p. 31.

4 *Ibid.*, p. 37.

5 Mark Kingwell, *In Pursuit of Happiness: Better Living from Plato to Prozac*, New York: Crown, 1998, p. 107.

6 Kingwell, *op. cit.*, p. 51.

7 John Ralston Saul, *Voltaire's Bastards: The Dictatorship of Reason in the West*, Toronto: Penguin Books, 1993, p. 480.

8 Kingwell, *op. cit.*, p. 35.

9 *Ibid.*, p. 64.

10 See: Jackson Lears, *Fables of Abundance: A Cultural History of Advertising in America*, New York: Basic Books, 1994, especially chapter 1, pp. 17ff.

11 Kingwell, *op. cit.*, p. 225.

12 *Ibid.*, p. 259.

13 Anthony Storr, *The School of Genius*, London: Deutsch, 1988, chapters 2 and 4.

14 Kingwell, *op. cit.*, p. 335.

15 Christopher Lasch, *The Culture of Narcissism: American Life in an Age of Diminishing Expectations*, New York: Columbia University Press, 1979, p. 30.

16 Lasch, *op. cit.*, p. 35.

17 *Ibid.*, p. 42.

18 See: Joel Parris, *Psychotherapy in an Age of Narcissism: Modernity, Science and Society*, Basingstoke: Palgrave Macmillan, 2013, p. 64 for a discussion on how therapy replaced religion, and 74ff for Narcissistic Personality Disorders (NPD).

19 *Ibid.*, p. 397.

20 Peter Watson, *A Terrible Beauty: The People and Ideas That Shaped the Modern Mind*, London: Weidenfeld & Nicolson, 2001, p. 601.

21 Christopher Lasch, *The Minimal Self: Psychic Survival in Troubled Times*, New York: W.W. Norton, 1995, p. 94.

22 Dale Jacquette (ed.), *Cannabis: Philosophy for Everyone*, New York and Oxford: Wiley-Blackwell, 2010, p. 39.

23 Jacquette, *op. cit.*, pp. 44–5.

24 Martin Booth, *Cannabis: A History*, London: Doubleday, 2003, chpater 24, pp. 292ff.

25 Frank Furedi, *Therapy Culture: Cultivating Vulnerability in an Uncertain Age*, London and New York: Routledge, 2004, p. 5.

26 Furedi, *op. cit.*, p. 7.

27 *Ibid.*, p. 100.

28 *Ibid.*, p. 17.

29 K.M. Sargeant, *Seeker Churches: Promoting Religion in a Nontraditional Way*, New Brunswick, NJ: Rutgers University Press, 2000, p. 45.

30 Furedi, *op. cit.*, p. 31.

31 *Ibid.*, p. 33.

32 *Ibid.*, p. 73.

33 *Ibid.*, p. 91.

34 *Ibid.*, p. 155.

35 Patrick Bracken, *Trauma: Culture, Meaning and Philosophy*, London: Whurr Publishers, 2002, p. 14.

36 Kenneth J. Gergen, 'Therapeutic Professions and the Diffusion of Deficit', *Journal of Mind and Behavior*, vol. 11, nos 3–4, 1990, p. 356.

37 Furedi, *op. cit.*, p. 204.

24: Faith in Detail

1 Seamus Heaney, *The Government of the Tongue*, London: Faber and Faber, 1988, p. xiii.

2 Heaney, *op. cit.*, p. xvi.

3 Czeslaw Milosz, *The Witness of Poetry*, Cambridge, Mass.: Harvard University Press, 1983, p. 16.

4 Milosz, *op. cit.*, p. 19.

5 *Ibid.*, p. 25.

6 *Ibid.*, p. 110.
7 *Ibid.*, p. 108.
8 Iris Murdoch, *Metaphysics as a Guide to Morals*, London: Chatto & Windus, 1992, p. 181.
9 Eva Hoffmann, review of Steiner's *Real Presences, New York Times*, 9 August 1989.
10 George Steiner, *Real Presences: Is There Anything in What We Say?*, London: Faber and Faber, 1989, p. 17.
11 Steiner, *op. cit.*, p. 53.
12 Heaney, *op. cit.*, pp. 93–4.
13 *Ibid.*, p. 124.
14 *Ibid.*, p. 168.
15 *Ibid.*, p. 16.
16 For Heaney on later Auden see: Arthur Kirsch, *Auden and Christianity*, London: Yale University Press, 2005, pp. 170.
17 Heaney, *op. cit.*, p. 122–3.
18 Michael Hamburger, *The Truth of Poetry: Tension in Modern Poetry from Baudelaire to the 1960s*, Manchester: Carcanet New Press, 1982, p. 267.
19 Hamburger, *op. cit.*, p. 215.
20 *Ibid.*, p. 118.
21 Michael Hamburger (ed. and with an Introduction by), *An Unofficial Rilke*, London: Anvil Poetry Press, 1981, p. 16.
22 Milosz, *op. cit.*, pp. 56–7.
23 Hamburger, *Truth of Poetry*, p. 39.
24 Wallace Stevens, *Collected Poems and Prose*, New York: Literary Classics of the United States, 1997, p. 104.
25 Hamburger, *Truth of Poetry*, p. 131.
26 James Wood, *The Broken Estate: Essays on Literature and Belief*, Jonathan Cape, 1999, p. 225.
27 Richard Rorty, *Achieving Our Country: Leftist Thought in Twentieth-century America*, Cambridge, Mass.: Harvard University Press, 1998, p. 132.
28 Rorty, *op. cit.*, p. 136.
29 *Ibid.*

25: 'Our Spiritual Goal Is the Enrichment of the Evolutionary Epic'

1 Richard Dawkins, *Unweaving the Rainbow*, London: Penguin Books, 1998, p. x.
2 Dawkins, *op. cit.*, p. xi.
3 *Ibid.*, p. 29.
4 *Ibid.*, pp. 312–13.
5 Richard Dawkins, *The Blind Watchmaker*, London: Penguin Books, 1986, p. 6.
6 Dawkins, *Blind Watchmaker*, appendix.
7 Daniel Dennett, *Breaking the Spell: Religion as a Natural Phenomenon*, London: Allen Lane, 2006, p. 14.
8 Dennett, *op. cit.*, p. 14.
9 *Ibid.*, p. 101.
10 *Ibid.*, p. 232.
11 For a possible explanation, see: Olivier Roy, *Holy Ignorance: When Religion and Culture Part Ways*, trans. Roy Schwartz, London: Hurst, 2010, *passim.*
12 Dennett, *op. cit.*, p. 303.
13 *Ibid.*, p. 268.
14 David Sloan Wilson, *Darwin's Cathedral: Evolution, Religion, and the Nature of Society*, Chicago and London: University of Chicago Press, 2002.
15 Sam Harris, *The Moral Landscape: How Science Can Determine Human Values*, London: Bantam, 2010, p. 32.
16 Matt Ridley, *The Origins of Virtue*, London: Viking, p. 264.
17 Steven Pinker, *The Better Angels of Our Nature: Why Violence Has Declined*, New York: Viking, 2011. See also Steven Pinker, 'Saturday Essay, Violence Vanquished', *Wall Street Journal*, 23 September 2011.
18 George Levine, *Darwin Loves You: Natural Selection and the Re-enchantment of the World*, Princeton and Oxford: Princeton University Press, 2006, p. 44.
19 E.O. Wilson, *On Human Nature*, Cambridge, Mass.: Harvard

University Press, 1979, p. 6.

20 Wilson, *op. cit.*, p. 171.

21 *Ibid.*, p. 201.

22 Stephen R. Kellert and Edward O. Wilson, *The Biophilia Hypothesis*, Washington DC: Island Press, 1993, p. 21.

23 Kellert and Wilson, *op. cit.*, p. 454.

24 Edward O. Wilson, *Consilience: The Unity of Knowledge*, New York: Knopf, 1998, p. 12.

25 Wilson, *Consilience*, p. 232.

26 *Ibid.*, p. 248.

27 *Ibid.*, p. 265.

28 Theodore Roszak, *Where the Wasteland Ends: Politics and Transcendence in Postindustrial Society*, London: Faber and Faber, 1973, p. 63.

29 Roszak, *op. cit.*, pp. 159, 162.

30 *Ibid.*, p. 159.

31 Mary Midgley, *Evolution as a Religion: Strange Hopes and Stranger Fears*, London: Methuen, 1985, p. 13.

32 Midgley, *op. cit.*, p. 63.

33 *Ibid.*, p. 140.

34 Mary Midgley, *Science as Salvation*, London: Routledge, 1992, p. 124.

35 Mary Midgley, *The Solitary Self: Darwin and the Selfish Gene*, Durham UK: Acumen, 2010, p. 92.

36 Paul Davies, *The Mind of God: Science and the Search for Ultimate Meaning*, London: Simon & Schuster, 1992, p. 153.

37 Davies, *op. cit.*, pp. 204, 209, 214.

38 David Deutsch, *The Fabric of Reality*, London: Penguin Books, 1997, pp. 352ff.

39 Deutsch, *op. cit.*, p. 358. See also Frank J. Tipler, *The Physics of Immortality: Modern Cosmology, God and the Resurrection of the Dead*, London: Macmillan, 1995.

26: 'The Good Life Is the Life Spent Seeking the Good Life'

1 T.S. Eliot, *Notes Towards the Definition of Culture*, London: Faber and Faber, 1948, p. 19.

2 Eliot, *op. cit.*, p. 88.

3 *Ibid.*, p. 105.

4 David Harvey, *The Condition of Postmodernity: An Enquiry into the Origins of Cultural Change*, Oxford: Blackwell, 1989, p. 53.

5 Steven Connor (ed.), *The Cambridge Companion to Postmodernity*, Cambridge UK: Cambridge University Press, 2004, p. 171.

6 Connor, *op. cit.*, p. 172.

7 Michael Cole et al., *What Is New Age?*, London: Hodder, 1990, p. 10.

8 MacIntyre's publications include *After Virtue: A Study in Moral Theory* (1981), *Whose Justice? Which Rationality?* (1988), *Three Rival Versions of Moral Enquiry* (1990) and *Dependent Rational Animals: Why Human Beings Need the Virtues* (1999), all published by Duckworth, London. The discussion here relates mainly to *After Virtue* and *Dependent Rational Animals, passim*.

9 John Rawls, *A Theory of Justice*, New York and Oxford: Oxford University Press, *passim*.

10 Robert J. Dostall (ed.), *The Cambridge Companion to Gadamer*, Cambridge UK: Cambridge University Press, 2002, p. 149. See also Hans-Georg Gadamer, *The Relevance of the Beautiful and Other Essays*, Cambridge UK: Cambridge University Press, 1986, trans. Nicholas Walker; ed. and with an Introduction by Robert Bernasconi; and Hans-Georg Gadamer, *Truth and Method*, trans. and ed. Garrett Barden and John Cumming, London: Sheed & Ward, 1975.

11 Dostall, *op. cit.*, p. 163.

12 *Ibid.*

13 A.C. Grayling, *The Choice of Hercules: Pleasure, Duty and the Good Life in the Twenty-first*

Century, London: Weidenfeld &
Nicolson, 2007, p. 25.

14 Terry Eagleton, *The Meaning of
Life*, Oxford: Oxford University
Press, 2007, *passim*.

15 Thomas Nagel, *The View from
Nowhere*, Oxford and New York:
Oxford University Press, 1986,
pp. 8–11.

16 Nagel, *op. cit.*, p. 108.

17 Thomas Nagel, *Mind & Cosmos:
Why the Materialist Neo-
Darwinian Conception of Nature
Is Almost Certainly False*, Oxford
and New York: Oxford University
Press, 2012, p. 7.

18 Nagel, *Mind & Cosmos*, p. 50.

19 *Ibid.*, p. 115.

20 Nagel, *View from Nowhere*, p. 223.

21 Richard Rorty, *Philosophy and
Social Hope*, New York and
London: Penguin Books, 1999,
p. xxv.

22 Rorty, *op. cit.*, p. 150.

23 *Ibid.*, p. 158.

24 *Ibid.*, p. 86.

25 Richard Rorty, *Philosophy as
Cultural Politics*, Cambridge UK:
Cambridge University Press, 2007,
p. 108.

26 Robert Nozick, *Invariances*,
Cambridge, Mass.: Belknap Press/
Harvard University Press, 2001,
p. 280.

27 Nozick, *op. cit.*, p. 300.

28 Robert Nozick, *The Examined Life:
Philosophical Meditations*, New
York: Simon & Schuster, 1989,
p. 12.

29 Nozick, *Examined Life*, p. 264.

30 *Ibid.*, p. 302.

31 Ronald Dworkin, *Justice for
Hedgehogs*, Cambridge, Mass.:
Belknap Press/Harvard University
Press, 2011, p. 13.

32 Dworkin, *op. cit.*, pp. 197–8.

33 *Ibid.*, p. 206.

34 *Ibid.*, p. 217.

35 Ronald Dworkin, 'Religion
without God', *New York Review
of Books*, 4 April 2013. See also

Dworkin's three Einstein lectures
delivered at the University of Bern,
Switzerland, on 12–14 December
2011, at http://www.law.nyu.edu/
news.Ronald Dworkin.

36 Jürgen Habermas,
*Postmetaphysical Thinking:
Philosophical Essays*, Cambridge
UK: Polity Press, 1992, p. xv.

37 Jürgen Habermas, *Between
Naturalism and Religion*,
Cambridge: Polity Press, 2008,
p. 29.

38 Jürgen Habermas, *Philosophical
Essays*, trans. Ciaran Cronin:
Cambridge UK: Polity Press, 2008.
And *Postmetaphysical Thinking*.

39 Jürgen Habermas, *An Awareness of
What Is Missing: Faith and Reason
in a Post-secular Age*, Cambridge
UK: Polity Press, 2010, p. 211.

40 Habermas, *Awareness of What Is
Missing*, p. 142.

41 *Ibid.*, pp. 139–40.

42 *Ibid.*, p. 37.

43 Alain de Botton, *Religion for
Atheists: A Non-believer's Guide
to the Uses of Religion*, London:
Hamish Hamilton, 2012, p. 44 and
passim.

**Conclusion: The Central Sane
Activity**

1 Salman Rushdie, *Joseph Anton*,
London: Jonathan Cape, 2012,
p. 476.

2 Harold Bloom, *The Anatomy of
Influence: Literature as a Way
of Life*, New Haven and London
(2011). Robert Bellah et al., *Habits
of the Heart: Individual and
Commitment in American Life*,
Berkeley, Los Angeles, London:
University of California Press
(1985). Richard Sennett, *The Fall of
Public Man* (2002), *Respect* (2003),
Craftsmanship (2008), *Together:
The Rituals, Pleasures and Politics
of Cooperation* (2012), all London
and New York: Allen Lane,
Penguin Press. Alan Dershowitz,

Rights from Wrongs: A Secular Theory of the Origin of Rights, New York: Basic Books (2004).

3 George Levine (ed.), *The Joy of Secularism: Eleven Essays for How We Live Now*, Princeton and London: Princeton University Press, 2011, p. 4.

4 John Gray, *Straw Dogs: Thoughts on Humans and Other Animals*, London: Granta Books, 2002, p. 74.

5 Gordon Graham, *The Re-enchantment of the World: Art versus Religion*, Oxford: Oxford University Press, 2007, pp. 82–5. Simon Blackburn, *Think: A Compelling Introduction to Philosophy*, Oxford and New York: Oxford University Press, 1999, p. 298.

6 Christopher Hitchens, *God Is Not Great: How Religion Poisons Everything*, New York: Twelve, 2007.

7 Gray, *op. cit.*, p. 43.

8 Jonathan Lear, *Happiness, Death and the Remainder of Life*, Cambridge, Mass., and London: Harvard University Press, 2000, p. 138.

9 Cynthia Ozick, *The Din in Our Head*, Boston: Houghton Mifflin, 2006, ch. 14.

10 Seamus Heaney, *The Government of the Tongue*, London: Faber and Faber, 1988, p. 189.

11 Rebecca Stott, 'The Webfooted Understorey: Darwinian Immersions', in Levine (ed.), pp. 216–21.

12 Gray, *op. cit.*, p. 198.

13 Richard Kearney, *Anatheism (Returning to God After God)*, New York: Columbia University Press, 2010, pp. 73, 80, 180.

ACKNOWLEDGEMENTS

I would like to thank those colleagues and friends who have helped me with *The Age of Nothing*, making suggestions for improvements, offering helpful criticisms, correcting errors, providing hospitality, loaning (and in some cases giving) books, reading parts or all of the text.

Pride of place goes to Alan Samson, Publisher of Weidenfeld & Nicolson, with whom the original idea was worked out and who has offered invaluable guidance on the book's shape and structure, and has been a support throughout. I am also grateful to the following: David Ambrose, Robert Arnold, Richard Ellis, Ian Gordon, David Henn, Charles Hill, Nicola Hodgkinson, James Joll, William Kistler, Thomas Lebien, Gerard Leroux, George Loudon, Constance Lowenthal, Sarah Macalpine, Brian MacArthur, Leighton Macarthy, Carolyn Mavroleon, Guislaine Vincent Morland, Bryan Moynahan, Andrew Nurnberg, Kathrine Palmer, Nicholas Pearson, Rüdiger Safranski, Alan Scott, Michael Stürmer, Mark Tompkins, Donna Ward, Anthony Wigram, David Wilkinson.

The literature on this subject keeps growing exponentially, beyond the grasp of any one individual: I come across a relevant new publication almost every week. I accept sole responsibility for the text as published, knowing only too well how much pertinent material has been left out.

INDEX

Abbey theatre, Dublin, 174
absolutism: Santayana on, 68; Husserl
    dismisses, 76; and Vienna Circle, 281-2;
    human desire for, 465
Abstract Expressionism, 403, 406, 409–10
Adam, Villiers de l'Isle: *Axel*, 167
Adler, Alfred, 378–9, 447
Adler, Viktor: influenced by Nietzsche, 33
Adorno, Theodor, 146, 380, 387
afterlife: Nietzsche on, 25; Rilke on, 236; in
    Christianity, 493
Agassiz, Louis, 57
Aiken, Conrad, 67
Akhmatova, Anna, 458
Al-Rawandi, 24
Alexander, Eben: *Proof of Heaven*, 11, 562–3
alienation, 509
Alldeutsche Verband, 52
Allen, Frederick Lewis: *Only Yesterday*, 247
Allison, Dorothy, 475
Altenesch, battle of (1234), 329
Altizer, Thomas, 392
ambiguity: in arts, 125
American Foundation of Religion and
    Psychiatry (AFRP), 369–70
American Society for Psychical Research, 180
Amour, L' (film), 564
amphetamines, 432
anatheism, 7
Anderson, Sherwood, 245; *Beyond Desire*,
    246–7, 552; *Winesburg, Ohio*, 248–9
Andre, Carl, 400
Andreas, Friedrich Carl, 232
Andreas–Salomé, Lou, 232, 445
Andrew, Joe, 109
Andronnik, Archbishop of Perm, 221

anima and animus, 296
Anouilh, Jean: *Antigone* (play), 347
anthroposophy, 217, 294, 326
anti–Semitism: and Nazism, 321–4, 328–9,
    381; in Poland, 339; *see also* Holocaust
anxiety: increase in, 452–3
Apollinaire, Guillaume, 124
Apostles (Cambridge group), 79, 311
archetypes: Jung on, 293, 296–7; God as,
    388–9
Arendt, Hannah, 196, 231, 449
Aristotle, 64, 88
Arnold, Matthew, 476; *Dover Beach* (poem),
    24
Aron, Raymond, 347
Arp, Hans, 119
art: inadequacy compared with religion,
    11; and salvation, 75; and Bloomsbury
    Group, 81; social importance, 91–2, 111–
    12, 148; modernist, 112–14; 'new spirit'
    in, 123–4; rivalry with reality, 125; Wells
    on inadequacy of, 137; Proust idealizes,
    146; and disappointment, 164–5; Yeats
    on religion and, 167; spiritual in, 184;
    Freud on as palliative, 291; Malraux on
    self-regarding, 350, 395; minimalism,
    399–400; in post-war USA, 405–8;
    Steiner on, 463–5; Iris Murdoch on, 474;
    E.O. Wilson on, 493; Gadamer on, 514
Asahara, Shoko, 451
Aschheim, Steven: on Nietzsche, 25, 33,
    38–9, 50; on Gottfried Benn, 50; on
    distribution of Nietzsche's *Thus Spake
    Zarathustra* to German troops, 192
Ascona (Switzerland): community and
    ideals, 40–7, 49

498; enlargement as aim of life, 526; and individuation, 535; plurality, 547–8; sense of, 547
self-actualization, 372–3, 379, 423
self-help, 366–7
Sennett, Richard, 543
Seurat, Georges, 112, 114, 116; *Port of Gravelines Channel* (painting), 114–15; *A Sunday Afternoon on the Island of La Grande Jatte* (painting), 115
Seventh Day Adventists, 180
Sewell, Elizabeth, 473
sex: Freud on, 291
shadow: as Jungian archetype, 296
shadow culture: in USA, 179–81
Shakers (movement), 179
Shakespeare, William, 158, 274, 462
Shattuck, Roger, 123–5
Shaw, George Bernard: visits Ascona, 44; beliefs, 100–6, 166, 546; on hope, 105; Wells and, 137; and Yeats, 168; and androgyny, 274; *Androcles and the Lion* (play), 105; *Back to Methuselah* (play), 102, 104, 106; *Candida* (play), 104; *Don Juan* (play), 104; *Heartbreak House* (play), 102; *Major Barbara* (play), 105; *Man and Superman* (play), 102; *The Quintessence of Ibsenism*, 101
Sheen, Monsignor Fulton, 370; *Peace of Soul*, 375
Shelley, Percy Bysshe, 152; 'Defence of Poetry', 474
Shestov, Lev, 210–12
short stories, 92–3
Signac, Paul, 116; *In the Time of Harmony* (painting), 116
Simmel, Georg, 37, 42
singing: Rilke exalts, 235–6
Sisley, Alfred, 114
Sisyphus (legendary figure), 357–8
situation ethics, 374–5
Skinner, B.F., 497
social Darwinism, 52
social hope, 66–7
socialism: Wells on, 140; Utopian, 180; and Great War, 198, 204; Nietzsche criticises, 213
society: as a machine, 92; *see also* community
Society for God Knowledge (German), 332
sociobiology, 488
Socrates, 24, 528
Solanas, Valerie, 433
solidarity, 135, 526, 539
solitude, 350, 445

Somme, Battle of the (1916), 191
soul: Musil defines, 241; Freud on, 287; Wittgenstein on, 310; belief in, 486
Soulé, Michael E., 492
Soutine, Chaim, 123
speaking in tongues, 15
Spencer, Herbert, 24, 76, 169
Spengler, Oswald: on Nietzsche, 34; *The Decline of the West*, 324
Spicer, Jack, 412
Spiegelberg, Frederic, 423; *The Religion of No Religion*, 423
Spinoza, Benedict de, 303
spiritual, the: Santayana on, 68–70, 130; Gide on, 130; common belief in need for, 482; and self-made beliefs, 510
spiritualism: Yeats's interest in, 175; strength, 180; in Great War, 200–1
Spitteler, Carl, 85
Spock, Benjamin, 364–6, 368
spontaneity, 395, 402–3, 410–12, 414
Stalin, Josef: adopts name, 210; favours Gorky, 214; anti-religious policy, 219–20, 223; purges and Great Terror, 223, 390, 396
Stanley, Augustus Owsley III, 431
Steigmann–Gall, Richard, 322
Stein, Gertrude, 244
Steiner, George: on seeking meaning, ix, 548; idealizes high art, 463–5; on science, 549; on aesthetic truths, 561; on imagination, 563; *Grammars of Creation*, 462; *Real Presences*, 462
Steiner, Rudolf, 217, 287, 319, 326, 331
Stella, Frank, 400
Stephen, Adrian, 79
Stephen, Sir Leslie, 24, 79, 275
Stephen, Thoby, 79
Stevens, Wallace: taught by Santayana, 67, 251; on infinity, 114; Wells and, 137; life and ideas, 148–9, 250–5; on poetry, 148–9, 467, 473; imagination, 179, 563; breaks hand in fight with Hemingway, 250; on importance of particulars, 546; on attaining meaning, 549; on embracing ideas like a woman, 557
Stewart, H.L.: *Nietzsche and the Ideals of Germany*, 192
Stewart-Williams, Steve: *Darwin, God and the Meaning of Life*, 7
Storr, Anthony, 445
Stott, Rebecca, 561
Strachey, Lytton, 80, 311
Strassman, Rick, 450